THE BOX
ENCYCLOPEDI
DETECTIVES

THE BOXTREE ENCYCLOPEDIA OF TV DETECTIVES

Geoff Tibballs

First published 1992 by
Boxtree Limited
36 Tavistock Street
London WC2E 7PB

© (text) Geoff Tibballs 1992

1 3 5 7 9 10 8 6 4 2

Design and computer page make up by Penny Mills
Cover illustration by Heléne Burrows
Printed in England by Clays Ltd, St Ives plc

A CIP catalogue record for this book
is available from the British Library

ISBN 1 85283 129 4

CONTENTS

ACKNOWLEDGEMENTS

Any detective starting out on a case as big as this needs a few breaks. I got lucky. I met people who were prepared to talk. And if they couldn't talk, they faxed. Soon I was building up the evidence – cast lists, fact sheets, transmission dates. I knew I was going to crack it. So to the following who helped me with my inquiries, I express my grateful thanks.

To Barry Macdonald and Jan Kacperek of the ITC Library, a national treasure on a par with the Tate Gallery; John Jordan of BBC Written Archives, another invaluable source of information; the British Film Institute; to Hilary Kingsley for her words of wisdom; Carole Grimes (Anglia Television) for archive material; the ITC Information Department for endless dates; Nathan Hasson, WGBH Boston; Judy Grant, NBC (New York); John Behrens (CBS, New York); Ed Cintron (ABC, New York); Penny Craig, MCA TV; Pam Wright, Paramount Television; Celia Reynolds, Twentieth Century Fox Television; Delores Sangster, Viacom; Shelley Groves, Warner Bros; Lisa Sanders, the Walt Disney Company Ltd; Angeline Burton (TVS); Chris Bell (STV); Wendy Taylor (The Bill); Heather Powell (Yorkshire Television); Margaret Duerden (Central Television); and to Naomi Phillipson (Anglia) for defying the call of the gas man and providing information on P.D. James and The Chief.

Thanks also to all at Boxtree for having faith in the idea, and to my family, especially my wife Carol, for feeding me intravenously for the past six months while I slaved over a hot word processor, and to my daughters, Nicola for filling me in on Inspector Gadget, and Lindsey for not getting doughnut jam on the finished manuscript.

I would like to dedicate this book to my parents, whose love of crime and detective shows meant that the first numbers I knew were Ten-four.

INTRODUCTION

We've seen them all. Fat detectives, scruffy detectives, a lollipop-sucking detective, an orchid-loving detective, a Confucius-spouting detective, a snuff-taking detective, a poetry-quoting detective, a horse-riding detective, a clock-mending detective, a priest detective with a streetwise nun, a ghost detective, a robot detective, an alien detective, a witch detective and a former-alcoholic-with-a-limp detective. Then there have been the defective detectives – sleuths with one arm, one eye, gammy leg, blind, wheelchair-bound, dwarf. Detectives have come in all nationalities – Belgian, Chinese, French, Dutch, German, Swiss, Red Indian, Aborigine, Scottish, even Geordie. Not to mention geriatric detectives, teenage detectives, aristocratic detectives, bimbo detectives, Victorian detectives, a singing detective, an ex-con, an ex-fireman, an ex-jockey, a disc jockey, a gypsy, a rabbi, one who had a pet cockatoo, another who kept an ocelot, and a seventh-century Chinese judge detective.

Mystery stories have long been a popular form of literature, from the days of Edgar Allan Poe and Conan Doyle through Agatha Christie, Dashiell Hammett, Raymond Chandler and Mickey Spillane, to present-day practitioners such as P.D. James, Ruth Rendell and Colin Dexter. Television has recognized the potential in transferring the printed page to the small screen as well as inventing its own sleuthing heroes. The first police serial was America's Police Patrol back in 1931 but it is since the Second World War, as global television expanded beyond its primitive origins, that the detective has become such an essential TV character.

The majority of the early post-war heroes were American, like Charlie Wild, Dick Tracy and Rocky King, as was the programme that changed the face of crime shows forever, Dragnet. This was the first attempt to paint an in-depth portrait of the day-to-day working lives of the police. The accent was on realism not sensationalism. Without Dragnet, there would have been no Hill Street Blues. While Britain answered with Dixon of Dock Green, No Hiding Place and Maigret, the late 1950s saw the US switch to a new breed of swinging private eyes in Peter Gunn, 77 Sunset Strip and Hawaiian Eye.

There followed classic shows including The Untouchables, Hawaii Five-O and our own Z Cars but it was the 1970s which produced a wave of highly imaginative TV-created American detectives – Columbo, Kojak, Cannon, McCloud, The Rockford Files and so on. Until recently, Britain's response had been relatively muted, but in the latter half of the 1980s we have seen a veritable resurgence in home-grown detective programming, spearheaded by quality adaptations of Sherlock Holmes, Miss Marple, Poirot, Adam Dalgliesh and the current sensation, Inspector Morse. The TV detective has never been more popular.

So why are we so addicted? Is it because good always triumphs over evil, that foul play is ultimately followed by a sense of fair play? Could it be that, with rising crime figures, detective shows provide a certain reassurance? Because no matter how hopelessly inept the police are, a helpful amateur or a seasoned professional sleuth is always on hand to bail them out. We know the murderer will be brought to justice at the end of each episode; there are no unsolved crimes in TV land. It will be safe to walk the streets again – until next week.

Television enables us to be detectives in the comfort of our own lounges without having to dodge a hail of bullets, or turn our coat collars up against the wind and rain, down some sleazy side street. And there is an immense feeling of satisfaction in correctly identifying the murderer before the first commercial break, while Dalgliesh labours on for another five weeks. Maybe it's just that we love a good murder mystery – as long as it takes place in the safety of a TV studio hundreds of miles away.

Then, of course, there are the heroes themselves, specially designed to appeal to all tastes. What girl could resist ironing Magnum's Hawaiian shirt, washing Sonny Crockett's boxer shorts or sharing the Times crossword with Morse? Someone somewhere must even love Taggart.

This book, the most comprehensive yet to be compiled on the subject, features every major (and most of the minor) detective series to have been screened on British and American TV since the war; a total of around 500 – many wonderful, some downright woeful.

Basically, there are three categories of detective: private eyes (Holmes, Philip Marlowe, Cannon etc), amateur sleuths (Miss Marple, Lord Peter Wimsey, Jessica Fletcher) and the police (Morse, Columbo, Cagney and Lacey). The hardest part in putting together this encyclopedia was defining the grey areas, those who fought crime but were not true detectives. Thus there is no place here for secret agents, courtroom dramas (with the honourable exception of Perry Mason who sneaks in via Paul Drake), superheroes (save Batman who was virtually an extension of the Gotham City Police Department) and factual series like Crimewatch UK and Police 5. Chisholm and Rycott from Minder don't make it either (the overall series was not a detective show) and much as I would like to have included The Invisible Man so that I could claim an invisible detective, I decided that he did not qualify either, at least not in his original concept.

What about Lassie, Champion the Wonder Horse, Rin Tin Tin, Flipper and all those other animal crime-busters who proved themselves eminently superior to their human owners? Who's to say Lassie wasn't more capable than Frank Cannon? Could Cannon wash between his legs like that? And would Starsky have achieved more if he had been paired with Skippy the bush kangaroo? But I felt purists might object to the inclusion of the likes of a dolphin detective even though a couple of toucans have made it.

Nor have I listed mini series, TV movies and single plays, simply because there are so many of them that the book would have grown to the size where it could have been used as a murder weapon in an episode of Inspector Morse. But it was tempting to include such one-off gems as Policewoman Centerfold, the title of which necessitates no further explanation. All I can say is that if your favourite show isn't included here...tough!

But if you were a fan of Kookie or Columbo, Hill Street Blues or Hawaii Five-0, Dragnet or Department S, or still rave over Taggart and Twin Peaks, Morse and Moonlighting, you'll find all you need to know about them in this volume.

ACE CRAWFORD, PRIVATE EYE

Criminals, beware! Innocent bystanders, take cover! Ace Crawford, private eye, is on the loose – and no one is safe from his comic confusion.

In his familiar hat and trench coat, Ace Crawford was Sam Spade played for laughs. Ace was tough, scrupulously honest and irresistible to women. Unfortunately he left almost as much disaster in his wake as the average hurricane.

Ace was totally inept, yet defying all the rules of logic, he somehow always managed to solve the case in what amounted to a detective version of the spy spoof Get Smart. Like all the best gumshoes, Ace had his favourite watering-hole, in this instance The Shanty, a sleazy wharfside club owned by the appropriately-named Inch, played by midget Billy Barty. There Ace enjoyed the kind of adulation normally reserved for Michael Jackson. His intellectually compatible part-time assistant, Toomey, hung on his every word, while sexy club singer, Luana, carried a torch that burned so fiercely as to be a fire risk. Even police Lieutenant Fanning had to admit to a grudging admiration for Ace's results although, like everyone else, he was baffled by his methods. Incidentally, Luana's blind piano accompanist, Mello, was played by jazz great, Bill Henderson.

Ace Crawford, Private Eye, was by no means the worst attempt at such a caper but it was relatively short-lived. Perhaps by the 1980s, the bumbling detective had been so brilliantly created by Peter Sellers as Inspector Clouseau, that there was simply little room for improvement.

REGULAR CAST

Ace Crawford Tim Conway   *Toomey* Joe Regalbuto
Luana Shera Danese   *Inch* Billy Barty
Mello Bill Henderson   *Lt Fanning* Dick Christie

Creators: Ron Clark, Tim Conway
Producer: Ron Clark

A Conway Enterprises Production for Viacom

13 colour 30-minute episodes
US: CBS 15 March 1983 - 12 April 1983
UK: ITV From 7 April 1984 (Yorkshire TV)

ADAM 12

Every Los Angeles Police Department squad car bears the motto: 'To protect and Serve.' Filmed in co-operation with the L.A.P.D., Jack

Webb's Adam 12 showed devoted police officers protecting and serving the city, whether it was tackling armed robbers or rescuing a little old lady's ginger tom cat from up a tree.

With Dragnet, Webb had proved himself to be a pioneer of portraying the everyday lives of police officers. His aim has always been realism, not glamorous cop shows rife with chaotic car chases and blonde bimbos. Adam 12 was Webb's successor to the adventures of Joe Friday and it became nearly as popular as Dragnet in the US, running for seven seasons.

It was very much the American counterpart of Z Cars, concentrating on the day to day work of two patrol car cops with the Los Angeles Police Department. The principal characters were senior officer Pete Malloy and probationary rookie Jim Reed, who were rewarded for services rendered to the city and viewers alike, with promotion. During the 1970-1 season, Reed was upgraded from rookie to officer and the following year Malloy was raised to Policeman 3, one rank below sergeant. They had earned it.

REGULAR CAST

Officer Pete Malloy Martin Milner   *Officer Jim Reed* Kent McCord
Sgt MacDonald William Boyett   *Officer Ed Wells* Gary Crosby
Dispatcher's voice Shaaron Claridge

Creators: Jack Webb, Robert A. Cinader
Music: Frank Comstock
Producer: Tom Williams
Executive producers: Jack Webb, Herman S. Saunders

A Universal Television Production

174 colour 30-minute episodes
US: NBC (Season 1) 21 Sept 1968 - 5 April 1969 (26 eps)

(Season 2) 20 Sept 1969 - 9 May 1970 (26 eps)
(Season 3) 19 Sept 1970 - 5 April 1971 (26 eps)
(Season 4) 15 Sept 1971 - 15 March 1972 (24 eps)
(Season 5) 13 Sept 1972 - 21 March 1973 (24 eps)
(Season 6) 12 Sept 1973 - 13 March 1974 (24 eps)
(Season 7) 24 Sept 1974 - 20 May 1975 (24 eps)

NEW ADAM 12

Adam 12 was revived in 1989 with two new young officers, Gus Grant and Matt Doyle, patrolling the streets of Los Angeles in their black and white squad car. Grant is a former American footballer while Doyle, played by Ethan Wayne, youngest son of John Wayne, comes from a long line of cops.

REGULAR CAST

Officer Gus Grant Peter Parros   *Officer Matt Doyle* Ethan Wayne

Co-executive producers: Burton Armus, Craig Kellem
Executive producer: Arthur L. Annecharico

An Arthur Company Production for WWOR-TV
52 colour 30-minute episodes (continuing)
US: Syndicated from 4 October 1989

THE ADVENTURES OF FU MANCHU

Dr Fu Manchu was the original Yellow Peril. Created by Sax Rohmer in a series of stories and novels first published around 1910, Fu was a brilliant Chinese scientist who became the personification of evil towards the west.

The character starred in numerous silent movies and on American radio from 1929. Gradually the racial element was toned down as Christopher Lee played him in a batch of 1960s films while Peter Sellers' final big screen appearance was in The Fiendish Plot of Dr Fu Manchu in 1979.

The first attempts to turn Fu into a TV moneyspinner came in 1952 when John Carradine played Fu and Sir Cedric Hardwicke appeared as his long-time adversary, Sir Dennis Nayland-Smith of Scotland Yard, in a pilot programme for American television. However it was deemed so awful that it was scrapped without being transmitted. But three years later, Republic Pictures paid four million dollars to Sax Rohmer for the rights to the characters and the result was The Adventures of Fu Manchu.

The series was set in London, beginning with Fu's wicked genius being aroused after his wife and son were accidentally killed by a British officer, Jack Petrie, during the Boxer Rebellion. Fu became deranged and vowed to destroy not only the Petrie family but the entire white race. He clearly bore quite a grudge. He retreated to his hideaway in Tibet where he established SUBTLY , a sinister organization bent on wrecking western democracies. More dastardly than Dick, each week he sent his agents on missions of hate but his every scheme was thwarted in the nick of time by the redoubtable Nayland-Smith, the epitome of the 1950s British police commander.

Of course for all his police training, Sir Dennis was never able to capture Fu himself, leaving the oriental one free to wreak further havoc in the following week's episode. It was just as well because it would have made for a fairly dull series if Fu had been thrown in prison after the first programme. It's not too easy to plot the overthrow of mankind from a cell in Wormwood Scrubs.

REGULAR CAST

Dr Fu Manchu Glen Gordon   *Sir Dennis Nayland-Smith* Lester Matthews
Dr John Petrie Clark Howat

A Republic Pictures Production

39 monochrome 30-minute episodes
US: Syndicated 1956

THE ADVENTURES OF SHERLOCK HOLMES

'It's strange, but when I play Holmes my whole body changes shape. I become long and lean and my skull seems to shrink.' – JEREMY BRETT

When the Allies reached Berlin in 1945, they found two movies in Hitler's bunker. Both were German Sherlock Holmes adventures – The Hound of the Baskervilles and The Man Who Was Sherlock Holmes. Such is the popularity of the world's greatest detective that he appeals to good and evil alike, although thankfully not all fans are tempted to go out and annexe Poland.

Holmes has been portrayed on the big screen by some 70 different actors (including one black, Sam Robinson, in 1918) and has appeared in just under 200 films. No other character has enjoyed such exposure in the history of the cinema. Yet for all the accomplished actors who have played Sir Arthur Conan Doyle's creation in the past (Basil Rathbone, John Barrymore, Peter Cushing etc), it is Jeremy Brett in the Granada Television series who has been hailed as the ideal Holmes.

Brett modestly maintains: 'The definitive Sherlock Holmes is in everyone's head. No actor can fit into that category because every reader has his own ideal. Sherlock Holmes is a free spirit, you cannot pin him down – he is probably the most complicated character I've played in my life.

'My Sherlock Holmes streaks through the night sky – not naked, you understand, but like a magnesium flare, with all the world trying to keep up with him. A man of utter genius.

'Some people see me as the Sherlock who twitches and looks stoned. They tell me I manage to get the combination of genius and madness. But there is another type of Holmes, the thinking man's Holmes who works things through logically, spasmodically puffing on his pipe as ash tumbles down his waistcoat. That's the one I've never been able to capture.'

It is the many facets of the resident of 221B Baker Street that make him such a compelling character. He hails from a line of English country squires but claims Huguenot blood. He remains secretive about his personal history, notably his education, but there is evidence to suggest he took science exams at London University. He is by no means the brains of the family – that honour belongs to his brother Mycroft, a Civil Service auditor. The only woman in his life is housekeeper Mrs Hudson although he did nearly fall for the beautiful but deadly Irene Adler, the one woman to outwit him. Now he leads a celibate existence, disliking women , and people in general.

Apart from Mrs Hudson, the sole person he can tolerate (and sometimes only barely) is his regular companion, retired army doctor John Watson. Always marvelling at the great sleuth's prowess and deductions, the amiable Watson is Holmes' straight-man.

Holmes is a man of many moods, some induced by his cocaine habit. Watching Jeremy Brett wild-eyed and haunted, it is easy to believe that Holmes has just had a sniff of something stronger than snuff. He also loves whisky and soda, playing the violin and tobacco. Indeed his legendary powers of observation enable him to distinguish between 120 different cigar ashes, 75 perfumes and 42 different impressions left by bicycle tyres. Astounding, Holmes!

Holmes was based in part on Dr Joseph Bell, a surgeon at Edinburgh University under whom Conan Doyle had studied. The author began work on the first Sherlock Holmes adventure, A Study in Scarlet, in 1886. It was rejected by Chamber's Journal as being 'both too short and too long' and was turned down by other publishers before Ward, Lock and Co. paid Conan Doyle £25 for the privilege. However, they said they couldn't publish it immediately as 'the market is flooded at present with cheap fiction' and so A Study in Scarlet was held over until 1887. Over the years, there were to be three more Holmes novels and 56 short stories, many of them serialized in Strand Magazine, accompanied by splendid illustrations from Sidney Paget. Conan Doyle tried to kill Holmes off in 1892, when he and the dreaded Moriarty plunged over the Reichenbach Falls, but after the people took to the streets of London in black arm bands in protest, the author was forced to bring his hero back from the grave, Dallas-like.

Meanwhile the Baker Street detective's fame was spreading beyond the printed page. In 1899, American actor/writer William Gillette played Holmes in a stage production, causing Conan Doyle to enthuse: 'He changed a creature of thin air into an absolutely convincing human being.' Gillette later became the first radio Holmes, on NBC in 1930. The character's first screen appearance was in 1900, a 30-second American silent called Sherlock Holmes Baffled.

Holmes came to television in 1937, seven years after Conan Doyle's death, with Louis Hector in an NBC production of The Three Garridebs. The New York Herald Tribune called it 'an interesting welding of film with studio production' but added that it would offer 'no serious challenge to the contemporary stage or screen.'

But it was at the cinema that Holmes blossomed, with Basil Rathbone delivering the most famous version. Rathbone's debut was in The Hound of the Baskervilles in 1939 but, as Jeremy Brett was to discover, Holmes can take over an actor's life. In 1947, Rathbone lamented: 'When Doyle invented Holmes, he created a Frankenstein. It got him and now it's killing me. I've been Holmes in fourteen films and hundreds of broadcasts. People think I am Holmes. Everybody has forgotten Basil Rathbone.'

Overall, Jeremy Brett is the 117th actor to play Holmes. He has followed the likes of Stewart Granger, Raymond Massey, Christopher Lee, Roger Moore, Leonard Nimoy, Peter Cook and John Cleese. Alan Napier (Batman's butler, Alfred) was Holmes in a 1949 US TV production, and among assorted Watsons has been John Steed himself, Patrick Macnee. Holmes has been translated into many languages on screen – Russian, Italian, Hungarian, French, Danish and German to name but a few. Good gracious, Holmes!

For Granada's Adventures of Sherlock Holmes, producer Michael Cox went back to the early Strand magazine stories and carefully recreated Sidney Paget's illustrations. For added authenticity, a Victorian Baker Street was built at Granada's Manchester studios, near the set of the long-running soap opera, Coronation Street. Now anybody having one too many in the Rover's Return risks being mown down by a Hansom cab.

Jeremy Brett researched the role by studying footage of Basil Rathbone. 'I got very depressed,' says Brett, 'because he looks exactly like the drawings by Sidney Paget. The part fitted Rathbone like a glove whereas I always need three quarters of an hour in make-up.

'But none of the previous film versions stuck as closely to the original as we have done. For example my Holmes, like Conan Doyle's, never wears a deerstalker in town, only in the country. And he only smokes a long, thin cherrywood pipe when he's in a disputative mood. In a meditative mood, he smokes a short clay pipe.

'Sticking to the text sometimes takes nerve. There is a scene in The Dancing Men when Holmes hurls himself to the ground and wriggles through the bracken like a golden retriever. I felt a complete fool doing it and I thought the audience might laugh. But they didn't, because it was perfectly in character – Holmes was using his animal intuition to find a clue and, needless to say, he came up with one. The fascinating thing about playing Holmes is that he keeps his mystery. I haven't got to the bottom of him yet.'

Brett wasn't always as keen on Holmes. At school at Eton, he had studied the books and admitted to not really enjoying them. 'I thought Holmes was a terrible know-all. I much preferred Dr Watson.' In the early days of the series, Brett was even quoted as saying: 'I found Holmes cold, chilling, a walking brain without emotion. Not the sort of person I'd cross the street to meet.'

There were other difficulties too. 'I found after a time that Holmes was threatening me,' continues Brett. 'He became the dark side of the moon because he is moody and solitary and I am sociable and gregarious. It got dangerous for me. I began to feel there was nothing in my life but Holmes.' Ultimately the anxiety about the part, coming shortly after the death of his second wife, resulted in Brett suffering a nervous breakdown in 1986 and spending eight weeks in hospital. But after a two-month convalescence, he was back playing Holmes.

And what of Watson? Played first by David Burke (in The Adventures) and subsequently by Edward Hardwicke (in The Return and The Case-Book), Watson has emerged as far less of a dozy doc than when portrayed by Nigel Stock. Hardwicke defends the faithful practitioner: 'I don't think Watson is stupid. After all, you have to be fairly bright to be a doctor. He is quite a humorous character and adds a lot of banter to the working relationship. I like to think Watson always had a slight smile in contrast with the emotionless Holmes. But Watson knows his place – he recognizes that in Holmes, he is in the presence of an expert.'

This latest and most elaborate production of Sherlock Holmes is without doubt the closest to Conan Doyle's original. Jeremy Brett has certainly captured the dark side of Holmes better than any of his predecessors. This Holmes may not be as likeable as, say, Peter Cushing's, but Holmes was never intended to be a clean-cut hero. And it's nice to see dear old Mrs Hudson getting a line or two, answering the door and ensuring that Holmes eats properly. For even the greatest detectives need nourishment. Alimentary, my dear Watson. (SEE ALSO THE CASES OF SHERLOCK HOLMES, THE HOUND OF THE BASKERVILLES, SHERLOCK HOLMES, YOUNG SHERLOCK)

* Jeremy Brett actually played Watson once, in a 1981 Los Angeles stage production of The Crucifer of Blood. Charlton Heston was Holmes.

* Edward Hardwicke is the son of distinguished actor Sir Cedric Hardwicke. Young Edward was raised in Hollywood and, through his father, knew Basil Rathbone.

REGULAR CAST

Sherlock Holmes Jeremy Brett
Dr Watson (Adventures) David Burke *(Return, Case-Book)* Edward Hardwicke
Mrs Hudson Rosalie Williams *Inspector Lestrade* Colin Jeavons

The Adventures of Sherlock Holmes

Season One

A Scandal in Bohemia

A masked nobleman visits Holmes and Watson in a state of distress. He reveals himself to be the King of Bohemia and tells of his affair with beautiful former opera singer Irene Adler who is now threatening to blackmail him on the eve of his wedding to a Scandinavian princess. But Holmes knows only too well that Miss Adler is a formidable adversary.

GUEST STARS:

Gayle Hunnicutt, Michael Carter, Wolf Kahler
Dramatized by Alexander Baron
Director: Paul Annett

The Dancing Men

Elsie Cubitt, the young wife of a Norfolk squire, is terrified by the peculiar matchstick men drawn in chalk on a garden seat. She tries to hide her fear but when more appear, Holmes is summoned. He deduces that the figures are a code which he duly cracks – but not before a tragic death.

GUEST STARS:

Tenniel Evans, Betsy Brantley
Dramatized by Anthony Skene
Director: John Bruce

The Naval Treaty

Copying a secret Anglo-Italian treaty late at night at the Foreign Office, a young diplomat leaves his desk for a few seconds. When he returns, the document has gone. The man, a friend of Watson's, asks Holmes to find out whether the treaty has fallen into enemy hands.

GUEST STARS:

David Gwillim, Alison Skilbeck
Dramatized by Jeremy Paul
Director: Alan Grint

The Solitary Cyclist

Each week Violet Smith cycles six miles along a lonely road to visit her mother. Whenever she gets to a certain stretch, a bearded stranger follows at a distance. If she slows, he slows. If she stops, he stops. As yet, he has done nothing untoward, but Holmes is asked to step in before he does.

GUEST STARS:

Barbara Wilshere, John Castle
Dramatized by Alan Plater
Director: Paul Annett

The Crooked Man

The morning after hearing a violent quarrel, the servants find Colonel Barclay dead from a gash in the back of his head, his face a mask of horror. His wife is stretched out unconscious on the sofa. Holmes deduces that there was a third person in the room.

GUEST STARS:

Norman Jones, Lisa Daniely
Dramatized by Alfred Shaughnessy
Director: Alan Grint

The Speckled Band

Engaged and in love, Helen Stoner fears for her life in her tyrannical stepfather's remote house, where her sister died screaming, 'The Speckled Band'. Holmes and Watson have faced some pretty fearsome foes in their time but few as lethal as the band, a highly poisonous snake prone to attacking people in their beds.

GUEST STARS:

Jeremy Kemp, Rosalyn Landor
Dramatized by Jeremy Paul
Director: John Bruce

The Blue Carbuncle

The precious stone known as the Blue Carbuncle is a bad omen. Two of its previous owners have committed suicide, so Holmes is alarmed to learn that it is on the loose again, having been stolen from the hotel suite of the Countess of Morcar.

GUEST STARS:

Frank Middlemass, Ken Campbell
Dramatized by Paul Finney
Director: David Carson

Season Two

The Copper Beeches

Violet Hunter is delighted to be appointed governess to Jephro Rucastle's young son – until she learns that the post is only hers provided she agrees to crop her long chestnut hair. She consults Holmes before accepting, but it is not long before she sends the great sleuth an urgent telegram: 'Please be at Black Swan Hotel, Winchester, midday tomorrow. Do come, I am at my wits' end. Violet Hunter.'

GUEST STARS:

Natasha Richardson, Joss Ackland
Dramatized by Bill Craig
Director: Paul Annett

The Greek Interpreter

Melas, a Greek interpreter, is taken by night in a carriage with the windows covered and made to interpret for a man being held prisoner. Afterwards Melas is dumped at the roadside. Mycroft Holmes becomes involved and knows that only one man can get to the root of the mystery – his famous brother Sherlock.

GUEST STARS:

Charles Gray (as Mycroft), George Costigan
Dramatized by Derek Marlowe
Director: Alan Grint

The Norwood Builder

Shortly after visiting Holmes, young solicitor John McFarlane is pulled in by Scotland Yard's Inspector Lestrade on a charge of murder. Jonas Oldacre, a Norwood builder, has vanished and McFarlane's blood-stained stick has been found at Oldacre's house. But Holmes is convinced that McFarlane is innocent.

GUEST STARS:

Matthew Solon, Jonathan Adams
Dramatized by Richard Harris
Director: Ken Grieve

The Resident Patient

Mr Blessington sets a brilliant young medical student, Trevelyan, up in practice at Brook Street in the West End of London. Blessington sees it as an investment and then moves in as resident patient. But news of the other patients terrifies him and makes for a startling case for Holmes.

GUEST STARS:

Patrick Newell, Nicholas Clay
Dramatized by Derek Marlowe
Director: David Carson

The Red-Headed League

It sounds too good to be true. A salary of £4 a week for easy work where the only qualification is to have red hair. But Jabez Wilson discovers there is more to the job than meets the eye, particularly when one day he finds that his employers have disappeared into thin air. He calls in Holmes in a desperate attempt to save the day.

GUEST STARS:

Roger Hammond, Eric Porter (as Moriarty)
Dramatized by John Hawkesworth
Director: John Bruce

The Final Problem

Following on from The Red-Headed League, Holmes realizes that arch criminal, Professor Moriarty, must be stopped once and for all. But Moriarty's brain has the same capacity for evil genius as Holmes' has for detection. The two men battle it out in Switzerland on the edge of the watery torrents of the Reichenbach Falls.

GUEST STARS:

Eric Porter (as Moriarty), Claude Le Sache
Dramatized by John Hawkesworth
Director: Alan Grint

The Return of Sherlock Holmes

Season One

The Empty House

'It is now three long years,' writes Watson, 'since my dear friend plunged to his death in the seething cauldron of the Reichenbach Falls, locked in the arms of his arch enemy. There, deep down under that swirling water, the infamous Professor Moriarty and the foremost champion of the law of his generation will lie together for all time.' With Holmes apparently dead, Watson has struggled on as a police surgeon. Then one day the Doctor finds himself in the middle of a baffling murder mystery, that of the Hon. Ronald Adair. If only Holmes were around to help out. Then suddenly he is, risen from the dead.

GUEST STARS:

Patrick Allen, Colin Jeavons
Dramatized by John Hawkesworth
Director: Howard Baker

The Abbey Grange

When drunken brute, Sir Eustace Brackenstall, is clubbed to death, his long-suffering wife, who had recently been beaten by him, maintains that the culprits were burglars. Holmes comes to another conclusion after studying three wine glasses, a blood-stained poker, a broken bell-rope and the frozen pond in the park.

GUEST STARS:

Conrad Phillips, Anne Louise Lambert
Dramatized by Trevor Bowen
Director: Peter Hammond

The Musgrave Ritual

What secret lies behind the death of Reginald Musgrave's trusty retainer? Musgrave gets more than he bargained for when he calls in Holmes to investigate, as the great man displays a profound knowledge of trigonometry and even uncovers the whereabouts of the missing crown of King Charles I.

GUEST STARS:

Michael Culver, James Hazeldine
Dramatized by Jeremy Paul
Director: David Carson

The Second Stain

The contents of a letter stolen from Westminster are of grave national importance. The Prime Minister personally asks Holmes to retrieve it. Failure to do so could result in the loss of many lives.

GUEST STARS:

Harry Andrews, Patricia Hodge
Dramatized by John Hawkesworth
Director: John Bruce

The Man with the Twisted Lip

Asked to track down missing husband, Neville St. Clair (curiously last seen at the window of a room in London's vilest opium den), Holmes' attention is drawn to a tramp who is pestering Mrs St. Clair. Holmes discovers that the 'tramp' is Neville – but what is the reason behind his double identity?

GUEST STARS:

Clive Francis, Eleanor David
Dramatized by Alan Plater
Director: Patrick Lau

The Priory School

Holmes takes on a case which must be conducted with the utmost secrecy. The Duke of Holdernesse's nine-year-old son has been kidnapped from his dormitory in the dead of night and Holmes and Watson embark on an eerie adventure high on the bleak Derbyshire moors.

GUEST STARS:

Alan Howard, Christopher Benjamin
Dramatized by T.R.Bowen
Director: John Madden

The Six Napoleons

Even Holmes is baffled by the seemingly pointless destruction of six stolen busts of Napoleon. But the discovery of a body near one emaciated Emperor throws new light on the case.

GUEST STARS:

Eric Sykes, Gerald Campion
Dramatized by John Kane
Director: David Carson

The Sign of Four

A two-hour film to mark the centenary of Holmes' first appearance. Following the strange disappearance of her father, the beautiful Miss Morstain has received each year a mysterious present of a rare and lustrous pearl. Now, on the day of the summons to meet her anonymous benefactor, she arrives at 221B Baker Street to consult Holmes. With Watson's help, Holmes pieces together a series of clues, and the pair embark on a thrilling chase down London's streets and waterways, in pursuit of a priceless hoard of Indian treasure and a murderer whose ominous trademark is 'the sign of four'.

GUEST STARS:

Jenny Seagrove, John Thaw, Ronald Lacey
Dramatized by John Hawkesworth
Director: Peter Hammond

Season Two

The Devil's Foot

Watson insists that Holmes takes a holiday in a small Cornish country cottage. But there is no rest for the great detective when a young woman is found dead.

Guest stars:

Denis Quilley, Damien Thomas
Dramatized by Gary Hopkins
Director: Brian Mills

Silver Blaze

A valuable racehorse, Silver Blaze, disappears mysteriously on the eve of a big race. Holmes sets off on the track of the horse and its kidnappers.

GUEST STARS:

Peter Barkworth, Malcolm Storry, Russell Hunter
Dramatized by John Hawkesworth
Director: Brian Mills

Wisteria Lodge

What is the secret of Wisteria Lodge? Holmes and Watson enter into a baffling case. A foreign tyrant, an English governess and an unorthodox police inspector lead them on a wild goose chase which starts with murder.

GUEST STARS:

Freddie Jones, Kika Markham, Donald Churchill
Dramatized by Jeremy Paul
Director: Peter Hammond

The Bruce-Partington Plans

A young man is found brutally beaten to death on a railway line. The plans of a secret submarine are found in his pocket. Is he a hero or a traitor?

GUEST STARS:

Charles Gray, Denis Lill, Geoffrey Bayldon
Dramatized by John Hawkesworth
Director: John Gorrie

The Hound of the Baskervilles

A two-hour film of the most famous of all Sherlock Holmes stories. A bizarre death and a missing boot lure Holmes to darkest Dartmoor to investigate the strange events at remote Baskerville Hall, particularly the legend regarding the Hound of Hell. Holmes' mission is to protect Sir Henry Baskerville from falling prey to the curse and the murderous greed of one of the locals who has a very good reason for wanting this latest Baskerville dead.

GUEST STARS:

Kristoffer Tabori, Ronald Pickup, James Faulkner
Dramatized by T.R. Bowen
Director: Brian Mills

The Case-Book of Sherlock Holmes

The Disappearance of Lady Frances Carfax

On holiday at a hotel in the Lake District, Watson becomes fascinated by one of his fellow guests, the enigmatic Lady Frances Carfax. When he relates to Holmes, 200 miles away in Baker Street, that Lady Frances's every move is observed from the fells by a strange black-bearded horseman, Holmes dashes north – just as Lady Frances disappears.

GUEST STARS:

Cheryl Campbell, Michael Jayston, Jack Klaff

Dramatized by T.R. Bowen
Director: John Madden

The Problem of Thor Bridge

Neil Gibson is prepared to spend a fortune to save Grace Dunbar from the gallows. But the evidence against her is overwhelming – until Holmes takes on the case.

GUEST STARS:

Daniel Massey, Catherine Russell, Celia Gregory

Dramatized by Jeremy Paul
Director: Michael Simpson

Shoscombe Old Place

If Sir Robert Norberton's horse loses in the Champion Stakes, he will be a ruined man. But who is the mysterious man that he meets in the church crypt?

GUEST STARS:

Robin Ellis, Frank Grimes
Dramatized by Gary Hopkins
Director: Patrick Lau

The Boscombe Valley Mystery

When an Australian-born farmer is murdered, his son stands accused of the crime. The local police inspector considers the case to be 'as plain as a pikestaff' but Alice Turner is convinced of the son's innocence and begs Holmes to investigate.

GUEST STARS:

Peter Vaughan, Joanna Roth, James Purefoy
Dramatized by John Hawkesworth
Director: June Howson

The Illustrious Client

The Austrian murderer, Baron Gruner, is considered to be the most dangerous man in Europe. Holmes is asked to help prevent him marrying a young English girl, but the great detective's intervention puts his own life at risk.

GUEST STARS:

Anthony Valentine, David Langton, Abigail Cruttenden
Dramatized by Robin Chapman
Director: Tim Sullivan

The Creeping Man

A dark, hunched silhouette at her bedroom window and the howling of her family's pet dog have terrified Edith Presbury, daughter of an eminent widowed professor. At first there seems little in the case to interest Holmes but a closer examination of the professor's engagement to a much younger girl reveals a deadly opponent. Miss Presbury must keep her door locked at all times.

GUEST STARS:

Charles Kay, Sarah Woodward, Adrian Lukis
Dramatized by Robin Chapman
Director: Tim Sullivan

THE ADVENTURES OF SHERLOCK
   HOLMES
Music: Patrick Gowers
Producer: Michael Cox
13 colour 60-minute episodes
(Season 1) UK: ITV 24 April - 5 June 1984
   (7 eps)
US: WGBH Boston 'Mystery' 14 March - 25
   April 1985
(Season 2) UK: ITV 25 Aug - 29 Sept 1985
   (6 eps)
US: WGBH 6 Feb - 13 March 1986

THE RETURN OF SHERLOCK HOLMES
Producer: June Wyndham Davies
Executive producer: Michael Cox
11 colour 60-minute episodes
(Season 1) UK: ITV 9 July - 20 Aug 1986
   (7 eps)
US: WGBH 5 Feb - 19 March 1987
(Season 2) UK: ITV 6 - 27 April 1988 (4 eps)
US: WGBH 27 Oct - 8 Dec 1988
The Sign of Four (colour 120-minutes)
UK: ITV 29 Dec 1987

THE HOUND OF THE BASKERVILLES
one colour 120-minute episode
UK: ITV 31 Aug 1988

THE CASE-BOOK OF SHERLOCK
   HOLMES
Producer: Michael Cox
6 colour 60-minute episodes
UK: ITV 21 Feb - 28 March 1991
A Granada Television Network Production

* Probably the most unusual TV characterization of the Baker Street sleuth was Tales of the Rodent Sherlock Holmes...starring Roland Rat. For cocaine, substitute cheese.

AFRICAN PATROL

This eminently forgettable series followed the exploits of British Patrol Inspector Paul Derek, who enforced the law in the East African jungle. He fought ivory poachers, gun runners and implausible scripts. The programme did have one good point. It was filmed entirely on location in East Africa, which at least meant that any animals seen were real and not cardboard cut-out wildebeest on a back lot at Shepperton. The star, John Bentley, later went on to play Hugh Mortimer, Meg's ill-fated husband in the much-mocked British soap opera, Crossroads, which must have made the jungle seem positively inviting by comparison.

REGULAR CAST

Inspector Derek   John Bentley

Music: Phil Green
Producer: Michael Sadler for *M.E. Productions*

Filmed by *Kenya Productions Ltd*

39 monochrome 30-minute episodes
UK: ITV 5 April 1958 - 6 February 1959
   (ATV)
US: Syndicated 1957

AGATHA CHRISTIE'S POIROT

'Poirot is the greatest lateral-thinking detective created in literature, far greater than Sherlock Holmes. He is a man of supreme intelligence, a walking brain.'   – DAVID SUCHET

Hercule Poirot is destined to be remembered as the only famous Belgian in history. The diminutive detective first appeared in The Mysterious Affair at Styles, Christie's debut novel published in 1920, and subsequently featured in 33 novels and 56 shorter stories, before returning to Styles in 1975 for the novel Curtain in which he died. It is believed that Christie came to actively dislike Poirot and that is why she had him killed off. Such is the power of the pen!

He has been played in movies by such illustrious names as Albert Finney and Peter Ustinov, although the latter was told in no uncertain terms by Christie's daughter, 'You're not Poirot. He is supposed to be small, dapper and bald.' But, as with Jeremy Brett and Holmes, it is a recent British television performance, by David Suchet, that has been hailed as the definitive portrayal of the character.

Poirot began detective work in Brussels but at the end of the First World War moved to London and shared rooms with his old friend Arthur Hastings. Soon he set up as a private detective, operating from a service flat in the splendid Whitehaven Mansions. He is 5ft 4ins tall and his egg-shaped head is carried slightly to the left-hand side. It is probably all those little grey cells weighing it down. His stick is embossed with a gold band, his watch keeps time exactly and he claims that his perfectly curled and generously waxed moustache is the finest in London. To say the least, he is eccentric.

In April 1936, Christie wrote a letter to her American publisher, purporting to come from Poirot. In it, 'he' summed up his idiosyncracies. 'Order and method are my Gods. In a bookcase I arrange the tallest books at the end, then the next tallest and so on. Medicine bottles are placed in a neatly graduated row. If your necktie were not correct, I should find it irresistible not to make it straight for you. For my breakfast, I have only toast which is cut into neat little squares. The eggs – there must be two – they must be identical in size.'

Poirot is a confirmed bachelor although he did once fall for a Russian countess and an English girl who made him fluffy omelettes. Not only would kissing a girl spoil his moustache but, he reasons: 'The marriage is not for me because in my time I have known five cases of women murdered by devoted husbands but twenty-two cases of men murdered by devoted wives...'

The part was a real challenge for David Suchet, brother of British newsreader, John. On filming days, he had to keep up Poirot's soft French accent throughout – even during meal breaks. 'If I had to keep going in and out of the voice, it would add an hour to my day,' he says. Once, after rehearsing his lines in the car on the way home, he greeted his family in Poirot-speak, unable to shake it off! Suchet is as meticulous in his preparation as the world-famous detective and read all the Poirot stories beforehand. He also concedes: 'I have the same eye for order as Poirot. I like things to be symmetrical. If I put two things on the mantelpiece, they have to be exactly evenly spaced.'

Suchet's assertion of Poirot's ability is difficult to dispute but it could be argued that the appearance of genius is heightened by the fact that, with the exception of his equally fastidious secretary Miss Lemon, Poirot's principal acquaintances are two men with barely a brain cell between them. Most clowns settle for one stooge; Poirot has two. First there is former army officer Captain Hastings, a ladies' man and accomplished sportsman with a passion for cars (he drives a dark green Lagonda). His upper lip is so stiff he could well have swallowed a packet of starch. The hard-of-thinking Hastings marvels at everything Poirot does. In that respect, he is not unlike a junior version of Dr Watson. The bombastic Belgian's friendly adversary is Inspector Japp who manages to turn up on virtually every case that Poirot investigates but never reaches the correct solution. His speciality is arresting everyone in sight before Poirot steps in to put him right. Japp secretly admires Poirot but understandably is irritated at constantly being beaten. If only he had some little grey cells of his own... Curiously David Suchet played a cockney Inspector Japp to Ustinov's Poirot in the film Thirteen at Dinner.

A former real Scotland Yard detective has poured scorn on Poirot's methods, pointing out that not only would he be thrown off the case by the police for interfering, but also that his habit of rounding up half a dozen suspects for the revelatory finale would never work in practice. 'You'd never get them all there voluntarily,' he explained. 'You'd have to arrest them. Then when the real culprit was exposed, the other five would sue for wrongful arrest!'

Notwithstanding these minor gripes, Agatha Christie's Poirot has been an outstanding success. It has been screened in over forty countries, including being dubbed into Turkish and Japanese. Suchet receives letters from all over the world, many of which he can't read because they are in Chinese.

The episodes take place in 1935, except for The Mysterious Affair at Styles which was set in 1917, and transmitted in September 1990 to celebrate the centenary of Christie's birth.

* Observe, 'Astings. The prototype for Poirot is believed to be Ignatius Paul Pollaky, a famous Austro-Hungarian detective who moved to England in 1850. He, too, had a splendid music-hall moustache.

* Ironically Christie herself never owned a television. She used to sneak into the back room where her housekeeper had a black and white set.

REGULAR CAST

Hercule Poirot David Suchet   *Captain Hastings* Hugh Fraser
Insp. (later Chief Insp.) Japp Philip Jackson   *Miss Lemon* Pauline Moran

Season One

The Adventure of the Clapham Cook

A respectable cook does not return to work in suburban London from a day's holiday. A city bank clerk absconds with £50,000. Poirot can find no apparent connection between the two incidents – until he discovers that a lodger in the cook's house works in the same bank as the vanished clerk. Putting his little grey cells to work, Poirot finds that the seemingly virtuous lodger had good reason for wanting the cook to leave in such haste.

GUEST STARS:

Brigit Forsyth, Dermot Crowley
Dramatized by Clive Exton
Director: Edward Bennett

Murder In The Mews

Against the background of Guy Fawkes Night, Poirot and Japp investigate what at first appears to be the suicide of a young widow, Mrs Allen. Her engagement to aspiring Member of Parliament, Charles Laverton-West, draws the case into the areas of scandal – something Poirot is always sensitive to avoid. But Mrs Allen's unhappy past is the key to a most unusual murder.

GUEST STARS:

David Yelland, Juliette Mole, James
    Faulkner
Dramatized by Clive Exton
Director: Edward Bennett

The Adventure of Johnnie Waverly

Poirot is called in by wealthy landowner, Marcus Waverly, to safeguard the security of his three-year-old son, Johnnie, who has been threatened with kidnap. Despite precautions at Waverly's country home, the boy is seized. Poirot realizes the crime had to be the work of a close relation.

GUEST STARS:

Geoffrey Bateman, Julia Chambers,
    Patrick Jordan
Dramatized by Clive Exton
Director: Renny Rye

Four and Twenty Blackbirds

While dining in his favourite London restaurant, Poirot is fascinated to hear a waitress describe how one of her regular customers has suddenly and completely changed the habits of a lifetime. The customer, whose practice it is to dine on Tuesdays and Thursdays, unexpectedly appears on a Monday and orders dishes he wouldn't normally touch. Naturally Poirot feels impelled to follow this story which leads him on a trail of murder and an ill-gotten inheritance.

GUEST STARS:

Richard Howard, Holly De Jong, Tony
    Aitken
Dramatized by Russell Murray
Director: Renny Rye

The Third Floor Flat

Poirot is disturbed one night in his London apartment by two young couples who have stumbled across the murdered body of Mrs Ernestine Grant, in the third-floor flat below. The police are convinced it is the work of an outsider but Poirot's suspicions are aroused by the seemingly innocent quartet who first awoke him. It transpires that bigamy is the issue and revenge the motive.

GUEST STARS:

Suzanne Burden, Amanda Elwes, Josie
    Lawrence, Robert Hines, Nicholas
    Pritchard
Dramatized by Michael Baker
Director: Edward Bennett

Triangle At Rhodes

Poirot is on holiday in Rhodes when one of his fellow hotel guests, Mrs Valentine Chantry, is murdered by a poisoned pink gin. Gradually our hero unravels a complicated set of love and hate relationships between assembled guests, culminating in the most unlikely romantic culprits.

GUEST STARS:

Peter Settelen, Annie Lambert, Frances
    Low, Angela Down
Dramatized by Stephen Wakelam
Director: Renny Rye

Problem At Sea

Relaxing on a Mediterranean cruise, Poirot's professional interest is aroused by some of his travelling companions, especially Colonel and Adeline Clapperton and the admiring Miss Ellie Henderson. When the boat docks for a day visit to Alexandria, the Colonel goes ashore, only to discover on his return that his wife has been murdered in their cabin.

GUEST STARS:

Sheila Allen, John Normington, Ann
    Firbank
Dramatized by Clive Exton
Director: Renny Rye

The Incredible Theft

Lord Mayfield, a first-class engineer and aircraft manufacturer, hosts a weekend party in his country house as a front to trap Mrs Vanderlyn, a suspected spy, into stealing the specifications for a new bomber. The plan backfires when the documents disappear. Against her husband's wishes, Lady Mayfield summons Poirot who reveals a truth not entirely to their liking.

GUEST STARS:

John Stride, John Carson, Phyllida Law, Carmen De Sautoy, Ciaren Madden
Dramatized by David Reid
Director: Edward Bennett

The King of Clubs

Starlet Valerie Saintclaire is the sole witness to the killing of unsavoury impressario Henry Reedburn. Valerie's fiance, Prince Paul of Maurania, asks Poirot to visit the scene of the crime and absolve her from suspicion. Poirot comes up trumps when he proves that an alibi of a game of bridge is false, with the King of Clubs the vital clue.

GUEST STARS:

Niamh Cusack, David Swift, Gawn Grainger, Jack Klaff
Dramatized by Clive Exton
Director: Renny Rye

The Dream

Can a man be induced by hypnosis to dream so clearly of suicide that he is driven to commit the act against his own wishes? This is the problem posed to Poirot by eccentric millionaire Benedict Farley – a fantasy which becomes all too real when Farley is later found dead, supposedly by his own hand. Poirot unearths a more plausible explanation.

GUEST STARS:

Alan Howard, Joely Richardson, Mary Tamm
Dramatized by Clive Exton
Director: Edward Bennett

Season Two

Peril At End House

Poirot and Hastings are holidaying on the Cornish Riviera when a chance meeting with Miss Buckley of nearby End House, provides Poirot with the stimulation on which his little grey cells thrive.

GUEST STARS:

Jeremy Young, John Harding, Polly Walker
Dramatized by Clive Exton
Director: Renny Rye

The Veiled Lady

While Japp is concerned with a daring jewel robbery, Poirot and Hastings have a meeting with a lady determined to keep her anonymity. But Poirot finds unexpected secrets behind the veil.

GUEST STARS:

Frances Barber, Terence Harvey, Carole Hayman
Dramatized by Clive Exton
Director: Edward Bennett

The Lost Mine

The game of Monopoly is the latest fashion and Hastings is determined to prove to Poirot that skill is the secret of winning...which probably means that Hastings will struggle to get past Go. But a visit to the bank makes Poirot realize that there are London streets not featured on the Monopoly board – and different skills are required.

GUEST STARS:

Anthony Bate, Gloria Connell
Dramatized by Michael Baker and David Renwick
Director: Edward Bennett

The Cornish Mystery

The village of Polgarwith is not a place where

secrets can be kept. But when Mrs Pengelley believes her life is in danger and sends for Poirot and Hastings, the pair find that the villagers swiftly close ranks against outsiders.

GUEST STARS:

Amanda Walker, Tilly Vosburgh, Jerome
   Willis
Dramatized by Clive Exton
Director: Edward Bennett

The Disappearance of Mr Davenheim

Japp believes he's on to easy money when Poirot accepts his wager to solve the mysterious disappearance of City banker, Matthew Davenheim, without ever leaving Whitehaven Mansions. But his bet is not so safe when Hastings pursues Poirot's oblique questions with commendable conviction.

GUEST STARS:

Mel Martin, Kenneth Colley
Dramatized by David Renwick
Director: Andrew Grieve

Double Sin

Whitcombe is the place for health. But when Poirot takes Hastings on a rest cure, the climate is more bracing than they expect and the locals more complex than they appear.

GUEST STARS:

Elspet Gray, David Hargreaves, Michael
   J. Shannon
Dramatized by Clive Exton
Director: Richard Spence

The Adventure of The Cheap Flat

Plans for a new submarine are stolen from the US Navy and Japp is detailed to assist the FBI in its investigations. Although he abhors American crime-busting techniques, Poirot finds the case irresistible.

GUEST STARS:

Samantha Bond, William Hootkins, John
   Michie
Dramatized by Russell Murray
Director: Richard Spence

The Kidnapped Prime Minister

The Prime Minister's speech at the Disarmament Conference is eagerly anticipated. But when Poirot is summoned to the Foreign Office, he learns that the political stability of his adoptive country is at stake.

GUEST STARS:

David Horovitch, Henry Moxon, Ronald
   Hines, Lisa Harrow
Dramatized by Clive Exton
Director: Andrew Grieve

The Adventure of The Western Star

Society magazine The Tatler is full of the news of the rival diamonds belonging to Lady Yardly and Marie Marvelle. However, Poirot finds himself involved in more than society scandal when both ladies receive threatening letters.

GUEST STARS:

Caroline Goodall, Rosalind Bennett,
   Bruce Montague
Dramatized by Clive Exton
Director: Richard Spence

The Mysterious Affair at Styles

The very first Poirot story. A two-hour production, it is set in 1917 with the then Lt Hastings recovering from war injuries. He receives an invitation to visit his friends, the Cavendish family, at Styles St Mary and staying nearby as their guests, is a group of Belgian refugees including, to Hastings' surprise, an old acquaintance – Hercule Poirot. So when a grisly murder occurs, Hastings immediately calls in Poirot to help, and the pair pit their wits against family machinations, manipulation, greed and betrayal. It is the start of an enduring working friendship.

GUEST STARS:

David Rintoul, Beatie Edney, Anthony
   Calf, Morris Perry
Dramatized by Clive Exton
Director: Ross Devenish

Season Three

How Does Your Garden Grow?

When Poirot has a rose named in his honour at the Chelsea Flower Show, the ceremony attracts more than casual interest. But a packet of seeds donated by an admirer, a wheelchair-bound old lady, sets the sleuth on a baffling case. For when the old lady is found poisoned by oysters laced with strychnine, the packet of Catherine the Great stock seeds provides a vital clue. She knew her life was in danger, but was it from an expatriate Russian girl fleeing from Stalin's regime or from the greed of those speculating in stocks and shares?

GUEST STARS:

Catherine Russell, Anne Stallybrass, Tim Wylton, Margery Mason
Dramatized by Andrew Marshall
Director: Brian Farnham

The Million Dollar Bond Robbery

The future of the London and Scottish Bank is riding on its shipment of liberty bonds to New York, on the inaugural sailing of the Queen Mary. Poirot endeavours to overcome the dreadful curse of sea-sickness to accompany them and so ensure their safe passage. But the bonds are switched before boarding.

GUEST STARS:

David Quilter, Ewan Hooper, Paul Young
Dramatized by Anthony Horowitz
Director: Andrew Grieve

The Plymouth Express

Poirot's advice is sought by an Australian shipping magnate worried about fortune hunters chasing his newly-separated daughter. But he soon finds himself involved in the chase to find vicious killers who have greed as a motive.

GUEST STARS:

John Stone, Marion Bailey, Alfredo Michelson

Dramatized by Rod Beacham
Director: Andrew Piddington

Wasps' Nest

Hastings finds intrigue and mystery in the picture when he experiments with a new camera at a garden fete he visits with Poirot and Japp. The little Belgian is soon caught up in a tale of jealousy, revenge and wasps, while Japp ends up in hospital with appendicitis.

GUEST STARS:

Martin Turner, Melanie Jessop, Peter Capaldi
Dramatized by David Renwick
Director: Brian Farnham

The Tragedy At Marsdon Manor

Ghost stories abound in the Norfolk village of Marsdon Leigh. The locals take their legends very seriously and so does Poirot. When murder strikes this rural backwater, the detective is drawn into the supernatural. The key to the killing turns out to be a disturbed blackbird's nest.

GUEST STARS:

Ian McCulloch, Geraldine Alexander, Neil Duncan
Dramatized by David Renwick
Director: Renny Rye

The Double Clue

For the first time in his life Poirot, normally impervious to womanly wiles, falls in love. The object of his unaccustomed affection is a beautiful Russian, the Countess Vera Rossakoff, newly arrived from the Soviet Union. They meet during his investigation into four jewel robberies and go for a picnic in the country. But the course of true love does not run smooth as the lady has criminal intent.

GUEST STARS:

Kika Markham, David Lyon, Nicholas Selby
Dramatized by Anthony Horowitz
Director: Andrew Piddington

The Mystery of the Spanish Chest

On a visit to the opera, Poirot learns of a society love tangle. Later at a party, he dances the Charleston unaware that a few yards away a body has been concealed in a chest. He is thus an unwitting witness to murder and Chief Inspector Japp must do his duty and interview him.

GUEST STARS:

John McEnery, Pip Torrens, Antonia Pemberton
Dramatized by Anthony Horowitz
Director: Andrew Grieve

The Theft of the Royal Ruby

Poirot intends spending Christmas alone but is accosted outside a chocolate shop by a drunken Prince Farouk of Egypt and driven to the Foreign Office. Farouk's precious ruby has been stolen by a female companion and the solution to the theft could lie at the stately home of a British colonel. It is in the national interest that Poirot should spend the festive season there to unravel the crime.

GUEST STARS:

Nigel Le Vaillant, Frederick Treves, Stephanie Cole
Dramatized by: Anthony Horowitz and Clive Exton
Director: Andrew Grieve

The Affair at the Victory Ball

Viscount Cronshaw and beautiful actress Coco Courtney have a blazing row at a society ball. Just before midnight, with the party in full swing, Cronshaw is discovered in the supper room with a table knife through his heart. Japp arrives to investigate but Poirot is already on the case.

GUEST STARS:

Haydn Gwynne, Nathaniel Parker, Mark Crowdy
Dramatized by: Andrew Marshall
Director: Renny Rye

The Mystery of Hunter's Lodge

Hastings and Poirot are invited to take part in a grouse shoot on the estate of Harrington Pace. But their stay is marred when firstly Harrington is accidentally injured and then later that night he is shot dead by a mysterious bearded stranger. And the housekeeper suddenly disappears. Poirot sets out on the trail of the ruthless killer – with a little help from man's best friend.

GUEST STARS:

Roy Boyd, Bernard Horsfall, Jim Norton
Dramatized by: T.R. Bowen
Director: Renny Rye

Music: Christopher Gunning
Producer: Brian Eastman
Executive producers: Nick Elliott and Linda Agran (Season One) Nick Elliott (Seasons Two and Three)

London Weekend Production

one colour 120-minute episode and 29 colour 60-minute episodes
(Season 1): UK: ITV 8 Jan - 19 March 1989 (10 eps)
US: WGBH Boston 'Mystery' 18 Jan - 15 March 1990
(Season 2): UK: 7 Jan - 4 March 1990 (9 eps)
US: 10 Jan - 14 March 1991
The Mysterious Affair at Styles: UK: 16 September 1990
(Season 3): UK: 6 Jan - 10 March 1991 (10 eps)

* In 1982, Thames Television produced a 13-week series The Agatha Christie Hour, but these tended to be love stories and psychological studies rather than mysteries, and are therefore not included here. For the record, they were screened in Britain on ITV 7 September - 16 November 1982 and in the States somehow qualified for WGBH Boston's 'Mystery' (I suspect on the author's name alone). Four episodes were shown there between 17 February and 10 March 1983 and six more from 31 January to 7 March 1985.

ALIEN NATION

'What I want to do here is explore the conflicting conditions of justice and prejudice that we've all experienced, but in a way that is one step removed from reality.'   – CREATOR KEN JOHNSON

Alien Nation is a science-fiction series, a cop show and a soap opera all rolled into one. A spin-off from the 1988 movie of the same name, Alien Nation is set in 1995 Los Angeles and explores the assimilation process of alien 'newcomers' into the California of the future.

The newcomers' spaceship crash-landed in the Mojave desert in 1992 and in the ensuing three years they had mastered the English language and adopted many of man's best – and worst – traits. The story centres on the complex and strained relationship between Matthew Sikes, a blunt and streetwise L.A. cop, and the more refined George Francisco, the first alien to achieve the rank of detective (although some would say that Columbo looked as if he came from another planet).

The series blends a futuristic police drama with the cultural clash between the two men. Also featured are Francisco's family – dedicated wife, Susan, rebellious teenage son, Buck, and nine-year-old daughter, Emily – as they strive to be accepted by the human population. Americans warmed to the series immediately. Emmy Magazine called it 'adventurous, innovative, thought-provoking.' They clearly thought it was out of this world.

REGULAR CAST

Detective Matthew Sikes Gary Graham
Detective George Francisco Eric Pierpoint
Susan Francisco Michele Scarabelli   *Buck Francisco* Sean Six
Emily Francisco Lauren Woodland

Creator: Ken Johnson
Producer: Ken Johnson

A Kenneth Johnson Production in association with Twentieth Century Fox Television

One colour 120-minute episode and 21 colour 60-minute episodes US: FBC 18 Sept 1989 - 17 Sept 1990
UK: British Sky Broadcasting From 3 October 1990

THE AMAZING CHAN AND THE CHAN CLAN

One of the worst cartoons from the prolific Hanna-Barbera stable, this was an ill-advised attempt to do a kiddies' version of the stories of Charlie Chan. The plot (if that's not too strong a word) concerned the efforts of Charlie's myriad offspring to help him crack cases. The only point of interest was that the voice of Chan was provided by Keye Luke who once played his Number One Son.

Music: Hoyt Curtin

A Hanna-Barbera Production

16 colour 25-minute episodes
US: CBS 9 Sept 1972 - 22 Sept 1974

THE AMAZING MR. MALONE

Even in the grey days of the early 1950s there was a tendency to spice up shows for television. A prime example was The Amazing Mr Malone, a live series about criminal lawyer John J. Malone created in the novels by Craig Rice. In print, Malone had been a heavy- drinking, irresponsible Chicago lawyer, on American radio (where he had been heard since 1947) he was cynical and humourless, but for TV he suddenly acquired a personality and became a wise-cracking dude with a girl on each arm. Malone was played by Lee Tracy who went on to become better known as Martin Kane. The Amazing Mr Malone alternated on ABC with Mr District Attorney.

REGULAR CAST

John J. Malone Lee Tracy

Director: Edgar Peterson
Producer: Edward Peterson

13 monochrome 30-minute episodes
US: ABC 24 Sept 1951 - 10 March 1952

An ABC Production

AMY PRENTISS

When the Chief of Detectives of the San Francisco Police Department died suddenly, the person at the head of the list of succession was Amy Prentiss, a 35-year-old widow with a young daughter. She was the first woman Chief of Detectives in the history of the department and a number of the male officers resented her promotion. But dogged Amy won them over, which is more than she did with the viewers, as only three episodes were made. They were screened in the US as part of the NBC Sunday Mystery Movie along with Columbo, McCloud and McMillan and Wife.

REGULAR CAST

Amy Prentiss Jessica Walter   *Detective Tony Russell* Steve Sandor
Detective Rod Pena Arthur Metrano   *Detective Contreras* Johnny Seven
Jill Prentiss Helen Hunt   *Joan Carter* Gwenn Mitchell

Mystery Movie Theme: Henry Mancini
Producer: Cy Chermak

A Universal Television Production

One colour 90-minute episode, 2 colour
120-minute episodes
US: NBC 1 Dec 1974 - 2 Feb 1975
UK: ITV 30 May 1976

THE ANDY GRIFFITH SHOW

Andy Griffith has been one of America's most popular performers for years, although in Britain he has only recently attracted attention as an ace TV lawyer (SEE MATLOCK). The Andy Griffith Show was a long-running comedy favourite in the States, spanning eight years.

It was very much a borderline cop show because, although Griffith played a present-day small-town sheriff, there was so little crime that the action was more domestic than detective.

The setting was the North Californian town of Mayberry whose law enforcer was Sheriff Andy Taylor, a thoughtful widower with a young son, Opie. The pair lived with Andy's Aunt Bee. Andy's dim deputy was his cousin, the daydreaming Barney Fife. The only thing he ever put behind bars was a crate of beer. Fife was played by Don Knotts who, along with another of the show's regulars, Jim Nabors, went on to star in series of their own.

Note that Opie was played by little Ronny Howard, later to become a stalwart of Happy Days.

REGULAR CAST

Andy Taylor Andy Griffith   *Opie Taylor* Ronny Howard
Barney Fife Don Knotts   *Gomer Pyle* Jim Nabors
Aunt Bee Taylor Frances Bavier

Music: Earle Hagen
Producers: Aaron Ruben, Richard O. Linke, Bob Ross
Executive producer: Sheldon Leonard

A Mayberry Production for CBS

149 monochrome 30-minute episodes
100 colour 30-minute episodes
US: CBS 3 Oct 1960 - 16 Sept 1968

ARCHER

Based on the private eye hero of Ross MacDonald's successful mystery novels, Archer should have been a big hit. It wasn't. That in itself is a mystery but the popular belief is that, because it was screened in the 1970s at a time when every TV detective had a gimmick (like wearing a shabby mac, riding a horse or sucking a lollipop), poor old Archer was simply too normal to catch on.

The series was set in Melrose, California, among the idle rich. Lew Archer was an ex-cop who preferred brain to brawn when it came to solving crimes. He was basically a pretty decent sort of chap although he wasn't beyond bending the law a little – but all in the cause of seeing that justice was done. In the pilot for the series, Peter Graves played Archer but was hopelessly mis-cast and Brian Keith took over. Earlier in 1966, MacDonald's character had been adapted for the Paul Newman film, Harper, the name being changed from Archer to comply with Newman's apparent liking for titles beginning with an H!

REGULAR CAST

Lew Archer Brian Keith   *Lt Barney Brighton* John P. Ryan

Music: Jerry Goldsmith
Producers: Jack Miller, Leonard B. Kaufman
Executive producer: David Carp

A Paramount Television Production

7 colour 60-minute episodes
US: NBC 30 Jan 1975 - 13 March 1975

ARMCHAIR DETECTIVE

This was an early attempt to turn sleuthing into a game show. Each week, the chosen few from the audience watched two one-act whodunnits which contained clues to the solution. At the end, all was revealed by H. Allen Smith, a member of the California State Legislature. The person who solved the mystery correctly won a prize. It's an incentive that even Shaw Taylor hasn't tried – catch a crook, win a washer.

REGULAR CAST

Mr Crime Interrogator John Milton Kennedy   *Mr Crime Authority* H. Allen Smith

Producer: Mike Stokey

A CBS Production

13 monochrome 30-minute episodes
US: CBS 6 July - 28 Sept 1949

ARREST AND TRIAL

The innovative Sixties series Arrest and Trial can take the credit – or blame – for the format adopted by so many of the TV movies of today. Each 90-minute programme was split into two halves. The first segment showed the crime, the police investigation and the arrest; the second featured the trial. The principal character in the first half was always Los Angeles police detective Nick Anderson, while the second half was dominated by defence attorney, John Egan, who was intent on getting Anderson's arrestee off the hook. It was simple and effective and the combination of police action and courtroom drama has been imitated ever since. The latest show to copy the idea is Law and Order.

REGULAR CAST

Det. Sgt Nick Anderson Ben Gazzara   *Attorney John Egan* Chuck Connors
Deputy District Attorney Jerry Miller John Larch
Assistant Deputy D.A. Barry Pine John Kerr   *Det. Sgt Dan Kirby* Roger Perry

Producer: Frank P. Rosenberg

A Revue Production for Universal

30 monochrome 90-minute episodes
US: ABC 15 Sept 1963 - 19 April 1964
UK: BBC1 24 April - 3 Nov 1964

THE ASPHALT JUNGLE

This hard-hitting cop show bore little relation to the 1950 film of the same title. It starred Jack Warden as Deputy Police Commissioner Matthew Gower, a man determined to break the organized crime rings that were plaguing the unnamed city under his jurisdiction. To this end, he appointed a special squad of select officers headed by Captain Gus Honochek and Sergeant Danny Keller. The pair took part in plenty of undercover operations and were regularly joined by Gower who, despite his lofty rank, was not one to sit behind a desk all day, playing with his crime statistics. It was adequate enough fare but is probably best remembered for Duke Ellington's classy background music.

REGULAR CAST

Dep. Commissioner Matthew Gower Jack Warden
Captain Gus Honochek Arch Johnson   *Sgt Danny Keller* Bill Smith

EPISODE TITLES

The Burglary Ring
The Lady and the Lawyer
The Friendly Gesture
The Gomez Affair
The Sniper
The Last Way Out
The McMasters Story
The Nine-Twenty Hero
The Professor
The Fighter

The Kidnapping
Dark Night
The Scott Machine

An MGM Production for ABC

13 monochrome 60-minute episodes
US: ABC 2 April - 24 Sept 1961

AUTOMAN

It had to happen in this computer age – a hologram detective. Its creator was Los Angeles police computer expert, Walter Nebicher, who thought up computer games in his spare time. It was an innocuous enough pursuit until one day an example of his handiwork, called Automan, leaped from the screen and changed Walter's life. Before this momentous event, Walter's superiors had considered him far more suited to software than the hardware needed to tackle crime on the streets but, thanks to Automan, he was able to combat the most ruthless international villains.

Neither Walter's irascible boss, Captain Boyd, nor his minder on the force, Lieutenant Curtis, knew of Automan's existence and were bewildered by Nebicher's remarkable success rate. Since Walter had programmed everything, the handsome Automan was really his alter-ego. Automan had certain advantages over mere mortals – like the ability to walk through walls and make objects appear and disappear. He was assisted by Cursor (the tiny dot on the screen) which accompanied Walter and his invention and, at their request, would outline a getaway car which would then promptly materialize. On a more human side, Automan had a smile so broad as to make Liberace look sour-faced. He could bring women to their knees at a thousand paces. But there was one drawback. Automan used so much energy that lights around him dimmed and he faded away completely at dawn, when the city's electrical consumption started to rise. This left Walter in the mire. For without Automan, he had lost his byte.

REGULAR CAST

Automan Chuck Wagner   *Walter Nebicher* Desi Arnaz Jr
Lt Jack Curtis Robert Lansing   *Capt. E.G. Boyd* Gerald S. O'Loughlin
Roxanne Caldwell Heather McNair

Creator: Glen A. Larson
Producer: Glen A. Larson

A Glen A. Larson Production for ABC

One colour 90-minute episode 12 colour 60-minute episodes
US: ABC 15 Dec 1983 - 2 April 1984
UK: BBC1 12 May - 28 August 1984

B.A.D. CATS

A show which lived up to the first half of its contrived title. Ocee James and Nick Donovan were two free-wheeling, stock car racing cops who worked for 'Burglary Auto Detail, Commercial Auto Thefts' (B.A.D. CATS, geddit?) in the Los Angeles Police Department. They were helped out by a young Michelle Pfeiffer, as beautiful back-up cop 'Sunshine' Samantha Jensen and by their resident informant Rodney Washington, owner of a car repossession agency. With endless car chases, it came over as a pale imitation of Starsky and Hutch. Yes, it was that bad.

REGULAR CAST

Ocee James Steven Hanks   *Nick Donovan* Asher Brauner
Samantha Jensen Michelle Pfeiffer   *Capt. Skip Nathan* Vic Morrow
Rodney Washington Jimmie Walker

Music: Barry De Vorzon, Mundell Lowe
Andrew Kulberg
Producer: Everett Chambers
Executive producers: Aaron Spelling,
Douglas S. Cramer *A Spelling-Cramer
Production for ABC*

6 colour 60-minute episodes US: ABC
4 Jan - 8 Feb 1980
UK: ITV From 11 Dec 1980

B.L. STRYKER

No, not an old series about industrial unrest at the Longbridge car plant but a new, light detective show backed financially by Tom 'Magnum' Selleck and starring Burt Reynolds. B.L. Stryker is a character with whom Reynolds himself can identify. He admits: 'Stryker has a history like mine. His failings have been my failings.' Stryker is a one-time college footballer (like Reynolds) who went on to serve in Vietnam, was an amateur boxer and had a distinguished career with the New Orleans Police Department. In fact he is macho man personified.

He left the force after an altercation with a serial killer and returned to his home town of Palm Beach, Florida, with his pal Oz, a former heavyweight boxing champion. Stryker lives on a rundown houseboat and drives a battered old Cadillac, his lifestyle and principles immediately clashing with those of the rich and powerful in Palm Beach. Stryker would just as soon spend his time fishing but, to pay the rent, satisfy his investigative mind and, usually, to help out a friend, he takes on cases as a private eye. Besides, he's still a good detective even though he can't knit like Miss Marple. As Oz says: 'The man sure can hit.'

The other regular is award-winning actress, Rita Moreno, as Stryker's ex-wife Kimberly. Since their divorce, she has re-married four times, each of her husbands being wealthier than the last – as she reminds Stryker whenever possible.

REGULAR CAST

B.L. Stryker Burt Reynolds   *Oz Jackson* Ossie Davis
Kimberly Baskin Rita Moreno

Producer: Alan Barnette
Executive producers: Tom Selleck, Burt
  Reynolds

12 colour 120-minute episodes
US: ABC From 13 Feb 1989
UK: ITV 27 April - 25 May 1991

*A TWS Production in association with
  Universal Television*

BANACEK

Banacek's gimmick was that the central character was ethnic, from that much-maligned group the Polish-Americans. Played by George Peppard some ten years before The A-Team, the super-smooth Thomas Banacek was a modern-day bounty hunter. He made his living by collecting rewards from insurance companies, as a result of solving crimes involving valuable stolen property. The more the goods were worth, the more Banacek, on a ten per cent finder's fee, was able to pocket.

It was a lucrative business, providing him with a home in the exclusive Beacon Hill area of Boston. He was driven around in style by his chauffeur, Jay, while his other pal, Felix, ran a local bookshop. For the second season, Carlie, an insurance agent, was brought in to add some romantic interest. The series stemmed from a 1971 pilot titled Detour to Nowhere and, in the US, was part of NBC's Wednesday Mystery Movie. Banacek may not have been a world-beater, but Polish-Americans, the butt of so many Stateside jokes, loved it. Perhaps it was the liberal sprinkling of Polish proverbs in the show, that earned it an award from the Polish-American Congress for portraying Polish-Americans in a positive manner. It wasn't exactly an Emmy but it's the thought that counts.

REGULAR CAST

Thomas Banacek George Peppard   *Jay Drury* Ralph Manza
Felix Mulholland Murray Matheson   *Carlie Kirkland* Christine Belford

EPISODE TITLES

The Greatest Collection of Them All
Let's Hear it for a Living Legend
A Million the Hard Way
No Sign of the Cross
Project Phoenix
To Steal a King
The Two Million Clams of Cap'n Jack
Ten Thousand Dollars a Page
A Horse of a Slightly Different Colour

If Max Is So Smart, Why Doesn't He
  Tell Us Where He Is?
Rocket to Oblivion
Fly Me - If You Can Find Me
No Stone Unturned
Now You See It, Now You Don't
The Three Million Dollar Piracy
The Vanishing Chalice

Creator: Anthony Wilson
Producer: Howie Horowitz
Executive producer: George Eckstein

A Universal Television Production

16 colour 90-minute episodes
US: NBC 13 Sept 1972 - 3 Sept 1974
UK: ITV 8 July 1975 - 23 Dec 1977

BANYON

Operating out of Los Angeles in the late 1930s, Miles C. Banyon was a tough but fair private eye, who took on any case for twenty dollars a day. His running costs were reduced by the helpful Peggy Revere, whose secretarial school was situated in the same building as Banyon's office, and who provided him each week with a new secretary – free. Mind you, the quality of the girls was variable, ranging from bright city types, who had all their diplomas on show, to country farm girls who thought Pitman's shorthand was a mining injury.

Banyon resisted the tempting temps as well as the clutches of his girlfriend Abby, a nightclub singer whose favourite tune was the wedding march. Banyon was a pretty humourless guy which is probably why the series never really took off. But all was not wasted. The show's successor, City of Angels, which fared a little better, was able to use the same building for the hero's office.

REGULAR CAST

Miles C. Banyon Robert Forster   *Peggy Revere* Joan Blondell
Abby Graham Julie Gregg   *Lt Pete McNeil* Richard Jaeckel

Producer: Richard Allen Simmons
Executive producer: Quinn Martin

A Quinn Martin Production for Warner Bros

13 colour 60-minute episodes
US: NBC 15 Sept 1972 - 12 Jan 1973
UK: ITV From 26 Aug 1975

BARETTA

'If all of TV was Mary Tyler Moore and The Waltons, we'd have the same or more violence in the country.'   – ROBERT BLAKE

Blake was the star of Baretta, a show repeatedly accused of being too violent. Sure, there was plenty of rugged action but Blake, who actually opposed wanton violence on TV, was unnecessarily pilloried. Compared to Miami Vice and some German cop shows, it was like a genteel vicar's tea party.

A former child actor, Blake was originally asked to take over the lead in the police drama, Toma, after its star, Tony Musante, had quit. However Toma was only a moderate success, not a big enough vehicle for Blake, and so the title, the setting and a few other details were changed, and Toma became Baretta. ABC wanted to call the show Johnny Baretta but Blake said that sounded like a pizza parlour. So the network settled for just Baretta and anyway his christian name changed to Tony.

It was Blake's actress wife, Sondra, who made occasional guest appearances during the programme's three-year run, that invented the background for her husband's character. And so Baretta became the orphaned son of poor Italian immigrants, his dad was a street hustler, his mum a prostitute. When Tony came out of the navy, he had two options – earn a living off the streets, in which case he would probably end up in prison, or become a cop. He chose the latter and turned into one of the most unconventional police detectives in Los Angeles.

He was certainly an unlikely-looking law enforcer, dressed in T-shirt and jeans and usually with a cap pulled down over his forehead. But his scruffy appearance, which at times made Columbo look like Donald Trump, worked to his advantage, as he was able to infiltrate gangs of downbeats with total plausibility. Neither did he retire to some fancy apartment off-duty, instead staying at the run-down King Edward Hotel. It had one star... which you could see through the ceiling. Baretta knew the city like the back of his hand and was a master of disguise, even dressing up as an old lady when the need arose.

From the first episode he set out to nail the gangsters who shot his girlfriend in mistake for him. He always worked alone, disregarding the advice of his boss, Inspector Schiller (for the first season) and then Lieutenant Brubaker. Like all the best cops on the street, Baretta needed good contacts. These included Billy Truman, a retired cop who became house detective at the King Edward Hotel, and Rooster, a jive-talking pimp. Rooster provided comic relief along with Fred, Baretta's pet cockatoo, which became the show's trademark. Another feature was Baretta's distinctive pronunciation – he always said 'Eye-talian' for Italian and 'dat' for that, all of which helped to give the series a strong youth appeal, to the extent that it rose to the ninth ranked show in the US and won Blake an Emmy for Best Actor.

The anti-violence brigade would doubtless have been pleased to learn that Robert Blake himself was a victim of an attack on the show – from his supposed pet. On one occasion the cockatoo chased the actor all around the set, pecking him furiously because Blake had been waving his arms about, pretending to issue bird commands. The bird's trainer sprang to his feathered friend's defence, stating that Blake was 'trying to impress the crew and Fred gets mad if he thinks people handling him don't know what they're doing!'

REGULAR CAST

Detective Tony Baretta Robert Blake   *Inspector Schiller* Dana Elcar
Lt Hal Brubaker Edward Grover   *Billy Truman* Tom Ewell
Rooster Michael D. Roberts   *Fats* Chino Williams

Creator: Stephen J. Cannell
Theme song: *Keep Your Eye on the Sparrow* sung by Sammy Davis Jnr
Music: Dave Grusin, Tom Scott
Producer: Jo Swerling Jnr
Executive producers: Roy Huggins, Bernard L. Kowalski, Anthony Spinner for *Public Arts/Universal*

81 colour 60-minute episodes
US: ABC (Season 1) 17 Jan 1975 - 30 April 1975 (13 eps)
(Season 2) 10 Sept 1975 - 24 March 1976 (21 eps)
(Season 3) 22 Sept 1976 - 6 April 1977 (24 eps)
(Season 4) 28 Sept 1977 - 18 May 1978 (23 eps)
UK: ITV 6 Jan 1978 - 3 March 1979

BARLOW AT LARGE

The aggressive Charlie Barlow had risen rapidly through the ranks of TV detectives since the days when he was a uniformed Sergeant in The Days of Vengeance and then an Inspector on Z Cars. The character was so popular (although not with the real police) that he had grown too big for both Z Cars and its successor, Softly, Softly. So Elwyn Jones, the driving force behind Softly, Softly, promoted cheerless Charlie to the Home Office in Barlow At Large.

By now he was a Detective Chief Superintendent, but a lofty perch didn't make him any less obstinate, and he endured a difficult relationship with his new superior, the smarmy A.G. Fenton. Barlow didn't suffer fools gladly. In fact, he didn't suffer anyone gladly.

This was followed by a further spin-off, Barlow, but although both series were of the immaculate standard expected from BBC drama, the central character looked a little lost without his old mate John Watt, who was still with Softly, Softly. (SEE ALSO SOFTLY, SOFTLY, Z CARS)

REGULAR CAST

Det. Chief Supt Barlow Stratford Johns   *A.G. Fenton* Neil Stacy
Det. Sgt Rees Norman Comer   *Det. Insp. Tucker* Derek Newark

Creator: Elwyn Jones
Producer: Keith Williams
Executive producer: Leonard Lewis

A BBC Television Production

Barlow at Large
14 colour 50-minute episodes
UK: BBC1 15 Sept 1971 - 11 April 1973

Barlow
16 colour 50-minute episodes
UK: BBC1 23 Jan 1974 - 26 Feb 1975

BARNABY JONES

'I had just been booked to guest on Cannon as a private eye, a character similar to Barnaby, with hopes that it might be a spin-off.When CBS had a gap in their schedule, programme boss Fred Silverman made an executive decision, and instead of my appearing as a guest on Cannon, Bill Conrad became a guest on the first of 13 Barnabys.' –   BUDDY EBSEN

After his tremendous success as ole Jed Clampett in the Beverly Hillbillies, Buddy Ebsen created another enduring favourite in Barnaby Jones. Barnaby had enjoyed a long and illustrious career as a private detective but had retired, leaving the Los Angeles-based business to his son Hal. But when Hal was murdered on a case, Barnaby stepped out of retirement to help track down the killer.

Hal's widow, Betty, assisted Barnaby with his enquiries, and when he inevitably decided to keep the agency going, she stayed on as his assistant. In the fifth season, Barnaby's young cousin J.R., who was studying to become a lawyer, also joined the family firm to gain some practical experience.

Barnaby Jones was an amiable old codger. He seemed to have the speed of thought of the average sea slug, but appearances can be deceptive as his adversaries found to their cost. For his vague exterior was just a ploy to lull the guilty into a false sense of security. In fact, Barnaby was one of the most accomplished of all TV detectives and even set up his own home crime laboratory, where he analysed clues and evidence. In all, Barnaby Jones ran for eight seasons and was said to be President Nixon's favourite detective show. I wonder if he ever asked for any tapes...

REGULAR CAST

Barnaby Jones Buddy Ebsen   *Betty Jones* Lee Meriwether
Jebediah Romano (J.R.) Jones Mark Shera   *Lt Biddle* John Carter

Music: Jerry Goldsmith
Producers: Gene Levitt (Season 1) Philip Salzman (2-6) Robert Sherman (7,8)

Executive producer: Quinn Martin

A Quinn Martin Production for CBS

174 colour 60-minute episodes
US: CBS (Season 1) 28 Jan 1973 - 6
    May 1973 (13 eps)
(Season 2) 16 Sept 1973 - 31 March
    1974 (24 eps)
(Season 3) 10 Sept 1974 - 15 April 1975
    (24 eps)
(Season 4) 19 Sept 1975 - 18 March
    1976 (24 eps)

(Season 5) 7 Oct 1976 - 19 May 1977
    (23 eps)
(Season 6) 15 Sept 1977 - 2 March 1978
    (21 eps)
(Season 7) 21 Sept 1978 - 19 April 1979
    (24 eps)
(Season 8) 20 Sept 1979 - 3 April 1980
    (21 eps)
UK: ITV 4 April 1974 - 20 Feb 1980

BARNEY BLAKE: POLICE REPORTER

NBC proudly claims that this was television's first regularly scheduled mystery series. It was a live show which saw newspaper reporter, Barney Blake, and his secretary, Jennifer, emerge as a formidable crime-fighting team specializing in murder cases. But for all its merits, it soon went up in smoke, being cancelled by sponsors American Tobacco Company after just 13 weeks.

REGULAR CAST

Barney Blake Gene O'Donnell   *Jennifer Allen* Judy Parrish

Producer: Wynn Wright

An NBC Production

13 monochrome 30-minute episodes
US: NBC 22 April - 8 July 1948

BARNEY MILLER

Barney Miller has been described as the M*A*S*H of cop shows. That may be flattering it considerably, but it did have a certain quirky appeal. The series originated from a rejected pilot, The Life and Times of Capt. Barney Miller, which was part of a 1974 ABC anthology called Just for Laughs. The pilot was set in Barney's police precinct house, where his family (wife Elizabeth, son David and daughter Rachael) featured prominently. But when the series proper began, the setting switched to the 12th precinct station house in Greenwich Village, where Barney and his police squad worked. The result was that Barney's domestic life diminished to the point that his nearest and dearest were rapidly written out.

The station house became a haven for all manner of weirdos wanting to use it as a restaurant, a meeting-place or somewhere to shelter from the rain. Occasionally someone even came in to report a crime. Throughout the frenzied activity, Miller usually found himself in the role of straight man, trying to retain his dignity while all around lost theirs. Yet though the format may sound far-fetched and an excuse for easy laughs, genuine policemen praised the show for its realism.

Miller certainly worked with a motley crew. There was fast-talking Puerto Rican Amenguale, the naive Wojo, the know-all Dietrich, 5ft 3in Levitt who was desperate to be a detective but was 'too short', Harris, the dapper ambitious black who eventually wrote a best-selling novel, the outdated boss Luger, the philosophical Yemana, noted for making appalling coffee and the hit of the show, the decrepit Fish, an ageing Jewish cop who looked as if he would be lucky to see out the shift. His greatest crisis was when the station house toilet was out of order. Not for the first time, the officers of the 12th had nothing to go on. The character became so popular that actor Abe Vigoda got his own spin-off series, imaginatively titled Fish.

There were some touching moments. When Jack Soo, who played Yemana, died in 1979, a special episode was screened as a tribute, containing clips from previous shows and reminiscences from the cast. At the end they all raised their coffee cups in a toast. Barney Miller was named outstanding comedy series in America for 1982 but by then ratings had started to dwindle and it was time to call it a day. The series ended when the precinct house was discovered to be a listed building, the very one that had been the headquarters of Teddy Roosevelt during his term as President of the New York Police Board in the 1890s. So the precinct had to move out. Miller was promoted to Deputy Inspector and Levitt finally made Sergeant, but the team were spread far and wide across New York. The city's waifs and strays would have to find somewhere else to go.

REGULAR CAST

Capt. *Barney Miller* Hal Linden   Det. *Phil Fish* Abe Vigoda
Det. *Sgt Chano Amenguale* Gregory Sierra
Det. *Stanley 'Wojo' Wojohowicz* Maxwell Gail
Det. *Nick Yemana* Jack Soo   Det. *Ron Harris* Ron Glass
Insp. *Frank Luger* James Gregory   Officer *Carl Levitt* Ron Carey
Det. *Arthur Dietrich* Steve Landesberg

Creators: Theodore J. Flicker, Danny Arnold
Producer: Chris Hayward

Executive producers: Theodore J. Flicker, Danny Arnold for *Columbia*

168 colour 30-minute episodes
US: ABC 23 Jan 1975 - 9 Sept 1982
UK: ITV 11 July 1979 - 7 Dec 1983
(Thames Television)

BATMAN

'I had the simple idea of overdoing it, of making it so square and so serious that adults would find it amusing. I knew kids would go for the derring-do, the adventure, but the trick would be to find adults who would either watch it with their kids or, to hell with the kids, and watch it anyway.' – EXECUTIVE PRODUCER WILLIAM DOZIER

OK, so if there's no place for crime-fighters like Superman and Spiderman in this book, what is the Caped Crusader doing here? For a start it's my book and I like him and, secondly, the show is worth including for two of the finest comic policemen in the history of television, Commissioner Gordon and Chief O'Hara. The pair were so hopelessly inept, it was little wonder that all of the world's arch villains flocked to Gotham City. And heaven knows where the crime figures would have been without the Commissioner's direct line to the Bat-cave! The Commissioner was even blissfully unaware that his own daughter, Barbara, was Batgirl.

The history and basic premise of Batman have been too well chronicled to warrant repetition here, but it is worth pointing out to those who do not consider him to be a true detective, that the elaborate crimes he had to solve, particularly some of the Riddler's rhymes, would have taxed the powers of deduction of such renowned intellectuals as Inspector Morse. And somehow I can't see Morse's dedication to combatting crime extending to prancing around Oxford in a cape, pointed ears and tights. Also, although Batman appeared to have a mighty armoury at his disposal, it should be noted that the Batmobile had a top speed of only 32 mph. It was, in fact, based on a 1955 Chrysler Futura, used to publicize the film Forbidden Planet.

The idea for the TV series certainly raised a few eyebrows in high places. William Dozier recalled: 'I explained to ABC executives how we were going to do it – that we were going to have "ZAP" and "POW". And ABC president Leonard Goldenson said, "We are going to have, right on the screen, 'ZAP' and 'POW'?" I said, "Yeah, and a lot more, Leonard." "Oh my," he said.'

Much of the show's success was down to Adam West's dead-pan performance. Dozier added: 'Adam was quick to grasp that it had to be played as though we were dropping a bomb on Hiroshima, with that kind of deadly seriousness.'

For two seasons it was a runaway hit, but gradually Batmania began to wane. And despite the introduction of Batgirl, fresh villains played by the likes of Joan Collins, Eartha Kitt and Zsa Zsa Gabor, and the abandonment of the twice-a-week format, the show finished after the third season. However, the Caped Crusader and the Boy Wonder lived on in cartoon form, most notably in 1977 in The New Adventures of Batman, for which Adam West and Burt Ward supplied the voices. The original TV series has since gone on to delight new generations of fans and is still seen in over a hundred countries today. Quite simply when it comes to escapism, there are only two words to describe it. Holy superior!

REGULAR CAST

Batman/Bruce Wayne Adam West   *Robin/Dick Grayson* Burt Ward
Alfred Alan Napier   *Aunt Harriet* Madge Blake
Commissioner Gordon Neil Hamilton   *Chief O'Hara* Stafford Repp
Batgirl Yvonne Craig   *Narrator* William Dozier

GUEST VILLAINS

The Riddler Frank Gorshin/John Astin   *The Penguin* Burgess Meredith
The Joker Cesar Romero
Mr Freeze George Sanders/Otto Preminger/Eli Wallach
Zelda the Great Anne Baxter   *The Mad Hatter* David Wayne
False-Face Malachi Throne
Catwoman Julie Newmar *(Season 1,2)* Eartha Kitt *(Season 3)*
King Tut Victor Buono   *The Bookworm* Roddy McDowall
The Archer Art Carney   *The Minstrel* Van Johnson
Ma Parker Shelley Winters   *The Clock King* Walter Slezak
Egghead Vincent Price   *Chandell* Liberace
Marsha Carolyn Jones   *Shame* Cliff Robertson
The Puzzler Maurice Evans   *Sandman* Michael Rennie
Colonel Gumm Roger C. Carmel   *The Black Widow* Tallulah Bankhead
The Siren Joan Collins   *Lola Lasagne* Ethel Merman
Louie the Lilac Milton Berle   *Lord Ffogg* Rudy Vallee
Nora Clavicle Barbara Rush   *Dr Cassandra* Ida Lupino
Minerva   Zsa Zsa Gabor

Music: Neal Hefti (theme), Nelson Riddle
Producer: Howie Horowitz
Executive producer: William Dozier

A Greenaway Production for 20th Century-Fox Television

120 colour 30-minute episodes

US: ABC (Season 1) 12 Jan 1966 - 5 May 1966 (34 eps)
(Season 2) 7 Sept 1966 - 30 March 1967 (60 eps)
(Season 3) 14 Sept 1967 - 14 March 1968 (26 eps)
UK: ITV (Season 1) 21 May 1966 - 11 Sept 1966 (UK ABC)
(Season 2) 17 Sept 1966 - 2 April 1967 (UK ABC)
(Season 3) 14 Sept 1974 - 8 March 1975 (LWT)

THE BEIDERBECKE AFFAIR

Trevor Chaplin was a woodwork teacher at a Leeds comprehensive school where his live-in lover, Jill Swinburne, taught English. Their lives were fairly uneventful until Trevor ordered a set of LPs by the jazz great, Bix Beiderbecke, from a platinum blonde selling mail order door to door. After a considerable delay, a package arrived, but was found to contain An Evening with Wolfgang Amadeus Mozart, Living Legends of the Cinema Organ, The George Formby Songbook Volume 3 and Everyday Spanish for Beginners. Anxious to determine the whereabouts of his order, Trevor set out to do some amateur detective work which involved Jill and himself in a web of corruption.

The series, with Kenny Baker recreating the sounds of Beiderbecke, proved so popular with critics and viewers alike, that the pair of unlikely heroes featured in two further adventures – The Beiderbecke Tapes, a tale of nuclear waste dumping in the Yorkshire Dales, and The Beiderbecke Connection, where they found themselves under police observation after giving sanctuary to a mysterious stranger.

Alan Plater's witty scripts threw forth a fund of colourful characters – their cynical teaching colleague Carter, pompous headmaster Mr Wheeler, the Batman and Robin of Leeds – Big Al and Little Norm – and bemused policemen Forrest and Hobson. The last-named began as an officious Detective Sergeant, but by the Beiderbecke Connection he had become a Detective Inspector with his own computer terminal. A thoroughly enjoyable trilogy – even if you don't like jazz.

The Beiderbecke Affair

Trevor Chaplin James Bolam
Jill Swinburne Barbara Flynn
Mr Carter Dudley Sutton
Mr Wheeler Keith Smith
Big Al Terence Rigby
Little Norm Danny Schiller
Chief Supt Forrest Colin Blakely
Det. Sgt Hobson Dominic Jephcott

Creator: Alan Plater
Music: Frank Ricotti
Director: David Reynolds
Producer: Anne W. Gibbons
Executive producer: David Cunliffe
6 colour 60-minute episodes
UK: ITV 6 Jan - 10 Feb 1985

The Beiderbecke Tapes

Trevor Chaplin James Bolam
Jill Swinburne Barbara Flynn
Mr Carter Dudley Sutton
Mr Wheeler Keith Smith

Paterson Malcolm Storry
Sylvia Beryl Reid

Director: Brian Parker
Producer: Michael Glynn
Executive producer: David Cunliffe
2 colour 90-minute episodes
UK: ITV 13 - 20 Dec 1987

The Beiderbecke Connection

Trevor Chaplin James Bolam
Jill Swinburne Barbara Flynn
Mr Carter Dudley Sutton
Mr Wheeler Keith Smith
Big Al Terence Rigby
Little Norm Danny Schiller
Det. Insp. Hobson Dominic Jephcott

Director: Alan Bell
Producer: Michael Glynn
Executive producer: Keith Richardson
4 colour 60-minute episodes
UK: ITV 27 Nov - 18 Dec 1988

*A Yorkshire Television Network
   Production*

BELLAMY

Not many Australian detective series have sold well overseas, and looking at Bellamy it was easy to see why. Steve Bellamy was billed as 'the toughest cop in town', 'a man with a mission' and various other cliches to mask the fact that he was exactly the same as countless other screen cops over the years. He and his partner, Mitchell, were part of a Special Crime Squad, dedicated to tracking down the hardest villains. It wasn't particularly successful in Australia and even less so in Britain, where it surfaced only sporadically and usually in the wee small hours of the morning.

REGULAR CAST

Bellamy John Stanton   *Mitchell* Tim Elston

Executive producer: Don Battye

A Grundy Organization Production
26 colour 60-minute episodes

Australia: Ten Network From 26 June 1981
UK: ITV 1 Sept 1984 - 4 April 1987 (LWT)

BERGERAC

'In fact, Jersey's a pretty quiet place where very little happens of a criminal nature.'   – PRODUCER JONATHAN ALWYN

You would never think it from watching Bergerac! Each week Jim stumbles over some major crime on the small millionaire's island so that, by now after ten years, he must have questioned every single one of the residents. Yet, far from being put off Jersey by the prospect of staying at a hotel with a corpse in the pool twice daily in high season, holidaymakers have flocked there, enchanted by the magnificent scenery they see on television. Quite simply, Bergerac is the best thing to happen to Jersey since Donald Peers stopped doing summer seasons.

Created by Robert Banks Stewart in the wake of Shoestring, Bergerac started out working for the Channel Islands' Bureau des Etrangers, the local police force. He was a Detective Sergeant with a past drink problem, a gammy leg and a broken marriage. In fact the only thing in his life that ran smoothly was his maroon vintage Triumph sports car. His leg injury was of particular interest. Actor John Nettles, who plays Jim Bergerac, once broke his right leg falling from a motorbike. It caused him to limp. But Bergerac limped on the left...

Bergerac is a decent sort of bloke, but he knew that his go-it-alone approach didn't meet with the approval of his senior officers and, therefore, despite his unparalleled success at solving cases, there was little chance of promotion. He had frequent altercations with his crusty boss, Chief Inspector Barney Crozier.

Another stumbling block to Bergerac's career prospects is his father-in-law Charlie Hungerford, a millionaire cigar-smoking businessman, who has managed to become entangled in all of the 84 crimes Bergerac has investigated to date. From the outset, viewers know that, no matter what the crime, it will somehow involve Charlie. Terence Alexander, who plays Hungerford, says: 'Bergerac disapproves of everything Charlie does, but he also admires his native cunning and is very happy to use Charlie's contacts and immense local knowledge. Charlie is a bit of a fly boy, a loveable rogue – but he never does anything that is totally dishonest.'

Charlie's daughter, Deborah, was the first in a long line of women for love-lorn Bergerac. After their marriage fell apart, he had a succession of girl-friends. There was Francine who worked for the tourist office, Marianne Bellshade and estate agent Susan Young, plus the occasional fling with glamorous jewel thief Philippa Vale. And when Bergerac finally quit the Bureau to become a private detective in Provence, he moved in with a new French girl, Danielle Aubry.

Of course his girl-friends would always be mixed up in the investigations. When Susan Young was the love of his life, every villain in Jersey appeared to have bought a house through the firm she worked for. It didn't bother actress Louise Jameson – at least it got her out and about. As she said: 'At the start, the producers didn't know what to do with me. During one series, I never seemed to be out of bed!'

In the early episodes there were a few other recurring characters who had to be included each week in addition to Charlie Hungerford and Jim's girl. These included Bureau secretary Charlotte (she was later replaced by the less prominent Peggy) and a local restaurateur who rejoiced in the name of Diamante Lil. Even if it was just to watch her freshly-served cod mornay splattered up the wall in the course of the final chase sequence, Lil would be featured.

Bergerac and Jersey have become inextricably linked, like Steve McGarrett and Hawaii. Even when he left for Provence (a move which coincided with Crozier being succeeded by the even more unpleasant Inspector Victor Deffand), Bergerac's cases still always managed to involve the island and its inhabitants. John Nettles' own love affair with Jersey has lasted longer than any of Bergerac's relationships, although he too had a bumpy ride when some island residents, who do not habitually welcome outsiders, tried to stop him buying a property there.

Nettles has even written a couple of books about Jersey. Most of the islanders have entered into the spirit. Millionaires have loaned their Rolls-Royces and their palatial homes for filming, and often pop up as extras. There are even stickers going around on Jersey proclaiming, 'My house hasn't been used for Bergerac'...

REGULAR CAST

Det. Sgt Jim Bergerac John Nettles   *Charlie Hungerford* Terence Alexander
Chief Insp. Barney Crozier Sean Arnold   *Deborah* Deborah Grant
Francine Cecile Paoli   *Marianne Bellshade* Celia Imrie
Susan Young Louise Jameson   *Philippa Vale* Liza Goddard
Danielle Aubry Therese Liotard   *Insp. Victor Deffand* Roger Sloman
Det. Con. Willy Pettit John Telfer   *Det. Con. Ben Lomas* David Kershaw
Diamante Lil Mela White   *Charlotte* Annette Badland
Peggy Masters Nancy Mansfield

Creator: Robert Banks Stewart
Title music: George Fenton
Producers: Robert Banks Stewart,
  Jonathan Alwyn, George Gallaccio

*A BBC Television Production in
  association with Seven Network,
  Australia*

80 colour 50-minute episodes and 4
  colour 90-minute episodes
UK: BBC1 (Season 1) 18 Oct - 20 Dec
  1981 (10 eps)

(Season 2) 9 Jan - 6 March 1983 (9 eps)
(Season 3) 3 Dec 1983 - 4 Feb 1984 (10
  eps)
(Season 4) 11 Oct - 20 Dec 1985 (9 eps)
(Season 5) 26 Dec 1986 - 21 Feb 1987
  (9 eps)
(Season 6) 26 Dec 1987 - 13 Feb 1988
  (8 eps)
(Season 7) 27 Dec 1988 - 18 March
  1989 (9 eps)
(Season 8) 14 Jan - 18 March 1990 (10
  eps)
(Season 9) 26 Dec 1990 - 9 March 1991
  (10 eps)

BERT D'ANGELO, SUPERSTAR

A spin-off from The Streets of San Francisco, poor old Bert D'Angelo was no superstar of the ratings and was cancelled in the States after just half a season. Bert was an Italian-American cop transferred to San Francisco after ten years with the New York City force. His fiery Latin temperament often landed him in hot water with his superiors but created a surge of apathy among viewers. The trouble was that although there was a fair quota of action, there was precious little else.

REGULAR CAST

Sgt Bert D'Angelo Paul Sorvino   *Insp. Larry Johnson* Robert Pine
Capt. Jack Breen Dennis Patrick

Music: Paul Williams
Producer: Morton Fine
Executive producer: Quinn Martin

A Quinn Martin Production

13 colour 60-minute episodes
US: ABC 21 Feb - 10 July 1976

BEVERLY HILLS BUNTZ

Dennis Franz's Norm Buntz was one of the outstanding characters in Hill Street Blues. With the build, looks and charm of a rampant rottweiler, Buntz stood no nonsense from anyone – whether they be crooks or fellow cops. In the final episode on the Hill, he earned everyone's eternal gratitude by flooring the obnoxious Chief Daniels.

Not unreasonably, that outburst would have heralded the end of his police career so, after the demise of Hill Street, Jeffery Lewis and David Milch, who had developed the character, transplanted him to Beverly Hills where he set up as a private eye. His office was suitably seedy, all the more so since he was joined by the hideous Sid the snitch who had been his principal informant on Hill Street. Sid, who had more oil on his hair than J.R. Ewing could ever dream of, could lower the tone of a meths drinkers' party. So he and Buntz were hopelessly out of place in Beverly Hills.

It was a good idea to continue the pair's love/hate relationship against this unlikely backdrop but it never really took off and the show was soon axed. The reason was probably that in California, Norm only tackled minor cases, nothing too dangerous. The great appeal in Hill Street was watching him sweat profusely as he stared down the barrel of a gun. But here he was wasted investigating cases of shoplifting. It was like putting Starsky and Hutch on traffic duty.

REGULAR CAST

Norm Buntz Dennis Franz   *Sid* Peter Durasik

Creators: Jeffery Lewis, David Milch
Executive producers: Jeffery Lewis,
   David Milch

An NBC Production

4 colour 30-minute episodes
US: NBC 17 March - 7 April 1988

Big Guns (see Charlesworth)

Big Shamus, Little Shamus

Suffering from a severe dose of saccharin, Big Shamus, Little Shamus was so poorly received in the US, that it was dropped after just two of the scheduled 13 episodes. Set in Atlantic City's Ansonia Hotel, the central figures in this comedy/drama were the hotel's veteran house detective, Arnie Sutter, and his smart 13-year-old son, Max. With unexpected help from the boy, Arnie attempted to cope with the increase in crime brought about by the legalization of gambling in Atlantic City, a move which had attracted thieves, conmen and prostitutes, all hoping to strike it rich. Arnie's boss was Korman, the hotel security chief, Stephanie Marsh was the new assistant manager, and one Jingles Lodestar was an undercover security agent posing as a cocktail waitress. But it proved too sentimental even for a nation raised on The Waltons.

Regular Cast

Arnie Sutter Brian Dennehy   *Max Sutter* Doug McKeon
George Korman George Wyner   *Stephanie Marsh* Kathryn Leigh Scott
Jingles Lodestar Cynthia Sikes

Creators: Tracy Hotchner, Christopher Knopf
Music: Mike Post, Pete Carpenter
Producer: Fred Freiburger

A Lorimar Production

13 colour 60-minute episodes
US: CBS 29 Sept - 6 Oct 1979
UK: ITV From 14 May 1981 (LWT)

The Bill

'Burnside just believes in nicking people if they've broken the law. If it means bending a few rules, that's what he'll do. In truth , there isn't much difference between him and some of the villains.'
– Christopher Ellison

The Bill is the natural successor to Z Cars – a first-rate, twice-weekly drama about the workings of a British inner-city police station. Every face of the force is represented, from the small-minded Chief Superintendent Brownlow, through the mavericks of CID, Frank Burnside (played by Christopher Ellison) and Ted Roach, to the bobbies on the beat, led by the fatherly Bob Cryer.

Set at Sun Hill police station (call sign Sierra Oscar) in the uncompromising East End of London (the building used in the series is an old factory), The Bill concentrates exclusively on the officers at work. Their private lives remain just that – and there is a rule that there must never be a scene without a police character in it. Most of the programmes are self-contained, although occasionally a major storyline will run on to the following episode.

The Bill began as part of the Thames Television series Storyteller, in an episode entitled Woodentop, CID slang for uniformed police. At first its one-hour format was as plodding as the sturdy feet of the WPC and her partner in the opening titles. Nor was it popular with the real police. After seeing previews, they refused to attend the launch party. The Police Federation went on to attack it for showing racism within the force.

Even when the pace quickened and the episodes were split into half-hours from the summer of 1988, Scotland Yard objected to the extensive publicity campaign. They claimed that newspaper advertisements resembled recruitment posters, except that they didn't like the implication that some policemen were 'liars, cheats and bullies'.

The senior officer at Sun Hill is Chief Superintendent Charles Brownlow, a stern, shallow, 'corporate man' whose main concern is the image of the force. He is not worried about right and wrong, just as long as nothing reflects badly on him. He attends a lot of meetings.

Under him are Chief Inspector Derek Conway, a gruff but fair old-fashioned copper, and Inspector Andrew Monroe, a stickler for discipline who might even put the wind up Charlie Barlow. The principal uniformed sergeants are Bob Cryer, experienced and respected with an unshakeable moral-code, and the jollier Alec Peters. Among the current crop of PCs are the caring June Ackland, the tactless but conscientious Tony Stamp and the hypochondriac Reg Hollis, who is also the station's Federation rep, a job he only got because nobody else wanted it.

The latest head of CID is Detective Chief Inspector Kim Reid, calm and assured but a woman who needs to put her foot down – preferably on Frank Burnside's windpipe. For trying to control DI Burnside is no easy task. The successor to hot-headed, red-headed Roy Galloway, Burnside is devious, manipulative and with a taste for tarty blondes. And they're his good points.

The other CID officers are DS Ted Roach, a rebellious tearaway, who has long since blown any chance of promotion but who knows street life like he knows the inside of a whisky bottle; the meticulous DS Alistair Greig who is very much in line for promotion; acting WDC Viv Martella, a cockney girl who combines toughness with femininity; solid and dependable young DC Jim Carver; the immaculately groomed DC Mike Dashwood, who would never dream of making an arrest if the crease was wrong in his trousers; and chubby 'Tosh' Lines, the complete opposite to Dashwood. He has a wife, five kids and a mortgage to support, and he owns one suit, one pair of cheap shoes and changes his shirt less frequently than some people change their cars.

Despite police objections in the past, The Bill is a thoroughly authentic series with the technique of hand-held cameras making the viewer feel he is actually in the thick of the action. And the acting is beyond reproach. Peter Ellis's Brownlow is more convincing than the real thing!

REGULAR CAST (present)

Chief Supt Charles Brownlow Peter Ellis   *Chief Insp. Derek Conway* Ben Roberts
Insp. Andrew Monroe Colin Tarrant   *Det. Chief Insp. Kim Reid* Carolyn Pickles
Det. Insp. Frank Burnside Christopher Ellison   *Det. Sgt Ted Roach* Tony Scannell
Det. Sgt Alistair Greig Andrew Mackintosh   *Det. Con. Alfred 'Tosh' Lines* Kevin Lloyd
Det. Con. Mike Dashwood Jon Iles   *WDC Viv Martella* Nula Conwell
Det. Con. Jim Carver Mark Wingett   *Sgt Bob Cryer* Eric Richard
Sgt Alec Peters Larry Dann   *Sgt John Maitland* Sam Miller
PC Reg Hollis Jeff Stewart   *PC Tony Stamp* Graham Cole
WPC June Ackland Trudie Goodwin   *PC Dave Quinnan* Andrew Paul
WPC Cathy Marshall Lynne Miller   *PC Steven Loxton* Tom Butcher
WPC Norika Datta Seeta Indrani   *PC George Garfield* Huw Higginson
WPC Delia French Natasha Williams   *WPC Suzanne Ford* Vikki Gee-Dare
PC Ron Smollett Nick Stringer

REGULAR CAST (PAST)

Det. Insp. Roy Galloway John Salthouse   *PC 'Taffy' Edwards* Colin Blumenau
PC Dave Litton Gary Olsen   *PC 'Yorkie' Smith* Robert Hudson
Sgt Tom Penny Roger Leach   *Insp. Kite* Simon Slater
PC Melvin Mark Powley   *Insp. Christine Frazer* Barbara Thorn
Det. Chief Insp. Gordon Wray Clive Wood   *PC Phil Young* Colin Aldridge

Creator: Geoff McQueen
Theme music: Andy Pask, Charlie Morgan
Producers: Michael Chapman, Peter Cregeen, Pat Sandys, Tony Virgo, Peter Wolfes
Executive producers: Michael Chapman, Lloyd Shirley

Over 350 colour episodes, 35 colour 60-minute, the rest colour 30-minute episodes
UK: ITV (Season 1) 16 Oct 1984 - 22 Jan 1985 (11 eps)
(Season 2) 11 Nov 1985 - 10 Feb 1986 (12 eps)
(Season 3) 21 Sept - 7 Dec 1987 (12 eps)
30-minute episodes from 19 July 1988

A Thames Television Network Production

BLACKE'S MAGIC

'Blacke's Magic presents two flamboyant personalities, one a sophisticated master of illusion, the other a folksy old con artist. Each week the two of them attempt to piece together a seemingly impossible crime.' – EXECUTIVE PRODUCER PETER S. FISCHER

The man responsible for Murder, She Wrote, Peter S. Fischer, enjoyed considerably less success with this short-lived show about an unusual father and son detective team. It turned out to be one of those 'let's think of a catchy title then build a story around it' series. Fischer certainly couldn't blame the casting, with Hal Linden of Barney Miller fame as retired magician turned private investigator, Alexander Blacke, and Harry Morgan (Colonel Potter in M*A*S*H) as Leonard Blacke, Alex's wise-cracking father and his undeniable source of inspiration.

In the pilot programme, a magician died, shot through the chest, in a sealed coffin at the bottom of a swimming pool. The police were suitably baffled but Alexander Blacke used his wit and charm to solve this and 12 other mystifying capers, each staged in the world of magic.

To ensure that the show had a ring of realism, Jim Steinmeyer, an associate of master illusionist Doug Henning, served as the show's technical adviser. But the most remarkable feat was the way in which Blacke's Magic made viewers disappear – just like that.

REGULAR CAST

Alexander Blacke Hal Linden   *Leonard Blacke* Harry Morgan

Creators: Peter S. Fischer Richard Levinson, William Link
Producer: Robert F. O'Neill
Executive producer: Peter S. Fischer

An MCA TV/Universal Production

13 colour 60-minute episodes
US: NBC 5 Jan - 8 May 1986
UK: ITV 7 April - 23 June 1987

BLOOD MONEY

Arden Winch's thriller was intended to be about a ten-year-old earl, seventeenth in line to the throne, who is kidnapped and held to a £1 million ransom. It was to be called Blood Royal but Buckingham Palace objected, fearing that it might put children of the Royal Family at risk as potential targets. So to the dismay of Winch, who justifiably reasoned that terrorists hardly needed him to give them ideas, the story and title were changed and the boy was demoted to being the son of a United Nations official. After a year's delay and the pulping of a book to accompany the original series, it appeared as a straightforward, but nonetheless meritorious police drama, with outstanding performances from Bernard Hepton as the police chief, Michael Denison as an intelligence officer and Juliet Hammond-Hill as a German terrorist.

MAIN CAST

Chief Supt Meadows Bernard Hepton   *Capt. Percival* Michael Denison
Irene Kohl Juliet Hammond-Hill

Writer: Arden Winch
Director: Michael E. Briant
Producer: Gerard Glaister

A BBC Television Production

6 colour 30-minute episodes
UK: BBC1 6 Sept - 11 Oct 1981

BLOOD RIGHTS

'Sammy Dean may not have a gun, a fast car or the romanticism of other tecs but I hope he gives more insight into the way some people live. He's not a stereotype or an angel, but a thinking person.'
– BRIAN BOVELL

Sammy Dean is very much a hero of today. A black investigative journalist who agreed to turn private eye purely to pay the bills, he is light years away from flashy operators like Magnum. Sammy comes from a tough background and already has a broken marriage to his name. This means he is separated from his young mixed-race son but he still does his utmost to behave like a responsible father. But in Sammy's line of work, that is not always easy.

Unlike previous black detectives such as Shaft, Sammy is a realist rather than a romantic. His creator, Mike Phillips (also a black journalist) says: 'Sammy differs from earlier investigators in that his own personal morality is more important than a simplistic view of law and order. His world isn't a stable one, there are no given standards or morals. I've always been fond of mysteries, from Christie and Hammett to the American modernists, but I wanted to write about modern preoccupations, class, race and changing society.'

Adapted from Phillips' best-selling novel of the same name, Blood Rights took Sammy Dean into the sleazy world of London drug-dealers, as he set out to find a wealthy Conservative MP's daughter who had apparently been kidnapped by a black youth. But Sammy finished up developing a certain sympathy for his prey. With a powerful performance from Brian Bovell in the lead role, it is to be hoped that further tales of Sammy Dean will make it to the screen.

REGULAR CAST

Sammy Dean Brian Bovell

Writer: Mike Phillips
Director: Lesley Manning
Producer: Caroline Oulton

A BBC Television Production

3 colour 55-minute episodes
UK: BBC2 24 Oct - 7 Nov 1990

THE BLUE KNIGHT

Bumper Morgan, alias the Blue Knight, was a Los Angeles version of Dixon of Dock Green. Bumper was an honest, old-fashioned foot-patrol cop who knew everyone, and whose main concern was to maintain harmony on his inner-city beat, even to the point of sometimes turning a blind eye to prostitutes with a hard-luck story. He was dedicated but stubborn, which from time to time brought him into conflict with his boss, Sergeant Newman. Bumper was happiest on the streets and his use of informants such as Wimpy, underlined the value of a good community cop.

The Blue Knight started out as a book by Joseph Wambaugh, a former member of the Los Angeles Police Department, and a consultant on the highly-praised Police Story. As with all of Wambaugh's work, it contained that vital ingredient, realism. The title first appeared on screen as a 1973 NBC mini series, for which William Holden, as Bumper, won an Emmy. It didn't make a series until two years later when, with different casting, it unaccountably enjoyed only a short life.

REGULAR CAST

Bumper Morgan George Kennedy   *Sgt Newman* Phillip Pine
Wimpy John Steadman   *Sgt Cabe* Charles Siebert
Lt Hauser Lin McCarthy

Creator: Joseph Wambaugh
Music: Henry Mancini
Producer: Joel Rogosin
Executive producers: Lee Rich, Philip Capice

A CBS Production

13 colour 60-minute episodes
US: CBS 17 Dec 1975 - 27 Oct 1976
UK: ITV From 5 Jan 1985 (Central)

Blue Thunder

The hero of this police adventure series, based on the 1983 movie Blue Thunder (with Roy Scheider), was a super-helicopter that fought crime with its sophisticated arsenal of aerial technology, weaponry and surveillance systems.

Blue Thunder was part of a special unit assembled by APEX, an agency of the federal government, to deal with particularly serious crimes. Its beat was the sprawling metropolis of Los Angeles, although the police department's AstroDivision would often send it on additional assignments for the FBI or the Treasury Department. Its pilot was former Vietnam veteran Frank Chaney, whose unorthodox methods frequently ruffled the feathers of his captain Ed Braddock. Chaney's sidekick was computer whiz Clinton C. Wonderlove and the unit also included ex-football player "Ski" Butowski, who drove the ground support van, and another computer king, "Bubba" Kelsey.

Blue Thunder was certainly no ordinary helicopter. It prowled the city at 250 mph, protecting its occupants with inch-thick armour. Its two locator lights, each three times as bright as the sun, enabled the chopper to pinpoint any vehicle or person on the ground. It could even see and hear through walls. It made the Batmobile look like the Clampetts' truck.

REGULAR CAST

Frank Chaney James Farentino   *Clinton C. Wonderlove* Dana Carvey
Ed Braddock Sandy McPeak   *Richard "Ski" Butowski* Dick Butkus
Lyman "Bubba" Kelsey Bubba Smith

Music: Frank Denson
Producers: Jeri Taylor, Donald A. Baer
Executive producers: Roy Huggins,
   David Moessinger

Rastar and Public Arts Production for Columbia Pictures Television

11 colour 60-minute episodes
US: ABC 6 Jan - 7 Sept 1984
UK: BBC1 6 Feb - 16 April 1984

Bluey

A 1970s police drama from Australia which proved surprisingly popular in Britain. Made by Crawford Productions, who also unleashed such other law enforcement spectacles as Homicide, Division 4 and Matlock

Police, it centred upon the adventures of 'Bluey' Hills, a tough cop with unorthodox methods.

REGULAR CAST

'Bluey' Hills Lucky Grills

Producers: Don Battye, Tom Hegarty
Julian Pringle

A Crawford (Australia) Production

One colour 90-minute episode and 38 colour 60-minute episodes
Australia: Seven Network From 2 Aug 1976
UK: ITV 9 Feb 1978 - 19 July 1979 (Granada)

BOGNOR

As a setting for fun and merriment, the Department of Trade would seem about as likely as the dentist. But Thames Television bravely tried to convert Tim Heald's novels about hapless D.O.T. special investigator Bognor into a twice-weekly series which saw the hero, aided by assistant Monica, risking life and limb as he probed such bizarre crimes as corruption at a dog show. Unfortunately, he didn't attract many viewers, principally because the producers appeared unsure as to whether it was supposed to be a comedy or a drama.

REGULAR CAST

Bognor David Horovitch   *Monica* Joanna McCallum
Parkinson (Head of Special Investigations) Ewan Roberts

Music: Mike Steer
Producer: Bernard Krichefski
Executive producer: John Frankau

A Thames Television Network Production

18 colour 30-minute episodes
UK: ITV 10 Feb - 9 April 1981

BONEY

This could well go down in history as the only Australian TV series to top the ratings in Scotland! Taken from the books by Arthur Upfield, it told of the cases of Aborigine Detective Inspector Napoloeon Bonaparte, or 'Boney' to his mates. Boney's beat was not the standard inner-city sleaze pit but the outback, that vast wilderness where the only people you meet are rival film crews, making The Flying Doctors. But Boney found enough crime to keep him in a series, what with scattered farmers and itinerant travellers. In their wisdom, the producers decided to black up a white man, New Zealand actor James Laurenson, as the Aborigine hero, which meant there was a constant struggle to prevent his make-up running under the heat so as to stop him ending up with a face like a zebra.

REGULAR CAST

Det. Insp. Napoleon Bonaparte   James Laurenson

Producer: John McCallum
Executive producers: Bob Austin, Lee
    Robinson

26 colour 60-minute episodes Australia:
    From 21 Jan 1972
UK: ITV From 2 Jan 1975 (LWT)

A Norfolk International Production

BOON

'Ex-fireman seeks interesting work - ANYTHING LEGAL CONSIDERED'

That advert in a local newspaper heralded the start of Boon, arguably the best thing to come out of Birmingham since the M6 motorway.

Ex-fireman Ken Boon had to accept early retirement from the brigade after damaging his lungs in a typically brave rescue attempt. He hatched up a number of unsuccessful money-making schemes until in desperation and debt, he turned for help to his old fire department colleague turned small hotelier, Harry Crawford. The result was Boon setting himself up as a freelance troubleshooter, prepared to help anyone in distress.

He saw himself as an urban cowboy and duly climbed aboard his trusty steed, a 650cc BSA Norton motorcycle, White Lightning, to embark on a series of light-hearted adventures across the Midlands prairies, ranging from child-minding to sorting out a protection racket gang. After an uncertain opening, the series began to catch on with even the theme song, Hi Ho Silver sung by Jim Diamond, reaching number five in the UK charts.

By the start of the second season, Harry had moved into a larger hotel and Ken had set up his own team of motorcycle despatch riders, The Texas Rangers, employing two teenagers, Rocky Cassidy and

Debbie Yates. Slow-witted Rocky dressed like a Hell's Angel but his heart was as soft as his head. He became a popular addition, attracting a large female following from girls who wanted to smother him and women who wanted to mother him. Meanwhile a little light briefly came into Ken's life in the shapely form of Margaret Davy, played by Amanda Burton.

For the fifth season, Ken, Harry and Rocky headed for Nottingham, where Harry opened a superior country house hotel and Ken went into business as a private eye, in which he was aided and abetted by Rocky as well as Debbie's replacement, the pretty Laura Marsh. Inevitably, Harry's hotel went bankrupt and the pair were last seen as Crawford-Boon Security.

While Harry and Ken have had more ups and downs than the Dow Jones, the series has gone from strength to strength despite some dodgy scripts. Much of its success is down to the charismatic Michael Elphick who, as Boon, has struck such a chord with the public that he receives as many as 1,000 letters a year. 'Boon is a man of the people,' says Elphick, 'and some fans think I'm just like him. That's why a lot of the letters I get are asking for help. They write to me but really they want a sort of "Ken Boon" answer, which I find quite weird. A lot of them need professional, serious help and I try to encourage them to get that.' Some of the writers seek Elphick's advice on alcoholism, following the star's own much-publicized battle with the bottle, which at one stage put the show in jeopardy – ironically while he was appearing in commercials for alcohol-free lager.

The series is pretty far-fetched at times (I mean, who in their right mind would go into financial partnership with Harry Crawford?) but Ken Boon deserves an award, even if it was just for his one-man campaign to make Birmingham seem interesting.

REGULAR CAST

Ken Boon Michael Elphick   *Harry Crawford* David Daker
Rocky Cassidy Neil Morrissey   *Debbie Yates* Lesley-Anne Sharpe
Laura Marsh Elizabeth Carling

Creators: Jim Hill, Bill Stair
Music: Dean Friedman
Producer: Kenny McBain (Season 1)
  Esta Charkham (Seasons 2,3,4)
  Michele Buck (Season 5) Simon
  Lewis (Season 6,7)
Executive producer: Ted Childs
  (Seasons 1,2,3,5,6,7)William
  Smethurst (Season 4)

*A Central Independent Television
  Production*

78 colour 60-minute episodes
UK: ITV 14 Jan - 8 April 1986 (13 eps)
17 Feb - 31 March 1987 (7 eps)
27 Oct - 1 Dec 1987 (6 eps)
1 Nov 1988 - 24 Jan 1989 (13 eps)
2 Oct - 20 Dec 1989 (13 eps)
25 Sept - 19 Dec 1990 (13 eps)
From 24 Sept 1991 (13 eps)

BOSTON BLACKIE

'Enemy of those who make him an enemy, friend of those who have no friend.'

Created by Jack Boyle in the early part of the century, Boston Blackie began his life as a burglar and bank robber, in magazines such as Cosmopolitan and Redbook. But after a spell in jail, he decided to go straight and solve crimes instead. Played by Chester Morris, Blackie became the hero of a dozen or so 1940s B movies and a star of American radio. The dapper ex-crook lived in Los Angeles where, assisted by his girlfriend Mary, his powers of detection proved infinitely superior to those of the police, not too difficult a task with the dense Inspector Faraday as competition.

Although some episodes were almost more comic than dramatic, this syndicated series was considered suitable only for adult viewing and was usually screened immediately before the 11pm news. It was also expensive for its day, costing some $21,000 per episode. There were two unusual features. Firstly, hardly any of the crimes involved stabbings, because production company boss Fred Ziv hated knives and secondly, sports broadcaster Tom Hanlon would appear as a news vendor half-way through the story and announce 'We'll be right back', to introduce the commercial break.

REGULAR CAST

Boston Blackie Kent Taylor   *Mary Wesley* Lois Collier
Insp. Faraday Frank Orth

Music: Joseph Hooven

A Ziv Production

58 monochrome 30-minute episodes
US: Syndicated 1951 - 1953

BOURBON STREET BEAT

In the late 1950s and early 1960s, Warner Bros enjoyed such a world-wide hit with 77 Sunset Strip, that they began churning out a run of almost identical shows – Surfside 6, Hawaiian Eye and Bourbon Street Beat. Like "77", Bourbon Street Beat starred two handsome detectives,

Cal Calhoun and Rex Randolph, who teamed up with a young junior-grade sleuth, Kenny Madison, and a pretty girl, Melody Lee Mercer, to form an agency (Randolph and Calhoun, Special Services) in an interesting location – this time New Orleans. It was formula television at its most blatant.

Another thing that Bourbon Street had in common with 77 Sunset Strip was that it stemmed from an episode of a series called Conflict. The episode was The Money, in which Andrew Duggan played murderous private eye Michael Austin, who killed a character by the name of Lila Prescott. Duggan went on to star in Bourbon Street which had a re-make of The Money entitled Twice Betrayed, in which Duggan, as Cal Calhoun, found himself on the other side of the law. This time he didn't strangle Lila Prescott for her money, but instead he caught the person who did!

Warner Bros searched long and hard for a trendy gimmick on Bourbon Street Beat, eventually coming up with the idea that the characters should greet each other by rubbing the soles of their shoes together. But, possibly due to the rising cost of shoe repairs, it never really took off and soon the show's leading lights headed for Warner Bros pastures new – Rex Randolph moved to Los Angeles and joined 77 Sunset Strip, while Kenny Madison departed to Miami Beach as one of the stars of Surfside 6.

Waste not, want not was clearly the company motto and that applied to the scripts, too, which were constantly re-cycled between the various shows, particularly during a lengthy writers' strike. One Warner regular recalled: 'They'd take a script for Sunset Strip and move it to Hawaiian Eye, Bourbon Street and The Roaring Twenties and just change the character names!' The hardest thing for the actors must have been not remembering their lines, but remembering which show they were in.

REGULAR CAST

Cal Calhoun Andrew Duggan   *Rex Randolph* Richard Long
Kenny Madison Van Williams   *Melody Lee Mercer* Arlene Howell

EPISODE TITLES

The Taste of Ashes
Melody in Diamonds
The Mourning Cloak
The House of Ledezan
Torch Song for Trumpet
Target of Hate
Woman in the River
The Missing Queen
Girl in Trouble
Neon Nightmare
The Tiger Moth

Wall of Silence
Secret of Hyacinth Bayou
Twice Betrayed
Invitation to a Murder
Swampfire
Mrs Viner Vanishes
If a Body
Light Touch of Terror
Six Hours to Midnight
The Golden Beetle
Last Exit
The Black Magnolia
Deadly Persuasion

Portrait of Lenore
Suitable for Framing
Kill With Kindness
False Identity
Inside Man
Green Hell
Find My Face
Ferry to Algiers
Knock on Any Tombstone
Wagon Show
Key to the City
Interrupted Wedding
The 10% Blues Reunion
Teresa

Theme music: Mack David, Jerry Livingston
Producers: William T. Orr, Charles Hoffman

A Warner Bros Production

39 monochrome 60-minute episodes
US: ABC 5 Oct 1959 - 26 Sept 1960
UK: ITV 29 June - 21 Sept 1963 (ABC)

THE BOYS FROM THE BUSH

Reg is the archetypal whingeing Pom. He has lived in Australia for twenty years, but the only bush he is interested in is Shepherds Bush, back in London, home of his beloved football team, Queens Park Rangers. Reg's business is Melbourne Confidential – part marriage bureau, part detective agency, part anything to make money. His partner is Dennis, a determined Aussie fighting middle-age, reality and his ex-wife. Reg's wife, Doris, longs for a world more like her favourite soaps, while their man-hungry daughter, Arlene, soon gets her claws into Reg's newly-divorced second cousin, Leslie, who in turn finds himself thrust into the unfamiliar role of private eye.

This gently amusing series saw the boys tackle some bizarre cases (such as a stuffed platypus containing a rare aphrodisiac) and presented a vastly different view of Melbourne from that seen on Neighbours. For that alone it deserves to succeed.

REGULAR CAST

Reg Toomer Tim Healy   *Dennis Tontine* Chris Haywood
Leslie Mark Haddigan   *Arlene* Nadine Garner
Doris Pat Thomson

Creator: Douglas Livingstone
Producer: Verity Lambert

10 colour 50-minute episodes
UK: BBC1 19 Jan - 5 April 1991

A Cinema Verity/Entertainment Media Production for BBC and Seven Network Australia

BRENNER

Brenner marked a shift from the traditional police shows of the 1950s because it showed that America's esteemed law enforcers were actually fallible. Filmed on location in New York, it was the story of two generations of officers – Roy Brenner, whose twenty years' service had seen him rise to Lieutenant, and his rookie patrolman son, Ernie. Roy's experience meant that he knew the kind of pressure cops were under and he strove to keep his men in line, not always successfully. Meanwhile young Ernie worked undercover with the vice squad. The two had contrasting approaches to the job (dad was battle-hardened and streetwise, son was idealistic) but they were able to learn from each other.

Sponsors Lever Brothers withdrew their backing because of what they considered to be the show's controversial nature, but CBS kept faith and five years after the initial 16 episodes, ten more were screened. But Brenner still didn't set the ratings alight – it was simply too far ahead of its time.

REGULAR CAST

Det. Lt Roy Brenner Edward Binns   *Officer Ernie Brenner* James Broderick

Creator: Herb Brodkin

A CBS Production

26 monochrome 30-minute episodes
US: CBS 6 June 1959 - 13 Sept 1964

BRONK

Normally associated with playing the sort of psychopaths that make Anthony Perkins look like a boy scout, Jack Palance cropped up as thoughtful Lieutenant Alex Bronkov, in this routine police show. Bronk had good reason to ponder, his daughter Ellen having been confined to a wheelchair by the accident that had killed his wife. The series was set in Ocean City, Southern California, where the Mayor was an old pal of Bronk's, Pete Santori. The Mayor wanted Bronk to rid the town of corruption and he did just that, with the valuable help of Sergeant Webber and occasional assistance from another old buddy, Harry Mark, who, on retiring from the police force, had found that his true vocation

lay in scrap metal. Alas, even the presence of the redoubtable Palance
was not enough to sustain pipe-smoking Bronk beyond a single season.
He simply ran out of puff.

REGULAR CAST

Lt Alex Bronkov Jack Palance   *Mayor Pete Santori* Joseph Mascolo
Sgt John Webber Tony King   *Harry Mark* Henry Beckman
Ellen Bronkov Dina Ousley

Creator: Carroll O'Connor
Producer: Leigh Vance
Executive producers: Carroll O'Connor,
  Bruce Geller

24 colour 60-minute episodes
US: CBS 21 Sept 1975 - 18 July 1976
UK: ITV 31 March 1977 - 31 May 1986

An MGM Television Production

THE BROTHERS BRANNAGAN

These two Phoenix, Arizona, private eyes were so hard to tell apart that
one American reviewer had to identify them by their suit colours! An
innocuous syndicated show in which the brothers' similarity served to
confuse the criminals as well as the critics. It also brought the pair a
complicated romantic life since, as is the wont with brothers, they kept
falling in love with the same girl.

REGULAR CAST

Mike Brannagan Steve Dunne   *Bob Brannagan* Mark Roberts

Producer: Wilbur Stark

39 monochrome 30-minute episodes
US: Syndicated 1960

BULMAN

George Bulman was television's only Shakespeare-quoting, nasal-
inhaling, glove-wearing, clock-mending detective. Three years after

starring in another worthy police series (SEE STRANGERS), Bulman re-surfaced having resigned from the force and set himself up as the proprietor of a small antique shop, which specialized in repairing clocks. But when an extra pair of hands arrived in the form of wee Scot Lucy McGinty, the criminologist daughter of an ex-colleague, Bulman soon began to get increasingly involved in private eye work. Even if he had wanted to devote his time to the mechanics of Big Ben, Lucy wouldn't have let him. She chided: 'You wrote the book on detection in this city, George. You were born to be a detective, not a clock mender.'

The pair became embroiled in some hair-raising escapades such as combatting KGB assassins, mostly the result of Bulman's connection with the mysterious Dugdale of the British Secret Service.

Where the series rose above the norm was actor Don Henderson's portrayal of the quirky Bulman, down to the gold-rimmed 'Edwardian' reading glasses and the plastic shopping bag which accompanied him everywhere. Yet many of the props came about by accident. When Henderson first played the unmarried Bulman, he couldn't get his own wedding ring off, so he decided to cover it up with a pair of gloves. 'When we went to buy clothes for the show, I said I wanted something very square and ordinary, and as we were going out of the shop, with an ill-fitting suit in the bag, I saw a pair of grey woolly gloves. It got more reaction from viewers than anything else, so I kept them. At the same time I had a sniffly cold. I couldn't hide it so I started using an inhaler. That was another thing that seemed to stick.'

But other gimmicks masked a more serious problem. His scarf hid the burns from Henderson's throat cancer treatment, and the fact that Bulman sometimes spoke in a whisper, attributed in the script to that permanent cold, was also due to the disease. Happily, it's cured now.

Henderson was able to inject some of his own experiences into the role, as before turning to acting, he had been an officer with Essex CID. In a line worthy of the eccentric Bulman, he explains: 'I packed it in because I felt so sorry for some of the villains I was nicking...'

REGULAR CAST

George Bulman Don Henderson   *Lucy McGinty* Siobhan Redmond
William Dugdale Thorley Walters

Based on characters created by
  Kenneth Royce
Principal writer: Murray Smith
Music: Dick Walter
Producer: Steve Hawes (Season 1) Sita
  Williams (Season 2)
Executive producer: Richard Everitt

*A Granada Television Network
  Production*

20 colour 60-minute episodes
UK: ITV (Season 1) 5 June - 28 Aug
  1985 (13 eps) (Season 2) 20 June -
  8 Aug 1987 (7 eps)

BURKE'S LAW

> 'It was my grandmother who helped me believe in myself. It was from her I got the kind of confidence I represent in Burke's Law – the elegant guy who seems to know about things, all about life, a sophisticated man of the world.'   – GENE BARRY, 1963

Amos Burke came as something of a culture shock in 1963. On both sides of the Atlantic we had been accustomed to seeing under-paid, hard-working policemen who arrived at the scene of a crime by no more luxurious a form of transport than a dented squad car or a push-bike. But Burke, a millionaire playboy who also happened to be Los Angeles' Chief of Detectives, thought nothing of turning up to a homicide in a Rolls-Royce driven by his chauffeur Henry.

The character of Burke first appeared in an episode of Dick Powell Theatre, titled Who Killed Julia Greer?, in which he was played by Powell himself. In the hands of Gene Barry, Burke was suave and witty, the most eligible bachelor in town. He lived in a luxurious mansion, visited by a steady stream of beautiful women, with the result that the long arm of the law reached some pretty erogenous zones.

Despite his generally amiable disposition, Burke could act tough when necessary and kept a close watch on his officers, including the veteran, Sergeant Hart, and fresh-faced Tilson. And he showed particular interest in glamorous policewoman Ames, the original fair cop. Every episode title began 'Who Killed...' (among them were: Who Killed What's His Name?, Who Killed the Eleventh Best Dressed Woman in the World?, Who Killed Vaudeville?, Who Killed the Rabbit's Husband? and Who Killed Mr Colby in Ladies' Lingerie?) and featured a wide array of guest stars; Zsa Zsa Gabor, Sir Cedric Hardwicke, Sammy Davis Jnr, Dorothy Lamour, Diana Dors and Mickey Rooney all plied their trade in Burke's Law.

After two successful seasons, the format was unwisely changed. Burke left the police force and became a globe-trotting secret agent for US intelligence, in a none too subtle imitation of James Bond. The title was changed to Amos Burke – Secret Agent and, apart from Barry, the only other regular was Carl Benton Reid, playing a spymaster known as 'The Man'. The new look was a flop. It was a shame that a highly enjoyable character had to bow out on such a low note.

REGULAR CAST

Capt. Amos Burke Gene Barry   *Det. Sgt Les Hart* Regis Toomey
Det. Tim Tilson Gary Conway   *Henry* Leon Lontoc
Sgt Ames Eileen O'Neill   *'The Man' (Season 3)* Carl Benton Reid

Creators: Ivan Goff, Ben Roberts
Music: Herschel Burke Gilbert
Producer: Aaron Spelling

A Four Star Production for ABC

81 monochrome 60-minute episodes

US: ABC (Season 1) 20 Sept 1963 - 8
    May 1964 (32 eps)
(Season 2) 16 Sept 1964 - 5 May 1965
    (32 eps)
Season 3) 15 Sept 1965 - 12 Jan 1966
    (17 eps)
UK: ITV 20 Sept 1963 - 12 Jan
    1966(ABC)

CADE'S COUNTY

Set in Madrid County, California, this modern Western police drama revolved around the work of Sheriff Sam Cade, portrayed by Hollywood star Glenn Ford. Cade was joined by ageing deputy J.J. Jackson and three younger deputies, Arlo, Rudy and Pete, the last-named being played by Glenn Ford's son Peter. The other regular role was that of police dispatcher. The first was Joanie Little Bird but she soon flew off to be replaced by Betty Ann Sundown. Both the actresses who took the parts were genuine American Indians. Cade's County was a pleasant enough diversion, but the central character was all work and no play, and therefore too one-dimensional to really grasp the public's imagination.

REGULAR CAST

Sam Cade Glenn Ford   *J.J. Jackson* Edgar Buchanan
Arlo Taylor Lacher   *Rudy* Victor Campos
Pete Peter Ford   *Joannie Little Bird* Sandra Ego
Betty Ann Sundown Betty Ann Carr

Music: Henry Mancini
Producer: Charles Larson
Executive producer: David Gerber

A TCF Production for CBS

24 colour 60-minute episodes
US: CBS 19 Sept 1971 - 9 April 1972
UK: ITV 1 March - 6 Sept 1972 (ATV)

CAGNEY AND LACEY

'Cagney and Lacey was a breakthrough series. We showed women doing a so-called "man's job" without ever forgetting they were women.' –   SHARON GLESS

Until Cagney and Lacey, American women detectives were usually little more than mindless bimbos in the Charlie's Angels mould, more likely to trap criminals by revealing three inches of thigh than a gun. But Christine Cagney and Mary Beth Lacey were different. They had brains. They were real people with real problems. True, Cagney was always being chased by her male colleagues, but first and foremost she was an outstanding detective. She was never portrayed as a sex symbol.

Because Cagney and Lacey was pioneering, the tussles the two New York cops faced on screen were nothing compared to the behind-the-scenes struggles to get the show accepted. Created by Barney Rosenzweig (ironically a producer on Charlie's Angels) with Barbara Avedon and Barbara Corday, the format had been rejected by all three US networks until it finally appeared in an October 1981 TV movie, with Loretta Swit as Cagney and Tyne Daly as Lacey. On the strength of healthy ratings, CBS commissioned a six-part series, but Loretta Swit was unavailable, as she was still heavily involved as Major 'Hotlips' Houlihan in M*A*S*H. Her place was taken by Meg Foster but, faced with dwindling viewing figures, CBS decided Meg was too butch for the part.

Attempting to explain the unpopularity of the Foster/Daly combination, one CBS executive (presumably male) said: 'They were too tough, too hard and not feminine. The American public doesn't respond to the bra burners, the fighters, the women who insist on calling manhole covers peoplehole covers. We perceived them as dykes.' Not surprisingly this last remark caused a storm of protest. But CBS was adamant that Foster had to go, and she in turn was succeeded by Sharon Gless, who in fact was the original choice for the part before Loretta Swit, but had been too busy to accept.

The arrival of the softer Gless led to more complaints, this time from gay groups, about her being 'too kittenish and too feminine.' By now many American viewers were so confused by Cagney having almost as many faces as Lon Chaney that they continued to desert the show and it was cancelled in September 1983.

However, women in particular had warmed to the characters, and a letter-writing campaign, partly co-ordinated by the National Organization for Women, resulted in huge publicity urging CBS to reconsider. All the hype boosted the ratings for the repeats and when Tyne Daly, who had researched the part by driving around Los Angeles' toughest districts in real patrol cars, unexpectedly won an Emmy in 1983, CBS relented and ordered further episodes for the following year. The girls had earned a reprieve. TV Guide advertized their American return in March 1984 with the headline: YOU WANT THEM! YOU'VE GOT THEM! Cagney and Lacey never looked back.

The strength of the series lay in the chemistry between the two principals. They were as different as chalk and cheese. In the squad room, where the pair were the first female detectives and consequently faced a battle to overcome initial male prejudice, the extrovert Cagney liked to be thought of as one of the boys. She gave as good as she got from the men officers and gradually won their respect. But her often carefree exterior masked a miserable private life. Unlucky in love, she spent many an evening alone in her apartment, behind the most heavily-fortified door this side of Fort Knox. In contrast, Lacey was quieter, less volatile and with a stable home life. She was happily married to supportive husband, Harvey, who worked in the construction industry. When he was laid off sick, he looked after their sons Harvey Junior and Michael. And when Mary Beth became pregnant with their third child, Alice, (Tyne Daly's real-life pregnancy being written into the plot) and beavered away at home, Harvey went back to construction. They seemed the perfect couple – even when Mary Beth was wheeled into the delivery-ward she was clutching Harv's bowling trophy. Ironically, John Karlen, who played this model husband, later blamed the stresses of the show for the break-up of his own 21-year marriage.

Cagney and Lacey were good friends, like a female Starsky and Hutch. Any crisis at home or at work and they would repair to the precinct's grimy ladies' loo. Many of the show's most poignant scenes took place in those unlikely surroundings. And they had plenty of problems to talk about, with storylines that frequently veered towards soap opera. It is surely no coincidence that co-creator Barbara Corday made her name with American daytime soaps such as The Days of Our Lives. Thus Lacey had a breast cancer scare, it was revealed that she had an abortion at 19, and she regularly encountered difficulties from teenage son, Harvey junior, who became a growing pain. Meanwhile, Cagney had an awkward relationship with the one man she worshipped, her retired-cop father Charlie, and experienced tremendous traumas when she discovered he was an alcoholic and a dying one at that. She too turned to the bottle (as incidentally, did Sharon Gless) and suffered further agonies when she was raped. And she was flashed at every week in the opening titles!

Besides her partner, Cagney always found an ample shoulder to cry on in the shape of her tough but protective boss, Lieutenant Samuels. The remaining men in the squad room often served as just a backdrop. Isbecki was a cocky womanizer; Petrie was serious-minded and married; Esposito was a computer buff; and LaGuardia was the wise elder statesman. The relative impotence of the men did not always go down well with the actors. In 1985 Martin Kove, who played Victor Isbecki, moaned: 'I'm fed up with the way the producers have castrated every male character on the show. My gun is rusty and there's dust on the trigger. The two women get all the best cases. In 59 episodes so far, I've arrested the bad guy just once – and that was by accident.'

Cagney and Lacey were finally taken off in 1988 after 125 episodes. Tyne Daly had won further Emmys in 1984 and 1985, with Sharon Gless stepping in for 1986. The programme also picked up the Best

Drama award that year. It became a huge hit on both sides of the Atlantic. All this from a show the networks didn't want...

REGULAR CAST

Det. Mary Beth Lacey Tyne Daly
Det. Christine Cagney Loretta Swit *(pilot)*   Meg Foster *(Season 1)*   Sharon Gless
Harvey Lacey John Karlen   *Lt Samuels* Al Waxman
Det. Isbecki Martin Kove   *Det. LaGuardia* Sidney Clute
Det. Petrie Carl Lumbly   *Det. Esposito* Robert Hegyes
Sgt Dory McKenna Barry Primus   *Harvey Lacey Jr* Tony La Torre
Michael Lacey Troy Slaten   *Desk Sergeant* Harvey Atkin
Charlie Cagney Dick O'Neill

Creators: Barney Rosenzweig, Barbara Avedon, Barbara Corday
Music: Nelson Riddle
Producer: Richard A. Rosenbloom
Executive producer: Barney Rosenzweig

A Mace Neufeld Production for Filmways and CBS

125 colour 60-minute episodes
US: CBS 25 March 1982 - 3 Aug 1988

UK: BBC1 9 July - 20 Aug 1982
21 Jan - 8 July 1983
21 April - 9 June 1984
16 Oct 1984 - 1 Jan 1985
3 Sept 1985 - 28 Jan 1986
5 April - 19 July 1986
3 Jan - 18 April 1987
16 May - 11 July 1987
14 Nov 1987 - 13 Feb 1988
19 Mar - 14 May 1988
20 Aug - 27 Aug 1988

CAIN'S HUNDRED

Once a gangland lawyer, Nick Cain switched sides, to become a federal government agent determined to bring to justice the hundred most important men behind organized crime in the USA. Presumably if there had only been ninety-six, it wouldn't have made for such a snappy title. Based on real case histories and presented in a semi-documentary format, this tedious series saw the able Cain tour the country with a special squad of assistants, to gain the necessary incriminating evidence. His intention was to prosecute one each week. Mercifully, he was stopped at thirty.

REGULAR CAST

Nick Cain Peter Mark Richman

Music: Jerry Goldsmith, Morton Stevens
Producer: Paul Monash

30 monochrome 60-minute episodes
US: NBC 19 Sept 1961 - 15 May 1962

An MGM Television Production

CALL THE GUN EXPERT

A fascinating series of dramatized reconstructions about the work of Churchill's, the celebrated London gunsmiths, and the expertise that Robert Churchill used to offer the CID, when they were investigating crimes involving firearms. It was presented by Macdonald Hastings, who would wander in and out of the re-enactments of the old cases that Churchill had helped to solve. The first investigation was that of the notorious murder of PC Gutteridge in 1927 Essex. Call the Gun Expert was a landmark in the early career of renowned TV and film director Jack Gold.

REGULAR CAST

Robert Churchill Wensley Pithey

Producer/Director: Jack Gold

6 monochrome 25-minute episodes
UK: BBC1 2 July - 6 Aug 1964

A BBC Television Production

CAMPION

'I once played the murderer in an episode of Miss Marple and there were so many red herrings, the evidence pointed to everyone but me. I like to think Allingham is more honest than Christie.' – PETER DAVISON

Described as the 'easiest of men to overlook or underestimate', Margery Allingham's gentlemanly amateur detective, Albert Campion, was born into that genteel age of crime-solving, the 1930s. In his 'enormous horm-rimmed spectacles', Campion looks rather vague but, as with Lord Peter Wimsey, he has hidden depths.

Campion is something of a mysterious character. He is the black sheep of an English aristocratic family, who was once offered the governorship of a British colony but rejected the post so that he could continue his sleuthing. Campion is not his real name, either. In Allingham's first book, a jeweller referred to him as 'Christopher Twelvetrees', while gypsies have been known to call him ' Orlando'. In total, there have been 26 Campion books and Allingham claimed that the character was modelled loosely on King George VI while he was still Duke of York.

In the TV series, Campion drove around East Anglia in his beautiful vintage Lagonda, dealing with murders and young ladies in dire straits. He was assisted on his cases by manservant Magersfontein Lugg, a reformed burglar who is less than deferential to his master. Lugg was played by former professional wrestler, Brian Glover. Campion's police contact is Chief Inspector Stanislaus Oates of the Metropolitan Police.

Campion is a throwback to what some observers have christened the 'Golden Age' of detective fiction, although the characters are not as obviously commercial as, say, Miss Marple. And making the series wasn't necessarily a bed of roses for Peter Davison. He explains: 'Campion always dresses for dinner, so I had to do quite a lot of detection in a wing collar which was very uncomfortable.'

* All the stories were two-parters.

REGULAR CAST

Albert Campion Peter Davison   *Magersfontein Lugg* Brian Glover
Chief Insp. Stanislaus Oates Andrew Burt

EPISODE TITLES

Season One

Look to the Lady
Police at the Funeral
The Case of the Late Pig
Death of a Ghost

Season Two

Sweet Danger
Dancers in Mourning
Flowers for the Judge
Mystery Mile

Music: Nigel Hess
Producer: Ken Riddington (Season 1)
Jonathan Alwyn (Season 2)

A BBC Television Production with WGBH Boston, Consolidated Productions

16 colour 55-minute episodes
(Season 1): UK: BBC1 22 Jan - 12 March 1989
US: WGBH Boston 'Mystery' 12 Oct - 30 Nov 1989
(Season 2): UK: 12 Jan - 16 March 1990
US: 15 Nov 1990 - 3 Jan 1991

CANNON

'I like to think that Cannon was the first with a gimmick. After me
came Kojak's lollipops, Columbo's raincoat and McCloud's horse. Not
to mention Charlie's Angels' unmentionables.'   – WILLIAM CONRAD

Frank Cannon's gimmick was there for all to see – he was TV's fattest
private eye. Played by 19-stone William Conrad, Cannon puffed and
panted his way through chases, while the suspension on his beloved
Lincoln convertible sagged alarmingly whenever he got in. Cannon
dreaded two things in life – a closed restaurant and a case where the bad
guy lived at the top of a flight of stairs. But in the 1970s, the golden era
for American detective shows, Cannon's popularity was as huge as his
waistline.

It all came as something of a surprise to William Conrad. His career
had begun in radio and for eleven years he had been the voice of Matt
Dillon on Gunsmoke. But when the series transferred to television,
Conrad was considered to be the wrong shape for the part (they would
have had to re-name it Podge City) and James Arness took over. Conrad
became a producer/director in TV and films and remained unseen as the
narrator of The Fugitive. He laments: 'For 15 years before Cannon, I
couldn't get much work as an actor because I was too fat and
unattractive. I'm five foot nine and look like an overfed walrus – and
I'm bald to boot. Producers took one look at me and ran. Then someone
came up with the bright idea that TV detectives were too clean-cut and
glamorous. It was decided to build a series around one who looked and
acted like any other guy with a weight problem. It sounded crazy to me.
Whoever heard of a cops and robbers chase with the hero wheezing?'

But it did take off – and in an American season where 70 per cent of
all new shows bit the dust. The reason the public warmed to the gravel-
voiced, Los Angeles-based P.I. was because he was a human being. He
wasn't a superhero – he got hurt in fights and bled when he was shot.
And his car ended up as a bit of a battered wreck too. At first, Conrad
did his own stunts but found it too painful. 'Did it hurt? You bet your
ass it hurt. My hide was a network of scars. So they hired a stunt man.
And his hide was a network of scars. I liked that a whole lot better!'

Cannon certainly had his faults but beneath the gruff exterior he had
a conscience. So although he habitually charged big fees (so that he
could afford to eat at the best restaurants and re-stock his fridge), he was
not above occasionally waiving payment to a deserving cause or a
damsel in distress.

Cannon and Conrad were good for one another, although even five
years after the show ended the actor claimed: 'My poor feet are still
hurting from all the running I did in Cannon. I was always running or
wrestling or hitting somebody or getting hit. I think I was the only

television detective who didn't have an assistant to take on some of the work. But I really enjoyed it. I liked filming it so much that I put on 20lb. in a season. It was one programme where I could eat and drink to my heart's content and call it "keeping in shape."'

* In the UK, Cannon aired under the BBC's umbrella title The Detectives, along with Harry O, The Rockford Files and A Man Called Ironside. A TV Movie, The Return of Frank Cannon, was made in 1980.

REGULAR CAST

Frank Cannon William Conrad

Music: John Parker, John Cannon
Producer: Anthony Spinner
Executive producer: Quinn Martin

A Quinn Martin Production for CBS

121 colour 60-minute episodes
US: CBS (Season 1) 14 Sept 1971 - 14 March 1972 (24 eps)

(Season 2) 13 Sept 1972 - 21 March 1973 (24 eps)
(Season 3) 12 Sept 1973 - 20 March 1974 (25 eps)
(Season 4) 11 Sept 1974 -2 April 1975 (24 eps)
(Season 5) 10 Sept 1975 -3 March 1976 (24 eps)
UK: BBC1 27 Oct 1972 - 30 Sept 1978

CAPTAIN ZEP – SPACE DETECTIVE

Dubbed a kind of 'Doctor Whodunnit', this children's series invited viewers to find the solutions to assorted space-age crimes. It was set in the year 2095 at the SOLVE Academy for student space detectives, which was under the command of Captain Zep, the Sherlock Holmes of the solar system. Each week he and his crew (in their spaceship Zep One) featured in some intergalactic mystery, and viewers attempted to guess the culprit before it was revealed on screen. The lucky winners received SOLVE badges as prizes. What more could any budding detective ask for?

REGULAR CAST

Captain Zep Paul Greenwood *(Season 1)* Richard Morant *(Season 2)*
Jason Brown Ben Ellison   *Professor Spiro* Harriet Keevil *(Season 1)*
Professor Vana Tracey Childs *(Season 2)*

Writer: Dick Hills (Season 1) Colin
   Bennett (Season 2)
Director: Christopher Pilkington
   (Season 1) Michael Forte (Season 2)
Producer: Christopher Pilkington

A BBC Television Production

12 colour 30-minute episodes
UK: BBC1 (Season 1) 5 Jan - 9 Feb
   1983
(Season 2) 9 March - 13 April 1984

CAR 54, WHERE ARE YOU?

'Car 54 gives a poor and inaccurate picture of a New York policeman in the '60s. I can tell you for a fact that police chiefs around the country are saddened to see a couple of buffoons masquerading as policemen.'
   – WALTER ARM, DEPUTY NEW YORK POLICE COMMISSIONER

That particular policeman's lot was not a happy one, as he singularly failed to see the joke in one of the funniest American comedies of the 1960s. At its best, Car 54 was reminiscent of Bilko, hardly surprising since it was created and produced by Nat Hiken, the man behind The Phil Silvers Show.

The connection didn't end there. Joe E. Ross and Bea Pons, who were Rupert and Emma Ritzik in Bilko, were also husband and wife in 'Car 54'. Ross was stumpy and stupid Officer Toody, patrol car partner to Fred Gwynne (who later went on to be the level-headed Herman Munster) as the lanky, contemplative Muldoon. Toody and Muldoon were hopelessly naive. Cruising the streets of New York's 53rd precinct, a derelict area in the Bronx, they merely succeeded in driving into trouble, to the despair of their boss, Captain Block.

Filming for the series was done on location, and their car had to be painted red and white to distinguish it from the green and white ones of the real New York Police Department. Of course on black and white TV they looked identical. However, some New Yorkers did have problems in separating fact from fiction. Much of the filming took place at an old movie studio with the exterior altered to resemble a police station, until one day a hysterical woman raced onto the set screaming: 'Help! Police! My husband is beating me!' The exterior was promptly changed.

Since Car 54 was in the best traditions of slapstick comedy, it was hard to understand why real cops should have taken offence. But many did. The police in San Antonio even went as far as registering an official complaint about the show, because it 'makes us look stupid.' If the show didn't, the complaint did. Meanwhile the Dayton, Ohio, Police Department dropped its patrol car 54 because nobody would drive it! Yet Joe E. Ross found that not all of the police were hostile, commenting: 'Policemen often lead me to the front of movie lines. And I get less traffic tickets than I used to.'

* Fred Gwynne was not the only future Munster to star in 'Car 54'. Al Lewis, who went on to play streaky-haired Grandpa, appeared as Officer Leo Schnauser.

REGULAR CAST

Officer Gunther Toody Joe E. Ross   *Officer Francis Muldoon* Fred Gwynne
Lucille Toody Bea Pons   *Capt. Martin Block* Paul Reed
Officer Leo Schnauser Al Lewis   *Officer Steinmetz* Joe Warren
Officer Kissel Bruce Kirby   *Officer Ed Nicholson* Hank Garrett
Desk Sgt Abrams Nathaniel Frey

Creator: Nat Hiken
Music: John Strauss
Producer: Nat Hiken

A Euopolis Production for NBC

60 monochrome 30-minute episodes
US: NBC 17 Sept 1961 - 8 Sept 1963
UK: ITV 9 July 1964 - 6 Nov 1965
  (Anglia)
Channel 4 (repeats) 19 May - 25 Aug
  1983
14 Feb 1986 - 13 March 1987

CARIBE

Exotic location, handsome lead, exciting boat chases. What more could you ask for? – How about a sensible script, for a start? Having spent all the budget on a Caribbean setting and star, Stacy Keach, the producers seemed to have forgotten about the necessity for providing him with half-decent lines. The idea was reasonable enough. Lieutenant Ben Logan and his black partner, Sergeant Mark Walters, worked for an international crime-fighting agency called Caribbean Force, designed to protect the interests of Americans. Their boss was Ed Rawlings of the Miami Police Department. But it was all so badly done that this nautical cops and robbers show quickly sank without trace.

REGULAR CAST

Lt Ben Logan Stacy Keach   *Sgt Mark Walters* Carl Franklin
Deputy Commissioner Ed Rawlings Robert Mandan

Music: John Elizade, Nelson Riddle
Producer: Anthony Spinner
Executive producer: Quinn Martin

13 colour 60-minute episodes
US: ABC 17 Feb - 11 Aug 1975
UK: ITV From 3 April 1975

A Quinn Martin Production

CARTER COUNTRY

When Jimmy Carter was United States President, American television tried to cash in with a situation comedy set in the small Georgia town of Clinton Corners. It was supposed to be near Plains, the former peanut-seller's home town, hence the title. That was about as funny as it got. The law in Clinton Corners was upheld by police chief Roy Mobey, an amiable redneck, and his sharp black deputy Curtis Baker, a graduate of big-city police practice, having trained in New York. This not only resulted in jokes about the colour of each other's skin, but also about their different attitudes to crime-fighting. Other regulars included Cloris Phebus, a man-eating policewoman, Teddy Burnside, the weak-willed mayor who was only elected because nobody else wanted the job, and Lucille, the mayor's secretary and the apple of Curtis Baker's eye. Sadly even the ever-smiling Jimmy Carter must have been hard pushed to laugh at this.

* Early in her career, Oscar-nominated actress Melanie Griffith (star of Working Girl) was sacked from her role as a newspaper reporter after just two episodes of Carter Country. She probably looks back on it as a lucky break.

REGULAR CAST

Chief Roy Mobey Victor French   *Sgt Curtis Baker* Kene Holliday
Mayor Teddy Burnside Richard Paul   *Cloris Phebus* Barbara Cason
Lucille Banks Vernee Watson

Music: Pete Rugolo
Producers: Douglas Arango, Phil Doran
Executive producers: Bud Yorkin, Saul
  Turteltaub Bernie Orenstein

An ABC Production

12 colour 30-minute episodes
US: ABC 15 Sept 1977 - 23 Aug 1979

THE CASE BOOK OF SHERLOCK HOLMES (SEE THE ADVENTURES OF SHERLOCK HOLMES)

CASE HISTORIES OF SCOTLAND YARD (US TITLE SCOTLAND YARD)

Noted British journalist and criminologist Edgar Lustgarten, author of a number of books on infamous crimes and trials, presented this classic filmed series based on real cases from the files of Scotland Yard. The cast varied from week to week, the nearest to a regular police character being Inspector Duggan, who appeared in some half a dozen episodes. The stories were particularly popular in the US.

SEMI-REGULAR CAST

Insp. Duggan Russell Napier   *Insp. Ross* Ken Henry
Sgt Mason Arthur Mason

Producer: Jack Greenwood

An Anglo Amalgamated Films Production

39 monochrome 30-minute episodes
UK: Syndicated 1955
US: ABC 17 Nov 1957 - 6 April 1958

THE CASE OF THE DANGEROUS ROBIN

A gallant attempt to turn the work of insurance investigators into compelling drama. In this syndicated series, karate expert, Robin and his partner, Phyllis, went where few had dared to go before – to track down and expose those who defraud insurance companies with false claims. Excitement was at a premium.

REGULAR CAST

Robin Scott Rick Jason   *Phyllis Collier* Jean Blake

Music: David Rose

A Ziv Production

38 monochrome 30-minute episodes
US: Syndicated 1961

THE CASES OF EDDIE DRAKE

Eddie Drake was a New York private detective whose help was enlisted by psychologist, Dr Karen Gayle, to acquire information for a book she was compiling on criminal behaviour. One of the earliest crime series, it was shown on CBS in 1949 but dropped after nine episodes. When it was later syndicated in 1952, it became a moderate hit.

REGULAR CAST

Eddie Drake Don Haggerty   *Karen Gayle* Patricia Morrison

Producers: Harlan Thompson, Lindsley Parsons

13 monochrome 30-minute episodes
US: Syndicated 1952

A CBS Production

THE CASES OF SHERLOCK HOLMES

Three years after starring alongside Douglas Wilmer (SEE SHERLOCK HOLMES), Nigel Stock's bumbling Dr Watson found a new partner in distinguished actor, Peter Cushing, for a typically affectionate BBC adaptation of 15 of Conan Doyle's stories. Cushing's Holmes reflected the image of the Baker Street sleuth with which most children had been brought up, even if it was not necessarily the one which Conan Doyle had intended. He came across as a great detective and basically a kind man (even to Watson), not prone to the wild-eyed excesses and black moods of Jeremy Brett's subsequent creation.

Cushing revealed that his fondness for Holmes dated back to his childhood. 'An uncle of mine was an absolute devotee of the adventures and I always remember him telling me about a friend of his who had been accused of molesting a lady on a train. My uncle said the man proved the lady was telling a lie rather as Holmes would have done. He called the guard and repeated what the lady had accused him of doing. "But it is absolutely impossible," the man insisted, "for look at my cigar – it has only about half an inch of ash on it. There was not enough time for me to have committed what she alleges." After that I thought Holmes must be a wonderful person and became a confirmed fan.'

REGULAR CAST

Sherlock Holmes Peter Cushing   *Dr Watson* Nigel Stock
Insp. Lestrade William Lucas   *Mrs Hudson* Grace Arnold
Mycroft Holmes   Ronald Adam

EPISODE TITLES

The Second Stain
A Study in Scarlet
The Dancing Men
The Hound of the Baskervilles (2 parts)
The Boscombe Valley Mystery
The Greek Interpreter
The Naval Treaty
Thor Bridge
The Musgrave Ritual
Black Peter
Wisteria Lodge

Shoscombe Old Place
The Solitary Cyclist
The Sign of Four
The Blue Carbuncle

Producer: William Sterling

A BBC Television Production

16 monochrome 50-minute episodes
UK: BBC1 9 Sept - 23 Dec 1968

CASSIE AND COMPANY

Following the euphoria of Police Woman, much was expected of Angie Dickinson's follow-up series Cassie and Company, particularly since her character, Cassie Holland, was virtually an exact replica of Pepper Anderson. But it didn't work out and the adventures of Cassie, a former police officer turned private detective, lasted a mere 13 episodes.

Cassie had taken over the business of 'Shack' Shackelford (none of the budget was wasted on dreaming up original nicknames) who, although officially retired, stayed on to help out with particularly awkward cases. The other members of the company were secretary Meryl, a young ex-con, and Benny, part-time manager of a local gymnasium who also acted as Cassie's legman and physical guardian. If the going got tough for Cassie, Benny would flex his pectorals and save the day. The other regular was Mike Holland, the City District Attorney, who just happened to be our heroine's former husband. If nothing else, he came in useful for providing snippets of information.

REGULAR CAST

Cassie Holland Angie Dickinson   *Lyman 'Shack' Shackelford* John Ireland
Meryl Dori Brenner   *Benny* A. Martinez
Mike Holland Alex Cord

A Carson Production for Columbia Pictures Television

13 colour 60-minute episodes
US: NBC 29 Jan - 20 Aug 1982

C.A.T.S. Eyes

The series that showed that whatever America could do with Charlie's Angels, the British could do equally badly. This action drama certainly had viewers on the edges of their seats – but in most cases it was just to switch off.

Pru Standfast, Maggie Forbes and Frederica 'Fred' Smith formed the Eyes Enquiry Agency, a cover for a Home Office security squad known as C.A.T.S. (Covert Activities Thames Section). This gave the three girls an excuse to race around England's Medway Towns (Rochester, Chatham and Gillingham) in pursuit of Russian spies and CIA plots – all in an area which had seen little activity since the threat of the Spanish Armada. The real reason for the location was that producers TVS wanted to utilize the north of their franchise region, in the light of their new Maidstone studios.

The leader of the pack was Pru Standfast, a tall University graduate with a War Office background. She was backed by former CID officer Maggie Forbes, who had spent five years having her hair permed on The Gentle Touch (SEE THE GENTLE TOUCH), and young computer buff Fred Smith. Keeping an eye on them was 'the man from the Ministry' Nigel Beaumont. For the second season, Pru was replaced by Tessa Robinson (played by Tracy-Louise Ward, younger sister of Thorn Birds' star Rachel Ward) with Maggie Forbes placed in charge.

C.A.T.S. Eyes promised 'pure entertainment without social statements.' It achieved neither. These British Charlie's Angels didn't so much turn my head as turn my stomach.

Regular Cast

Pru Standfast Rosalyn Landor   *Maggie Forbes* Jill Gascoine
Fred Smith Leslie Ash   *Nigel Beaumont* Don Warrington
Tessa Robinson Tracy-Louise Ward

Creator: Terence Feely
Music: John Kongos (Season 1)
   Barbara Thompson (Seasons 2,3)
Producers: Dickie Bamber, Frank Cox
   (Season 1) Raymond Menmuir
   (Seasons 2,3)
Executive producer: Rex Firkin

A TVS Network Production

One colour 90-minute and 30 colour 60-minute episodes
UK: ITV (Season 1) 12 April - 26 June 1985 (13 eps)
(Season 2) 5 April - 14 June 1986 (11 eps)
(Season 3) 25 April - 6 June 1987 (7 eps)

CHARLESWORTH

A fine upstanding Metropolitan Policeman of the 1950s who, according to his creator, Berkely Mather, 'combines the gentle pedantry of a Cambridge don with a penchant for clipping unlawful characters over the ear'ole for failure to address him as Mister Charlesworth.' He made his debut as a Chief Detective Inspector in Tales From Soho, six stories about London's famous square half-mile, and was elevated to Detective Superintendent for his own series, Big Guns, in which he did battle with the evil J. Philimore Sparkes. Here, Charlesworth was played by a totally different actor, but nobody minded about things like that in those days.

Tales from Soho

REGULAR CAST

Chief Det. Insp. Charlesworth John Welsh

Creator: Berkely Mather
Producer: Tony Richardson

A BBC Television Production

7 monochrome 30-minute episodes
UK: BBC 21 Jan - 3 March 1956

Big Guns

REGULAR CAST

Det. Supt Charlesworth Wensley Pithey
J. Philimore Sparkes Walter Fitzgerald
Sgt Spence Nigel Davenport

Creator: Berkely Mather
Producer: Gerard Glaister

A BBC Television Production

6 monochrome 30-minute episodes
UK: BBC 1 Jan - 5 Feb 1958

CHARLIE

British film actor David Warner (Tom Jones, Morgan etc) made a rare excursion into television as private detective Charlie Alexander, in this worthy four-part adventure. Charlie, described by Warner as 'a decent fellow', was minding his own business when he stumbled across a dying man, whose address book contained Charlie's name and phone number. Yet Charlie had never set eyes on the man before. So he began investigating the stranger's past and became enmeshed in a series of murders.

MAIN CAST

Charlie Alexander David Warner   *Harry Ainsworth* Frank Windsor
Susan Alexander Marion Bailey

Creator: Nigel Williams
Director: Martin Campbell
Producer: Graham Benson

A Central Television Production

4 colour 60-minute episodes
UK: ITV 26 March - 4 April 1984

CHARLIE WILD, PRIVATE DETECTIVE

'He's hard-boiled and dedicated to the proposition that crime does not pay. He's a man's man – but the ladies, too, go for Charlie Wild, Private Eye. Follow him into adventure.' – PROGRAMME TRAIL

Charlie Wild's origins lay with Dashiell Hammett's archetypal private detective Sam Spade. The Adventures of Sam Spade was once a highly popular American radio series, but when Hammett was branded a communist by McCarthyite witch-hunters, Spade's name was changed to Charlie Wild across the airwaves. In spite of his identity crisis, Charlie became a big hit in the late 1940s and graduated to his own live television show, where he was played first by Kevin O'Morrison and, from 1951, by John McQuade.

Assisted by his faithful secretary Effie, Charlie was a tough New York private eye who got involved in a punch-up nearly every week. He saw the world too, appearing on no fewer than three different American networks – CBS, ABC and DuMont. The series was sponsored by a wine company, although in truth the hero was more of a bar-room brawler than a Champagne Charlie. It is difficult to imagine that he did much for the sales of Chablis.

REGULAR CAST

Charlie Wild Kevin O'Morrison *(1950-1)* John McQuade *(1951-2)*
Effie Perrine Cloris Leachman

Producers: Carlo De Angelo, Herbert Brodkin

US: CBS/ABC/DuMont 22 Dec 1950 - 19 June 1952

Approx. 60 monochrome 30-minute episodes

CHARLIE'S ANGELS

'Once upon a time, there were three girls who went to the police academy and they were each assigned very hazardous duties. But I took them away from all that and now they work for me. My name is Charlie.'

The show that did for women's lib what myxomatosis did for the rabbit. Charlie's Angels was farcical, feeble, far-fetched and phenomenally successful. It illustrated that scantily-clad girls not only sell newspapers, they also work wonders for TV ratings. The plots were skimpier than the girls' outfits and the acting was so wooden it could have been taken from a Forestry Commission training film, yet western civilization was hooked. Indeed episodes were still being repeated on ITV in 1991, 15 years after the show's less than immaculate conception.

For those fortunate enough never to have sat through Charlie's Angels, it revolved around three extremely attractive police-trained detectives working for an unseen boss by the name of Charlie, who phoned in their latest assignments. Their only tangible point of contact with Charlie was his dull assistant, Bosley. Every case tended to have a glamorous backdrop like a night club or a swimming pool where the girls could go undercover and wear the bare minimum of clothing. Having created sex symbols, the producers naturally saw little point in wrapping them in donkey jackets and wellington boots, to investigate some construction site scam.

The original trio were leader Sabrina Duncan (played by Kate Jackson), ex-showgirl Kelly Garrett (Jaclyn Smith) and the athletic Jill Munroe (Farrah Fawcett-Majors). Farrah was the last to be cast (the programme needed a blonde since the other two were dark-haired) and was relatively unknown compared to Kate Jackson. But it was Farrah who quickly became the star of the show, following a series of daring publicity photos in a swimsuit. Whether they worked in a beauty salon or the Co-op, girls on both sides of the Atlantic copied her shaggy blonde hair-style (reminiscent of an Afghan Hound on heat) and Farrah dolls were marketed amidst rumours that they were better actresses than the real thing. Farrah herself felt that her talents were wasted on the show and walked out to pursue a career in films where, incidentally, she has turned in some surprisingly capable performances. Her exit prompted a rush of law suits for breach of contract and the acrimony was only resolved when she finally agreed to make a limited number of guest appearances on the show, over the ensuing three seasons.

Thereafter Angels came and went. Jill Munroe's replacement was her younger sister Kris (Cheryl Ladd); for the fourth season Sabrina was succeeded by Tiffany Welles, the daughter of a Connecticut police chief; and a year later for the fifth and final season, Tiffany was in turn ousted by street-wise Julie Rogers. Kate Jackson and Jaclyn Smith both blamed their real-life divorces on the pressures of doing Charlie's Angels. Jackson admitted afterwards: 'I didn't consider it was acting. We might as well have been Barbie Dolls in some store window.' One who wasn't complaining was John Forsythe (later Blake Carrington in Dynasty) who provided the voice of Charlie. His role gave him ample opportunity to play golf. He said at the time: 'I must be the only actor in Hollywood who can phone in his lines!'

Charlie was happy to be heard but not seen. Perhaps I would have been happier if the Angels had just been seen and not heard

REGULAR CAST

Sabrina Duncan Kate Jackson   *Jill Munroe* Farrah Fawcett-Majors
Kelly Garrett Jaclyn Smith   *Kris Munroe* Cheryl Ladd
Tiffany Welles Shelly Hack   *Julie Rogers* Tanya Roberts
John Bosley David Doyle   *Charlie Townsend (voice)* John Forsythe

Music: Jack Elliott, Allyn Ferguson
Producers: Rick Huskey, David
  Levinson, Barney Rosenzweig
Executive producers: Aaron Spelling,
  Leonard Goldberg

A Twentieth Century-Fox Production

109 colour 60-minute episodes US: ABC
  (Season 1) 22 Sept 1976 - 4 May
  1977 (22 eps)

(Season 2) 14 Sept 1977 - 10 May 1978
  (24 eps)
(Season 3) 13 Sept 1978 - 16 May 1979
  (22 eps)
(Season 4) 12 Sept 1979 - 7 May 1980
  (24 eps)
Season 5) 16 Nov 1980 - 24 June 1981
  (17 eps)
UK: ITV 3 Jan 1977 - 8 May 1982

CHARTERS AND CALDICOTT

Charters and Caldicott were a couple of eccentric old buffers who believed that the world was divided into those who played cricket and those who did not. Non-cricketing nations were definitely not to be trusted.

They first appeared in Hitchcock's 1938 classic comedy thriller The Lady Vanishes, where they were played by Basil Radford and Naunton Wayne, and went on to star in two sequels, Night Train to Munich and Crooks' Tour (both 1940).

For television, they were brought up to date, older and recently retired from the diplomatic service. Charters was a widower living in Surrey, while Caldicott lived in Viceroy Court, Kensington. On the first

Friday of each month, Charters would hail a Green Line bus like a taxi, and journey to London for lunch with his old friend at their gentlemen's club, the Pall Mall. The idea was that afterwards they would go to the cinema but instead, they ended up as amateur detectives, having always somehow managed to become involved in a criminal plot. This they duly solved in the finest traditions of British fair-play. Their innings was all too short.

REGULAR CAST

Charters Robin Bailey   *Caldicott* Michael Aldridge

Original creators: Frank Launder, Sidney Gilliat
Writer: Keith Waterhouse
Director: Julian Amyes
Producer: Ron Craddock

A BBC Television Production with Network Seven Australia

6 colour 50-minute episodes
UK: BBC1 10 Jan - 14 Feb 1985
US: WGBH Boston 'Mystery' 20 March - 24 April 1986

CHASE

So many police series have been set in Los Angeles, that there would appear to be a unit created to cater for every possible criminal permutation in the city. Somewhere there must be an elite squad, which deals only with murders committed on Mondays and Tuesdays, by bearded Frenchmen with a shoe size 8 and a half and under.

Captain Chase Reddick commanded one such group of men. They were a plainclothes division of the Los Angeles Police Department, accountable only to the Chief of Detectives, and were called in to crack cases that none of the rest of the city's cops could deal with. There were four men in Reddick's unit and each had a special ability – Sam MacCray was a police dog handler, Steve Baker a hot rod car driver, Fred Sing an ace motorcyclist and Norm Hamilton had been a helicopter pilot in Vietnam. But even with Jack Webb on the case, there was one phenomenon this multi-talented crew couldn't handle – low ratings. This Chase was soon over.

* The unsung hero of Chase was German Shepherd dog Farouk who played police dog Fuzz. Even though he was only four, Farouk was a TV veteran, having previously appeared on Ironside, The Mod Squad and Mission Impossible. He actually won a Patsy Award (a kind of four-

legged Oscar) for giving the best animal performance on television, in Ironside! And what's more he did it all without the help of a stunt double, as producers were unable to find another German Shepherd with a similar coat. What a star.

REGULAR CAST

Capt. Chase Reddick Mitchell Ryan   *Officer Norm Hamilton* Reid Smith
Officer Steve Baker Michael Richardson   *Officer Fred Sing* Brian Fong
Sgt Sam MacCray Wayne Maunder   *Chief Frank Dawson* Albert Reed

Music: Oliver Nelson
Producer: James Schmerer
Executive producer: Robert A. Cinader

*A Universal Television Production in
association with Mark VII Ltd*

23 colour 60-minute episodes
US: NBC 11 Sept 1973 - 28 Aug 1974
UK: ITV From 1 Nov 1975

THE CHEATERS

A dreary drama about the work of John Hunter and his assistant Walter, claims investigators with the Eastern Insurance Company. The pair were committed (and so they should have been) to thwarting fraudulent claims, usually involving relatively serious cases such as fire or theft, rather than broken roof tiles or buckled guttering. It merely served to underline that the life of an insurance man is not one of glamour and unbridled excitement. The best policy was to switch off.

REGULAR CAST

John Hunter John Ireland   *Walter* Robert Ayres

A Danziger Production

UK: ITV 10 Dec 1960 - 23 June 1962
US: Syndicated 1960

39 monochrome 30-minute episodes

CHECKMATE

Checkmate Inc. of San Francisco was an investigative agency with a difference. Its aim was to prevent crime, thereby removing the need to solve it. The outfit was run by Don Corey and Jed Sills, the latter played by Doug McClure just before he starred in The Virginian. Corey and Sills invariably found themselves trying to protect people threatened by criminals. Their intention was to checkmate the crooks who were menacing their clients. It was an intelligent series, aided by the presence of Carl Hyatt, a bearded former Oxford professor of criminology, who was employed as special consultant to the firm. Another investigator, Chris Devlin, was added to the team in the show's final year.

REGULAR CAST

Don Corey Anthony George   *Jed Sills* Doug McClure
Carl Hyatt Sebastian Cabot   *Chris Devlin* Jack Betts

Creator: Eric Ambler
Producers: Dick Berg, Herb Coleman
  Maxwell Shane

A Revue/J and M Production

70 monochrome 60-minute episodes
US: CBS (Season 1) 17 Sept 1960 - 24
  June 1961 (36 eps)
(Season 2) 4 Oct 1961 - 13 June 1962
  (34 eps)
UK: ITV 29 June - 27 Nov 1963 (ATV)

CHICAGOLAND MYSTERY PLAYERS

Criminologist Jeffrey Hall and his sidekick, Sergeant Holland, pursued the bad guys in this early crime drama. The series had actually been shown on Chicago television for two years before it was networked, and in its local days, it featured a novel twist in the tail . The solution was not divulged on screen, but instead viewers were told to buy the following day's Chicago Tribune to discover whodunnit. It was a clever commercial tie-in but one which, for obvious reasons, was not repeated nationally.

REGULAR CAST

Jeffrey Hall Gordon Urquhart   *Sgt Holland* Bob Smith

A DuMont Production   26 monochrome 30-minute episodes
US: DuMont 18 Sept 1949 - 30 July 1950

THE CHIEF

'Stafford goes in where angels fear to tread. He's a liberal who shoots
from the hip.'
– TIM PIGOTT-SMITH

It sounds like something from Miami Vice. But The Chief is set in
rural East Anglia. And John Stafford is no Morris dancing version of
Sonny Crockett. The Chief is not about bobbies on the beat and car
chases – it deals with the concepts of policing in modern Britain,
focussing on the higher echelons of the force.

The stories revolve around John Stafford, the outspoken newly-
appointed Chief Constable of Eastland. Played by Jewel in the Crown
star Tim Pigott-Smith, Stafford is a fighter. He is tough, blunt and his
vigorous enthusiasm for law and order is vital to combat a high crime
rate. But there is a rude awakening for those who appointed him. They
grow to dislike the maverick newcomer who refuses to play the game
by their rules. He ousts a sergeant for drinking on duty, calls a halt to
dangerous car chases by over-zealous rookie constables, refuses to
send in his men when a prison riot threatens to erupt, and insists that
students have a legal right to voice their protests to a visiting
Government minister. Consequently Stafford soon finds himself under
severe pressure, and ultimately suspension, from the Home Office but
nothing will divert him from his principles.

He came to Eastland from Nottinghamshire and brought with him
Anne Stewart who was head of CID there. She is swiftly promoted to
head of Crime and Operations, to the resentment of fellow officers.
Confronted with the prejudices of a predominantly male organization,
she has to fight hard to assert her authority. There are problems too
with her husband, Martin, when he is left at home wearing the apron.
Stafford is more fortunate in that he can count on the support of his
GP wife, Elizabeth, although wayward teenage offspring Tim and
Emma ensure that home life can often be as fraught as that at the
office.

Much of the credit for the series' authenticity must go to former
Chief Constable of Devon and Cornwall John Alderson who acted as
advisor. A police officer with 36 years experience, he says: 'In all the
television dramas about the police, we have not seen what goes on
around a Chief Constable. The Chief is breaking new ground.'

REGULAR CAST

Chief Constable John Stafford Tim Pigott-Smith
Asst Chief Const. Anne Stewart Karen Archer   *Dr Elizabeth Stafford* Judy Loe
Det. Chief Supt Jim Gray Eamon Boland   *Emma Stafford (Season 1)* Sara Griffiths
Tim Stafford (Season 1) Ross Livingstone   *Martin Stewart* David Cardy

Creator: Jeffrey Caine Music: Nigel
   Beaham-Powell, Bella Russell
Director: Brian Farnham (Season 1)
   Desmond Davis (Season 2)
Producer: Ruth Boswell
Executive producer: Brenda Reid

An Anglia Films Production

12 colour 60-minute episodes
UK: ITV (Season 1) 20 April - 25 May
   1990 (6 eps)
(Season 2) 5 April - 10 May 1991 (6 eps)

CHIEF OF DETECTIVES (US TITLE: EISCHIED)

Earl Eischied was the uncompromising Chief of Detectives of the New York City Police Department. Played by the mountainous Joe Don Baker, he was not a man to mess with. He was a hard task-master, too – any praise was restricted to the occasional grudging 'you done good' in his familiar Southern drawl. But whatever his lack of social graces, Eischied was a good cop, ready to bend the rule book if necessary. This practice worried Deputy Commissioner Kimbrough, not because he wanted to read the book next but because he had clear-cut political ambitions. Fortunately Eischied's friend and colleague, Chief Inspector Ed Parks, was usually around to keep the two men apart.

Eischied was in charge of his own special squad which included Carol Wright, Rick Alessi and the loyal Captain Finnerty. Police detection meant everything to Earl Eischied. He was a bachelor and his only companion was his cat, P.C., which even came to work with him.

Originating from an impressive mini series, To Kill a Cop, and with a charismatic actor like Joe Don Baker in the lead, Eischied should have been a huge success. Maybe the reason it wasn't was that nobody could pronounce his name.

* This was promotion indeed for Eddie Egan who played Chief Inspector Ed Parks. As a real-life New York cop, he only reached the rank of Detective First Grade.

REGULAR CAST

Chief Earl Eischied Joe Don Baker   *Chief Insp. Ed Parks* Eddie Egan
Capt. Finnerty Alan Oppenheimer   *Deputy Com. Kimbrough* Alan Fudge
Carol Wright Suzanne Lederer   *Rick Alessi* Vincent Bufano

Producers: Matthew Rapf, Jay Daniel
Executive producer: David Gerber

Gerber Productions/Columbia Pictures TV

13 colour 60-minute episodes
US: NBC 21 Sept 1979 - 29 Aug 1980
UK: ITV 17 Jan - 10 April 1980

THE CHINESE DETECTIVE

'Johnny Ho does have a wonderful sense of humour – humour is the Chinese outlet. But their humour is weird. I don't understand it.'–
DAVID YIP

Half-Chinese actor, David Yip, (he was born in Liverpool but his dad was Chinese) played scruffy loner Detective Sergeant Johnny Ho, in the first British police drama to have an ethnic hero.

Ho joined up partly to clear his father's name but had to overcome innumerable obstacles. For a start he was too short to be accepted by the Metropolitan Police, but having obtained a posting elsewhere, he encountered a great deal of antagonism and racism from within the force. His boss, the burly no-nonsense, Detective Chief Inspector Berwick, became so fed up with his slovenly attitude that he teamed him up with Detective Sergeant Donald Chegwyn, in the hope that the wayward Ho might toe the line. But the Chinese detective still took plenty of blows, although they tended to be emotional and moral rather than physical.

Penned by Ian Kennedy Martin who created The Sweeney, this hard-hitting series did not always go down well with the real boys in blue, particularly the suggestions of racism. But it did show that Chinese detectives were not all like Charlie Chan.

REGULAR CAST

Det. Sgt Johnny Ho David Yip   *Det. Chief Insp. Berwick* Derek Martin
Det. Sgt Donald Chegwyn Arthur Kelly

Creator: Ian Kennedy Martin
Producer: Terence Williams

A BBC Television Production

14 colour 50-minute episodes
UK: BBC1 (Season 1) 30 April - 4 June
 1981 (6 eps)
(Season 2)10 Sept - 5 Nov 1982(8 eps)

CHiPS

CHiPS was by no means the most intellectually demanding of police shows but it won a vast teenage following, who tuned in for the all-action motorbike chases and to catch a glimpse of the boyish heroes Jon and Ponch. The Latin looks of Erik Estrada as the carefree Ponch, replaced David Cassidy on girls' bedroom walls, with fair-haired Larry Wilcox as the more serious Jon not far behind.

Naturally enough, the producers built the show around the appeal of the two stars, who were thus given ample opportunity to flash their sparkling white teeth and pose into the camera before, after and during each chase. Their smiles were usually infinitely more dazzling than the plots but the show's legions of fans didn't care.

Jon and Ponch were state motorcycle patrolmen with the California Highway Patrol (abbreviation CHiPS) and it has to be admitted they were better looking than Broderick Crawford! However, Ponch's laid-back manner didn't always endear him to their boss Sergeant Getraer. Other characters included Harlan, a mechanic, and Sindy Cahill, a female 'Chippie' who operated from a patrol car. But she was replaced after a year by Bonnie Clark, in a bid to set young male pulses racing too. Other recruits arrived, the prime requisite for acceptance seeming to be a perfect profile and a grin wider than the Golden Gate Bridge, rather than any particular law-enforcing ability.

In the autumn of 1981, Erik Estrada was locked in a contractual dispute with MGM and his place was temporarily filled by former Olympic decathlon champion Bruce Jenner, as Officer Steve McLeish. When Estrada returned, Jenner left. A year later Larry Wilcox quit and Tom Reilly was introduced as Ponch's new partner, Bobby Nelson. In that same final season, professional racing motorcyclist Bruce Penhall joined as Bobby Nelson's younger brother, Bruce. The producers clearly didn't want to take any risks with him forgetting his character name.

Ironically for two who were such good buddies on screen, Larry Wilcox and Erik Estrada didn't get on at all once the cameras had stopped rolling. Yet they always managed to hide it from the viewers. Some observers believe it was the only decent bit of acting in the show.

REGULAR CAST

Officer Jon Baker Larry Wilcox   *Officer Frank 'Ponch' Poncherello* Erik Estrada
Sgt Joe Getraer Robert Pine   *Officer Sindy Cahill* Brianne Leary
Harlan Lou Wagner   *Officer Bonnie Clark* Randi Oakes
Officer Bobby Nelson Tom Reilly   *Cadet Bruce Nelson* Bruce Penhall

Creator: Rick Rosner
Music: Mike Post, Pete Carpenter
Theme: John Parker
Producers: Cy Chermak, Rick Rosner, Ric Randall

An MGM Television Production

138 colour 60-minute episodes
US: NBC 15 Sept 1977 - 17 July 1983
UK: ITV 6 Jan 1979 - 14 March 1987
(LWT)

CHOPPER ONE

An above-average but short-lived adventure series about two young cops, Don Burdick and Gil Foley, on police helicopter duty in Los Angeles. They were called in to deal with any crimes committed in the open – muggers in parks and rooftop snipers were particular favourites. Captain McKeegan was their boss and Mitch their mechanic.

REGULAR CAST

Officer Don Burdick Jim McMullan   *Officer Gil Foley* Dirk Benedict
Captain McKeegan Ted Hartley   *Mitch* Lou Frizzel

Music: Dominic Frontiere
Producers: Ronald Austin, James Buchanan
Executive producer: Aaron Spelling

An Aaron Spelling Production for ABC

13 colour 30-minute episodes
US: ABC 17 Jan - 11 July 1974

CHRISTINE CROMWELL

Jaclyn Smith proved there is some life after Charlie's Angels, by playing Harvard Law School graduate, Christine Cromwell, in a glossy new addition to the detective ranks. Christine is a partner in Blain &

Knapp, a prestigious San Francisco management firm that only accepts new clients with a net worth of $15 million plus. And when these clients become involved in murder cases, inevitably it is Christine who steps in to provide an extra professional service by getting them off the hook.

Described as 'a light English Country House-style mystery without graphic violence', Christine Cromwell held intimate appeal for Jaclyn. 'My character has led a charmed life', she explained. 'She's very glamorous and I was kind of excited about that. Also I got the chance to wear beautiful clothes and be in very luxurious surroundings.'

Another bonus is the show's strong supporting cast, with Celeste Holm as Christine's eight-times-married mother, Samantha, and Ralph Bellamy as Christine's paternal boss, Cyrus Blaine. Guest stars include Dennis Franz (Hill Street's Norm Buntz, playing a typically bullish police detective), Bradford Dillman and Mel Ferrer.

In the US, Christine Cromwell aired as part of the new Mystery Movie with B.L. Stryker, New Columbo and New Kojak. At the time of writing, the episodes are awaiting transmission in Britain.

REGULAR CAST

Christine Cromwell Jaclyn Smith   *Samantha Cromwell* Celeste Holm
Cyrus Blain Ralph Bellamy

Creator/Executive producer: Dick Wolf

A Wolf Films Production in association with Universal Television

4 colour 120-minute episodes
US: ABC From 11 Nov 1989

CITY DETECTIVE

Gangling Rod Cameron was just another minor star of the 1940s – until he discovered syndicated television. Cameron became the undisputed king of American syndicated series in the Fifties, appearing in State Trooper, Coronado 9 and, first of all, City Detective. Cameron was no fool. While other actors enjoyed the glamour of a regular network spot, he was able to pocket $200,000 a year in residuals, as the shows sold overseas.

In City Detective, he played tough but witty cop Bart Grant, a man who fought crime from Mexico to New York and found a beautiful girl in every city along the way. At one time the writer and associate producer of City Detective was Blake Edwards, who went on to guide the career of a more famous but considerably less competent detective in Inspector Clouseau, for the Pink Panther movies.

REGULAR CAST

Det. Lt Bart Grant   Rod Cameron

Producer: Richard Irving

A Universal/MCA Production

65 monochrome 30-minute episodes
US: Syndicated 1953 - 1955

CITY OF ANGELS

Much was expected of City of Angels, Wayne Rogers' first role since Trapper John in M*A*S*H, but it proved more popular with critics than viewers and was cancelled after 13 episodes. Inspired by the movie, Chinatown, City of Angels was set in the corrupt Los Angeles of the 1930s. Rogers played hard-bitten private investigator Jake Axminster, a man alone, a man who trusted nobody completely, not even his attorney, Michael Brimm, and certainly not devious Lieutenant Quint, who delighted in beating him with a truncheon and threatening to kill him. Jake's trouble was he ruffled too many feathers while waging his one-man war against the system. But he could look after himself and was quite prepared to lie or steal to keep out of jail.

Wayne Rogers did his utmost to inject some humour into the series, which otherwise relied on his zany secretary, Marsha, and the switchboard she operated in the adjoining office for call girls. But it never really took off. Rogers later blamed the show's failure on sloppy scripts and bad production. 'Sometimes we'd have a script only at the last minute. And I never heard of a TV show where you shot through the night and ran out of darkness, but that's what happened to us!'

REGULAR CAST

Jake Axminster Wayne Rogers   *Lt Quint* Clifton James
Marsha Elaine Joyce   *Michael Brimm* Philip Sterling

Creators: Roy Huggins, Stephen J. Cannell
Music: Nelson Riddle, Hal Mooney
Producer: Roy Huggins
Executive producer: Jo Swerling Jnr

A Universal Production with Public Arts

13 colour 60-minute episodes
US: NBC 3 Feb - 10 Aug 1976
UK: ITV 1 Sept - 6 Oct 1981
20 July - 31 Aug 1982 (Thames)

CLUEDO

If your knowledge of murder and mystery extends no further than guessing that it was Colonel Mustard with the candlestick in the library, then this is the show for you. Based on the world-famous board game invented by solicitor's clerk Anthony Pratt in 1944, and now sold in 73 countries, Cluedo is the latest television whodunnit quiz.

Two teams of celebrities attempt to solve a weekly murder at stately Arlington Grange, by watching a playlet and then quizzing the six suspects. The cast performs with great gusto, notably June Whitfield who made a splendid Mrs White, but I was disappointed that a few of the original weapons were omitted. Is there no place in the 1990s for a length of lead piping? My only other complaint is that in the entire first series the culprit is never the Rev. Green, whereas anybody who has played Cluedo knows only too well that the murderer is nearly always the Rev Green!

Still it was good fun and led to a Christmas special when for some reason the entire cast was changed. And then when a new six-part series began, the cast was changed yet again, prompting speculation that the originals had all been murdered...

* David McCallum, who played the third Professor Plum, confessed that after 30 years as an actor, Cluedo finally brought him a role which impressed his children. 'When I told them I was playing Plum, the response was amazing,' he says. 'It brought back lots of happy memories of all the times when we used to sit down and play the game for hours.'

CAST SEASON ONE

Mrs Peacock Stephanie Beacham   *Mrs White* June Whitfield
Ms Scarlett Tracy-Louise Ward   *Colonel Mustard* Robin Ellis
Rev Green Robin Nedwell   *Professor Plum* Kristoffer Tabori
Host James Bellini

Director: John Kaye Cooper   *Executive producer:* Dianne Nelmes
Producer: Stephen Leahy

CHRISTMAS SPECIAL

Mrs Peacock Kate O'Mara   *Mrs White* Joan Sims
Ms Scarlett Toyah Wilcox   *Colonel Mustard* David Robb
Rev Green Derek Nimmo   *Professor Plum* Ian Lavender
Host James Bellini

Studio producer: Caroline Gosling   *Producer/Director:* Mary McMurray

SEASON TWO

Mrs Peacock Rula Lenska   *Mrs White* Mollie Sugden
Ms Scarlett Koo Stark   *Colonel Mustard* Michael Jayston
Rev. Green Richard Wilson   *Professor Plum* David McCallum
Host Chris Tarrant

Producer: Brian Park
Executive producer: Dianne Nelmes

A Granada Television Production in association with Waddingtons and Action Time

12 colour 30-minute episodes and one colour 45-minute episode
UK: ITV (Season 1) 25 July - 29 Aug 1990 (6 eps)
26 Dec 1990
(Season 2) 24 April - 5 June 1991 (6 eps)

CLUFF

Pipe in mouth, stick in hand, hat on head, dog at heels, Detective Sergeant Caleb Cluff strode across the moors to ensure that good honest Yorkshire folk stayed that way. Cluff had lived in the small fictional town of Gunnarshaw all his life, and preferred to stay there rather than be promoted elsewhere. There was very little crime in Gunnarshaw in the 1960s – a broken milk bottle would have made front page headlines in the local paper. There was the occasional theft but by and large Cluff was able to go about his duties at his leisure. To the disapproval of his punctilious superior, Inspector Mole, Cluff liked to take his time – he didn't believe in rushing into things. He had probably only just taken down the wanted posters for Crippen.

Cluff knew everyone and everyone knew him, a typical country bobby. He lived alone with his dog, Clive, apart from visits from daily help, Annie Croft, and enjoyed nothing more than long walks and imparting his wisdom to his protege in the force, young Detective Constable Barker.

Actor Leslie Sands, who played Cluff, had previous police experience when he appeared as Superintendent Miller in Z Cars. He chose all of Cluff's accessories personally – the tweed suits, the brown boots, the broad ties, the pipes and the two chestnut walking sticks, which cost Sands 4s6d each. He even had a broad-rimmed tweed hat specially made for the part, and in the fashion-conscious 1960s, it set an unlikely trend.

* Cluff originated from an episode of Detective (SEE DETECTIVE).

REGULAR CAST

Det. Sgt Caleb Cluff Leslie Sands
Insp. Mole (Season 1) Eric Barker *(Season 2)* Michael Bates
Det. Con. Barker John Rolfe   *PC Harry Bullock* John McKelvey
Annie Croft Olive Milbourne

Creator: Gil North
Music: Harry Dexter
Producer/Director: Terence Dudley

19 monochrome 50-minute episodes
UK: BBC1 (Season 1) 3 Aug - 7 Sept
1964 (6 eps)
(Season 2) 15 May - 15 Aug
1965(13 eps)

CODE THREE

Based on actual case files, this 1950s crime caper was centred on the investigations of Assistant Sheriff Barrett, of the Los Angeles County Sheriff's office, into offences designated Code Three – murder, robbery and kidnapping. It was pretty routine fare, notable only for the guest appearance of one Eugene W. Bissculuce, the real Sheriff of Los Angeles County at the time.

REGULAR CAST

Asst Sheriff Barrett Richard Travis   *Lt Bill Hollis* Fred Wynn
Sgt Murchison Denver Pyle

Executive producer: Hal Roach

39 monochrome 30-minute episodes
US: Syndicated 1957

COLONEL MARCH
OF SCOTLAND YARD

Sixty-eight-year-old Boris Karloff in a black eye patch made for one of the most bizarre sights on Fifties television. Everything about this filmed series was odd. For a start, Karloff's Colonel March was chief investigator for Scotland Yard's Department of Queer Complaints. And the eerie cases he looked into were far from run-of-the-mill – his adversaries included the Abominable Snowman and the Missing Link. Even Joe Friday would have been mildly disturbed by those two!

But the strangest thing by far was that the set never collapsed on March's head. For this was primitive TV, where the walls shook when a door opened and bannisters looked as if they were held in place by sellotape. In many respects, Colonel March of Scotland Yard was Karloff's biggest horror film of all.

REGULAR CAST

Colonel March Boris Karloff   *Insp. Ames* Ewan Williams

EPISODE TITLES

Passage of Arms	**The Silent Vow**
The Sorcerer	**Death and the Other Monkey**
The Abominable Snowman	**Strange Event at Roman Fall**
Present Tense	**The Stolen Crime**
At Night All Cats Are Grey	**The Silver Curtain**
The Invisible Knife	**Error at Daybreak**
The Case of the Kidnapped Poodle	**Hot Money**
The Headless Hat	**The New Invisible Man**
The Missing Link	**Death in the Dressing Room**
The Second Mona Lisa	
The Case of the Misguided Missal	*Producer:* Hannah Weinstein
Death in Inner Space	
The Talking Head	*A Sapphire Films Production*
The Deadly Gift	
The Case of the Lively Ghost	26 monochrome 30-minute episodes
The Devil Sells his Soul	UK: ITV 22 Feb 1956 - 11 April 1957
Murder Is Permanent	US: Syndicated 1957

COLUMBO

'Before we did Columbo, I was in New York on 57th Street one day and it started raining, so I went into a store and bought this cheap raincoat. When we started shooting, I wanted to wear my own clothes, not the stuff in the wardrobe department. That's all there is to it.' –
PETER FALK

That is how just about the most famous television-created cop came to acquire his most famous prop. And it was probably the only thing that ever happened to Columbo by chance. For despite resembling a refugee from cardboard city, Columbo has the keenest eye for detail of any detective bar Holmes.

Peter Falk, the man who has made Columbo an international star, enjoys comparing the modus operandi of the able Lieutenant and Sherlock Holmes. 'I do think of Columbo as an American Sherlock Holmes. He uses his mind – not bullets. Holmes was tall, Columbo is short. Holmes had a long neck, Columbo has no neck. Holmes smoked an expensive Meerschaum pipe, Columbo puffs on cheap cigars. Holmes is articulate, lucid and uses elegant words. Columbo is still working on his basic English. But both of them have this insatiable curiosity – in that sense they are like children because what you and I take for granted, they find interesting. Both are obsessed with getting answers to questions.'

Columbo is the most unlikely member of the Los Angeles Police Department. He has only one good eye (Falk lost his right eye when he was three and has been wearing a glass one ever since). He drives around in a battered old Peugeot that doesn't even look as if it would make good scrap. The average flasher wouldn't be seen dead in his raincoat, his shoes are scuffed, his trousers crumpled and his shirt stained. He is a loner. He doesn't trust other cops. He is rarely seen at the office, never at home. His only companion is his bassett hound. Columbo doesn't even have a first name although in the play, Prescription: Murder, in which the character first appeared, he was referred to as 'Philip'. He smokes a cigar stub, waves his hands around a lot, keeps scratching his forehead, gazing at his feet then staring at the sky. This bizarre behaviour indicates that his brain is working.

But from the moment he shambles on to the screen, flips out his badge and announces 'Lieutenant Columbo. Homicide,' we know that he is going to nail the murderer.

The character of Columbo was based on Porfiry Petrovich, a police inspector in Dostoevsky's Crime and punishment. His debut in Prescription: Murder was inauspicious, the play folding before it even reached Broadway. Instead it became a 1967 TV movie. Amazingly the original choice for the part was Bing Crosby, but he turned it down because it wouldn't have left him enough time to play golf.

Falk and Columbo became TV regulars in 1971, as part of the NBC Sunday Mystery Movie, in company with McMillan and Wife and McCloud. The show's format has remained unchanged ever since. And why not? You don't change a winning team.

Each episode opens with a particularly devious murder, the setting for which is usually one of beauty and opulence, to contrast with the down-at-heel detective. We know the identity of the killer, and since Columbo never seems to have more than one suspect, it must be assumed that either he is clairvoyant or he has read the script. But the joy of the shows is watching him grind the culprits down until finally it is a great relief for them to confess, if only to get Columbo out of their hair.

It all starts amicably enough. The killer (usually played by a star name – these have included William Shatner, Patrick McGoohan, who also directed some episodes, and Leonard Nimoy) makes the understandable mistake of thinking he is intellectually superior to the Lieutenant, and is lulled into a false sense of security. He is always extremely patient in the face of Columbo's endless questions (be downright rude to Columbo and you're off the hook) and is even helpful enough to offer a theory of his own, principally to frame someone else. For his part, Columbo is unfailingly polite to, even in awe of, the suspect. Either he or the unseen (but oft-mentioned) Mrs Columbo is invariably a big fan of the murderer (be he a musician, TV producer or actor) which probably accounts for why Columbo feels a certain amount of regret when he does eventually extract a confession. His opening gambit is usually: 'Wonder if you might be able to help me, sir.' He always apologizes for taking up their time. Thereafter the steady questioning begins, arising from the significant little messages he keeps on scraps of paper in his raincoat pocket. And there's his master-stroke, the devastating habit of seeming to leave, then pausing at the door when his opponent is off guard, with a key question beginning, 'Ah, just one more thing...' Before long, the killer starts to lose his cool. He becomes less obliging as he realizes Columbo is no bungling fool after all. But by then it is too late.

Happily, the murderers are an honourable breed and don't see fit to threaten Columbo and make a run for it. Thus Columbo has no need ever to carry a gun.

Peter Falk is glad about that. Speaking recently to launch the return of Columbo, nearly 20 years after the first series began, he said: 'There's still very little violence in the show and certainly nothing gratuitous. I wouldn't do it if there was. There's still that feeling with American cop shows that if you don't have 40 dead, 15 wrecked cars and two helicopters blown up in the first 15 minutes, it's too slow. And if the script gets bogged down, throw in a car chase. And if you can't think of an ending, then kill everyone. I'm not interested in programmes like Miami Vice which is the same thing over and over again. How many times can you watch someone get out of a car with a machine-gun blazing? It's very boring. I couldn't do it.'

Falk likes Columbo. He admits: 'There's a lot of me in Columbo, I know that. I'm as sloppy as him but not as smart. My own car is like a junk yard and as for clothes, I may be even worse than he is. I could wear the same stuff day after day, it wouldn't worry me.' And like Columbo, Falk is no pushover. On the original series he was reportedly earning £125,000 per episode but still refused to make more than a few a year. Now to entice him back, the fee has been upped to £600,000 per show. The only other thing that has changed is the raincoat. The old £15 faithful which served him for six years and some 50 episodes has been retired – and replaced by an exact replica. As Columbo would say with a puff on his cigar and a scratch of his head: 'That's progress for you.'

* Just one more thing. The very first episode was directed by Steven Spielberg. I wonder what happened to him?

REGULAR CAST

Lt Columbo Peter Falk

Creators: Richard Levinson William Link
Producers (1971-7): Edward K. DoddsEverett Chambers, Richard Alan Simmons
Producer (1989): Stanley Kallis
Executive producers (1971-7): Roland Kibbee Dean Hargrove
Executive producer (1989): Richard Alan Simmons

A Universal Television Production

Columbo
27 colour 90-minute and 18 colour 120-minute episodes
US: NBC 15 Sept 1971 - 4 Sept 1977
UK: ITV 14 Oct 1972 - 10 June 1979

New Columbo
18 colour 120-minute episodes
US: ABC From 27 Feb 1989
UK: ITV 23 Feb - 16 March 1991

COOL MILLION

A former CIA agent, Jefferson Keyes had become such a successful private investigator that he was able to charge a cool million dollar fee for his services. Mind you, if he didn't deliver the result, he promised to refund the money. Keyes had his own executive jet but no office as such. Instead he used the Lincoln, Nebraska, home of a woman called Elena as his base. Prospective clients dialled a special phone number, 30-30100, and Elena, the only person able to contact him, would duly relay the message. For all his wealth, Keyes couldn't buy success, and Cool Million closed after just four contributions to the NBC Wednesday Mystery Movie.

REGULAR CAST

Jefferson Keyes James Farentino   *Elena* Adele Mara

Producers: Jo Swerling Jnr, Gene Levitt
Executive producer: Roy Huggins

A Universal Television Production

4 colour 90-minute episodes
US: NBC 25 Oct 1972 - 11 July 1973
UK: ITV 6 Feb 1973 - 13 July 1976

The Cop and the Kid

A hideously sentimental American sit-com about Frank Murphy, an ageing cop who suffered an asthma attack while chasing shoplifting suspect Lucas Adams, a young black streetwise orphan. Realizing that Murphy's asthma could get him thrown out of the force, Lucas blackmailed him into pleading for leniency at the trial. Murphy was so convincing that the court made him Lucas's guardian. The network showed mercy too, and passed only a short sentence – six episodes.

Regular Cast

Officer Frank Murphy Charles Durning   *Lucas Adams* Tierre Turner
Mrs Brigid Murphy Patsy Kelly

Creator: Jerry Davis
Music: Jerry Fielding
Executive producer: Jerry Davis

A Playboy Production for Paramount Television

6 colour 30-minute episodes
US: NBC 4 Dec 1975 - 4 March 1976

Cop Rock

A unique blend of gritty drama, humour and rock music, Cop Rock was the latest product from the prolific Steven Bochco, the award-winning writer/producer of such hits as Hill Street Blues, L.A. Law and Hooperman. Set against the backdrop of the Los Angeles Police Department, Cop Rock juxtaposed the raw world of inner-city law enforcement with a musical score that ranged from rock to rap, gospel to ballads. The series spotlighted a group of urban cops as they battled street crime, the city's political bureaucracy and the criminal justice system, and their feelings were frequently expressed in song, to the tune of five numbers per episode.

The Cop Rock team was headed by Chief of Police Roger Kendrik, an effective leader with a penchant for the Old West. Captain John Hollander was the department's no-nonsense, yet compassionate, commanding officer, backed up by the young and enthusiastic Detective Joseph Gaines, and the veteran forensics expert, Ralph Ruskin. With his waistline expanding as fast as his hair was receding, Ruskin was an unlikely husband for Officer Vicki Quinn, some 25 years his junior. Vicki sought solace from her partner, handsome Officer Andy Campo.

Inevitably the cast also included Steven Bochco's wife Barbara Bosson (she was a regular in Hill Street and Hooperman), this time as Louise Plank, L.A.'s 'iron lady' mayor.

Given an interesting format and Bochco's track record, it was a surprise when Cop Rock was cancelled in the US after just 11 episodes. Of course the basic idea of combining drama and music has long been practised in the UK by playwright Dennis Potter (SEE THE SINGING DETECTIVE). It certainly provided a new slant on police procedurals, although I'm not sure it should be allowed to spread to other cop shows. Who could bear the thought of Kojak bursting into My Boy Lollipop or Columbo singing I Only Have Eye For You?

REGULAR CAST

Officer Andy Campo David Gianopoulos   *Officer Vicki Quinn* Anne Bobby
Chief Roger Kendrik Ronny Cox   *Capt. John Hollander* Larry Joshua
Ralph Ruskin Ron McLarty   *Det. Joseph Gaines* Mick Murray
Mayor Louise Plank Barbara Bosson

Creators: Steven Bochco, William M Finkelstein
Theme song *Under the Gun* Randy Newman
Producer: Gregory Hoblit
Executive producer: Steven Bochco

A Steven Bochco Production for Twentieth Century-Fox Television

11 colour 60-minute episodes
US: ABC 1 Sept - 26 Dec 1990
UK: BBC1 From 30 Sept 1991

COPPERS END

A moderate British sit-com about the country's laziest police station, run by the less than capable Sergeant Sam Short. Fighting crime took a back seat as Short hired out squad cars for weddings, funerals, driving lessons and even stock car racing. But all that was threatened by the arrival of enthusiastic policewoman Penny Pringle who was more interested in training school than card schools. Coppers End was the brainchild of Dixon of Dock Green creator Ted Willis. George Dixon would definitely not have been amused by their antics. Nor were many viewers.

REGULAR CAST

Sgt Sam Short Bill Owen   *PC Eddie Edwards* Richard Wattis
WPC Penny Pringle Josephine Tewson   *PC Chipper Collins* George Moon
PC Dinkie Dinkworth Royce Mills   *Chief Supt Ripper* Kevin Brennan

Creator: Ted Willis
Producer: Shaun O'Riordan

13 colour 30-minute episodes
UK: ITV 19 Feb - 14 May 1971

An ATV Network Production

CORONADO 9

Another of Rod Cameron's money-spinning syndicated series (SEE CITY DETECTIVE, STATE TROOPER). In this one he played a former Naval Intelligence Officer turned private eye. The setting was the Coronado Peninsular near San Diego, and the title sprang from his telephone exchange – Coronado 9.

REGULAR CAST

Dan Adams Rod Cameron

Producer: Richard Irving

39 monochrome 30-minute episodes
US: Syndicated 1959 - 60

A Revue Production with Universal Television

THE CORRIDOR PEOPLE

A short-lived thriller that leaned more towards the surrealism of The Avengers, than the traditional British police shows of the 1960s. The central characters were Scrotty, a Bogart-obsessed private detective, and Krock, a bluff CID man who was assisted in his enquiries by the unlikely pairing of Inspector Blood and Sergeant Hound! Scrotty was hired to trace the millionaire owner of a large cosmetics company, which had developed a perfume that deprived people of their senses for 24 hours. But the mogul had been kidnapped by glamorous international villainess Syrie Van Epp, who wanted to get her hands on the secret formula to further her sadistic scientific ambitions.

REGULAR CAST

Phil Scrotty Gary Cockrell   *Krock* John Sharp
Insp. Blood Alan Curtis   *Sgt Hound* William Maxwell
Syrie Van Epp   Elizabeth Shepherd

Creator: Edward Boyd
Director: David Boisseau
Producer: Richard Everitt

*A Granada Television Network
Production*

4 monochrome 60-minute episodes
UK: ITV 26 Aug - 16 Sept 1966

THE COURT OF LAST RESORT

In the early 1950s, mystery writer Erle Stanley Gardner, the creator of Perry Mason, founded a committee of crime experts in America, known as the Court of Last Resort. They were called upon to look into cases where there was some doubt as to the guilt of a convicted prisoner. This moderately successful series dramatized the real-life cases taken on by the distinguished group.

REGULAR CAST

Sam Larson Lyle Bettger   *Erle Stanley Gardner* Paul Birch

Producers: Elliott Lewis, Jules
Goldstone

26 monochrome 30-minute episodes
US: NBC 4 Oct 1957 - 17 Feb 1960

A Paisano Production for NBC

CRAIG KENNEDY, CRIMINOLOGIST

Scientific detective Craig Kennedy started life in a novel entitled The Silent Bullet, written by Arthur B. Reeve in 1912. He became so popular that by the time the final book, The Stars Scream Murder, was published in 1936, Kennedy was labelled the "American Sherlock Holmes." Not for the first, nor the last time, was such a claim grossly exaggerated. Kennedy appeared in half a dozen movies between 1915 and 1936, and transferred to television in the early 1950s where he was seen as the criminologist of Columbia University, probing gangland crimes in New York. The show had the distinction of being the first filmed TV series ever to be shown in US Army hospitals abroad.

REGULAR CAST
Craig Kennedy Donald Woods

Producer: Adrian Weiss

26 monochrome 30-minute episodes
US: Syndicated 1952

CRAZY LIKE A FOX

'Death is something every living organism on this planet tries to avoid...except my father.' — HARRISON K. FOX

A competent crime caper starring veteran actor Jack Warden, and John Rubinstein, son of the late concert pianist Arthur Rubinstein, as father and son Harry and Harrison K. Fox. Fifty-five-year-old Harry was an irascible San Francisco private eye, who insisted in involving his smart lawyer son in a series of hair-raising escapades.

All Harrison wanted was to be able to live a decent law-abiding existence with his wife Cindy and their son Josh. But he should have known better than to ask his crusty old dad to turn up evidence for a case he was working on, because from then on, Harrison's routine day at the office turned into a roller-coaster of adventure. He was constantly railroaded in to help Harry, who was in his element now that father and son were working together (not that you'd have known it from the amount of gratitude he showed). But Harrison was far too conservative for such moments of wild abandon. He would only take part in car chases if they were conducted well within the speed limit.

And all the while Cindy was no longer worrying about her husband being late for dinner – she was worried about him being her late husband.

REGULAR CAST
Harry Fox Jack Warden *Harrison K. Fox* John Rubinstein
Cindy Penny Peyser *Josh* Robby Kiger

Creators: Roger Shulman, John Baskin
George Schenck, Frank Cardea
Executive producers: George Schenck,
Frank Cardea

35 colour 60-minute episodes
US: CBS 16 Dec 1984 - 3 May 1986
UK: ITV 19 Jan - 9 March 1986 (Thames)

*A Columbia Pictures Television
Production for CBS*

CRIBB

'Cribb never uses violence to help solve crime, which he does despite constant interference from his superiors.' – ALAN DOBIE

Back in the 1960s, British college lecturer Peter Lovesey spotted that a publishing firm was offering a £1,000 prize for the best first crime novel. He wrote his inaugural Cribb story and, from 250 entries, it won. Thus the following year, Cribb appeared on the bookstalls in Wobble to Death.

Lovesey's stories were set in Victorian London around the 1880s, at a time when the dim, gas-lit streets were menaced by Jack the Ripper. Cribb was a Detective Sergeant with the recently-formed Criminal Investigation Department, an obstinate officer but with a dry sense of humour and absolutely no respect for Scotland Yard. He knew he would never be in line for promotion, solely because, like his contemporary, Sergeant Cork, he faced a constant battle with his superiors, in this case the surly Inspector Jowett.

Cribb was married to Millie but he still had an eye for the ladies, which he put to good practice when he and his loyal sidekick, Constable Thackeray, probed such 19th century pastimes as bare-fisted pugilism, the music hall, walking marathons (hence Wobble to Death) and spiritualism in the drawing rooms of high society. An excellent series which captured perfectly the feel of the period.

REGULAR CAST

Sergeant Cribb Alan Dobie   *Con. Thackeray* William Simons
Insp. Jowett David Waller

EPISODE TITLES

Waxwork (pilot)
Swing, Swing Together
Abracadaver
The Detective Wore Silk Drawers
The Horizontal Witness
Wobble to Death
Something Old, Something New
A Case of Spirits
Mad Hatter's Holiday
The Last Trumpet
The Hand That Rocks the Cradle
The Choir That Wouldn't Sing
Murder Old Boy
Invitation to a Dynamite Party

Producer: June Wyndham Davies
Executive producer: Peter Eckersley

A Granada Television Network Production

One colour 90-minute episode and 13 colour 60-minute episodes UK: ITV (Season 1) 13 April - 25 May 1980 (Season 2) 29 March - 10 May 1981 US: WGBH Boston 'Mystery' 6 - 20 May 1980
21 April - 19 May 1981
13 Jan - 10 Feb 1983

CRIME PHOTOGRAPHER

Based on the Casey novels by George Harmon Coxe, Crime Photographer, like so many of its contemporaries, was initially dramatized as a radio series in the 1940s. Set in and broadcast from New York, this live series centred around the assignments of Casey, campaigning crime photographer for The Morning Express newspaper and a man who would take a negative but not a no for an answer. Casey's habitual haunt was the Blue Note Cafe, where he enjoyed recounting tales of homicides and sieges he had covered, to the barman Ethelbert.(Have you ever heard of a barman named Ethelbert?) Other characters included Express reporter, Ann Williams, Casey's girlfriend, and cub reporter Jack Lipman, who dutifully penned the copy to accompany Casey's world-shattering exposes.

The first Casey was Richard Carlyle, but he and the original Ethelbert were substituted after just two months. The role of the hero was played thereafter by Darren McGavin, who went on to make a name for himself as Mike Hammer (SEE MICKEY SPILLANE'S MIKE HAMMER). Crime Photographer is only really memorable for one thing – it was directed by 27-year-old Sidney Lumet, now one of Hollywood's most celebrated movie makers.

REGULAR CAST

Casey (April - June 1951) Richard Carlyle *(June 1951 - 1952)* Darren McGavin
Ethelbert (April - June 1951) John Gibson *(June 1951 -1952)* Cliff Hall
Ann Williams Jan Miner   *Captain Bill Logan* Donald McClelland
Jack Lipman Archie Smith

Announcer: Ken Roberts
Music: Morton Gould
Blue Note Cafe musicians: The Tony Mottola Trio
Director: Sidney Lumet
Producers: Charles Russell, Martin Manulis

A CBS Production

Approx. 40 monochrome 30-minute episodes
US: CBS 19 April 1951 - 5 June 1952

CRIME SHEET

This was the middle segment in the trilogy of first-rate British police dramas featuring Raymond Francis as Tom Lockhart (SEE ALSO MURDER BAG and NO HIDING PLACE). It followed on directly from Murder Bag and saw Lockhart promoted from Detective Superintendent to Chief Detective Superintendent. The only other change was that his brief now extended to all types of major crime – not just murder. As with its predecessor, Crime Sheet proved enormously popular, to the extent that, after five months, its half-hour stories were replaced by hour-long episodes in No Hiding Place.

REGULAR CAST

Chief Det. Supt Lockhart Raymond Francis

Creator: Glyn Davies
Producer: Barry Baker

An Associated Rediffusion Network Production

17 monochrome 30-minute episodes
UK: ITV 8 April - 9 Sept 1959

CRIME STORY

Hailed by NBC as 'a latter-day Untouchables', Crime Story won a cult following in the States, with its clever implementation of 1960s rock music. It was set first in Chicago and latterly Las Vegas, at the very start of the 1960s, with the music of the time, heralded by the theme, Del Shannon's Runaway, frequently tied in to the on-screen action. This has become the trademark of the show's producer, Michael Mann, who employed a similar technique on Miami Vice.

Crime Story was the battle of a squad of tough, honest cops against a ruthless but charismatic gangster, Ray Luca, who, having started out as a small-time jewel thief, had progressed through the ranks to obtaining his full mobster's membership card, the one that says more about you than a hail of machine-gun bullets ever can. Crime Story's equivalent of Eliot Ness was the rugged Lieutenant Michael Torello, who was understandably dedicated to nailing Luca, having had several friends murdered by him. Luca's henchmen were Pauli Taglia and attorney David Abrams, son of gangster Izzy 'the Dancer' Abrams. David Abrams was initially on the side of law and order but defected to Luca's camp for the second season.

The casting for the show was highly imaginative. Torello was played by Dennis Farina, himself an ex-cop having actually been a member of the now-defunct unit on which Torello's group was based. Co-creator Chuck Adamson spent 17 years with the Chicago force and Farina served under him on the Criminal Intelligence Unit. A great deal of the character of Torello was based on Adamson, with elements of Farina also thrown in for good measure. His adversaries were pretty authentic too. Anthony Denison, who played Luca, had once been a professional gambler, while Taglia was played by former jewel thief John Santucci.

The first season ended with Luca and Pauli surviving a ferocious gun battle with Torello and his men, only to flee into an atomic test in the desert near Las Vegas. We all thought that was the end of the baddies but, when a second series was unexpectedly commissioned, they had to be miraculously brought back to life!

REGULAR CAST

Lt Michael Torello Dennis Farina   *Ray Luca* Anthony Denison
Pauli Taglia John Santucci   *David Abrams* Stephen Lang

Creators: Chuck Adamson, Gustave
  Reininger
Producer: Michael Mann

48 colour 60-minute episodes
US: NBC 18 Sept 1986 - 23 April 1988
UK: ITV 4 May - 20 Sept 1989 (Anglia)

CRIME SYNDICATED

A live American series of the early 1950s, presenting dramatizations of real cases drawn from the files of the Senate Crime Investigating Committee, the FBI and local law-enforcement agencies. The original host was Rudolph Halley, former chief counsel for the SCIC, but when he was appointed President of New York City Council towards the end of 1951, he decided to alternate with Herbert R. O'Conor, an ex-chairman of the SCIC.

Narrators: Rudolph Halley, Herbert R.
  O'Conor
Producer: Jerry Danzig

Approx. 45 monochrome 30-minute
  episodes
US: CBS 18 Sept 1951 - 23 June 1953

CRIME WITH FATHER

Three decades before the father and son in Crazy Like a Fox, there was a father and daughter detective team in Crime With Father. Captain Jim Riland was a senior homicide detective who found that his daughter, Chris, was better at solving crime than the men in his squad. So she ended up helping out on his cases. A half-baked idea matched by its execution.

REGULAR CAST

Capt. Jim Riland Rusty Lane   *Chris Riland* Peggy Lobbin

Producer: Wilbur Stark

An ABC Production

16 monochrome 30-minute episodes
US: ABC 31 Aug 1951 - 18 Jan 1952

THE D.A.'S MAN.

A forgettable Jack Webb series about Shannon, an ex-private eye who was taken on as an undercover investigator for the New York City District Attorney's Office. Thus he became The D.A.'s Man. In the course of his duties, Shannon succeeded in infiltrating the city's underworld and unearthed incriminating evidence on 'mob' income from such activities as prostitution and drug-pushing. His contact at the District Attorney's office was First Assistant D.A. Al Bonacorsi.

REGULAR CAST

Shannon John Compton   *Al Bonacorsi* Ralph Manza

Music: Frank Comstock
Executive producer: Jack Webb

A Universal Television Production

26 monochrome 30-minute episodes
US: NBC 3 Jan - 29 Aug 1959

DAN AUGUST

'How did I get the part? They asked me if I could jump over a car. I said, "Sure I can jump over a car." They said, "You're our boy."' –
BURT REYNOLDS

Burt Reynolds starred as Detective Lieutenant Dan August, preserver of the peace in Santa Luisa, California. Since it was his home patch, Dan knew most of the inhabitants and consequently became personally involved in the majority of the cases. His local knowledge paid dividends and there weren't many crimes he couldn't crack. He certainly pulled in crooks faster than he pulled in viewers, because the show was initially so poorly received that ABC dropped it. However, shortly afterwards, Reynolds became a big star, and two years after its cancellation, CBS aired repeats which drew larger audiences than the originals.

* The pilot for the series was The House on Greenapple Road, in which Christopher George played Dan.

REGULAR CAST

Det. Lt Dan August Burt Reynolds   *Sgt Charles Wilentz* Norman Fell
Sgt Joe Rivera Ned Romero   *Chief George Untermeyer* Richard Anderson
Katy Grant Ena Hartmann

EPISODE TITLES

In the Eyes of God
Murder by Proxy
The Murder of a Small Town
Quadrangle for Death
The Soldier
Love Is a Nickel Bag
The Law
The Colour of Fury
The King Is Dead
Epitaph for a Swinger
When the Shouting Dies
Passing Fair
Invitation to Murder
The Union Forever
Death Chain
Trackdown
Days of Rage
The Titan Dead

Witness to a Killing
Bullet for a Hero
Circle of Lies
Prognosis Homicide
The Assassin
The Worst Crime
The Meal Ticket
The Manufactured Man

Music: Dave Grusin
Producer: Adrian Samish
Executive producer: Quinn Martin

A Quinn Martin Production
26 colour 60-minute episodes
US: ABC 23 Sept 1970 - 8 April 1971
UK: ITV 9 June 1976 - 13 June 1978

DAN RAVEN

From the era of 77 Sunset Strip came Dan Raven, a lively cop show which surprisingly ran to only 13 episodes. Raven's beat was also Sunset Strip (it's a wonder he didn't bump into Stu, Jeff and Kookie) which he patrolled with his partner Sergeant Burke. The duo worked for the West Hollywood Division of the Los Angeles sheriff's office and spent most of their time gathering information in the clubs and coffee houses along the

Strip. A regular thorn in their side was magazine photographer, Perry Levitt, who covered Hollywood and had a nasty habit of ending up in the thick of the action. As an added attraction, Raven's investigations frequently involved celebrities who were working on the Strip. Among those who put in guest appearances were Bobby Darin and Paul Anka.

REGULAR CAST

Lt Dan Raven Skip Homeier *Det. Sgt Burke* Dan Barton
Perry Levitt Quinn Redeker

*A Columbia Pictures Television
Production for NBC*

13 monochrome 60-minute episodes
US: NBC 23 Sept 1960 - 6 Jan 1961

DAVID CASSIDY, MAN UNDERCOVER

A desperate attempt to cash in on the waning popularity of teen heart-throb David Cassidy. Turning the clean-cut Cassidy into a cop was a ridiculous piece of casting, the equivalent of picking Cliff Richard to play Al Capone. What's more, he was just about the only cop I've ever seen who didn't look old enough to shave.

It sprang from an episode of Police Story, and saw Shay as part of a Los Angeles undercover team led by Sergeant Abrams. The stories had Shay infiltrating a gang of young bank robbers, or posing as a student to break an illegal adoption racket – anything with teenage appeal. Shay was actually supposed to be in his late twenties and had a wife, Joanne, and young daughter, Cindy, to prove it. But whether or not his fans objected to his having a home life, after four episodes and a stack of bad reviews, the show was unceremoniously dumped.

REGULAR CAST

Officer Dan Shay David Cassidy   *Joanne Shay* Wendy Rastatter
Cindy Shay Elizabeth Reddin   *Sgt Abrams* Simon Oakland

Creator: Richard Fielder
Producers: Mark Rodgers, Mel Swope
Executive producer: David Gerber

*A Columbia Pictures Television
Production*
4 colour 60-minute episodes
US: NBC 2 Nov 1978 - 2 Aug 1979

DEAR DETECTIVE

Based on the French comedy-thriller film Tendre Poulet (in Britain it was known as Dear Inspector), this short-lived American series centred around Detective Sergeant Kate Hudson of the Los Angeles Police Department. Kate led a full life. She had to raise her daughter, Lisa, single-handed after divorce, and then fell in love with Professor Richard Weyland who taught English literature. But it was a rocky romance, as Weyland disapproved of the police and her irregular working hours. It was a gallant attempt to show the complications of being a working mum, particularly on the police force, but nobody seemed sure whether to play it as drama or comedy.

REGULAR CAST

Det. Sgt Kate Hudson Brenda Vaccaro   *Prof. Richard Weyland* Arlen Dean Snyder
Det. Brock Michael McRae   *Det. Schwartz* Ron Silver
Lisa Jet Yardum

Music: Dick and Dean de Benedictis
Executive producers: Dean Hargrove, Roland Kibbee

A Viacom Production for CBS

4 colour 60-minute episodes
US: CBS 28 March - 18 April 1979

DECOY

The adventures of glamorous undercover policewoman Casey Jones who, like her train-driver namesake, had a tender behind. Casey was an all-action New york cop, in a series that was fairly violent for its time, most of the stories being rife with sex maniacs, serial killers and psychos. Among the irregular supporting cast was a young Ed Asner, now best known as Lou Grant. The series also goes under the title of Police Woman Decoy.

REGULAR CAST

Casey Jones Beverly Garland

Producer: David Alexander

An Official Films Production with Pyramid

39 monochrome 30-minute episodes
US: Syndicated 1957
UK: 1962 (ATV)

DELVECCHIO

Dominick Delvecchio combined brains and brawn. A law school graduate, he turned hard-nosed police detective, much to the dismay of his Italian father, Tomaso, who ran a Los Angeles barber's shop and had grander ideas for his son.

Dominick and his partner Paul Shonski, were stationed at the Washington Heights Division of the L.A.P.D. where their boss was Lt Macavan. They dealt with all manner of big city crime, in what turned into a highly competent show. Judd Hirsch (later to find fame in Taxi) was a solid lead, and received sound back-up from three future Hill Street Blues stars, Charles Haid, Michael Conrad and George Wyner (also Steven Bochco was one of the co-creators). It deserved a longer run.

* Delvecchio's badge number was 425

REGULAR CAST

Sgt Dominick Delvecchio Judd Hirsch   *Sgt Paul Shonski* Charles Haid
Lt Macavan Michael Conrad   *Tomaso Delvecchio* Mario Gallo
Asst D.A. Dorfman George Wyner

Creators: Sam Rolfe, Joseph Polizzi, Steven Bochco
Music: Billy Goldenberg, Richard Clements
Producer: Michael Rhodes
Executive producers: William Sackheim, Lane Slate

A Universal Television Production

20 colour 60-minute episodes
US: NBC 9 Sept 1976 - 17 July 1977

DEMPSEY AND MAKEPEACE

'Dempsey was a survivor who came up from the gutter and worked his way through the ranks to become a homicide detective. I grew up on the streets of New York and was able to incorporate aspects of my past into the character.' – MICHAEL BRANDON

The character of New York Lieutenant James Dempsey was originally going to be a smooth womanizer, but actor Michael Brandon changed him into a tough guy, so that he could draw on his own experiences. As a teenager, Brandon had been a Brooklyn gang member. 'I had to fight a lot,' he says, and still bears a seven-inch battle scar on his arm, a stiletto wound from a gang fight on Long Island – '300 of us all armed with clubs, knives and zip guns. But then I started to realize I was involved in some kind of war in which people could be killed. These days in New York and Los Angeles, the gangs shoot each other. It makes my blood run cold just to think about it now.'

Maybe the producers should have simply screened The Michael Brandon Story, because it would undoubtedly have been far more believable and would probably have made for better viewing than the ludicrous series that went out under the title Dempsey and Makepeace.

Dempsey was a streetwise cop from Manhattan's tough 9th Precinct, who had shot dead his partner after allegations of police corruption. Fearing reprisals from his fellow officers, the NYPD decided to dump Dempsey on the British and he was seconded to a crack undercover unit, SI (Special Intelligence) 10. Dempsey called himself a 'Lootenant' and even in England's leafy lanes would carry his .357 Magnum. He had yet to differentiate between Broadstairs and the Bronx.

Dempsey didn't rate the British police, a situation exacerbated by his pairing with Detective Sergeant Harriet Makepeace, a chocolate box blonde with a hard centre. Plummy Harriet (she had a titled 'deddy') let it be known that the feeling was mutual. She hated the brash American. But as the two of them raced around this green and pleasant land, tackling a weekly diet of international terrorists and drug dealers, a reluctant attraction started to develop. Unfortunately, the silly storylines meant that the on-screen relationship between Dempsey and Makepeace was never as interesting as the off-screen romance between Brandon and co-star Glynis Barber.

The head of SI 10 was Chief Superintendent Gordon Spikings, a rude Liverpudlian who did nothing other than shout a lot, a complete waste of a fine actor, Ray Smith. But the biggest tragedy was that, having blown away one partner, Dempsey didn't immediately do the same to Makepeace and spare us all.

REGULAR CAST

Lt James Dempsey Michael Brandon   *Det. Sgt Harriet Makepeace* Glynis Barber
Ch. Supt Gordon Spikings Ray Smith   *Det. Sgt Chas Jarvis* Tony Osoba

Creator: Tony Wharmby
Music: Alan Parker
Producer: Tony Wharmby
Executive producer: Nick Elliott

A Golden Eagle Films Production for London Weekend Television

One colour 105-minute episode and 29 colour 60-minute episodes UK: ITV (Season 1) 11 Jan - 15 March 1985 (10 eps)
(Season 2) 31 Aug - 2 Nov 1985 (10 eps)
(Season 3) 30 Aug - 1 Nov 1986 (10 eps)

DEPARTMENT S

A series that has rightly gone on to acquire cult status, although most people's recollections of it tend to dwell more on the state of Peter Wyngarde's wardrobe than the complexity of the plots. Wyngarde's Jason King was, shall we say, a flamboyant dresser. With his droopy moustache and flower-power clothes, he could have stepped straight out of Woodstock.

King was the senior investigator for Department S, a branch of Interpol which was called in to solve crimes that had defeated the finest brains in the land. In his spare time, he was a highly successful writer of detective fiction, and would address each case by considering how his hero would tackle it. Contrasting with the wildly imaginative King was Stewart Sullivan, whose more contemplative approach meant the two men were often at loggerheads. There was nothing Sullivan enjoyed more than ridiculing King's ideas. Completing the trio of investigators was the one female member (unless you count Jason King), the scientifically-orientated Annabelle Hurst. The Department Head was Sir Curtis Seretse.

Department S probed a wide variety of baffling cases. In addition to murders, they tackled such unnatural phenomena as a crashed car driven by a tailor's dummy, a pilotless aircraft and the mystery of a ghost village. They would have been the ideal people to track down the crew of the Marie Celeste.

Episodes took them as far afield as Naples, Paris and Beirut, and among the guest stars lending weight to the already substantial stories were Anthony Hopkins, Stratford Johns, Alexandra Bastedo, Sue Lloyd and Kate O'Mara. A superb series all round, but I still reckon the most baffling crime was how King was allowed to get away with wearing those shirts. (SEE ALSO JASON KING)

REGULAR CAST

Jason King Peter Wyngarde   *Stewart Sullivan* Joel Fabiani
Annabelle Hurst Rosemary Nicols   *Sir Curtis Seretse* Dennis Alaba Peters

---

EPISODE TITLES

Six Days	**The Treasure of the Costa del Sol**
The Trojan Tanker	**The Man Who Got a New Face**
A Cellar Full of Silence	**Les Fleurs du Mal**
The Pied Piper of Hambledown	**The Shift That Never Was**
One of Our Aircraft is Empty	**A Ticket to Nowhere**
The Man in the Elegant Room	**The Man From X**
Handicap Dead	**Dead Men Die Twice**
Black Out	**The Perfect Operation**
Who Plays the Dummy?	**The Duplicated Man**

The Mysterious Man in the Flying
Machine
The Double Death of Charlie Crippen
Death on Reflection
The Last Train to Redbridge
A Small War of Nerves
The Bones of Byrom Blain
Spencer Bodily is 60 Years Old
The Ghost of Mary Burnham
A Fish Out of Water
The Soup of the Day

Creators: Monty Berman, Dennis
Spooner
Music: Edwin Astley
Producer: Monty Berman

An ITC Production

28 colour 60-minute episodes
UK: ITV 9 March 1969 - 4 March 1970
US: Syndicated 1971

DERRICK

Derrick is a middle-aged German detective in a similar vein to that other
continental crimebuster Van der Valk. He specializes in serious crimes
such as armed robbery, terrorism and murder. A handful of episodes are
currently being shown on the ITV regions, usually just as the milkman
starts his early-morning round. But a 4am timeslot hasn't stopped
Derrick from catching on. There is even a fan club in a London pub!
And he's big business overseas. He is the top imported programme in
Holland and has acquired something approaching cult status in Italy.

REGULAR CAST

Chief Insp. Derrick Horst Tappert

Creator: Herbert Reinecker

A ZDF Production

140 colour 60-minute episodes
UK: ITV 15 Jan - 7 Oct 1987 (8 eps)
8 Jan 1991 - (20 eps) (Yorkshire)

DETECTIVE

The most distinguished collection of detective talent ever assembled
graced our screens for this BBC anthology series of the 1960s. Each
episode was introduced by Rupert Davies in the guise of Maigret, and
went on to feature a case involving a sleuth, either famous from
literature or created specially for television. Some characters cropped up
in more than one season.

There were early TV portrayals of Campion and Father Brown, while Douglas Wilmer presented his version of Sherlock Holmes investigating that sinister serpent The Speckled Band (SEE SHERLOCK HOLMES). Many inquiries before The Equalizer and Over My Dead Body, Edward Woodward appeared twice – as Francis Didelot's Commissaire Bignon and Edgar Allan Poe's Auguste Dupin. The latter's case was The Murders in the Rue Morgue, set in 1841 Paris and which has the distinction of being the first true detective story ever written.

Glynn Edwards (best known as Dave from The Winchester in the hit comedy/drama Minder) starred as Detective Chief Inspector Dew in the hunt for Crippen, brilliantly played by Bernard Hepton. Alan Dobie, later to play Cribb, was John Trench's archaeologist detective, Martin Cotterell, and Leslie Sands' performance as a dour Yorkshire policeman led to a spin-off series (SEE CLUFF).

Among other detectives called into action were extrovert barrister Sir Henry Merrivale, dotty Oxford don Professor Gervase Fen, cosmopolitan connoisseur Philip Trent, American attorney Bob Race, Bow Street Runner Jasper Shrig, the pretty Eve Gill (whose father was a smuggler), husband and wife team Jane and Dogobert Brown, plump, jolly Reggie Fortune and Detective Chief Inspector Dover, best described as lazy, fat, middle-aged and thick.

A cracking idea. How about a new series?

* There were plans to include Michael Innes' aristocratic Inspector Appleby, but they never materialized.

CAST

Sir Henry Merrivale David Horne
(Season 1)
Martin Wyldeck (3)
(*Creator* Carter Dickson)

Philip Trent Michael Gwynn
(*Creator* E.C. Bentley)

Professor Gervase Fen Richard Wordsworth
(*Creator* Edmund Crispin)

Det. Sgt Caleb Cluff Leslie Sands
(*Creator* Gil North)

Nigel Strangeways Glyn Houston (1)
Bernard Horsfall (2)
(*Creator* Nicholas Blake, alias poet Cecil Day Lewis)

Martin Cotterell Alan Dobie
(*Creator* John Trench)

Inspector Rason Michael Hordern (1)
John Welsh (2)
(*Creator* Roy Vickers)

Sherlock Holmes Douglas Wilmer
(*Creator* Sir Arthur Conan Doyle)

Bob Race Frank Lieberman
(*Creator* Douglas Sanderson)

Jasper Shrig Patrick Troughton (1)
Colin Blakely (2)
(*Creator* Jeffery Farnol)

Eve Gill Jane Merrow (1)
Penelope Horner (2)
(*Creator* Selwyn Jepson)

Dr Thorndyke Peter Copley
(*Creator* Austin Freeman)

Jane and Dogobert Brown Joan Reynolds, Leslie Randall
(*Creator* Delano Ames)

Father Brown Mervyn Johns
(*Creator* G.K. Chesterton)

Det. Ch. Insp. Dover Paul Dawkins
(*Creator* Joyce Porter)

Reggie Fortune Denholm Elliott
(*Creator* H.C. Bailey)

Auguste Dupin Edward Woodward
(*Creator* Edgar Allan Poe)

Ch. Det. Insp. Roderick Alleyn Michael
Allinson
(*Creator* Ngaio Marsh)

Det. Ch. Insp. Dew Glynn Edwards
(*Creator* Colin Morris)

Albert Campion Brian Smith
(*Creator* Margery Allingham)

Miss Pye Angela Baddeley
(*Creator* Ethel Lina White)

Commissaire Bignon Edward Woodward
(*Creator* Francis Didelot)

Music: John Addison
Producer: David Goddard (Season 1)
Verity Lambert (Season 2)
Jordan Lawrence (Season 3)

A BBC Television Production

46 monochrome 50-minute episodes UK:
BBC1
(Season 1) 30 March - 27 July 1964 (18
eps)
(Season 2) 17 May - 1 Sept 1968 (18
eps)
(Season 3)7 Sept - 9 Nov 1969
(10 eps)

THE DETECTIVE

Tom Bell, an actor who could make Jackanory sound chilling, starred as ramrod-straight Commander Ken Crocker, head of Scotland Yard's Special Intelligence Branch, in this compelling serial about corruption in high places. Crocker was as honest as they come, a man who saw the police as servants of the community and was appalled when they fell short of the high standards expected of them. His investigations ruffled plenty of feathers and strained loyalties to breaking point. But the single-minded Crocker was determined to root out evil in the force even if it meant jeopardizing his home life.

MAIN CAST

Ken Crocker Tom Bell   *Supt Wilf Penfold* Mark Eden
Det. Insp. Vera Harris Vivienne Ritchie

Writer: Ted Whitehead from the novel
by Paul Ferris
Director: Don Leaver
Producer: Sally Head

A BBC Television Production

5 colour 50-minute episodes
UK: BBC1 10 May - 7 June 1985

DETECTIVE IN THE HOUSE

Judd Hirsch, Cassie Yates and Connie Stevens starred in this unhappy union of mystery and comedy. Hirsch played a much-married engineer who solved his mid-life crisis by making a serious career move and setting up as a private detective. Daily Variety described it as 'a mix of Father Knows Best and the private eye genre. It offers the worst elements of each.'

Creators: Judy Merl, Paul Eric Myers
Producer: William L. Young
Executive producers: Gary Adelson, Gil Grant

A Lorimar Production for CBS

7 colour 60-minute episodes
US: CBS 15 March - 26 April 1985

DETECTIVE SCHOOL

Whereas most people take evening classes in Spanish, rug-making or pottery, Nick Hannigan's pupils went to night school to learn how to become detectives. Needless to say, the lessons spilled over from the classroom and his students regularly found themselves involved in real cases, leaving Nick to bail them out. Or sometimes they demonstrated their new-found expertise by bailing him out. The students in this sit-com were a bizarre bunch including an old guy called Robert Redford. Alas that was just about the show's only joke, and it quickly folded.

REGULAR CAST

Nick Hannigan James Gregory   *Eddie Dawkins* Randolph Mantooth
Charlene Jenkins LaWanda Page   *Robert Redford* Douglas V. Fowley
Leo Frick Pat Proft   *Silvio Galindez* Taylor Negron

Music: Peter Matz
Producer: Hank Bradford
Executive producers: Bernie Kukoff, Jeff Harris, Caryn Sneider

10 colour 30-minute episodes
US: ABC 31 July - 24 Nov 1979

DETECTIVE'S WIFE

This live show was the summer replacement for Man Against Crime in 1950. Adam Conway was a private detective who wanted a relatively quiet life, investigating routine domestic cases. Unfortunately he attracted so much publicity after once solving a murder that he became in great demand to tackle homicides. As an added complication, his tiresome wife, Connie, always managed to get herself involved too.

REGULAR CAST

Adam Conway Donald Curtis   *Connie Conway* Lynn Bari

A CBS Production   US: CBS 7 July - 29 Sept 1950

13 monochrome 30-minute episodes

THE DETECTIVES

Screen star Robert Taylor (real name Spangler Arlington Brugh – no wonder he changed it) starred as po-faced Captain Matt Holbrook in this invigorating American big-city police drama. Matt Holbrook was a no-nonsense kinda guy, a widower whose strict moral code at work and at play was in sharp contrast to those of his contemporaries on 77 Sunset Strip, Hawaiian Eye, Bourbon Street Beat etc. Taylor, once regarded as the most handsome man in the world, permitted Holbrook to have just one brief dalliance in the show's three-year run – and that was with his real-life wife, German actress Ursula Thiess, who played police reporter Lisa Bonay.

Holbrook commanded a team of three plainclothes detectives who would take it in turns to delve into a major crime. The original trio were Lieutenant Otto Lindstrom, an old-timer who exposed con artists; the uncompromising, cigar-chewing Lieutenant John Russo of burglary; and young ladies' man Lieutenant James Conway of homicide. Had he but known it, Holbrook had an even more accomplished crime-fighter at his disposal for the final season. Adam West played Sergeant Steve Nelson five years before becoming the scourge of the Gotham City underworld. What a recruit Batman would have made to Holbrook's squad!

For that third and last season, the show moved to NBC, became an hour-long format instead of half an hour and the title was changed to Robert Taylor's Detectives.

REGULAR CAST

Capt. Matt Holbrook Robert Taylor   *Lt Otto Lindstrom* Russell Thorson
Lt John Russo Tige Andrews   *Lt James Conway* Lee Farr
Sgt Steve Nelson Adam West   *Sgt Chris Ballard* Mark Goddard
Lisa Bonay Ursula Thiess

Music: Herschel Burke Gilbert

A Hastings Production with Four Star

67 monochrome 30-minute episodes and 30 monochrome 60-minute episodes

US: ABC (Season 1) 16 Oct 1959 - 27 May 1960 (33 eps) (Season 2) 16 Sept 1960 - 19 May 1961 (34 eps) NBC (Season 3) 29 Sept 1961 - 18 May 1962 (30 eps)
UK: ITV 11 Aug 1964 - 16 Feb 1965 (Anglia)

DIAL 999

'We weren't allowed any humour. One day I ad-libbed a joke and the American series adviser was furious. He rushed over to me and yelled: "Cops don't make jokes!"' –   ROBERT BEATTY

There may not have been any humour in Dial 999 but that did not prevent it from being one of the finest police shows of the day. Robert Beatty starred as a tough Canadian Mountie, Mike Maguire, attached to Scotland Yard to study British policing methods. He was given the acting rank of Detective Inspector and teamed with Detective Inspector Winter and Detective Sergeant West. The series was made in co-operation with Scotland Yard (ex-Superintendent Tom Fallon was the show's British police consultant) and its realism was considerably enhanced by the fact that virtually every scene was shot on location.

It was filmed with more than one eye on the American market. Looking back, Robert Beatty says: 'It was a co-production with the States and was modelled on Highway Patrol, so there always had to be a chase at the end. It was hard work because we did two episodes a week and I did a lot of the stunts myself, like chasing over rooftops. Fortunately the only time I was hurt was when I sprained my ankle in a chase sequence at Brighton and anyway for anything really daredevil, we used a stunt man. Popular though it was, Dial 999 put me out of television for ten years. I was type-cast – my face was too well-known for being a cop.'

REGULAR CAST

Mike Maguire Robert Beatty   *Det. Insp. Winter* Duncan Lamont
Det. Sgt West John Witty

EPISODE TITLES

The Killing Job
Old Soldiers Sometimes Die
Thames Division
Commando Crook
Robbery with Violence
Night Mail
Illegal Entry
77 Bus
Exception to the Rule
Gun Rule
Motor Bike Bandits
Special Branch
The Big Fish
Barge Burglars
Escape
Rat Trap
Mechanical Watchman
Living Loot
50,000 Hands
Payroll Job
Hunter Hunted
Inside Job
Extradition
Radioactive
Honeymoon

Key Witness
Rolling Racketeers
Picture Puzzle
Mined Area
Deadly Blackmail
Down to the Sea
Ghost Squad
22 Hours
Heads or Tails
Death Ride
Missing Persons
Special Edition
The Great Gold Robbery
Fashions in Crime

Music: Sidney Torch
Producer: Harry Alan Towers

*A Towers of London Production in
    association with Ziv Productions*

39 monochrome 30-minute episodes
UK: ITV 8 June 1958 - 13 June 1959
US: Syndicated 1959

THE DIAMOND BROTHERS

'South by South East' were the last words spoken by secret agent Jake McGuffin. Unfortunately for him, Tim Diamond, Camden Town's least competent detective, was the one who heard them and he hadn't a clue what they meant. Diamond was a uniquely unsuccessful private eye – his only salvation was his 15-year-old kid brother Nick, the brains of the outfit. McGuffin's last words plunged the Diamond brothers into a world of bluff and counter-bluff, of MI6, secret agents, murder and a host of characters that could have walked straight out of a Hitchcock movie. And all the while the pair were pursued by suspicious policemen

Snape and Boyle. For most detectives, it would have been all in a day's work but there was some doubt as to whether Tim Diamond would survive beyond lunch.

This highly imaginative young people's comedy drama was based on the film Just Ask For Diamond and Anthony Horowitz's book South By South East, the latest of his Diamond brothers novels.

REGULAR CAST

Tim Diamond Dursley McLinden   Nick Diamond Colin Dale
Snape Michael Feast   Boyle Gordon Winter

Creator/Director: Anthony Horowitz
Producer: Richard Turner
Executive producers: J. Nigel Pickard
   Linda James, Stephen Bayly

A Red Rooster Production for TVS

6 colour 30-minute episodes
UK: ITV 26 March - 30 April 1991

DICK AND THE DUCHESS

Dick Starrett was an American insurance investigator living in London and his wife, Jane, was the daughter of an English earl (but Dick always called her 'Duchess' – hence the title). This amiable comedy adventure, which proved popular on both sides of the Atlantic, revolved around Dick's difficulties in adapting to his well-bred in-laws and Jane's habit of interfering with his investigations. Other characters included Dick's boss, Peter Jamison, and Inspector Stark of Scotland Yard, with whom Dick often joined forces.

REGULAR CAST

Dick Starrett Patrick O'Neal   Jane Starrett Hazel Court
Peter Jamison Richard Wattis   Insp. Stark Michael Shepley

Executive producer: Nicole Milinair

A Sheldon Reynolds Production

26 monochrome 30-minute episodes
UK: ITV 21 May 1959 - 8 July 1960
US: CBS 28 Sept 1957 - 16 May 1958

DICK BARTON – SPECIAL AGENT

The famous British radio detective of the 1940s made an uneasy transition to television. In his heyday, former soldier Barton was a national hero on a par with Churchill, keeping 15 million listeners on tenterhooks between 1946 and 1951. Above all, he adhered to 13 codes of conduct including one which stated that violence must be restricted to 'clean socks on the jaw'. (A funny place to wear socks, you might think!) Another rule affirmed that 'sex, in the active sense, plays no part in Barton adventures' and there could be no bad language or any reference ever made to alcohol. Noel Johnson, who played the first radio Dick Barton, said: 'Once when the script provided me with a glass of whisky in a saloon bar, it had to be changed and I went to a milk bar for a cup of cocoa instead.' When Johnson quit, there were over 1,000 applicants for the part, among them a policeman who wrote that he was 'experienced in all branches of crime detection' and a seven-year-old boy who listed his qualifications as: 'I have a gruff voice and I can shout.'

Alas when Barton and his old army colleagues, Snowey White and Jock Anderson, came to television in 1979, they upset the purists. This was principally because, far from being clean-cut, the TV Barton, Tony Vogel, looked decidedly unsavoury. One was left with the distinct impression that he swore, drank, fought dirty and probably regularly indulged in funny business. It was no way to treat a hero.

REGULAR CAST

Dick Barton Tony Vogel   *Snowey White* Anthony Heaton
Jock Anderson James Cosmo

Producer: Jon Scoffield
Executive producers: Terence Baker, Lewis Rudd

A Southern Television Network Production
26 colour 15-minute episodes
UK: ITV 6 Jan - 8 April 1979

DICK TRACY

Forget Warren Beatty. To millions of Americans in the Thirties, Forties and Fifties, Dick Tracy meant only one man – Ralph Byrd. Chester Gould created his lantern-jawed comic-strip hero in 1931 and it was

Byrd who starred in a collection of 15-episode black and white film serials for Republic Pictures, including Dick Tracy (1937), Dick Tracy Returns (1938), Dick Tracy's G-Men (1939) and Dick Tracy vs Crime Inc. (1941) where he tackled such international evildoers as The Spider, Zarnoff and The Ghost. Tracy also appeared on American radio between 1935 and 1948 before, albeit briefly, coming to television in a live 1950 production, again with Ralph Byrd in the title role.

It began at a time when Congress was expressing growing concern about screen violence and orders went out to tone down the mayhem. Accordingly, the first two episodes were relatively mild but by the fifth programme, the halo had started to slip. That edition produced two murders, a gun fight and a fist fight, and the sixth show opened with a hanging.

The TV Tracy continued on his violent way but also remained faithful to the original with such familiar faces as his sidekick Sam Catchem and Police Chief Murphy, as well as a gang of typically inventive villains like The Mole, a counterfeiter who tunnelled underground. It is doubtful whether Dick Tracy would have run to a second season, but that became hypothetical when Ralph Byrd died in 1952.

REGULAR CAST

Dick Tracy Ralph Byrd   *Sam Catchem* Joe Devlin
Police Chief Murphy Dick Elliott

Producers: Dick Moore, Keith Kalmer

An ABC Production

23 monochrome 30-minute episodes
US: ABC 11 Sept 1950 - 12 Feb 1951

A UPA Production

130 colour 5-minute episodes
US: Syndicated 1961
UK: ITV 30 June 1980 - 30 July 1982
   (Thames)

* As recently as 28 March, 1983, Central Television screened the old black and white Republic serial Dick Tracy Returns, starring Ralph Byrd with Charles Middleton as public enemy Pa Stark. The 15 episodes were transmitted daily over a period of three weeks.

*There was also an animated Dick Tracy series in which, for some reason, Tracy stayed at home and sent his assistants (who included Hemlock Holmes and The Retouchables Squad) out on the cases. Everett Sloane supplied the voice of Tracy and among the assorted villains were classic Gould creations Pruneface, Flat-Top and Mumbles.

DIXON OF DOCK GREEN

'He's a solid, dependable sort of bloke. People have seen so much of
these phoney American-type detectives that Dixon makes a nice
change. He's got no fancy ideas on detection and no idea of
promotion. He's just trying to do his job.' –   JACK WARNER, 1955

Yes, solid and dependable that was old George, the epitome of the
friendly London bobby in the days when you could park your car in the
West End and not have to retrieve it, minus radio and hub-caps, from
the East End. Played by Jack Warner, brother of music-hall stars Elsie
and Doris Waters, George Dixon was unique in the history of the police
force. For a start he was killed five years before the series began and
secondly he was still in the force at the ripe old age of 80!

Dixon's debut was in the 1950 film, The Blue Lamp, in which he
was gunned down after just 21 minutes by a young Dirk Bogarde. Five
years later, writer Ted Willis administered the kiss-of-life and created a
series that was to span 21 years and 367 episodes and become a British
institution. Yet after being commissioned to write the initial six-part
series, Willis was worried. 'I didn't know how I'd be able to find six
good stories,' he later admitted. So he embarked on a period of thorough
research. 'I spent six or eight weeks at a police station in Paddington
Green, riding round in police cars, sitting behind the counter, talking to
policemen. And I decided that the series would be non-violent. It would
concentrate on marriages being more important than murder.'
Eventually Willis had no fewer than 250 policemen on his payroll who
fed him incidents and true stories for the scripts.

Each episode opened with what became Dixon's trademark, a salute
and a matey greeting of 'Evenin' all', and concluded with him standing
outside the station, updating the viewers on what had happened to the
characters in that evening's programme. This would always be a happy
ending, more along the lines of 'And little Johnny's promised to
remember to cross the road safely from now on' rather than 'And little
Johnny's now serving life for topping the lollipop lady.'

George Dixon was based on a real policeman once stationed at
Leman St. in the East End of London. Dixon reflected the public's
image of the police at the time – he was the friendly, local bobby with a
kind word for everyone. He started off as a Constable but on 19
September 1964, amidst scenes of national rejoicing, he was promoted
to Sergeant. As he grew too old to pound the beat, he defied the years
and the Met's rules about retirement by continuing to work behind the
desk at Dock Green, allowing the CID, headed by his son-in-law Andy
Crawford, to take the lion's share of what action there was. Andy was
married to George's daughter Mary (she made George a granddad by
having twins) which permitted cosy family scenes away from the

station. Other favourites at Dock Green were PC (later Detective Constable) Lauderdale, known to all as 'Laudy', and Desk Sergeant Flint played by Arthur Rigby. Apparently absent-minded Rigby put the desk sergeant's blotting pad to good use by writing his lines on it.

Jack Warner identified so closely with George Dixon that in later years he seemed to think he was a real policeman and would wander round London in uniform. He even walked like a copper on the beat. Years earlier, he had damaged his back while playing a train driver in a film and the injury caused him to walk with his feet spread apart, like a penguin. In his relentless quest for authenticity, Warner discovered that back in the 1950s a policeman was not supposed to remove his helmet when entering a house, but he should take it off when asking an old lady about her dog licence. And the helmet had to be held under the arm when addressing a bishop.

Especially in the early days there was very little serious crime in Dock Green and therefore precious little action as we know it today. George was more likely to be found spraying his tomatoes than spraying bullets. He wouldn't have dreamed of using the rough-house tactics employed by British policemen in Z Cars and later The Sweeney. Somehow it would have been inappropriate for old George to rugby-tackle a suspect, put him in an arm-lock, spreadeagle him against a wall and bellow 'you're nicked, sunshine' just for riding a bicycle without an effective rear light.

As times changed and crime became more violent, Dixon of Dock Green seemed further and further removed from reality. He was living in an ideal world, not the one inhabited by most of the population. How would he have coped as desk sergeant at Hill Street? If the officers at Dock Green did have their fingers on the pulse, it was only to check they were still alive.

Even Ted Willis conceded: 'I think Dixon did run out of steam and become a bit tired and cosy.' Z Cars was a particular thorn in the side of both him and Jack Warner. When the upstarts from Newtown arrived on the scene in 1962, observers were quick to point out how tame it made Dixon look. Jack Warner sprang to his show's defence: 'When Z Cars have worn out as many tyres as I have worn out boots pounding the beat, they'll have something to crow about. Rough stuff? We've had our moments before Z Cars was thought of. I have been coshed and a boy has been murdered.' But that was in seven years...

Ted Willis became so irritated by the comparisons, that he 'borrowed' a Z Cars script in which Barlow was shaking the life out of a juvenile delinquent, and inserted the scene word for word in Dixon. Willis remembered: 'Whereas Stratford Johns as Barlow kept saying "Come on!", Jack Warner would say, "Now, come on" and it came out as cosy as if I had written it. I realized then that there was no way you could change Jack.'

Dixon finally retired in 1976 and Jack Warner died five years later at the age of 85. At his funeral was a wreath in the shape of a blue lamp, and the show's theme tune, An Ordinary Copper, was played over the public address system. His coffin was borne by officers from Paddington Green, where Ted Willis had conducted his research all those years ago. A Scotland Yard tribute described him as 'a charming character who served the Metropolitan Police and public so well. His warmth and understanding of the problems of London PCs will long be remembered with affection.' Sadly, it seems the likes of George Dixon are destined never to be seen again.

* The very first episode of Dixon of Dock Green was entitled PC Crawford's First Pinch.

REGULAR CAST

PC George Dixon Jack Warner   *Det. Sgt Andy Crawford* Peter Byrne
Mary Crawford (1955) Billie Whitelaw *(From 1955)* Jeannette Hutchinson
PC Lauderdale Geoffrey Adams   *Desk Sgt Flint* Arthur Rigby
PC Willis Nicholas Donnelly   *PC Tubb Barrell* Neil Wilson
Sgt Grace Millard Moira Mannion   *Cadet Jamie MacPherson* David Webster
PC Bob Penney Anthony Parker   *WPC Kay Shaw* Jocelyne Rhodes

---

Creator: Ted Willis
Producers: Douglas Moodie, Ronald Marsh,Philip Barker, Joe Waters

367 monochrome/colour 25-minute and 45-minute episodes
UK: BBC1 9 July 1955 - 1 May 1976

A BBC Television Production

* At the time of writing there are plans for a new series built around Dixon's grandson, Charles Dixon Crawford, a Falklands War veteran turned cop.

DOG AND CAT

Before Kim Basinger became a hot box office property, she played Officer J.Z. Kane in the light American cop show, Dog and Cat. Even there she made men's pulses race faster than the average squad car. Dog and Cat was slang for male and female police teams. Kane was The Cat, 'a beautiful, hip, Southern college graduate', and veteran plainclothes cop Jack Ramsey was The Dog. Together these unlikely partners fought crime with the 42nd division of the Los Angeles Police

Department. But it didn't take off, and suffice to say that Ms Basinger has subsequently gone on to considerably better things. It would have been difficult not to.

REGULAR CAST

Det. Sgt Jack Ramsey Lou Antonio   *Officer J.Z. Kane* Kim Basinger
Lt Arthur Kipling Matt Clark

Creator: Walter Hill
Music: Barry De Vorzon
Producer: Robert Singer
Executive producer: Lawrence Gordon

A Paramount Television Production

10 colour 60-minute episodes
US: ABC 5 March - 14 May 1977

DOROTHY L. SAYERS MYSTERY

'Wimsey is a complex character who's not always aware of how he appears. But sometimes the comic veneer is intentional. If he just sat there looking like the world's greatest detective, nobody would give anything away to him.' –   EDWARD PETHERBRIDGE

Following the widely-acclaimed performance of Ian Carmichael, fifteen years earlier (SEE LORD PETER WIMSEY), Edward Petherbridge starred in further adventures of Dorothy L. Sayers' aristocratic period sleuth, Peter Death Bredon Wimsey, second son to the Duke of Denver. Petherbridge's Wimsey was less 'frightfully jolly ho' than Carmichael's, and physically more as Sayers intended – tall, slim, athletic and in his thirties. The other difference with this version was that joining Wimsey and his ex-army sergeant manservant, Bunter, was the formidable Harriet Vane who appeared in four Wimsey novels and who is generally thought to be Sayers herself. Wimsey and Harriet first met when she was on trial at the Old Bailey, accused of murdering her lover and after he had saved her from the gallows, she responded by falling in love with him.

A fine series, with faithful adaptations and characterizations, although not as strong in entertainment value as the 1972 production.

REGULAR CAST

Lord Peter Wimsey Edward Petherbridge   *Bunter* Richard Morant
Harriet Vane Harriet Walter

Strong Poison

(3-part story)
Famous mystery writer, Harriet Vane, is on trial for her life. Did she or did she not poison her lover? Lord Peter Wimsey has just 30 days to save her from the rope.

GUEST STARS:

Margaretta Scott, Clive Francis, David Quilter
Dramatized by   Philip Broadley
Director: Christopher Hodson

Have His Carcase

(4-part story)
Cleared of murder, Harriet Vane goes on a walking tour of the West Country, but her peace is shattered when she stumbles across a corpse on a rock. The man's throat had been cut and further inquiries reveal him to be a notorious gigolo. A letter found on his body provides the most vital clue as to the identity of his killer.

GUEST STARS:

Rowena Cooper, Ray Armstrong

Dramatized by   Rosemary Anne Sisson
Director: Christopher Hodson

Gaudy Night

(3-part story)
Harriet Vane is invited to the annual 'gaudy' of her old Oxford college but she finds herself investigating, and being a victim of, bizarre acts of violence. Lord Peter is asked to assist in solving the mystery.

GUEST STARS:

Sheila Burrell, Charmian May, Dilys Hamlett
Dramatized by   Philip Broadley
Director: Michael Simpson

Music: Joseph Horowitz
Producer: Michael Chapman

A BBC Television Production

10 colour 55-minute episodes
UK: BBC2 25 March - 27 May 1987
US: WGBH Boston 'Mystery' 1 Oct - 3 Dec 1987

DRAGNET

'When I took the original tape to NBC, they weren't impressed. "No blondes, shots, blood or thrills," they said. They gave the show a four-week trial.' –   JACK WEBB

Dragnet went on to become arguably the most successful police series ever. Back in 1951, it broke new ground with its realism, documentary-style narration and the fact that the cases were drawn from the actual files of the Los Angeles Police Department. The effect was to reduce contemporaries like Martin Kane and Dick Tracy to the realms of sensational melodramas. From the moment the opening titles ran and Sergeant Joe Friday intoned: 'This is the city...Los Angeles...California ...I work here...I carry a badge,' viewers were hooked. Then followed Walter Schumann's evocative Dum De Dum Dum music and the announcer declaring: 'Ladies and gentlemen, the story you are about to see is true...only the names have been changed to protect the innocent.' America had never seen or heard anything quite like it.

Dragnet was the brainchild of Jack Webb. He created it, produced it, directed most of the episodes, acted as narrator and starred in it. The origins date back to a 1948 documentary-style police movie, He Walked By Night, in which Webb played a laboratory technician. The word 'dragnet' was even used in the dialogue. The film's technical adviser was a Los Angeles police sergeant, Marty Wynn, who complained to Webb about the inaccuracy of Hollywood's cop movies. Webb set out to rectify the situation and research a realistic account of police work, by riding around on patrol with Wynn and his partner. This was how he obtained the feel for the minutia which symbolized Dragnet – the constant use of dates, times and venues – and the flat hypnotic dialogue which was to become a rich source of parody for comedians. Friday's staccato catchphrases – 'My name's Friday, I'm a cop' and 'Just the facts, ma'am, ' – swept the nation, as did such police jargon as 'Book him on a 358', which could have been a bus for all we knew.

Right from the start, Webb had a clear picture of his central character. 'I wanted Friday to be the steady, plodding kind of cop the public never really understood or appreciated or ever heard about...an honest, decent home-loving guy, the image of 50,000 real officers who do their work without the help of beautiful, mysterious blondes, hefty swigs from an ever-present bottle and handy automatics thrust into their belts or hidden in their socks.' He never included anything in Dragnet that he wouldn't have wanted his own children to see, and introduced a rule allowing only one bullet to be fired every four episodes.

Dragnet began on radio in 1949, where Friday emerged as a quiet, hard-working cop who pursued every lead, interviewed every witness and eventually apprehended the wrongdoer. It became the highest-rated radio show and duly switched to American television in December 1951, on a programme called Chesterfield Sound Off Time, with Barton Yarborough appearing as Friday's partner, Sergeant Ben Romero. But after just three episodes had been filmed, Yarborough died of a heart attack, and a succession of actors went on to play Friday's sidekick. For the rest of the first season, it was Barney Phillips as Sergeant Ed Jacobs. Then Herb Ellis, briefly, and Ben Alexander took over for six years as Officer Frank Smith, named after Webb's own uncle. And for the Dragnet revival in 1967, Harry Morgan filled the breach as Officer Bill Gannon. These partners were on hand to provide the occasional moment of light relief. Indeed, Gannon was practically a re-incarnation of Smith – both were gourmet hypochondriacs intent on persuading bachelor Friday to get hitched.

Dragnet was gritty not glamorous. The crimes investigated were often relatively minor, and much of the police work was seen to be routine and unrewarding. There wasn't a serial killer on every street corner. Since the stories were based on real cases, at the end of each episode when the criminal had been caught, the announcer reported what had happened at the trial. This, plus Webb's regular tendency to use amateurs – occasionally people involved in the actual case – all helped to enhance the sense of authenticity. Then there was the famous music which provided the perfect background, conveying tension and desperation whenever necessary. In fact in 1953 Dragnet produced two hits – a record of the theme music and a send-up by Stan Freberg. The following year Webb directed a successful movie spin-off and Dragnet remained on American TV until 1959 by which time Friday and Smith had earned promotions to Lieutenant and Sergeant respectively. The show was revived eight years later as Dragnet 67, with a greater emphasis placed on community involvement. It ran for two and a half seasons. Syndicated versions also did the rounds under the title Badge 714 (Friday's number).

One thing more than any other has puzzled Dragnet fans over the years. Why did Webb choose the name Friday? Some thought it came from Robinson Crusoe and his man Friday, or that Webb thought of it on a Friday. Neither was true. Webb explained: 'I wanted a name that had no connotations at all. He could be Jewish or Greek or English or anything. He could be all men to all people in their living rooms.'

REGULAR CAST

Sgt Joe Friday Jack Webb
Sgt Ben Romero Barton Yarborough   *Sgt Ed Jacobs* Barney Phillips
Officer Frank Smith (1952) Herb Ellis   *(1953-9)* Ben Alexander
Officer Bill Gannon (1967-70) Harry Morgan
Announcers: George Fenneman, Hal Gibney   *Narrator:* Jack Webb

Creators: Jack Webb, Richard Breen
Theme music: Walter Schumann
Producer: Jack Webb

An MCA Television Production

263 monochrome 30-minute episodes
US: NBC (Season 1) 16 Dec 1951 - 19 June 1952 (14 eps)
(Season 2) 11 Sept 1952 - 18 June 1953 (33 eps)
(Season 3) 3 Sept 1953 - 27 May 1954 (39 eps)
(Season 4) 26 Aug 1954 - 26 May 1955 (39 eps)
(Season 5) 1 Sept 1955 - 31 May 1956 (39 eps)
(Season 6) 27 Sept 1956 - 30 May 1957 (34 eps)

(Season 7) 26 Sept 1957 - 26 June 1958 (39 eps)
(Season 8) 23 Sept 1958 - 24 March 1959 (26 eps)

98 colour 30-minute episodes
US: NBC (Season 1) 12 Jan 1967 - 11 May 1967 (17 eps)
(Season 2) 14 Sept 1967 - 4 April 1968 (29 eps)
(Season 3) 19 Sept 1968 - 17 April 1969 (26 eps)
(Season 4) 18 Sept 1969 - 16 April 1970 (26 eps)
UK: ITV 15 Sept 1961 - 23 Aug 1968 (Anglia)
(In some ITV regions, Dragnet started much earlier. The premiere date in London was 23 September 1955)

* Although Jack Webb died in 1982, Dragnet is not forgotten. There was a spoof movie in 1987 starring Dan Aykroyd and, in 1989, another TV series emerged with two new younger cops, Sergeant Vic Daniels and Detective Carl Molina. Daniels is single and diligent while Molina is married with five children, and possesses a certain irreverence which masks his intensity and devotion to the job. The famous introduction, the documentary-style, the basing of stories on genuine L.A.P.D. cases, all faithfully follow the traditions of the original Dragnet. Only the names have been changed...

REGULAR CAST

Sgt Vic Daniels Jeffrey Osterhage   *Det. Carl Molina* Bernard White
Capt. Lussen Don Stroud   *Capt. Bolz* Thalmus Rasulala

Executive producer: Arthur L. Annecharico
Co-executive producers: Burton Armus, Craig Kellem

An Arthur Company Production for WWOR-TV

78 colour 30-minute episodes
US: Syndicated from 4 October 1989

THE DUKE

Ageing prizefighter, Oscar 'Duke' Ramsey was an unlucky kind of guy. He was unlucky in losing a bout to a much younger opponent, so he packed up boxing. Instead, he thought he would devote his time to running Duke and Benny's Corner, a Chicago bar. But just as it was about to open, Duke had another bit of bad luck – Benny was murdered. Game to the last, Duke tracked down his would-be partner's killer and found a new career as a private detective. He was helped by all his old boxing cronies, including the curiously-named Joe Cadillac, a flash young bookmaker. And with the attentions of beautiful jet-setter Dedra Smith, it appeared that Duke's luck had finally changed. But then after just four dismal episodes, the network dropped his show. It was our turn to be lucky.

REGULAR CAST

Oscar 'Duke' Ramsey Robert Conrad   *Joe Cadillac* Larry Manetti
Sgt Mick O'Brien Red West   *Dedra Smith* Patricia Conwell

Music: Mike Post, Pete Carpenter
Producers: Alex Beaton, Don Carlos
   Dunaway
Executive producer: Stephen J. Cannell

*A Stephen J. Cannell Production for
   Universal Television*

One colour 120-minute episode, 3 colour
   60-minute episodes
US: NBC 5 April - 18 May 1979

ECHO FOUR-TWO

Detective Sergeant Harry Baxter built up such a fervent female following in No Hiding Place, that he was given his own spin-off series, Echo Four-Two, and promoted to Detective Inspector. Baxter assumed command of London's E Division squad of unmarked Q-cars (a sort of undercover police car) and, with his assistant, Detective Sergeant Joe York, set about fighting crime in the very heart of London. Alas, before he could make too many inroads, an actors' strike curtailed production and only ten of the planned 13 episodes were ever made. It was no great loss. Older and probably wiser for the experience, Harry Baxter duly returned to No Hiding Place where he was happiest.

REGULAR CAST

Det. Insp. Baxter Eric Lander   *Det. Sgt York* Geoffrey Russell
Acting Supt Dean Geoffrey Chater

Music: Laurie Johnson
Producer: Richard Matthews

*An Associated Rediffusion Network
   Production*

10 monochrome 30-minute episodes
UK: ITV 24 Aug - 25 Oct 1961

THE EDDIE CAPRA MYSTERIES

A traditional, but nonetheless entertaining, whodunnit series featuring young lawyer-sleuth Eddie Capra, junior partner with the prominent law firm of Devlin, Linkman and O'Brien. Each programme opened with a murder and over the next hour, viewers would watch Eddie slowly but steadily sift through the clues to unmask the killer. Helping him out were his keen legman, Harvey Winchell, and lovely secretary, Lacey Brown, with whom he established quite a romantic rapport. It was just a pity she had an appallingly precocious daughter, Jennie, the sort of child that makes you think King Herod wasn't such a bad guy after all. But the real bane of Eddie's life was the firm's senior partner, the crusty J.J. Devlin, with whom his unconventional approach frequently clashed. Eddie may have only been the junior but he had one big advantage over Devlin – it was his name in the show's title.

REGULAR CAST

Eddie Capra Vincent Baggetta   *Lacey Brown* Wendy Phillips
J.J. Devlin Ken Swofford   *Harvey Winchell* Michael Horton
Jennie Brown   Seven Ann McDonald

Creator: Peter S. Fischer
Producer: James McAdams
Executive producer: Peter S. Fischer

A Universal Television Production

11 colour 60-minute and 2 colour 120-minute episodes US: NBC 8 Sept 1978 - 7 Sept 1979
UK: BBC1 8 Feb - 30 April 1980

EDGE OF DARKNESS

Yorkshire police detective Ronald Craven's investigation into the murder of his own daughter, Emma, sparked off a first-rate political thriller which embroiled any number of organizations – NATO, NASA, the CIA. Virtually the only one not involved was BAFTA but they made up for it by festooning Edge of Darkness with a trio of well-deserved awards. Bob Peck played Craven, a role he was eminently suited to since his brother Geoff was a Yorkshire policeman, and Joe Don Baker was cast as mountainous CIA agent, Jedburgh, to obtain American backers for the serial. Indeed he was paid more than any of the British actors, but was so enamoured with the production that he later said he would have done it for nothing. If only they had known...

Edge of Darkness did not please everyone, however. MI5 was annoyed at the disclosure of their precious security codes, while GAIA, the fictional underground terrorist group, was discovered to be the name of a respectable ecological publishing firm backed by Prince Philip. They were not amused to be associated with the CIA, guns and sabotage.

MAIN CAST

Det. Ronald Craven Bob Peck   *Darius Jedburgh* Joe Don Baker
Emma Craven Joanne Whalley   *Det.Chief Supt Ross* John Woodvine

Creator: Troy Kennedy Martin
Music: Eric Clapton, Michael Kamen
Director: Martin Campbell
Producer: Michael Wearing

A BBC Television Production

6 colour 55-minute episodes UK: BBC2 4 Nov - 9 Dec 1985

87TH PRECINCT

With stories taken from Ed McBain's enduring crime novels, 87th Precinct was one of the classiest American cop shows of the 1960s. The action took place in Manhattan's 87th precinct, and showed the police at work and at play. As detectives of an inner-city zone, they had to deal with the familiar cases of murder and robbery as well as more minor transgressions. The four principals were moody Steve Carella, the young and enthusiastic Bert Kling, and two older officers – Roger Havilland, a tough pro, and the cynical Meyer Meyer ('my parents had a sense of humour'), who had seen it all and injected wry, dry humour into the otherwise grim proceedings.

It was Norman Fell as Meyer Meyer who stole the show, along with Gena Rowlands as Carella's pretty, deaf mute wife, Teddy. The scenes in which she featured lifted 87th Precinct way above the norm.

* Ed McBain is a pseudonym of Evan Hunter.

REGULAR CAST

Det. Steve Carella Robert Lansing   *Det. Meyer Meyer* Norman Fell
Det. Bert Kling Ron Harper   *Det. Roger Havilland* Gregory Walcott
Teddy Carella Gena Rowlands

Creator: Ed McBain
Music: Morton Stevens

A Hubbell Robinson Production with MCA TV

30 monochrome 60-minute episodes
US: NBC 25 Sept 1961 - 10 Sept 1962
UK: ITV 5 Jan - 30 Aug 1962 (Anglia)

EL C.I.D.

'When you're tailing someone, you're not supposed to have lunch with them.'
– BLAKE TO BROMLEY

Bromley and Blake were the heroes of a classy comedy/drama about two Scotland Yard policeman who decided to give up a life of fighting crime and retire to Spain. Douglas Bromley was the Yard's pen-pusher and genius of the filing system but a man whose idea of action was to fit a new blotting pad. In contrast, Bernard Blake was a rugged gangbuster, like Bodie and Doyle of The Professionals rolled into one. Unfortunately he spent much of his time recuperating in hospital beds after his latest beating. Faced with re-location to Derbyshire, a prospect he did not relish, Bromley decided to take early retirement, and persuaded his unlikely pal, Blake, to opt for a quiet life abroad. So they set sail on Bromley's boat, the appropriately-named El C.I.D., and headed for the Costa del Sol.

They soon discovered it is not all sun, sea and sangria, and also why the area is dubbed the Costa del Crime. After falling foul of villains, the pair teamed up with Spanish father and daughter private eyes, Delgado and Mercedes, who sent them off on a series of strange assignments.

Much of the comedy derived from Bromley's hapless attempts to behave like a detective, when his entire police career had been spent behind a desk. But thanks to the subtle under-playing of both John Bird (Bromley) and Alfred Molina (Blake), the humour always managed to stay the right side of farce. There was an excellent supporting cast too, notably Donald Churchill as the pompous British marina-owner, Metcalf, and Tony Haygarth as another ex-pat, restaurateur Frank (proprietor of Chez Frank's). During the second season, Robert Reynolds arrived as Blake's wayward brother Stevie.

REGULAR CAST

Blake Alfred Molina   *Bromley* John Bird
Frank Tony Haygarth   *Metcalf* Donald Churchill
Delgado Simon Andreu   *Mercedes* Viviane Vives
Stevie Robert Reynolds

* For the third series in 1992, Blake (Alfred Molina) will be replaced by Amanda Redman *as Douglas' estranged daughter, Rosie.*

Creators: Chris Kelly, Iain Roy
Producer: Matthew Bird
Executive producer: Sally Head

*A Granada Television Network
Production*

13 colour 60-minute episodes
UK: ITV (Season 1) 7 Feb - 14 March 1990 (6 eps) (Season 2) 1 Jan - 12 Feb 1991(7 eps)

ELLERY QUEEN

Ellery Queen served as the prototype for a particular strand of TV detective, the mystery writer turned sleuth, paving the way for the likes of Jessica Fletcher in Murder, She Wrote and Max Beckett in Over My Dead Body. Queen first appeared in print in a 1929 novel, The Roman Hat Mystery, written by Frederic Dannay and Manfred Bennington Lee, before graduating to nine 'B' movies and earning his own CBS radio series from 1939. Ellery was the all-American boy – tall, athletic and, despite his somewhat vague manner, supremely intelligent. His father, Inspector Richard Queen of the New York Police Department, was astounded by Ellery's unerring ability to solve the most baffling of cases. But then again he wasn't as clever as his know-all son.

In total there have been no fewer than five different Ellerys on American TV. The first was Richard Hart in The Adventures of Ellery Queen in 1950, but within a year he had died of a heart attack and been replaced by Lee Bowman. After that short-lived series, a syndicated film version appeared in 1954, also titled The Adventures of Ellery Queen (although it later changed to Mystery Is My Business), and starring Hugh Marlowe, one of four actors who had played Ellery on radio.

In 1958, Ellery popped up on the US network again, this time with George Nader in the lead role and Les Tremayne as his father. The series was initially called The Further Adventures of Ellery Queen and then shortened to just Ellery Queen. But when production transferred from Hollywood to New York, Nader and Tremayne quit, so Lee Philips came in as Ellery and the poor Inspector was dropped altogether.

Finally in 1975, by which time Ellery had made more comebacks than Sinatra, Jim Hutton starred in a one-season series set in New York in the late 1940s, entitled simply Ellery Queen. This was the least numbing of the adaptations, as Hutton did actually attempt to inject a little humour into the character and make for a warmer relationship with his father. Added to the cast were Sergeant Velie, a dependable plainclothes assistant to Inspector Queen, who had been in the novels and on radio but had been omitted from the previous TV versions; Simon Brimmer, an arrogant radio detective who set himself up in competition with Ellery; and newspaper columnist Frank Flannigan, who also tried to solve the murder-of-the-week before Queen. In an effort to encourage viewer participation, Ellery would turn to the camera just before revealing the culprit and ask: 'Have you figured it out? Do you know who the murderer is?' No, but sure as hell Ellery did.

* Ellery's address was 212-A West 87th Street, a flagrant imitation of Sherlock Holmes.

The Adventures of Ellery Queen (1950)

REGULAR CAST

Ellery Queen (1950-1) Richard Hart *(1951-2)* Lee Bowman
Insp. Richard Queen (1950-2) Florenz Ames

Producers: Norman Pincus, Irving
   Pincus
Approx. 50 monochrome 30-minute
   episodes

US: DuMont/ABC

14 Oct 1950 - Dec 1952

The Adventures of Ellery Queen(1954)

REGULAR CAST

Ellery Queen Hugh Marlowe   *Insp. Richard Queen* Florenz Ames

A Norvin/Arrow Production

32 monochrome 30-minute episodes US:
Syndicated 1954

The Further Adventures of Ellery Queen

REGULAR CAST

Ellery Queen (1958-9) George Nader *(1959)* Lee Philips
Insp. Richard Queen (1958-9) Les Tremayne

Producer: Albert McCleery

26 monochrome 60-minute episodes
US: NBC 26 Sept 1958 - 5 June 1959

Ellery Queen (1975)

REGULAR CAST

Ellery Queen Jim Hutton   *Insp. Richard Queen* David Wayne
Sgt Velie Tom Reese   *Simon Brimmer* John Hillerman
Frank Flannigan Ken Swofford

Creators: Richard Levinson, William
   Link
Music: Elmer Bernstein
Producers: Peter S. Fischer, Michael
   Rhodes
Executive producers: Richard Levinson,
   William Link

A Fairmont-Foxcroft Production with
   Universal Television
One colour 120-minute episode and 22
   colour 60-minute episodes US: NBC
   11 Sept 1975 - 4 April 1976
UK: BBC1 6 Jan - 7 April 1976 9 Aug -
   23 Aug 1976

THE ENIGMA FILES

Heard the one about the doctor, the comedian and the girl from the coffee ads? Well they all teamed up in a worthy BBC crime show, The Enigma Files. It starred Tom Adams, who had made ladies' hearts flutter as a doctor in the British afternoon soap opera, General Hospital. He played Detective Chief Inspector Nick Lewis who, very much against his wishes, was transferred to an apparently harmless desk job with the Prisoners' Property Office. This was a bit like demoting Shakespeare to the stationery department. But old habits die hard, and any hopes his superiors had that he would settle down to a life of boring paperwork were destroyed when he began looking through some old files. To the surprise of the PPO's laboratory technician (played by stand-up comedian Duggie Brown) and the irritation of its executive officer (played by Sharon Maughan, later to star in those hideously smug Gold Blend coffee commercials), Lewis stirred up a veritable hornets' nest, as the contents of the files led him to investigate a series of unsolved cases. And there were plenty of villains out there intent on ensuring that those cases remained unsolved.

REGULAR CAST

Det. Chief Insp. Nick Lewis Tom Adams   *Kate Burton* Sharon Maughan
Phil Strong Duggie Brown

Creator: Derek Ingrey
Music: Anthony Isaac
Producer: Joe Waters

15 colour 50-minute episodes
UK: BBC2 15 April - 22 July 1980

A BBC Television Production

ENOS

A moderate comedy spin-off from The Dukes of Hazzard, featuring the gullible Enos Strate who had been deputy sheriff of Hazzard County. The Los Angeles Police Department was so impressed by his capture of two wanted crooks (it had, of course, been a complete fluke) that he was offered a post with the new Special Branch of the city's Metro Squad. What laughs there were arose from the juxtaposition of country bumpkin Enos and his streetwise black partner Turk Adams. Yet dim though he appeared (and in this case looks weren't deceiving), Enos unaccountably always got his man. Each episode was narrated by Enos in the form of a letter written to the sorely-missed Daisy Duke, informing her of his escapades in the big city.

REGULAR CAST

Officer Enos Strate Sonny Shroyer   *Officer Turk Adams* Samuel E. Wright
Lt Jacob Broggi John Dehner

Creator: Gy Waldron
Executive producer: Gy Waldron

A Warner Bros Production

17 colour 60-minute episodes
US: CBS 5 Nov 1980 - 19 Sept 1981

THE EQUALIZER

'It's astonishing. Even when I went to Nigeria, tribes called out, "Equalizer! Equalizer!"'   – EDWARD WOODWARD

Death Wish comes to television! Edward Woodward played New York's avenging angel Robert McCall, a man so tough and ruthless he made Charles Bronson look like one of The Osmonds. McCall was a cynical former FBI agent who, possibly out of a sense of guilt over the nature of his previous work, decided to offer his services to help those in trouble – for free. Accordingly he placed an advert in the small ads section of a newspaper, volunteering to 'equalize' matters for anyone finding the odds stacked against them. This sounded very dignified and amicable on paper but what it meant in practice was that McCall would hunt whoever was causing the grief and mow them down in a hail of bullets. For his 'equalizer' was his gun. He didn't always ask many questions before taking on a case, either, which meant that if you complained to him in a fit of pique about your husband's snoring, you could wake up in the morning and find your beloved lying on the bed in a pool of blood.

For the most part his quarry were the New York low-life, the muggers and scum who prey on the subway system and down dark alleys. But they met their match in Robert McCall.

The Equalizer's violence prompted predictable outrage on both sides of the Atlantic, but Woodward was quick to defend the charges. 'McCall is hard and ruthless but he's also very gentle, soft-hearted and compassionate. And I think that's what makes him an interesting character – he's full of contradictions. And I cut an awful lot of violence out if I think it's gratuitous.'

Anyway the objectors were well and truly equalized by the show's fans. Woodward received thousands of congratulatory letters and was even voted the sexiest man on American TV, which came as something of a surprise to the affable actor at the age of 54. The citizens of New York, in particular, took the street vigilante to their hearts. While on location, Woodward was regularly asked for help by distraught members of the public. 'They'd say, "Hey man, can you help me? I've got some bother, it's just up the block." I had to say that I was just a character in a series but I did have a list in my trailer provided by the police so I asked them what the problem was and referred them to the right person.'

And Woodward has a ready argument for those who insist that New York really isn't that violent, that the series is far-fetched. For once while filming in the city, two actors who were playing a victim and a terrorist in a hostage scene went off for lunch and were involved in a real hostage drama. Woodward recalls: 'The area was sealed off and we were without our central characters for about five hours!'

REGULAR CAST

Robert McCall Edward Woodward   *Control* Robert Lansing

Creators: Michael Sloan, Richard Lindheim
Music: Stewart Copeland
Producer: Alan Barnette
Executive producer: James McAdams

A Universal Television Production

88 colour 60-minute episodes
US: CBS 11 Sept 1985 - 24 Aug 1989
UK: ITV From 29 Oct 1986

EUROCOPS

If you think Switzerland has as much use for a police force as it does coastguards, or that the Austrian police are about as busy as the Dutch mountain rescue team, Eurocops will have put matters straight. With stories originating from six other European countries, it showed that crime on the continent can be just as gruesome as in Britain and with one additional deadly menace – sub-titles.

Eurocops is a praiseworthy enough venture by which each country submits a police story in its native tongue. Murder may be an international language, but naturally some contributions work better than others. Personally I have never been able to adjust to the Austrians having a female detective called Bigi. She would get an awful lot of stick down at Sun Hill. Even allowing for patriotic bias, the British trilogy, featuring John Benfield's powerful performance as trouble-torn Detective Constable George Jackson, was a fine piece of television, worthy of a longer run.

PRINCIPLE CHARACTERS (UK)

Det. Con. George Jackson John Benfield
(Italy) Commissioner Corso Diego Abatantuono
(France) Luc Bertrand Lacy *Nicolas* Patrick Raynal
(Germany) Inspector Dorn Heiner Lauterbach
(Switzerland) Insp. Peter Brodbeck Wolfram Berger
(Austria) Insp. Peter Brucker Bernd Jeschek *Bigi Herzog* Bigi Fischer
(Spain) Inspector Crespo Alberto Closas

Producers:
  Picture Palace Productions, Channel 4 (UK), *RAI* (Italy)
  Antenne 2 (France), *ZDF* (Germany)
  SRG Zurich (Switzerland)
  ORF (Austria), *RTVE* (Spain)

19 colour 60-minute episodes
UK: Channel 4 (Season 1) 8 Nov -
  13 Dec 1988 (6 eps)
(Season 2) 5 March - 16 April 1990
  (7 eps)
(Season 3) 29 Jan - 5 March 1991
  (6 eps)

THE EXPERT

Years before Quincy's ridiculous ranting and raving gave pathologists a bad name, Marius Goring starred as Dr John Hardy, in a fondly-remembered series rich in authenticity and BBC quality. The Expert was inspired by the work of Professor John Glaister, a Professor of Forensic Medicine at Glasgow University. He also happened to be the uncle of BBC drama producer Gerard Glaister, veteran of the Detective Superintendent Charlesworth stories, and ultimately the man responsible for Howards' Way.

It was set in Warwickshire where Hardy, sometimes with help from his wife Jo, who was also a doctor, and his assistant/receptionist Jane, would unravel murder cases with his unsurpassed knowledge of forensic science. The police were always grateful for his expertise. Detective Chief Inspector Fleming and he became good friends. There was no professional animosity – just a mutual respect.

But the keynote to the series was its realism. Goring went to great lengths to obtain an accurate portrayal of a pathologist's work, conducting hours of research at Guy's Hospital, London. 'I went along there almost every week,' he said. 'I watched them work, studied their methods and practised. If necessary, I got out anatomy books and made anatomical drawings.'

REGULAR CAST

Dr John Hardy Marius Goring   *Jo Hardy* Ann Morrish
Det. Chief Insp. Fleming Victor Winding   *Jane Carter* Sally Nesbitt

Creators: Gerard Glaister, N.J. Crisp
Producer: Gerard Glaister

A BBC Television Production

52 colour 50-minute episodes
UK: BBC2 (Season 1) 5 July - 27 Sept
  1968 (13 eps)
(Season 2) 4 April - 26 Sept 1969 (26
  eps)
(Season 3) 3 Jan - 28 March 1971 (13
  eps)

EYE TO EYE

Oscar Poole had virtually retired from the private detective business and
was a happy-go-lucky regular at O'Malley's Bar, until he bumped into
Tracy Doyle, the daughter of his former partner. She quizzed him about
the mysterious circumstances under which her father died, and
reluctantly Oscar was winched off his bar stool and teamed up with her
to investigate. And would you believe it, other equally dangerous cases
came their way, so the overweight, middle-aged Oscar and the
vivacious, blonde Tracy set up as partners. Someone must have thought
it was a good idea.

REGULAR CAST

Oscar Poole Charles Durning   *Tracy Doyle* Stephanie Faracy

Creators: Rich Eustis, Michael Elias
Producer: Steven A. Vail

A Skorpios Production with Warner Bros

6 colour 60-minute episodes
US: ABC 21 March - 25 April 1984

FABIAN OF THE YARD

An immensely popular British filmed series of the 1950s, which
introduced Inspector Robert Fabian of Scotland Yard, played by noted
character actor Bruce Seton, in semi-fictional re-creations of police
cases. Fabian was typically British – courteous with a clipped reserve –

but he was quite a trailblazer in his day, as he strove to drag policing methods into the 20th century. For he was a great advocate of modern scientific techniques, an approach which led to him being considered somewhat unorthodox by his colleagues. Fabian concentrated on major crimes – robberies, kidnappings and murders, the same type of cases that Tom Lockhart would investigate during his lengthy TV career. Fabian of the Yard was syndicated to the US, where it ran for one season on CBS under the title Patrol Car. The series was also sometimes known as Fabian of Scotland Yard.

* The real Robert Fabian was the first Scotland Yard detective to become a TV personality when, on retiring from the force, he was appointed 'custodian of the questions' on the quiz show The 64,000 Question.

REGULAR CAST

Det. Insp. Fabian Bruce Seton

39 monochrome 30-minute episodes   US: Syndicated 1956
UK: BBC 13 Nov 1954 - 26 Sept 1956

FARADAY AND COMPANY

A brief addition to NBC's Wednesday Mystery Movie series, Faraday and Company offered an early opportunity for actress Sharon Gless, later to star in Cagney and Lacey. Private detective Frank Faraday had been wrongly imprisoned for 25 years in a South American jail, and when he was finally released, his first job was to track down the real culprit and bring him to justice. There was another change in Frank's life too – he had acquired a son Steve, born to his secretary Lou Carson after his imprisonment. Steve had also gone into the detective business, so what better way for father and son to get to know one another than to join forces in a Los Angeles agency specializing in security investigations? Fortunately the relationship did not overdose on saccharin. Indeed the two were often at loggerheads, principally because of their different styles. Steve preferred the patient approach while Frank's idea of diplomacy was a right hook.

REGULAR CAST

Frank Faraday Dan Dailey   *Steve Faraday* James Naughton
Holly Barrett Sharon Gless   *Lou Carson* Geraldine Brooks

Creators: Leonard B. Stern, Ken Pettus, Burt Prelutsky
Music: Jerry Fielding
Producers: Tony Barrett, Stanley Kallis
Executive producer: Leonard B. Stern

A Universal Television Production

4 colour 90-minute episodes
US: NBC 26 Sept 1973 - 13 Aug 1974
UK: ITV 10 Jan 1974 - 30 Aug 1977

FATHER BROWN

Father Brown was television's priest detective. Adapted from the stories of G.K. Chesterton, this beautifully-crafted series made a refreshing change from the blood and thunder approach of many crime shows of the 1970s. Father Brown, motto 'Have Bible... Will Travel', was described as having a face 'as round and dull as a Norfolk dumpling'. But he possessed plenty of guile and solved mysteries by his insight into the workings of the human mind. He had no need for a Magnum secreted in his cassock.

Kenneth More played the thoughtful Father but only after a great deal of pressure from ATV boss Lew Grade. The celebrated impresario was determined to persuade More to take the part and to this end made regular early-morning phone calls to the actor, addressing him as 'Father'. More was not sure he was the right man for the role but after three years of Lew's heavy hints, he eventually agreed. Lew knew he had got his man when he greeted More with the customary 'Morning, Father' and heard the reply, 'God bless you, my son.'

It is hard to believe that such a gentle programme could offend anybody, but in one episode Muhammed was referred to as a 'dirty old humbug' and 2,000 Bradford Muslims promptly marched in protest.

REGULAR CAST

Father Brown Kenneth More   *Flambeau* Dennis Burgess

EPISODE TITLES

The Hammer of God
The Oracle of the Dog
The Curse of the Golden Cross
The Quick One
The Man with Two Beards
The Head of Caesar
The Eye of Apollo
The Dagger with Wings
The Actor and the Alibi
The Arrow of Heaven
The Secret Garden

Music: Jack Parnell
Producer: Ian Fordyce

An ATV Network Production

11 colour 60-minute episodes
UK: ITV 26 Sept - 5 Dec 1974
US: WGBH Boston 'Mystery' 2 - 23 Nov 1982

FATHER DOWLING INVESTIGATES

Lord preserve us! A Chicago parish priest detective and a streetwise nun! Taken from the books by Ralph McInerny, Father Frank Dowling, played here by cuddly Tom Bosley from Happy Days, is a kindly inner-city priest who cannot resist poking his nose into the baffling crimes which conveniently turn up on the steps of his church. His average congregation would more than likely contain three men with gunshot wounds and one with a knife in his back, the flower arranger would be on the F.B.I.'s Most Wanted list, half a dozen choir boys would have ski masks hidden in their hymn books, while the substitute organist would find his playing restricted by the ball and chain around his ankles.

The character of Father Dowling is crazy enough but what really makes this series laughable (and it's not supposed to be) is young Sister Steve, the swinging nun. She can crack jokes, pick locks, drive fast cars, play pool, deal a mean hand of poker and mix great cocktails, presumably known as Bloody Hail Marys...

The pair operate out of St. Michael's and involve themselves in cases which often require Sister Steve to shed her nun's attire and go undercover. They are on good terms with the police and are tolerated by Dowling's housekeeper, Marie, but not always by the Bishop who is understandably concerned about seeing his priest's face in the papers almost as much as George Bush's. The Bishop dearly wanted to post Father Dowling to Alaska but relented at the last minute. Please, Bishop, it's not too late to reconsider. We have done penance enough for our sins without another series of Father Dowling.

* In the US, the programmes are known as The Father Dowling Mysteries. To date, three seasons have been completed, a total of over 30 episodes.

REGULAR CAST

Father Frank Dowling Tom Bosley   *Sister Steve* Tracy Nelson
Marie Mary Wickes

Creator: Ralph McInerny
Developed for TV by Dean Hargrove,
   Joel Steiger
Theme music: Dick DeBenedictis
Producer: Barry Steinberg
Executive producers: Fred Silverman,
   Dean Hargrove

A Viacom Production

Colour 105-minute episodes
US: NBC/ABC From 1 April 1990
UK: ITV 28 Dec 1990 - 14 July 1991
   (LWT)

THE F.B.I.

'The F.B.I. A Quinn Martin Production.'

Somehow those words were more frightening than the activities of the F.B.I. agents themselves, who in this series were just about the nicest guys you could wish to meet. It amounted to a party political broadcast on behalf of the Federal Bureau of Investigation. And because it always portrayed them in a favourable light, the show won the approval of real F.B.I. Director J. Edgar Hoover, who blessed it with full governmental co-operation (stories were supposed to be based on cases from authentic F.B.I. files) and even allowed a few scenes to be filmed at Bureau headquarters in Washington. In return, the programme frequently finished with a plea to viewers for information on the F.B.I.'s most wanted criminals, as well as constantly reminding the American public what a fine body of men were responsible for national security.

It starred a post-Sunset Strip Efrem Zimbalist Jnr as Inspector Lew Erskine, a dedicated government agent who was so immaculately dressed he could have stepped straight out of a shop window. Unfortunately he also had the personality of a tailor's dummy. For the first season he did have a daughter, Barbara, but she was written out, presumably on the grounds that there wasn't room in his life for both the F.B.I. and a family. And he could never be seen displaying human emotions. Erskine reported to Arthur Ward, assistant to the F.B.I. Director, and had a succession of sidekicks – Jim Rhodes, Tom Colby (for six years) and, for the final season, Chris Daniels – who helped him tackle anyone from Communist spies to hippies. Somehow I don't think Lew Erskine believed in flowers, beads and brown rice.

* The series was sponsored by the Ford Motor Company, which was why the agents were always seen driving Fords.

REGULAR CAST

Insp. Lew Erskine Efrem Zimbalist Jnr   *Arthur Ward* Philip Abbott
Barbara Erskine Lynn Loring   *Special Agent Jim Rhodes* Stephen Brooks
Special Agent Tom Colby William Reynolds   *Agent Chris Daniels* Shelly Novack
Narrator Marvin Miller

F.B.I. Theme Bronislau Kaper
Music: Richard Markowitz John Elizade
Producer: Charles Lawton
Executive producer: Quinn Martin

A Quinn Martin Production for Warner Bros

238 colour 60-minute episodes
US: ABC (Season 1) 19 Sept 1965 -
    1 May 1966 (31 eps)
(Season 2) 8 Sept 1966 - 16 April 1967
    (29 eps)
(Season 3) 17 Sept 1967 - 28 April 1968
    (27 eps)

(Season 4) 22 Sept 1968 - 30 March
1969 (25 eps)
(Season 5) 14 Sept 1969 - 8 March
1970 (26 eps)
(Season 6) 20 Sept 1970 - 21 March
1971 (26 eps)
(Season 7) 12 Sept 1971 - 19 March
1972 (26 eps)

(Season 8) 17 Sept 1972 - 1 April 1973
(26 eps)
(Season 9) 16 Sept 1973 - 28 April 1974
(22 eps)
UK: ITV From 3 Oct 1965 (ATV)

FEARLESS FOSDICK PUPPET SHOW

Fearless Fosdick was an American, early 1950s send-up of Dick Tracy. The idea came from Al Capp's comic strip 'Li'l Abner' and was a clever blend of animation and puppets, the latter provided by The Mary Chase Marionettes. According to Li'l Abner, Fosdick was the world's greatest detective, but his boss on the police force treated him with utter contempt. Nevertheless he was a determined crime-fighter who didn't know the meaning of the word defeat. In fact there were quite a few words the dim Fosdick didn't know the meaning of. But he certainly proved popular with children and adults alike. For after starting on Sunday afternoons, he was soon promoted to an evening slot.

Producer: Charles Buggenheim

12 monochrome 30-minute episodes
US: NBC 13 July - 28 Sept 1952

THE FEATHER AND FATHER GANG

One that Stefanie Powers probably keeps quiet about on her Curriculum Vitae. It was an uninspired offering in which Stefanie played 'Feather', a beautiful young attorney with the Los Angeles firm of Huffaker, Danton and Binkwell. Her father was a suave reformed con man and, together with their ill-assorted gaggle of underworld associates, they made up a crack investigative team. In the course of their work, they used a lot of disguises. But the audience saw through them and the show was axed after 13 episodes.

REGULAR CAST

Toni 'Feather' Danton Stefanie Powers   *Harry Danton* Harold Gould
Enzo Frank Delfino   *Margo* Joan Shawlee
Michael Monte Landis   *Lou* Lewis Charles

Creator: Bill Driskill
Music: George Romanis
Producers: Robert Mintz, Bill Driskill
Executive producer: Larry White

*A Columbia Pictures Television
Production*

13 colour 60-minute episodes
US: ABC 7 March - 6 Aug 1977

THE FELLOWS

This spin-off series (SEE THE MAN IN ROOM 17) reunited crusty criminologists Oldenshaw and Dimmock. Having resigned from his Government crime-fighting department, Oldenshaw teamed up with his former colleague when the two were jointly appointed by the Home Office to the Peel Research Fellowship at All Saints College, Cambridge. Their brief was: 'To investigate the general proposition that in a period of rapid social change, the nature of crime – and therefore criminals – would change.' But no matter how adaptable crooks became, they were unable to match the brainpower of The Fellows who, on a good day with the wind at their backs, could have given Poirot and Holmes a run for their money.

REGULAR CAST

Oldenshaw Richard Vernon   *Dimmock* Michael Aldridge

Creator: Robin Chapman
Producers: Robin Chapman, Peter
  Plummer

*A Granada Television Network
Production*

12 monochrome 60-minute episodes
UK: ITV 19 May - 11 Aug 1967

THE FELONY SQUAD

A good solid 1960s police drama filmed around Los Angeles. It starred three generations of cops – young Detective Jim Briggs, his partner, Detective Sergeant Sam Stone, who boasted 20 years on the force, and Jim Briggs' father, Dan, the kindly Desk Sergeant who kept a paternal eye on all the young officers at the station house. During the first and third seasons, their commanding officer was Captain Nye but for the middle series he was temporarily replaced by Captain Franks.

The Felony Squad's final US season was 1968-9, a period of great upheaval in the States, with the assassinations of Martin Luther King and Bobby Kennedy. The television networks were anxious not to show excessive violence on screen and so The Felony Squad's producers were asked to tone down the number of killings. Whereas previously, murderous mayhem had been rife, the first episode of that third series contained just one punch and one shooting. And even then, Sam Stone leaned over the victim and said, 'He's still alive.'

REGULAR CAST

Det. Sgt Sam Stone Howard Duff   *Det. Jim Briggs* Dennis Cole
Desk Sgt Dan Briggs Ben Alexander   *Capt. Nye* Frank Maxwell
Capt. Franks Barney Phillips

Theme music: Pete Rugolo
Producer: Walter Grauman

A TCF Production with ABC

73 colour 30-minute episodes

US: ABC (Season 1) 12 Sept 1966 -
10 April 1967 (30 eps)
(Season 2) 11 Sept 1967 - 18 March
1968 (26 eps)
(Season 3) 27 Sept 1968 - 31 Jan 1969
(17 eps)
UK: ITV 4 July 1967 - 9 May 1969 (ATV)

THE FILES OF JEFFREY JONES

With the same star and producer as The Cases of Eddie Drake, this was another cheaply-produced American syndication series of the 1950s. Here the central character was sport-loving detective Jeffrey Jones.

REGULAR CAST

Jeffrey Jones Don Haggerty

Producer: Lindsley Parsons

26 monochrome 30-minute episodes
US: Syndicated 1953

FINDER OF LOST LOVES

'There is so much love in this series, you almost wish for some violence.'   – TV GUIDE

A borderline detective show which bore the Aaron Spelling trademark of slushy, happy endings – witness Love Boat and Fantasy Island. Cary

Maxwell was a wealthy widower who, following the sudden death of his wife, decided he would bring romance back into the lives of others by reuniting parted lovers. He was assisted by the glamorous Daisy Lloyd, young trainee, Brian Fletcher, and his highly-organized office manager Rita Hargrove. But Maxwell's most important ally was Oscar, the computer he programmed to track down those poor, love-torn, long-lost souls. Yuk! Eat your heart out, Cilla Black.

REGULAR CAST

Cary Maxwell Tony Franciosa	*Daisy Lloyd* Deborah Adair
Rita Hargrove Anne Jeffreys	*Brian Fletcher* Richard Kantor

Creators: Jill Baer, Christopher Vane
  Bill and Jo LaMond
Executive producer: Aaron Spelling

37 colour 60-minute episodes
US: ABC 22 Sept 1984 - 24 Aug 1985

An Aaron Spelling Production for Warner Bros

FOR THE PEOPLE

An early vehicle for William Shatner, but one that was barely roadworthy and was consigned to scrap after 15 weeks. Shatner was David Koster, a keen young New York City district attorney, whose fervour for justice frequently landed him in hot water, both with his superiors (notably bureau chief, Anthony Celese) and the criminal fraternity who took exception to some guy who was hell-bent on locking them up – even if he was going to be in Star Trek the following year. Koster's wife Phyllis was a classical viola player. This brought further conflict into the life of the zealous prosecutor, who was only interested in his own work and objected to his wife having another string to her bow. He finished up spending more time with his leg man, detective Frank Malloy – but it was purely platonic.

REGULAR CAST

David Koster William Shatner	*Anthony Celese* Howard Da Silva
Frank Malloy Lonny Chapman	*Phyllis Koster* Jessica Walter

Executive producer: Herbert Brodkin

15 monochrome 60-minute episodes
US: CBS 31 Jan - 9 May 1965

A CBS Production

FOUL PLAY

Based on the 1978 movie of the same name starring Chevy Chase and Goldie Hawn, Foul Play was a zany comedy about a chat show hostess, Gloria Munday, who joined forces with Tucker Pendleton, a concert violinist-turned-cop to solve crimes in San Francisco. Other characters were Captain Lombardi, Tucker's boss, and Ben and Beau, a couple of midgets who provided a little help. However, the series was a pale imitation of the original and was soon cancelled.

REGULAR CAST

Gloria Munday Deborah Raffin   *Det. Tucker Pendleton* Barry Bostwick
Capt. Lombardi Richard Romanus   *Ben* Greg Rice
Beau John Rice

Creator: Hal Sitowitz

A Miller/Milkis/Boyett Production for Paramount Television

6 colour 60-minute episodes
US: ABC 26 Jan - 23 Aug 1981

THE FOUR JUST MEN

This star-studded quartet qualify as detectives on the strength of Jack Hawkins' character, Ben Manfred, an MP who dabbled in amateur sleuthing. Manfred, American newspaperman, Tim Collier, lawyer, Jeff Ryder and wealthy Italian hotelier, Ricco Poccari were all in the same World War Two unit. Having gone their separate ways, they were reunited by their old commander, Colonel Bacon, on his deathbed and asked to form a secret crime-fighting society. They called themselves The Four Just Men. But it wasn't just men. Each of Manfred's men was joined on their crusades by his personal secretary; Collier was accompanied by the beautiful Nicole, Poccari by Guilia and Ryder by Vicky.

Among the strong list of guest stars were young pretenders such as Judi Dench and Alan Bates, while the writers included Leon Griffiths who, some 20 years later, was to create Minder. Despite Vittorio De Sica's dodgy English, The Four Just Men was an international hit but one which, surprisingly, only ran to one season of syndication in the US.

REGULAR CAST

Ben Manfred Jack Hawkins   *Tim Collier* Dan Dailey
Jeff Ryder Richard Conte   *Ricco Poccari* Vittorio De Sica
Nicole Honor Blackman   *Guilia* Lisa Gastoni
Vicky June Thorburn

Producers: Sidney Cole, Jud Kinberg
Executive producer: Hannah Weinstein

A Sapphire Films Production for ATV

39 monochrome 30-minute episodes
UK: ITV 17 Sept 1959 - 22 June 1960
(ATV)
US: Syndicated 1957

FRANCIS STORM INVESTIGATES

A British children's drama series of the Sixties about a private detective whose deeds were as invigorating as his name. Storm's additional eye was his friend Robin, played by William Simons, who later went back in time as assistant to a more famous sleuth, Cribb.

REGULAR CAST

Francis Storm Brian Worth   *Robin* William Simons
Sgt Pilcher Robin Wentworth

Creator: Peter Elliott Hayes
Director: Grahame Turner

*An Associated Rediffusion Network
Production*

5 monochrome 30-minute episodes
UK: ITV 8 March - 5 April 1960 (ATV)

FRAUD SQUAD

Forgers, con artists, embezzlers and any other fraudsters were the province of Detective Inspector Gamble and his assistant Detective Sergeant Vicky Hicks, members of Scotland Yard's Fraudulent Crimes Squad. A splendid series which managed to make even the most routine cases entertaining, it was all the more worthy for allowing a woman to break into the hitherto male-dominated ranks of British TV police. Guest stars included Michael Gambon, Martin Shaw, Colin Welland and, on the wrong side of the law, for once, as a master-forger, Rupert 'Maigret' Davies.

REGULAR CAST

Det. Insp. Gamble Patrick O'Connell   *Det. Sgt Hicks* Joanna Van Gyseghem

Creator: Ivor Jay
Producer: Nicholas Palmer

An ATV Network Production

26 colour 60-minute episodes
UK: ITV (Season 1) 20 May - 12 Aug
1969 (13 eps)
(Season 2) 19 Sept - 12 Dec 1970
(13 eps)

FREEBIE AND THE BEAN

A cleaned-up version of the 1974 box office hit starring James Caan and Alan Arkin. Freebie and the Bean were two plainclothes police officers, assigned to special duties for San Francisco District Attorney Walter W. Cruikshank. They were complete opposites. Detective Sergeant Tim Walker (Freebie) was a carefree bachelor not averse to bending the law, while Detective Sergeant Dan Delgado (the Bean) was a doom-laden introvert with a wife and two kids and a propensity for doing things by the book. But Freebie's more forceful personality invariably won the day and his reluctant partner was forced to take part in some hairy car chases, most of which resulted in the destruction of a considerable amount of police property. This tendency did not always endear them to the D.A. Alas the mix of slapstick comedy and drama that had worked so well on the big screen, failed to transfer to TV and the show flopped in the States.

REGULAR CAST

Det. Sgt Tim Walker (Freebie) Tom Mason
Det. Sgt Dan Delgado (the Bean) Hector Elizondo
D.A. Walter W. Cruikshank William Daniels

Creator: Dick Nelson
Producer: Philip Saltzman

A Warner Bros Production

6 colour 60-minute episodes
US: CBS 6 Dec 1980 - 17 Jan 1981
UK: BBC1 27 July - 1 Sept 1981

FRONT PAGE DETECTIVE

'Presenting an unusual story of love and mystery on Front Page
Detective starring Mr Edmund Lowe as the famed newspaper
columnist and amateur detective, David Chase. And now for another
thrilling adventure as we accompany David Chase and watch him
match wits with those who would take the law into their own hands.'
—PROGRAMME ANNOUNCER

Gripping stuff, eh? They don't make them like that any more. Suave
American film star of the Twenties and Thirties, Edmund Lowe
played principled journalist David Chase, the man who 'couldn't be
bought.' Chase not only reported on murders, he solved them too,
sometimes with the help of his fashion designer girl-friend. Front
Page Detective was a filmed series which was mainly syndicated to
local American stations, but it did also briefly appear on the DuMont
network.

REGULAR CAST

David Chase Edmund Lowe   *The homicide detective* Frank Jenks
David's girlfriend Paula Drew

Producers: Riley Jackson, Jerry
Fairbanks

30 monochrome 30-minute episodes
US: DuMont 6 July 1951 - 13 Nov 1953

THE FUGITIVE

'I was dining in a London restaurant when the waiter brought me a
note. It read: "Kimble is in the kitchen." – BARRY MORSE

Back in the mid-1960s, the world wondered whether the Beatles would
last, whether the mini-skirt would catch on and whether Dr Richard
Kimble would ever track down the one-armed man. The Fugitive had us
hooked. It was a classic drama serial which maintained the suspense
right up until the 120th and final episode.

For the uninitiated, the story was that Dr Richard Kimble (played
by David Janssen) had been sentenced to death for the murder of his
wife, a crime of which he was wholly innocent. He was being
escorted to a prison by Lieutenant Philip Gerard (Barry Morse) for
the execution when the train in which they were travelling was

derailed. Gerard was rendered unconscious and Kimble saw his chance to escape. For the next four years, Gerard pursued Kimble across the length and breadth of America, while Kimble in turn searched for the elusive one-armed man who he had actually seen murder his wife. To stay one step ahead of the police, Kimble adopted a host of new identities. Then in the final two-parter, Kimble at last found the one-armed man and in a dramatic chase they confronted one another at the top of a tower. Gerard, who was also closing in on his quarry, realized he had been wrong about the good doctor and, in the nick of time shot the one-armed man who plunged to his death. Justice had been done.

The Fugitive had a phenomenal impact. Prisoners wrote to David Janssen saying they had been framed too, and convicts on a chain-gang in the Deep South threatened to riot, when a warder said he would prevent them watching the show. Old ladies reported sightings of one-armed men and, when in Britain, Granada Television suddenly stopped screening the series half-way through, 600 Liverpool factory-girls formed an action committee to persuade the company to reconsider. Granada backed down.

The final two-parter in August 1967 caused uproar, because so many viewers were on holiday. Having seen the first part, holidaymakers rang TV stations to ask if the second half was being shown where they were staying. Many pleaded for private screenings as they were going abroad. Others cancelled their holidays altogether. To keep the outcome secret, the second segment was televised all over the world on the same day (although with time changes, it wasn't always the same date). Barmaids and waiters were given time off to watch it as it was thought that bars and restaurants would be empty anyway. In the US it drew record viewing figures, not surpassed until the famous Dallas episode revealing who shot J.R.

The most important man in Britain was Granada's despatch officer Bert Dye. He travelled down to London to collect the final reel, but by the time he returned to Manchester, the studios were locked. So he dutifully took it home and, in case his house was burgled that night, he hid the reel in the loft. The next day he took it to the studios on the bus, earning some puzzled looks from his fellow passengers for carrying a can marked 'The Fugitive'.

* The Fugitive won an Emmy in 1965 for Outstanding Dramatic series.

REGULAR CAST

Dr Richard Kimble David Janssen   *Lt Philip Gerard* Barry Morse
Fred Johnson, the One-Armed Man Bill Raisch   *Narrator* William Conrad

---

Creator: Roy Huggins
Music: Pete Rugolo
Producer: Wilton Schiller
Executive producer: Quinn Martin

A Quinn Martin Production for ABC
90 monochrome and 30 colour 60-minute
    episodes

US: ABC (Season 1) 17 Sept 1963 -
    21 April 1964 (30 eps)
Season 2) 15 Sept 1964 - 20 April 1965
    (30 eps)
(Season 3) 14 Sept 1965 - 26 April 1966
    (30 eps)
(Season 4) 13 Sept 1966 - 29 Aug 1967
    (30 eps)
UK: ITV 7 Jan 1964 - 30 Aug 1967
    (Anglia)

FUTURE COP

Also known as Cleaver and Haven, this was the deeply unlikely tale of
an old-fashioned cop, Joe Cleaver (played by a wasted Ernest
Borgnine), who was given an android rookie, John Haven, as a partner.
The joke (and there was only the one) was that a third L.A.P.D. officer,
Bill Bundy, didn't know that Haven was a robot. Haven had been
programmed to be the perfect cop. He was capable of almost anything.
It was just a shame his talents didn't extend to coming up with a half-
decent script.

REGULAR CAST

Officer Joe Cleaver Ernest Borgnine   *Officer Bill Bundy* John Amos
Officer John Haven Michael Shannon   *Captain Skaggs* Herbert Nelson

Producer: Everett Chambers
Executive producers: Anthony Wilson,
    Gary Damsker

A Paramount Television Production

6 colour 60-minute episodes
US: ABC 5 March - 6 Aug 1977

THE FUZZ

A British police comedy which, despite a strong cast and the writing
talents of Willis Hall (Budgie, Billy Liar etc), was not in the least
arresting. The principals were the long-suffering Detective Sergeant
Marble and, the reasons for his misery, over-enthusiastic PCs Cordwainer
and Dickinson. These two created mayhem around town in the station's
only Panda car, as they daydreamed about tackling a really big case – like
a nice juicy murder. The nearest they got was when a pantie thief plunged

them into the underwear underworld. Meanwhile, the only crime figure that oily Chief Superintendent Allardyce was interested in was that of glamorous WPC 'Purrfect' Purvis. Cagney and Lacey would have had him in an arm-lock before you could say 'sexual harassment'.

REGULAR CAST

Det. Sgt Marble Michael Robbins   *PC Cordwainer* Nigel Lambert
PC Dickinson Mike Savage   *WPC Purvis* Lynda Bellingham
Supt. Allardyce Colin Jeavons

Creator: Willis Hall
Producer/Director: Stuart Allen

7 colour 30-minute episodes
UK: ITV 8 Sept - 20 Oct 1977

A Thames Television Network Production

THE GALLERY OF MME LUI-TSONG

Described by America's DuMont network as 'a good girl against bad men,' Mme Lui-Tsong was the first woman detective to have her own show. Played by Chinese-American actress Anna May Wong (whose real name was Wong Lui-Tsong), she owned a world-wide chain of art galleries and doubled up in her spare time as an exotic sleuth full of Eastern promise. Her cases frequently involved the art world but also took in international intrigue. After six episodes she lost 'The Gallery Of' from the title. Seven episodes later she lost the lot.

REGULAR CAST

Mme Lui-Tsong Anna May Wong

A DuMont Production
13 monochrome 30-minute episodes

US: DuMont 3 Sept - 21 Nov 1951

GANGBUSTERS

With its stories taken from real police and F.B.I. files and its semi-documentary presentation, Gangbusters was a mainstay of American radio for 21 years, between 1936 and 1957. Yet its TV life was relatively short, principally because it was only ever intended as a stop-gap for the weeks when Dragnet was not on. It alternated on Thursday nights with Dragnet, and Jack Webb even used to plug next week's adventure, with Joe Friday, at the finish of Gangbusters. Between them, the two programmes were so popular that the other networks virtually threw in the towel and scheduled political debates as opposition. Then when Webb was able to produce Dragnet on a weekly basis, Gangbusters simply drifted away.

Gangbusters had no regular cast but a feature of the show was its 'most wanted' spot at the end. A photo of one of the nation's most sought-after criminals was put on screen, accompanied by an appeal for information. On radio (presumably without the photo!) this measure resulted in several hundred arrests.

Narrator/creator/producer: Phillips H. Lord

An NBC Production

21 monochrome 30-minute episodes
US: NBC 20 March - 25 Dec 1952

THE GENTLE TOUCH

Introducing Detective Inspector Maggie Forbes who, by five months (Juliet Bravo followed in August), became British television's first starring female detective, when she hit the screen in April 1980. It was not a happy start for the woman who had worked her way up through the ranks, after joining the Metropolitan Police as a young cadet – in the first episode her PC husband, Ray, was shot dead during a robbery by two brothers. This left Maggie to raise her surly teenage son, Steve. She bore it through gritted teeth.

Played by Jill Gascoine, Maggie was based at London's Seven Dials police station near Soho. Her boss was grumpy, baggy-eyed Detective Chief Inspector Russell, and her fellow DI was Scottish male chauvinist boar, Bob Croft. The Detective Sergeants were more amiable – kindly Jake Barratt, young Jimmy Fenton and for the last two series, another fresh-faced recruit, Peter Philips. It seemed to be written into Jill Gascoine's contract that in the course of virtually every episode someone (either one of the sergeants, a crook or a witness) had to remark how attractive Maggie Forbes was. It reached the stage where one expected a bank raid in full swing to be interrupted by the wailing of police sirens then the gang to stop, drop the loot and lift up their masks to coo at the approaching DI Forbes, 'Cor what a smasher.'

Mind you, at first she did very little crime-busting. Her working routine appeared to consist of a hard day at the hairdresser's, having her perm done. Eventually the action did pick up. Jill Gascoine admitted: 'The series and Maggie got tougher.' Not that her fans cared either way – they mobbed her on location and were quite jealous when Maggie had a fling with Mike Turnbull. The fourth season ended with Seven Dials' answer to Wonder Woman being carted out of the station on a stretcher, after a villain's wife had hurled a hand grenade at her. In a wonderful understatement, Jill Gascoine remarked of Maggie at the start of the next series : 'Being blown up has changed her.' It probably meant she had to spend even more time at the hairdresser.

After five years, Maggie Forbes was packed off to join C.A.T.S. Eyes. She may have had her faults, but nobody deserved that. (SEE C.A.T.S. EYES)

* In The Gentle Touch, because Jill Gascoine couldn't drive, Maggie was always seen at the wheel of a stationary car!

REGULAR CAST

Det. Insp. Maggie Forbes Jill Gascoine	*Det. Ch. Insp. Russell* William Marlowe
Det. Sgt Jake Barratt Paul Moriarty	*Det. Sgt Jimmy Fenton* Derek Thompson
Det. Insp. Bob Croft Brian Gwaspari	*Det. Sgt Peter Philips* Kevin O'Shea
Steve Forbes Nigel Rathbone	*Mike Turnbull* Bernard Holley

Music: Roger Webb
Producers: Kim Mills, Jack Williams (Seasons 1, 2) Michael Verney-Elliott (2 - 5)
Executive producer: Tony Wharmby (1 - 4) Nick Elliott (5)

An LWT Network Production

56 colour 60-minute episodes
UK: ITV

(Season 1) 11 April - 23 May 1980 (7 eps)
(Season 2) 5 Sept - 7 Nov 1980 (10 eps)
(Season 3) 6 Nov 1981 - 5 Feb 1982 (13 eps)
(Season 4) 22 Oct 1982 - 28 Jan 1983 (13 eps)
(Season 5) 1 Sept - 24 Nov 1984 (13 eps)

GET CHRISTIE LOVE

Christie Love was a sexy black undercover cop (played by Laugh-In's Teresa Graves) working for the Special Investigations Division of the Los Angeles Police Department. She was described by ABC as 'an upbeat, together young lady with charm and humour.' Her tough boss was Lieutenant Matt Reardon (later replaced by Captain Arthur Ryan) and her partner in fighting crime was Sergeant Pete Gallagher. The reason Christie used to like working undercover, in a variety of disguises, was not because of any great bravery or calling but because she hated the police uniform. It's a good job they don't all think like that.

* The show's technical adviser was Detective Olga Ford of the New York police Department.

REGULAR CAST

Det. Christie Love Teresa Graves   *Lt Matt Reardon* Charles Cioffi
Capt. Arthur P. Ryan Jack Kelly   *Sgt Pete Gallagher* Michael Pataki

Producer: Paul Mason
Executive producer: David L. Wolper

22 colour 60-minute episodes
US: ABC 11 Sept 1974 - 18 July 1975

A Universal Television Production

GHOST SQUAD

A classic British crime series based on former police detective John Gosling's book, The Ghost Squad, which described the activities of Scotland Yard's real-life undercover unit. They were no ordinary undercover cops, seconded for a day or two as supplementary store detectives. The men and women of Ghost Squad were an elite band of agents whose mission was to infiltrate and eliminate the international underworld. They often worked alone and always in total secrecy. Only their controllers knew their identity. It was a dangerous job and one with a high casualty rate, illustrated by the assassination of the squad's leading operator, American master of disguise Nick Craig, at the end of the second series.

Before his untimely demise, Craig's colleagues had been the rugged Tony Miller and secretary-turned-agent, Jean Carter. In contrast, Craig's replacement was the quiet, studious but equally effective Peter Clarke. Ghost Squad started out under the control of Sir Andrew Wilson, but when he and his secretary, Helen Winters, were posted elsewhere, Geoffrey Stock took over the running of the department. For the third and final season, the series was re-titled GS5.

REGULAR CAST

Nick Craig Michael Quinn   *Sir Andrew Wilson* Sir Donald Wolfit
Tony Miller Neil Hallett   *Helen Winters* Angela Browne
Geoffrey Stock Anthony Marlowe   *Jean Carter* Claire Nielson
Peter Clarke Ray Barrett

Music: Philip Green
Producer: Connery Chappell (Season 1) Anthony Kearey (Season 2) Dennis Vance (Season 3)

A Rank Organization TV Film in association with ATV (Season 1)

An ATV Network Production (Seasons 2, 3)
52 monochrome 60-minute episodes

UK: ITV (Season 1) 9 Sept - 11 Nov 1961 (13 eps)
(Season 2) 22 Dec 1962 - 4 May 1963 (26 eps)
(Season 3) 22 Feb - 27 June 1964 (13 eps)
US: Syndicated 1960 (10 eps from season 1)

GIDEON OLIVER

Professor Gideon Oliver can lay claims to being the cleverest man on television. A teacher of Anthropology, a subject which has made him an authority on world cultures, he possesses an inquiring mind that leads him to some of the world's most puzzling crimes. He does not carry a gun, but his athletic skills include kick-boxing, a potentially deadly karate-like sport which has saved his life on more than one occasion. Gideon Oliver is divorced and in his forties. He knows that for better or worse he is a role model to his students. His lecture room has the indefinable air of relaxed attention that is the hallmark of a great teacher. Gideon makes learning exciting because he can communicate the joy of the search for knowledge. And he is never satisfied with incomplete information – once he has got the bit between his teeth, he will keep going until all the loose ends are tied up. His criminal investigations have been known to take him half-way round the world.

The two constants in Gideon's life are Catherine Fraker, his secretary and personal assistant for the past 20 years, and his pretty daughter Zina, a graduate student in clinical psychology.

* Gideon Oliver is one of the new Mystery Movies from Universal.

REGULAR CAST

Gideon Oliver Louis Gossett Jr   *Zina Oliver* Shari Headley

Producer: Kevin Donnelly
Executive producers: William Sackheim, Dick Wolf

5 colour 120-minute episodes
US: ABC From 20 Feb 1989

A Universal Television Production

GIDEON'S WAY

Commander George Gideon of Scotland Yard was a steady reliable copper, with the responsibility of maintaining law and order on the streets of London in the often-turbulent mid-Sixties. He and Chief Inspector David Keen stalked murderers and robbers galore, in a series that created considerable concern over its level of violence for an 8pm time slot. Ultimately some particularly gruesome scenes were ordered to be cut.

Each week Gideon's Way paraded a fine supporting cast. Michael Cashman, best known as gay Colin in the soap opera EastEnders, was a child actor in one episode, while Derren Nesbitt (later of Special Branch) and John Hurt played a couple of escaped prisoners, Hurt's character having robbed a fur store. The series was based on the stories by John Creasey.

REGULAR CAST

Commander Gideon John Gregson   *Chief Insp. Keen* Alexander Davion

Music: Edwin Astley
Producers: Robert S. Baker, Monty Norman

26 monochrome 60-minute episodes
UK: ITV 18 March 1965 - 10 May 1966

An ATV Presentation

GLYNIS

Built around the appeal of comedy actress Glynis Johns, this American sit-com featured the exploits of high-powered attorney, Keith Granville, and his wacky wife, Glynis, a mystery writer. Both had an unfortunate tendency to play amateur detective which frequently landed them in hot water. But predictably, despite their decidedly unorthodox approach, they somehow succeeded in solving every crime they tackled.

REGULAR CAST

Glynis Granville Glynis Johns   *Keith Granville* Keith Andes

Producers: Jess Oppenheimer, Edward
   H. Feldman

A Desilu Production

13 monochrome 30-minute episodes
US: CBS 25 Sept - 18 Dec 1963
UK: BBC1 1 June - 8 Oct 1964

THE GOLD ROBBERS

Actor Peter Vaughan is capable of injecting menace into the most innocent situations. He could make The Tales of Peter Rabbit sound like a Hammer horror story. So he was perfectly cast as the steely-eyed Detective Chief Superintendent Cradock, destined to spend 13 weeks tracking down a gang who had lifted five and a half million pounds of gold bullion in 'the crime of the century'. This was a superior cops and robbers series, full of action and all the better for an eminent list of guest stars, including Peter Bowles, Ian Hendry, Joss Ackland and George Cole as a small-time conman. It was good practice for playing Arthur Daley in Minder, as well as being a nice little earner.

REGULAR CAST

Det. Chief Supt Cradock Peter Vaughan   *Det. Sgt Toms* Artro Morris
Insp. Tompkins Michael Wynne

Creators: John Hawkesworth, Glyn
   Jones
Music: Max Harris
Producer: John Hawkesworth

An LWT Network Production

13 colour 60-minute episodes
UK: ITV 6 June - 29 Aug 1969

THE GREEN HORNET

Hot on the heels of The Caped Crusader came The Green Hornet, from the same Batproducer, William Dozier. Yet the Hornet was no brash new interloper onto the superhero scene – he was created by George W. Trendle, the man behind The Lone Ranger, as far back as 1936 and was a popular diversion on American radio in the Thirties and Forties. Like all the best crime-fighters, he led a double existence. When there were no dastardly deeds to be undone, he was Britt Reid, campaigning editor and publisher of The Daily Sentinel. Only his faithful manservant Kato (an inspiration for the Pink Panther?) and District Attorney Scanlon knew that in times of stress, Reid became The Green Hornet. Even

Reid's adoring secretary, 'Casey' Case, and hard-bitten crime reporter, Mike Axford, never cottoned on.

In the television version, Reid's existence was modernized and instead of running a newspaper, he owned a TV station. And Kato was played by an unknown oriental actor named Bruce Lee.

The equivalent of the Batmobile was the Black Beauty, complete with a built-in TV camera which could see four miles ahead, and a contraption capable of spreading ice over the road so that any pursuers would come to a slippery end. In reality the car was a customized Chrysler Imperial. The Green Hornet also brandished a gas gun to immobilize his enemies, and a sting gun that penetrated steel. He fought more conventional criminals than Batman's bizarre baddies, and perhaps this was one of the reasons the show never caught on to the same extent. Or maybe he should have stuck to being unseen on radio. For on TV he merely looked like an overgrown grasshopper.

* The Green Hornet's theme music was an arrangement of The Flight of the Bumble Bee played by Al Hirt.

REGULAR CAST

Britt Reid/The Green Hornet Van Williams   *Kato* Bruce Lee
Leonore 'Casey' Case Wende Wagner   *Mike Axford* Lloyd Gough
District Attorney F.P. Scanlon Walter Brooke   *Announcer:* Gary Owens

Music: Billy May
Producer: William Dozier

26 colour 30-minute episodes
US: ABC 9 Sept 1966 - 14 July 1967

A TCF Production for ABC

GRIFF

There was a distinct Western feel to Griff since it starred Lorne Greene, late of Bonanza, and Ben Murphy in his first series since Alias Smith and Jones. Greene played Wade Griffin, a distinguished police captain with 30 years' service to his credit, who decided to resign from the force on a point of principle. Thereupon he set up business as Wade Griffin Investigations, in the Westwood area of Los Angeles where he was assisted by Mike Murdoch and a secretary called Gracie. Much of the interest lay in watching the veteran Griff cope with the many youngsters in the neighbourhood. Unfortunately, neither that nor the presence of its two stars was sufficient to sustain the show, and it quickly perished in competition with Barnaby Jones, which had much the same idea but did it considerably better.

REGULAR CAST

Wade Griffin Lorne Greene   *Mike Murdoch* Ben Murphy
Gracie Newcombe Patricia Stich   *Capt. Barney Marcus* Vic Tayback

Creator: Larry Cohen
Music: Elliott Kaplan, Mike Post, Pete
  Carpenter
Producer: Steven Bochco
Executive producer: David Victor

A Universal Television Production

12 colour 60-minute episodes
US: ABC 29 Sept 1973 - 5 Jan 1974
UK: ITV 27 Aug 1974 - 18 March 1976
  (LWT)

THE GROWING PAINS OF PC PENROSE (SEE ROSIE)

HAGEN

What could be more natural than a tracker detective? Paul Hagen was a mountain man, an accomplished hunter. Carl Palmer was a San Francisco attorney. What could be more natural than for them to combine their diverse talents to tackle tough criminal investigations? Hagen did the legwork prowling around the city, while Palmer sorted out the legal side. What could be more natural than to take it off after nine episodes?

REGULAR CAST

Paul Hagen Chad Everett   *Carl Palmer* Arthur Hill

Creators: Charles Larson, Frank
  Glicksman
Music: George Romanis
Producer: Jack Sowards
Executive producer: Frank Glicksman

9 colour 60-minute episodes
US: ABC 29 Sept 1973 - 5 Jan 1974

A TCF Production

HALF NELSON

Rocky Nelson was not only one of the shortest private eyes on TV, his show had just about the shortest-ever run on the network – two episodes. Seven were made in all but the first couple were so poorly received that the remainder were shelved. It was intended to be an old-fashioned gangster comedy about a pint-sized New York cop who went to Hollywood to film his own life story. Turned down for the part because he was too small, he became a private eye instead. If nothing else, Half Nelson certainly disproved the theory that the best things come in small packages.

REGULAR CAST

Rocky Nelson Joe Pesci   *Annie O'Hara* Victoria Jackson

Creators: Glen Larson, Lou Shaw
Producer: Harker Wade
Executive producer: Glen Larson

A Glen Larson Production for TCF

One colour 120-minute episode and 6 colour 60-minute episodes (Only 2 transmitted)
US: NBC 24 March, 10 May 1985

HARBOUR COMMMAND

Highway Patrol at sea. This syndicated police action series was set in the harbour of a large American city, with Captain Ralph Baxter, the plainclothes chief of Harbour Command, fighting an assortment of waterside villains – drug smugglers, murderers, deckchair attendants etc.

REGULAR CAST

Capt. Ralph Baxter Wendell Corey

A United Artists production

39 monochrome 30-minute episodes

US: Syndicated 1957
UK: ITV 8 Aug 1958 - 13 May 1960
(ATV)

HARBOURMASTER

Peaceful Scott Island off the coast of New England was the setting for the adventures of harbourmaster David Scott. His principal duty was arranging dock space for boats and repairing craft with the aid of young Jeff Kittridge, but he also served as a one-man rescue squad and police force in his vessel Blue Chip II. And even though the locals seemed to lead a tranquil existence, there was enough crime around to keep him going for 26 weeks. When the series switched from CBS to ABC midway through, the title was altered to Adventures at Scott Island.

REGULAR CAST

Capt. David Scott Barry Sullivan   *Jeff Kittridge* Paul Burke

Producers: Jon Epstein, Leon Benson
Eddie Davis, Henry Kessler

A United Artists Production

26 monochrome 30-minute episodes
US: CBS/ABC 26 Sept 1957 - 29 June
1958

HARDBALL

That old ploy of pairing two cops who have absolutely nothing in common was given a fresh airing in this pacey American crime drama. Charlie Battles was a tough, baseball-loving, veteran cop who had no intention of adhering to his superiors' wishes and going quietly into either a desk job or early retirement. Joe 'Kaz' Kaczierowski was a young, carefree, long-haired, undercover cop, the son of a former police officer, who loved his job almost as much as he loved his powerful Harley Davidson motorcycle.

The pair were teamed together to protect a woman and her son from her Los Angeles mobster husband, against whom she was about to testify. Battles made it clear from the start that he despised much about his new partner including his youth, clothes, pony-tail, opinions, taste in food – and especially his tongue-tying surname. For his part, the laid-back Kaz admired his irascible colleague and thought they would get along just fine. They needed to because their everyday policing activities brought them into contact with hit-men, international terrorists and even the KGB. It was never like that down at Dock Green.

REGULAR CAST

Charlie Battles John Ashton   *Joe 'Kaz' Kaczierowski* Richard Tyson

Creator: Robert Palm
Music: Sylvester Levay
Executive producers: Frank Lupo, John
  Ashley

*A Columbia Pictures Television
  Production in association with NBC*

One colour 90-minute epiosode and 17
  colour 60-minute episodes US: NBC
  28 Sept 1989 - 29 June 1990
UK: ITV 10 Jan - 30 May 1991 (Thames)

HARDCASTLE AND MCCORMICK

Milton G. Hardcastle was a judge with a grudge. He strongly objected to the fact that anyone had walked free from his courtroom (and that probably included the usher), particularly those who had been let off through lack of evidence or because their lawyers had discovered a legal loophole. He called them 'the ones that got away'.

After 30 years on the bench, Hardcastle came out to play. He may have officially retired but there was no respite for criminals, because he was determined to track down those who had escaped on a technicality. He was a well-preserved 65-year-old but he needed help with the legwork, and that's where wayward hotrod racing driver Mark 'Skid' McCormick came in. McCormick had a string of convictions to his name and was on a charge of car theft. The judge made him an offer, laced with blackmail. If McCormick helped him hunt down those who had cheated justice, the judge would get him off the hook when he appeared in court. Anyone in their right mind would have told the old man to forget it, but 'Hardcastle' wouldn't have made such a good series title. So the pair teamed up for a succession of comic action adventures with a positive plethora of car crashes.

The judge was certainly a colourful character. He leaned pretty heavily on his old bench-mates to solve the cases and liked nothing better than a weekly game of poker, to the amazement of his acid-tongued housekeeper Sarah. He used to wear loud shirts and tennis shorts under his robes in court and now resorted to T-shirts bearing such subtle slogans as 'Find 'Em and Hang 'Em'. He also drove around in a red sports car bearing the number plates DE JUDGE. In fact there was a fair case for suggesting he was the one who wanted locking up.

REGULAR CAST

Judge Milton G. Hardcastle Brian Keith   *Mark 'Skid' McCormick* Daniel Hugh-Kelly
Sarah Wicks Mary Jackson

Music: Mike Post, Pete Carpenter
Producers: Les Sheldon, Larry Hertzog
Executive producers: Stephen J.
  Cannell, Patrick Hasburgh

65 colour 60-minute episodes
US: ABC 18 Sept 1983 - 16 July 1986
UK: ITV 16 Oct 1983 - 31 March 1985

A Paramount Production

THE HARDY BOYS/NANCY DREW MYSTERIES

The adventure stories of juvenile sleuths, The Hardy Boys, and their female counterpart, Nancy Drew, had been a popular part of American teenage literature for most of the century. The Hardy Boys mystery books were supposedly written by Franklin W. Dixon but no such person existed. They were actually produced by a writing factory founded in the early 1900s by Edward Stratemeyer who, with his daughter, Harriet Adams, wrote or oversaw the writing of every story. They used the pseudonyms of Franklin W. Dixon for Hardy and Carolyn Keene for Nancy Drew. In the late 1930s there was a series of second feature Nancy Drew films starring Bonita Granville.

Initially on American TV, The Hardy Boys alternated on Sunday nights with The Nancy Drew Mysteries (SEE THE NANCY DREW MYSTERIES) but the two series then joined forces to tackle such innocuous cases as searching for missing people and pets or acting as ghostbusters. The mainstays of the Hardy family were 16-year-old Joe and 18-year-old Frank, sons of renowned private investigator Fenton Hardy. They were helped out by Callie, who worked part-time at their father's agency, and by Aunt Gertrude. Joe was played by Shaun Cassidy, younger brother of David, and after he sang the old Crystals hit Da Do Ron Ron in one episode, it shot to the top of the US charts.

The original Nancy Drew was Pamela Sue Martin who went on to undergo all manner of weird experiences as Fallon in Dynasty. But she quit when the two shows merged and was replaced briefly by Janet Louise Johnson before, in an act of unsurpassed chauvinism, poor old Nancy Drew was dropped altogether and the title shortened to The Hardy Boys.

REGULAR CAST

Joe Hardy Shaun Cassidy   *Frank Hardy* Parker Stevenson
Fenton Hardy Edmund Gilbert   *Callie Shaw* Lisa Eilbacher
Aunt Gertrude Edith Atwater   *Nancy Drew* Janet Louise Johnson

Creator: Glen A. Larson
Producers: Joyce Brotman, B.W. Sandefur
Executive producer: Glen A. Larson

A Universal Television Production
46 colour 60-minute episodes US: ABC

(Season 1) 30 Jan 1977 - 22 May 1977 (14 eps)
(Season 2) 11 Sept 1977 - 7 May 1978 (22 eps)
(Season 3) 1 Oct 1978 - 3 Dec 1978 (10 eps)
UK: BBC1 25 April - 23 May 1981
21 Dec 1981 - 8 Jan 1982 (transmitted daily)

HARRY O

Harry Orwell was not a happy man. He suffered a lot, physically and mentally. First he was pensioned off from the police force after being shot in the back, and he remained in pain from the bullet that was still lodged in his body. But he managed to set up as a private detective, using his former partner, Lieutenant Manny Quinlan of the San Diego Police Department, as a point of contact. But then Quinlan was killed and so a distraught Harry took his business to Santa Monica. Life there was even worse. He had lost one of his few friends and instead had to deal with the permanently sarcastic Lieutenant Trench. Harry could cheerfully have buried him in one .

Despite his sea-front cottage, Harry O was definitely a graduate of the downbeat school of private eyes. Even the first-person narrative smacked of Raymond Chandler and Mickey Spillane. He was often forced to travel around by bus because his car was in an almost permanent state of disrepair. He led a lonely existence, punctuated by occasional assistance from amateur criminologists Lester Hodges and Dr Fong, and saw most of his life through the bottom of a whisky glass. The one thing Harry did have was beautiful neighbours like Farrah Fawcett and Linda Evans. At least their appearance spread a flicker of a smile across his lugubrious face.

Played by *Fugitive* star David Janssen, the series looked a sure-fire winner, yet it took two pilots, *Harry O* and *Smile Jenny, You're Dead* (the latter featuring 12-year-old Jodie Foster), before it got off the ground. It was generally worth waiting for although Harry's dour demeanour meant that as a tonic it was about as effective as a Leonard Cohen LP.

REGULAR CAST

Harry Orwell David Janssen   *Det. Lt Manny Quinlan* Henry Darrow
Lt K.C. Trench Anthony Zerbe   *Lester Hodges* Les Lannom
Dr Fong Keye Luke

EPISODE TITLES

Harry O
Smile Jenny, You're Dead
Gertrude
The Admiral's Lady
Mortal Sin
Guardian at the Gate
Eye Witness
Coinage of the Realm
Material Witness
Shadows at Noon
Ballinger's Choice
Second Sight
Accounts Balanced
Forty Reasons to Kill
Elegy for a Cop
Silent Kill
For the Love of Money
The Counterfeit People
The Last Heir
Double Jeopardy
Sound of Trumpets
Street Games
Lester
Lester Two
Anatomy of a Frame
Portrait of a Murder
Book of Changes Shades
One for the Road
Tender Killing Care
The Madonna Legacy
APB Harry Orwell

The Acolyte
Reflections
Mayday
Mister Five and Dime
Group Terror
Exercise in Fatality
Forbidden City
The Amazing Case of Lester and Dr
   Fong
Ruby
Death Certificate
Past Imperfect
Hostage
Victim

Creator: Howard Rodman
Producers: Robert E. Thompson,
   Robert Dozier, Buck Houghton, Alex
   Beaton
Executive producer: Jerry Thorpe

A Warner Bros Television Production

2 colour 120-minute episodes and 43
   colour 60-minute episodes US: ABC
(Season 1) 12 Sept 1974 - 13 March
   1975 (23 eps)
(Season 2) 11 Sept 1975 - 29 April 1976
   (22 eps)
UK: BBC1 8 Nov 1974 - 24 June 1977

HART OF THE YARD

Known in the US as Nobody's Perfect, this situation comedy starred
that fine actor, Ron Moody, as a clueless Scotland Yard detective in San
Francisco. The Clouseau-like Inspector Roger Hart was notoriously
clumsy, liable to self-ignite at a moment's notice, but he also possessed
hidden talents. He was an accomplished swordsman, a master of

disguise and a bomb expert – providing he remembered to cut the correct wire. But he was a headache to his boss, Lieutenant Vince de Gennaro, who responded by teaming him with another odd ball, Detective Jennifer Dempsey. With a strong cast and a reasonable scenario, Hart of the Yard should have been a roaring success.

But unfortunately somebody forgot to include any jokes.

REGULAR CAST

Det. Insp. Roger Hart Ron Moody   *Det. Jennifer Dempsey* Cassie Yates
Lt Vince de Gennaro Michael Durrell

Creators: Arne Sultan, Chris Hayward
Music: Tom Scott
Producer: Lew Gallo

10 colour 30-minute episodes
US: NBC 26 June - 28 Aug 1980
UK: ITV 3 Sept 1980 - 5 Jan 1981

A Universal Television Production

HART TO HART

The show that borrowed everything, even the dog, from The Thin Man. Jonathan and Jennifer Hart had money, style, money, glamour and more money. He was a self-made millionaire, the head of Hart Industries, and she was an internationally famous freelance journalist. They were blissfully happily married and lived with their dog, Freeway, in a huge Beverly Hills mansion overflowing with the trappings of success. Yet they yearned for something more in life – excitement. For as their gravel-voiced chauffeur, Max, informed us at the start of each episode, the Harts' hobby was murder.

So the wisecracking couple became amateur sleuths, touring the playgrounds of the wealthy in their private jet and solving crimes en route. Inevitably most of their cases involved Jennifer being placed in mortal danger either side of the second commercial break.

Hart to Hart was a resounding success, principally due of course to the appeal of its two stars, Robert Wagner and Stefanie Powers, who were glossiness personified. Stefanie Powers was always Wagner's first choice for the part but she had her doubts, simply because her previous excursions into television, The Girl From U.N.C.L.E. and The Feather and Father Gang, had been less than memorable.

Created by best-selling novelist,Sidney Sheldon, Hart to Hart has been widely vilified for its derivative format, but in fairness it was a pretty good piece of escapism in its own right. The interplay between the leads was outstanding and the scripts were generally slick and witty. But above all, Hart to Hart looked good, which was more than could be said for Max. That is the one thing that has always puzzled me. How could a couple who loved to be surrounded by the beautiful things in life, employ a driver with a face like a dried prune?

REGULAR CAST

Jonathan Hart Robert Wagner   *Jennifer Hart* Stefanie Powers
Max Lionel Stander

Creator: Sidney Sheldon
Producer: Mart Crowley
Executive producer: Aaron Spelling

An Aaron Spelling Production for ABC

110 colour 60-minute episodes
US: ABC (Season 1) 29 Sept 1979 - 3 June 1980 (22 eps)

(Season 2) 11 Nov 1980 - 26 May 1981 (20 eps)
(Season 3) 6 Oct 1981 - 18 May 1982 (24 eps)
(Season 4) 28 Sept 1982 - 10 May 1983 (22 eps)
(Season 5) 27 Sept 1983 - 22 May 1984 (22 eps)
UK: ITV 3 Feb 1980 - 14 April 1985 (LWT)

HAWAII FIVE-O

'He takes orders only from the Governor...or God. And sometimes even they have trouble.'

That was a Five-O colleague's irreverent assessment of Steve McGarrett, the most self-righteous law enforcer in the history of television. Unsmiling and unemotional, Jack Lord's McGarrett was the pinnacle of law and order on Hawaii. There is more chance of the island winning the 1994 World Cup than there was of getting McGarrett to break into a laugh. In comparison, he made Inspector Morse look like a court jester.

The only man on Hawaii to wear a suit, McGarrett was the head of Five-O, a group which worked out of the Iolani Palace in Honolulu as part of the Hawaiian State Police and was accountable directly to the Governor. To say he was dedicated is like calling Cannon 'chubby' – the mere mention of crime made his eyes narrow into that famous steely stare. The only time McGarrett ever showed the slightest hint of satisfaction was when he whispered to his second-in-command, Detective Danny Williams, the three little words that meant everything to him: 'Book 'em, Danno'. After a wry pause, he sometimes added, 'Murder, one'. For McGarrett, that was the perfect climax to a perfect day.

But there was one master criminal that McGarrett couldn't throw the book at – evil genius Wo Fat. Just when poor old Steve thought he'd got crime on the island well under control, Wo Fat would pop up with one of his devilish plots, designed to destroy mankind as well as McGarrett's hopes of a full night's sleep. There was precious little else to disturb McGarrett's sleep, since any private life he had was never featured, allowing him to concentrate his mind fully on cracking crime.

Hawaii Five-O ran for 12 seasons, making it the longest continuously running police show in the annals of American T V. And eventually in that final season, McGarrett nailed Wo Fat, trapping his arch enemy by disguising himself as a scientist. Wo Fat was put behind bars.

During those dozen years, there were surprisingly few cast changes. At the end of the first season, McGarrett did swap secretaries, from May to Jenny, and Detective Kono departed in 1972. But otherwise, the leads remained intact, until Kam Fong became disillusioned with playing Chin Ho and was killed off in the final episode of the 1977-8 season. At the end of the following season, James MacArthur, who played Danny Williams, tired of cricking his neck while looking up to McGarrett and also departed for pastures new. Three new members were added to the team, 'Kimo' Carew, Truck Kealoha and Lori Wilson, but falling ratings sounded the show's death knell.

It was little wonder that the cast had been content for so long with the programme being filmed entirely on location, against the idyllic Hawaiian backdrop of palm trees, sun and sea. Jack Lord even decided to live in Hawaii, where he is said to have considered himself an important local figure. To some extent that belief is justified. Throughout the 1970s, Steve McGarrett was the best-known figure on the island and the show did wonders for local tourism. McGarrett epitomized Hawaii – he even wore his hair in a wave – and, although it had its critics, there have been few better series of its type than Hawaii Five-O.

REGULAR CAST

Det. Steve McGarrett Jack Lord   *Det. Danny Williams* James MacArthur
Det. Chin Ho Kelly Kam Fong   *Det. Kono* Zulu
Governor Philip Grey Richard Denning   *Wo Fat* Khigh Dhiegh
Coroner Che Fong Harry Endo   *Doc* Al Eban
May Maggi Parker   *Jenny* Peggy Ryan   *Duke Lukela* Herman Wedemeyer
James 'Kimo' Carew William Smith   *Truck Kealoha* Moe Keale
Lori Wilson Sharon Farrell

Creator: Leonard Freeman
Music: Morton Stevens, Pete Rugolo
Producers: Bill Finnegan, Bob Sweeney, Richard Newton, Philip Leacock
Executive producer: Leonard Freeman

A Leonard Freeman Production for CBS

268 colour 60-minute episodes
US: CBS (Season 1) 26 Sept 1968 - 19 March 1969 (22 eps)

(Season 2) 24 Sept 1969 - 11 March 1970 (25 eps)
(Season 3) 16 Sept 1970 - 10 March 1971 (23 eps)
(Season 4) 14 Sept 1971 - 7 March 1972 (23 eps)
(Season 5) 12 Sept 1972 - 13 March 1973 (24 eps)
(Season 6) 11 Sept 1973 - 26 Feb 1974 (24 eps)
(Season 7) 10 Sept 1974 - 25 March 1975 (24 eps)
(Season 8) 12 Sept 1975 - 4 March 1976 (22 eps)
(Season 9) 30 Sept 1976 - 5 May 1977 (23 eps)
(Season 10) 15 Sept 1977 - 3 Aug 1978 (23 eps)
(Season 11) 28 Sept 1978 - 5 April 1979 (20 eps)
(Season 12) 4 Oct 1979 - 5 April 1980 (15 eps)
UK: ITV 19 July 1970 - 29 Aug 1982 (Anglia)

HAWAIIAN EYE

When 77 Sunset Strip was at its peak, Warner Bros wanted to set a similar show in the Caribbean. But producer William Orr believed Hawaii was a better proposition and so Hawaiian Eye emerged as little more than 77 Sunset Strip with louder shirts, surfing and extra palm trees. In the finest traditions of Warner Bros circa 1960, the two shows were, to the untrained eye, almost impossible to tell apart. There were two handsome young detectives who alternated as leads, a bevy of beautiful girls and, to add to the confusion, Stu Bailey used to pop over occasionally from the mainland.

Hawaiian Eye's trendy tecs, Tom Lopaka and Tracy Stele, were based at a poolside office of the Hawaiian Village Hotel – no seedy basement rooms here, with a view of broken guttering and graffiti-desecrated walls. Their sidekicks were singer-photographer Cricket Blake, who was groomed as the show's answer to Kookie, and Kazuo Kim, a colourful straw-hat-wearing, ukelele-playing one-man taxi service. Kim was extremely useful, as all his relatives lived on the island, and were more than willing to help out the boys if they were short-handed on a case. Cricket was played by Connie Stevens, whose stint on the show led to a lucrative singing career.

A new detective, Greg McKenzie, arrived during the second season as did Quon, their contact on the Honolulu Police Force. For the final season, teen idol, Troy Donahue, joined as the hotel's social director, Philip Barton. Ironically, in a series which slipped in a surfing scene whenever the action faltered, Donahue couldn't surf and had to use a stunt double. This would have come as something of a blow to his fans – it is like discovering that Batman is afraid of the dark!

* Bob Conrad, who played Tom Lopaka, laid claim to one of the world's most unusual fans. He revealed: 'Three times a week when the

show was on, I used to get a letter from a woman in Indiana thanking me for the happiness I was bringing into her life. Along with each letter, she sent me a one-dollar bill. The money ran into hundreds of dollars. I tried to return it to her after 11 letters by sending her 11 dollars. But by return of post, I received 12 dollars!'

REGULAR CAST

Tom Lopaka Bob Conrad   *Tracy Stele* Anthony Eisley
Cricket Blake Connie Stevens   *Kazuo Kim* Poncie Ponce
Greg MacKenzie Grant Williams   *Philip Barton* Troy Donahue
Quon Mel Prestidge

Music: Mack David, Jerry Livingston
Producers: Charles Hoffman, Stanley Niss, Ed Jurist
Executive producer: William T. Orr

A Warner Bros Television Production

133 monochrome 60-minute episodes
US: ABC (Season 1) 7 Oct 1959 - 25 May 1960 (33 eps)

(Season 2) 14 Sept 1960 - 31 May 1961 (38 eps)
(Season 3) 27 Sept 1961 - 20 June 1962 (38 eps)
(Season 4) 2 Oct 1962 - 2 April 1963 (24 eps)
UK: ITV 31 Dec 1960 - 29 March 1963 (Anglia)

HAWAIIAN HEAT

Fed up with the Chicago weather and the hustle and bustle of the city, cops Andy Senkowski and Mac Riley sought a posting to Hawaii, where they worked as undercover detectives for the Honolulu Police. They were considered 'Mainland snowbirds' by their tropical contemporaries, until they proved themselves in a drugs bust. From then on, they took to their new surroundings like a duck takes to orange sauce, and moved into a beach house which they shared with a number of girls who seemed to be taking part in a non-stop swimwear parade. These included a highly desirable helicopter pilot by the name of Irene Gorley, who kept a pet parrot, Pakalolo.

Andy and Mac were unlikely buddies. Andy was rather reserved while Mac had a brash, impulsive nature that made John McEnroe look like a shrinking violet. At headquarters they reported to Harker, a local cop in his forties, and assistant to Major Oshira, head of the Detective Division. Harker was wary of the newcomers but Oshira liked them, since they always got their man. However, Andy and Mac were unable to win over the viewers as easily and Hawaiian Heat was frozen out after 11 episodes.

Regular Cast

Andy Senkowski Jeff McCracken   *Mac Riley* Robert Ginty
Irene Gorley Tracy Scoggins   *Major Taro* Oshira Mako
Harker Branscombe Richmond

Producers: Dan Nichols, Dean Zanetos
Executive producer: James D. Parriott

An MCA Television Production

One colour 120-minute episode and 10
colour 60-minute episodes US: ABC
14 Sept - 7 Dec 1984

HAWK

Here's a novelty – a Red Indian detective. A young Burt Reynolds, who
is himself part-Indian, played John Hawk, an Iroquois Indian who
worked nights for the New York District Attorney's office with his
partner Detective Dan Carter. Hawk was very much at home on the
dimly-lit streets and honed his traditional Indian tracking skills to hunt
down the city's nocturnal criminals. The series was actually filmed on
location in and around New York at night. It was first screened by ABC
in 1966 but NBC repeated it ten years later to cash in on Reynolds'
upsurge in popularity, just as CBS had done with his other cop show,
Dan August, also originally shown on ABC .

Regular Cast

Lt John Hawk Burt Reynolds   *Det. Dan Carter* Wayne Grice
Asst D.A. Murray Slaken Bruce Glover   *Asst D.A. Ed Gorton* Leon Janney

---

Creator: Allan Sloane
Producer: Paul Bogart
Executive producer: Hubbell Robinson

*A Columbia Pictures Television
    Production*

17 colour 60-minute episodes
US: ABC 8 Sept - 29 Dec 1966
UK: ITV From 18 Jan 1973 (Granada)

HAWKINS

Slow-talking James Stewart entered the detective field as amiable Billy
Jim Hawkins, who quit his job as a Deputy District Attorney to go into

private legal practice in rural West Virginia. He specialized in murder cases and his reputation drew clients from all over America, who were only too aware that his vague shambling exterior camouflaged a steely determination. He was helped by his cousin, investigator R.J. Hawkins, and the pair were prepared to travel miles to obtain evidence necessary to clear Billy Jim's client and nail the guilty party. Surprisingly, Hawkins failed to capture the American public's imagination and was soon cancelled.

REGULAR CAST

Billy Jim Hawkins James Stewart   *R.J. Hawkins* Strother Martin

Producer: Jud Taylor
Executive producer: Norman Felton

An MGM Television Production

7 colour 90-minute episodes
US: CBS 2 Oct 1973 - 3 Sept 1974

HAZELL

'He's a bit like Marlowe, certainly more cheerful than Frank Marker. I would describe him as a Jack the Lad.'   – TERRY VENABLES, 1978

Former England footballer and manager of Tottenham Hotspur, Terry Venables, was the co-creator of the adventures of cocky Cockney private eye James Hazell, 33, divorced and invalided out of the police force with a dodgy ankle. Hazell's pride had been injured, too, on being booted out of the police. He turned to the bottle for comfort and that was when his marriage fell apart.

He pulled himself round by setting up as a private detective in one of the meaner areas of London, helped by his cousin Tel. Hazell enjoyed the glamour of being a private detective – it helped to pull the birds. What he didn't enjoy were the regular beatings he was subjected to in the course of his inquiries. He fancied himself as one of the big boys and owned a .44 Magnum. But it scared him to death.

Hazell also had trouble with the police, in the shape of dour Scottish CID man, 'Choc' Minty, who didn't like Hazell's flash wide-boy attitude. Consequently he held a grudge against our hero and was always threatening to withdraw his investigator's licence.

Although it was a little too violent for some tastes, Hazell was a first-class series, perfectly capturing the London low-life with witty cockney repartee. In the end though, what 'Choc' Minty couldn't achieve, the

BBC did – they dealt a massive blow to Hazell by scheduling a season of Robert Redford films in opposition. It was enough to make him go back on the bottle...

* Terry Venables and Gordon Williams wrote the Hazell books under the joint pseudonym of P.B.Yuill

REGULAR CAST

James Hazell Nicholas Ball   *'Choc' Minty* Roddy McMillan
Cousin Tel Desmond McNamara

EPISODE TITLES

Hazell Plays Solomon
Hazell Pays a Debt
Hazell and the Walking Blur
Hazell Settles the Accounts
Hazell Meets the First Eleven
Hazell and the Rubber-heel Brigade
Hazell Goes to the Dogs
Hazell and the Weekend Man
Hazell Works for Nothing
Hazell and the Maltese Vulture
Hazell and the Baker Street Sleuth
Hazell and the Deptford Virgin
Hazell Bangs the Drum
Hazell Gets the Boot
Hazell Gets the Bird
Hazell and the Big Sleep

Hazell and the Suffolk Ghost
Hazell and Hyde
Hazell and the Happy Couple
Hazell Gets the Part
Hazell and the Greasy Gunners
Hazell and the Public Enemy

Producer: June Roberts (Season 1) Tim Aspinall (Season 2)

A Thames Television Network Production

22 colour 60-minute episodes
UK: ITV (Season 1) 16 Jan - 20 March 1978 (10 eps)
(Season 2) 19 April 1979 - 30 Jan 1980 (12 eps)

HEART OF THE CITY

Wes Kennedy had more on his plate than most cops. In addition to his day-to-day work on the streets of Los Angeles with partner Rik Arno, he had to raise, single-handed, his two teenagers, Robin and Kevin. Needless to say, they presented him with more problems than all of the city's crooks put together. A gallant attempt to breathe new life into the police show format, but it soon folded.

REGULAR CAST

Wes Kennedy Robert Desiderio   *Rik Arno* Kario Salem
Robin Kennedy Christina Applegate   *Kevin Kennedy* Jonathan Ward

Creators: Michael Zinberg, E. Arthur
 Kean
Producer: David M. Balkan
Executive producer: Michael Zinberg

*A Michael Zinberg and American Flyer
 Television Ltd Production in
 association with 20th Century Fox*

One colour 90-minute episode and 13
 colour 60-minute episodes US: ABC
 27 Sept 1986 - 2 July 1987
UK: ITV 16 Jan - 9 May 1989 (LWT)

HEC RAMSEY

Hec Ramsey was a pioneering detective, a rugged Western hero at the turn of the century, who had become fascinated by the new-fangled science of criminology. The series opened with him arriving in New Prospect, Oklahoma, to begin work as deputy to young Sheriff Oliver B. Stamp. Soon old Hec was teaching his boss everything he knew about fingerprinting techniques, magnifying glasses and all the other detective equipment. Since not everyone was as enlightened, Hec still carried a gun to be on the safe side but preferred to solve crimes by more peaceful means. Originating from a pilot entitled The Century Turns, Hec Ramsey aired as part of the NBC Sunday Mystery Movie in the US.

REGULAR CAST

Hec Ramsey Richard Boone   *Sheriff Oliver B. Stamp* Richard Lenz

Music: Fred Steiner, Lee Holdridge
Producers: William Finnegan, Douglas
 Benton, Harold Jack Bloom
Executive producer: Jack Webb

A Universal Television Production

7 colour 120-minute and 3 colour 90-
 minute episodes
US: NBC 8 Oct 1972 - 25 Aug 1974
UK: ITV 10 March 1973 - 19 May 1974

THE HIDDEN TRUTH

An ITV forerunner to The Expert, The Hidden Truth revealed a team of pathologists at work on investigations into such crimes as arson and insurance fraud. The Chief pathologist was Professor Robert Lazard and he was assisted by Dr Henry Fox, Dr Ruth Coliton and Ceylonese Dr Hamavid de Silva. Professor Lazard's rule was, 'Stay clear of involvement' which meant that they were not permitted to discuss amongst themselves any of the cases they were handling.

REGULAR CAST

Professor Lazard Alexander Knox   *Dr Henry Fox* James Maxwell
Dr Ruth Coliton Elizabeth Weaver   *Dr Hamavid de Silva* Zia Mohyeddin

Creators: John Whitney, Geoffrey Bellman
Producer: Stella Richman

A Rediffusion Network Production

4 monochrome 60-minute episodes
UK: ITV 24 Sept - 13 Oct 1964

HIGHWAY PATROL

'Whenever the laws of any state are broken, a duly authorized organization swings into action. It may be called the State Police, State Troopers, militia, the Rangers or the Highway Patrol. These are the stories of the men whose training, skill and courage have enforced and preserved our state laws.'   – PROGRAMME ANNOUNCER

Highway Patrol was the most successful syndicated series of the 1950s. Viewers across the world became familiar with the rotund figure of Broderick Crawford, as fast-talking Chief Dan Mathews, leaning on the side of his patrol car, microphone in hand and uttering the immortal words, 'Ten-four'.

As with all Ziv productions, the keyword was cheap. Even the show's theme music was lifted from Ziv's huge library of royalty-free tunes. Indeed it had earlier been used to introduce the radio version of Mr District Attorney! But after starting out as a minor filler, Highway Patrol became Fred Ziv's biggest-ever money-spinner and had the distinction of becoming the first American show to be screened on West Germany's commercial TV channel.

All the action revolved around Crawford – and there was quite a lot of him to revolve around. Whatever his appeal, it certainly wasn't his handsome looks, as he possessed one of the few faces that could actually be improved by the addition of a stocking mask. There were no other regular characters, although William Boyett did pop up from time to time as his assistant, Sergeant Williams.

Crawford was in his element as the tough cop. He said at the time: 'I'd acted the gangster in so many movies that when I first came to play in Patrol, I was faced with the problem of how to win over an audience instead of making them hate me. I like Mathews. His cold hard exterior doesn't fool me one bit. I know that he's more concerned than he'll ever show over the safety and welfare of his men. In other words, he's a "good guy".'

Highway Patrol adopted something of a campaigning air, with Crawford using the programme to hit out at bad drivers. 'Leave your blood at the Red Cross, not on the highway,' he warned. Ironically at around this time, Crawford himself was twice booked by highway patrols for dangerous driving...

REGULAR CAST

Chief Dan Mathews Broderick Crawford

Music: Richard Llewellyn
Asst producer: Joe Wonder
Executive producer: Vernon E. Clark

A Ziv Production

156 monochrome 30-minute episodes
US: Syndicated Sept 1955 - 1959
UK: ITV 20 Nov 1960 - 14 Sept 1962
(Anglia)
(In the London ITV region, Highway Patrol started airing as early as the first part of 1956.)

HILL STREET BLUES

'One of the biggest professional thrills of my life was the night the cast gathered to watch the pilot. There was no music, no titles, just this wonderful work on the screen. Everyone was saying, "It's good, isn't it? We're good, aren't we?" Then we said, "Hey, but this is television, they won't want anything this good!"'

– DANIEL J. TRAVANTI

But they did. Hill Street Blues went on to be showered with accolades over the next seven seasons, and justifiably came to be regarded as the finest police series television has ever produced. Quite simply, it was a masterpiece. The acting and production were superlative. It was also revolutionary with its huge cast of regulars, the multiple soap-opera-style storylines and the camera technique that followed the characters around so that the viewer felt part of the action. We could almost taste the atmosphere in the station house, smell Belker and touch Buntz's sweat.

Hill Street Blues was the brainchild of Steven Bochco and Michael Kozoll. Looking back on its origins, Kozoll says: 'NBC chief Fred Silverman wanted to make a cop show and Steven Bochco and I were invited to do a pilot. I didn't particularly want to do it. But because I was given autonomy to do what I wanted to do and because I didn't care about the show getting on the air, I wrote something that I had some feeling for – and that's how Hill Street Blues came into being.' The pilot was called Hill Street Station, but NBC rejected that and came up with The Blue Zoo, which Bochco and Kozoll hated. Eventually the title Hill Street Blues was thought up...by an employee in NBC's Business Affairs department!

In terms of ratings, the new show couldn't have made a less auspicious start. At the end of the first US season, it ranked 87th out of 96 peak-time shows. It was the lowest-rated programme NBC had ever renewed. But the critics loved it and by the close of the second season it had turned into a hit. For that second season, NBC laid down a single stipulation to programme-makers MTM, that at least one story-line must be concluded in each episode.

Hill Street was a run-down inner-city area of a large unnamed metropolis (the station house seen in exterior shots was Maxwell Street Precinct, Chicago). The station house was a constant hive of activity as it played host to the city's low-life, some of whom were wearing police uniforms. For this was no whitewashed portrayal of law enforcers – they were on display warts and all. There was alcoholic vice cop, J.D. LaRue, who had more vices than most of the hoods he was chasing; wild-man undercover detective, Mick Belker, who needed very little disguise to become a thoroughly convincing tramp and who was prone to barking at dogs and biting suspects; prissy Howard Hunter, the trigger-happy leader of the precinct's SWAT team; and latterly, abrasive Norm Buntz whose manners were as appalling as his dress sense. Yet although these were all policemen we wouldn't dream of asking the time from, deep down we couldn't help but like them because, for all their faults, they were dedicated to doing a good job. It was just that their methods couldn't always be found in the rule book.

In the midst of the general mayhem, standing like a nobleman above the peasants, was Captain Frank Furillo, magnificently played by Daniel J. Travanti. Steven Bochco describes the character thus: 'Furillo was a pragmatist. Furillo was very rooted in the real world – he understood that he was not going to solve crime. By and large that wasn't what he was there for. He negotiated truces; he kept the peace to some extent. He negotiated survival on the hill.' Travanti himself has great respect for Furillo. He says: 'Here was a fellow who could control events and people without trying to muscle them and, because he always played by the rules, he had the respect of everybody. He's the way I'd like to be.'

Furillo encountered more problems per day than most of us do in a year. For a start he was constantly badgered for more alimony by his highly-strung ex-wife Fay. Then there was his relationship with strong-willed public defender Joyce Davenport. Their work frequently placed them in direct opposition as she tried to free on a technicality, some blatantly guilty scumbag that Furillo's officers had risked life and limb to apprehend. Yet they became lovers, secretly at first, then they went public and eventually got married one lunch-hour. They continued to have their altercations at work, where they treated each other as professionals rather than husband and wife. Joyce, played by Veronica Hamel, was a stunning woman. Clive James wrote of her: 'She has Clarence Darrow's sense of justice, the figure of Cyd Charisse and the face of an angel.' Frank liked her too, and the episodes invariably ended with Joyce and her 'pizza man', as she called him, in bed. Heaven knows where they got the energy from...

Furillo also had to cope with politics in the unpalatable form of Chief Fletcher P. Daniels, who worried about nothing more than his own smarmy image, particularly when he decided to stand for mayor. To the relief of everybody on the hill, he lost. To keep something resembling peace on the streets, Furillo held war councils with local gang leaders. The most notorious of these, the cocky Hispanic Jesus Martinez, actually became an ally of Furillo, who he referred to as 'Frankie'. He even took up practising law. Furillo was always a tower of strength to his officers, readily offering a shoulder to cry on. When LaRue's alcohol problems were worsening, Furillo persuaded him to attend a meeting of Alcoholics Anonymous. When LaRue arrived, he found Furillo there too (a neat touch, since in real life Travanti confesses to once being an alcoholic).

Just as the episodes finished with Furillo and Joyce in bed, so each show opened with a roll call, always at some unearthly hour like 5.37 am. For the first four seasons this was conducted by kindly father-figure Sergeant Phil Esterhaus (played by Michael Conrad) who closed each briefing with the much-imitated plea to his men: 'And hey – let's be careful out there.' When Michael Conrad died in 1984, Esterhaus was killed off too. He had been having an affair with Grace Gardner, the widow of a fellow officer , and it transpired that he expired from a heart attack half-way through a particularly frenetic bout of love-making. Everyone said it was the way Phil wanted to go.

His successor was Sergeant Stan Jablonski who coined the less memorable phrase, 'Let's do it to them before they do it to us.' Phil Esterhaus was a tough act to follow.

There were a multitude of other memorable characters. Affable black cop, Bobby Hill, and his country-boy partner, Andy Renko, were shot dead in the pilot but came back to life as a first-rate double act; Henry Goldblume, the intense community affairs officer who had a brief affair of his own with Fay Furillo; cool toothpick-chewing Detective Neal Washington, J.D.'s long-suffering partner; Lieutenant Ray Calletano, Furillo's second-in-command, and so proud of his Hispanic background that he ultimately pressed the self-destruct button by becoming too militant; and Fay Furillo herself, who wound up as a victims' rights representative – an appropriate post since she considered herself to be a perennial victim.

Hill Street Blues combined comedy, pathos and drama – tough-guy Belker being given a hard time by his mum for not ringing her regularly;

Lucy Bates' emotional heartache when she wanted to become guardian to a child offender; Assistant D.A. Irwin Bernstein's sudden declaration of love for Joyce; and Norm Buntz's terrifying ordeal at the hands of an armed madman. Held captive, Buntz psyched out the psycho by pretending to be unruffled and, although tied to a chair, he succeeded in shoving his captor through an upper-floor window. After this Buntz returned to the station house, threw up, popped a fresh piece of chewing-gum in his mouth and carried on with life as if nothing had happened. It was a remarkable episode in a remarkable series.

Steven Bochco left in 1985, apparently fired by MTM for going over budget. While he went on to help create L.A. Law and Hooperman, Hill Street continued until Travanti refused to do an eighth season. Travanti reflects: 'I thought we had slipped in terms of quality.' Fittingly, Hill Street Blues ended on a high, with Buntz decking Chief Daniels (SEE BEVERLY HILLS BUNTZ).

The series remains hugely popular in Britain, for although Channel 4 has finished screening it, episodes are currently being shown on British Sky Broadcasting. So what was the secret of its success? Bruce Weitz, who played Belker, offers his opinion : 'We portrayed law-enforcement people as they really are – they're not superheroes and they're not buffoons. TV and movies always show them as one or the other. We played them as ordinary people who had problems, who screwed up, who weren't perfect but who were out there trying to do a really difficult job.'

REGULAR CAST

Capt. Frank Furillo Daniel J. Travanti   Sgt Phil Esterhaus Michael Conrad
Joyce Davenport Veronica Hamel   Officer Bobby Hill Michael Warren
Officer Andy Renko Charles Haid   Det. Mick Belker Bruce Weitz
Lt Ray Calletano Rene Enriquez   Det. Johnny (J.D.) LaRue Kiel Martin
Det. Neal Washington Taurean Blacque   Lt Howard Hunter James B. Sikking
Sgt/Lt Henry Goldblume Joe Spano   Officer/Sgt Lucy Bates Betty Thomas
Grace Gardner Barbara Babcock   Fay Furillo Barbara Bosson
Det./Lt Alf Chesley Gerry Black   Officer Leo Schitz Robert Hirschfield
Officer Joe Coffey Ed Marinaro   Chief Fletcher P. Daniels Jon Cypher
Officer Robin Tataglia Lisa Sutton   Asst. D.A. Irwin Bernstein George Wyner
Sgt Stanislaus Jablonski Robert Prosky   Sgt Norman Buntz Dennis Franz
Det. Garibaldi Ken Olin   Det. Patricia Mayo Mimi Kuzyk
Jesus Martinez Trinidad Silva

Creators: Steven Bochco, Michael Kozoll
Music: Mike Post
Executive producers: Steven Bochco, Gregory Hoblit

145 colour 60-minute episodes
US: NBC 15 Jan 1981 - 19 May 1987
UK: ITV 22 Jan 1981 - 25 Oct 1984
Channel Four 3 Nov 1984 - 4 April 1989

An MTM Production

HOLLYWOOD BEAT

An action comedy about two Hollywood undercover cops, McCarren and Rado, with a penchant for dressing-up. Their impressive array of disguises plus an intricate network of street informants meant they were able to infiltrate successfully the Hollywood underworld. They had the best arrest rate on the force. One week the macho heroes would be disguised as old men, the next they'd be in drag. Sadly the series was a drag too – the L.A. Times went as far as to call it 'repulsive'.

REGULAR CAST

Det. Nick McCarren Jack Scalia   *Det. Jack Rado* Jay Acovone

Creator/Producer: Henry Rosenbaum
Executive producer: Aaron Spelling

An Aaron Spelling Production for Warner Bros Television

7 colour 60-minute episodes US: ABC 21 Sept - 2 Nov 1985

HOLLYWOOD OFF BEAT (US TITLE STEVE RANDALL)

A Fifties filmed series focussing on the activities of Steve Randall, a smooth disbarred lawyer, who had taken up private detective work in the hope that he might once again be permitted to practice law. After 13 weeks of toiling away manfully solving baffling cases of blackmail and murder, Randall was finally reinstated as a lawyer. But his joy was tempered by the fact that this change of environment also meant the end of his show. For nobody wanted another courtroom drama.

REGULAR CAST

Steve Randall Melvyn Douglas

Producers: Marlon Parsonett, Lester Lewis

13 monochrome 30-minute episodes US: DuMont 7 Nov 1952 - 30 Jan 1953

HOLMES AND YOYO

Richard B. Shull and John Schuck (dim Sergeant Enright from McMillan and Wife) were optimistically billed as the new Laurel and Hardy, but their show lasted just three months. Shull played Alexander Holmes, an accident-prone detective with an unfortunate knack of landing his partners in hospital. The only solution seemed to be to provide him with an indestructible partner, so the force came up with a lifelike robot named Yoyo. He had a photographic memory, his own power source and could produce colour prints almost as fast as a Polaroid. He also proved irresistible to Officer Maxine Moon, who was unaware that he was anything other than human. Such excitement was always likely to cause him to blow a fuse. Worse still was when a bullet short-circuited his rhythm system, making him tap dance out of control, half-way through a chase.

REGULAR CAST

Det. Alexander Holmes Richard B. Shull   *Gregory 'Yoyo' Yoyonovich* John Schuck
Officer Maxine Moon Andrea Howard   *Capt. Harry Sedford* Bruce Kirby

Creators: Jack Sher, Lee Hewitt
Producer: Arne Sultan
Executive producer: Leonard B. Stern

A Universal Television Production
13 colour 30-minute episodes
US: ABC 25 Sept - 11 Dec 1976
UK: BBC1 29 Oct 1976 - 9 Feb 1977

HOMICIDE

Long before we discovered that Bouncer the labrador was the most accomplished actor ever to come out of Australia, Homicide was the country's first big seller abroad. Indeed prior to Neighbours and Home and Away, it was the most successful drama series ever produced Down Under, running for 13 years and 509 episodes. And the stars became Australia's first TV-created celebrities.

It was inspired by the glossy American crime dramas which had been so popular on Australian television since the mid 1950s. But its birth was not without difficulties. One of the show's writers, Terry Stapleton, recalls: 'The Channel 7 network had been very nervous about buying Homicide, because they feared viewers would find it too much of a culture shock to hear serious-faced detectives in hats and raincoats speaking like they did, not like Americans. It took Crawfords 18 months to sell the first series.'

But once Homicide was accepted, it brought a new air of realism to Australian TV, particularly with the later episodes which were shot entirely on film. It was set in Melbourne among the Homicide Squad of the Victoria Police. The real Victoria force acted as consultants and even sponsored the programme for the first year. In all, 78 episodes were syndicated to the US.

* Devotees of old British television will remember Charles Tingwell, who played Inspector Lawson, as surgeon Alan Dawson from Emergency – Ward 10.

REGULAR CAST

Insp. Connolly Jack Fegan *Det. Sgt Mackay* Leonard Teale
Det. Peter Barnes George Mallaby *Det. Sgt Bronson* Terry McDermott
Insp. Lawson Charles Tingwell *Det. Harry White* Don Barker

Producers: Igor Auzins, Don Battye, Ian Crawford
Executive producers: Dorothy Crawford, Hector Crawford, Henry Crawford, Ian Crawford

A Crawfords (Australia) Production

376 monochrome episodes and 133 colour 60-minute episodes
Australia: Channel 7 20 Oct 1964 - 1977
US: Syndicated 1967

HONEY WEST

Honey West had a most definite claim to fame – she was television's only ocelot-keeping detective. She started life in a collection of quirky mystery novels, by a husband and wife writing team using the pseudonym G.G. Fickling, and was introduced to viewers in an episode of Burke's Law, in which she even managed to outfox the venerable Amos.

Honey became a private detective after inheriting the family agency and her partner, Sam Bolt, from her late father. She was a real femme fatale, an expert in the martial arts, with a veritable army of gadgets including a special lipstick that contained a radio transmitter. To add to her unorthodox approach, Honey's office was a specially-equipped van marked 'H.W. Bolt and Co, TV Service'.

Female detectives were a rarity in the Sixties which made Honey quite a catch. Sam Bolt certainly had designs on her, but to his chagrin, the only male she was interested in was Bruce, her pet ocelot.

REGULAR CAST

Honey West Anne Francis   *Sam Bolt* John Ericson

Music: Joseph Mullendore

A Four Star Production

30 monochrome 30-minute episodes
US: ABC 17 Sept 1965 - 2 Sept 1966

HONG KONG PHOOEY

Hong Kong Phooey was 'America's secret weapon against crime'. In the traditions of Batman and Superman, this cartoon series followed the adventures of a timid janitor, Henry, who led a double life as disaster-prone super-detective Hong Kong Phooey. Scatman Crothers provided the voice for Henry/Phooey.

A Hanna-Barbera Production

16 colour 25-minute episodes
US: ABC 7 Sept 1974 - 4 Sept 1976

HOOPERMAN

San Francisco Police Inspector Harry Hooperman was in as much danger at home as he was at work. On the job, he dodged bullets and the eagle eye of Captain C.Z.Stern, his decidedly superior officer, who seldom appreciated his unusual policing methods, while at home the run-down apartment building he inherited was filled with angry tenants demanding repairs he couldn't afford to make. And Bijoux, the dog he inherited along with the building, made life even more uncomfortable by biting anything that moved, including Hooperman.

Created by Steven Bochco and Terry Louise Fisher, the team behind L.A. Law (Bochco, of course, also co-created Hill Street Blues), Hooperman was a classy comedy that deserved much wider acclaim. John Ritter, son of the late country and western star Tex Ritter, played the nicest cop to be seen on TV in years. Anyone who had to put up with a manic boss like Stern (another job for Bochco's wife, Barbara Bosson) deserved the greatest sympathy. Where Hooperman went wrong was falling for one of his tenants, beautiful plumber Susan Smith, who lived in a downstairs apartment. They endured a true love/hate relationship which seemed doomed to failure. They were never able to spend any time together courting. Because everyone knows you can never get a plumber to come out at weekends.

REGULAR CAST

Insp. Harry Hooperman John Ritter *Captain C.Z. Stern* Barbara Bosson
Susan Smith Debrah Farentino *Mo Demott* Sydney Walsh
Rick Silardi Joseph Gian *Bobo Pritzger* Clarence Felder
Clarence McNeil Felton Perry

Creators: Steven Bochco, Terry Louise Fisher
Music: Mike Post
Executive producers: Robert Myman, Leon Tokatyan, Rick Kellard

An Adam Production in association with Twentieth Century Fox Television

42 colour 30-minute episodes
US: ABC 23 Sept 1987 - 6 Sept 1989
UK: ITV 17 April - 30 Dec 1988 then at various times throughout the network

THE HOUND OF THE BASKERVILLES

A worthy four-part adaptation of Conan Doyle's piece de resistance with one-time Dr Who, Tom Baker, as Holmes. There were certainly plenty of policemen about. Terence Rigby (former dog handler Henry Snow from Softly, Softly) was Watson while evil entymologist Stapleton, was played by Christopher Ravenscroft, now best known as Reg Wexford's sidekick, Burden, in the Ruth Rendell Mysteries. (SEE ALSO THE ADVENTURES OF SHERLOCK HOLMES, THE CASES OF SHERLOCK HOLMES, SHERLOCK HOLMES, YOUNG SHERLOCK)

MAIN CAST

Sherlock Holmes Tom Baker *Dr Watson* Terence Rigby
Sir Henry Baskerville Nicolas Wodeson *Stapleton* Christopher Ravenscroft

Dramatized by Alexander Baron
Director: Peter Duguid
Producer: Barry Letts

4 colour 30-minute episodes

UK: BBC1 3 - 24 Oct 1982

HUNTER

Detective Sergeant Rick Hunter is a man with a mission – to gun down as many crooks as possible in one hour (leaving time for commercial breaks and credits). To all intents and purposes, Hunter is the TV version of Dirty Harry. Like Clint Eastwood's 'shoot first, ask questions later' hero, former American football star Fred Dryer's Detective Sergeant Rick Hunter likes nothing better than producing his hefty Magnum revolver which he has affectionately christened 'Simon'. So when he tries to arrest a low-life who resists, demanding, 'Who says?', Hunter draws his gun and replies, 'Simon says'. A pretty convincing argument.

The similarities between Harry and Hunter don't end there. Harry Callahan's famous catchphrase was 'Make my day'. Hunter has his own – 'Works for me'. And both men have had to contend with incompetent interfering superiors intent on relieving them of their badge. Nothing bugs Hunter more than a desk-bound boss who is more concerned with paper-work than cleaning up the streets.

Hunter is a plainclothes detective in Los Angeles. His world is made up of pimps and psychopaths. He knows that these people do not respond to polite requests to accompany him to the station, so he adopts more aggressive tactics. And that is where he comes into conflict with his seniors.

Against all the odds, Hunter finds an ally in his constant battle to buck the system in the shape of tough policewoman Dee Dee McCall. Like Dirty Harry, Hunter didn't think much of female cops – until he met Dee Dee. For she is no ordinary policewoman, she is as unorthodox as Hunter. Together they make a formidable duo with a nice line in repartee. If they don't kill you with bullets, they'll wound you with sarcasm.

Despite the recent departure of Stepfanie Kramer as Dee Dee, Hunter has continued to go from strength to strength in the US and is about to begin its eighth season with well over 100 episodes to its name. It hasn't travelled well to Britain however, and after a brief spell on the ITV network, it was shown irregularly in local regions before transferring to British Sky Broadcasting.

REGULAR CAST

Det. Sgt Rick Hunter Fred Dryer   *Det. Sgt Dee Dee McCall* Stepfanie Kramer
Capt. Lester Cain Arthur Rosenberg   *Capt. Dolan* John Amos
Det. Bernie Terwilliger James Whitmore Jnr

Producer: Chuck Bowman
Executive producers: Stephen J.
  Cannell, Frank Lupo, Roy Huggins

*A Stephen J. Cannell Production for
  Lorimar*

60-minute colour episodes
US: NBC From 18 Sept 1984
UK: ITV 27 April - 13 July 1985

HUNTER'S WALK

A plodding police series from Ted Willis which bore many of the hallmarks of his most memorable creation, Dixon of Dock Green, but featured a set of characters who each appeared to have undergone a successful charisma by-pass operation. Set in the fictional town of Broadstone (filming was done at Rushden, Northants), Hunter's Walk depicted the routine work of the local force. Action was strictly limited – even car chases were conducted with the hand-brake on.

The principals were Detective Sergeant 'Smithy' Smith, an unsmiling CID man; Sergeant Ken Ridgeway, the station officer; Detective Constable 'Mickey' Finn, Smith's young protege; and eager Constables Fred Pooley and Harry Coombes. Also featured was Ruth Madoc (later to star in the British holiday camp comedy Hi de Hi) as Smith's wife, Betty. Hunter's Walk certainly couldn't be accused of over-glamorizing the police but neither could it be accused of being particularly exciting viewing.

REGULAR CAST

Det. Sgt Smith Ewan Hooper   *Sgt Ken Ridgeway* Davyd Harries
Det. Con. 'Mickey' Finn David Simeon   *PC Fred Pooley* Duncan Preston
PC Harry Coombes Charles Rea   *Betty Smith* Ruth Madoc

Creator: Ted Willis
Music: Derek Scott
Producer: John Cooper

An ATV Network Production 39 colour
  60-minute episodes

UK: ITV (Season 1) 4 June - 3 Sept 1973
(Season 2) 22 April - 22 July 1974
(Season 3) 1 June - 24 Aug 1976

I HAD THREE WIVES

Remington Steele meets Charlie's Angels. A ludicrous format about a supposedly suave private eye, who solved cases with the help of his trio of glamorous ex-wives. Jackson Beaudine was a romantic sleuth who, for some reason, felt obliged to involve all the women in his life with his work. They were Mary Beaudine Parker, a subsequently-remarried lawyer and mother of their ten-year-old son, Andrew; Samantha Collins Beaudine, an actress who also happened to be an expert in martial arts, motor racing and scuba diving; and Elizabeth Bailey Beaudine, an investigative reporter intent on winning a Pulitzer Prize, becoming editor of a big city newspaper, or both. Jackson just couldn't get along without them. But after six weeks, America got along just fine without I Had Three Wives.

REGULAR CAST

Jackson Beaudine Victor Garber   *Mary Beaudine Parker* Maggie Cooper
Samantha Collins Beaudine Teri Copley   *Elizabeth Bailey Beaudine* Shanna Reed
Andrew David Faustino

Creator/Executive producer: Donald A. Baer

A Brownstone Production for Warner Bros Television

6 colour 60-minute episodes
US: CBS 26 June - 6 Sept 1985

I'M THE LAW

Big screen tough guy, George Raft, who nearly always played a gangster, swapped sides to star as hard-bitten New York cop, Lieutenant George Kirby, in this powerful syndicated series. As would be expected from Raft, there was no pussy-footing around – Kirby was handy with his fists and his gun as he hunted dangerous criminals throughout the city. Raft also narrated the series, which was made by comedian Lou Costello's production company, Raft having been friends with Lou's brother, Pat, since they appeared together in vaudeville.

REGULAR CAST

Lt George Kirby George Raft

Executive producer: Pat Costello

A Cosman Production

26 monochrome 30-minute episodes
US: Syndicated 1953
UK: BBC 10 July 1954 - 18 July 1955

INCH HIGH, PRIVATE EYE

The cartoon adventures of the world's smallest detective. Helped and hindered by his niece, Laurie, master of disguise, Gator, and Braveheart, his cowardly dog, Inch tackled cases for the Finkerton Organization in his car, The Hugemobile. Short on stature, short on entertainment.

A Hanna-Barbera Production   13 colour 30-minute episodes

US: NBC 8 Sept 1973 - 31 Aug 1974

INSPECTOR GADGET

A popular American cartoon series about a bumbling semi-robot detective engaged in a constant battle with the evil Dr Claw, and the organization M.A.D. (Mean and Dirty). As his name implies, Inspector Gadget is a mass of technology including special springy legs and extending arms, bringing a new meaning to 'the long arm of the law'. He was assisted in his fight against crime by his niece, Penny, and the dopey little family dog, Brain. The original voice of the noble Inspector was Don Adams of Get Smart fame, but he left before the series finished and was replaced by an imitator.

A DIC Production   65 colour 30-minute episodes
UK: ITV From 25 Aug 1984

INSPECTOR MORSE

'When I was in America I was told that viewers like Morse because it is not all car chases and violence. They see it as an antidote. They like the tranquillity and the very English manner of Morse.' – JOHN THAW

Inspector Morse is a colossal hit in over 50 countries, giving it a world-wide audience of 75 million people. It has caught on fast in America, the Australians adore it, and now the Russians are coming to appreciate its quality. Morse mania has also reached such diverse lands as Bulgaria, Angola, Germany, Saudi Arabia and Zambia. In Britain, people hold Morse parties to guess the murderer, workers on North Sea oil rigs demand to have Morse on video and the US Department of Defense has purchased the series to show on closed circuit television to servicemen. Morse is the highest-rated detective series on British television for almost a decade, pulling an audience of over 16 million. Even knowing 'whodunnit' doesn't deter loyal Morse devotees, as repeats attract 12 million viewers. The result of this huge success is that both the series and actor John Thaw, who plays Morse, have been besieged with awards. And they have fans in high places – Princess Margaret is a confirmed aficionado.

But what is it about a programme in which the hero is a grumpy, middle-aged policeman who doesn't carry a gun, never gets the girl, has no first name and drinks real ale, that has millions glued to their seats for two hours at a time? John Thaw is in no doubt. 'I think Morse is so popular because people don't know what makes him tick. They're fascinated by the way he approaches things. I like him because he is not a "cliche copper". The guy's brain is working all the time. He has a mind like an intellectual grasshopper. Also the fact that he is not a slick character and has his own problems is a lot to do with his appeal. And people like his non-violent approach. He hates violence and goes out of his way to avoid it. I think viewers are fed-up with car chases and shoot-outs. They enjoy Morse because he is a more cerebral character who sees each case as a battle of wits. He is the thinking man's detective.'

Morse is the creation of Colin Dexter, a former classics teacher whose increasing deafness (the inspiration for the Morse episode The Silent World of Nicholas Quinn) forced him to leave the classroom 25 years ago and start working for Oxford University, overseeing classics exams for the Oxford and Cambridge Examination Board. He dreamed up Morse on a wet weekend in Wales. 'I was on holiday and was reading some pretty average crime books that I thought I might be able to improve upon. I had always liked detective fiction in my youth so I started writing it myself.'

Dexter's first Inspector Morse book, Last Bus to Woodstock, was published in 1975. He deliberately set out to make Morse an unashamedly intelligent and literate character, set against his own academic Oxford background. 'I wanted somebody who was extraordinarily clever – cerebrally alpha plus,' says Dexter. 'I wanted somebody who was free, unmarried and world-weary. I think Raymond Chandler, who is one of my greatest heroes, made a huge mistake when he married Philip Marlowe off. The state of marriage is tedious and uninteresting for a detective – it's better for him to fall in love with the women he meets. It also makes it easier for female readers and viewers to fall for him.'

And they have. John Thaw receives a huge postbag from female admirers who want to get to know Morse for his mind as well as his body. Thaw understands why women find Morse so attractive. 'It's nothing to do with the way he looks – just the way he is. He likes women, he's sensitive and romantic and he doesn't hide it if he is attracted to someone, but he's also a challenge. Women see him as the eternal bachelor, they think they can change him but he's so set in his ways it's impossible. With Morse, women either go along with his lifestyle or get out.'

The names of Morse and his sidekick, Sergeant Lewis, emanate from Colin Dexter's love of crosswords. Morse is Sir Jeremy Morse, chairman of Lloyds Bank, and an eminent figure amongst crossword-solving brethren. And Lewis is Mrs B. Lewis, the pseudonym used by Dorothy Taylor who sets the crossword in the Observer newspaper. 'They were the two people I admired most in the crossword world,' says Dexter, who has himself won several national competitions and compiles crosswords for the Oxford Times. A love of cross words is just one of the traits Dexter has passed on to Morse.

Dexter has now written nine Inspector Morse books (the other episodes are penned by outside writers) and, ironically, the success of the TV series has resulted in his having to modify certain aspects of the novels. In print, Lewis is Welsh and nearing retirement, but he is played on screen by 40-year-old Englishman, Kevin Whately. Dexter concedes: 'I still think of Lewis as I originally did, but I know the public think of Kevin, so now I tend not to mention his Welshness or his age in the novels.' And the famous red 1960 Mark 2 Jaguar, originally bought for £200, has become Morse's emblem to the extent that the Lancia he drove in the books has been altered to 'Jaguar' in recent editions.

The strength of the series (which should really be called 'Chief Inspector Morse' to reflect his rank) is that the entire production by Zenith oozes class. The intricate plots (a legacy of Colin Dexter's puzzle-solving ability), the haunting theme, the outstanding acting, the tranquil setting of the university city of Oxford, the country pubs, Morse's insistence on the correct use of the English language and his regular intake of classical music, all leave us with the feeling that we are watching something very special indeed. And the two-hour episodes give us time to get a feel for the characters. But it is the relationship between Morse and Lewis which brings the screen to life. Morse, Oxford-educated, silver-haired, single and brusque, teamed with the faithful Lewis, a bit slow on the uptake, married and amiable. How we have all sympathized with the poor sergeant after Morse has turned to him with a sarcastic 'Got that Lewis?' Morse's problem is that he is unable to accept that anyone of Lewis's limited education can ever be right. Yet Morse himself is often guilty of jumping to the wrong conclusion on a murder case while Lewis, for all his apparent sloth, has been known to come up trumps. Lewis seems to have begun to realize that for all his intellect, Morse is not infallible and after initially allowing himself to be treated like a doormat, has started to stand up for himself. It is also about time Morse bought Lewis a drink instead of constantly saying, 'Your round, I think, Lewis', thereby expecting his poorly-paid underling to keep him supplied with his beloved real ale. Lewis is more privileged than Morse in one respect though – he has a first name. For in the course of their Australian escapade in the fifth season, Lewis finally revealed that his friends call him Robbie.

It was quite a coup persuading John Thaw to play Morse, since after his long-running role as hard-living Jack Regan in The Sweeney, he had been reported as saying that he would never play another policeman. 'What I actually said was that I would never play another policeman like Jack Regan. If Morse had been like Regan, chasing and fighting villains, I would not have done it. But Morse is so far away from Regan. In fact I don't think there has ever been a fictional policeman like him, so I liked the idea of being first in the field. Really though there are only two things Morse and I have in common, a love of music and a hatred of the sight of blood – I can't stand hospitals.'

One characteristic they definitely do not share is a liking for real ale. 'I haven't acquired the taste,' admits Thaw, 'so every time we have to shoot a scene in a pub where I'm supposed to be drinking, I try and make sure I'm seen just downing the last few drops of a pint. The trouble is that on film nothing looks as good as the real thing so we can't fake it.' There was an occasion when a scene called for Morse to down a pint of beer in one. Thaw bravely went through with the ordeal only to learn that something was wrong in the shot and he had to do it all over again. He dutifully repeated the dose to find that the clock was showing the wrong time. So he had to drink a third pint. At the end, he received a hearty round of applause from the film crew.

An essential ingredient of the show is the music. Morse loves opera and orchestras (he finds they give him inspiration for unravelling mysteries) yet the authentic sounds heard wafting from his record collection are all fakes, specially recorded for the programme by top session musicians, simply because the royalties on using the original recordings would be too expensive. Barrington Pheloung, who composed the wonderful theme (a musical representation of Morse code) says: 'Not only is it cheaper to record it ourselves, it's better quality. We use some of the best players in the country. Morse loves string quartets. We can knock out a Beethoven Quartet in a sitting.'

Apart from Morse and Lewis there are no running characters, although Morse's old pathologist friend, Max, appeared in the first two series before being replaced by the vivacious Dr Grayling Russell, to whom Morse took quite a shine. Morse's first superior was Chief Superintendent Bell and recently he has been harangued by the overweight Chief Superintendent Strange.

One person who has cropped up in all but one of the Morse stories, however, is Colin Dexter. His Hitchcock-like walk-ons have included a mourner at a funeral, a man reading an atlas in a launderette, a college porter, a member of the chorus of The Magic Flute and a pub customer doing the crossword! 'I have become a sort of talisman for the series,' he explains.

Dexter is understandably delighted by the success of the television adaptations of Morse – not least because they have boosted sales of his books. 'Recently somebody complained that their copy of one of my books was signed by me and not by John Thaw. You wouldn't think someone would come up and tell you that! It made my day.'

MORSE TRIVIA

* Keen-eyed viewers have noticed that Morse limps occasionally. This is because John Thaw broke his foot when he was 12 and it didn't set properly. It still drags a little now when he is tired.

* Kevin Whately was first cast as a downtrodden police sergeant in the Miss Marple story A Murder Is Announced.

* Ironically for someone playing such an honest policeman, Whately himself was once arrested for illegal busking at London's Oxford Circus Underground station.

* Whately's actress wife, Madelaine Newton, appeared in the Morse episode Masonic Mysteries. But the two never had the chance to work together as such, since her character was fatally stabbed before Lewis arrived on the scene.

REGULAR CAST

Chief Insp. Morse John Thaw   *Det. Sgt Lewis* Kevin Whately
Max Peter Woodthorpe   *Dr Grayling Russell* Amanda Hillwood
Chief Supt Bell Norman Jones   *Chief Supt Strange* James Grout

Season One

The Dead of Jericho

Anne Staveley is found dead at her home in the run-down Jericho district of Oxford. The evidence suggests suicide, but Morse is unconvinced and has very personal reasons for believing that she was murdered. Morse belonged to the same choir as Anne and had hopes of romance. Shortly before her death she had accepted a supper invitation from him, so why should she suddenly commit suicide? Several suspects emerge – a peeping tom, a neurotic music student and a ruthless business man and father of Anne's unborn child.

GUEST STARS:

Gemma Jones, Patrick Troughton, James Laurenson
Screenplay: Anthony Minghella
Director: Alistair Reid

The Silent World of Nicholas Quinn

Nicholas Quinn is deaf. He is a junior member of the Foreign Examinations Syndicate which sets exam papers all over the world. Security within the department is vital. Quinn can lip-read and 'overhears' a conversation at a party which reveals that the Syndicate is corrupt. One of its seven members is accepting huge bribes from an

Arab Sheikh who is desperate for his son to receive a degree from Oxford. Within a few days Quinn is found murdered. All his colleagues are under suspicion, as Morse and Lewis seek to make sense of the flimsy clues.

GUEST STARS:

Barbara Flynn, Roger Lloyd Pack, Michael Gough
Screenplay: Julian Mitchell
Director: Brian Parker

Service of All the Dead

The body of a church warden has been found with a knife in his back, in the vestry. This proves to be just the first in a series of gruesome killings in and around the quiet country church. As the mystery deepens, Morse has five bodies on his hands. In a desperate race against time, he tries to track down the ruthless killer. Lives, and his own credibility, are at stake.

GUEST STARS:

Michael Hordern, Angela Morant, John Normington
Screenplay: Julian Mitchell
Director: Peter Hammond

Season Two

The Wolvercote Tongue

Laura and Eddie Poindexter, two retired Americans, are enjoying a cultural visit to Britain. Laura has inherited a precious jewel, known as the Wolvercote Tongue, which she plans to donate to the Ashmolean Museum in Oxford. But within an hour of her arrival in the city, Laura is found dead in her hotel room and the Wolvercote Tongue is missing. Morse suspects foul play despite the pathologist's report that she died of a heart attack.

GUEST STARS:

Simon Callow, Kenneth Cranham, Roberta Taylor
Screenplay: Julian Mitchell
Director: Alastair Reid

Last Seen Wearing

Valerie Craven, a schoolgirl from a wealthy family, has been missing for six months. Morse is convinced she has been murdered and his investigations reveal there is more going on at the exclusive Homewood School than meets the eye. The headmaster's idyllic family life turns out to be a sham and Valerie's favourite teacher, Miss Baines, knows a good deal more than she has admitted. But before he has unravelled the mystery, Morse finds another murder on his hands.

GUEST STARS:

Peter McEnery, Frances Tomelty, Suzanne Bertish
Screenplay: Thomas Ellice
Director: Edward Bennett

The Settling of the Sun

In the tranquil cloisters of an ancient Oxford college, Morse is called in to investigate a case of bloody revenge for war-time torture. A group of overseas students arrive in the city for summer school. Morse is asked to attend a dinner to present the prize to the winner of a crossword competition, but during the meal a Japanese student is brutally murdered, apparently the victim of a ritual killing. The principal suspects all have a perfect alibi – Morse himself was dining with them when the murder took place.

GUEST STARS:

Anna Calder-Marshall, Robert Stephens, Derek Fowlds
Screenplay: Charles Wood
Director: Peter Hammond

Last Bus to Woodstock

Morse is called in to investigate when 18-year-old Sylvia Kane's body is found in a pub car park in Woodstock. Sylvia worked at an insurance office and had hitched a lift to the pub to meet her boyfriend. The mystery deepens when Morse finds a coded letter in the girl's handbag, addressed to her boss. His inquiries uncover a tangled web of hidden passion and corruption at the insurance office.

GUEST STARS:

Anthony Bate, Holly Aird, Terence
  Hardiman
Screenplay: Michael Wilcox
Director: Peter Duffell

Season Three

The Ghost in the Machine

Morse and Lewis are summoned to the
magnificent stately home of Sir Julius and
Lady Hanbury. They have been called to
investigate the strange death of Sir Julius,
which followed the theft of several valuable
Victorian paintings. Even the beautiful Lady
Hanbury cannot be ruled out of Morse's list
of suspects.

GUEST STARS:

Patricia Hodge, Michael Godley, Amanda
  Hillwood
Screenplay: Julian Mitchell
Director: Herbert Wise

The Last Enemy

Morse is back on familiar territory – behind
the closed doors of the academic world, in
the university city of Oxford. A body is
found in the canal and the only clue to its
identity points to a connection with one of
the colleges. Morse discovers that intense
rivalry for a prestigious post in the university
has led to murder. But he must find which
contender is the killer.

GUEST STARS:

Barry Foster, Tenniel Evans, Amanda
  Hillwood
Screenplay: Peter Buckman
Director: James Scott

Deceived by Flight

What could be more peaceful than an old
boys' cricket match on a summer's day? But
before the first ball has been bowled, one of
the players meets an untimely death.
Sergeant Lewis gets the chance to
demonstrate his cricketing skills when he is
planted in the team to glean inside
information.

GUEST STARS:

Norman Rodway, Sharon Maughan,
  Daniel Massey, Nicky Henson,
  Amanda Hillwood
Screenplay: Anthony Minghella
Director: Anthony Simmons

The Secret of Bay 5B

A murder in a multi-storey car park leaves
only two clues – a diary and a parking ticket.
At first it seems to be a straightforward case
of an eternal triangle, but as Morse and Lewis
pursue their investigations, the crime
becomes increasingly baffling.

GUEST STARS:

Mel Martin, Marion Bailey, Amanda
  Hillwood
Screenplay: Alma Cullen
Director: Jim Goddard

Season Four

Infernal Serpent

Morse and Lewis tackle a particularly
unsavoury case involving child abuse. Their
enquiries into the murder of an eminent
environmentalist, killed minutes before he
was due to give a controversial lecture,
unearth skeletons in the cupboard of a
seemingly respectable academic family.

GUEST STARS:

Cheryl Campbell, Geoffrey Palmer,
  Barbara Leigh-Hunt
Screenplay: Alma Cullen
Director: John Madden

The Sins of the Fathers

Real ale buff Morse is in his element when
he investigates foul play at a family-run
brewery. The old-fashioned Radford Brewery
is the subject of an unwelcome takeover bid
by a huge multi-national, when a member of

the current board dies suspiciously. The two events seem connected.

GUEST STARS:

Lionel Jeffries, Isabel Dean, Lisa Harrow
Screenplay: Jeremy Burnham
Director: Peter Hammond

Driven to Distraction

Morse's attempts to solve the apparently motiveless murder of a young woman lead him to question his driving ability and to consider selling his coveted Mark 2 Jaguar. The chief suspect appears to be a brash car salesman but Morse discovers that the real killer is just along the road.

GUEST STARS:

Patrick Malahide, David Ryall, Mary Jo Randall
Screenplay: Anthony Minghella
Director: Sandy Johnson

Masonic Mysteries

Morse finds himself top of the list of suspects when his lady friend is found murdered. Even the loyal Sergeant Lewis has to admit that all the clues point to Morse, when Beryl Newsome is stabbed at a dress rehearsal for the local amateur dramatic society's production of The Magic Flute.

GUEST STARS:

Ian McDiarmid, James Grout, Diane Fletcher
Screenplay: Julian Mitchell
Director: Danny Boyle

Season Five

Second Time Around

Ex-Deputy Commissioner Charlie Hillian returns home after spending the evening as guest of honour at a dinner attended by Morse and Chief Inspector Patrick Dawson. Hillian is killed by an intruder, who also steals a chapter from his unpublished memoirs relating to the murder of a young girl eighteen years ago. Morse and Dawson were also involved in the fruitless search for the girl's killer, and old wounds are opened when the two deaths seem curiously related.

GUEST STARS:

Kenneth Colley, Ann Bell, Pat Heywood
Screenplay: Daniel Boyle
Director: Adrian Shergold

Fat Chance

Morse is probing the suspicious death of a woman deacon when he is attracted to cleric, Emma Pickford. The victim was a member of Emma's women's group, along with Hilary Dobson who is a strong candidate to become the first female chaplain of St Saviour's College, Oxford. The group's vociferous campaign supporting Hilary's bid for the chaplaincy has aroused strong feelings among a faction of Oxford's ultra-conservative clerics. But Morse finds it hard to believe that these feelings could turn to murder. And when a local slimming club comes into the frame, the mystery deepens.

GUEST STARS:

Zoe Wanamaker, Maggie O'Neill, Maurice Denham
Screenplay: Alma Cullen
Director: Roy Battersby

Who Killed Harry Field?

Harry Field was an artist, a raconteur, a drinker – and not averse to forging the odd painting or inventing an impressive coat of arms for a gullible tourist. When Harry is killed, Morse is plunged into the arty world of the dead man's Bohemian friends. At first Morse likes the sound of Harry, but eventually he discovers that perhaps Harry wasn't the lovable rogue he was painted.

GUEST STARS:

Trevor Byfield, Freddie Jones, Geraldine James
Screenplay: Geoffrey Case
Director: Colin Gregg

Greeks Bearing Gifts

When the chef at Sergeant Lewis's favourite Greek restaurant is found dead and a baby goes missing, the Greek community in Oxford closes ranks. Morse feels more at home with the city's other Greek connection, the classical scholars, and discovers that there could be a link between the two worlds. For several people with a motive for the crime, together with the cream of Oxford's scholars, attended an event involving ancient Greek naval ships the previous summer.

GUEST STARS:

Jan Harvey, Martin Jarvis, James Hazeldine, James Faulkner
Screenplay: Peter Nichols
Director: Adrian Shergold

Promised Land

Morse and Lewis head for Australia on the trail of supergrass Kenny Stone, whose evidence helped put away a gang of armed robbers responsible for killing a policeman friend of Morse several years earlier. One of the gang has died in prison of AIDS and the death sparks a media campaign to re-open the case. Morse's bid to find Stone and confirm his original evidence, turns into a race against time when the Oxford detectives learn that someone else is after him too.

GUEST STARS:

Con O'Neill, Rhondda Findleton, John Jarratt
Screenplay: Julian Mitchell
Director: John Madden
Creator: Colin Dexter
Music: Barrington Pheloung
Producers: Kenny McBain (Seasons 1,2), Chris Burt (Season 3), David Lascelles (Seasons 4,5)
Executive producer: Ted Childs

A Zenith Production for Central Independent Television

20 colour 120-minute episodes
UK: ITV (Season 1) 6 Jan - 20 Jan 1987
(Season 2) 25 Dec 1987 - 22 March 1988
(Season 3) 4 Jan - 25 Jan 1989
(Season 4) 3 Jan - 24 Jan 1990
(Season 5) 20 Feb - 27 March 1991
US: WGBH Boston 'Mystery' (Season 1) 4 Feb - 10 March 1988
(Season 2) 15 Dec 1988 - 2 Feb 1989
(Season 3) 3 May - 7 June 1990
(Season 4) 16 May - 20 June 1991

INTERNATIONAL DETECTIVE

'Though these stories are based on real cases from the secret files of the W.J.B. Detective Agency, the names of clients and locations have been changed to protect their privacy.' –   PROGRAMME ANNOUNCER

Just about everyone's privacy was protected in International Detective. Even William J. Burns, chief of W.J.B., was never seen properly as he assigned a case to ace investigator Ken Franklin, at the start of each episode. The scene was carefully shot so that we just saw the odd limb or the top of his head. The William J. Burns International Detective Agency was based in New York (although this popular syndicated series was filmed in Britain) and, from there, Ken Franklin set off to the corners of the globe to crack the most complex cases Burns could throw at him. Franklin, was an accomplished detective who fired nothing more lethal than probing questions...but for all his brainpower, he never managed to work out why his boss didn't have a face.

REGULAR CAST

Ken Franklin Arthur Fleming

EPISODE TITLES

The Conway Case
The Stevenson Case
The Carrington Case
The Raffael Case
The Dimitrios Case
The Bristol Case
The Cumberland Case
The Buxton Case
The Winthrop Case
The Joplin Case
The Whitley Case
The Santerno Case
The Prescott Case
The Bismark Case
The Dudley Case
The Marlowe Case
The Rose Bowl Case
The Rashid Case
The Broker Case
The Orlando Case
The Steibel Case
The Sheridan Case
The Bremner Case
The Somerset Case
The Dennison Case

The Anthony Case
The Barnaby Case
The Dolores Case
The Robbins Case
The Stanton Case
The Oakland Case
The Dunster Case
The Carter Case
The Martos Case
The Marino Case
The Washington Case
The Daniels Case
The Madonna Case
The Kempton Case

Theme music: Le Roy Holmes
Music: Edwin Astley, Harry Booth
Producer: Gordon L.T. Scott

A Delfry Production for ABC Television

39 monochrome 30-minute episodes
UK: ITV 26 Dec 1959 - 4 June 1961
US: Syndicated 1959

INTERPOL CALLING

'Set in a dignified building in Paris, lies the headquarters of the International Criminal Police Organization (Interpol for short). Some of the most extraordinary stories in the annals of crime have happened here. Interpol Calling tells just some of those stories.' –
PROGRAMME INTRODUCTION

It was a tough life being a crook in the 1960s. Time was when you could escape to another country and nobody could lay a finger on you.

Then Interpol came along and by an organized agreement between participating countries, legal borders no longer existed, so that a villain fleeing from Britain found that the tentacles of the law stretched right across Europe, to as far afield as Africa and beyond. It was hardly fair.

This fondly-remembered action series depicted the cases of Interpol inspectors Duval and Mornay as they unearthed more European criminal records than the Eurovision Song Contest.

REGULAR CAST

Insp. Paul Duval Charles Korvin   *Insp. Mornay* Edwin Richfield

Producers: Anthony Perry, Connery
   Chappell
Executive producer: F. Sherwin Green

A Rank/Wrather Production

39 monochrome 30-minute episodes
UK: ITV 14 Sept 1959 - 20 June 1960
  (ATV)
US: Syndicated 1961

IN THE HEAT OF THE NIGHT

'It is a natural for a TV series. A white chief of police for a small Mississippi town and a black Philadelphia detective, always at odds with each other, but always working together, an interesting dramatic team.'   – SCREENWRITER JAMES LEE BARRETT

Twenty-four years ago, Rod Steiger and Sidney Poitier teamed up to star in the hit motion picture In the Heat of the Night, a film that was to become a five-time Academy Award winner, including a Best Actor Award for Steiger, in the face of such formidable opposition as Warren Beatty (Bonnie and Clyde) and Dustin Hoffman (The Graduate). The adaptation of John Ball's novel was a screen landmark, graphically illustrating the uneasy collaboration between black and white, even as police colleagues.

The TV version, launched in 1988, features Carroll O'Connor (the American Alf Garnett from All in the Family) in the Steiger role of Police Chief Bill Gillespie, and Howard Rollins as Poitier's Detective Virgil Tibbs. It opened with Tibbs returning to his hometown of Sparta, Mississippi, for his mother's funeral. He was subsequently appointed Chief of Detectives by a politically-ambitious mayor, seeking a seat in Congress, who believed the presence of Tibbs would win him the black vote.

Tibbs and Gillespie investigated the murder of a white girl, the accused being a young black man. Gillespie was not happy about having Tibbs on his staff but nevertheless had a grudging respect for him and, as the case progressed, their camaraderie grew until Gillespie finally accepted him.

With the crime solved, Gillespie believed his new detective would return to Philadelphia, only to find Tibbs sharing his office. They have been together ever since.

The opening two-hour episode, penned by the late James Lee Barrett, beat Moonlighting in the US ratings, and has gone on to be a television rarity – a quality spin-off from a successful movie. The series concluded its fourth US season in spring 1991, by which time 72 episodes had been shown. Scheduling in the UK has been more haphazard. After an initial run on the ITV net work, it has been sucked into the abyss of late-night transmission around the regions. It deserves better.

REGULAR CAST

Chief Bill Gillespie Carroll O'Connor *Det. Virgil Tibbs* Howard Rollins
Sgt Bubba Skinner Alan Autry *Althea Tibbs* Anne-Marie Johnson
Det. Parker Williams David Hart *Det. Willson Sweet* Geoffrey Thorne

Creator: James Lee Barrett
Producers: Hugh Benson, Ed Ledding
Executive producers: Fred Silverman,
Juanita Bartlett, David Moessinger,
Jeri Taylor, Carroll O'Connor

An MGM Television Production Colour

60-minute episodes
US: NBC From 6 March 1988
UK: ITV 19 July 1988 - 19 Dec 1990

THE INVESTIGATOR

A live American summer replacement, featuring father and son Jeff and Lloyd Prior. Jeff was a cool, successful private investigator in his early thirties, who had picked up all manner of handy hints on detection from his dad, Lloyd, a retired newspaperman. When Lloyd was a young reporter back in the 1920s, he himself had earned a considerable reputation for solving mysteries. Now he passed on his wisdom to his son. The pair worked together on cases, with Jeff acting as legman while Lloyd adopted a more thoughtful, less energetic approach.

REGULAR CAST

Jeff Prior Lonny Chapman *Lloyd Prior* Howard St John

An NBC Production

13 monochrome 30-minute episodes
US: NBC 3 June - 2 Sept 1958

THE INVESTIGATORS

Russ Andrews, Steve Banks and Bill Davis were insurance investigators for the prestigious New York firm of Investigators Inc. which had plush offices on the wealthy East Side. Assisted from time to time by their secretary, Maggie Peters, who specialized in going undercover, the trio sought evidence to ascertain whether or not certain large insurance claims were legitimate. Their inquiries brought them into contact with the underworld and the police, as they did everything in their power to avoid paying out. They could have proved that Little Bo Peep lost her sheep deliberately, as part of an insurance fiddle.

Andrews was played by James Franciscus who, a decade later, starred as a more famous insurance investigator (SEE LONGSTREET).

REGULAR CAST

Russ Andrews James Franciscus   *Steve Banks* James Philbrook
Bill Davis Al Austin   *Maggie Peters* Mary Murphy

A Revue Production for CBS

13 monochrome 60-minute episodes
US: CBS 5 Oct - 28 Dec 1961

IRONSIDE (SEE A MAN CALLED IRONSIDE)

IT'S DARK OUTSIDE

The middle segment in the splendid trilogy of series featuring the acidic Chief Inspector Rose (SEE ALSO THE ODD MAN AND MR ROSE). As in The Odd Man six months earlier, Rose was initially teamed with the pensive Detective Sergeant Swift, played by a young Keith Barron. They were joined for the first eight episodes by barrister Anthony Brand, a friend of Rose's, and his wife Alice. But for the second eight, Swift was replaced by Detective Sergeant Hunter, while Brand and Alice made way for Hunter's girlfriend Claire and her drunken journalist friend, Fred Blaine.

It's Dark Outside was not only responsible for a number one hit Where Are You Now? by Jackie Trent, it also furthered the career of an up-and-coming actor by the name of Oliver Reed. In the second series, he played a young gang-leader whose criminal activities brought him into conflict with Rose and Hunter.

REGULAR CAST

Chief Insp. Rose William Mervyn   *Det. Sgt Swift* Keith Barron
Brand John Carson   *Alice* June Tobin
Det. Sgt Hunter Anthony Ainley   *Claire* Veronica Strong
Blaine John Stratton   *Sebastian* Oliver Reed

Producer: Derek Bennett

A Granada Television Network Production

16 monochrome 60-minute episodes
UK: ITV (Season 1) 3 Jan - 21 Feb 1964 (8 eps)
(Season 2) 26 Feb - 23 April 1965 (8 eps)

JACKS AND KNAVES

Liverpool folk-lore has it that such was the presence of Detective Sergeant Bill Prendergast, that any thieves he had put in the dock used to stand up in court and practically shout 'guilty'. Prendergast, or 'Mr P' as he was known in the city, spent 28 years with Liverpool CID, during which time he earned a reputation for being able to extract confessions even from suspects with watertight alibis. His interrogation methods became legendary, especially his practice of never taking notes.

Jacks and Knaves (in Liverpool, a detective is known as a 'jack') was a series of light dramas based on Prendergast, whom producer Gilchrist Calder described as being 'tough but with a great sense of humour and much humanity.' The central character was Detective Sergeant Tom Hitchin, but the programme's major contribution to detective television was that it served as a forerunner to the long-running and immensely popular Z Cars.

REGULAR CAST

Det. Sgt Tom Hitchin John Barrie

Creator: Colin Morris
Producer/Director: Gilchrist Calder

A BBC Television Production

4 monochrome 45-minute episodes
UK: BBC 16 Nov - 7 Dec 1961

JAKE AND THE FATMAN

Following Cannon and Nero Wolfe, William Conrad has again demonstrated his appetite for a good detective yarn, with the highly successful Jake and the Fatman. No prizes for guessing which one Conrad plays – he is J.L. 'Fatman' McCabe, a former Hawaiian cop who, many years on, has returned to his home state as Honolulu's district attorney. McCabe is rough, tough and cunning and, if necessary, is even prepared to go outside the law to get to the truth. And he doesn't spend all his time behind a desk – he likes to be out there on the streets fighting crime. His almost constant companion is his pet bulldog, Max. And when Max sits on McCabe's lap, I defy anyone to tell the two apart.

McCabe's private investigator is the suave Jake Styles. The pair met after Jake's vacation in Hawaii turned sour when he was framed for his best friend's murder. As a stranger to the island, he had nobody to turn to – until he bumped into McCabe. Jake is a ladies' man with an expensive taste in clothes and fast cars. In contrast, McCabe's clothes are only expensive because they require so much material. Jake is also a pretty determined operator and ends up in some hair-raising scrapes, although his designer suit usually manages to emerge unscathed. Completing the line-up is Derek Mitchell, McCabe's eager young assistant prosecutor, who sometimes acts as reluctant caretaker of Max.

As Hawaii Five-0 and Magnum P.I. proved, Hawaii is an ideal setting for a crime show and, with two contrasting but equally charismatic leads, Jake and the Fatman swings along nicely. In the US it has so far totalled five seasons and some 100 episodes. In Britain it has been scattered across the ITV network, invariably late at night. Perhaps it is just as well it is not screened earlier, since the sight of Conrad in a Hawaiian shirt and baseball cap is definitely not for the squeamish.

REGULAR CAST

J.L. 'Fatman' McCabe William Conrad   *Joe Penny* Jake Styles
Derek Mitchell Alan Campbell

Creators: Dean Hargrove, Joel Steiger
Music: Dick DeBenedictis
Producers: Ron Satlof, Fred McKnight
Executive producers: Fred Silverman, Dean Hargrove, David Moessinger, Ed Waters

60-minute colour episodes
US: CBS From 15 Sept 1987
UK: ITV From 20 May 1989

A Viacom Production

P.D. JAMES

'I have had Adam Dalgliesh living with me intimately for 35 years. I don't think I have fallen in love with him, which is an occupational hazard for women writers. But I have a great respect and affection for him as a character.'   – P.D. JAMES

Along with Morse and Ruth Rendell's Wexford, Adam Dalgliesh represents the new era of British literary police detectives. To date, six of P.D. James' best-selling Dalgliesh novels have been adapted for television, each with loving care and precision...and lots and lots of horrible murders. The body count runs at almost one per episode which means that after 36 programmes, Miss James has wiped out virtually half the population of East Anglia. What were once peaceful country lanes echoing to the song of the skylark, now seem to hide a mutilated corpse behind every hedgerow.

Its blood-thirsty nature has not prevented the series selling to over 60 countries including Holland, Iceland, Finland and the United States. Indeed Dalgliesh has become a cult figure in the US, with a thriving fan club who visit Britain to watch him filming on location.

Adam Dalgliesh began as a Chief Superintendent at Scotland Yard but was promoted to Commander for the story The Black Tower. Played by 6ft 3in Roy Marsden, Dalgliesh is an acclaimed poet and the son of an Anglican vicar. A widower, following the tragic death of his wife, he has two homes – one in London, the other a converted windmill in Norfolk. He is aloof yet eloquent, steely-eyed yet courteous. When necessary he can also be ruthless, a man to strike fear into the most cunning of murderers. 'He is a very moral man,' says Marsden. 'He respects old-fashioned values, believes in the triumph of good. He is quiet and private and this shows in the way he dresses.'

Marsden himself turned detective in preparation for the role – but with less success than Dalgliesh. 'I wanted to know how high-ranking policemen talk to each other, the clubs they belong to, their interests, where they socialize. But I found them reluctant to talk about themselves.' He admits that at first he was unsure how to play the character. 'I'm a shoe person. If I can decide what shoes a character would wear, I can get inside him. But Dalgliesh's shoes did not help at all. Then I noticed how many high-ranking cops wore moustaches. And I thought, that's it. It gave Dalgliesh the right amount of sternness and strength, with a hint of secrecy too.' And topping it off was the familiar Roy Marsden toupee (the balding actor has worn a variety of hairpieces in his different TV roles).

P.D. James, whose initials stand for Phyllis Dorothy, is one of the world's leading mystery writers. Now 71, she has been dubbed the 'Queen of Crime' after being awarded the Cartier Diamond Dagger by the Crime Writers' Association for a lifetime's achievement in the world of crime fiction. She was a hospital administrator in the National Health Service before working for the Home Office in the forensic science and criminal departments, from where she drew much of her inspiration and technical expertise. Her first novel, Cover Her Face, was published in 1962 and she eventually took early retirement from the Home Office in 1979, to devote her energies to writing.

She plots her murders meticulously. 'Planning a murder is a very disciplined and detailed exercise,' she says, 'and the author must remember at all times where her suspects were at the time of the murder. I need to know not only where they were, but where they told the police they were and I make two lists of these different facts for every 15 minutes of the hours before and after the murder.'

P.D. James is impressed with the way her creation has transferred to screen. 'To many millions of people all over the world now, Roy Marsden is Adam Dalgliesh. I think Roy's interpretation of Dalgliesh is a marvellous piece of acting. He has that quiet authority at the heart of the story which is totally convincing. You can believe he is a poet, you can believe he is a policeman. The height and the lovely voice are very much part of my idea of Dalgliesh.'

Since the death of his wife, Dalgliesh has been a melancholy, lonely individual, obsessed by work. Apart from the first three stories when he was assisted by the ambitious John Massingham, he has been a solitary figure. Yet in the most recent adaptation, Devices and Desires, he mellowed a little. Not only was he wearing a leather jacket and cords instead of his customary sombre suit (this was simply because he was on holiday) but keen observers actually noticed a flicker of a smile. What's more, he began to show quite an interest in a housekeeper played by Susannah York. Could this at last lead to a hint of happiness for Dalgliesh?

Roy Marsden certainly hopes so. 'Since his wife died, Dalgliesh has been carrying the hurt around. He's never got between the sheets with anyone, though once someone did get him on the bed and began taking his tie off, but that was as far as it got. But with Susannah, we were seen walking along almost hand in hand. It's a start!'

REGULAR CAST

Adam Dalgliesh Roy Marsden   *John Massingham* John Vine *(Seasons 1-3)*

Death of an Expert Witness

A police pathologist is roused from sleep by an early morning phone call, alerting him to a murder in East Anglia's isolated and secretive Fenland. The victim, a fun-loving girl of 19, lies strangled on the back seat of a car. Local police are jubilant when her boy friend quickly confesses to the killing but Dalgliesh senses it is not quite so straightforward. He is hunting an elusive 'back-seat strangler' who has already notched up four murders. Is the girl the fifth? Dalgliesh decides not, particularly when another murder takes place at a science laboratory, where the detective finds himself embroiled in a complex web of jealousy, desperation, revenge and blackmail.

GUEST STARS:

Barry Foster, Geoffrey Palmer, Ray
    Brooks
Dramatized by Robin Chapman
Director: Herbert Wise

Shroud for a Nightingale

Dalgliesh's murder inquiries take him to the bedside of a dying patient at the John Carpendar Hospital, and to gloomy Nightingale House, the adjoining training wing and young nurses' home where, suddenly, the risk of death seems greater than on any ward. A nurse is poisoned and Dalgliesh is ordered to suspend his investigation. Suspecting a high-level cover-up, he refuses to do so, thereby putting his career at risk. In the intrigues, jealousies and secretive loves of this tight-knit community, Dalgliesh discovers more than one motive – but then there's more than one murder.

GUEST STARS:

Joss Ackland, Liz Fraser, Sheila Allen
Dramatized by Robin Chapman
Director: John Gorrie

Cover Her Face

Dalgliesh is called in to track down the killer of a Greek Cypriot drugs racketeer, found strangled in the basement of a respectable book club. His key witness in the case turns out to be Sally Jupp, a young unmarried mother on a day visit to London from rural Suffolk, so his inquiries switch between a dangerous urban drugs scene, where one detective has been killed already, and a middle-class society where the girl is a mysterious new face. Dalgliesh has his suspicions about Miss Jupp but only another murder will disclose her part in the proceedings.

GUEST STARS:

Kim Thomson, Mel Martin, Phyllis Calvert
Dramatized by Robin Chapman
Director: John Davies

The Black Tower

Newly promoted to the rank of Commander, Dalgliesh is facing a crisis in his career. Dissatisfied with his work, restless and vulnerable, he contemplates resigning from the Force. So an invitation to visit an old family friend, Father Baddeley – chaplain to Toynton Grange, a private nursing home – appeals to him, especially when his curiosity is aroused by the elderly priest's misgivings about recent events at the home. On arriving at Toynton, Dalgliesh learns of two sudden deaths, one apparently accidental and the other supposedly from natural causes. But Dalgliesh is uneasy and tensions are heightened by a series of poison pen letters and inexplicable deaths. His presence increasingly resented by some in the community, Dalgliesh puts his own safety at risk, as the violence becomes more open and dangerous.

GUEST STARS:

Pauline Collins, Art Malik, Maurice
    Denham
Dramatized by William Humble
Director: Ronald Wilson

A Taste For Death

An old acquaintance, Sir Paul Berowne, a prominent Government minister, asks Dalgliesh to investigate a series of unpleasant anonymous letters. Events escalate swiftly when one of Berowne's servants dies in strange circumstances, and soon Dalgliesh finds himself investigating a gruesome double murder. Everyone connected with the Berowne household falls under suspicion. Behind their seemingly respectable facade lurk the ugly emotions of lust, greed, hatred and fear. One by one, the characters reveal their darkest secrets as the search proceeds towards its terrifying conclusion.

GUEST STARS:

Dame Wendy Hiller, Simon Ward, Fiona
Fullerton
Dramatized by Alick Rowe
Director: John Davies

Devices and Desires

Dalgliesh is taking a break from his Scotland
Yard duties. In her will, his elderly aunt has
left him her windmill on the North Norfolk
coast and it seems the perfect refuge for the
poetic policeman. But his solitude is
shattered when he discovers there is a
psychopathic killer on the loose, known as
the Whistler, and he is quickly drawn into the
murder hunt. He also becomes entangled in
the locals' passionate protests against the
presence of a nuclear power station. Are the
murders linked to the drama at the power
station? Dalgliesh must find the answer
before there are further killings.

GUEST STARS:

Susannah York, Gemma Jones, James
Faulkner
Dramatized by Thomas Ellice
Director: John Davies

Music: Richard Harvey
Producer: John Rosenberg

*An Anglia Films Production for Anglia
Television Limited*

DEATH OF AN EXPERT WITNESS
7 colour 60-minute episodes
UK: ITV 8 April - 20 May 1983
US: WGBH Boston 'Mystery' 24 Oct - 28
Nov 1985
SHROUD FOR A NIGHTINGALE
4 colour 60-minute episodes and one
colour 90-minute episode
UK: ITV 9 March - 6 April 1984
US: 'Mystery' 9 Oct - 6 Nov 1986
COVER HER FACE
6 colour 60-minute episodes
UK: ITV 17 Feb - 24 March 1985
US: 'Mystery' 26 March - 30 April 1987
THE BLACK TOWER
6 colour 60-minute episodes
UK: ITV 8 Nov - 13 Dec 1985
US: 'Mystery' 28 April - 2 June 1988
A TASTE FOR DEATH
6 colour 60-minute episodes
UK: ITV 14 Oct - 18 Nov 1988
US: 'Mystery' 22 March - 26 April 1990
DEVICES AND DESIRES
6 colour 60-minute episodes
UK: ITV 4 Jan - 8 Feb 1991

JANGO

Described as a cross between Jacques Tati's Monsieur Hulot and G.K.
Chesterton's Father Brown, Jango also had something of the flavour of
an early Columbo. A professor of criminology, he was amiable,
intelligent but scruffy, with a dirty raincoat and a gnarled walking stick.
As a private detective, he looked a pushover but that was to be the
downfall of many a villain. For once Jango had got his teeth into a case,
he wouldn't let go. A lovable eccentric, Jango was divorced from his
wife, Dee, a boutique owner, but still bedded down on her settee.

The character was created by the show's star, Robert Urquhart, and
originally appeared in a comedy mystery titled Murder Stamp, before
being brought back two months later in this series by public demand.

REGULAR CAST

Jango Smith Robert Urquhart   *Dee Smith* Moira Redmond

Creator: Robert Urquhart
Producer/Director: Cyril Coke

*An Associated Rediffusion Network
Production*

8 monochrome 30-minute episodes
UK: ITV 25 Jan - 22 March 1961

JASON KING

Having given up his career as an international investigator (SEE DEPARTMENT S), the flamboyant Jason King concentrated on writing more of his acclaimed Mark Caine novels, to the delight of his publisher, Nicola Harvester. Although officially he was no longer involved in crime-busting, he still worked occasionally for British Intelligence (which was often a contradiction in terms) at the behest of high-ranking civil servant, Sir Brian, and his assistant, Ryland. Naturally King wound up in any number of scrapes, usually involving beautiful girls who had spent almost as long in make-up as he had. This spin-off series wasn't as successful as Department S but it was enjoyable nonetheless. And colour television was simply made for Jason King's shirts...

REGULAR CAST

Jason King Peter Wyngarde   *Nicola Harvester* Ann Sharp
Sir Brian Dennis Price   *Ryland* Ronald Lacey

Creators: Dennis Spooner, Monty
   Berman
Music: Laurie Johnson
Producer: Monty Berman

A Scroton Production for ITC

26 colour 60-minute episodes
UK: ITV 15 Sept 1971 - 5 May 1972

JEMIMA SHORE INVESTIGATES

'They made Jemima use bad language and I had to put my foot down because I felt it was something a forceful, self-confident woman like her would never do.'   – ANTONIA FRASER

Author Antonia Fraser made sure that the television adaptation of her Jemima Shore novels didn't stray far from the originals. But even with the talented Patricia Hodge in the title role, it was at best only moderate.

Antonia Fraser's upper-class heroine was very much a privileged career woman of the 1980s. Educated abroad, she went on to write and present her own series for Megalith Television, Jemima Shore Investigates, as well as indulging in a spot of spare-time amateur sleuthing. Cat-loving, music-loving Jemima lived in West London and mixed in the highest circles of society, from where she found herself plunged into cases of murder, blackmail and general intrigue.

Antonia Fraser and her creation have a number of things in common. They are both university graduates, neither touch alcohol except for white wine and they even share the same hairdresser. Yet Fraser insists she is not like Jemima. 'She is single with no children and no living relatives, whereas I have a tribe. But I will admit that perhaps Jemima is my fantasy lady.'

* Antonia Fraser made a Hitchcock-like, one-line appearance in the first episode, A Splash of Red.

REGULAR CAST

Jemima Shore Patricia Hodge

Creator: Antonia Fraser
Producer: Tim Aspinall

12 colour 60-minute episodes
UK: ITV 8 June - 24 Aug 1983

A Thames Television Network Production

JESSIE

Bionic Woman, Lindsay Wagner, produced and starred in this short-lived series about a staff psychiatrist working for a Southern California police department. But she would have needed the special powers she had as Jaime Sommers to have made it a hit. It wasn't entirely her fault. She wanted the show to be a quiet, realistic view of psychiatry, but ABC chiefs decided the pilot was too boring and ordered the rest of the episodes to be beefed up with car chases and gun fights. So the psychiatric angle was played down. They needed their heads examined.

Wagner played Dr Jessie Hayden, an understanding medic who helped the police in their dealings with psychopathic killers and other mentally unstable criminals, as well as counselling victims of crime. So far so good, but every case had to place her in grave physical danger, to the concern of her mother, Molly, with whom she lived, and the police department's Lieutenant Ascoli. The result was that what started out as a reasonable idea, ended up like too many other police series.

REGULAR CAST

Dr Jessie Hayden Lindsay Wagner   *Lt Alex Ascoli* Tony Lo Bianco
Molly Hayden Celeste Holm

Music: John Cacavas
Producers: Lindsay Wagner, Richard
   Michaels

10 colour 60-minute episodes
US: ABC 18 Sept - 13 Nov 1984
UK: ITV 6 Oct - 27 Nov 1986 (TVS)

An MGM Television Production

JIGSAW

Lieutenant Frank Dain was a special investigator for the California State Department's Bureau of Missing Persons. He had already put his talents to good use by tracking down an elusive witness who saved him from a murder charge and here he took on the Bureau's toughest cases – and cracking the lot. Dain was tough and rebellious and didn't mind breaking the rules to get results. There is no doubt that his ability for finding long-lost souls and bringing them back alive, would have made him a natural as a researcher on This Is Your Life.

In the US, Jigsaw was screened as part of the umbrella series The Men (the other components were the spy shows Assignment Vienna and The Delphi Bureau).

REGULAR CAST

Lt Frank Dain James Wainwright

Creator: Robert Thompson
Music: Robert Drasnin, Harper McKay
Producer: Stanley Kallis

8 colour 60-minute episodes
US: ABC 21 Sept 1972 - 11 Aug 1973
UK: ITV 17 Jan 1974 - 22 Aug 1975

A Universal Television Production

JIGSAW JOHN

As a senior investigator with the Los Angeles Police Department, John St John earned the nickname 'Jigsaw' because of his aptitude for steadily fitting together the pieces of a murder inquiry. With his partner, Sam Donner, Jigsaw (played by Crazy Like a Fox star Jack Warden) solved no end of baffling murders, although his unique methods didn't always endear him to his superiors. He was dedicated to his work, even at the expense of his long-standing romance with pretty nursery-school teacher, Maggie Hearn. Jigsaw must have had a piece missing.

REGULAR CAST

John St John Jack Warden   *Sam Donner* Alan Feinstein
Maggie Hearn Pippa Scott

Creator: Al Martinez
Producers: Ronald Austin, James Buchanan

An MGM Television Production

13 colour 60-minute episodes
US: NBC 2 Feb - 8 Sept 1976

JIMMY HUGHES, ROOKIE COP

America was proud of Jimmy Hughes. A young soldier, just back from the Korean War, he learned that his cop father had been killed in a shoot-out. So what did he do? Why, he joined the police force to avenge his dad's death. Under the eagle eye of his hard-nosed boss, Inspector Ferguson, and the loving eye of sister, Betty, rookie Jimmy hunted down the killers and won his father's badge. He then proceeded to tackle the most dangerous cases around and came through them all with flying colours. Wadda guy!

* The original Jimmy Hughes, William Redfield, was replaced by Conrad Janis for the last few episodes.

REGULAR CAST

Officer Jimmy Hughes William Redfield, and later Conrad Janis
Insp. Ferguson Rusty Lane   *Betty Hughes* Wendy Drew

A DuMont Production

US: DuMont 8 May - 3 July 1953

8 monochrome 30-minute episodes

JOE FORRESTER

Lloyd Bridges, forever remembered as Mike Nelson in Sea Hunt, surfaced 20 years later minus wet suit and snorkel, as honest Joe Forrester, a friendly cop on the beat. Like an American version of George Dixon (SEE DIXON OF DOCK GREEN), Joe was a father figure to the residents of the tough city area he had been patrolling for years. Everybody knew him and respected him and in return, he was occasionally prepared to turn a blind eye to minor misdemeanours. He was an outstanding advertisement for community relations, having broken down many of the barriers between the police and ethnic groups. He was particularly friendly with a young black student, Jolene Jackson. Other characters included his immediate boss, Sergeant Bernie Vincent (played by former New York cop Eddie Egan), and Joe's girlfriend, Georgia Cameron. That was one thing he didn't have in common with George Dixon!

Joe Forrester was a good steady show, but suffered from being launched in the same American season as a similar series, The Blue Knight.

REGULAR CAST

Joe Forrester Lloyd Bridges   *Georgia Cameron* Patricia Crowley
Sgt Bernie Vincent Eddie Egan   *Jolene Jackson* Dawn Smith

Creator: Mark Rodgers
Producers: Mark Rodgers, James H. Brown
Executive producer: David Gerber

13 colour 60-minute episodes
US: NBC 9 Sept 1975 - 30 Aug 1976
UK: ITV 23 Oct 1976 - 11 Sept 1977

A Columbia Pictures Television Production

JOHNNY MIDNIGHT

One-time Hollywood star, Edmond O'Brien, played Manhattan actor turned detective, Johnny Midnight, in this syndicated action series. Johnny, whose police contacts at the NYPD were Sergeant Sam Olivera and Lieutenant Geller, concentrated his sleuthing activities around Times Square – the same area of the city where he had enjoyed the highspots of his acting career. An interesting feature was that Johnny had a Japanese houseboy, Aki. These were commonplace in 1930s crime stories but were rare in the 1960s.

For all his reputation, Edmond O'Brien was brought down to earth with a bump before the series even started. Executive producer, Jack Chertok, flatly refused to let him step before the cameras until he had lost weight.

REGULAR CAST

Johnny Midnight Edmond O'Brien   *Sgt Sam Olivera* Arthur Batanides
Lt Geller Barney Phillips   *Aki* Yuki Shemoda

Music: Joe Bushkin, Stanley Wilson   39 monochrome 30-minute episodes
Executive producer: Jack Chertok   US: Syndicated 1960

A Revue Production for MCA

JOHNNY STACCATO

An extremely stylish crime series, a cut above most of the programmes around at the time. Originally just called Staccato (under which banner it was screened in Britain on Channel 4 recently), it was set in New York and combined first-rate stories with a tremendous jazz flavour. The central character was Johnny Staccato, who supplemented his miserly wages as a jazz pianist, by taking on cases as a private detective. He picked up most of his assignments at Waldo's, a claustrophobic club in Greenwich Village, where he spent much of his free time. For added authenticity, the jazz combo playing in the club was that of Pete Candoli, and included such noted musicians as Barney Kessel and Red Norvo. After NBC cancelled the show, ABC picked it up and showed repeats.

REGULAR CAST

Johnny Staccato John Cassavetes   *Waldo* Eduardo Ciannelli

Music: Elmer Bernstein   27 monochrome 30-minute episodes
Producer: Everett Chambers   US: NBC/ABC 10 Sept 1959 - 25 Sept
Executive producer: William Frye   1960
                                       UK: Channel 4 17 Feb - 27 April 1988

A Revue Production for MCA/Universal

JUDGE DEE

Presenting indubitably the only 7th century Chinese judge detective. Adapted from the novels by Robert Van Gulik, this was a most unusual production for an ITV company.

Judge Dee himself was a real person, a philosophical, all-powerful, investigative magistrate, who lived in China from 630 to 700 A.D., serving as a Minister for State in the Tang Empire. He was feared throughout the land by the criminal fraternity. But the series proved somewhat less omnipotent, running to just six episodes, only five of which were transmitted.

It was almost worth tuning in to witness such honorary Chinamen as Welshman Garfield Morgan and Cockney Michael Robbins (Arthur from the sit-com On the Buses). I suspect his experiences of the Orient are confined to the soccer team that plays in East London. Confucius he say: get it off.

* In 1974, Khigh Dhiegh (Wo Fat from Hawaii Five-O) starred in an American TV movie, Judge Dee and the Monastery Murders.

REGULAR CAST

Judge Dee Michael Goodliffe   *Tao Gan* Garfield Morgan

Writer: John Wiles
Music: Derek Hilton
Producer: Howard Baker

A Granada Television Network Production

5 colour 60-minute episodes
UK: ITV 8 April - 13 May 1969

JULIET BRAVO

'A major crime in Hartley? Nine people hacked to death outside 't' Co-op? I'll just put 't' kettle on, ma'am.' That was the usual reaction both Inspector Jean Darblay and her successor, Kate Longton, got from their unflappable plainclothes colleagues at Hartley police station.

Brewer in chief was Sergeant Joe Beck, hewn from solid Northern rock, and a pillar of the community in the fictional small Lancashire town. Mind you, he could occasionally show signs of emotion – if there was a particularly gruesome murder, he'd slip in an extra tea bag.

But for the most part life was fairly peaceful in Hartley. Indeed the pace of life was so slow it was hard to believe that the programme was created by Ian Kennedy Martin, the man behind The Sweeney.

Most viewers spent the first ten weeks waiting for Juliet Bravo herself to appear, before they realized it was a police call-sign. The series spotlighted the problems and prejudices faced by a woman arriving to take charge at a male stronghold, in this instance as an Inspector at the local police station. And for all its parochialism, it did it pretty well – it was certainly streets ahead of its Southern rival The Gentle Touch.

The first incumbent was Inspector Jean Darblay, senior police officer and housewife (she was married to Tom). As she got her feet under the desk and introduced her own ideas, she had to win over long-serving officers such as Joe Beck and his fellow sergeant, George Parrish. But both were good men and, although they still had their reservations about a woman boss, they were happy enough to serve under her. More difficult to convert were the chauvinistic CID officers, most of whom were portrayed as objectionable bunglers.

After three seasons, Jean Darblay, played by Stephanie Turner, was promoted and left to be replaced by Inspector Kate Longton (Anna Carteret). Researching the role took Anna to a number of local police stations where she was given advice on how a woman uniformed police Inspector should behave. It was suggested that she should smile more and cut her hair so that it didn't touch the collar. She was also told that policewomen should look feminine and that if they tried to be tougher than the men, they would risk being branded neurotic.

Although it may have proved a mite slow to those raised on Starsky and Hutch, Juliet Bravo proved enormously popular , particularly among female viewers. It offered honest realism, never feeling the need to introduce sensational storylines just for the sake of it. It was quality television – never more so than when young PC Danny Sparks was trapped in a blazing nightclub, his life ebbing away to the resonant beat of U2's Sunday, Bloody Sunday. Juliet Bravo may have been much-mocked but TV police series have produced few more poignant scenes than that.

REGULAR CAST

Insp. Jean Darblay (Seasons 1-3) Stephanie Turner
Tom Darblay (Seasons 1-3) David Hargreaves
Insp. Kate Longton (Seasons 4-6) Anna Carteret
Sgt Joe Beck David Ellison   *Sgt George Parrish* Noel Collins
PC Danny Sparks Mark Botham   *PC Brian Kelleher* C.J. Allen

Creator: Ian Kennedy Martin
Producers: Terence Williams, Peter Cregeen

A BBC Television Production

82 colour 50-minute episodes
UK: BBC1 (Season 1) 30 Aug - 13 Dec 1980 (10 eps)
(Season 2) 5 Sept - 5 Dec 1981 (14 eps)

(Season 3) 4 Sept - 4 Dec 1982 (14 eps)
(Season 4) 3 Sept - 3 Dec 1983 (14 eps)
(Season 5) 1 Sept - 1 Dec 1984 (14 eps)
(Season 6) 7 Sept - 21 Dec 1985 (16 eps)

KATTS AND DOG

Hank Katts had the world at his feet. Freshly graduated from Police Academy (the institution not the movie), he dreamed the American cop series dream of fighting crime in the streets with a partner. What he didn't know was that his partner would be a dog. For Hank was assigned to the K-9 Corps and teamed up with Alsatian Rinty. Aimed primarily at a young audience, the age group who used to lap up The Adventures of Rin Tin Tin in the 1950s, this was harmless enough fare, although I must express doubt about the billing of the dog as Rin Tin Tin III. The original Rin Tin Tin made his film debut way back in 1923 and died nine years later. This would make the latest claimant to that title at least 30.

REGULAR CAST

Hank Katts Jesse Collins   *Maggie* Cali Timmins
Stevie Andrew Bednarski   *Capt. Murdoch* Ken Pogue
Rinty Rin Tin Tin III

Producer: Barry Pearson

A Pearson Lamb Production with Bert Leonard Films for CBS (Canada)

Colour 30-minute episodes
Canada: From 16 Sept 1988
UK: ITV 20 Jan - 5 May 1990 (13 eps)
(LWT)

KAZ

Essentially a courtroom drama, Kaz qualifies as a detective series on the strength of the hero's unconventional background. For attorney Martin Kazinsky earned his law degree while in prison and his inside knowledge of the criminal mind gave him a head start over his new partners in the reputable Los Angeles law firm of Bennett, Rheinhart and Alquist. Kaz was a whizz at unearthing vital fresh evidence, sometimes with the help of his girlfriend, court reporter Katie McKenna. He lived in a flat over the Starting Gate jazz club, owned by his friend Mary Parnell, and used to drum with the resident band.

Kaz was a competent enough show but it only ran to 13 episodes. It obviously did actor George Wyner no favours. Here he played District Attorney Frank Revko but shortly afterwards was demoted to Assistant D.A., as Irwin Bernstein in Hill Street Blues.

REGULAR CAST

Martin 'Kaz' Kazinsky Ron Leibman   *Samuel Bennett* Patrick O'Neal
Katie McKenna Linda Carlson   *Mary Parnell* Gloria Le Roy
D.A. Frank Revko George Wyner

Music: Fred Karlin
Producers: Peter Katz, Sam Rolfe
Executive producers: Lee Rich, Marc
Merson

13 colour 60-minute episodes
US: CBS 10 Sept 1978 - 19 Aug 1979
UK: ITV 20 Nov - 11 Dec 1980
26 Jan - 13 July 1982 (Thames)

A Lorimar Production

KHAN

This series goes down in American television history as the only one in which the star (Khigh Dhiegh) refused billing. Maybe he knew something because it was axed after four weeks. Based in San Francisco's Chinatown, private detective Khan was a modern Charlie Chan. He unravelled intricate mysteries with the help of student offspring, Anna, and number one son, Kim. They were a formidable team but were unable to combat the great God Apathy.

REGULAR CAST

Khan Khigh Dhiegh   *Anna Khan* Irene Yah-Ling Sun
Kim Khan Evan Kim   *Lt Gubbins* Vic Tayback

Creator: Chet Gould
Producers: Laurence Heath, Joseph
Henry

4 colour 60-minute episodes
US: CBS 7 Feb - 28 Feb 1975

KING OF DIAMONDS

Broderick Crawford's follow-up to Highway Patrol saw him travelling the world as John King, Chief of Security for the diamond industry. With his young sidekick, Al Casey, King solved all manner of crimes involving the diamond trade, his sworn enemy being the Illegal Diamond Buyers' Syndicate. But this series was no gem and was not helped by an unsavoury hero whose violence extended to beating up women. King of Diamonds was not a girl's best friend.

REGULAR CAST

John King Broderick Crawford   *Al Casey* Ray Hamilton

A Ziv Production for United Artists

39 monochrome 30-minute episodes
US: Syndicated Sept 1961

KODIAK

Many moons after his adventures as Cheyenne, Clint Walker starred as Cal 'Kodiak' McKay, stalwart of the Alaska State Patrol. His beat was just about the largest of any police show – 50,000 square miles of barren Alaskan land – which he often crossed on skis or snowshoes. Kodiak liked to work alone but sometimes sought the advice of his Eskimo friend, Abraham Lincoln Imhook, in tracking down criminals. Fortunately crime was a rarity (there weren't many banks to rob) and much of Kodiak's time was spent rescuing avalanche victims or acting as peacekeeper in mining disputes. The series was filmed in Alaska.

REGULAR CAST

Cal 'Kodiak' McKay Clint Walker   *Abraham Lincoln Imhook* Abner Biberman

Creators: Stan Shpetner, Anthony
    Laurence
Music: Morton Stevens
Producer: Stan Shpetner

A Kodiak Production

13 colour 30-minute episodes
US: ABC 13 Sept - 11 Oct 1974

KOJAK

'All Kojak's catch-phrases come from me. They come from living in New York most of my life. I figure I know better than any scriptwriter how a cop like him talks.' – Telly Savalas

'Who loves ya, baby?' – Over 100 countries in Kojak's heyday in the 1970s. The lollipop-sucking Greek cop in the three-piece suit, who called everybody 'pussycat' became one of the success stories of the decade, to the ironic amusement of the show's star, Telly Savalas, previously a bad guy in countless films.

'It's amazing,' he says, 'I made more than 70 movies without making it. Once I was cast as Kojak, suddenly everybody in the world wanted me.' Yet he very nearly turned down the part. 'I'm always thought of as tough and sinister and I've been unable to get away from a police badge or killer's knife. The interrogation rooms, the sirens, the whole stereotype were endangering my career.'

Kojak was first seen in a gritty 1972 TV movie, The Marcus-Nelson Murders, based on a real case in which he tried to help a black youth who had been wrongly arrested for the murder of two women. For the series itself, Lieutenant Theo (short for Theopodophilous) Kojak was based at the 13th Precinct in Manhattan South, where the Chief of Detectives was his erstwhile partner, Frank McNeil. Kojak had repeatedly been overlooked for promotion, partly because of his tendency to bend the rules but more importantly because he wasn't prepared to play political games.

Kojak was a bitter man. Not through missing out on a bigger desk and his own rubber plant but because he cared about people, he cared about the city. Above all, he detested corruption, particularly at the highest level. On the outside Kojak was tough and streetwise, but this hid a tender streak which brought Savalas an army of adoring female fans who all thought that bald was beautiful.

Savalas was very concerned about violence. 'What you do on screen can obviously be copied. That is why Kojak was never allowed to use excessive violence. You only ever saw him pull his gun as a last resort. In fact he used his lollipop as his gun. It's because of that cops all over the world love the character, for being an honest portrayal of the way they work.'

As with the famous catchphrases and the waistcoats, it was Savalas' idea to introduce the lollipop, originally as a cigarette substitute when Kojak tried to give up smoking. As a result lollipop sales increased 500 per cent – and not just to children.

There was a fine back-up team in Kojak, notably Bobby Crocker, a hard-nosed young detective played by Kevin Dobson, and plant-loving Detective Stavros, played by Telly Savalas' brother George. For the first two seasons, George Savalas was billed as simply 'Demosthenes' (his middle name) so that he could be judged as an actor not just as Telly's brother.

Awarded the Purple Heart as a war hero, Telly Savalas worked as a senior director for ABC News, before turning to acting in his late thirties. He first shaved his head for Burt Lancaster's 1962 film, Birdman of Alcatraz, and this of course became his trademark. He was 49 when Kojak started and its five-season run made him a big star. He branched out into a recording career and, displaying even more nerve than Kojak in a sleazy alley full of hoods, went to the top of the charts by mumbling his way through David Gates' classic love song If (it sounded as if he was still sucking his lollipop).

Although it deteriorated towards the end of its run, when Savalas seemed more interested in playing the romantic warbler than the cop with a conscience, Kojak was undoubtedly one of the best shows of its type. And it has remained popular, to the point of being revived 12 years after the original series finished. Savalas has reportedly been paid £8 million to recreate the character.

'Kojak just won't die,' says Savalas, now 67, 'although he has mellowed. These days he uses razzle dazzle instead of his fists.' Maintaining the programme's family tradition, Telly's daughter Candice comes in to play his secretary, to give a more feminine touch to the precinct house. And Savalas is thinking about bowing to dental pressure and dropping the lollipop. 'Dentists kept complaining that I encouraged children to rot their teeth, so maybe the lollipop will have to go.' When you've been paid £8 million, you can afford to lose a little lolly.

REGULAR CAST (Original Series)

Lt Theo Kojak Telly Savalas   Frank McNeil Dan Frazer
Lt Bobby Crocker Kevin Dobson   Det. Stavros George Savalas
Det. Saperstein Mark Russell   Det. Rizzo Vince Conti

Creator: Abby Mann
Theme music: Billy Goldenberg
Producers: James MacAdams, Jack Laird
Executive producer: Matthew Rapf

A Universal Television Production

One colour 180-minute episode, 3 colour 120-minute and 112 colour 60-minute episodes
US: CBS (Season 1) 24 Oct 1973 - 8 May 1974 (22 eps)

(Season 2) 15 Sept 1974 - 9 March 1975 (24 eps)
(Season 3) 14 Sept 1975 - 7 March 1976 (24 eps)
(Season 4) 26 Sept 1976 - 22 March 1977 (24 eps)
(Season 5) 2 Oct 1977 - 18 March 1978 (22 eps)
UK: BBC1 (Season 1) 24 Aug 1974 - 23 June 1975
(Season 2) 23 Aug 1975 - 21 Feb 1976
(Season 3) 9 Sept 1976 - 9 Feb 1977
(Season 4) 16 April 1977 - 11 June 1977
(Season 5) 18 March 1978 - 19 Aug 1978

KOLCHAK: THE NIGHT STALKER

Carl Kolchak was a crime reporter with the Chicago-based Independent News Service. He was a dangerous man to know as whenever he roamed the streets, he stumbled across hideous supernatural monsters – vampires, werewolves and hounds from hell – as well as the comparatively civilized

Jack the Ripper. Unfortunately, although Kolchak repeatedly came up with these sensational scoops, his boss, Tony Vincenzo, always spiked them. So his stories never appeared in print.

Kolchak was played by the first Mike Hammer, Darren McGavin, who narrated these tales of the unexpected in a first person, private eye-style voice-over. The monsters he unearthed remained in the shadows, not only to maintain the mystique but also to appease US network bosses, who were paranoid about anything too horrific appearing on screen.

It became something of a cult series but finished prematurely, after Jeff Rice, on whose novel the original TV movie The Night Stalker had been based, took legal action, claiming that he had not given permission for a regular series to be made from his creation.

REGULAR CAST

Carl Kolchak Darren McGavin   *Tony Vincenzo* Simon Oakland

Creator: Jeff Rice
Music: Gil Melle
Producers: Paul Playdon, Cy Chermak
Executive producer: Darren McGavin

Francy Productions for Universal Television

20 colour 60-minute episodes
US: ABC 13 Sept 1974 - 30 Aug 1975
UK: ITV 15 Oct - 10 Dec 1983
14 Nov 1984 - 4 March 1985 (Central)

LADY BLUE

Detective Katy Mahoney was arguably the toughest female cop there's ever been. This Dirty Harriet worked on the seedier side of Chicago, tracking down drug pushers, money launderers, rapists and other slime. Her method of arrest was simple – immobilize them by blowing a hole in their heart with a .357 Magnum.

As a result, Internal Affairs were none too keen on her, and men in general were rather wary, too. For although she could be sexy, the overriding violence in her life tended to interfere with any truly sensitive relationships. Probably the only way for a man to walk out on her was in a bullet-proof vest.

REGULAR CAST

Det. Katy Mahoney Jamie Rose   *Chief Det. Terry McNichols* Danny Aiello
Sgt Gina Ginelli Ron Dean   *Capt. Flynn* Ralph Foody

Creator: Robert Vincent O'Neill
Producer: Mark Rodgers
Executive producer: David Gerber

An MGM Television Production

One colour 120-minute episode and 12
colour 60-minute episodes
US: ABC 14 April 1985 - 25 Jan 1986

LANIGAN'S RABBI

David Small was television's rabbi detective. He was such an accomplished amateur criminologist that his friend, Paul Lanigan, police chief of Cameron, California, sought his assistance whenever he was faced with an awkward case. The pair worked in tandem and socialized in the evenings, to the despair of their wives who became bored by incessant crime talk. Lanigan was played by Art Carney whose daughter, Barbara, appeared as dogged local newspaper reporter, Bobbie Whittaker.

In the US, Lanigan's Rabbi was screened in the NBC Sunday Mystery Movie slot, rotating with Columbo, McCloud and McMillan and Wife. The series was based on the novels by Harry Kemelman, the first of which was Friday The Rabbi Slept Late.

REGULAR CAST

Chief Paul Lanigan Art Carney *Rabbi David Small* Bruce Solomon
Kate Lanigan Janis Paige *Miriam Small* Janet Margolin
Bobbie Whittaker Barbara Carney *Lt Osgood* Robert Doyle

Music: Don Costa
Producers: David J. Connell, Gordon Cotler, Don Mankiewicz
Executive producer: Leonard B. Stern

A Universal Television Production

4 colour 90-minute episodes
US: NBC 30 Jan - 3 July 1977
UK: ITV 16 Feb 1978 - 16 Nov 1979

THE LAW AND HARRY MCGRAW

Created by Peter S. Fischer (the brains behind Murder, She Wrote), The Law and Harry McGraw was set in the historical city of Boston, Massachusetts – a pleasant change from all those American detective shows which journey no further than the suburbs of Los Angeles. The central characters were the refined Ellie Maginnis, a recently-widowed criminal lawyer, and Harry McGraw, a small-time private investigator who was, shall we say, rather gross. Ellie was a model of courtesy and breeding, Harry's idea of a cultural outing was a baseball game followed by corned beef and cabbage served up at his favourite eating place, Gilhooley's Little Bit O' Heaven. The only thing the two had in common was that their offices were in the same block – across the corridor, to be precise.

Cynical Harry had little patience with Ellie's sympathy for underdogs – except when they were his underdogs she was defending. Yet, incredibly, they were strangely drawn to each other. This did not please Ellie's nephew, Steve Lacey, a smart tax lawyer who, although he was hoping for some return on his interest in Harry's secretary and niece, Emma Jean, was not enamoured at the prospect of his aunt linking up with Harry, professionally or romantically.

Harry also had a rival for Ellie's affections, oily district attorney Tyler Chase, a man so conceited he made Narcissus look modest.

The Law and Harry McGraw was a diverting comedy/drama from a successful stable. To underline the point, Harry teamed up with Jessica Fletcher for an episode of Murder, She Wrote.

REGULAR CAST

Harry McGraw Jerry Orbach   *Ellie Maginnis* Barbara Babcock
Emma Jean Brunson Juli Donald   *Steve Lacey* Shea Farrell
Tyler Chase Peter Haskell

Creator: Peter S. Fischer
Producer: Robert F. O'Neill
Executive producer: Peter S. Fischer

A Universal Television Production

One colour 120-minute episode and 15 colour 60-minute episodes
US: CBS 27 Sept 1987 - 10 Feb 1988
UK: ITV 1 July - 4 Dec 1990 (TVS)

LAW AND ORDER (1)

One of the most controversial ever British crime series and one which led to the BBC being banned from filming inside jails for a year by the Prison Officers' Association. Meanwhile the police stated that they were not prepared to co-operate on any future series until the Corporation gave certain assurances as to their content.

Law and Order consisted of four hard-hitting fictional plays by G.F. Newman, looking at crime and punishment through the respective eyes of a detective, a criminal, a lawyer and a prison officer. It suggested that corruption was rife among cops as well as robbers, and showed the police taking bribes and 'fitting up' villains. The police objections were fuelled by the fact that the programmes were shot in a drama/documentary format, and looked so realistic that they feared viewers would confuse fact with fiction.

Newman had made his views on the police known once before, when he attended a production meeting with the intention of writing an episode for the popular series Softly, Softly. His opening idea to the producer was, 'Sergeant Watt takes this bribe of £500...' He was swiftly shown the door.

Writer: G.F. Newman
Director: Leslie Blair
Producer: Tony Garnett

4 colour 75-minute episodes
UK: BBC2 6 April - 27 April 1978

A BBC Television Production

LAW AND ORDER (2)

An updated version of Arrest and Trial with each episode divided into two halves – the first being the investigation and the arrest , the second the trial.

The opening segment is set on the mean streets of New York, where Detective Sergeant Max Greevey and his young partner, Detective Mike Logan, are called to a crime and end up making an arrest. Then the focus switches to the criminal courts where Assistant District Attorneys Ben Stone and Paul Robinette, the two prosecutors, work within a complicated justice system, where solutions are frequently only provided by the striking of cynical deals.

Actor Christopher Noth, who plays Logan, visited a tough 'training school' for his research into the part. He said: 'Logan is based on observations of the New York detective squad at the 34th Precinct on 184th Street which has the dubious honour of having the most homicides of any precinct in Manhattan – and for that matter perhaps the entire country.'

REGULAR CAST

Asst D.A. Ben Stone Michael Moriarty   *Det. Sgt Max Greevey* George Dzundza
Det. Mike Logan Christopher Noth   *Asst D.A. Paul Robinette* Richard Brooks

Producers: Robert Palm, Dan Sackheim
Executive producer: Dick Wolf

US: NBC From Sept 1990
UK: BBC1 8 April 1991 - 23 Sept 1991

*A Wolf Films Production in association
with Universal Television 60-minute
colour episodes*

LAWBREAKER

Lee Marvin hosted dramatizations of real criminal cases in this unintentionally hilarious drama series. The problem was that instead of hiring proper actors, the producers decided to allow the crime victims and the police to play themselves, with the police also doubling up as the crooks. The aim was authenticity, but the result was some abysmally amateurish acting. There was even one memorable moment when, during a supposedly tension-packed scene, two kidnap victims were to be seen sniggering.

Host: Lee Marvin
Executive producer: Maurice Unger

32 monochrome 30-minute episodes
US: Syndicated 1963

A Latimer Production for United Artists

THE LAWLESS YEARS

In The Lawless Years, the names were changed to protect the guilty. Whereas the chief crime-buster kept the name Barney Ruditsky, a real-life New York cop on whose cases the stories were based, the gangsters used pseudonyms.

Set in New York in those Roaring Twenties' days of speakeasies and mobsters, with the battle-hardened Ruditsky fearlessly combatting the evils of organized crime, NBC's The Lawless Years was compellingly realistic. It would have enjoyed a much longer life but for the arrival six months afterwards, of ABC's legendary show The Untouchables, a virtually identical programme but set in Chicago. The Lawless Years was soon dropped but the success of its rival did prompt a new series two years later.

The real Barney Ruditsky, who had retired from the force in 1941 and was running a detective agency on the west Coast, acted as technical adviser on The Lawless Years. He was also a friend of TV producer Danny Arnold who, in the 1970s, named his own famous cop, Barney Miller, after him.

REGULAR CAST

Barney Ruditsky James Gregory   *Max* Robert Karnes

Executive producer: Jack Chertok

47 monochrome 30-minute episodes
US: NBC (Season 1) 16 April - 3 Sept
  1959 (19 eps)

(Season 2) 1 Oct - 17 Dec 1959 (8 eps)
(Season 3) 12 May - 22 Sept 1961
  (20 eps)
UK: ITV 27 Sept 1987 - 24 April 1988
  (LWT)

LAZARUS AND DINGWALL

Some detective show parodies are about as rewarding as being related to
Jessica Fletcher, but Lazarus and Dingwall, starring Stephen Frost and
Mark Arden from the popular British TV commercials for Carling Black
Label lager, is an honourable exception.

Steve Lazarus and Mark Dingwall ('Laz and Ding' to their mates) are
unlikely members of the Really Serious Crime Squad. Almost as funny as
Dempsey and Makepeace, their methods are at best chaotic, but somehow
they get results. Also in the team are the sultry Detective Beverly
Armitage, constantly fighting pig rustlers and Dingwall's amorous
advances; clothes-conscious Detectives One and Two who spend much of
their time debating the superiority of Lycra over Polyester and who want
to go undercover at an Acid House party but can't find suitably trendy
footwear; and Detective Clinton Clinton, a black undercover cop who is
so good at posing as a drug dealer that he's always being arrested as a
drug dealer. Their Chief is an eccentric father-figure, whose office is
equipped with all the essential modern crime-fighting technology –
stowaway bed, freezer filing cabinet and microwave oven.

There were some good jokes as they tackled cases ranging from the
smuggling of cocaine in the bellies of Colombian haddock, to an anti-
intellectual mutant rabbit which murders novelists. And because of
financial cutbacks, when they take out weapons Lazarus and Dingwall
are given just one bullet each and told: 'Be thrifty out there.'

Laz and Ding may be remarkably successful crime-fighters but I'm
sure Inspector Morse wouldn't want them on his team. I bet they don't
drink real ale.

REGULAR CAST

Lazarus Stephen Frost   *Dingwall* Mark Arden
Chief Peter Bland   *Armitage* Race Davies
Clinton Jim Findley   *Detective One* Simon Godley
Detective Two Neil Mullarkey

Creators: Kim Fuller, Vicky Pile
Director: Bob Spiers
Producer: Geoff Posner

A BBC Television Production

6 colour 30-minute episodes
UK: BBC2 1 Feb - 8 March 1991

LEGMEN

Other students work their way through college by finding jobs as waiters or barmen. Not Jack Gage and David Taylor. They wanted excitement as well as cash, so they became legmen for a seedy private eye named Oscar Armismendi. After a few episodes he was replaced by the more ruthless Tom Bannon, whose employment technique came straight out of Oliver Twist. He saw the boys as slave labour able to do his dirty work, which meant that, having started out on mundane chores like car re-possession, they found themselves dodging bullets. There were compensations, however, since as with the majority of private eye capers, the more dangerous the case, the more glamorous the women.

REGULAR CAST

Jack Gage Bruce Greenwood   *David Taylor* J.T. Terlsky
Oscar Armismendi Don Calfa   *Tom Bannon* Claude Akins

Producers: April Kelly, Alex Baton
Executive producers: Richard
  Chapman, Bill Dial, Andrew Mirisch

A Universal Television Production

8 colour 60-minute episodes
US: NBC 20 Jan - 16 March 1984
UK: ITV 21 Aug - 4 Dec 1984 (Thames)

LEG WORK

> 'Television is ready to stretch itself with a new creative concept which allows us to bring a true sense of reality to the world of the private investigator. It is art imitating life within the confines of commercial television.' – EXECUTIVE PRODUCER FRANK ABATEMARCO

Claire McCarron was witty, young and beautiful. But there was nothing glamorous about her job. A law school graduate, she gave up her post as an Assistant District Attorney to open her own private detective agency. And she soon discovered that the work isn't the endless diet of swimming pools, car chases, shoot-outs and champagne that some TV shows would have us believe. For her day consisted of endless meetings, interviews, paperwork, telephone calls, follow-ups on tips and scrounging for information – in short, leg work.

Her clients varied from understaffed district attorneys to defence attorneys; from insurance companies to major corporations; from private citizens to owners of small businesses. And first there was the task of being awarded an assignment and afterwards the even tougher one of getting paid.

Filmed entirely in New York, Leg Work also encompassed Claire's private life, spotlighting the problems and pressure s facing a single girl in New York in the late 1980s. Claire was played by Margaret Colin, whose own father spent 26 years as a member of the New York police Department. Indeed the show's technical adviser was a police officer who once worked with her father. The other principals were Claire's brother Fred, a public information officer with the NYPD, and her Assistant D.A. pal, Willie Pipal.

Leg Work was a valiant attempt to bring a little more realism into the world of the American private eye than had been displayed in the likes of Magnum and Remington Steele. Even if only for that reason it deserved a much longer life than the ten episodes it mustered. And the delightful Ms Colin alone was worth the admission money.

REGULAR CAST

Claire McCarron Margaret Colin   *Willie Pipal* Frances McDormand
Fred McCarron Patrick James Clarke

Creator: Frank Abatemarco
Producer: John Starke
Executive producer: Frank Abatemarco

10 colour 60-minute episodes
US: CBS 3 Oct - 5 Dec 1987
UK: ITV 15 April - 20 May 1988 (LWT)

*A Frank Abatemarco and Treasure Island
Production in association with
Twentieth Century Fox Television*

LIME STREET

After It Takes a Thief, Switch and Hart to Hart, the mere presence of Robert Wagner should have guaranteed success. It didn't with Lime Street. Wagner was James Greyson Culver, dapper investigator with an international insurance agency, whose main office was on Lime Street in London. Culver ran the Washington end while his British partner, Edward Wingate, once Culver's roommate at Oxford, looked after the London bureau.

Culver's job sent him on the trail of international criminals, jet-set embezzlers and killers rolling for high stakes – you wouldn't find him chasing those who had fallen behind with their 50p a week endowment insurance premiums. His cases took him to the playgrounds of the world but he was happiest back home on his sprawling ranch in Virginia, with his father, Henry, and daughters, Elizabeth and Margaret Ann.

The show also featured a number of British actors, notably John Standing as Wingate and Patrick Macnee. With big stars, exotic locations and plenty of action, it had all the ingredients. But someone got the recipe wrong and it folded after eight weeks.

REGULAR CAST

James Greyson Culver Robert Wagner   *Edward Wingate* John Standing
Elizabeth Culver Samantha Smith   *Margaret Ann Culver* Maia Brewton
Henry Wade Culver Lew Ayres   *Sir Geoffrey Rimbatten* Patrick Macnee

Creator: Linda Bloodworth Thomason
Producer: E. Jack Kaplan
Executive producers: Robert Wagner, Harry Thomason, Linda Bloodworth Thomason

An R.J./Mozark Production for Columbia Pictures Television

One colour 90-minute episode and 7 colour 60-minute episodes
US: ABC 21 Sept - 26 Oct 1985

THE LINEUP (SEE SAN FRANCISCO BEAT)

LOBO

A predictable slapstick spin-off from B.J. and the Bear, featuring the devious Sheriff Elroy P. Lobo of Orly County, Georgia. The first-season title was The Misadventures of Sheriff Lobo, but for the second season it was shortened to Lobo and the action moved to Atlanta, where the Sheriff, his inept brother-in-law, Deputy Perkins, and the naive, college-educated 'Birdie' Hawkins, were given jobs with a special city task force. Apparently the Governor of Atlanta had sent for the trio because he had been impressed by the low crime rate in Orly under Lobo's rule. But the reason there appeared to be little crime was because Lobo had forgotten to send in the figures. Needless to say, the country boys proved amazingly successful in their new surroundings, much to the irritation of the city cops.

* The Ballad of Sheriff Lobo was sung by Frankie Laine.

REGULAR CAST

Sheriff Elroy P. Lobo Claude Akins   *Deputy Perkins* Mills Watson
Deputy Birdwell 'Birdie' Hawkins Brian Kerwin

Executive producers: Glen A. Larson,   38 colour 60-minute episodes
   William P. D'Angelo   US: NBC 18 Sept 1979 - 25 Aug 1981

A Universal Television Production

LONGSTREET

Longstreet was television's blind detective, and it would have been better for all of us if we hadn't been able to see him either. For a show which purported to treat sensitively a serious issue, merely ended up as the most tasteless of all the Seventies' gimmick detective series. Far from evoking sympathy, Longstreet encouraged only laughter, as he prodded his way round the streets of New Orleans with his electronic cane and his Alsatian guide dog, Pax, still determined to track down the bad guys.

Mike Longstreet was an insurance-company investigator who, we were led to believe, was so expert at solving crimes that a gang of jewel robbers went to the trouble of trying to wipe him out before they pulled their next job, in case he put the finger on them. This was like Ronnie Biggs deciding to eliminate Shaw Taylor before the Great Train Robbery! But the resultant explosion killed Longstreet's wife, Ingrid, instead and left the investigator blinded for life. So with a sense of blind justice, Longstreet continued in business and set off on the trail of the killers, as if he had no greater inconvenience than a nasty cold.

He was helped by Nikki, his girl Friday, and by Duke Paige, his friend and workmate. Martial arts king Bruce Lee also put in an appearance, as Longstreet's self-defence instructor. But it was impossible to defend Longstreet and it was given the chop after one season.

* Longstreet's address in New Orleans was 835 Charters Street

REGULAR CAST

Mike Longstreet James Franciscus   *Nikki Bell* Marlyn Mason
Duke Paige Peter Mark Richman

Music: Billy Goldenberg, Robert Drasnin   24 colour 60-minute episodes
Producer: Joel Rogosin   US: ABC 9 Sept 1971 - 10 Aug 1972
Executive producer: Stirling Silliphant   UK: ITV 27 Jan - 24 March 1973 (ATV)

A Paramount Television Production

LORD PETER WIMSEY

'I am often asked why I like Wimsey so much. Well the answer is
because I identify so closely with him. In fact, to be absolutely truthful
I wish I had been him. He is such a bloody fine character.'
— IAN CARMICHAEL

It took Ian Carmichael five years to persuade a British television
company to adapt Dorothy L. Sayers' aristocratic sleuth, Lord Peter
Wimsey. Finally the BBC agreed. It was worth waiting for. Carmichael
had made a career out of playing upper-class twits such as P.G.
Wodehouse's Bertie Wooster and although he didn't exactly convey the
athletic prowess of the printed Wimsey, his interpretation was a delight.

The actor had been a Wimsey fan since 1938 when he saw the play
Busman's Holiday. 'We have a lot in common,' said Carmichael. 'Both
Lord Peter and I love good food, good wine, good music, good wit. And
cricket, of course. Wimsey has such a great sense of humour and depth
of character. He is a highly-educated man with a most erudite mind and
an encyclopedic knowledge of classical music. But there are times when
it does not suit him to look too intelligent. So I sometimes wear the
famous eyeglass. It serves a practical purpose when Wimsey wants to
look like a complete nincompoop.

'To Dorothy L. Sayers, Wimsey was a very real person. I was sent a
copy of The Papers Pertaining to the Family Wimsey which traced his
ancestry right back to the Duke Of Denver. All totally fictitious of
course.'

Clergyman's daughter Dorothy L. Sayers used to work in an
advertising agency where she thought up the famous slogan, 'Guinness
is good for you'. Lord Peter Wimsey was good for her, too, because
following his debut in Whose Body? in 1923, he went on to appear in 11
novels and 21 short stories up until In the Teeth of Evidence in 1940.

On the surface, Wimsey is the archetypal English aristocrat with the
monocle, the Savile Row suits and gormless sayings like 'Cheer-
frightfully-ho!' No wonder villains never regard him as much of a
threat. Yet as with Margery Allingham's Campion, the vacant exterior
hides a surprisingly sharp mind, able to unravel the most devious
criminal plan.

Wimsey solves crime for the sheer hell of it. His family motto is: 'As
my Whimsey takes me'. He certainly doesn't need the money but he
sees detection as a pastime which brings a little excitement into his life,

because being frightfully rich can be terribly dull. He lives in London at 110A Piccadilly, where his every whim is attended to by his manservant, Bunter, who had served under Lord Peter as a sergeant during the First World War. Bunter is Wimsey's equivalent of Dr Watson. The other regular character in this series was Detective Inspector Charles Parker, Wimsey's brother-in-law. But missing was Harriet Vane, although she did take a bow in a 1980s adaptation of the Wimsey stories (SEE DOROTHY L. SAYERS MYSTERY). Carmichael had wanted to include Harriet and had hoped to shoot a dramatization of Strong Poison, in which she was introduced, but a strike by BBC production assistants restricted the choice to a novel that could be filmed mainly on location. So Five Red Herrings was chosen instead, with Strong Poison eventually being adapted as a BBC radio play starring Carmichael. Even so the producers did indulge in a little poetic licence with Five Red Herrings. The book was set in high summer but the TV version was shot in mid-winter in the wilds of Galloway in Scotland.

Lord Peter Wimsey was the perfect antidote to all those detective series with screeching tyres and screeching cops. It harked back to the golden days of detective writing where even murderers had manners. Where else would a killing be described as an 'unpleasantness'? It was gentle, refined, terribly English and a credit to all concerned.

REGULAR CAST

Lord Peter Wimsey Ian Carmichael   *Bunter* Glyn Houston
Det. Insp. Parker Mark Eden

Clouds of Witness

Wimsey's brother, Gerald, Duke of Denver, is accused of the murder of their sister Mary's fiance. On hearing the news, Lord Peter at once flies over from Paris.

GUEST STARS:

David Langton, Georgina Cookson
Dramatized by Anthony Steven
Director: Hugh David

The Unpleasantness at the Bellona Club

During the two-minute silence on Armistice Day, old General Fentinan is murdered in his favourite armchair at his private club.

Wimsey steps in to solve this frightfully bad show.

GUEST STARS:

Terence Alexander, John Welsh, Clifford Rose
Dramatized by Anthony Steven
Director: Ronald Wilson

Murder Must Advertise

When a young man falls to his death down a spiral staircase at Pym's Publicity, it transpires that foul play was afoot. Lord Peter sets out to trap the killer, by going undercover as a copywriter in the world of advertising.

GUEST STARS:

Peter Bowles, Shirley Cain, Christopher
  Timothy
Dramatized by Bill Craig
Director: Rodney Bennett

GUEST STARS:

John Junkin, James Copeland, Russell
  Hunter
Dramatized by Anthony Steven
Director: Robert Tronson

Producer: Richard Beynon

A BBC Television Production

The Nine Tailors

Wimsey finds himself involved in the
mystery of a dead man's identity, when an
unknown corpse is found in someone else's
grave. The corpse is bound with bell-ringer's
ropes (the title refers to the nine bells that toll
when a man dies).

GUEST STARS:

Patrick Jordan, Gail Harrison
Dramatized by Anthony Steven
Director: Raymond Menmuir

Five Red Herrings

Wimsey and Bunter head for a peaceful
holiday in the Galloway Hills. Wimsey
intends to fish and Bunter plans to paint.
Instead they stumble over a body.

UK: BBC1 CLOUDS OF WITNESS
5 colour 45-minute episodes
5 April - 3 May 1972
THE UNPLEASANTNESS AT THE
  BELLONA CLUB
4 colour 45-minute episodes
1 - 22 Feb 1973
MURDER MUST ADVERTISE
4 colour 50-minute episodes
30 Nov - 21 Dec 1973
THE NINE TAILORS
4 colour 55-minute episodes
22 April - 13 May 1974
FIVE RED HERRINGS
4 colour 50-minute episodes
23 July - 13 Aug 1975
US: 'Masterpiece Theatre' From 1972

MACGRUDER AND LOUD

A half-baked idea about two US police officers, Malcolm MacGruder and
Jenny Loud, who teamed up as detectives to investigate the death of Mac's
ex-partner and thereafter got themselves into all sorts of crazy situations.
What made their situation even more chaotic was that they were trying to
keep the fact that they were married a secret, because it contravened
departmental policy. A pity they didn't keep this series to themselves too.

REGULAR CAST

Malcolm MacGruder John Getz   *Jenny Loud* Kathryn Harrold

Producer: Jerry London
Executive producers: Aaron Spelling,
  Douglas S. Cramer

An Aaron Spelling Production

One colour 120-minute episode and 12
  colour 60-minute episodes US: ABC
  20 Jan - 10 Sept 1985
UK: ITV 8 April 1988 (LWT) (TV movie
  only shown)

MADIGAN

Sergeant Dan Madigan was one of the most miserable men on television. By nature, the New York police detective was a loner. Not that he had much choice, for his cold, abrasive exterior hardly made him the ideal party guest. He would have been as out of place as the Pope on a Club 18-30 holiday. Yet rumour had it that beneath the surface lay a heart of gold, not granite, and it was just that Madigan didn't like to indicate that he might have character flaws like emotions. As it was, his whole life revolved around work – home was nothing more than a spartan one-room apartment.

In the US, Madigan aired as part of the NBC Wednesday Mystery Movie, with Banacek and Cool Million. The character was actually based on a 1968 film (also starring Richard Widmark) in which Madigan died. Sometimes it was hard to tell whether or not he was still dead.

REGULAR CAST

Sgt Dan Madigan Richard Widmark

EPISODE TITLES

The Manhattan Beat
The Midtown Beat
The Lisbon Beat
The London Beat
The Naples Beat
The Park Avenue Beat

Producer: Roland Kibbee
Executive producers: Dean Hargrove, Frank Rosenberg

A Universal Television Production

6 colour 90-minute episodes
US: NBC 20 Sept 1972 - 22 Aug 1973
UK: ITV From 17 Feb 1973

MAGNUM, P.I.

'I did eight years of Magnum and I was totally committed to it – so committed that I turned down the Harrison Ford role in Raiders of the Lost Ark.'
— TOM SELLECK

The reason for the popularity of Magnum, P.I. lay firmly with its star. Tom's Selleck's casual shirts, moustache and performing eyebrows brought him a vast female following, up to 10,000 fan letters a week.

The actor became one of America's prime-time sex symbols, even though he admits his screen image was far removed from his private persona. 'I've never been terribly outgoing and being what is called a "sex symbol" brings a lot of unknown factors you'd never imagine into your life. Enough to say that being quite a shy kind of guy in a profession where you spend all the time in the limelight allegedly sipping champagne can be quite strenuous.'

Selleck was a virtual unknown when he appeared in a couple of episodes of The Rockford Files as smug P.I. Lance White. His comic talents caught the eye and scriptwriters were sent away to think of a suitable vehicle for him. Some six months later, he was former Vietnam Naval intelligence veteran-turned-private eye Thomas Magnum.

The pilot show for Magnum, Don't Eat the Snow in Hawaii, was full of Vietnam flashbacks, but the series proper knew its place was beneath the palm trees of Honolulu. It replaced Hawaii Five-O in the CBS schedule (Magnum occasionally referred to Steve McGarrett) and had an immediate financial appeal to CBS, who were thus able to make further use of the splendid Hawaiian production facilities that they had built for Five-O.

Although a lot of ladies wanted to see him on his back, Thomas Magnum landed on his feet. In return for helping with the security on the palatial Oahu estate of wealthy writer Robin Masters (who remained forever unseen), Magnum was given a rather pleasant roof over his head, a beachfront abode on Oahu's north shore. It was part of the estate and what's more, it was free. The bad news was that Masters was always away somewhere, leaving his pompous British manservant Higgins (a dreadful stereotype, played by American actor John Hillerman) in charge of the estate. Higgins and Magnum did not see eye to eye, possibly because Hillerman was 5 ft. 7in. and Selleck 6ft. 4in. Higgins was an ex-sergeant major and his military precision conflicted sharply with Magnum's laid-back approach. Higgins also objected to the way in which Magnum drove around in Masters' $60,000 red Ferrari as if he owned it. But Higgins did extract some satisfaction by quietly encouraging his two Dobermann pinschers, Zeus and Apollo, who guarded the estate, to take lumps out of Magnum at every available opportunity.

When he wasn't surrounded by beautiful women, Magnum was surrounded by two of his wartime buddies, T.C. and Rick, who helped on his investigations. T.C. was a helicopter pilot who ran his own chopper service, Island Hoppers, and Rick, who understandably detested his real name, Orville, owned a Honolulu nightclub modelled on Bogart's in Casablanca. Soon, however, he sold it and went into partnership with the elusive Robin Masters in the exclusive King Kamehameha Beach Club.

Tom Selleck's enormous appeal and flair for comedy guided the show through what were, at times, some pretty mediocre scripts. After seven successful seasons, he decided enough was enough but was persuaded back for an eighth. By then, Three Men and a Baby had established him as a major Hollywood attraction too, and this time Magnum really did bite the bullet.

* Frank Sinatra made a guest appearance in an episode of Magnum, P.I. as a New York cop.

REGULAR CAST

Thomas Magnum Tom Selleck   *Jonathan Quale Higgins III* John Hillerman
Theodore 'T.C.' Calvin Roger E. Mosley   *Orville 'Rick' Wright* Larry Manetti
Robin Masters (voice) Orson Welles   *Lt MacReynolds* Jeff McKay
Lt Tanaka Kwan Hi Lim   *Lt Poole* Jean Bruce Scott

Creators: Donald P. Bellisario, Glen Larson
Executive producers: Donald P. Bellisario, Glen Larson

A Universal Television Production

150 colour 60-minute episodes and 6 colour 120-minute episodes US: CBS 11 Dec 1980 - 2 May 1988
UK: ITV 23 May 1981 - 14 Sept 1987 (Thames)

MAIGRET

'At last I have found the perfect Maigret.' – book inscription from
GEORGES SIMENON to RUPERT DAVIES

On Monday evenings in the early 1960's, millions of British viewers tuned in to watch actor Rupert Davies strike a match on a wall and light up his pipe, to herald another adventure for Georges Simenon's illustrious Parisian detective, Maigret. In his trilby hat and belted mac, Davies looked every inch the part – and Simenon agreed wholeheartedly. Before filming, Davies and series producer Andrew Osborn went to France to meet the author. Simenon took one look and beamed: 'He is Maigret!' His only reservation was that the actor's hair was too long.

Davies certainly had one thing in common with Maigret – he was an inveterate pipe-smoker, with over 40 pipes and a dozen different kinds of tobacco. At the height of his fame, he became mildly irritated by the public continually writing to him and asking for pipes, pouches and tobacco. 'People must think I chew up two pipes an episode,' he moaned.

Chief Inspector Maigret was a thoughtful police detective who obtained results by studying character rather than clues. One of his favourite ploys was to interview suspects by calling on them at their homes, in preference to bringing them to his off ice. He found he learned more about them in their own surroundings. He was a devoted husband and there was always room on his desk for a framed photograph of Mme Maigret. His colleagues at the Surete included his sidekick Lucas, the young and eager Sergeant Lapointe and Inspector Lognon.

Simenon's books had been translated into 25 languages and in France had actually been responsible for a change in the public's attitude towards the police. French policemen had once been regarded with very little sympathy or affection but Maigret came along and changed all that. Aware of the BBC's reputation for quality drama, Simenon encouraged them to make a series. He was not disappointed.

Apart from his delight at the central casting (he also sent Davies a bottle of liqueur inscribed 'To the English Maigret from the French Maigret. Bravo!'), Simenon was rewarded for his faith by a classy production, right down to Ron Grainer's familiar theme music. The long-defunct Reynolds News described the show as being 'as French as Gauloises and garlic'.

Whether it would bear repeating today is another matter. There were some unfortunate moments. I well remember a close-up of a corpse with a knife in his chest and the 'dead' actor was breathing so heavily that the lethal weapon visibly moved up and down on screen. And not everyone was impressed by Maigret's lifestyle; the Reverend George Boffin of Cleckheaton, Yorkshire, launched a stinging attack on the drinking habits of both Maigret and that other reprobate, George Dixon. 'Maigret drinks such a lot it's surprising he doesn't fall flat on his face in the middle of every programme,' he said. 'It amazes me he can stay sober enough to arrest anyone. And Dixon spends too much of his off-duty time in the local. I see no reason why Dixon and Maigret shouldn't drink tea and ginger pop instead of pints of ale and bottles of wine.' Quite.

Maigret made Rupert Davies a household name. In 1963, the series' final season, he was voted TV Actor of the Year. He bought the black Citroen used in the programme and the study of his London home was crammed with Maigret memorabilia, including a bowl of pipes. But then things started to go downhill; he starred in a Maigret play in the West End but it folded after 20 performances, and he walked off the set of a Maigret film after ten days, disagreeing with the script and choice of director. Maigret was to end up haunting Rupert Davies. He had become completely typecast and found work worthy of his talents difficult to come by, right up until his death from cancer in 1976.

REGULAR CAST

Chief Insp. Maigret Rupert Davies   *Lucas* Ewen Solon
Mme Maigret Helen Shingler   *Sgt Lapointe* Neville Jason
Insp. Lognon Henry Oscar

Creator: Georges Simenon
Music: Ron Grainer
Producer: Andrew Osborn

A BBC Television Production

52 monochrome 50-minute episodes
UK: BBC (Season 1) 31 Oct 1960 - 23
Jan 1961 (13 eps)
(Season 2) 23 Oct 1961 - 15 Jan 1962
(13 eps)
(Season 3) 24 Sept - 17 Dec 1962 (13
eps)
(Season 4) 1 Oct - 24 Dec 1963 (13 eps)

* On 21 May 1988, Richard Harris starred in a Maigret television film made by HTV. The critics dubbed it 'McGray' because of the Irish actor's failure to come up with anything remotely resembling a French accent.

* Maigret is set to return in 1992 starring Michael Gambon.

MAN AGAINST CRIME

'Somebody must be murdered, preferably early, with the threat of more violence to come.'   – INSTRUCTION TO WRITERS

The anti-violence lobby would have had a field day with Man Against Crime, a rough and raw live American crime series from the early 1950's. It made Miami Vice look like Sesame Street. The 'man' in the title was rugged New York private eye, Mike Barnett, so tough he didn't need to carry a gun. Instead he fought with fists that would have reduced Mike Tyson to rubble. Barnett had plenty of opportunity to practise since the show's writers were also told that he 'must be menaced early and often.' For the first three years the adventures of loner Barnett were transmitted live from the CBS studios at Grand Central Station, New York, with Ralph Bellamy as the lead, although he did take a break in the summer of 1951, during which Robert Preston stood in as Barnett's brother, Pat. From 1952, the series was filmed and then it left CBS and took the unprecedented step of being scheduled simultaneously on two different networks, NBC and DuMont, at 10.30 pm on a Sunday. This situation prevailed for six months until, following another rest, Man Against Crime returned as a live show in 1956, with Frank Lovejoy taking over the role of Mike Barnett.

A feature of Man Against Crime in its live days was that every episode contained a search scene towards the end, in which Barnett would comb a room for a vital clue. Because it was live, signals from the production crew told him how long he should take – if the show was under-running, he could take his time, if it was over-running, he would find the clue straight away!

The programme sponsor was Camel cigarettes, which accounted for why only the good guys smoked, always doing so gracefully. And nobody ever coughed.

REGULAR CAST

Mike Barnett (1949 - 54) Ralph Bellamy
Mike Barnett (1956) Frank Lovejoy
Pat Barnett (1951) Robert Preston

Producers: Edward J. Montagne, Paul Nickell
82 monochrome 30-minute episodes

US: CBS/NBC/DuMont 7 Oct 1949 - 19 Aug 1956

THE MAN BEHIND THE BADGE

A live semi-documentary series which presented dramatized reconstructions of real cases. Most of the stories concentrated on the police but the 'badge' also referred on occasions to park rangers, public defenders and parole officers, and sometimes the 'man' was a policewoman or lady judge. Among the actors who appeared were Jack Warden and a young Leslie Nielsen.

Host/narrator: Norman Rose
Producers: Jerry Robertson, Bernard Prockter

Approx. 26 monochrome 30-minute episodes US: CBS 11 Oct 1953 - 3 Oct 1954

A CBS Production

* After the CBS series went off the air, a syndicated film version of The Man Behind the Badge was produced, narrated by Charles Bickford.

A Buckeye Production

38 monochrome 30-minute episodes US: Syndicated Jan 1955

A MAN CALLED IRONSIDE (US TITLE: IRONSIDE)

'I received scores of letters from fans convinced that I was disabled. There was a story that I had a war wound. People were amazed to see me stand up.'
— RAYMOND BURR

Having spent nine years as Perry Mason, Raymond Burr vowed that he would never become involved in another long-running TV series. But 18 months after Perry conducted his final defence, Burr found himself in a role that would necessitate him spending the best part of the next eight years in a wheelchair. Burr, whose accumulated wealth from Perry Mason had brought him his own personal Pacific island, Naitauba near Fiji, had initial misgivings. 'After Mason I thought I'd never do another TV series. Then I did a two-hour TV play about a detective who got shot and had to spend the rest of his waking and working life in a wheelchair. Afterwards I forgot about it because I'd gone back to my island. But when the TV play was shown it was a fantastic success. Before I knew it, I was back in Hollywood and into Ironside.'

Ironside's wheelchair 'gimmick' really came about by accident. Burr explains: 'What happened was that we never thought that Ironside would make a series. We just did the movie in which he was paralyzed. But it was so successful they wanted to make a series out of the character and there was no way we could suddenly have him walking about again. So he stayed in the wheelchair. But it turned out a plus because it gave a whole new edge to the character.'

Robert T. Ironside had been a member of the San Francisco Police Department for 25 years and had risen to the rank of Chief of Detectives when a potential assassin's bullet grazed his spine, leaving him paralyzed from the waist down. He could no longer continue on the force as a regular cop but he managed to persuade Police Commissioner Randall to employ him as a special consultant. In effect, the wheelchair-bound Ironside did exactly the same work as before, except he now solved all his cases sitting down.

Conveniently, he was allowed to keep his two assistants, Detective Sergeant Ed Brown and Policewoman Eve Whitfield, and added to the team was reformed tearaway, Mark Sanger, who acted as Ironside's bodyguard and wheelchair-pusher-in-chief, as he hauled his boss in and out of the specially-equipped police van that was used for transport. Barbara Anderson, who played Eve Whitfield, left after four seasons over a contractual dispute and was replaced by Elizabeth Baur as Fran Belding. Ironside lived and worked in a converted attic at the police headquarters and, even in a wheelchair, was such an imposing figure that Ed and Eve only ever dared call him 'Chief'.

Although this was one of the ultimate defective detective shows, it was infinitely more acceptable than Longstreet (SEE LONGSTREET). Much of that was due to its charismatic star but the scripts, especially at first, were much sharper too, marred only by those irritating finales where Ironside adopted the drawing-room style favoured by so many sleuths, to explain precisely what had been going on for the previous hour.

Raymond Burr's declining health was the principal reason for the show's eventual termination. In 1974 he suffered a heart attack on a plane as it was about to take off, and lay in a coma for two days. He said: 'As soon as I came round, the doctors told me to quit chain-smoking and lose 100lb.' He fought a constant battle with his weight and confessed at the time: 'Twenty stone is a lot to carry around even with the help of a wheelchair when I'm working.' Further illness resulted in another spell in hospital, causing several episodes to be hastily re-written to feature him as little as possible.

So, not surprisingly, Burr decided he had seen enough of Ironside and retreated to his island. Universal chiefs briefly contemplated taking the mountain to Mohammed and setting a series on Naitauba called Ironside in Paradise, but thankfully it was not to be. Burr reflected: 'We had six marvellous years of Ironside but after that the scripts were only acceptable, not great.'

REGULAR CAST

Chief Robert T. Ironside Raymond Burr   Det. Sgt Ed Brown Don Galloway
Eve Whitfield Barbara Anderson   Fran Belding Elizabeth Baur
Mark Sanger Don Mitchell   Commissioner Dennis Randall Gene Lyons
Lt Carl Reese Johnny Seven

Creator: Collier Young
Music: Monty Paich, Oliver Nelson
Executive producers: Cy Chermak, Joel
   Rogosin

A Harbour Production for Universal
   Television

188 colour 60-minute episodes and 7
   colour 120-minute episodes US: NBC
   14 Sept 1967 - 16 Jan 1975
UK: BBC1 8 Oct 1967 - 27 Feb 1976

MANCUSO FBI

Nick Mancuso was the cynical FBI agent who solved international crises at the drop of his hat. He tackled Asian drugs barons, government corruption and the Israeli secret service, each case having the potential to destroy civilization as we know it. And he cracked every one in 50 minutes. He could probably have sorted out Watergate before the first commercial break.

Mancuso was a throwback to the days of J. Edgar Hoover – he even dressed as if he was from a bygone age. Yet despite the changes to the Bureau over the years, he still managed to survive in Washington DC, always heading off at a tangent but coming up with the right solution. Mancuso was his own man. He didn't take kindly to advice, particularly from his new boss, the ambitious Eddie McMasters, who regarded him as something of a dinosaur. McMasters was furious that Mancuso never adhered to the rules but old Nick had forgotten more than the young upstart ever knew. McMasters may have been running the department but he was barely capable of running a bath.

Naturally Mancuso worked alone, which rendered his loyal secretary, Jean St John, fairly inactive. So, with nothing else to do, Jean just used to hang around looking tall. The other regulars were young lawyer Kristin Carter, who acted as liaison between the Justice department and the FBI, and forensic expert Dr Paul Summers, Mancuso's friend and occasional confidant.

Mancuso was not dissimilar to Quincy in that he infuriated his superiors, didn't mind whose feathers he ruffled to get at the truth and always ended up being proved right. He was my kinda guy.

REGULAR CAST

Nick Mancuso Robert Loggia   *Eddie McMasters* Frederic Lehne
Jean St John Randi Brazen   *Kristin Carter* Lindsay Frost
Dr Paul Summers Charles Siebert

Creator: Steve Sohner
Music: Dennis McCarthy
Producers: Jacob Epstein, Ken Solarz
Executive producers: Steve Sohner,
    Jeff Bleckner

A Steve Sohner Production for NBC

19 colour 60-minute episodes
US: NBC 13 Oct 1989 - 18 May 1990
UK: BBC1 3 Sept 1990 - 18 March 1991

THE MAN FROM INTERPOL

Son of Interpol Calling! Rightly consigned to anonymity, this 'no expense spent' crime drama was shot in front of sets that looked as if they had been rustled up by a class of five-year-olds. The action purported to relate the adventures of a high-ranking Interpol agent, Commander Anthony Smith, on secondment to Scotland Yard. Tedious in the extreme – The Man From Interflora would have been more exciting.

REGULAR CAST

Anthony Smith Richard Wyler   *Det. Insp. Mercer* John Longden

Music: Tony Crombie

A Danziger Brothers Production

39 monochrome 30-minute episodes
UK: Syndicated 1960
US: NBC 30 Jan - 22 Oct 1960

MANHUNT

Police and Press are sometimes sworn enemies but here they worked hand in hand. Detective Lieutenant Howard Finucane of the San Diego Police Department and Ben Andrews of the Chronicle were old friends, both hard-nosed professionals who knew the score. They needed each other in the constant battle against mobsters and murderers. Added to which, Finucane must have been glad to hear the voice of experience because, for the rest of the time, he was helped out by a succession of young detectives. Each appeared in a dozen or so episodes, part of Screen Gems' drive to discover new talent, a sort of Opportunity Cops. A measure of its success can be judged by the fact that none have been heard of since.

REGULAR CAST

Det. Lt Howard Finucane Victor Jory   *Ben Andrews* Patrick McVey
Det. George Peters (eps 1 - 13) Charles Bateman
Det. Bruce Hanna (14 - 23) Rian Garrick
Det. Dan Kramer (24 - 39) Chuck Henderson
Det. Paul Kirk (40 - 52) Michael Steffany
Det. Phil Burns (53 - 65) Robert Crawford
Det. Carl Spencer (66 - 78) Todd Armstrong

Producer: Jerry Briskin

A Screen Gems/Columbia Production

78 monochrome 30-minute episodes
US: Syndicated Sept 1959 - 1960

THE MANHUNTER

Dave Barrett became a private investigator to avenge the death of his best friend. A former Marine, Dave ran a farm in Idaho during the Depression years of the 1930s but, when his pal was killed by bank robbers, he decided to exchange rounding up sheep for rounding up criminals just like the ones who shot his buddy. So he trekked back and forth across America, only lingering long enough in any one town to bring the baddies to justice. He was so successful that he was in danger of putting the police out of a job. He did occasionally pause between expeditions though, to see his sister Lizabeth and his folks back home.

* Dave's second best friend was his dog, Beau.

REGULAR CAST

Dave Barrett Ken Howard   *Sheriff Paul Tate* Robert Hogan
Lizabeth Barrett Hilary Thompson

Music: Duane Tatro
Producer: Sam Rolfe
Executive producer: Quinn Martin

24 colour 60-minute episodes
US: CBS 11 Sept 1974 - 9 April 1975
UK: ITV From 4 March 1976 (LWT)

A Quinn Martin Production

MANIMAL

Arrant nonsense about Jonathan Chase, a New York professor of criminology, with the ability and apparently the desire, to transform himself into the animal of his choosing, so that he could solve crimes. As his breathing intensified, his hands contracted and whiskers and fangs sprouted from his face. Well, it's one way of making sure you get a seat on the bus. His piece de resistance was his panther but he also did a jolly passable cobra. But for all Chase's crime-busting skills, one mystery remained unsolved during his manic metamorphosis – what happened to his clothes?

Only two people knew about his quick-change act – Ty Earle, his black helper and Brooke McKenzie, a pretty police detective. But they didn't have to keep the secret for long because, after eight totally unremarkable episodes, Jonathan Chase transformed himself into a dodo.

REGULAR CAST

Jonathan Chase Simon MacCorkindale   *Brooke McKenzie* Melody Anderson
Ty Earle Michael D. Roberts   *Lt Rivera* Reni Santoni

Creator/Producer: Glen A. Larson

A Glen Larson Production

One colour 90-minute episode and 7
colour 60-minute episodes
US: NBC 30 Sept - 31 Dec 1983
UK: BBC1 4 June - 23 July 1984

THE MAN IN ROOM 17

A terribly British series about a pair of academic criminologists who were able to solve the most baffling crimes purely by logic, without ever leaving their room. The 'man' in the title was Oldenshaw, a former barrister who had been asked to form 'Room 17', a special government department designed to explore crime and the criminal mind. His colleague in the first season was Dimmock, once a student at Ohio University's Institute for Criminology. He was replaced during the second season by the splendidly-named Imlac Defraits but re-joined Oldenshaw in a spin-off series (SEE THE FELLOWS).

The team were given cases which had defeated the police and other supposedly finely-tuned minds, and ranged from espionage to intricate whodunnits. And through it all they remained in their room, the only contact with the outside world being civil servant Sir Geoffrey Norton.

REGULAR CAST

Oldenshaw Richard Vernon *Dimmock* Michael Aldridge
Defraits Denholm Elliott *Sir Geoffrey* Willoughby Goddard

Creator: Robin Chapman
Producer: Richard Everitt

*A Granada Television Network
Production*

26 monochrome 60-minute episodes
UK: ITV (Season 1) 11 June - 3 Sept
1965 (13 eps)
(Season 2) 8 April - 1 July 1966(13 eps)

MAN IN A SUITCASE

McGill was a travelling salesman with menaces. He journeyed across Europe carrying nothing more than a leather suitcase. But the contents were not lavatory brushes and dusters but a change of clothes and a gun. For McGill was a modern-day bounty hunter, yet he never enjoyed the taste of paradise – he was too busy looking over his shoulder, fearful of being betrayed by his ex CIA colleagues.

McGill had been thrown out of American Intelligence after being wrongly accused of failing to stop an eminent scientist from defecting to Russia. It was a treasonable offence. Forced to find a new means of income, he turned private investigator at a fee of $500 a day plus expenses. He became known as the Man in a Suitcase.

McGill was a tough cookie and while scouring the European underworld in search of the evidence that could establish his innocence, he took on a whole host of cases, even the most innocuous of which invariably ended in a fight.

A good action series in its day, Man in a Suitcase unfortunately tends to be overlooked now, in favour of that other 'loner' series of the 1960s, The Fugitive.

* Guest stars included Donald Sutherland and Edward Fox

REGULAR CAST

McGill Richard Bradford

An ITC Production

Creators: Richard Harris, Dennis
  Spooner
Title music: Ron Grainer
Producer: Sidney Cole

30 colour 60-minute episodes
UK: ITV 27 Sept 1967 - 17 April 1968
US: ABC 3 May - 20 Sept 1968 (28 eps)

MANNIX

'What's wrong with fighting for what is right? John Wayne always did it in the movies. It's the American way. You stand up for what you believe in. I certainly don't consider the manly art of self-defence to be violent.'   – MIKE CONNORS

Despite its star's protestations to the contrary, Mannix did overdo the violence. Not even Muhammad Ali had as many fights as Joe Mannix. If there wasn't a full-scale punch-up in the first 15 minutes, you thought you were watching the wrong programme.

For the first season, Mannix was a Los Angeles private eye employed by a large detective agency called Intertect. The company had installed all the latest computer equipment but Mannix preferred more traditional detection methods. His tried and trusted way of obtaining answers was by hitting people – hard.

At the beginning of the second season, he had set up on his own in an office in the building at 17 Paseo Verde where he lived. His secretary was Peggy Fair, a classy black lady whose husband, a former police officer and friend of Joe's, had been killed in action. Peggy was trouble. Instead of sticking to her secretarial duties, she was forever becoming involved in cases and had an alarming habit of getting herself kidnapped. This of course served as an excuse for Mannix to thump a few people.

Other arrivals on the scene were L.A.P.D. Lieutenants Adam Tobias (played by Robert Reed of The Defenders) and George Kramer (played by Larry Linville, soon to be promoted to Major as the incomparable Frank Burns in M*A*S*H). Lou Wickersham, Mannix 's old boss at Intertect, also put in the odd appearance, but the most celebrated guest was in the first season, when the cameo role of a night-club singer was taken by Neil Diamond.

As the fists continued to fly almost as fast as the cliches, the show came under increasing fire. CBS ordered the producers to reduce the violence until eventually, after eight seasons, Mannix was cancelled. In spite of its shortcomings, it was a popular series in the US, mainly due to the athletic Connors. But it flopped in the UK.

REGULAR CAST

Joe Mannix Mike Connors   *Peggy Fair* Gail Fisher
Lt Adam Tobias Robert Reed   *Lt George Kramer* Larry Linville
Lou Wickersham Joseph Campanella

Creators: Richard Levinson, William Link
Music: Lalo Schifrin
Producers: Ivan Goff, Ben Roberts
Executive producer: Bruce Geller

A Paramount Television Production

193 colour 60-minute episodes
US: CBS (Season 1) 16 Sept 1967 - 16 March 1968 (24 eps)
(Season 2) 28 Sept 1968 - 12 April 1969 (25 eps)
(Season 3) 27 Sept 1969 - 21 March 1970 (25 eps)

(Season 4) 19 Sept 1970 - 13 March 1971 (24 eps)
(Season 5) 15 Sept 1971 - 8 March 1972 (24 eps)
(Season 6) 17 Sept 1972 - 11 March 1973 (24 eps)
(Season 7) 16 Sept 1973 - 31 March 1974 (24 eps)
(Season 8) 29 Sept 1974 - 13 April 1975 (23 eps)
UK: ITV 13 Feb - 27 March 1971 (ATV)
ITV 14 Nov 1980 - 19 Oct 1983 (LWT)

MAN WITH A CAMERA

Memorable solely for the fact that a young Charles Bronson played the lead. Mike Kovac (Bronson) had been a war photographer before turning freelance in which guise he accepted jobs from a variety of sources – insurance companies, newspapers and the police. But unlike most press photographers, who don't hang around a second longer than they have to in case they miss opening time, Kovac found himself enmeshed in cases of mystery and murder and thus operated more as a detective than a humble snapper. When he was really in the dark, he sought the help of his father, Anton. Suffice it to say that this was by no means the highspot of Bronson's career.

REGULAR CAST

Mike Kovac Charles Bronson   *Anton Kovac* Ludwig Stossel
Lt Donovan James Flavin

Producers: Warren Lewis, Don Sharpe

An MCW Production

29 monochrome 30-minute episodes
US: ABC (Season 1) 10 Oct 1958 - 23 Jan 1959 (15 eps)
(Season 2) 19 Oct 1959 - 8 Feb 1960 (14 eps)

MARKHAM

That fine actor, Ray Milland, starred in this convincing series about Roy Markham, a polished and wealthy attorney who fancied a little more excitement than the courtroom could provide, and decided to set up as a private investigator. Markham was so rich that he didn't really have to work for a living and was thus able to vary his charges according to the client's circumstances. If he was looking into a case of corporate fraud for a big company, he could charge an astronomical fee, but if he was trying to get a poor girl's husband off a murder rap, he would more than likely provide his services free.

Markham was based in New York but his cases took him all over the world. For the first two months he had an assistant, John Riggs, to do the legwork but once he left, Markham conducted very much a solo operation. Ray Milland also narrated the series.

REGULAR CAST

Roy Markham Ray Milland   *John Riggs* Simon Scott

Producers: Joe Sistiam, Warren Duff

A Universal Television Production

60 monochrome 30-minute episodes
US: CBS 2 May 1959 - 22 Sept 1960

MARK SABER

Mark Saber underwent more personality changes than Dr Jekyll. He started out as a British cop working for the homicide team of a big-city US police department, but ended up as a one-armed private detective in London.

The first Mark Saber series was American and starred Tom Conway, with James Burke as his sidekick, the loyal but not awfully bright Sergeant Tim Maloney. This Saber reflected the American view of the British at the time – he was dapper with a pencil-thin moustache and wore smart pinstriped suits. It was initially known as Mystery Theatre before being re-named Inspector Mark Saber – Homicide Squad, in 1952.

It ended in 1954 and then production switched to Britain for 52 programmes known as 'Mark Saber' in the UK and 'The Vise' in the US. Saber mark two had lost a limb and gone private, and most of his cases were set in London. The cast had changed too. South African-born Donald Gray, who had lost an arm in the war, took over as Saber, with Michael Balfour as his leg man, Barny O'Keefe. Other characters included his vivacious blonde secretary, Stephanie, and Scotland Yard Inspectors, Brady and Chester.

Next came Saber of London, in which our hero's adventures took him to the glamour spots of Europe, including Paris and the French Riviera. With the departure of O'Keefe, he got through three more assistants – Peter Paulson, Bob Page and Eddie Wells, the latter a reformed crook. Stephanie also vanished and the female interest was briefly provided by Saber's girlfriend, Ann Summers. There was a new Scotland Yard detective too – Inspector Parker – although he was played by Colin Tapley, who had previously been Chester.

Despite, or possibly because of his disability, Donald Gray was a popular actor of the time and managed to sustain the show through some dreadful storylines. The public took to the gallant Saber as, even with the odds stacked against him, he always managed to defeat the able-bodied. Somehow he typified that British bulldog spirit.

* Just to add to the complications, Saber of London was syndicated in the US as Detective's Diary.

INSPECTOR MARK SABER – HOMICIDE SQUAD

REGULAR CAST

Mark Saber Tom Conway   *Sgt Tim Maloney* James Burke

Director: Eugene Forde
Producers: J. Donald Wilson, Roland Reed

78 monochrome 30-minute episodes
US: ABC 5 Oct 1951 - June 1954

MARK SABER (US TITLE THE VISE)

REGULAR CAST

Mark Saber Donald Gray   *Barny O'Keefe* Michael Balfour
Stephanie Ames Diana Decker   *Insp. Brady* Patrick Holt
Insp. Chester Colin Tapley

Producers: Edward and Harry Lee
   Danziger
52 monochrome 30-minute episodes

UK: ITV 18 Sept 1957 - 22 June 1959
US: ABC Dec 1955 - June 1957

SABER OF LONDON

REGULAR CAST

Mark Saber Donald Gray   *Peter Paulson* Neil McCallum
   Bob Page Robert Arden   *Eddie Wells* Jerry Thorne
      Insp. Parker Colin Tapley

Producers: Edward and Harry Lee
   Danziger
83 monochrome 30-minute episodes

UK: ITV 12 Aug 1959 - 30 Aug 1961
US: NBC 13 Oct 1957 - 15 May 1960

MARLOWE – PRIVATE EYE

'Too often he has been played as a seedy man in a raincoat. That's not the man that was written by Chandler. Marlowe was tough but not a tough guy. He was not middle-aged, he was not world-weary. He always had hope. So I went back to the stories, stripped away all that I'd seen on screen before and started from the essence.'
                                    – PRODUCER DAVID WICKES

It is a brave man that attempts to tamper with the public's image of a character as well-known as Philip Marlowe. It is rather like doing a remake of Lassie with a dachshund. But David Wickes' gamble paid off with a splendidly atmospheric re-creation of Raymond Chandler's celebrated private eye.

Marlowe is one of the world's truly great detectives. He first appeared in print in the late 1930s and graduated to big screen prominence in films such as Farewell My Lovely with Dick Powell (1944), The Big Sleep, first with Humphrey Bogart in 1946 and then with Robert Mitchum in 1977, and Marlowe with James Garner (1969).

This TV version starred American actor, Powers Boothe, of whom one critic wrote: 'He has a wide-jawed face that can endure a savage beating-up with only a swollen lip and a few grazes to show for it next day.' Boothe excelled as the compassionate Marlowe in a production of which surely Chandler himself would have been proud. Like many London Weekend dramas, it was aimed very much at the American market. It was filmed partly in London, partly in California (the final story dealt with the death of a Hollywood movie star) and picked up fans on both sides of the Atlantic. At five episodes, it was all too short. (SEE ALSO PHILIP MARLOWE)

REGULAR CAST

Philip Marlowe Powers Boothe   *Lt Magee* William Kearns
Annie Riordan Kathryn Leigh Scott

EPISODE TITLES

The Pencil
Nevada Gas
Finger Man
The King in Yellow
Smart-Aleck Kill

Based on stories by Raymond Chandler
Music: John Cameron
Producer: David Wickes

A David Wickes Television Production in association with London Weekend Television

5 colour 60-minute episodes
UK: ITV 27 April - 25 May 1984
US: Cable 27 April - 25 May 1986

* A further six episodes were made in 1986. This was a Canadian production filmed in Toronto and LWT were not involved. In Britain, Granada Television transmitted them from 16 March 1991.

MARTIN KANE, PRIVATE EYE

In 1950, Martin Kane, Private Eye reached number 12 in the American ratings, thus making it television's first hit detective show. Kane had already been a popular radio character and his fame did not alter in this live TV series. His face did though – three times.

The first Kane was William Gargan, himself a former detective, who brought a certain amount of wit and charm to the less than glamorous work of solving New York murders. In the early days Kane also liaised closely with the police, particularly Lieutenant Bender. But subsequent Kanes were less able. Lloyd Nolan, Lee Tracy and Mark Stevens all gave him a tougher edge and as a result did not enjoy such a close working relationship with Bender's successors.

For the first four years, Kane was a regular customer at Happy McMann's tobacconists, which enabled him casually to plug the products of the show's sponsor. The conversation invariably worked its way round to the merits of Sano and Encore cigarettes, or Old Briar pipe tobacco. The American Kane finally ran out of puff the following year, but was soon resurrected in Britain (SEE MARTIN KANE, PRIVATE INVESTIGATOR).

* The real Martin Kane was actually an executive with the advertising agency J. Walter Thompson, who produced the series. He had never done a day's sleuthing in his life.

REGULAR CAST

Martin Kane (1949 - 51) William Gargan *(1951 - 2)* Lloyd Nolan
(1952 - 3) Lee Tracy *(1953 - 4)* Mark Stevens
Lt Bender (1949 - 50) Fred Hillebrand   *Happy McMann* Walter Kinsella
Capt. Burke (1951 - 2) Frank Thomas   *Lt Grey (1952 - 4)* King Calder

Announcer: Fred Uttal
Music: Charles Paul
Producers: Frank Burns, Ed Sutherland
  Edward C. Kahan

An NBC Production

Approx. 120 monochrome 30-minute
  episodes
US: NBC 1 Sept 1949 - 17 June 1954

MARTIN KANE, PRIVATE INVESTIGATOR (US TITLE: THE NEW ADVENTURES OF MARTIN KANE)

It must have seemed like a good idea to bring the original and best Martin Kane, William Gargan, over for a new series set in London. It wasn't. The sturdy British policemen of the 1950s were simply not interested in wise-cracking smart alec American private detectives – and it showed. Whereas American cops liked to throw themselves into the action on the streets, Kane's new contact, Superintendent Page of Scotland Yard, rarely ventured further than his office – and that was only to fetch some more digestive biscuits.

REGULAR CAST

Martin Kane William Gargan   *Supt Page* Brian Reece

Producer: Harry Alan Towers

A Towers of London Production for ABC TV

39 monochrome 30-minute episodes
UK: ITV 14 Sept 1957 - 1 June 1958
US: Syndicated 1957

THE MASK

The only claim to fame of The Mask is that it was the first one-hour mystery series on TV. Other than that, it was fairly forgettable. It centred around two brothers who were attorneys and partners in the legal firm of Guilfoyle and Guilfoyle. The melodramatic title came from the way these brothers-in-law went around unmasking gangsters and saving damsels in distress. But nobody cared about saving their show and it was axed after four months.

REGULAR CAST

Walter Guilfoyle Gary Merrill
Peter Guilfoyle William Prince

An ABC Production

14 monochrome 60-minute episodes
US: ABC 10 Jan - 16 May 1954

MATLOCK

Ben Matlock is a rural Perry Mason. Played by the enduring Andy Griffith, he comes across as a simple country lawyer who looks about as sophisticated as his rumpled suit. But he's a wily old fox and beneath that charming, often vague exterior, lurks a razor-sharp mind ready to cut prosecution cases to ribbons.

His adversaries tend to underestimate him but his clients don't. From Senators to rock stars, the rich and famous in trouble pay big money for the best defence lawyer around.

Gentle Ben is backed up by a crack investigative team. There are his assistants, Michelle Thomas and Cassie Phillips, his own daughter, Charlene, a junior partner of Matlock and Matlock and keen to follow in her father's footsteps, and the firm's private investigator, Tyler Hudson. Tyler is a successful stock market businessman in his own right and would happily concentrate his energies in that direction. But he finds himself repeatedly lured back to detection by Matlock's gentle persuasion.

The show doesn't exactly break new ground but what it does, it does well. And Andy Griffith is so convincing, you get the feeling he could have got the Boston Strangler off with a fine. It has completed five seasons in the US so far, totalling over 100 episodes.

REGULAR CAST

Ben Matlock Andy Griffith Les Calhoun Don Knotts
Michelle Thomas Nancy Stafford Tyler Hudson Kene Holliday
Cassie Phillips Kari Lizer Charlene Matlock Linda Purl

Creator: Dean Hargrove
Music: Dick De Benedictis
Producer: Rich Collins
Executive producers: Dean Hargrove, Fred Silverman

A Strathmore Production in association with Viacom

Colour 60-minute episodes
US: NBC From 16 Sept 1986
UK: ITV From 1 May 1987

MATT HELM

Matt Helm was a graduate of the playboy school of private eyes. Based on the novels by Donald Hamilton and the films starring Dean Martin, Helm was a one-time CIA agent, who had become a depressingly standard, wisecracking Los Angeles detective. He lived the good life, eating at the finest restaurants, driving the fastest foreign sports car and going out with the fastest girl in town, attorney Claire Kronski. In keeping with his image, he only took on glamorous cases with an abundance of swimming pools – you wouldn't have caught him doing a stint as a store detective. Sergeant Hanrahan was his police contact and 'Ethel' was an answering-service operator.

Despite using expensive locations on private Californian estates, the series was a pale imitation of the movies and ultimately came over as being about as natural as formica.

REGULAR CAST

Matt Helm Anthony Franciosa Claire Kronski Laraine Stephens
Sgt Hanrahan Gene Evans Ethel Jeff Donnell

Developed for TV by Sam Rolfe
Music: Morton Stevens
Producers: Charles Fitzsimmons, Ken Pettus

A Columbia Pictures Television Production

13 colour 60-minute episodes
US: ABC 20 Sept 1975 - 3 Jan 1976
UK: ITV 19 June 1980 - 31 May 1983 (Thames)

MATT HOUSTON

Matt Houston was rich, rich, rich. The son of a Texas oil millionaire, he was refined rather than crude. He flew his own helicopter, owned a luxurious penthouse pad and he drove fast cars, his favourite being a cream-coloured Excalibur, which is quite a few steps up from a Volkswagon Beetle.

Matt had been responsible for managing his father's oil business back in Texas, but now he had moved to California (more convenient for the TV studios) to oversee off-shore drilling operations. The business virtually ran itself, leaving Matt with plenty of spare time in which to indulge his fantasies. So he realized his life-long ambition and became a private detective.

That he made little money from his hobby was immaterial. He enjoyed himself. Hardly surprising since he usually had at least one woman on each arm, notably beautiful Harvard-trained lawyer C.J. Parsons. For the first season, two feuding cowboys, Bo and Lamar (the latter played by Paul Brinegar, old Wishbone from Rawhide), journeyed over from Texas to give Matt a helping hand. At that time Matt also had a useful ally in Lieutenant Vince Novelli of the police department – so much so that Mama Novelli used to invite Matt round to taste her Italian cooking. It was an offer he couldn't refuse.

But in the second season Novelli and his mum were replaced by the less co-operative Lieutenant Michael Hoyt, and Matt handed over his oil interests to business partner Murray so that he could devote his time solely to detective work.

REGULAR CAST

Matt Houston Lee Horsley   *C.J. Parsons* Pamela Hensley
Murray George Wyner   *Bo* Dennis Frimple
Lamar Paul Brinegar   *Lt Vince Novelli* John Aprea
Mama Novelli Penny Santon   *Det. Lt Michael Hoyt* Lincoln Kilpartick

Creator: Lawrence Gordon
Producer: Michael Fisher
Executive producer: Aaron Spelling

An Aaron Spelling Production for Warner Bros

66 colour 60-minute episodes
US: ABC 26 Sept 1982 - 19 July 1985
UK: BBC1 28 Feb - 15 Aug 1983 (23 eps)
9 May - 27 Aug 1985 (14 eps)
6 Aug 1986 - 19 Feb 1987 (21 eps)
20 March - 30 May 1987 (8 eps)

MAX MONROE: LOOSE CANNON

Another tale of unlikely partners, with the wildly unconventional Max Monroe teamed up with conservative veteran cop, Charlie Ivers. Played by Shadoe Stevens, host of the United States' most listened-to radio show, American Top 40, Max is a cool customer with a flamboyant lifestyle. A grandmaster at chess, he is so unpredictable at work that many of his fellow officers with the Los Angeles Police Department refuse to work with him. There could be another reason – they are probably worried about being seen in the company of a man whose long tresses of blonde hair would look a good deal better on a Sindy doll than on a tough cop. He ended up resembling Kojak in a Farrah Fawcett wig.

The scripts, some penned by Brian Clemens of The Avengers and The Professionals fame, gave Max plenty of scope for eccentricity. One week he would be diving from a sixth-floor hotel room into a swimming pool below, or driving through a restaurant window, the next he would be subjecting himself to a monastic existence, in order to crack a murder among a small religious order of monks. Utterly implausible but quite enjoyable.

REGULAR CAST

Max Monroe Shadoe Stevens   *Charlie Ivers* Bruce A. Young

Creators/Executive producers: Fred Silverman, Dean Hargrove

A Viacom Production

One colour 120-minute episode and 6 colour 60-minute episodes
US: CBS 5 Jan - 19 April 1990
UK: ITV From 1 June 1991

MCCLAIN'S LAW

Back in 1952, John Wayne had starred in the Warner Bros film Big Jim McClain. Nearly 30 years on, another famous screen cowboy (James Arness from Gunsmoke) re-created the role on television.

A leg injury had forced Jim McClain to retire from the San Pedro police at the age of 39, and since then he had worked as a fisherman. But when his fishing partner was robbed and murdered, Big Jim insisted on being re-instated as a police detective so that he could apprehend the killer. Incredibly, the police department agreed to his demands and, at 52, he resumed his career, gammy leg and all.

Naturally McClain's new colleagues, particularly his boss, Lieutenant DeNisco, were somewhat dubious as to his effectiveness but, in the finest traditions of television he quickly earned the respect of his young partner, Harry Gates, and fellow detective, Jerry Cross. He proved that there is no substitute for experience or a gimmick.

* In his spare time Jim used to hang out at Vangie Cruise's dockside cafe.

REGULAR CAST

Det. Jim McClain James Arness   *Det. Harry Gates* Marshall Colt
Lt Edward DeNisco George DiCenzo   *Det. Jerry Cross* Carl Franklin
Vangie Cruise Conchata Ferrell

Creator: Eric Bercovici
Music: James Di Pasquale
Producers: Mark Rafters, Robert H. Justman

13 colour 60-minute episodes
US: NBC 20 Nov 1981 - 24 Aug 1982
UK: BBC1 19 Feb - 11 June 1982

An MGM Television Production

McCLOUD

'McCloud was the kind of role I left Gunsmoke to get. I wanted to be a leading man instead of a second banana.'   – DENNIS WEAVER

Inspired by the 1968 Clint Eastwood movie Coogan's Bluff, the quirky McCloud, starring Dennis Weaver, was among the best of the Seventies' gimmick shows. McCloud's gimmick was one of location – a rural Western lawman plunged into a big-city way of life which was completely foreign to him.

Deputy Marshal Sam McCloud hailed from Taos in New Mexico, as near to the old Wild West as existed in 1970. The pursuit of an escaped prisoner took him to New York where his strong-arm tactics, not to mention his horse, raised more than a few eyebrows among the officers of the NYPD. Having captured his man, instead of simply returning to New Mexico, McCloud somehow wound up doing further training on temporary attachment to Manhattan's 27th Precinct, under the watchful eye of Chief Peter B. Clifford.

The general idea was that McCloud would pick up metropolitan policing methods, but the Marshal was too set in his ways to learn fancy techniques. Besides, he was happy doing things his way. So despite the protestations of the hapless Clifford and his subordinates, McCloud went his own way – often on horseback, thereby creating total mayhem on the streets of New York and bringing rush-hour traffic to a standstill. And he insisted on dragging Sergeant Joe Broadhurst along on his cases which, although the two became quite pally, didn't do Broadhurst's chances of promotion much good. Also featured occasionally was McCloud's girlfriend, writer Chris Coughlin.

In his cowboy hat and sheepskin jacket, McCloud stuck out like a sore thumb in New York. And he was always ready with a little homily from down south as well as his infuriating catchphrase, 'There you go.'

The popularity of McCloud was very much down to Dennis Weaver, who had built up such a following as the limping Chester in Gunsmoke and deserved a hit of his own. McCloud was exactly that. Now Weaver was top banana.

* McCloud aired in the US as part of NBC's Mystery Movie, in company with Columbo and McMillan and Wife.

* The pilot show for McCloud, which took him to New York in the first place, was Who Killed Miss USA? (in Britain the title was changed to Who Killed Merri-Ann?)

* Dennis Weaver was reportedly paid £100,000 per episode of McCloud.

* One notable McCloud episode featured singer John Denver making his acting debut and Farrah Fawcett playing a hooker.

REGULAR CAST

Sam McCloud Dennis Weaver	*Chief Clifford* J.D. Cannon
Sgt Joe Broadhurst Terry Carter	*Chris Coughlin* Diana Muldaur

---

Music: Richard Clements
Creator/Executive producer: Glen A. Larson

A Universal Television Production

6 colour 60-minute episode, 19 colour 90-minute episodes and 21 colour 120-minute episodes
US: NBC 16 Sept 1970 - 28 Aug 1977
UK: ITV 16 Sept 1972 - 9 Oct 1976

McMILLAN AND WIFE

Like Hart to Hart, this engaging series owed more than a little to Nick and Nora Charles from The Thin Man. Here the happily-married husband and wife sleuths were San Francisco Police Commissioner Stewart McMillan and his scatter-brained wife, Sally. Any hopes Mac had of leaving his work at the office were repeatedly dashed by Sally's remarkable habit of stumbling over major crimes. Wherever she went, whatever she did, trouble was never far away. If she went to the supermarket, she'd find the checkout girl slumped over the frozen food counter with a knife in her back. Having discovered a corpse, she then spent the rest of the episode being kidnapped, attacked or threatened (sometimes all three) until Mac stepped in to save the day. He really must have loved her to put up with all that, week in, week out.

McMillan and Wife was very much a vehicle for Rock Hudson, who was paid £170,000 per episode and whose light comic touch neatly complimented the beautiful, husky-voiced Susan Saint James as Sally. She won the part after being spotted in an episode of McCloud. However, the real strength of McMillan and Wife was that not only did it have excellent leads, but also the supporting characters were exceptionally strong. Nancy Walker was wonderful as the McMillans' acid-tongued maid, Mildred. She was good protection, too – she could wound an intruder just by talking to him. Then there was John Schuck as Mac's assistant, the plodding Sergeant Charles Enright, a man with a face like a benevolent potato – and a brain to match.

The problem for the production team was that Schuck and Walker became so popular that eventually they wanted to leave. At the end of the 1975-6 season, Susan Saint James quit over a contractual dispute and Nancy Walker departed to star in her own series. But John Schuck did stay after being promoted to Lieutenant. So with no Wife, (Sally was hastily killed off in a plane crash – no half measures when you've fallen out with the producers) the title was shortened to McMillan and the widowed Commissioner acquired a new maid, Mildred's sister Agatha, a new sergeant, Steve DiMaggio, and a new secretary, Maggie. But the old sparkle had gone and that was to be the last season. McMillan without his Wife was like Columbo without his mac.

* The pilot for McMillan and Wife was Once Upon a Dead Man

REGULAR CAST

Commissioner Stewart McMillan Rock Hudson   *Sally McMillan* Susan Saint James
Sgt Charles Enright John Schuck   *Mildred* Nancy Walker
Agatha Martha Raye   *Sgt Steve DiMaggio* Richard Gilliland
Maggie Gloria Strook

Creator: Leonard B. Stern
Producer: Jon Epstein
Executive producer: Leonard B. Stern

24 colour 90-minute episodes and 16
colour 120-minute episodes US: NBC
29 Sept 1971 - 21 Aug 1977
UK: ITV 10 April 1972 - 18 April 1979

A Universal Television Production

Me and Mom

A ghastly comedy/drama about a mother and daughter detective team. Six-times-married Zena Hunnicutt decides on the day of her seventh wedding, that she would have much more fun and excitement poking her nose into daughter Kate's private eye business. So she abandons the ceremony and instead joins Kate and her sleuthing partner, ex-cop Lou Garfield (played by James Earl Jones who should have known better). And before long the domineering Zena has taken the practice and its clientele up-market and has even hired a new 'office boy' in the muscular shape of ex-football pro Vince Caladori. Thereafter mother and daughter proceeded to take it in turns to be placed in peril. Sadly, they were always rescued.

Regular Cast

Kate Morgan Lisa Eilbacher   *Zena Hunnicutt* Holland Taylor
Vince Caladori Bruce Jenner   *Lou Garfield* James Earl Jones

Creator: Marsha Miller
Producer: Hal Sitowitz

A Viacom Production

One colour 90-minute episode and 6 colour 60-minute episodes
US: ABC 1984 - 5

Meet McGraw

McGraw had no gun, no Christian name and no qualms about tackling the toughest cases. He would accept any job, no matter how dangerous, as long as it paid well, and he was quite happy slugging his way out of hazardous situations. He worked alone and didn't even have the perk of a pretty girl – more often than not he left one behind in a town because he couldn't allow himself to be tied down. The man was clearly unstable. A routine 'loner' series.

* After six months the title changed to The Adventures of McGraw.

Regular Cast

McGraw Frank Lovejoy

Producers: Warren Lewis, Don Sharpe

33 monochrome 30-minute episodes

US: NBC (Season 1) 2 July - 17 Sept
1957 (12 eps)
(Season 2) 24 Sept 1957 - 1 April 1958
(21 eps)-

MIAMI UNDERCOVER

Private investigator Jeff Thompson was hired by the Miami Hotel Owners' Association to keep the city crime-free. Posing (and I use the word advisedly) as a sophisticated man about town, Thompson was given physical assistance by Rocky, played by former boxer Rocky Graziano. Together they met dozens of gorgeous girls and still had enough energy left to cleanse the city – although thoughtfully they left enough criminals behind for Miami Vice.

REGULAR CAST

Jeff Thompson Lee Bowman   *Rocky* Rocky Graziano

Executive producers: Aubrey Schenck,
Howard W. Koch

38 monochrome 30-minute episodes
US: Syndicated 1961

A United Artists Production

MIAMI VICE

'Ricardo Tubbs' brother has been blown away. Sonny Crockett's marriage has fallen apart. Now, the only ones they can count on are each other!'   – SERIES PROMOTION

Crockett and Tubbs were television's designer detectives – slicked-back hair, three-day stubble, Armani suits and pastel shades. Hoods would never shoot at Sonny Crockett until they could see the whites of his socks. Wise to this, Sonny stopped wearing socks altogether.

Crockett was an undercover detective with the Miami Vice Squad, living on a houseboat called St Vitus Dance, which was guarded by his pet alligator, Elvis. Tubbs was a black cop from New York who had gone south to seek out the drug dealer that had murdered his brother. Together (under the command of moody Lieutenant Martin Castillo) they combed the city's sweaty and seedy alleyways as well as the gaudy Gold Coast, to rip out the underbelly of Miami's vice rings, usually in a hail of bullets. Sonny was worried about shooting people – in case the blood splattered onto his suit.

What set Miami Vice apart from its peers was the vibrant contemporary rock music background, responding to NBC's desire for a 'Hill Street MTV'. It received no fewer than 15 Emmy nominations in its first year and made stars out of Don Johnson (Crockett) and Philip Michael Thomas (Tubbs). Both actors lived up to their screen images. It was reported that Thomas, a former star of Hair!, was the father of eight children (six born out of wedlock) by several different mothers. Johnson appeared on the cover of a thousand magazines and admitted: 'There's plenty of Sonny Crockett in me. He enjoys plenty of hard partying. We both enjoy life in the fast lane.' Crockett's designer stubble created a trend among international poseurs. Joe Friday would not have been impressed.

With the music, the clothes and Crockett's flashy, black, Ferrari Spider sports car, Miami Vice became the show on which to be seen. Phil Collins played a con man in one episode, Princess Stephanie of Monaco tested for a part but was judged too inexperienced as an actress and Sheena Easton appeared as a singer, Caitlin, who became the new Mrs Crockett. The marriage didn't last long – Caitlin was soon gunned down (rumour had it that the killer was a music-lover). Even George Bush, then American Vice-President, asked to do a guest spot. Executive producer Michael Mann had to reject the idea, explaining: 'We couldn't have someone just walk on. There has to be a character.' Others to miss out were George Michael and Andrew Ridgeley of Wham! – they turned down the chance to play waiters.

However, the show wasn't popular with everyone. Some episodes were excessively violent, so much so that the then BBC chief, Michael Grade, rejected four episodes, including one about an IRA terrorist. And the police were none too pleased either. They claimed Miami Vice was totally unrepresentative. In one series alone, Crockett killed 32.5 bad guys and Tubbs 13.5 (they both shot the same cocaine-dealer) whereas the real Miami police are only responsible for about eight deaths a year. Gerald Avenberg, head of the 21,000-strong Association of Chiefs of Police, bitterly objected to the programme giving the impression that drug-dealing was a 'great career'. But the thing that miffed America's lawmen most, was that they had to wear tatty jeans to work, not $600 suits...

REGULAR CAST

Det. James 'Sonny' Crockett Don Johnson
Det. Ricardo Tubbs Philip Michael Thomas   *Lt Martin Castillo* Edward James Olmos
Det. Gina Navarro Saundra Santiago   *Det. Trudy Joblin* Olivia Brown
Det. Stan Switek Michael Talbott   *Det. Zito* John Diehl

Creator: Anthony Yerkovitch
Music: Jan Hamer
Executive producer: Michael Mann

A Universal Television Production

108 colour 60-minute episodes and three
colour 120-minute episodes
US: NBC 16 Sept 1984 - 26 July 1989
UK: BBC1 12 Feb 1985 - 20 Aug 1990

MICHAEL SHAYNE

Also hailing from Miami was Michael Shayne, hero of over 60 novels, a radio series (starring Jeff Chandler), a monthly mystery magazine and a dozen 1940s 'B' movies, featuring first Lloyd Nolan then Hugh Beaumont. Shayne made his debut in 1939 in the book Dividend on Death, written by Davis Dresser under the more glamorous pen name of Brett Halliday. In that, Shayne was a tall red-head but he shrank considerably in the films, where he was played by the stocky Lloyd Nolan. However, for the TV series Dresser acted as technical consultant, so the hero, in the guise of Richard Denning, looked much more like the original.

Shayne was a happy-go-lucky private eye, who nevertheless regularly seemed to end up in the middle of a murder. His trouble was he just couldn't resist a pretty face – nor the body that went with it. And this landed him in all sorts of bother. Happily, on television at least, there were plenty of people willing to bail out the affable detective, including Will Gentry, the Miami police chief, Tim Rourke, a young newspaper reporter, and Dick Hamilton, brother of Shayne's secretary-cum-girlfriend Lucy. Shayne flirted with so many girls that he didn't always pay much attention to Lucy. He didn't even notice when she grew a new head half-way through the series...

REGULAR CAST

Michael Shayne Richard Denning   *Tim Rourke* Jerry Paris
Lucy Hamilton (1960-1) Patricia Donahue   *(1961)* Margie Regan
Will Gentry Herbert Rudley   *Dick Hamilton* Gary Clarke

EPISODE TITLES

Dolls Are Deadly
A Night With Nora
Die Like a Dog
Framed in Blood
Call for Michael Shayne
Shoot the Works
This is it, Michael Shayne

The Poison Pen Club
Blood on Biscayne Bay
Murder Plays Charades
Murder and the Wanton Bride
Death Selects the Winner
Murder in Wonderland
Man with a Cane

Spotlight on a Corpse
Murder Round My Wrist
The Badge
The Heiress
Final Settlement
Four Lethal Ladies
The Ancient Art of Murder
Murder at the Convention
Strike Out
Murder Is a Fine Art
The Body Beautiful
Marriage Can Be Fatal
The Boat Caper
Date with Death

The Trouble with Ernie
No Shroud for Shayne
It Takes a Heap O'Dyin'
Dead Air

A Four Star Production

32 monochrome 60-minute episodes
US: NBC 30 Sept 1960 - 22 Sept 1961
UK: ITV 25 March 1962 - 15 Dec 1963
   (Anglia)

MICKEY SPILLANE'S MIKE HAMMER

'Hammer's appeal is in the same genre as John Wayne's but his weakness is that he finds women irresistible.'   – STACY KEACH

Wisecracking, womanizing, weapon-wielding Mike Hammer is one of the most formidable private detectives in the history of popular fiction. Created in Mickey Spillane's novel, I The Jury, published in 1947, Hammer is a blend of those two old reliables, sex and violence. It is a mix which has certainly worked since with worldwide book sales of over 100 million, he is probably the most successful private eye ever.

Hammer is mean but so is the company he keeps. He is usually cast as an avenging angel, looking to exact full and bloody retribution for some crime committed against a friend. He also has an insatiable lust for women. Both of these characteristics were to the fore in the first Mike Hammer TV series in the 1950s, a syndicated show starring Darren McGavin and set in New York. It has been said that if Hammer wasn't kissing them, he was killing them – Angie Dickinson came to an untimely end in the opening episode. These programmes brandished as much violence as the novels and caused quite an outrage at the time. Spillane defended the level of violence but later confessed that he hadn't really had that much to do with the show. 'I just took the money and went home,' he said.

Over 20 years later, Hammer reappeared on TV in an updated version, with Stacy Keach as a Vietnam veteran, giving him plenty of opportunity to vent his spleen, and sometimes other people's, all over the screen. After two TV movies (Murder Me, Murder You and More than Murder), it graduated to a series, and Keach's Hammer became a favourite on both sides of the Atlantic.

In modern-day New York, the background was understandably still violent, and there remained a steady stream of wisecracks and an even steadier stream of voluptuous girls who made Madonna look shy. The most prominent of these was Velda, Hammer's busty secretary, who gave the distinct impression that she was concealing a portable typewriter about her person. When he could prize himself away from this bevy of beauties, Hammer was in his element among the street low-life to whom he used to deliver such endearing greetings as 'Hey, giant lizard breath'. His principal contact was Ozzie the Answer, and he also obtained information and untold pleasure from Jenny, the sexy bartender at the Light 'n' Easy, his favourite watering-hole.

Hammer's often brutal approach brought him into conflict with Assistant District Attorney Lawrence D. Barrington, who liked to operate by the book, but he had a slightly more sympathetic ear in Captain Pat Chambers of the N.Y.P.D.

No case was too tough for Mike Hammer, who tackled and solved everything from murder to drug dealing, ironic because a year into the series, Stacy Keach was imprisoned for possessing drugs. So after 24 episodes had been screened, production was halted while Keach served his time. It returned in 1986, titled in the US The New Mike Hammer.

Mike Hammer is a larger than life character, almost in the realms of superhero, and living proof that some girls do like a bit of rough. As Keach himself said: 'Hammer is tough, charming and romantic – the classic American detective.'

* In the UK, episodes have transferred from ITV to British Sky Broadcasting.

REGULAR CAST (Series 1)

Mike Hammer Darren McGavin   *Capt. Pat Chambers* Bart Burns

Music: David Kahn, Melvyn Lenard

A Revue Production for MCA

78 monochrome 30-minute episodes
US: Syndicated 1957 - 1960

REGULAR CAST (Series 2)

Mike Hammer Stacy Keach   *Capt. Pat Chambers* Don Stroud
Velda Lindsay Bloom   *Asst D.A. Barrington* Kent Williams
Ozzie the Answer Danny Goldman   *Jenny* Lee Benton

Theme music 'Harlem Nocturne': Earle Hagen
Producer: Lew Gallo
Executive producer: Jay Bernstein

A Columbia Pictures Television Production

One colour 120-minute episode and 46 colour 60-minute episodes
US: CBS 26 Jan 1984 - 13 May 1987
UK: ITV 13 Feb - 9 April 1984
12 Sept 1985 - 27 Aug 1986

MIDNIGHT CALLER

'This is your host Jack Killian on KJCM 98.3 FM, "Goodnight America wherever you are."'
— PROGRAMME CLOSE

Jack Killian is a cross between Dr Ruth and Philip Marlowe. First he advises people on their problems and then he goes out and hunts down those responsible for causing them. He is a DJ detective, America's Eddie Shoestring (SEE SHOESTRING), who hosts the midnight to 3am radio talk-show on KJCM, San Francisco. He is known as the Nighthawk.

Played by Gary Cole, who turned down the role of Sonny Crockett on Miami Vice, Killian is an ex-cop who quit the force after inadvertently gunning down his own partner, a fact of which he is regularly reminded by his more outspoken listeners. Although there is animosity towards him in certain quarters, he still has a good police contact in Lieutenant Carl Zymak, while newspaper reporter, Deacon Bridges, also helps out on tricky cases. These are usually a matter of life and death since, although Jack receives a wide variety of calls asking for help, we don't often see him going round to somebody's house to unblock a drain.

Jack Killian is moody and unpredictable, a nightmare for the beautiful station boss, Devon King, who would rather he toe the line a little more. This is despite what must be phenomenal ratings, because everyone in San Francisco seems to listen to his show, no matter what else they are doing at the time. Passionate lovers will always have the radio competing with the bedsprings and, no doubt, a gang about to blow a bank safe would insist on total silence – except for Jack's show.

In his relaxed moments, Jack is flip and hip, but deep down he is an intense kinda guy, still haunted by his past. He cares so much it hurts. And it hurts us when we have to listen to those sentimental homilies at the end of each programme, which are in danger of spoiling an otherwise excellent series.

One puzzling thing is the staffing level at KJCM. Apart from Devon, the only other member of personnel ever seen was engineer/producer Billy Po, who did little more than say 'Call for you, Jack' and grin, until he was replaced by Lindy Ross. But how can a successful radio station in a vast city like San Francisco, be run with just two members of staff? I think I'll ring Jack and ask him.

* To date, Midnight Caller has completed three seasons in the US, a total of some 60 episodes

---

REGULAR CAST

Jack Killian Gary Cole   *Devon King* Wendy Kilbourne
Billy Po Dennis Dun   *Lt Carl Zymak* Arthur Taxier
Deacon Bridges Mykel T. Williamson

Creator: Richard Di Lello
Theme music: Brad Fiedel
Producer: John F. Perry
Executive producer: Robert Singer

A December 3rd Production for Lorimar

60-minute colour episodes
US: From Oct 1988
UK: BBC1 28 Jan - 1 April 1989 (8 eps)
30 Dec 1989 - 24 March 1990 (12 eps)
5 Jan - 23 Feb 1991 (8 eps)

THE MIND OF MR J G REEDER

Mr J.G. Reeder was an unlikely crime-fighter. He was certainly no Mike Hammer. He was the sort of insignificant, bespectacled little man, who gets sand kicked in his face by seven-stone weaklings. But hidden beneath that meek exterior lay a sharp criminal mind, dedicated to outwitting villains.

Based on the stories by Edgar Wallace, Reeder was a mild-mannered clerk for the Department of Public Prosecutions in the 1920s. This charming series pitted him against such diverse adversaries as a Chicago gangster, confidence tricksters and bank robbers. With the help of Mrs Houchin, Miss Belman and department head, Sir Jason Toovey, Mr J.G. Reeder proved more than a match for them all.

REGULAR CAST

J.G. Reeder Hugh Burden   *Sir Jason Toovey* Willoughby Goddard
Mrs Houchin Mona Bruce *(Season 1)*   *Miss Belman* Gillian Lewis *(Season 2)*

Producers: Kim Mills (Season 1) Robert
   Love (Season 2)
Executive producer: Lloyd Shirley

A Thames Television Network Production

16 colour 60-minute episodes
UK: ITV (Season 1) 23 April - 11 June
   1969 (8 eps)
(Season 2) 19 April - 7 June 1971 (8 eps)

MISS ADVENTURE

Miss Adventure was miscast, because such a splendid comedy actress as Hattie Jacques should not have wasted her talents in this rather weak private eye escapade. She played Stacey Smith, a confidential investigator for the lowly Stanton Detective Agency, whose boss Henry sent her off on what appeared to be routine assignments, but which turned out to be unbelievable adventures. Fortunately, they didn't carry on for long.

REGULAR CAST

Stacey Smith Hattie Jacques   *Henry Stanton* Jameson Clark

Creators: Peter and Marjorie Yeldham
Producer: Ernest Maxim

13 monochrome 45-minute episodes
UK: ITV 5 July - 13 Oct 1964

An ABC Weekend Network Production

MISS MARPLE

'Christie's audience likes its murders scented with magnolia blossoms and does not care to be reminded that murder is an act of infinite cruelty.'
                                                    – RAYMOND CHANDLER

When the BBC first attempted a Miss Marple mystery in 1949, a piece of scenery collapsed and a corpse got up and wandered off set. Thankfully standards had improved immeasurably by the time Joan Hickson came to play the world-famous sleuth of St Mary Mead, 35 years later, in a production that was an example of British television at its finest.

Joan Hickson was no stranger to the works of Christie. Back in 1946 she had played 'a little spinster' in a Christie play. It was only a minor part but had so impressed the watching author, that she sent Joan a congratulatory letter. Joan says: 'Around the time I was picked to do Miss Marple, my daughter was rummaging through a box of old letters and found one from Agatha Christie in which she wrote: "I do hope one day you will play my dear Miss Marple." I remember when I received it, I was shattered that one day I would be old enough to play her.'

When Joan finally fulfilled Christie's dream, she confessed to having initial reservations. 'When I was offered the part, I said, "Oh no, I can't.

I'm not the right shape." I thought she ought to be smaller – she was a fluffy old lady with a shawl. But it seems to have worked.' There were, however, modifications, for at 79 Joan was so young-looking that she had to dye the edges of her hair white and wear grey wigs to pass off as Miss Marple, who was supposed to be only about 70!

Jane Marple was a busybody spinster who lived in the quaint English village of St Mary Mead in the Thirties and Forties. (For the TV series, Nether Wallop in Hampshire doubled as St Mary Mead.) Hers was a world of afternoon tea, vicars and immaculately manicured lawns. It was a genteel existence, where social acceptance often hinged on the ability to crook one's finger around the handle of a bone china tea-cup.

But behind this peaceful facade lurked murder. For foul play followed Miss Marple as sure as the weather follows the news. And whenever there was a murder, she simply had to solve it, although she liked to continue knitting while she did so. She was a bossy individual and never hesitated to point out to the police the error of their ways. Her ally was usually the appropriately-named Detective Inspector Slack, who was continually outshone by Miss Marple's brilliant powers of analysis and deduction. And she enjoyed nothing more than gathering all the suspects around her for the grand revelation. It was her supreme moment of triumph, which the police seemed quite prepared to tolerate. They clearly recognized the fact that they would never have wrapped up a case without her intervention.

Of course the stories were all in the best Christie tradition – no gore, no car chases, no gruesome sights – for, as Raymond Chandler said, she believed in gentle murders, all carried out quietly and efficiently. Christie's interest in murder began as a teenager, when she read crime reports from newspapers to her elderly grandmother and discussed ways in which the victims had died. Then her First World War training, as a chemist's dispenser in Torquay, gave her a professional knowledge of poisons. Miss Marple's first appearance was in Murder at the Vicarage in 1930, and Angela Lansbury, who has played the character on screen in The Mirror Crack'd and also stars in the Marple-orientated Murder She Wrote, believes that Miss M was really Christie's aunt. This has never been substantiated, however.

The other noted movie Marple was Margaret Rutherford, whose portrayal Christie disliked as being too all-action. Coincidentally, Margaret Rutherford was a friend of Joan Hickson's – in fact she was godmother to Joan's son. And Joan even played the daily woman in one of Rutherford's Marple films, the 1961 production of Murder She Said.

The Miss Marple television series was a worldwide success. When the Russians were sent a shopping list for British programmes to be screened there, Miss Marple was top of their list. Joan Hickson was awarded the OBE in 1987, and at the presentation, the Queen said that she, too, was a fan of the show.

The programmes were made with such loving care and even tempted Roy Boulting, one of the celebrated film-making twins, to direct his first

TV drama at the age of 71, with The Moving Finger. An example of the programme-makers thoughtful attention to detail is A Caribbean Mystery. It was filmed in Barbados at the same Coral Reef holiday complex where Christie had written the actual book, and the owners, Budge and Cynthia O'Hara, not only remembered her stay, but are immortalized as characters in the story. This was the tenth adaptation of Christie's stories and proved to be splendid entertainment.

It almost goes without saying that Joan Hickson is a great Christie fan and has read many of her novels. 'I do like Miss Marple. I like her high standards. Most of all, she isn't condemning. She always sees the villain's point of view. As for the television series, I hope that wherever Agatha may be, she'll think it was a good idea.'

* The unlikeliest people derived inspiration from the stories. Two Staffordshire boys who sent letters to their headmaster, threatening to burn down the school unless he paid them £2,500, admitted that they got the idea from the Miss Marple series!

REGULAR CAST

Miss Marple Joan Hickson *Det. Insp. Slack* David Horovitch

The Body in the Library

One morning the Bantrys wake up to find everything far from ordinary. They call their friend and neighbour, Miss Marple, to unravel the mystery, and the investigation takes them to a strange seaside hotel.

GUEST STARS:

Gwen Watford, Andrew Cruickshank, Moray Watson
Dramatized by T.R. Bowen
Director: Silvio Narizzano

A Murder Is Announced

Among the classified advertisements in a local paper is one announcing the time and place of a forthcoming murder. The residents of the small village of Chipping Cleghorn think it's harmless fun – at first.

GUEST STARS:

Ursula Howells, Renee Asherson, Sylvia Syms
Dramatized by Alan Plater
Director: David Giles

The Moving Finger

Accompanied by his sister, Joanna, Gerry Burton has gone to the village of Lymston in East Anglia, to convalesce after an accident. But dark undercurrents are at work in the village.

GUEST STARS:

Michael Culver, Andrew Bicknall, Sabina Franklyn
Dramatized by Julia Jones
Director: Roy Boulting

A Pocketful of Rye

Why are members of the Fortescue household being poisoned? Can the deaths really be connected by a nursery rhyme? Miss Marple investigates.

GUEST STARS:

Fabia Drake, Timothy West, Peter Davison
Dramatized by T.R. Bowen
Director: Guy Slater

Murder at the Vicarage

Miss Marple's debut in print. The elderly sleuth abandons her knitting when a murder at the local vicarage shatters the peace and calm of St Mary Mead.

GUEST STARS:

Paul Eddington, Cheryl Campbell
Dramatized by T.R. Bowen
Director: Julian Amyes

Sleeping Murder

A young couple move into an old house in Devon, and soon Miss Marple has to tackle a murder that has gone undetected for twenty years.

GUEST STARS:

Jean Anderson, John Bennett, Terence Hardiman
Dramatized by Ken Taylor
Director: John Davies

At Bertram's Hotel

Miss Marple has not visited Bertram's since her childhood and yet it seems unchanged. Then Canon Pennyfather disappears and there is a shooting.

GUEST STARS:

Joan Greenwood, Caroline Blakiston, George Baker
Dramatized by T.R. Bowen
Director: Mary McMurray

Nemesis

Millionaire Jason Rafiel, about to die on his private island, dictates his final instructions to his secretary and talks of Nemesis. Miss Marple, recruited by his solicitors to solve a crime as yet unknown, is sent on a coach tour of historic homes and gardens, where she encounters tales of lost love, prodigal sons and jealous lovers before trapping a killer.

GUEST STARS:

Peter Tilbury, Helen Cherry, Margaret Tyzack
Dramatized by T.R. Bowen
Director: David Tucker

4.50 From Paddington

Mrs McGillicuddy witnesses a murder on a passing train, while travelling on the 4.50 from London's Paddington station. She reports the crime, but the absence of a body causes everyone to dismiss what she has seen as the imaginings of an elderly woman – everyone that is, except Miss Marple.

GUEST STARS:

Mona Bruce, Maurice Denham, Joanna David
Dramatized by T.R. Bowen
Director: Martyn Friend

A Caribbean Mystery

Miss Marple plans a quiet holiday at the Golden Palm Hotel in Barbados. But her stay is soon disrupted by a series of most unpleasant murders.

GUEST STARS:

Donald Pleasence, T.P. McKenna, Frank Middlemass
Dramatized by T.R. Bowen
Director: Christopher Petit

They Do It With Mirrors

At the insistence of an old schoolfriend, Miss Marple agrees to visit Carrie Louise Serrocold at her rambling country house, Stoneygates. When her stepson is found murdered, it is revealed that someone has been trying slowly to poison Carrie.

GUEST STARS:

Jean Simmons, Joss Ackland, Faith Brook
Dramatized by T.R. Bowen
Director: Norman Stone

Music: Ken Howard, Alan Blaikey
Producers: Guy Slater, George Gallacio

A BBC Television Production

THE BODY IN THE LIBRARY
3 colour 50-minute episodes
UK: BBC1 26 - 28 Dec 1984
US: WGBH Boston 'Mystery' 2 - 16 Jan
   1986
THE MOVING FINGER
2 colour 50-minute episodes
UK: BBC1 21 - 22 Feb 1985
US: 'Mystery' 23 - 30 Jan 1986
A MURDER IS ANNOUNCED
3 colour 50-minute episodes
UK: BBC1 28 Feb - 2 March 1985
US: 'Mystery' 1 - 15 Jan 1987
A POCKETFUL OF RYE
2 colour 50-minute episodes
UK: BBC1 7 - 8 March 1985
US: 'Mystery' 4 - 11 Dec 1986
MURDER AT THE VICARAGE
One colour 110-minute episode
UK: BBC1 25 Dec 1986
US: 'Mystery' 9 Feb 1989

SLEEPING MURDER
2 colour 50-minute episodes
UK: BBC1 11 - 18 Jan 1987
US: 'Mystery' 7 - 14 Jan 1988
AT BERTRAM'S HOTEL
2 colour 50-minute episodes
UK: BBC1 25 Jan - 1 Feb 1987
US: 'Mystery' 21 - 28 Jan 1988
NEMESIS
2 colour 50-minute episodes
UK: BBC1 8 - 15 Feb 1987
US: 'Mystery' 10 - 17 Dec 1987
4.50 FROM PADDINGTON
One colour 110-minute episode
UK: BBC1 25 Dec 1987
US: 'Mystery' 16 March 1989
A CARIBBEAN MYSTERY
One colour 110-minute episode
UK: BBC1 25 Dec 1989
THEY DO IT WITH MIRRORS
One colour 100-minute episode
UK: BBC1 Xmas 1991

MR AND MRS NORTH

A husband and wife amateur detective team created by Richard and
Frances Lockridge for the magazine New Yorker. They went on to
establish quite a following on American radio, and their adventures
also spawned a Broadway hit and a 1941 film starring Gracie Allen.
The TV series was a light-hearted mystery about a seemingly
ordinary Greenwich Village couple, who stumbled over bodies at
every turn. This greatly appealed to Jerry North who published
mystery stories and had visions of himself as an amateur sleuth. But
somehow he was always upstaged by his deceptively sharp wife,
Pamela, who managed to nail the culprit ahead of either him or the
police.

REGULAR CAST

Pamela North Barbara Britton   *Jerry North* Richard Denning
Lt Bill Weigand Francis De Sales

Executive producer: Bernard L.
  Schubert

57 monochrome 30-minute episodes
US: CBS/NBC 3 Oct 1952 - 20 July 1954

MR DISTRICT ATTORNEY

'Mr District Attorney! Champion of the people! Guardian of our
fundamental rights to life, liberty and the pursuit of happiness!' - -
PROGRAMME INTRODUCTION

A fine upstanding citizen, crusading District Attorney Paul Garrett was
modelled on a real-life counterpart, New York crime-fighter, Thomas E.
Dewey, who was twice a Republican candidate for US President.
Garrett's career began in the Forties on American radio, before
switching to television for a live show which alternated with The
Amazing Mr Malone. The cast and characters remained the same as on
radio, Garrett being assisted by his secretary, Miss Miller, and
investigator Harrington, a former cop.

REGULAR CAST

D.A. Paul Garrett Jay Jostyn   *Harrington* Len Doyle
Miss Miller Vicki Vola

Announcer: Fred Uttal
Creator/Executive producer: Edward C.
Byron

An ABC Production

13 monochrome 30-minute episodes
US: ABC 1 Oct 1951 - 23 June 1952

* Two years after the demise of the live ABC show, a low-budget,
syndicated version of Mr District Attorney was produced.

REGULAR CAST

D.A. Paul Garrett David Brian   *Miss Miller* Jackie Loughery

A Ziv Production

78 monochrome 30-minute episodes
US: Syndicated 1954

MR ROSE

The return of William Mervyn as Chief Inspector Rose (SEE THE ODD
MAN AND IT'S DARK OUTSIDE) although now that he had retired
from the force, he was known simply as Mr Rose. The rotund Rose had
been left a sizeable amount of money following the death of two maiden
aunts, but instead of sitting back and wallowing in his new-found wealth
and growing his beloved roses, his restless spirit demanded that he

continued to investigate crime, this time as a civilian. His new-found status meant that he was no longer restricted by the police rule-book and could act as his conscience dictated. He could either inform the law of his findings or just keep quiet about them.

Many of Rose's escapades arose from his decision to write his revelatory memoirs. Certain members of the underworld, with whom he'd had dealings in the past, were alarmed to think they might be included and were prepared to go to any lengths to halt publication.

Rose worked from his country cottage in company with manservant Halifax, an ex-detective, and prissy secretary Drusilla. A new secretary, Jessica, arrived at the start of the second season and another male assistant, Trent, appeared in season three.

REGULAR CAST

Mr Rose William Mervyn   *John Halifax* Donald Webster
Drusilla Lamb Gillian Lewis   *Jessica Dalton* Jennifer Clulow
Robert Trent Eric Woolfe

Creator: Philip Mackie
Producers: Philip Mackie (Season 1)
    Margaret Morris (Seasons 2 and 3)

*A Granada Television Network
    Production*

25 colour 60-minute episodes

UK: ITV (Season 1) 17 Feb - 12 May
    1967 (13 eps)
(Season 2) 31 May - 5 July 1968 (6 eps)
(Season 3) 7 Nov - 5 Dec 1968 (6 eps)

MRS COLUMBO (US TITLE: KATE LOVES A MYSTERY)

A foolhardy attempt to cash in on the popularity of Columbo, by making his hitherto unseen wife a detective in her own right. The story was that Peter Falk had become too expensive for NBC, so they decided on a spin-off starring Kate Mulgrew. At first Mulgrew said, 'Forget it' but then changed her mind. She should have stuck to her original decision.

Thus Kate Columbo freed herself from the shackles which had bound her to the kitchen sink for the previous seven years, and stepped out into the sunlight as a reporter for The Valley Advocate, a weekly newspaper edited by the irascible Josh Alden. Kate had a seven-year-old daughter, Jenny, and presumably somewhere a Lieutenant, but family ties failed to prevent her from becoming involved in a succession of murder mysteries, which she solved with the same aplomb as her illustrious husband but with slightly better clothes-sense.

However, the producers soon realized that they would have been better advised making a spin-off about Columbo's basset-hound. The original title of Kate Columbo was rapidly changed to Kate the Detective, then Kate Loves a Mystery, as they tried to disassociate her from Columbo. In fact she was eventually given a new surname, Callahan, and all references to her husband were dropped. But even with more titles than Burke's Peerage, the show still bombed.

REGULAR CAST

Kate Columbo/Callahan Kate Mulgrew	*Jenny Columbo/Callahan* Lili Haydn
Josh Alden Henry Jones	*Sgt Varrick* Don Stroud

Creators: Richard Levinson, William Link
Producers: Richard Alan Simmons,
   Richard Irving

A Universal Television Production

14 colour 60-minute episodes
US: NBC 26 Feb - 6 Dec 1979

THE MOD SQUAD

Take three young Americans. Give each one a rebellious past. Better still, put them on probation. Then make them undercover cops. What's the result? – A horribly contrived series called The Mod Squad.

The trio (who critics described as 'one black, one white and one blonde') all looked as if the most anarchic thing they had ever done was return a library book a day late. Yet Pete Cochran, Linc Hayes and Julie Barnes were supposed to be tough cookies. Mean and moody Cochran was on probation for stealing a car, after being thrown out by his wealthy Beverly Hills parents; Hayes, whose hairstyle suggested that he was wearing a bowling ball on his head, came from a ghetto family of 13, and had been arrested during the Watts riots in Los Angeles; and Barnes was the daughter of a San Francisco prostitute who had run away from home and been picked up for vagrancy. She behaved as if she was in one long trance.

These drippy hippies were all intent on going straight and so they jumped at the chance when L.A.P.D. Captain Adam Greer said that he wanted to recruit them for a special youth squad, aimed at weeding out crooks who preyed on youngsters in Southern California. For their first season as undercover operatives, they drove around in a clapped-out old station wagon christened Woody, but early in the second series it was driven over a cliff. Unfortunately the Mod Squad didn't meet a similar fate.

Incredibly, co-creator Bud Ruskin claimed to have based the show on his own experiences, when he had been part of an undercover drugs squad, made up of young officers with the Los Angeles Sheriff's department in the 1950s. A pilot programme had been made in 1960, but it took another eight years to hit the screen which, in spite of the show's inexplicable success, proves that some sensible TV executives had reservations.

The series ran for five years until 1973 and just when we thought it was safe to switch on the television again, the three drop-outs bounced back, in a 1979 TV movie The Return of the Mod Squad, in which they came out of 'retirement' in a bid to find out who was trying to murder their former chief. Luckily it passed away peacefully.

Incidentally, studio legend has it that none of the three leads had any acting experience before making The Mod Squad. It showed.

REGULAR CAST

Pete Cochran Michael Cole   *Linc Hayes* Clarence Williams III
Julie Barnes Peggy Lipton   *Capt. Adam Greer* Tige Andrews

Creators: Bud Ruskin, Sammy Hess Aaron Spelling
Music: Earle Hagen
Producers: Harve Bennett, Tony Barrett
Executive producer: Aaron Spelling

An Aaron Spelling Production for ABC

123 colour 30-minute episodes
US: ABC (Season 1) 24 Sept 1968 - 15 April 1969 (26 eps)

(Season 2) 23 Sept 1969 -7 April 1970 (26 eps)
(Season 3) 22 Sept 1970 - 23 March 1971 (24 eps)
(Season 4) 14 Sept 1971 -7 March 1972 (24 eps)
(Season 5) 14 Sept 1972 -1 March 1973 (23 eps)
UK: ITV From 31 Dec 1970

MOONLIGHTING

'Everybody just wanted to know when David and Maddie would get horizontal.'
– BRUCE WILLIS

Moonlighting was one of those programmes you either loved or hated. It was the great yuppie detective show, as much a part of the late Eighties as the filofax. Fans used to ring each other on their car phones to discuss the previous night's episode. But whether you found the repartee between the two principals witty and engaging or smug and insufferable, one fact is inescapable – Moonlighting made Cybill Shepherd and Bruce Willis big stars.

Apart from a role as a crook in Miami Vice, former lorry driver and barman, Willis, had found it tough going in the world of acting. Then he heard about the auditions for an untried series called Moonlighting. He was the last of 3,000 actors to read for the part of David Addison and turned up to the audition in a punk haircut, khaki army trousers and three ear-rings. Producer Glenn Caron was impressed by his interpretation – 'I wanted a guy who speaks his mind and deals with women as he deals with men.' And with Cybill Shepherd installed as Maddie Hayes, the stage was set for one of the most sizzling small screen relationships ever. As Shepherd later remarked: 'Sparks flew. It's chemistry baby. Either you got it or you don't. And David and Maddie had it.'

The plot revolved around one-time international model, Maddie Hayes, who had been swindled by her advisers and left in deep trouble financially. Among her assets was the small City of Angels Detective Agency, which had deliberately been running at a loss as a tax dodge. Instead of selling it, she teamed up with the reluctant incumbent, private eye David Addison, and proceeded to turn the business into a profit-making concern, as the Blue Moon Detective Agency.

Having inherited Addison, Maddie now had to work with him. That proved to be far from easy. She was icy, aloof and professional, he was wise-cracking with a permanent lop-sided smirk. It was very much a love/hate relationship, made all the more intriguing for viewers by reports that the two stars couldn't stand the sight of one another off set. Any affection was reserved strictly for the cameras.

Cybill Shepherd admits there were problems. She says: 'The premise of the series was that Bruce's character David would be a jerk – that's where the conflict came. But after a while Bruce didn't want to be a jerk. So the producer decided to make my character ridiculously unsympathetic. After that, it wasn't as much fun.

'There was a lot of tension. We were like two rats trapped in a cage. It's like being married to someone you don't love.'

Eventually, almost by public demand, there was on-screen affection and the two wound up in bed together. But the passionate love scenes on screen weren't all they were cracked up to be. Shepherd did not care for Willis's kissing technique. She complained: 'His idea of a romantic kiss was to go 'blaah' and gag me with his tongue.'

Another theory for the development of the romantic story-line is that Cybill was pregnant with twins at the time and because the producers wanted her to stay, they needed an explanation for the bulge. But she took time off anyway, a situation which displeased Willis. 'Not having Cybill on the show was like watching the Three Stooges with only one Stooge,' he said. 'Her absence made the writers go into these ridiculous situations with the kind of format all the other TV shows have. We'd always been different. We were innovative and there had never been any formula.' Not only was Willis upset, but his character Addison was, too, for when Maddie returned for the third season, she broke his heart by marrying a man she met on a train.

In its prime, Moonlighting certainly was different. The interplay between Maddie and David was quite outstanding, with an extra dimension added by their scatty receptionist, Miss Dipesto. It was quirky and loved to break the rules of television, by putting out shows which were anything but conventional. For example one episode, dealing with an unsolved Forties mystery, was shot in black and white for extra effect. And it showed the same events seen differently through the eyes of the various characters. Another edition, Atomic Shakespeare, was written in iambic pentameters, with Willis singing a storming version of True Love, to a bride trussed in bondage at the altar. Then there were all the asides to the camera, the show within a show – they all helped to give Moonlighting an individual flavour. The cases they were investigating became incidental. It was so refreshing to watch something that wasn't safe.

The gamble paid off handsomely. In the US it competed on Tuesday nights with the standard NBC police series, Riptide, which attracted a predominantly male audience. Moonlighting appealed to both sexes and duly won the day. For his part, Willis was rewarded with a Best Actor Emmy, a musical sideline (he had a hit with The Drifters' classic Under the Boardwalk) and a blossoming movie career which has led to him being just about Hollywood's hottest property. And all because he wore khaki trousers...

* Moonlighting was so popular in Britain, that after being shown on BBC, it was bought by British Sky Broadcasting and screened again right from the start.

REGULAR CAST

Maddie Hayes Cybill Shepherd   *David Addison* Bruce Willis
Agnes Dipesto Allyce Beasley

Creator: Glenn Caron
Theme song: Al Jarreau
Producer: Jay Daniel
Executive producer: Glenn Caron

A Picturemaker Production for ABC

One colour 120-minute episode and 66 colour 60-minute episodes US: ABC 5 March 1985 - 14 May 1989
UK: BBC2 29 May - 25 Sept 1986 and 23 Dec 1986 (19 eps)
26 Jan - 15 June 1987 and 22 Dec 1987 (19 eps)
4 Jan - 21 March 1988 (12 eps)
21 Feb - 13 June 1989 (17 eps)

THE MOST DEADLY GAME

The title of this glossy whodunnit referred to murder. For murder was the business of expert criminologists Arcane, Croft and Vanessa. They may sound like a troupe of jugglers but in fact they bore a greater resemblance to those extra-sensory buffoons The Champions, but without the moments of sublime contemplation. Arcane was the leader, a suave elder statesman who used to be guardian to the beautiful Vanessa. Completing the line-up was the husky Croft, a former military intelligence officer played by Route 66 star, George Maharis. It was a familiar escapist format but only lasted 12 weeks, by which time it had turned into The Most Deadly Bore.

REGULAR CAST

Jonathan Croft George Maharis   *Mr Arcane* Ralph Bellamy
Vanessa Smith Yvette Mimieux

Creators: David Fine, Mort Friedkin
Producer: Joan Harrison
Executive producer: Aaron Spelling

12 colour 60-minute episodes
US: ABC 10 Oct 1970 - 16 Jan 1971

An Aaron Spelling Production for ABC

MOST WANTED

The standard for this second-rate American cop show was set by the opening case, in which the Most Wanted unit of the Los Angeles Police Department stalked a maniac who raped and murdered nuns. Subsequent investigations were no more sensible. The squad was an elite task force which concentrated solely on bringing to justice the criminals on the mayor's most-wanted list. It starred a wasted Robert Stack as Captain Linc Evers, backed up by Sergeant Charlie Benson and Officer Kate Manners. It soon became apparent that what were really most wanted were better scripts.

REGULAR CAST

Capt. Linc Evers Robert Stack   *Sgt Charlie Benson* Shelly Novack
Officer Kate Manners Jo Ann Harris   *Mayor Dan Stoddard* Harry Rhodes

Music: Lalo Schifrin
Producer: Harold Gast
Executive producer: Quinn Martin

A Quinn Martin Production for ABC

22 colour 60-minute episodes
US: ABC 16 Oct 1976 - 25 April 1977

M SQUAD

The M stood for Murder in this action-packed 1950's show, which starred Lee Marvin as fearless Lieutenant Frank Ballinger. There have been few tougher nuts in the history of television than Ballinger as he led the M Squad, a crack unit of plainclothes detectives, in the ever-present battle against Chicago's maniacal killers. Ballinger was rugged, broody and unflappable with no personal life to distract him from the job in hand. His commanding officer was Captain Grey.

Marvin, who also narrated the series, was just beginning to establish a reputation as a screen tough guy and M Squad did him no harm at all. But rumours abounded at the time that he was difficult to work with, a charge the actor refuted by remarking: 'I just change bad scripts.'

* From the second season onwards, the Theme From M Squad was a fine jazzy piece composed by the legendary Count Basie.

REGULAR CAST

Lt Frank Ballinger Lee Marvin   *Capt. Grey* Paul Newlan

Theme music: Stanley Wilson (Season 1) Count Basie (Season 2)
Producer: John Larkin
Executive producer: Richard Lewis

A Latimer Production for Universal Television/MCA

115 monochrome 30-minute episodes
US: NBC (Season 1) 20 Sept 1957 - 13 June 1958 (37 eps)
(Season 2) 19 Sept 1958 - 3 July 1959 (39 eps)
(Season 3) 4 Sept 1959 - 28 June 1960 (39 eps)
UK: ITV 11 Jan 1958 - 7 May 1960 (ATV)

MURDER BAG

The series that introduced Raymond Francis as Superintendent Lockhart, a man who went on to become one of British TV's most popular policemen over the next ten years (SEE CRIME SHEET AND NO HIDING PLACE).

The central theme was the Murder Bag itself, a black leather briefcase which the police took to the scene of a murder. It contained some 80 items of equipment, which the officers would use to collect forensic evidence in the hope of trapping the killer. The idea grew out of discussions between the programme's writer/producer, Barry Baker, and a former Detective Sergeant with 20 years' experience who, at the time, was working as technical adviser on the ITV series Shadow Squad.

Murder Bag was meticulously authentic and proved a great success, even though it was originally intended only as a filler. It was made live, the only piece of film being in the titles, where a Scotland Yard detective checked the contents of the bag. But the production got off to a hesitant start when the first actor to speak in the opening episode 'dried' for several seconds. Francis himself was not immune to such lapses either. He used to hide his lines all over the set. One such crib card was placed inside his desk drawer and Francis would open it slightly and glance down. One day a studio technician played a joke on him by replacing the card with one which read: 'You will dry now.' And sure enough he did!

Lockhart's trademark was taking snuff, something Francis enjoyed too. On the show he used a snuffbox that had been given to him by Kenneth More.

In 1957, the contents of the Murder Bag were as follows:

1 bottle of disinfectant	2 pairs of rubber gloves
1 bottle of graphite powder	1 pair of handcuffs
2 glass bottles with stoppers	4 pairs of scissors
2 glass bottles with caps	1 metal probe
6 small cardboard boxes	1 case of lancets and pliers
1 soap box	2 towels
1 lens with spare bulb and battery	1 case of napkins
	3 pairs of tweezers
1 'Staybright' footprint former	6 large plastic bags, 6 small ones
1 2ft boxwood rule	1 box of Lysolite
1 66ft measuring tape	1 graphite powder duster
1 2 metre rule	1 clinical thermometer
1 sponge	1 standard thermometer
1 squeegee	1 boiler suit
1 tin of Vaprole	6 railway warrant forms
1 test tube	statement paper
1 pencil torch with reflector	adhesive paper
4 test tubes	transparent paper
2 rubber corks	envelopes
1 gauge	pocket books
2 magnifying glasses	labels
1 compass	1 copy of the Home Office circular about forensic
1 fingerprint outfit	science laboratories
1 rubber apron	

And not an egg and cress sandwich in sight...

REGULAR CAST

Supt Lockhart Raymond Francis

Creator: Glyn Davies
Producer: Barry Baker

An Associated Rediffusion Network Production

55 monochrome 30-minute episodes
UK: ITV (Season 1) 16 Sept 1957 - 31 March 1958 (30 eps)
(Season 2) 30 June 1958 - 1 April 1959 (25 eps)

MURDER, SHE WROTE

'Nobody thought it would go. I just happened to be the right person
for the part at the right time. And mystery happened to be what was
needed on CBS at 8.00 on a Sunday evening after Tonight.'
                                                    – ANGELA LANSBURY

Jessica Fletcher, played by London-born Angela Lansbury, is the
American Miss Marple. The similarities are unmistakeable – both are
sprightly though of pensionable age (Jessica is a few years younger than
Miss M), both are unattached (Jessica is a widow), both come from
small town/village backgrounds and both have an insatiable appetite for
solving murders. An extra link is that Angela Lansbury actually played
Miss Marple in the 1980 movie, The Mirror Crack'd.

Jessica lives in peaceful Cabot Cove (population 3,560 and falling)
on the Maine coast. Once a teacher, her life changed dramatically when
she became a successful, Christie-like, mystery novelist. At first she had
written purely for pleasure, to concentrate her mind on something
worthwhile following the death of her husband, until her favourite
relative, Grady Fletcher, submitted her manuscript, The Corpse Danced
at Midnight, to Coventry House Publishers. It became a best-seller and
Jessica hasn't looked back since.

She is so prolific and so popular that she is required to spend a
considerable amount of time away from Cabot Cove, either at signing
sessions or at TV studios where she acts as consultant for an up-coming
adaptation of one of her works. But wherever Jessica goes, there is a
murder. Her presence is a more certain sign of death than a waiting hearse.

Fortunately, Jessica has an inexhaustible supply of nephews and
nieces scattered throughout the land. In the seven years that the series
has been running to date, virtually every one of her relatives has either
been murdered or accused of murder. Indeed one nephew, a New York
accountant, has been a suspect on several occasions!

It then remains for Jessica to utilize the criminal knowledge which
she has built up through her writing to act as an amateur sleuth, and
steer the ever-incompetent police in the right direction. Some of the
police are fans of her books, others see her as a nosey nuisance; hardly
surprising since, although she claims, 'I'm the last person in the world
who'd want to interfere', that is precisely what she always does.
Sometimes she is even allowed to stand in on the interrogation at the
police station. But perhaps it's as well that she is around, otherwise
there would be an infinite number of miscarriages of justice. The
police have been known to arrest three wrong suspects in the course of
just one show. Finally the guilty party, having plotted an intricate
crime and bamboozled the police, surrenders to Jessica under the
mildest of questioning. And, as with Miss Marple, the culprit is rarely
truly heinous – the cases often almost amount to justifiable homicide.

As a break from getting friends and relatives off the hook, Jessica occasionally finds a nice murder to solve in her home town where Amos, the Sheriff of Cabot Cove, and her family doctor, Seth Haslett, are featured. Or Angela Lansbury will appear as Jessica's British cousin Emma, a former music hall singer, whose hobby is amateur detection. And for one episode, Jessica travelled to Hawaii to team up with Magnum in a murder inquiry. The story was concluded on the following week's Magnum, P.I., thereby boosting the ratings for both programmes.

Dubbed in one US paper 'a granny Mary Poppins' because she fixes everything, Jessica Fletcher has become one of the most popular of all TV-created detectives. The number of episodes screened in the US is rapidly approaching the 200 mark. Much of the credit is down to Angela Lansbury herself, who manages to combine Anglo-American tastes. She says, 'In America, they think I'm very English, in England they think I'm very American.' She wins both ways. After a few contractual skirmishes, mainly over the long hours, she is now reputed to be the highest-paid woman on American TV. 'I only work four days a week now,' says the 66-year-old actress. 'It used to be five with very long hours. It was relentless hard work.'

Just two things puzzle me. Jessica is so busy solving murders, how does she find time to write her books? By now she must have attended more funerals than she's written best-sellers. And if she is making such a vast amount of money, isn't it about time she got rid of that tatty old typewriter she uses in the opening credits?

REGULAR CAST

Jessica Beatrice Fletcher Angela Lansbury   *Amos* Tom Bosley
Seth Haslett William Windom

Creators: Peter S. Fischer, Richard Levinson, William Link
Producers: Robert F. O'Neill, Robert E. Swanson
Executive producer: Peter S. Fischer

A Universal Television Production
Colour 60-minute episodes
US: CBS From 30 Sept 1984
UK: ITV From 19 May 1985

MURPHY'S LAW

Daedelous Murphy was a reformed alcoholic detective. Played by George Segal (maybe it should have been called A Touch of Glass), Murphy had been on the wagon more times than Seth Adams. At the age of 42, he was working as a private investigator for a large insurance company, First Fidelity, looking into possible fraudulent claims.

Actually, working was too strong a word to describe Murphy's activities, because he had devoted his life to avoiding labour of any kind. He operated by his own set of rules but they tended to coincide with the original Murphy's Law – anything that can go wrong, will.

There were usually so many distractions to prevent him accepting a case – like his ex-wife engaging him in a custody battle; like the charms of his young oriental room-mate and fellow sleuth, Ms Fanucchi; and like remaining sober. Yet on the rare occasions when he did get his act together, the poetry-quoting investigator with the chaotic lifestyle was able to outwit the most devious of criminal minds. It's just that he would rather have stayed in bed.

REGULAR CAST

Daedelous Murphy George Segal   *Kimi Fanucchi* Maggie Han

EPISODE TITLES

The Room Above the Indian Grocery
Where Are My Socks and Other Mysteries of Love
If You Can't Win, Shoot For a Tie
Do Someone a Favour and It Becomes Your Job
Never Play Leapfrog With a Unicorn
Never Try to Teach a Pig to Sing
Two Wrongs Are Only the Beginning
Never Wear Earmuffs in a Bed of Rattlesnakes
Where There's a Will, There's a Won't
When You're Over the Hill, You Pick Up Speed
Experience Is Something You Don't Get Until Just After You Need It

Doing It the Hard Way Is Always Easier
If Anything Can Go Wrong, It Will

Creator: Lee Zlotoff
Producer: Lynn Raynor
Executive producers: Zev Braun, Michael Gleason

A New World Television Production

13 colour 60-minute episodes
US: ABC 22 Nov 1988 - 8 March 1989
UK: ITV 2 April - 23 July 1990 (Thames)

MY FRIEND TONY

A silly idea by any standards. Just after the Second World War, John Woodruff almost had his wallet stolen in Italy by a young street thief named Tony Novello. Years later the adult Tony came to New York to join Woodruff, now an eminent professor of criminology, in his private investigation set-up. While the solid and dependable Woodruff exercised his brilliant analytical mind, carefree romeo, Tony, acted as his legman and got him out of any spots of physical bother. Next...

REGULAR CAST

Professor John Woodruff James Whitmore   *Tony Novello* Enzo Cerusico

Executive producer: Sheldon B. Leonard

A Sheldon Leonard Production for NBC

16 colour 60-minute episodes
US: NBC 5 Jan - 31 Sept 1969

MYSTERIES OF CHINATOWN

As far as I am aware, Dr Yat Fu was the only TV detective who was also proprietor of a herb and curio shop in San Francisco's China town. For that alone, he has a place in history. Dr Fu was strictly amateur and was sometimes assisted by his niece, Ah Toy, in this live crime series of the late 1940s.

REGULAR CAST

Dr Yat Fu Marvin Miller   *Ah Toy* Gloria Saunders
Lt Hargrove Bill Eythe

An ABC Production

Approx. 35 monochrome 30-minute episodes
US: ABC 4 Dec 1949 - 23 Oct 1950

NAKED CITY

'There are eight million stories in the Naked City...this has been one of them.'   – PROGAMME CLOSE

The omnipotent narrator's pay-off line is the single thing most people remember about Naked City, one of the all-time great cop shows. Yet he wasn't the star – in truth no human was. The real star was the city itself. Illuminated and spread out before us, this vast metropolis controlled the lives of the inhabitants far more than any individual characters. The city could be hard and cold, it could be warm and welcoming. It could be all things to all men.

The series was based on the story by Mark Hellinger that was made into the 1948 movie, The Naked City, and in which Hellinger himself spoke the famous end line. In some respects Naked City even surpassed Dragnet because, realistic though Jack Webb's show was, it did only offer a one-dimensional view of the police – they were all good guys, whereas Naked City was quite prepared to air stories where the cops had faults and the crooks had the occasional redeeming feature.

The first 39 episodes were good old-fashioned cops and robbers shows. They starred James Franciscus as young Detective Jim Halloran and John McIntire as the paternal Detective Lieutenant Dan Muldoon. During that first season McIntire decided he wanted to leave, so Muldoon was killed off when his squad car ploughed into a petrol lorry during a chase sequence. This was one of the earliest examples of TV executives resorting to such extreme measures to rid themselves of discontented stars. In this respect too, Naked City was something of a trailblazer.

For the remainder of the season, Lieutenant Mike Parker filled the dead man's shoes as the department's rugged veteran cop, and he stayed when the programme returned after a 16-month lay-off, in a new one-hour format (the previous shows had been 30 minutes long). Halloran didn't stay, however, and so Parker acquired a new young partner in Detective Adam Flint, played by Paul Burke. Another arrival was Flint's girlfriend, Libby, while Patrolman Frank Arcaro was made up to Sergeant.

Not only did the hour-long programmes have different characters, they also had a different emphasis. They became more concerned with exploring the motives behind crimes such as why two out-of-town teenagers should kill 14 people on a visit to the big city (A Case Study of Two Savages) or why a respectable middle-aged man should shoot and murder five people one morning (Murder Is A Face I Know). The episode titles were very much a hallmark of Naked City, boasting such gems as Robin Hood and Clarence Darrow They Went Out With Bow and Arrow, Today the Man Who Kills Ants Is Coming and No Naked Ladies in Front of Giovanni's House.

The producers went to great lengths to ensure realism. It was the first police series to be filmed on the streets of New York, and passers-by were used as extras. During filming, to avoid confusion between police and actors, the TV police cars were painted maroon and yellow instead of the real police department's black and green – they looked identical on black and white television.

Naked City gave an early break to many young acting hopefuls, among them Robert Redford, Peter Fonda, Jon Voight, Martin Sheen, Gene Hackman, George Segal and Peter Falk. Paul Burke related this story about one aspiring thespian. 'I remember seeing a young actor go nuts in our squad room in one scene. He was so out of it, he was shaking. I ran over and grabbed him and I put my arms around him just to bring him back. I said, "You were marvellous! That's my REAL pay on this show, to see great talents like yours." And he says to me, "Oh Jeezuz, you really believe that?" I said, "Yes, sensational, you got a great talent, you belong in Hollywood!" He laughed. He said, "I'm from Hollywood. They would never put me in pictures. Look at me, I'm a little character guy." It was Dustin Hoffman.'

There were over 800 actors in the Naked City. Dustin Hoffman was one of them.

REGULAR CAST

Det. Lt Dan Muldoon John McIntire   *Det. Jim Halloran* James Franciscus
Janet Halloran Suzanne Storrs   *Lt Mike Parker* Horace McMahon
Det. Adam Flint Paul Burke   *Libby* Nancy Malone
Patrolman/Sgt Frank Arcaro Harry Bellaver

EPISODE TITLES (Hour-long episodes only)

A Death of Princes (with Eli Wallach)
The Pedigree Sheet (with Suzanne Pleshette)
A Succession of Heartbeats
Down the Long Night (with Leslie Nielsen)
To Walk in Silence (with Telly Savalas)
Killer with a Kiss
Debt of Honour
The Human Trap (with Jack Lord)
The Man Who Bit a Diamond in Half (with Walter Matthau)
Bullets Cost Too Much (with James Caan)
Murder Is a Face I Know
Landscape with Dead Figures
A Hole in the City (with Robert Duvall)
The Well Dressed Termite (with Jack Klugman)
The Day It Rained Mink
Button in the Haystack
Shoes for Vinnie Wineford (with Dennis Hopper)
Deadly Guinea Pig
Vengeance is a Wheel
Fault in Our Stars (with Roddy McDowall)
Tombstone for a Derelict (with Robert Redford)
A Memory of Crying
New York to LA (with Robert Blake)
A Very Cautious Boy (with Peter Falk)
An Economy of death
$C_3H_5(NO_3)_3$
Make Believe Man

To Dream Without Sleep
A Kettle of Precious Fish
Sweet Prince of Delancey Street (with Dustin Hoffman)
The Day the Island Almost Sank
Take and Put
Take Off Your Hat When a Funeral Passes (with Lee J. Cobb)
Dead on a Field of Honour
The Corpse Ran Down Mulberry Street
The Fingers of Henry Tourelle
A Wednesday Night Story (with David Janssen)
The Tragic Success of Alfred Tiloff
Which Is Joseph Creeley?
Show Me The Way To Go Home
The Hot Minerva (with Glynis Johns)
Requiem for a Sunday Afternoon
Oftus Goofus (with Mickey Rooney)
Bridge Party
The Face of the Enemy
Portrait of a Painter
The Night the Saints Lost Their Halo (with Peter Fonda)
The Contract
One of the Most Important Men in the World (with Richard Conte)
A Case Study of Two Savages (with Tuesday Weld)
Let Me Die Before I Wake
To Walk Like a Lion
Today the Man Who Kills Ants Is Coming
A Run for the Money
The One Marked Hot Gives Cold

Without Stick or Sword (with William Shatner)
Lament for a Dead Indian (with Peter Falk)
The Sweet Smiling Face of Truth
And If Any Are Frozen, Warm Them
Strike a Statue (with George C. Scott)
The Multiplicity of Herbert Konish
The King of Venus Will Take Care of You
The Rydecker Case
Memory of a Red Trolley Car (with Gladys Cooper)
Goodbye, Mama, Hello Auntie Maud (with James Coburn)
Hold for Gloria Christmas
Idylls of a Running Back
Daughter, Am I in My Father's House?
And By the Sweat of Thy Brow
Kill Me While I'm Young So I Can Die Happy
Five Cranks for Winter, Ten Cranks for Spring
Go Fight City Hall
Torment Him Much and Hold Him Long
Make It Fifty Dollars and Add Love to Nona
A Horse Has a Big Head, Let Him Worry (with Diahann Carroll)
Dust Devil on a Quiet Street
The Virtues of Madame Douvay
King Stanislaus and the Knights of the Round Stable
Spectre of the Rose Street Gang
Don't Knock It Till You've Tried It (with Walter Matthau)
Her Life in Moving Pictures
Robin Hood and Clarence Darrow, They Went Out With Bow and Arrow
The Apple Falls Not Far From the Tree
Beyond This Place There Be Dragons

Man Without a Skin (with George Segal)
Prime of Life (with Gene Hackman)
Bringing Far Places Together
The Highest of Prizes (with Robert Culp)
Alive and Still a Second Lieutenant (with Jon Voight)
Stop the Parade, a Baby Is Crying
On the Battlefront Every Minute Is Important
Howard Running Bear Is a Turtle
No Naked Ladies In Front of Giovanni's House
Colour Schemes Like Never Before
Carrier
The SS American Dream
Golden Lads and Girls
Barefoot on a Bed of Coals (with Dustin Hoffman)

Creator: Sterling Silliphant
Music: Nelson Riddle
Theme 'Somewhere in the Night': Billy May, Milton Raskin Executive producer: Herbert B. Leonard

A Columbia Pictures Television Production

39 monochrome 30-minute episodes and 99 monochrome 60-minute episodes
US: ABC (Season 1) 30 Sept 1958 - 23 June 1959 (39 eps)
(Season 2) 12 Oct 1960 - 21 June 1961 (32 eps)
(Season 3) 27 Sept 1961 - 27 June 1962 (35 eps)
(Season 4) 19 Sept 1962 - 29 May 1963 (32 eps)
UK: ITV 2 Jan 1962 - 13 May 1963 (57 eps)
(Associated - Rediffusion)
Channel Four 16 April 1983 - 4 Dec 1985

NAKIA

After years of portraying Indians as little more than rifle fodder with the battle tactics of the average lemming, American television attempted partially to redress the balance with a series which showed them in a more favourable light.

Nakia Parker was a modern-day deputy sheriff in a New Mexico city (the programme was filmed in Albuquerque). He was also part Navajo Indian and consequently found a conflict of interests between adhering to the ancient tribal customs and sticking to modern police methods. With no squad car, he often travelled around on horse back, investigating cases which ranged from town council warfare to demonstrations on the reservation. But viewers had their reservations, too, and Nakia was dropped after 15 episodes.

REGULAR CAST

Deputy Nakia Parker Robert Forster   *Sheriff Sam Jericho* Arthur Kennedy
Deputy Hubbel Martin Taylor Lacher

Producer: Charles Larson
Executive producer: David Gerber

15 colour 60-minute episodes
US: ABC 21 Sept - 28 Dec 1974

*A Columbia Pictures Television
Production*

THE NANCY DREW MYSTERIES

The girls' equivalent of The Hardy Boys with which it alternated in the US on Sunday nights. Eighteen-year-old Nancy, played by future Dynasty star, Pamela Sue Martin, was the daughter of celebrated criminal lawyer, Carson Drew, who lived in the plush New York suburb of River Heights. With the help of her friend, George (a girl) and, at first, Carson's law-student assistant, Ned Nickerson, Nancy acted as a teenage sleuth on a host of non-violent adventures. But when Ned became an investigator for the District Attorney's office, he was understandably less inclined to go ghost-busting at night and vainly tried to keep Nancy out of trouble. After ten episodes, this innocuous teenage fare merged with The Hardy Boys. It should have been a union made in Heaven, but sadly they soon split up. (SEE THE HARDY BOYS/NANCY DREW MYSTERIES)

REGULAR CAST

Nancy Drew Pamela Sue Martin   *Carson Drew* William Schallert
Ned Nickerson George O'Hanlon
George Fayne (1977) Jean Rasey *(1977 - 8)* Susan Buckner

Producers: Arlene Sidaris, B.W. Sandefur
Executive producer: Glen A. Larson

10 colour 60-minute episodes
US: ABC 6 Feb 1977 - 1 Jan 1978

A Universal Television Production

NASHVILLE 99

Country and western music is always associated with some kind of tragedy, but few tragedies were greater than Nashville 99, the country and western detective series. It was cancelled after just four episodes.

Veteran Detective Lieutenant Stonewall Jackson Huff, known to his friends as 'Stoney', maintained law and order in the country and western capital of the world, Nashville. Stoney's partner was Detective Trace Mayne, played by country music star Jerry Reed. The producers certainly did their best to make the show authentic, not only filming it in Nashville but also allowing real country music performers like Chet Atkins to play themselves. But it never struck the right chord with viewers.

* Nashville 99 was Stoney's badge number

REGULAR CAST

Det. Lt Stoney Huff Claude Akins   *Det. Trace Mayne* Jerry Reed

Producer: Richard Newton
Executive producer: Ernie Frankel

A TCF Production for CBS

4 colour 60-minute episodes
US: CBS 1 - 22 April 1977

NERO WOLFE

'Nero Wolfe is so much more restful than Frank Cannon. He rarely goes out of the house – maybe once in four or five shows.'
– William Conrad

Rex Stout's overweight, house-bound, orchid-loving detective, Nero Wolfe, was created in the 1930s. His novels sold more than 200 million copies worldwide but had not been adapted for television because Stout refused to sell the TV rights during his lifetime. Stout died in 1975, and six years later Wolfe finally hit the screen, with William Conrad the obvious choice for the title role.

Wolfe was a reclusive, wealthy eccentric. In addition he was a crime-solving genius and, to the delight of Conrad, after years of panting and puffing as Cannon, the most strenuous thing he ever did was eat a mountainous breakfast in bed and then be transported by elevator to the greenhouse on the roof of his New York home, where he spent most of the day tending the rare orchids he raised. When he fitted in detective work, all the running around was done by his assistants, Archie Goodwin and Saul Panzer. Goodwin was a particularly dogged legman in the Sam Spade mould. After the pair had collected the clues, Wolfe sat back and provided the deduction.

Wolfe's faithful retainers also included valued horticulturist, Theodore Horstman, and gourmet cook, Fritz Brenner. It was an idyllic existence – one which suited Wolfe and Conrad down to the ground. Even apart from the lack of physical exertion and the enormous culinary benefits, the actor was very fond of the character. 'He has a great sense of humour,' Conrad explained at the time, 'only he doesn't let people know it, which is the greatest sense of humour of all.'

REGULAR CAST

Nero Wolfe William Conrad   *Archie Goodwin* Lee Horsley
Saul Panzer George Wyner   *Theodore Horstman* Robert Coote
Fritz Brenner George Voskovec   *Inspector Cramer* Allan Miller

Creator: Rex Stout
Executive producers: Ivan Goff, Ben Roberts

A Paramount Television Production

13 colour 60-minute episodes
US: NBC 16 Jan - 25 Aug 1981
UK: ITV From 22 May 1983 (LWT)

THE NEW ADVENTURES OF CHARLIE CHAN

Charlie Chan he say, 'Don't alibi. Old excuse, like ancient goat, has whiskers.'

You can't argue with that. Nor with any of Charlie's other little homilies like, 'Man is not incurably drowned if he still knows he is all wet.' Or 'Be punctual. Cold omelette, like fish out of sea, does not improve with age.' Or even one of his all-time favourites, 'Don't talk too much. Words, like sunbeams, the more they are condensed the deeper they burn.' And Morse thinks *he's* a philosopher!

Earl Derr Biggers created the inscrutable Charlie Chan in the 1920s, but in fact only wrote six Chan stories, the remainder being penned by other writers following his death in 1933. The sage oriental sleuth with the impeccable manners and more patience than Dr Kildare, was popular in the 1930s and 1940s in movies, on American radio and in comic strips as well as books. He was originally modelled on a real person, Detective Chang Apana of the Honolulu police. Accordingly the early productions all featured Charlie as a Honolulu police Inspector, but for the British-made TV series he worked out of London along with Inspector Duff, played by Rupert Davies who was to become a famous sleuth in his own right, Maigret.

The heavily made-up New York Irishman J. Carrol Naish played Charlie, following a long line of non-orientals in the role. These included Warner Oland, Sydney Toler and Roland Winters in movies and Walter Connolly, Ed Begley and Santos Ortega on radio.

Charlie Chan had 14 children, which couldn't have left him much time or energy for detective work, and was always helped by his Number One Son, Barry.

It was passable at the time, but could have done with more action and fewer sayings of Confucius. Viewers they say, 'All talk no deed, like drill in oil-field, make for big bore.' (SEE ALSO THE AMAZING CHAN AND THE CHAN CLAN)

REGULAR CAST

Charlie Chan J. Carrol Naish   *Barry Chan* James Hong
Insp. Duff Rupert Davies   *Insp. Marlowe* Hugh Williams

EPISODE TITLES

Your Money or Your Wife
Secret of the Sea
The Lost Face
Blind Man's Buff
The Great Salvos
The Counterfeiters
Death of a Don
Charlie's Highland Fling
The Patient in Room 21
The Rajput Ruby
Final Curtain
Death at High Tide
Circle of Fear
Exhibit in Wax
Backfire
Patron of the Arts
Hamlet in Flames
Dateline – Execution
The Sweater
The Noble Art of Murder
Three Men on a Raft
No Holiday for Murder
No Future for Frederick
Safe Deposit
Voodoo Death

The Expatriate
Airport Murder Case
The Hand of Hera Dass
The Chippendale Racket
The Invalid
The Man in the Wall
Something Old, Something New
The Man With a Hundred Faces
Point of No Return
A Bowl by Cellini
Without Fear
Kidnap
Rhyme or Treason
Three for One

Producers: Sidney Marshall, Rudolph Flothow
Executive producer: Leon Fromkess

An ITC Production

39 monochrome 30-minute episodes
UK: ITV 28 Sept 1957 - 1961
US: Syndicated June 1957

THE NEW ADVENTURES OF PERRY MASON

It is bad enough when producers insist on re-casting a character half-way through a series, so that a short brunette suddenly appears as a leggy blonde with the same name. But to do it with a character like Perry Mason was sacrilege.

Raymond Burr is Perry Mason. End of story. But CBS wanted to capitalize on the 1970s upsurge in the popularity of detective shows and, with Burr wheeling and dealing as Ironside at the time, they decided to resurrect Perry played by a different actor – Monte Markham. He brought with him a new Della, a new Paul Drake, a new Hamilton Burger, and a new Lieutenant Tragg. Even the one new regular character, Perry's receptionist, Gertie, was played by a different actress (Brett Somers) than when she had made occasional appearances in the original series. Then, she was played by Connie Cezon.

Not surprisingly, the great American viewing jury were not impressed by the imposters. This was one case Perry lost. (SEE ALSO PERRY MASON)

REGULAR CAST

Perry Mason Monte Markham   *Della Street* Sharon Acker
Paul Drake Albert Stratton   *Lt Arthur Tragg* Dane Clark
Hamilton Burger Harry Guardino   *Gertrude Lade* Brett Somers

---

Creator: Erle Stanley Gardner   *A TCF Production for CBS*
Music: Earle Hagen
Producers: Ernie Frankel, Art Seid   15 colour 60-minute episodes
Executive producer: Cornwall Jackson   US: CBS 16 Sept 1973 - 27 Jan 1974

THE NEW BREED

These men were the 'new breed' of policemen, members of the crack Metropolitan Squad of the Los Angeles Police Department who were trained to fight crime with the latest electronic gadgetry. Their leader was Lieutenant Price Adams, played by Leslie Nielsen, and there were occasions when the show was unintentionally almost as funny as Nielsen's more recent outing, the manic Police Squad. But it had its moments and gave work to the likes of Peter Fonda, Charles Bronson, Telly Savalas and Peter Falk.

REGULAR CAST

Lt Price Adams Leslie Nielsen   *Sgt Vince Cavelli* John Beradino
Patrolman Joe Huddleston John Clarke   *Patrolman Pete Garcia* Greg Roman
Capt. Keith Gregory Byron Morrow

EPISODE TITLES

No Fat Cops
Prime Target
Death of a Ghost
To None a Deadly Drug
The Compulsion to Confess
'Til Death Do Us Part
The Butcher
Wave Goodbye to Grandpa
Sweet Bloom of Death
The Valley of the Three Charlies
Lady Killer
Blood Money
I Remember Murder
The All-American Boy
Cross the Little Line
To Sell a Human
Care Is No Cure
Policemen Die Alone (two-parter)
Mrs Weltschmerz
Wings for a Plush Horse
How Proud the Guilty
The Torch
All the Dead Faces

The Deadlier Sex
Edge of Violence
Echoes of Hate
The Man with the Other Face
Thousands and Thousands of Miles
Hail, Hail, The Gang's All Here
My Brother's Keeper
A Motive Named Walter
Wherefore Art Thou, Romeo?
Judgement at San Belito
So Dark the Night
Walk This Street Lightly

Executive producer: Quinn Martin

A Quinn Martin Production for ABC

36 monochrome 60-minute episodes
US: ABC 3 Oct 1961 - 25 Sept 1962
UK: ITV 1 April - 10 Dec 1963 (13 eps)
  (Anglia)

NEW SCOTLAND YARD

Chief Superintendent John Kingdom and Detective Sergeant Alan Ward were the new breed of British policemen in the early 1970s. Serious crime was escalating – armed robbery, murder and terrorism were all on the increase – it needed serious officers to deal with it. And were these two ever serious! I think they only smiled at Coronations.

But they were dedicated coppers, the backbone of New Scotland Yard's CID division. Their relationship was not always harmonious (Ward, in particular, was no loss to the diplomatic service) but they respected each other as policemen.

They remained in partnership for three seasons, but for the fourth and final series were replaced by Detective Chief Superintendent Clay and Detective Sergeant Dexter (the latter played by Clive Francis, son of No Hiding Place's Raymond Francis).

New Scotland Yard was impeccably produced, with fine acting (among those given an early break in a guest role was Bob Hoskins). But it never caught on in the same way that The Sweeney was to, because the central characters were so dull. In attempting to be ultra-realistic, somebody forgot that even life itself has humour.

REGULAR CAST

Det. Chief Supt Kingdom John Woodvine *Det. Sgt Ward* John Carlisle
Det. Chief Supt Clay Michael Turner *Det. Sgt Dexter* Clive Francis

Producer: Jack Williams
Executive producer: Rex Firkin

A London Weekend Television Production

45 colour 60-minute episodes

UK: ITV (Season 1) 22 April - 15 July 1972 (12 eps)
(Season 2) 13 Oct 1972 - 12 Jan 1973 (13 eps)
(Season 3) 23 June - 15 Sept 1973 (13 eps)
(Season 4) 13 April - 25 May 1974 (7 eps)

NIGHT HEAT

A hard-hitting Canadian police series about detectives O'Brien and Giambone working on the night shift in Toronto. Filmed on location in Toronto, Night Heat has proved one of Canada's most successful TV exports and is a mainstay of late-night viewing on the ITV regions.

Much of its popularity is down to authenticity – producers Sonny Grosso and Eddie Egan were both real-life cops who became overnight celebrities when they seized 32 million dollars' worth of heroin, smuggled into New York in a limousine owned by a French television personality. This spectacular coup inspired the 1971 hit movie The French Connection, with Egan serving as the role model for Gene Hackman's Popeye Doyle. So these guys know what they're talking about.

Indeed, Night Heat has been compared to Hill Street Blues – albeit unfavourably.

REGULAR CAST

O'Brien Scott Hylands *Giambone* Jeff Wincott
Lt Hogan Sean McCann

Producers: Sonny Grosso, Eddie Egan
Executive producers: Sonny Grosso,
  Larry Jacobson

A Grosso Jacobson Production for CBS

70 colour 60-minute episodes
Canada: CBS 7 Feb 1985 - 1989
US: 4 - 25 Aug 1987
UK: ITV From 5 Sept 1986 (LWT)

NO HIDING PLACE

Son of Crime Sheet and grandson of Murder Bag, No Hiding Place was
the third in the trilogy of series featuring Raymond Francis as snuff-
taking policeman, Tom Lockhart, now a Chief Detective Superintendent
with Scotland Yard. No Hiding Place was live, which meant that even
car chases took place in the studio!

Lockhart's first assistant was Detective Sergeant Harry Baxter (Eric
Lander) who proved so popular, especially with female viewers, that he
was promoted to Inspector and his own spin-off series (SEE ECHO
FOUR-TWO). In total he appeared in 141 episodes of No Hiding Place,
before handing over to Detective Sergeants Russell and Perryman,
played by Johnny Briggs (now better known as Mike Baldwin from
Coronation Street) and Michael McStay.

But Briggs nearly didn't measure up to the part. He is comparatively
short and Raymond Francis advised him that he stood a better chance of
getting the role if he wore lifts in his shoes. 'Give yourself an extra inch,
because you're a bit small,' said Francis. So Briggs did just that. Later
director Ian Fordyce suggested: 'Johnny, why don't you put a pair of
lifts in your shoes to give you a couple of inches?' Again he agreed,
duly took the screen test and, now growing steadily, was standing at the
bar with Michael McStay. Briggs says: 'I heard Raymond Francis
saying to producer Peter Willes and Ian Fordyce that he wanted to give
me the part. Ian said: "Yes, but Michael is 6ft. 1in. and Johnny is much
shorter." To which Peter Willes replied: "Well, that's not a problem. We
can give him some lifts!"' Once he had got the part, Briggs had a pair of
shoes specially made to make him three inches taller. Francis called
them his orthopaedic boots.

Michael McStay suffered an even more embarrassing experience.
While filming on the Embankment in London, McStay (in plain clothes)
was leading two uniformed policemen in a chase for an unseen villain.
A passer-by witnessed this, thought McStay was trying to escape from
two policemen and decided to have a go. He whacked the actor over the
head with a silver-knobbed cane and McStay had to be taken to hospital.

With a title guaranteed to instil fear into the criminal fraternity, No
Hiding Place never lost its appeal and when, in 1965, it was announced
that the series was to be dropped, both public and police protested. So it
was brought back for two more years (the final season saw the demise

of Russell and Perryman and the introduction of Detective Sergeant Gregg) before Lockhart finally laid his snuffbox to rest.

REGULAR CAST
Chief Det. Supt Lockhart Raymond Francis   *Det. Sgt/Insp. Baxter* Eric Lander
Det. Sgt Russell Johnny Briggs   *Det. Sgt Perryman* Michael McStay
Det. Sgt Gregg Sean Caffrey

Producers: Ray Dicks, Richard Matthews, Johnny Goodman, Peter Willes, Geoffrey Nugus, Michael Currer-Briggs

An Associated Rediffusion Production

236 monochrome 60-minute episodes
UK: ITV 16 Sept 1959 - 22 June 1967

N.O.P.D.

An American syndicated series of the 1950s featuring Beaujac, a detective based in New Orleans. Not even the jazz city setting could help a show which rarely hit the right note.

REGULAR CAST
Beaujac Stacy Harris

Producers: Minot films

39 monochrome 30-minute episodes
UK: Syndicated 1956

NOT FOR HIRE

This syndicated show had a bit more guts to it. Indeed it was pretty strong stuff for 1959, the first episode revealing that a policewoman's trigger-happy attitude stemmed from a pathological hatred of men, after she had been gang-raped as a teenager.

The central character was Steve Dekker, a Honolulu Sergeant with the US Army Criminal Investigations Division. With the aid of his sidekicks, Sonica Zametoo and Corporal Zimmerman, he tracked down those responsible for military crimes – principally deserters and saboteurs.

All the villains had one thing in common – they didn't smoke. This was because the show was sponsored by a tobacco company who didn't want its image tarnished by being associated with crooks. Presumably if it had been sponsored by a razor firm, all of the criminals would have had beards ...

REGULAR CAST

Sgt Steve Dekker Ralph Meeker   *Sonica Zametoo* Lizabeth Rush
Corporal Zimmerman Ken Drake

An NBC Production

39 monochrome 30-minute episodes

US: Syndicated 1959
UK: ITV 27 March - 1 May 1963 (Anglia)

N.Y.P.D.

Produced with the co-operation of the real New York Police Department and based on actual cases, this all-action drama series was a great favourite with the City governors. The Mayor at the time, John Lindsay, went out of his way to commend it and permitted filming to take place in the hallowed City Hall.

Set in the 27th Precinct, it followed three plainclothes detectives on the never-ending hunt for New York's assorted murderers, rapists, muggers and drug pushers. The trio were Lieutenant Mike Haines, an experienced cop with 18 years' service, black officer Jeff Ward and young Johnny Corso. With plenty of screeching tyres and gunfire, the show hardly acted as a tourist brochure for New York, which made it all the more remarkable that it was so warmly greeted by the City brethren.

REGULAR CAST

Det. Lt Mike Haines Jack Warden   *Det. Jeff Ward* Robert Hooks
Det. Johnny Corso Frank Converse

Creators: David Susskind, Arnold Perl
Producer: Robert Butler
Executive producers: Danny Melnick, Bob Markell

A Talent Associates Production for ABC

49 colour 30-minute episodes
US: ABC (Season 1) 5 Sept 1967 - 19 March 1968 (26 eps)
(Season 2) 1 Oct 1968 - 25 March 1969 (23 eps)

UK: ITV 5 April - 27 Dec 1968 (Anglia)

THE ODD MAN

'Edwin Richfield was a kind of East End Bogart – that was the strength of The Odd Man.'   – CREATOR EDWARD BOYD

A cult British crime drama of the 1960s which followed on from Edward Boyd's husband-and-wife detective teams on radio. It first introduced the character of Chief Inspector Rose (SEE ALSO IT'S DARK OUTSIDE AND MR ROSE) although he didn't actually appear until the second series, the grim Chief Inspector Gordon being the detective in the first season. But anyway the star of the piece was Edwin Richfield, as theatrical agent and part-time private eye, Steve Gardiner, a man who became involved in all manner of bizarre cases from murder to espionage. Richfield originally auditioned for a minor role but bluntly informed director Derek Bennett that he should be playing the lead. Bennett agreed.

Gardiner's wife, Judy (played by Sarah Lawson) was killed off during the first season by a mysterious mute killer, South, but the producers, Granada Television, received so much hate mail that they decided to resurrect her. So Lawson was re-cast as Judy's twin sister who had been working in central Africa!

A splendid off-beat series, some years ahead of its time. Incidentally, Rose was a deeply unpleasant policeman here – it was only in the subsequent spin-offs that he became jolly. Obviously having his own show agreed with him.

* Guest artists in The Odd Man included James Bolam as a pop star and Donald Sutherland as a drug-addicted drummer.

REGULAR CAST

Steve Gardiner Edwin Richfield   *Judy Gardiner* Sarah Lawson
Ch. Insp. Rose William Mervyn   *Ch. Insp. Gordon* Moultrie Kelsall
Det. Sgt Swift Keith Barron   *South* Christopher Quinee

Creator: Edward Boyd
Producer: Stuart Latham

24 monochrome 60-minute episodes

UK: ITV (Season 1) 11 May - 29 June
    1962 (8 eps)
(Season 2) 5 April - 24 May 1963 (8 eps)
(Season 3) 26 July - 13 Sept 1963
    (8 eps)

*A Granada Television Network
    Production*

OFFICIAL DETECTIVE

'We hope to show our audience that truth is not only stranger than fiction but more exciting.'   – PRODUCER MORT BRISKIN

Dramatizations of stories from Official Detective magazine, whose researchers vetted the show for accuracy. Each episode was also filmed in the presence of various technical advisers, including a policeman who instructed actresses on the finer points of judo.

Indeed the programme paid great attention to detail – the police were seen working in conjunction with forensics and diligently checking and cross-checking every fact. No sloppiness here! There was no Regular Cast, the only constant being host/narrator Everett Sloane. Before moving to television, Official Detective was a meritorious American radio series.

Producer: Mort Briskin

A Desilu Production with NTA

39 monochrome 30-minute episodes
US: Syndicated 1957
UK: ITV 20 May 1960 - 20 March 1962
   (ATV)

O'HARA, U S TREASURY

After years of being chased as The Fugitive, David Janssen did the pursuing as US Treasury Department agent, Jim O'Hara, a man intent on trapping those who chose to violate federal laws. He served all five of the department's enforcement agencies – Bureau of Customs; Secret Service; Internal Revenue Service Intelligence Division; Internal Revenue Service Inspection Division; and Internal Revenue Service Alcohol, Tobacco and Firearms Division. It took him longer to say where he was from than to solve the case.

* The show was made with the approval of the real US Treasury Department.

REGULAR CAST

Jim O'Hara David Janssen

Creators: Jack Webb, James E. Moser
Music: Ray Heindorf
Producer: Leonard B. Kaufman
Executive producer: Jack Webb

*A Mark VII Ltd Production in association
with Universal Television*

52 colour 60-minute episodes
US: CBS 17 Sept 1971 - 8 Sept 1972
UK: ITV 18 Sept 1971 - 28 March 1973
(ATV)

THE OLDEST ROOKIE

Ike Porter seemed to have the ideal job. As Head of Public Affairs for a big-city police department, he spent his days wining and dining with city officials, attending awards banquets and handling the occasional press inquiry. But he felt separated from 'real cops'. So when an old classmate from Police Academy was gunned down in the line of duty, Ike began to question the career path he had chosen and decided to return to his original goal – being a police officer on active duty. Starting at the bottom, he became the oldest rookie.

After years behind a desk, where his greatest exertion was lifting the telephone receiver, Ike had to complete the Police Academy's rigorous physical training programme all over again. He also faced resistance from superiors who doubted his ability to last the pace, and from his new young partner, Tony Jonas, a brash, street-wise cop with a basketball court in his living room and a penchant for Bruce Springsteen music, as opposed to Ike's liking for Glenn Miller.

In search of action, Ike managed to get him and Tony transferred to detective work. But there they found themselves reporting to Lieutenant Marco Zaga, a hard-nosed officer who resented Ike's years of free lunches, and repeatedly assigned the pair of them to mundane tasks such as babysitting a foreign delegation, interviewing every would-be psychic for murder leads or pursuing stolen avocados.

This comedy/drama may not have set the world alight but at least it was a different idea. And there aren't always too many of those around in television.

REGULAR CAST

Ike Porter Paul Sorvino   *Tony Jonas* D.W. Moffett
Lt Marco Zaga   Raymond J. Barry

Creators: Gil Grant, Richard Chapman
Executive producer: Richard Chapman

*A Touchstone Television Production for
the Walt Disney Company*

14 colour 60-minute episodes

US: CBS 16 Sept 1987 - 6 Jan 1988
UK: ITV 14 July - 8 Dec 1989 (Anglia)

THE OUTSIDER

Darren McGavin, the first TV Mike Hammer, played private eye David Ross, the ultimate loner. He made Howard Hughes look gregarious. Ross's life had been one long trauma. As a small child he was orphaned. He didn't finish high school. Then as an adult he was framed for murder and spent six years in jail before being pardoned. He really was an outsider.

As a detective, he was a graduate of the Philip Marlowe school. He lived and worked from a derelict Los Angeles apartment building where, for some reason, he kept the phone in the fridge. Perhaps he didn't fancy having a 'hot line'. And he finished the average day as beaten up and battered as his old wreck of a car. There was certainly nothing glamorous about Ross's solitary existence and his cases barely paid enough money to live on. But after everything he had been through, he had a compassionate streak to help others. All in all, a decent sort of chap but not somebody with whom you would want to spend your stag night.

* The Outsider was adapted from the 1949 private eye novel, The Double Take.

REGULAR CAST

David Ross Darren McGavin

Creator: Roy Huggins
Producer: Gene Levitt
Executive producer: Roy Huggins

A Public Arts Production in association with Universal Television

One colour 120-minute episode and 26 colour 60-minute episodes US: NBC 18 Sept 1968 - 3 Sept 1969

OVER MY DEAD BODY

The title of this comedy thriller had an ironic ring for actor Edward Woodward, who made his name with American viewers as Robert McCall, The Equalizer. That show's punishing 18 hours-a-day schedule for four years had resulted in Woodward suffering a massive heart attack in 1987. Even though he was back pounding the streets of New

York as The Equalizer a month later, he vowed that for his next series he was going to take things a little easier.

So when he was offered the role of mystery writer and sleuth, Max Beckett, he made Universal agree to shoot only four days a week, ten hours day. That way, it wouldn't be his dead body they were filming over.

In many ways Max Beckett was a male Jessica Fletcher but without the dead nephews. However, whereas Jessica was a widely-acclaimed murder-mystery writer, Max's last two novels had been dismal failures. Even the Rolls-Royce he drove was clapped out. Silver-haired, bespectacled and portly, Max looked reasonably distinguished, but in reality he was a con artist. He had built his reputation on having been a retired Inspector from Scotland Yard. His book publicity referred to him as a hard-bitten cop who had solved hundreds of murders. Yet far from being gunned out of London by irate mobsters, the truth emerged that Max was really only a back-office clerk at Scotland Yard, who twisted his knee on a flight of stairs. Woodward described him as 'A noisy, bombastic con artist. A crazy mixed-up mess, but quite a smart mess.'

As if he hadn't enough problems with an ailing career, an anxious publisher and an impending divorce, into his life stepped the vivacious motorcycle-riding Nicki Page, obituary writer for the San Francisco Union newspaper, under the name of Miss Black. She had witnessed the grisly murder of a call girl and, unable to obtain police interest, pestered Max until he agreed to help. Her boundless enthusiasm gave him a new lease of life and they joined together to form an entertaining, if brief, partnership.

Over My Dead Body was roundly panned on both sides of the Atlantic but I quite enjoyed it. Jessica Lundy as Nicki Page looked a most promising newcomer and there were some good jokes. If there was a fault, perhaps it was that Max Beckett was too over the top to be believable. Yet Edward Woodward insists: 'He was based on a man I know well and I played him the way he really is. But I'm not saying who he is.' A wise decision.

REGULAR CAST

Max Beckett Edward Woodward   *Nicki Page* Jessica Lundy

Creators: William Link, David Chisholm
Music: Lee Holdridge
Producer: Ken Topolsky
Executive producers: William Link, David Chisholm

One colour 120-minute episode and 7 colour 60-minute episodes

A Universal Television Production

US: CBS 26 Oct - 21 Dec 1990
UK: BBC1 4 Jan - 20 March 1991

PARIS

The loveliness of Paris was lost on the viewing public, simply because an intelligent idea was marred by hopeless miscasting. For classical Shakespearean actor James Earl Jones looked completely lost as diligent black police captain Woody Paris. It was like putting Olivier in Dixon of Dock Green.

Paris was a thoughtful cop, a born leader of men, who believed in the sanctity of the uniform. At night he taught criminology at the local university. He was head of the special Metro Squad, an inner-city team formed to crack the toughest cases. Under him were four young officers – Stacey Erickson, Charlie Bogart, Ernie Villas and Willie Miller.

Woody Paris was well-liked – by his boss, Deputy Chief Jerome Bench and, a rarity for TV cops, even by his own wife, Barbara. But despite good reviews, he wasn't as popular in the lounges of America and the show was axed after 13 episodes.

It was a pity because a couple of episodes were of outstanding quality. Dead Men Don't Kill was particularly powerful, with Georg Stanford Brown playing a wrongly-convicted murderer awaiting execution. Paris had discovered that he was innocent but the state governor refused to halt the proceedings. There was no familiar last-minute reprieve, the ultimate cop-out. Instead there was a graphic illustration of a prisoner's last moments of life as, eyes bulging, sweating profusely and strapped to a chair, he felt the cyanide capsule being released into the gas chamber. The watching Paris left in tears.

Paris also played a minor part in the birth of Hill Street Blues. It was created by Steven Bochco, the man behind Hill Street, and among the guest stars were future favourites on the Hill, Kiel Martin, Joe Spano, Taurean Blacque, James B. Sikking and Michael Conrad. But the failure of Paris nearly dissuaded Bochco from doing any more police series. Hill Street may never have happened. He admits: 'I was personally so dismayed with the work on Paris. I wasn't happy with what I did at all. And so I sure wasn't looking to do another cop show...'

REGULAR CAST

Woody Paris James Earl Jones   *Barbara Paris* Lee Chamberlain
Deputy Chief Jerome Bench Hank Garrett   *Stacey Erickson* Cecilia Hart
Charlie Bogart Jake Mitchell   *Ernie Villas* Frank Ramirez
Willie Miller Mike Warren

EPISODE TITLES

Pilot show
Dear John

Pawn
Friends and Enemies

Once More For Free
Dead Men Don't Kill
Burnout
Decisions
Fitz's Boys
The Price Is Right
The Ghost Maker
Pay The Two Bucks
America The Beautiful

Creator: Steven Bochco
Producers: Gregory Hoblit, Edward De Blasio
Executive producer: Steven Bochco

An MTM Production

13 colour 60-minute episodes
US: CBS 29 Sept 1979 - 15 Jan 1980
UK: ITV 21 Oct 1980 - 15 Dec 1981
(Thames)

PARIS PRECINCT

Beaumont and Bolbec were a couple of forerunners of Maigret – French Surete Inspectors, whose lot in life was to clean up crime on the streets of Paris. This French-produced 1950s export was inspired by the American police series of the time.

* In the US, Paris Precinct was syndicated under the title World Crime Hunt.

REGULAR CAST

Insp. Beaumont Louis Jourdan   *Insp. Bolbec* Claude Dauphin

An Etoile Production

26 monochrome 30-minute episodes
US: ABC 3 April 1953 - 18 Dec 1955

PARKIN'S PATCH

A gentle Yorkshire police drama created by Softly, Softly writer, Elwyn Jones. It followed the adventures of PC Moss Parkin, the friendly copper on the beat, and his CID colleague, Detective Constable Ron Radley. Their first investigation was a break-in at a tobacconist's. That just about set the tone for the rest of the series.

REGULAR CAST

PC Moss Parkin John Flanagan   *Det. Con. Ron Radley* Gareth Thomas
Beth Parkin Heather Page

Creator: Elwyn Jones
Producer: Terence Williams

A Yorkshire Television Network Production

26 colour 30-minute episodes
UK: ITV 19 Sept 1969 - 10 March 1972

THE PARTNERS

A below-average American sit-com about two police detectives, Robinson and Crooke, one black and one white, who, despite landing themselves in no end of chaotic scrapes, always managed to solve the crime – to the irritation of their boss, Captain Andrews, and his unctious underling, Sergeant Higgenbottom. The best character was Freddie Butler, a compulsive confessor, who would claim responsibility for everything from the sacking of Rome to being Jack the Ripper. But apart from him, it was a dismal affair. The Partners was created by and starred Don Adams of Get Smart fame. Afterwards he should have repeated his Get Smart catchphrase: 'Sorry about that.'

REGULAR CAST

Det. Lennie Crooke Don Adams   *Det. George Robinson* Rupert Crosse
Capt. Andrews John Doucette   *Sgt Higgenbottom* Dick Van Patten
Freddie Butler Robert Karvelas

Creator: Don Adams
Music: Lalo Schifrin
Executive producer: Don Lee

A Universal Television Production

20 colour 30-minute episodes
US: NBC 18 Sept 1971 - 8 Sept 1972
UK: ITV From 9 March 1972

PARTNERS IN CRIME (UK)

Following their one-off Agatha Christie adaptations, Why Didn't They Ask Evans? and The Seven Dials Mystery, London Weekend Television produced a glossy series about two of her lesser-known characters, Tommy and Tuppence Beresford. It opened with a two-hour version of Christie's thriller The Secret Adversary and took Tommy and Tuppence on a further ten weeks of adventures. The idea was that the pair met up again after the First World War, married and set up as private detectives.

They called their agency Blunt's and proceeded to do a spot of top-hole sleuthing among high society in the Twenties and Thirties. I'm not sure what Christie's reaction would have been to taking liberties with her characters, but Partners In Crime did well enough to sell overseas.

REGULAR CAST

Tuppence Beresford Francesca Annis   *Tommy Beresford* James Warwick
Insp. Marriott Arthur Cox

EPISODE TITLES

The Secret Adversary
The Affair of the Pink Pearl
The House of Lurking Death
The Sunningdale Mystery
The Clergyman's Daughter
Finessing the King
The Ambassador's Boots
The Man In the Mist
The Unbreakable Alibi
The Case of the Missing Lady
The Crackler

Music: Joseph Horowitz
Producer: Jack Williams

An LWT Network Production

One colour 120-minute episode and 10 colour 60-minute episodes UK: ITV 8 Oct 1983 - 14 Jan 1984
US: WGBH Boston 'Mystery' 29 Nov - 27 Dec 1984 (5 eps)
1 - 29 May 1986 (5 eps)
22 - 29 Jan 1987 (The Secret Adversary)

PARTNERS IN CRIME (US)

A feeble mystery series, starring Lynda Carter who made her name as Wonder Woman. This was a more a case of Wonder Why.

Leggy Lynda played Carole Stanwyck, a rich professional photographer who shared the same ex-husband as the equally glamorous Sydney Kovak, an effervescent blonde who played the bass in a jazz band and was a budding pickpocket. When their ex-husband, eccentric San Francisco private detective, Raymond Caulfield, was murdered, the two girls inexplicably teamed up to catch the killer. They then discovered that in his will Caulfield had left them half shares in his detective agency, and so they became two spare parts from Charlie's Angels.

In the real world, the police would have had absolutely nothing to do with them but this was prime-time television, so not only was the S.F.P.D.'s Lieutenant Ed Vronsky helpful, he was continually trying to chat up Sydney. Other characters were Harmon Shain, the girls' dense assistant, and Jeanine, Caulfield's mother, an interfering amateur sleuth who ran a mystery bookshop called Partners in Crime.

Regular Cast

Carole Stanwyck Lynda Carter   *Sydney Kovak* Loni Anderson
Lt Ed Vronsky Leo Rossi   *Harmon Shain* Walter Olkewicz
Jeanine Eileen Heckart

Creators: Bill Driskill, Robert Van Scoyk
Producer: Bill Driskill

A Carson Production for Columbia Pictures Television

12 colour 60-minute episodes
US: NBC 22 Sept - 5 Jan 1985
UK: ITV 25 March - 10 June 1986

PAUL TEMPLE

'Paul Temple hits people sometimes but when he does, he gets his knuckles cut and it hurts.'   – PRODUCER PETER BRYANT

In 1938 on a train from the Midlands to London, thriller writer Francis Durbridge sat opposite a man in his mid-thirties who, handsome, calm and smoking a pipe, looked to Durbridge as if he might be a private eye. The two men never spoke but unbeknown to the mystery passenger, he was to become the role model for Durbridge's elegant sleuth, Paul Temple.

The character was first introduced on British radio four years later and, in all, six different actors had played the part before Francis Matthews came along with the definitive version on TV, in 1969.

Paul Temple was the epitome of the suave Englishman. At 35, he drove a Rolls-Royce Silver Shadow drop-head Coupe, lived in a smart Chelsea pad with beautiful wife, Steve, and was so wealthy as an author that he only needed to write one book a year.

The TV series was brought up to date, set in the late 1960s and had the distinction of being one of the BBC's first major colour productions. It cost £630,000, more than twice the cost of the black and white classic, The Forsyte Saga.

The Temples were enthusiasts who carried on sleuthing for the fun of it. Many of their adventures took them abroad, which enabled them to compare the opulent lifestyles of European cities with their own. One thing that did ruffle Paul's calm was violence, particularly if he was on the receiving end. It was always such a chore having to take the tuxedo to the dry cleaner's.

The urbane Francis Matthews looked very much at home in the role. He even admitted at the time: 'I'm more or less playing myself.'

* Francis Durbridge's superior thriller serials were a mainstay of BBC

output in the 1950s and 1960s, with such offerings as The World of Tim Frazer, Bat Out of Hell and The Doll.

Paul Temple Francis Matthews   *Steve Temple* Ros Drinkwater

Creator: Francis Durbridge
Music: Ron Grainer
Producers: Alan Bromly, Peter Bryant
   Derrick Sherwin

A BBC Television Production

52 colour 50-minute episodes

UK: BBC1 (Season 1) 23 Nov 1969 -
   15 Feb 1970 (13 eps)
(Season 2) 5 April - 26 July 1970
   (13 eps)
(Season 3) 10 Jan - 11 April 1971
   (13 eps)
(Season 4) 9 June - 1 Sept 1971
   (13 eps)

PERRY MASON

'When I was originally asked to test for the Perry Mason series, it was not for the part of Mason but the prosecuting attorney!'

– RAYMOND BURR

How the course of television history would have been changed, had Raymond Burr played District Attorney Ham Burger, instead of defence counsel supreme, Perry Mason. Such was Burr's authority that surely the prosecution would have won every case instead. But as it happened, back in 1956, Burr insisted on auditioning for the role of Mason as well, in company with 200 other actors. Erle Stanley Gardner took one look and knew that he had found his ideal Perry Mason.

Strictly speaking, Perry Mason was not a detective series but a courtroom drama. However, in the course of 271 episodes, Paul Drake did more investigating than Columbo, Miss Marple and Jim Rockford put together.

Perry Mason was created by Erle Stanley Gardner in the 1933 novel, The Case of the Velvet Claws, and went on to appear in 82 further books, as well as on film and radio. But those adaptations did not meet with Gardner's wholehearted approval and he decided to take a closer interest in the TV series, especially the casting. His involvement was so great that in the final Mason story, The Case of the Final Fadeout, he played the judge.

During the show's nine-year run, its characters became household names – Perry's loyal secretary, Della Street; his trusted investigator, Paul Drake; and, on the prosecution side, long-suffering District Attorney Hamilton Burger and Lieutenant Tragg. The format was always the same – the victim was widely hated but all would look lost for the accused (usually a helpless damsel) until Paul walked into court with a vital piece of information and, in a dramatic finale, the real culprit would break down and confess in court, under Perry's relentless examination. I always felt sorry for the judge, who had nothing more to say than 'sustained', 'overruled' and 'case dismissed' or the juries who spent all those years in court and never got to deliver a verdict.

Perry's outstanding trait was an invincibility that bordered on the God-like. Out of those 271 cases, he lost only three. On one of those rare occasions, when a defendant refused to reveal the information that would have saved her, 30,000 Americans wrote to Burr urging: 'Don't do that again.' In Britain, a Glasgow bookmaker claimed to have been tipped off that Mason was going to lose that week's case and offered odds of 20-1 on him losing. 600 punters took up the challenge, but the bookie's information was wrong and he graciously donated his £100 takings to charity. Even when Burr was ill for The Case of the Constant Doyle, Bette Davis stepped in to play a lawyer friend and she duly triumphed.

Burr was as meticulous as Mason in his preparation. He used to live in a bungalow in the studio grounds and would get up at 3.30am to learn his lines. Immediately after being awarded the part, he spent six months sitting in court and studying real-life attorneys in action. And even when he was comfortably settled into the role, he used to confer regularly with six Superior Court judges, who were all friends of his, before delivering his speeches. If all six said something he was planning was technically incorrect, he would drop it.

This attention to detail helped make Perry Mason one of the most popular ever TV dramas. In the UK, the Bar Council reported that the programme had helped raise the standard of British juries, and Burr was so convincing that he was often invited to address lawyers' gatherings.

One of the burning issues was Perry's relationship with Della, played by Barbara Hale. Was the famous lawyer ever caught with his briefs around his ankles?

Burr says: 'Mr Gardner wouldn't allow us to show anything of any personal involvement between Perry Mason and his secretary. We couldn't dance together, nothing. But we used to try to sneak things in. Once I remember Paul, Della and Mason were in Mason's office at three in the morning. She was asleep and exhausted because we'd all been working very hard on a case and we were going out to see if we could find further clues.

'I said to the director: "Why don't we let Perry be a gentleman there?" I suggested he should start to carry his coat out, realize that Della had fallen asleep, that perhaps she's getting a bit chilly, then just put his coat over her and leave. The director said, "Great idea!"

'So I said to Barbara, "It's Mason's coat, his tobacco, his cologne and you've snuggled up into that coat many, many times. You're asleep but play the scene." She did it and it was subtle enough to get by the production office who probably wouldn't have let it go through if they had realized what we were trying to do. But the viewers did – and we got 35,000 letters about that scene saying, "Now we know..."'

The series came to an end in 1966, and Burr went on to star in A Man Called Ironside. There was an ill-fated revival with a different cast (SEE THE NEW ADVENTURES OF PERRY MASON) until Burr was persuaded back for a series of two-hour TV movies in 1986 (they were shown in Britain from 1990). Paunchier, grey-haired with a beard and sometimes walking with the aid of a stick, Mason had progressed to the rank of Appeal Court judge, while Della had become the top executive for one of the wealthiest men in the world. But when Della was conveniently charged with murder, there was only one man who could defend her, and so Perry resigned from the bench.

Barbara Hale returned as Della, with her real son, William Katt, taking over as Paul Drake Junior (the original Paul Drake, William Hopper, died in 1970). William Talman and Ray Collins, who played Burger and Tragg, were also dead, so Perry had a new, equally unsuccessful courtroom adversary, prosecutor Michael Reston, played by David Ogden Stiers (the pompous Charles Emerson Winchester in M*A*S*H). But with no disrespect to the new cast, somehow without the old faces the shows failed to have the same impact, particularly since they were not based on the Gardner novels. I object to them on the grounds that they risk diminishing the memory of a superb series – Sustained.

* Perry Mason may have been virtually unbeatable, but Raymond Burr did lose a court case when he conducted his own defence. In 1963 a court in Phoenix, Arizona, ordered him to pay £402 to a creditor who claimed that Burr had owed him money since 1949. The judge said that he would have dismissed the case because the debt was too old, but instead of answering the summons through a lawyer, as Arizona law required, Burr had followed the improper procedure of pleading his own case. This, remarked the judge, was not good law. Sometimes it doesn't pay an actor to identify too closely with a part...

REGULAR CAST

Perry Mason Raymond Burr   *Della Street* Barbara Hale
Paul Drake William Hopper   *Hamilton Burger* William Talman
Lt Arthur Tragg Ray Collins

Creator: Erle Stanley Gardner
Music: Richard Shores, Fred Steiner
Producers: Art Seid, Sam White, Ben Brady
Executive producers: Gail Patrick Jackson, Arthur Marks

A Paisano Production for CBS

271 monochrome 60-minute episodes (except the final programme which was in colour)

US: CBS (Season 1) 21 Sept 1957 - 28 June 1958 (40 eps)
(Season 2) 20 Sept 1958 - 27 June 1959 (31 eps)
(Season 3) 3 Oct 1959 - 11 June 1960 (27 eps)
(Season 4) 1 Oct 1960 - 24 June 1961 (27 eps)
(Season 5) 16 Sept 1961 - 26 May 1962 (29 eps)
(Season 6) 27 Sept 1962 - 16 May 1963 (27 eps)
(Season 7) 26 Sept 1963 - 21 May 1964 (30 eps)
(Season 8) 24 Sept 1964 - 13 May 1965 (30 eps)
(Season 9) 12 Sept 1965 - 22 May 1966 (30 eps)
UK: BBC 1 30 Jan 1961 - 14 July 1967

THE PERSUADERS

Following the success of The Saint, ATV chief Sir Lew Grade hoped Roger Moore would work his magic again in The Persuaders, a light international adventure series about two wealthy but reluctant crime-fighters. Moore played Lord Brett Sinclair, whose life to date had been devoted to fast cars and fast women. He teamed up with Tony Curtis as playboy oil millionaire Danny Wilde (Rock Hudson was approached first but was unavailable).

The pair operated under the jurisdiction of Judge Fulton who, although retired, was still determined to purge the world of crime, and persuaded Sinclair and Wilde to become his 'instruments of justice'. Thus they embarked on a new career of pulling in crooks and pulling girls in equal proportions.

Moore and Curtis struck up an instant rapport, both on and off screen (Moore even gave up smoking because Curtis was a fervent campaigner for the American Cancer Society) and this made the show one of the best of its type. Mind you, it wasn't cheap. At £2½ million, it was the most expensive British programme so far, but the outlay was offset by Sir Lew shrewdly pre-selling it to America's ABC network, for over £3 million.

Yet despite being unashamedly designed to cater for the transatlantic market, America was the one country where The Persuaders failed to take off, ABC axing it after 24 of the scheduled 26 episodes. The original intention was to make five series but, faced with US diffidence, the show was scrapped. Not that Moore and Curtis minded too much – the money they earned from it meant they were laughing all the way to the bank.

REGULAR CAST

Danny Wilde Tony Curtis   *Lord Brett Sinclair* Roger Moore
Judge Fulton Laurence Naismith

Creator: Robert S. Baker
Persuaders theme: John Barry
Music: Ken Thorne
Producer: Robert S. Baker

A Tribune Production

24 colour 60-minute episodes
UK: ITV 17 Sept 1971 - 25 Feb 1972
US: ABC 18 Sept 1971 - 14 June 1972

PETER GUNN

In 1958, Peter Gunn heralded a new era of trendy tecs on TV. Gone were the trenchcoats and trilbys, in came a hip, lady-killing breed of private eye. Producer Blake Edwards knew exactly how he wanted his creation to look and told the show's star, Craig Stevens, to get his hair styled in what amounted to a crew-cut. The image worked, as women swooned over the new hero.

And whereas his hard-boiled, mean-street predecessors worked out of grim downtown offices, Peter Gunn operated from a plush apartment at 351, Ellis Park Road, Los Angeles. Nor did Gunn drink at some cheap gin-joint, he spent most of his free time at a jazz club called Mother's, where the resident singer was his pretty blonde girlfriend Edie. Gunn was a cool customer even in the deadliest of situations. Next to him, James Bond looked sweaty. Gunn always won through, there wasn't a case he couldn't crack although sometimes he found himself in deep water and had to rely on the intervention of his friendly police adversary, Lieutenant Jacoby.

The interplay between Gunn and Jacoby was an essential ingredient of the show and so when actor Herschel Bernardi, who played Jacoby, was briefly hospitalized, Blake Edwards made sure that the character was still included in that episode. What happened was that a double moved in front of a brick wall to establish shots and Bernardi was then filmed in close-up from his bed, with a brick backdrop behind him. The ward must have had a very understanding Sister.

But the one feature that most people remember about Peter Gunn is Henry Mancini's aggressive theme music. This, coupled with the jazz sounds that punctuated the action, gave the show a really modern feel, one that was to be imitated many times over.

So in every respect this was a landmark detective programme which maintained its high standard for over 100 episodes. Even then, Gunn hadn't quite run out of ammunition. Edwards and Stevens teamed up for a 1967 movie, titled simply Gunn, but it paled in comparison with the TV series, mainly due to the absence of Herschel Bernardi, and Lola Albright who played Edie.

* Henry Mancini's jazz themes were so popular that RCA released two hit albums from the show, The Music from Peter Gunn and More Music from Peter Gunn. Why waste money thinking up catchy titles...?

* The second 'Mother' was Minerva Urecal, familiar at the time to viewers on both sides of the Atlantic as Tugboat Annie.

REGULAR CAST

Peter Gunn Craig Stevens   Edie Hart Lola Albright
Lt Jacoby Herschel Bernardi
'Mother' (Season 1) Hope Emerson (Season 2) Minerva Urecal

Creator/Producer: Blake Edwards
Theme music: Henry Mancini

A Spartan Production

110 monochrome 30-minute episodes

US: NBC (Season 1) 22 Sept 1958 - 15 June 1959 (36 eps)
(Season 2) 21 Sept 1959 - 13 June 1960 (37 eps)
ABC (Season 3) 3 Oct 1960 - 26 June 1961 (37 eps)

PETROCELLI

Barry Newman first played Italian-American lawyer, Tony Petrocelli, in the 1970 film The Lawyer. Four years later this intelligent spin-off appeared, set in the fictional Southwestern town of San Remo.

City-boy Tony had made a decision to practice law in the middle of nowhere, and so he set up shop in the heart of cattle country. Petrocelli was so idealistic that he took on cases regardless of whether his clients could afford to pay him, with the result that he was generally impoverished and he and his wife, Maggie, had to live in a caravan. To help out, he hired a local cowboy, Pete Ritter, as his investigator. The other major character was Lieutenant Ponce of the San Remo police. Outside working hours he was Petrocelli's friend but they were rivals in court.

There aren't too many legal eagles with a heart who don't mind waiving payment. Petrocelli was one. It's a shame he's not still in the business...

REGULAR CAST

Tony Petrocelli Barry Newman   Maggie Petrocelli Susan Howard
Pete Ritter Albert Salmi   Lt Ponce David Huddleston

Creators: Sidney J. Furie, Harold Buchman, E. Jack Newman
Producers: Thomas L. Miller, Edward J. Milkis
A Paramount Television Production

41 colour 60-minute episodes

US: NBC (Season 1) 11 Sept 1974 - 2 April 1975 (22 eps)
(Season 2) 10 Sept 1975 - 3 March 1976 (19 eps)
UK: BBC1 (Season 1) 21 April - 8 Sept 1978
(Season 2) 23 Feb - 2 Nov 1979

PHILIP MARLOWE

'Down these mean streets a man must go who is not himself mean, who is neither tarnished nor afraid. He is the hero, he is everything. A complete man and a common man and yet an unusual man. He is a very lonely man and his pride is that you will treat him as a proud man or be very sorry you ever saw him. He talks as the man of his age talks – that is, with rude wit, a lively sense of the grotesque, a disgust for sham and a contempt for pettiness. If there were enough like him, the world would be a very safe place to live in, without becoming too dull to be worth living in.'   – RAYMOND CHANDLER ON PHILIP MARLOWE

Not a patch on the Powers Boothe interpretation (SEE MARLOWE - PRIVATE EYE), this earlier Philip Marlowe was about as hard-bitten and fearless as Woody Allen. All the venom and violence from Chandler's novels had been removed, to leave a man with impeccable manners. In fact the only thing the actor had in common with the character was that they shared the same christian name.

REGULAR CAST

Philip Marlowe Philip Carey

An ABC Production

26 monochrome 30-minute episodes

US: ABC 6 Oct 1959 - 29 March 1960
UK: BBC 25 Jan - 12 Sept 1960

PHOTOCRIME

Genial Inspector Hannibal Cobb was the hero of this short-lived, early American cop show. It was produced in association with Look magazine and was sometimes also known as Look Photocrime.

REGULAR CAST

Insp. Hannibal Cobb Chuck Webster

An ABC Production

13 monochrome 30-minute episodes
US: ABC 21 Sept - 14 Dec 1949

PILGRIM STREET

In 1950, figures showed that out of 100,304 indictable crimes reported in London's Metropolitan Police district, only 18 were murders. These peaceful times were reflected in Pilgrim Street, an early BBC police series made in co-operation with the Met.

Created by Jan Read, who wrote the film The Blue Lamp which introduced George Dixon, it showed life at Pilgrim Street, a fictional, old-fashioned London police station, where most of the cases were nothing more serious than milk bottle thieving. Hardly worth calling in the S.W.A.T. brigade for! There was no regular cast but the producer, Robert Barr, went on to be one of the principal writers for Maigret, Z Cars and Softly, Softly.

Creator: Jan Read
Producer: Robert Barr

6 monochrome 30-minute episodes
UK: BBC 4 June - 9 July 1952

A BBC Television Production

THE PINK PANTHER SHOW

An ever popular cartoon series that crops up whenever there's a Bank Holiday or the snooker finishes early. It not only features 'the one and only truly original panther, Pink Panther from head to toes' but the world's most inept detective, the accident-prone Inspector Clouseau. The show originated from the inventive title sequence of the 1963 film of the same name, starring David Niven and, of course, Peter Sellers.

Music: Henry Mancini
Producers: David De Patie, Friz Freleng

Colour 30-minute episodes
US: NBC From 6 Sept 1969
UK: BBC1 From 12 Sept 1970

THE PLAINCLOTHESMAN

A long-running American big-city crime series of the late 1940s and early '50s, showing the ceaseless dedication of an unnamed Lieutenant on homicide, and his sidekick Sergeant Brady. Not only did the

Lieutenant remain anonymous, but in the programme's five-year lifespan he was seen only once – and that was in a flashback. This was because The Plainclothesman employed the technique of using the Lieutenant as a camera, with everything seen from his viewpoint. Thus, if he was knocked over, the viewer looked up from floor level, if he got something in his eye, the camera blinked. And if he was punched in the face, you probably had to buy a new TV set.

REGULAR CAST

The Lieutenant Ken Lynch   *Sgt Brady* Jack Orrison

Producers: John L. Clark, John Clarol

A DuMont Production

Monochrome 30-minute episodes
US: DuMont 12 Oct 1949 - 19 Sept 1954

POLICE RESCUE

'If you watched the soaps, you would begin to believe that Australia was in a time warp away from the rest of the world, where the toughest decision you have to make is what to throw on the barbie.'
– GARY SWEET

The guys on the Sydney-based police rescue unit deal with explosions, cliff and sea rescues, train, plane and helicopter crashes, suicides and sieges – and still find time to play detective. Yes, they can rescue just about anything...except a dodgy script and their mates' wooden acting.

For this action series is not the finest example of Australian drama. True it's a little grittier than Neighbours, but otherwise it's the same old mix of plenty of 'g'days', melodramatic acting and predictable stories that went out with Skippy. The only surprising thing about Police Rescue is that the BBC lashed out £3 million to co-produce it, the Corporation's biggest ever overseas commitment.

The central character is Sergeant Steve 'Mickey' McClintock, played by Gary Sweet, an all-Australian hero with wife problems and the eye of the squad's only girl, First Class Constable Georgia Rattray. Among Mickey's male buddies are romeo ex-con, Angel, and the amiable Sootie.

Police Rescue has turned Gary Sweet into Australia's hottest property since Dame Edna Everage, so naturally he is full of praise for the programme. 'It shows men and women doing a very unpleasant job under a lot of pressure in a big city,' he says. 'They moan, they have a few drinks, they argue and they worry. Just like real people.' Well, nearly.

REGULAR CAST

Sgt 'Mickey' McClintock Gary Sweet   *Angel* Steve Bastoni
Georgia Sonia Todd   *Sootie* Peter Browne

Music: Martin Armiger
Producers: Sandra Levy, John Edwards
Executive producers: Kim Williams,
  Penny Chapman

*A Southern Star Xanadu Production in
association with the Australian
Broadcasting Corporation and the
BBC*

One colour 90-minute episode and 12
colour 60-minute episodes
UK: BBC1 30 March - 17 July 1991

POLICE SQUAD

Too many police spoofs have possessed the entertainment value of a
night in the cells, with only a CHiPS video for company. Police Squad
was a notable exception. This was madcap comedy in the finest
traditions of Jerry and David Zucker and Jim Abrahams, the brains
behind the hilarious disaster movie send-up, Airplane.

Like Airplane, Police Squad starred Leslie Nielsen, an actor who
made his name in straight-laced cop shows like The New Breed and The
Protectors. Here he also kept a straight face as sober Detective Frank
Drebin, a man you wouldn't put in charge of a car boot sale, let alone a
murder inquiry.

Each episode began with a robotic Quinn Martin-style introduction,
'Tonight's episode...', whereupon a totally different title would appear
on screen. Also right at the start, that week's guest star was always
murdered, never to be seen again. And the closing credits were a parody
of Dr Kildare, with the actors freezing in mid-air.

It was all wonderfully silly, laden with running gags such as Drebin
pulling up in his squad car and knocking over a dustbin. The second
week he knocked over two bins, the third week three and so on. It was a
good job the show didn't run to a second series, his car would have been
a write-off.

Among the supporting characters were the loyal Captain Hocken,
lecherous police scientist, Ted Olson, and Johnny the Snitch, street
informant and just about the oldest shoeshine boy in town. Johnny
wouldn't talk until he had been paid, but once he had got the money in
his hand, he wouldn't shut up. Then there was Al, a 7ft cop whose face
was never seen, because he was too tall to fit on the screen.

Police Squad demanded the utmost concentration, because so many
gags, many of them visual, were packed into each half-hour. Blink and
you'd miss a couple. And Drebin used to become involved in the most

convoluted conversations. The whole thing was frantic and very funny. Yet in the midst of it all, Drebin was deadly serious. In fact, I'd go as far as to say Frank was earnest. Oh dear, that sounds like the beginning of one of Drebin's conversations.

* Police Squad led to a hit movie spin-off, Naked Gun.

REGULAR CAST

Det. Frank Drebin Leslie Nielsen   *Capt. Ed Hocken* Alan North
Ted Olson Ed Williams   *Johnny the Snitch* William Duell

Creators: Jerry Zucker, David Zucker, Jim Abrahams
Producer: Bob Weiss

A Zucker/Zucker/Abrahams Production for Paramount Television

6 colour 30-minute episodes
US: ABC 4 March - 2 Sept 1982
UK: ITV 5 Oct - 2 Nov 1985 (LWT)

POLICE STORY (1952)

A live series mainly composed of dramatized case histories drawn from the files of law-enforcement agencies, although some episodes were devoted to crime prevention rather than detection. There was no regular cast, with actors being selected on the strength of their physical similarity to the police officers who had worked on that particular case. Among those who passed the lookalike test was E. G. Marshall, later a stalwart of that classic courtroom drama The Defenders.

Narrator: Norman Rose

A CBS Production

16 monochrome 30-minute episodes
US: CBS 4 April - 1 Aug 1952

POLICE STORY (1973)

'I had quite a few guys in handcuffs who almost seemed proud to be arrested by me. They even asked for autographs.'
– JOSEPH WAMBAUGH

When Police Story began, its creator, best-selling author Joseph Wambaugh, was still a cop with the Los Angeles Police Department, and thus became quite a celebrity with colleagues and criminals alike. He had already penned two best-selling police novels, The New Centurions and The Blue Knight, the latter of which was also to become a TV series (SEE THE BLUE KNIGHT). But with Police Story, Wambaugh wanted to do something different from the standard cops and robbers fare – he wanted to emphasize the mental as well as the physical anguish of the job, to impress upon the public that police work is 'the most dangerous job in the world emotionally.'

He stressed that police rarely discharged their weapons but when they did, instead of purely concentrating on the effect on the victim, Wambaugh wanted to spotlight the traumas faced by the officer who fired the bullet. For especially if it is fatal, a shooting, no matter how justified, leaves a scar on the most battle-hardened cop. And what of policemen's families? How do they cope with the pressures of saying goodbye to someone in the morning, never sure whether they will ever see them alive again? Wambaugh was keen to explore the strain that being a cop puts on a marriage, as well as examining other personal problems such as alcoholism and enforced retirement. He wanted to look at every aspect of a policeman's life, to paint a picture of a person as a whole.

It was a revolutionary concept, all the more so since it would be an anthology series with no uniform cast. So inadequate scripts could not hide behind popular characters. Predictably, the idea ran into an immediate brick wall with certain narrow-minded American TV executives. It was rejected by all three major networks until producer David Gerber took an interest. Wambaugh laid down his conditions, Gerber added a little, but not too much, melodrama, to make it palatable for the masses and, just to ensure that the series didn't stray too far from his original synopsis, Wambaugh stayed on as consultant.

The outcome was one of the most penetrating police dramas ever. The authenticity arose not only from Wambaugh's own experiences but also from other members of the force who were encouraged to talk about their work and relate their feelings into cassette recorders. From these interviews, writers developed the stories, although the episodes were not strictly based on real case histories.

Police Story ran for five seasons, the last being a series of eight two-hour specials, which are still frequently screened as TV movies (they appeared on BBC1 in autumn 1990). Two of the programmes were so successful that they were turned into series. The Gamble starred Angie Dickinson as policewoman, Lisa Beaumont, but six months later her name was changed to Pepper Anderson and she became the redoubtable Police Woman (SEE POLICE WOMAN). And The Return of Joe Forrester, with Lloyd Bridges, also developed into a spin-off series (SEE JOE FORRESTER).

Although Police Story was an anthology, a few characters cropped up more than once, among them detectives Tony Calabrese (Tony Lo Bianco) and Bert Jameson (Don Meredith), while an impressive array of guest stars numbered the likes of Ed Asner, Robert Culp and James Farentino.

Police Story was a compellingly accurate portrayal of American cops in the 1970s. Starsky and Hutch it wasn't.

Creator: Joseph Wambaugh
Producers: Christopher Morgan, Liam O'Brien
Executive producers: David Gerber, Stanley Kallis

A Columbia Pictures Television Production

86 colour 60-minute episodes and 8 colour 120-minute episodes US: NBC (Season 1) 25 Sept 1973 - 26 March 1974 (21 eps)
(Season 2) 10 Sept 1974 - 11 March 1975 (21 eps)
(Season 3) 9 Sept 1975 - 12 March 1976 (22 eps)
(Season 4) 21 Sept 1976 - 10 May 1977 (22 eps)
(Season 5) 27 Sept 1977 - 2 April 1980 (8 eps)
UK: ITV 11 Sept 1974 - 7 July 1980

POLICE SURGEON (UK)

Young police surgeon Dr Geoffrey Brent was not satisfied with simply passing on his medical expertise to London's Bayswater police division, he couldn't resist turning detective, too, and trying to solve every case he dealt with. Of course this being television fiction, he was allowed to pursue his inquiries unhindered, although such interference would have had him rapidly thrown out of Sun Hill or Hill Street.

Police Surgeon's major claim to TV fame was that it provided early platforms for Michael Crawford as a young thief in the opening episode, Easy Money, and Ian Hendry as Brent. It also led indirectly to greater things, since shortly after Police Surgeon's life support machine had been switched off, Hendry was back in a white coat as Dr David Keel in The Avengers.

REGULAR CAST

Dr Geoffrey Brent Ian Hendry   *Inspector Landon* John Warwick

Producers: Julian Bond, Leonard White

An ABC Television Network Production

12 monochrome 30-minute episodes
UK: ITV 10 Sept - 3 Dec 1960

POLICE SURGEON (CANADA) (US TITLE: DR SIMON LOCKE)

The kindest thing that can be said about the transatlantic Police Surgeon series was that it was cheap. Production was switched from Hollywood to Toronto in order to save money; there were no dressing rooms on location – the stars had to change in the bushes; and to restrict the budget further, the cast were not shown the rushes at the end of each day's filming. When actor Jack Albertson eventually saw the shoddy results (with little things like microphones in shot), he quit on the spot. The producer reminded him of his contract. 'After what I just saw,' raged Albertson, 'there's not a jury in the world that would convict me!'

Albertson was duly pacified and continued to play the crusty Dr Sellers, guiding light to studious young physician Dr Simon Locke, who gave his name to the show's title for that first season. For a doctor in a small country town (Dixon Mills), Locke stumbled across an awful lot of murders, even more so in the second season, when he moved to the big city to join a police emergency unit and the title switched to Police Surgeon.

His first boss was the aggressive Detective Lieutenant Dan Palmer (handily transferred from Dixon Mills) and he was succeeded for the third and final season by Lieutenant Jack Gordon. Among the guest stars in that concluding season were William Shatner and Leslie Nielsen. The budget was obviously increased by two dollars.

* The series was sponsored by Colgate.

REGULAR CAST

Dr Simon Locke Sam Groom   *Dr Sellers* Jack Albertson
Det. Lt Dan Palmer Len Birman   *Lt Jack Gordon* Larry D. Mann

---

Producers: Wilton Schiller, Chester Krunholz
Executive producer: Murray Chercover

A CIV Production

52 colour 30-minute episodes
US: Syndicated 1971 - 74
UK: ITV 22 Feb 1972 - 11 Jan 1974
8 Oct 1978 - 10 Oct 1981 (LWT)

POLICE WOMAN

'There was a fantastic audience reaction to The Gamble. We convinced Angie that a series would not get dull because, as a vice squad officer, she does a different 'cover' character each week. She's not just playing a fantasy super-chick.' – EXECUTIVE PRODUCER DAVID GERBER

Legs apart, pistol pointed, Angie Dickinson as Police Woman 'Pepper' Anderson was TV's first female pin-up cop. Nicknamed 'Pepper' because she was hot stuff, she was the cop who literally worked undercover. For whether she was posing as a prostitute or a gangster's moll, the chances were that she would end up under the covers, either with a suspect or her boss, Lieutenant Bill Crowley.

Pepper worked on the vice squad of the Los Angeles Police Department along with two other undercover officers, Detectives Joe Styles and Pete Royster. But it was Crowley who caught her eye. It seemed they were more than just good cops.

The plots on Police Woman were largely irrelevant – just as long as Pepper was placed in mortal danger and was dressed provocatively enough to give men a hot flush. One critic said that the show's motto should have been: 'Shoot now, talk dirty later'. The producers tried to soften the initial blow by giving Pepper an autistic younger sister, Cheryl, presumably to show that the heroine was a tart with a heart. But that character was dropped at the end of the first season.

Yet, for all its failings, Police Woman was a ratings success and became the first hit police drama starring a woman. Not that feminists were exactly celebrating – Pepper was hardly their ideal role model. And Joseph Wambaugh, creator of Police Story from which the pilot episode The Gamble originated, wasn't even consulted about the spin-off series. Perhaps it was just as well.

REGULAR CAST

Sgt Suzanne 'Pepper' Anderson Angie Dickinson   *Lt Bill Crowley* Earl Holliman
Det. Joe Styles Ed Bernard   *Det. Pete Royster* Charles Dierkop
Cheryl Nichole Kallis

Creator: Robert Collins
Producer: Douglas Benton
Executive producer: David Gerber

A Columbia Pictures Television Production

91 colour 60-minute episodes
US: NBC (Season 1) 13 Sept 1974 - 14 March 1975 (22 eps)
(Season 2) 12 Sept 1975 - 9 March 1976 (24 eps)
(Season 3) 28 Sept 1976 - 22 March 1977 (23 eps)
(Season 4) 25 Oct 1977 - 30 March 1978 (22 eps)
UK: ITV 25 July 1975 - 4 Aug 1979

PRIVATE EYE

In 1956, Los Angeles was a city with an inescapable presence – a seductive, modern wasteland, where middle America had gone haywire with the cultural shift to rock 'n' roll. It was a time of Elvis, martinis, James Dean...cars, stars, bars and guitars.

The world was a dangerous place, especially for a man like Jack Cleary who had always lived according to the rules. His world had been turned upside down – he had been thrown off the police force on phony charges and his brother, a respected private detective, had been murdered.

Cleary met up with a street-wise young rockabilly named Johnny Betts, a friend of his dead brother. Betts knew his way around L.A. and together they scoured the city until they found the killer and cleared Jack's name in the process. But even with his reputation restored, Cleary couldn't go back to being a cop, so he took over his brother's detective agency...and Johnny Betts too.

What could have been just another tale of unlikely partners, was given an extra dimension by the background of 1950s music, with creator and executive producer, Anthony Yerkovich, exploiting his success on Miami Vice. But Cleary and Betts failed to emulate Crockett and Tubbs in other respects and the show was cancelled after 12 weeks.

Private Eye also featured Charlie Fontana, Cleary's former partner on the force, and Dottie Dworski, Cleary's gum-chewing secretary who dreamed of Hollywood stardom. She had to wait a little longer.

REGULAR CAST

Jack Cleary Michael Woods *Johnny Betts* Josh Brolin
Charlie Fontana Bill Sadler *Dottie Dworski* Lisa Jane Persky

Creator: Anthony Yerkovitch
Music: Joe Jackson
Producers: John Leekley, Fred Lyle
Executive producer: Anthony Yerkovitch

A Universal Television Production

One colour 120-minute episode and 11 colour 60-minute episodes US: NBC 13 Sept 1987 - 8 Jan 1988

PRIVATE INVESTIGATOR

This heavily-restrained British private eye series of the late 1950s was a far cry from the world of 77 Sunset Strip. The central character, John Unthank, was one of the least memorable heroes ever – but that was exactly how creator Arthur Swinson planned it.

Swinson explained: 'In my research I was told that a private investigator must look insignificant. His clothes, his manner, his general appearance must allow him to fade into the landscape. He does not go in for loud ties or loud wisecracks. He doesn't buy large whiskies for everyone in sight nor astonish the assembled company with his wit. Whatever he does, he does quietly and if no one notices him, he has usually succeeded.' To ensure authenticity, Swinson listened to the advice of the Q-Men, an organization of former Scotland Yard detectives.

Unthank, whose clipped Scottish tones answered the phone with the familiar 'Unthank speaking', had four assistants – Bill Jessel, James Wilson, Peter Clarke and Mrs Layton. His first case, a three-parter, looked into a French currency racket and his second, spread over six weeks, took him to the sunny Mediterranean on behalf of the National Canine Defence League. It wasn't always a dog's life for John Unthank.

REGULAR CAST

John Unthank Campbell Singer   *Bill Jessel* Douglas Muir
James Wilson Allan McClelland   *Mrs Layton* Ursula Camm
Peter Clarke Ian White

Creator/producer: Arthur Swinson

A BBC Television Production

9 monochrome 45-minute episodes
UK: BBC 4 Dec 1958 - 17 Dec 1959

THE PROFESSIONALS

To call those two boneheads Bodie and Doyle 'detectives', is sullying the name of a noble profession, but they qualify for inclusion on the back of their secret policing activities.

Albert Fennell and Brian Clemens, partners on The Avengers, originally signed plummy Anthony Andrews to play ex-SAS soldier William Bodie, with Jon Finch as former CID man Ray Doyle. Finch decided he couldn't play Doyle as an ex-cop, so the producers went back to auditioning every tough guy actor in town. They came up with Martin Shaw, but in screen tests he looked remarkably similar to Andrews. Then they remembered Lewis Collins who had appeared with Shaw in an episode of the Avengers. So Anthony Andrews was out (leaving him free to attain international stardom in Brideshead Revisited) and Martin Shaw and Lewis Collins were in. They were joined by Gordon Jackson as George Cowley, the limping taskmaster of CI5 (his dodgy limb was the legacy of an old war wound). CI5 stood for

Criminal Intelligence 5, an elite undercover crime-fighting squad formed to keep the streets of England safe.

The Professionals was bursting at the seams with gunfire, explosions and murders. Bodie was the original Action Man, while the only person who ever made a fool out of Doyle was his hairdresser. But complaints about the levels of violence meant that a rule was introduced restricting the number of explosions to two per episode. Lewis Collins seemed intent on proving that he was even tougher than Bodie and went parachute-jumping in his spare time. Unfortunately for him and the production, he broke an ankle and delayed filming for four months.

Bodie and Doyle thought nothing of abseiling down the side of an office-block but before long, Shaw and Collins didn't think much of it either. Shaw wanted out after the first year but was tied to a four-year contract. He described the series as 'a prison' and called Doyle a 'violent puppet'. He loathed his famous permed curls too. 'That awful haircut– Lewis used to call me the Bionic Golly,' he said. In 1988, Shaw blocked further repeats of the show, believing that the Doyle role was hindering his film career. For his part, Collins confessed that he was ashamed to watch some episodes.

There was never any shortage of excitement with The Professionals, although to most of us there was a marked absence of credibility. But the Libyans obviously saw it as realistic. After the People's Bureau shooting drama in London, they besieged the British embassy in Tripoli with cries of 'Down with CI5!'

For me, the series had one almighty failing. No matter how tough Collins and Shaw looked and how convincingly they leaped about the screen, the series fell apart the moment Gordon Jackson appeared. Not because he wasn't a fine actor but because, to 99.9 per cent of the British population, he was still Hudson from Upstairs, Downstairs. And somehow his commands to Bodie and Doyle to combat terrorism sounded no more menacing than a stern reprimand to Rose for not buttering the tea-cakes.

REGULAR CAST

George Cowley Gordon Jackson *Bodie* Lewis Collins
Doyle Martin Shaw

Creator: Brian Clemens
Music: Laurie Johnson
Producers: Sidney Hayers, Raymond Menmuir
Executive producers: Albert Fennell, Brian Clemens

An Avengers Mark 1 Production for London Weekend Television

57 colour 60-minute episodes
UK: ITV (Season 1) 30 Dec 1977 - 17 March 1978 (13 eps)
(Season 2) 7 Oct - 9 Dec 1978 (10 eps)
(Season 3) 27 Oct - 15 Dec 1979(8 eps)
(Season 4) 7 Sept - 27 Dec 1980 (15 eps)
(Season 5) 7 Nov 1982 - 6 Feb 1983 (11 eps)

THE PROTECTORS (UK)

At a time when glossy series were all the rage, The Protectors was glossier than most – exotic locations, beautiful girls, handsome men, champagne lifestyles and a star-studded cast headed by The Man From U.N.C.L.E., Robert Vaughn. As a viewing spectacle, it was devastatingly undemanding, but that didn't prevent it from becoming a huge success.

Vaughn, who later claimed he was sickened by the show's violence, played Harry Rule, a wealthy private detective who operated out of an ultra-smart London office. The other two Protectors were Lady Caroline Ogilvie, known as the Contessa di Contini, who lived in Roman luxury and ran a detective agency specializing in art and antiques, and Gallic charmer Paul Buchet, who had a string of girlfriends. Besides their dedication to detection and crime-fighting, the three had one other thing in common – they were all incredibly bland and looked like refugees from Thunderbirds. Was it just a coincidence that the producer was Gerry Anderson?

In more ways than one, the best part of The Protectors was the end, because that was when Tony Christie sang the show's hit theme, In the Avenues and Alleyways.

REGULAR CAST

Harry Rule Robert Vaughn   *Contessa Di Contini* Nyree Dawn Porter
Paul Buchet Tony Anholt

Music: John Cameron
End theme sung by Tony Christie
Producers: Gerry Anderson, Reg Hill

A Group Three Production for ITC

52 colour 30-minute episodes
UK: ITV (Season 1) 29 Sept 1972 -
   30 March 1973 (26 eps)
   (Season 2) 21 Sept 1973 - 15 March
   1974 (26 eps)
US: Syndicated 1972

THE PROTECTORS (US)

A US police drama that was one of three rotating shows in The Bold Ones for the 1969-70 season, along with The Lawyers and The New Doctors. The central characters in The Protectors were big-city deputy police chief Sam Danforth, and black District Attorney William Washburn. Danforth was a graduate of the old school, who liked to stick to tried and tested methods but Washburn was more progressively-minded, a skilled politician who saw the need to move with the times. Although both men were dedicated workers, their different beliefs meant that they were frequently at loggerheads. Honest but unremarkable.

REGULAR CAST

Sam Danforth Leslie Nielsen   *William Washburn* Hari Rhodes

Creators: Roland Wolpert, William Sackheim
Producer: Jerrold Freedman
Executive producer: Jack Laird

A Universal Television Production

6 colour 60-minute episodes
US: NBC 28 Sept 1969 - 6 Sept 1970

PUBLIC EYE

'Marker uses money as something to pay the rent, get his shoes repaired or his raincoat cleaned. Marker doesn't want anything, except to be left alone.'   – ALFRED BURKE

Private eyes didn't get much shabbier than Frank Marker. He operated at the very bottom of the detective ladder. There were no plush offices for him – he used any tatty room he could find, wherever the rent was cheapest. Nor was there much chance of him jetting off to the world's glamour spots on a case – not unless you consider that Birmingham falls into that category. As for girls, never mind about a beautiful blonde on each arm, Marker's idea of a good-looking woman was one who still had all her own teeth.

Marker never carried a gun, preferring to obtain results by sheer persistence, which usually necessitated trudging the streets for hours on end in pursuit of some hapless debtor remarkably similar to himself. His lack of defence made him an easy target for unscrupulous clients. He was a good man to frame – he had no friends, nobody cared about him. Who would bother if he carried the can? And so it was that Marker was jailed after being fitted up and caught in possession of stolen jewellery.

Marker may not have had any friends on screen but he had plenty among the British public. Seeing him in prison, worried viewers made him cakes and sent socks and cigarette papers. Eventually public demand for his release grew to the point where he was let out on parole with full remission.

Even more amazing, Marker had an army of teenage fans. Alfred Burke, whose portrayal of the sorry sleuth made Public Eye truly compelling, was equally mystified. He said at the time: 'Why young girls should identify themselves with a shabby, middle-aged character I don't know. But I think they're attracted by his loneliness, his unspoken experiences and a father-figure affection.'

Eventually, Marker did gain a couple of acquaintances – a police contact, Detective Inspector Firbank, and fellow investigator Ron Gash, who was keen to go into partnership with him. But to all intents and purposes, Frank Marker was still a classic loner.

REGULAR CAST

Frank Marker Alfred Burke   *Det. Insp. Firbank* Ray Smith
Ron Gash Peter Childs

Creators: Roger Marshall, Anthony Marriott
Theme music: Robert Earley
Producers: Don Leaver, John Bryce (Season 1), Richard Bates (2), Michael Chapman (3,7), Kim Mills (4,5), Robert Love (6)

An ABC Weekend Network Production (1-3)

A Thames Television Network Production (4-7)

28 monochrome 60-minute episodes and 59 colour 60-minute episodes
UK: ITV (Season 1) 23 Jan - 1 May 1965 (15 eps)
(Season 2) 2 July - 24 Sept 1966 (13 eps)
(Season 3) 20 Jan - 13 April 1968 (13 eps)
(Season 4) 30 July - 10 Sept 1969 (7 eps)
(Season 5) 7 July - 29 Sept 1971 (13 eps)
(Season 6) 8 Nov 1972 - 14 Feb 1973 (13 eps)
(Season 7) 6 Jan - 7 April 1975 (13 eps)

PUBLIC PROSECUTOR

An early American 1950s mystery quiz, in which detective-fiction writers and other guests attempted to work out the solutions to filmed whodunnits. The host for the first two shows was John Howard, but he was then replaced by Warren Hull with Howard appearing as an actor in some of the playlets. The series was sponsored by Crawford Clothes, and was also known as Crawford Mystery Theatre although it was under the title of Public Prosecutor that it continued to air locally in New York, after the finish of its brief network run.

Announcer: Bob Shepard

A DuMont Production

Monochrome 30-minute episodes (4 shows were networked)
US: DuMont 6 - 27 Sept 1951

THE PURSUERS

By the start of the 1960s, the likes of Lassie and Rin Tin Tin had done a great deal for Canine Lib. Dog owners had come to realize that their pooches were capable of more than rolling over on their backs and fouling footpaths. Lassie's talent was such that she not only fetched slippers, she could probably sole and heel them too.

The police were quick to recognize this potential and The Pursuers was one of the first series to cast the police dog in more than a mere supporting role. So it was that Scotland Yard's Detective Inspector Bollinger and Detective Sergeant Wall came to patrol the streets of London accompanied by a large black alsatian.

Alas the series flopped miserably because not only was the dog more intelligent than the two policemen, it was also a better actor.

REGULAR CAST

Det. Insp. Bollinger Louis Hayward   *Det. Sgt Steve Wall* Gaylord Cavallaro

Executive producer: Donald Hyde

A Crestview Production for ABC TV

39 monochrome 30-minute episodes
UK: ITV 1 April 1961 - 21 April 1962

QUINCY, M.E.

The sound of Quincy's voice was enough to wake the dead. The medical examiner for the Los Angeles County Coroner's Office roared, ranted and raved non-stop. To say he had strong principles was like calling Hitler 'unpleasant'.

Quincy (he never had a first name, although a business card seen fleetingly in one episode read 'Dr R. Quincy') had said goodbye to a thriving private practice to join the County Coroner's Office. And once there, he was determined to be heard. He objected to departmental policy, he objected to his boss, he objected to what day of the week it was. But most of all he objected to anybody else's opinion.

For Quincy, there was no such thing as death by natural causes. He could lay a 110-year-old man with a dodgy heart out on the slab and be convinced it was murder. Consequently he became more of a detective than a pathologist, as he sought the evidence to back up his contentious beliefs. This greatly irritated the police onto whose territory he was constantly straying, and whose judgment was therefore being questioned. Quincy's inquiries involved his disappearing for hours on end, usually just as his long-suffering boss, Dr Robert Astin, was about to be grilled by the press. Astin was undertandably peeved by Quincy at first but after a while he started to realize that, no matter how clear-cut the evidence seemed to the contrary, Quincy was always proved right. For Quincy was Perry Mason in a white coat.

The only one to be spared Quincy's icy blasts was his personable young assistant, Sam Fujiyama, who was always being roped in to help confirm a theory. Everyone else knew that if Quincy was off on a crusade, it was time to lie low. Astin and L.A.P.D. Lieutenant Frank Monahan bore the main brunt – and Monahan was Quincy's friend.

And for all his bullishness, 'Quince' (as he was affectionately known) had quite a few friends. He lived on a boat and spent most evenings at Danny's Place, a marina-side bar where he and his cronies would tuck into a meal and down a few beers. Most episodes ended with them sitting around a large table sharing a joke. After all the corpses, it was clearly felt each show should end on a light note.

Early on, he had a girlfriend, Lee Potter, but pressure of work meant they hardly saw one another, and then in the final sea son he married Dr Emily Hanover, an attractive psychiatrist. She obviously saw him as a professional challenge.

Quincy ran for seven highly successful seasons but, towards the end of the run, there were signs that he was beginning to mellow. He and Astin were no longer continually at each other's throats, with Astin actually taking the trouble to defend his pathologist's wayward actions to the press and police. Then of course there was his marriage. It was hard to imagine him being domesticated – woe betide the poor woman if she didn't iron his shirts properly or under-boiled his egg. And he was never one to leave work at the office. No doubt if she announced that their rubber plant had died, he would suspect it was poisoned and order an autopsy.

It was a highly watchable if sometimes predictable show, with Jack Klugman acting his socks off as Quincy. If only he had been fitted with a volume control...

* At first Quincy was part of NBC'S Sunday Mystery Movie in the US, but after five shows, it soon became a weekly series in its own right, on Friday nights.

REGULAR CAST

Quincy Jack Klugman   *Sam Fujiyama* Robert Ito
Lt Frank Monahan Garry Walberg   *Dr Robert Astin* John S. Ragin
Danny Tovo Val Bisoglio   *Lee Potter (Season 1)* Lynette Mettey
Dr Emily Hanover (Season 7) Anita Gillette

Creators: Glen A. Larson, Lou Shaw
Music: Glen A. Larson, Stu Phillips
Producers: Lou Shaw, Robert O'Neil, Michael Star
Executive producer: Glen A. Larson

A Universal Television Production

5 colour 120-minute and 143 colour 60-minute episodes
US: NBC Pilot show: 3 Oct 1976
(Season 1) 4 Feb - 27 May 1977 (12 eps)
(Season 2) 16 Sept 1977 - 10 March 1978 (20 eps)

(Season 3) 21 Sept 1978 - 12 April 1979 (22 eps)
(Season 4) 20 Sept 1979 - 10 Sept 1980 (22 eps)
(Season 5) 16 Sept 1980 - 6 May 1981 (19 eps)
(Season 6) 28 Oct 1981 - 12 May 1982 (24 eps)
(Season 7) 29 Sept 1982 - 11 May 1983 (24 eps)
UK: ITV Pilot show: 24 Feb 1977
Series: 8 Sept 1977 - 28 May 1985

THE RACING GAME

Much was expected of these adaptations of the best-sellers by jockey-turned-thriller author Dick Francis. But after starting out as a favourite, it quickly became a no-hoper, and finished way down the field in the detective stakes. The series followed the cases of Sid Halley, a former jockey who, forced to give up riding through injury, became a private investigator working mainly for the rich stables. With his companion, Chico Barnes, Halley probed betting coups and disappearing racehorses with such a lack of conviction that it was a mercy when, after six episodes, The Racing Game was consigned to the TV knacker's yard.

REGULAR CAST

Sid Halley Mike Gwilym   *Chico Barnes* Mick Ford

Music: Mike Moran
Producer: Jacky Stoller
Executive producer: David Cunliffe

A Yorkshire Television Network Production

6 colour 60-minute episodes
UK: ITV 21 Nov 1979 - 9 Jan 1980
US: WGBH Boston 'Mystery' 8 - 22 April 1980
31 March - 14 April 1981

RACKET SQUAD

'I'm closing this case now but there'll be others because that's the way the world is built. Remember there are people who can slap you on the back with one hand and pick your pocket with the other – and it could happen to you.'   – CAPTAIN JOHN BRADDOCK'S PROGRAMME CLOSE

Captain John Braddock was the sworn foe of America's con men in the early 1950s. Working in the racket squad of a big city police department, his job was to protect the public from various tricksters. The series was based on actual case records from police departments and described in considerable detail the methods of the con artist. The upright Braddock was played by Reed Hadley who also narrated the show. In addition, Hadley had been in a syndicated version of Racket Squad in 1950, a year before it was promoted to the CBS network.

REGULAR CAST

Capt. John Braddock Reed Hadley

Producers: Hal Roach Jnr, Carroll
Chase
Director: Frank McDonald

98 monochrome 30-minute episodes
US: CBS 7 June 1951 - 28 Sept 1953

RANDALL AND HOPKIRK (DECEASED) (US TITLE: MY PARTNER THE GHOST)

'There's something different about this pair of private eyes...one of them is dead!' – PROGRAMME BILLING

Marty Hopkirk was television's ghost detective, an invisible man to all but his partner, Jeff Randall. Together their private eye firm of Randall and Hopkirk had been ticking along nicely, until Marty was mown down by a car while crossing the road to his flat in London's Maida Vale. It transpired that the death was no accident – Marty had been mistaken for Jeff and was killed by a hit-man that Jeff had been investigating.

But when Jeff visited his pal's grave to pay his respects, he was confronted by the ghost of Marty and they set out to bring the murderer to justice. Unfortunately in doing so, Marty made the same mistake as Cinderella, and forgot to get back home in time.

In this instance, he omitted to return to his grave by daylight, thus violating an ancient curse, and was consequently trapped as a ghost on Earth for 100 years.

So, whether he liked it or not, Jeff was saddled with the ghostly Marty for a long, long time. It was quite a useful party-trick for a detective to be invisible, and he was repeatedly able to use it to extricate Jeff from some hair-raising predicaments. But he could be a nuisance too, particularly with regard to his widow, Jean, who had gone to work in Jeff's office. For Marty was a jealous spectre and if there was any hint of bachelor Jeff and Jean becoming a mite too friendly, their attention would suddenly be diverted by some ghost-induced disturbance.

Randall and Hopkirk formed an unusual partnership even by the standards of TV detective shows. It was a cracking good comedy /drama though, and Kenneth Cope was a fantastic phantom. But the expensive white suit he wore as Marty caused numerous headaches for the production team, who were so worried about keeping it spotless that they made Cope strip off after each 'take'!

Although it bombed in the States under the title My Partner the Ghost, the series is fondly remembered in many countries. There is even still an appreciation society. I wonder how many of the show's fans know that because of an inept Canadian hairdresser, Cope wore his wig on back to front in two episodes. He says: 'I looked like the middle one of The Three Stooges.'

REGULAR CAST

Jeff Randall Mike Pratt   *Marty Hopkirk* Kenneth Cope
Jean Hopkirk Annette Andre

EPISODE TITLES

My Late Lamented Friend and Partner
A Disturbing Case
That's How Murder Snowballs
Never Trust a Ghost
Who Ever Heard of a Ghost Dying?
The House on Haunted Hill
When Did You Start to Stop Seeing
    Things?
Just for the Record
Murder Ain't What It Used To Be!
But What a Sweet Little Room
Who Killed Cock Robin
The Ghost Who Saved the Bank at
    Monte Carlo
For the Girl Who Has Everything
You Can Always Find a Fall Guy
The Smile Behind the Veil
A Sentimental Journey
When the Spirit Moves You
The Trouble with Women
It's Supposed to be Thicker Than
    Water

The Man from Nowhere
Could You Recognize the Man Again?
Vendetta for a Dead Man
Money to Burn
The Ghost Talks All
Work and No Pay
Somebody Just Walked Over My
    Grave

Creator: Dennis Spooner
Music: Edwin Astley
Producer: Monty Berman

An ITC Production

26 colour 60-minute episodes
UK: ITV 26 Sept 1969 - 31 July 1971
US: Syndicated 1973

REDCAP

Actor John Thaw had plenty of rehearsal for being miserable as Inspector Morse, when back in the 1960s he played stern military policeman, John Mann, in Redcap. Just as Morse bullies Lewis, Mann seemed to delight in bawling out the lower ranks, although he did display a more tender side to his nature when dealing with families of the bereaved.

Sergeant Mann worked for the hated Special Investigation Branch of the Royal Military Police, where his duty was to crack down on any serious crime anywhere in the world that involved British troops. His cases took him to such exotic climes as Borneo and Cyprus, probing murder, bullying and desertion, but because he was an internal investigator, his presence was rarely welcomed.

Tough and uncompromising, it was hardly surprising that this Mann didn't have a best friend.

REGULAR CAST
Sgt John Mann John Thaw

Creator: Jack Bell
Producer: John Bryce

An ABC Weekend Network Production

26 monochrome 60-minute episodes
UK: ITV (Season 1) 17 Oct 1964 - 16 Jan 1965 (13 eps)
(Season 2) 2 April - 25 June 1966 (13 eps)

REMINGTON STEELE

Remington Steele was Mr Cool. He didn't pick his teeth in restaurants or blow his nose on the serviette. He didn't have dandruff, hiccups or excessive flatulence after eating cabbage. He had style. He was so handsome he made Robert Redford look like the Elephant Man. Glamorous girls swooned at his immaculately-manicured feet. There was only one tiny blemish on his perfection – he didn't really exist.

He was a figment of Laura Holt's imagination. When she opened her own investigation agency, she found that clients did not readily respond to a woman's name on the door, so she invented a non-existent male boss. She called him Remington Steele, presumably because she had liked the company so much she'd bought it.

Business boomed, but all her new-found customers were anxious to meet the elusive Mr Steele. There came a time when Laura could hold them off no longer so, when a suitably handsome chap with an appropriately mysterious background appeared on the scene, she christened him Remington Steele.

Fortunately he was only too willing to comply with the pretty Laura's desires and, although his real identity remained a secret, he quickly proved himself an adept private eye, much more than just a figurehead. In fact, more of a blockhead because, for all his elegance he had the personality of a plank of wood.

Together, Laura and Steele went around solving a series of baffling murders in the highest of high society, while their relationship continually threatened to boil over into something steamier than businesslike. Steele liked to wallow in old Hollywood movies and often carried out his investigations in the manner of a scene from one of his favourite films. Was he ever vain!

Steele was played by Pierce Brosnan, who used to be touted as the next James Bond, with Stephanie Zimbalist, daughter of Efrem Zimbalist Jnr, as Laura. Their secretary for the first season was Bernice Foxe, but she ran off with a saxophone player and was replaced by Mildred Krebs, a former Inland Revenue agent who had been sacked after allowing Steele to beat a charge of tax evasion. Another early departure was Laura's first legman, Murphy Michaels, who left to set up his own detective agency.

Remington Steele did well in the US, but its superficiality did not sit as comfortably with British audiences. All the episode titles contained the word Steele, such as Steele Waters Run Deep, Signed Steeled and Delivered, Thou Shalt Not Steele and Steele Crazy After All These Years. After 72 episodes they ran out of puns.

REGULAR CAST

Laura Holt Stephanie Zimbalist   *Remington Steele* Pierce Brosnan
Mildred Krebs Doris Roberts   *Bernice Foxe* Janet DeMay
Murphy Michaels James Read

Creators: Michael Gleason, Robert Butler
Producers: Glenn Caron, Gareth Davies, Lee Zlotoff
Executive producer: Michael Gleason

An MTM Production

72 colour 60-minute episodes
US: NBC 1 Oct 1982 - 9 March 1987
UK: BBC1 3 Sept - 12 Nov 1983
13 Jan - 18 April 1984
Channel Four 29 July 1986 - 20 Jan 1987

RENEGADES

This was a case of The Mod Squad Rides Again and was notable only for the fact that it starred a young Patrick Swayze. As one of seven hoodlum gang leaders, Swayze had been involved in a fair amount of dirty dealing, but now he and the other six were given the opportunity by police officials to wipe the slate clean and serve the community instead. The idea was that they could clear their own records by teaming up with hip cop Marciano, to fight big-city crime rather than each other.

Their undercover activities included infiltrating gangs and high schools in search of drugs operations and other youth-orientated felonies but, despite their success rate, they didn't impress Marciano's boss, Captain Scanlon...nor the viewers.

REGULAR CAST

Bandit Patrick Swayze   *Tracy* Tracy Scoggins
Eagle Randy Brooks   *J.T.* Paul Mones
Dancer Robert Thaler   *Gaucho* Fausto Bara
Dragon Brian Tochi   *Lt Marciano* James Luisi
Capt. Scanlon Kurtwood Smith

Producer: Chuck Gordon
Executive producer: Lawrence Gordon

6 colour 60-minute episodes
US: ABC 4 March - 8 April 1983

A Paramount Television Production

THE RETURN OF SHERLOCK HOLMES (SEE THE ADVENTURES OF SHERLOCK HOLMES)

THE RETURN OF THE SAINT

In the same way that The New Adventures of Perry Mason foundered with a new actor in the title role, so did The Return of The Saint.

Roger Moore was an impossible act to follow as his replacement, Ian Ogilvy, soon found to his cost. There was nothing wrong with Ogilvy's portrayal, although he did lack Moore's mischievous smile, it was simply that the public was not prepared to accept an imposter. After 24 episodes which were less than rapturously received, Ogilvy went off to appear in coffee commercials. What would Simon Templar have said? (SEE ALSO THE SAINT)

* US viewers had an opportunity to compare the respective merits of the two Saints in 1980, when the CBS Late Movie screened the Moore series on Wednesdays and the Ogilvy version on Fridays.

REGULAR CAST

Simon Templar Ian Ogilvy

Theme music: Brian Dane
Music: Johnny Scott
Producer: Anthony Spinner
Executive producer: Robert S. Baker

An ITC Production

24 colour 60-minute episodes
UK: ITV 10 Sept 1978 - 12 March 1979
US: CBS 21 Dec 1979 - 14 March 1980
10 May - 15 Aug 1980

RICHARD DIAMOND, PRIVATE DETECTIVE

Young Mary Tyler Moore got her big break on Richard Diamond, Private Detective – but you'd never have known it. She played Diamond's mysterious answering service called 'Sam' and, although her voice was heard, her body was seen only from the waist down. And there was no clue as to her identity in the end credits.

Richard Diamond (a pun on Sam Spade) had started life on American radio from 1949 to 1952. There he was played by Dick Powell, whose production company, Four Star, made the TV series. Played by David Janssen, Diamond was a young, former New York cop, who had become a wisecracking private eye using his old contacts on the force, principally Lieutenant McGough, to obtain privileged information.

After two years, he switched from New York to Hollywood and found himself a new police contact, Lieutenant Kile, a girlfriend, Karen Wells, as well as 'Sam' who, among other things, often used to reach Diamond on his car phone to warn him of trouble ahead. Yes, a car phone. Richard Diamond was a 1959 yuppie.

* In syndication, the show was known as Call Mr Diamond

REGULAR CAST

Richard Diamond David Janssen   *Lt McGough* Regis Toomey
Lt Kile Russ Conway   *Karen Wells* Barbara Bain
'Sam' (1959) Mary Tyler Moore   *(1959 - 60)* Roxanne Brooks

Creator: Blake Edwards

A Four Star Production

51 monochrome 30-minute episodes
US: CBS 1 July 1957 - 6 Sept 1960

RICHIE BROCKELMAN, PRIVATE EYE

Richie Brockelman boasted an impeccable background in more ways than one. Not only was he smart and college educated but his show was produced by three of the biggest names in the world of TV detection – Stephen J. Cannell (Baretta, The Rockford Files and Riptide), Steven Bochco (Hill Street Blues and Hooperman) and Peter S. Fischer (Ellery Queen and Murder, She Wrote).

Brockelman was actually a spin-off from The Rockford Files, although he had previously appeared in a Rockford-less pilot movie, Richie Brockelman: Missing 24 Hours, in 1976. Yet in spite of his pedigree, only five episodes were made and Richie bade farewell to stardom and a series of his own to lend Jim Rockford a hand in another of his adventures.

Richie was 23 and ran a small agency, relying on the help of his secretary, Sharon, and police contact Sergeant Ted Coopersmith. With his fresh college-boy looks, he was an unlikely detective, with none of the world-weariness usually associated with his trade. He didn't carry a gun, he didn't practise karate and even Joe Bugner could have beaten him in a fight. But his biggest problem was that he didn't have a gimmick. And in the 1970s that could be fatal.

REGULAR CAST

Richie Brockelman Dennis Dugan   *Sgt Ted Coopersmith* Robert Hogan
Sharon Deterson Barbara Bosson

Creators: Stephen J. Cannell, Steven Bochco
Music: Mike Post, Pete Carpenter
Producer: Peter S. Fischer
Executive producers: Stephen J. Cannell, Steven Bochco

A Universal Television Production

One colour 90-minute episode and 4 colour 60-minute episodes
US: NBC 17 March - 24 Aug 1978

RICHMOND HILL

From the land of Scott and Charlene, Alf and Ailsa and Rod Hull and Emu came Richmond Hill, a soppy, sentimental soap set in a Sydney suburb. It was centred around the local police force, principally fair and fatherly Sergeant Dan Costello, petite crackshot Constable Susan Miller, po-faced Warren Bryant and handsome, young Tim Shannon.

Being a soap opera, the show concentrated more on the characters' private lives than any real detective work. Kleenex did a roaring trade when Costello's wife, Alice, died of cancer, when Bryant's wife Janet left him in the aftermath of being raped and when Shannon revealed that he was illegitimate and had been abandoned by his parents. He went on to share a flat with Susan Miller, but got up to nothing more reckless than ruining the cooking.

Richmond Hill opened on Channel 10 in Australia in January 1988 but lasted less than a year, running to some 80 episodes. There was an embarrassing start when, with production already under way, it was discovered that there was a real Richmond Hill in New Zealand. After studying the electoral register, several character names were altered to protect the innocent.

* Students of Australian drama have observed that there only seem to be 20 or so actors in the entire country, and these switch between Neighbours/Home and Away/A Country Practice/The Flying Doctors and anything else that happens to be going. So it comes as little surprise to learn that Tim Elston, who played Bryant, was a leading light in another Oz cop export, Bellamy.

REGULAR CAST

Sgt Dan Costello Ross Higgins   *Susan Miller* Felicity Soper
Warren Bryant Tim Elston   *Tim Shannon* Robert Sampson

Creator: Reg Watson
Producer: Phil East

A Grundy Production

Approx. 80 colour 60-minute episodes
UK: ITV 5 Oct 1988 - 30 Aug 1989

RIKER

Expelled from the Los Angeles Police Department for a flagrant breach of the rules, Frank Riker was secretly appointed undercover operative for California's Deputy Attorney General, Brice Landis, Riker's former partner. Apart from the State Governor, Landis was the only person to know of Riker's special status. To everyone else, he was a disgraced cop and received a welcome that was not so much warm as heated. But he didn't have to put up with the abuse for long – the show was cancelled after four weeks.

REGULAR CAST

Frank Riker Josh Taylor   *Brice Landis* Michael Shannon

Creator: Jerry Ludwig
Executive producer: David Gerber

*A Columbia Pictures Television
  Production*

4 colour 60-minute episodes
US: CBS 14 March - 11 April 1981

RIPCORD

'This is the most danger-packed show on television. Every aerial manoeuvre is real, photographed just as it happened without tricks or illusions. All that stands between a jumper and death is his Ripcord.'
– PROGRAMME ANNOUNCER

They came from out of the sky, descending on some unsuspecting crook just as he was about to hold up a liquor store. They were television's parachuting detectives!

Ted McKeever and Jim Buckley ran Ripcord Inc., a firm which taught the art of skydiving. But whenever the boys landed, they came to earth with a bump, usually just as a crime was being committed. So they unstrapped their harnesses and got on with solving it.

The aeronautical Starsky and Hutch were helped out by their pilot, first Chuck Lambert and then, from mid-way through the opening season, Charlie Kern.

A feature of Ripcord were the spectacular flying scenes with some pretty impressive, mid-air fist-fights. And no filming was wasted. Once, when two planes crashed in the course of shooting scenes for the show, the footage of the accident was saved and used later in the series.

REGULAR CAST

Ted McKeever Larry Pennell   *Jim Buckley* Ken Curtis
Chuck Lambert Paul Comi *Charlie Kern* Shug Fisher

Producers: Maurice Ungar, Leon
  Benson

A United Artists Television Production

76 monochrome 30-minute episodes
US: Syndicated Sept 1961 - 1963
UK: BBC1 31 March 1964 - 20 Sept 1965

RIPTIDE

'They live on a yacht, on a helicopter – and on the edge of deadly danger! They're private eyes and public scandals who always get their man – and sometimes the girl!'

Nick Ryder and Cody Allen were two old Army buddies who were bored with life. All they ever did was lounge around the beach, eyeing up beautiful girls. They wanted a bit of excitement. So why not become private detectives?

The problem was that Nick and Cody were only half as bright as their shirts, so they realized that they needed some brains for their outfit. Accordingly, they recruited a third partner, Murray 'Boz' Bozinsky, an electronics wizard who tapped into computers and owned his own robot. Unfortunately the robot, named Roboz, had a mind of its own and rarely worked properly. Being a boffin (this was instantly recognisable as he wore glasses), Boz spoke a language all of his own. On the occasions he did make any sense, it was evident that he idolized Nick and Cody. He couldn't have been that clever after all.

The boys operated from the Riptide, an ageing 50ft fishing trawler, docked at Pier 56 in King's Harbour. However, this was hardly suitable for the many high-speed sea chases in which they became involved and so they utilized alternative modes of transport in the form of Cody's speedboat, the Ebbtide and Nick's broken-down helicopter, the Screaming Mimi, which was painted pink with a huge gaping mouth on the front. Inevitably the show paraded an abundance of sun-tanned beauties, including the all-girl crew of the Barefoot Contessa, a charter boat that was moored next to the Riptide. Sometimes Nick, Cody and Boz persuaded the boat's skipper, Mama Jo, and her girls, to help out on a case.

Riptide bore little resemblance to reality but it managed to entertain young Americans for three seasons. And Joe Penny, who played Nick, has gone on to co-star in Jake and the Fatman.

REGULAR CAST

Cody Allen Perry King   *Nick Ryder* Joe Penny
Murray 'Boz' Bozinsky Thom Bray   *Lt Ted Quinlan* Jack Ging
Mama Jo Anne Francis

Creators/Executive producers: Stephen J. Cannell, Frank Lupo

A Stephen J. Cannell Production for Paramount

55 colour 60-minute episodes
US: NBC 3 Jan 1984 - 15 Aug 1986
UK: ITV 5 June - 28 Aug 1986

THE RIVALS OF SHERLOCK HOLMES

Like the BBC's Detective a few years earlier, The Rivals of Sherlock Holmes presented a gallery of sleuths, including John Thaw of Inspector Morse fame, as Danish detective Lieutenant Holst.

The series was taken from an anthology by Sir Hugh Greene and featured the cases of Holmes' contemporaries. Among them were blind detective Max Carrados, Simon Carne, a popular man about town who became mysterious private detective Klimo, Lady Molly of Scotland Yard, conman investigator Romney Pringle, France's finest amateur detective, M. Valmont, forensic expert Dr Thorndyke, private enquiry agent Horace Dorrington, professional ghost-hunter Carnacki and gypsy detective (a definite first!) Hagar.

CAST

Dr Thorndyke John Neville *(Season 1)*   Barrie Ingham *(Season 2)*
(Creator: R. Austin Freeman*)*

Max Carrados Robert Stevens
(Creator: Ernest Bramah*)*

Horace Dorrington Peter Vaughan
(Creator: Arthur Morrison*)*

Simon Carne Roy Dotrice

Carnacki Donald Pleasence
(Creator: W. Hope Hodgson*)*

Dixon Druce John Fraser
(Creators: L.T. Meade, Robert Eustace*)*

Jonathan Pride Ronald Hines
(Creator: Arthur Morrison*)*

Lady Molly Elvi Hale
(Creator: Baroness Orczy*)*

Arthur Hewitt Peter Barkworth
(Creator: Arthur Morrison*)*

Romney Pringle Donald Sinden
(Creator: Clifford Ashdown*)*

Bernard Sutton Robert Lang
(Creator: Max Pemberton*)*

Polly Burton Judy Geeson
(Creator: Baroness Orczy*)*

Insp. Lipinzki Barry Keegan
(Creator: George Griffith*)*

Professor Van Dusen Douglas Wilmer
(Creator: Jacques Futrelle*)*

Laxworthy Bernard Hepton
(Creator: E. Phillips Oppenheim*)*

M. Valmont Charles Gray

Lt Holst John Thaw
(Creator: Palle Rosenkrantz*)*

Dabogert Trostler Ronald Lewis
(Creator: Baldwin Groller*)*

William Drew Derek Jacobi
(Creator: William Le Queux*)*

Mr Horrocks Ronald Fraser
(Creator: C.J. Cunliffe-Hyne*)*

Hagar Sara Kestelman
(Creator: Fergus Hume*)*

* In one of Horace Dorrington's cases, the supporting cast contained a young actor by the name of Jeremy Irons

Music: Bob Sharples
Producers: Robert Love, Jonathan Alwyn (Season 1), Reginald Collin, Jonathan Alwyn (2)
Executive producers: Lloyd Shirley (1), Kim Mills (2)

26 colour 60-minute episodes
UK: ITV (Season 1) 20 Sept - 9 Dec 1971 (13 eps)
(Season 2) 29 Jan - 16 April 1973 (13 eps)
US: PBS 1975 - 1976 (13 eps)

A Thames Television Network Production

RIVIERA POLICE

The glamorous backdrop of the sun-soaked French Riviera, playground for the rich and famous, was wasted on this inept 1960s cops and robbers show. Most of the cases revolved around such prestigious events as the Cannes Film Festival, the Nice Flower Festival or the Monaco Grand Prix, but would have been just as effective set on Bridlington seafront on the day of the annual Donkey Derby. And it would have been cheaper.

REGULAR CAST

Supt Johnson Noel Trevarthen   *Supt Hunter* Geoffrey Frederick
Lt Col Sorel Frank Lieberman   *Insp. Legrand* Brian Spink

Title music: Laurie Johnson
Producer: Jordan Lawrence

An Associated Rediffusion Network
  Production

13 monochrome 60-minute episodes
UK: ITV 2 Aug - 27 Oct 1965
US: Syndicated 1965

THE ROCKFORD FILES

'Hello, this is James Rockford. At the sound of the tone, please leave
your name and number. I'll get back to you as soon as possible.' –
ANSWERPHONE SEQUENCE AT PROGRAMME START

Jim Rockford was not the standard private eye. Whenever he walked down 'those mean streets', it would not be with a confident swagger, it would be with furtive glances over his shoulder, lest anyone should leap out of the shadows and hit him. In truth it was a wonder that Rockford ever ventured out at night, because he was a born coward, the very antithesis of everything that Spade, Hammer and Dick Tracy stood for.

Rockford had plenty in common with that earlier collaboration between actor James Garner and writer/producer Roy Huggins, Maverick. That show, in which Garner starred as Bret Maverick, broke the mould of TV Westerns, not only by being funny but also by having heroes that were lily-livered. The public identified with Rockford because he was human. He didn't possess the recovery powers of Tom and Jerry – if somebody hit him, it hurt and if it was he who was doing the hitting, the chances were that he would end up with a broken hand. He kept a gun in the biscuit jar, but only for emergencies. Garner admitted: 'The thing I like about Jim Rockford is that he's not a hero in the accepted sense of the word. I probably wouldn't have accepted the part if he had been, because I'm not the heroic type and I don't believe in heroic types.'

Jim Rockford was television's ex-con private detective, having been wrongly imprisoned for five years, before finally being freed when new evidence was unearthed to support his innocence. Consequently, although he was not one to bear a grudge, Rockford liked to put one over on the police in his new capacity as P.I. He found that the best method of one-upmanship was to take on cases (at a fee of $200 per day plus expenses) that the police considered closed, where they were positive they had apprehended the guilty party, and then to dig up new information which pointed to a different theory altogether. Besides, having been in the same position himself, he liked to help those who had been falsely accused. Needless to say, the police did not take kindly to seeing all their hard work undone, and Rockford was not exactly top of their Christmas card list. Most of his dealings were with

Detective Dennis Becker with whom he built up a surprising friendship, liberally interspersed with lively professional disagreements.

But the most important relationship in the show was between Jim and his dad, 'Rocky', a retired lorry driver, played by that Circus Boy stalwart Noah Beery (who was in fact only 12 years older than Garner!). Father and son lived together in a house trailer parked on the beach near Los Angeles, an arrangement that didn't always make for a harmonious co-existence. Rocky was set in his ways and tended to try to curb Jim's freewheeling spirit. What's more, he used to insist on helping out on assignments from time to time.

Rocky's presence certainly did nothing to help the course of true love run smooth, between Jim and his attorney girlfriend, Beth Davenport (possibly a distant relation of Joyce?). Beth was a useful friend to have, as she was able to bail Jim out whenever he landed himself in trouble with the law.

Like Bret Maverick at the poker table, Jim Rockford was a kindly con-man. He only tricked people who deserved it and it was usually to benefit his client. Assisting in these shady enterprises were some of his old prison friends, among them his former cellmate, Angel Martin, and the mighty Gandolph Fitch, who always called him 'Rockfish'. Another steady source of information in the later episodes was disbarred lawyer, John Cooper.

The Rockford Files succeeded thanks to some slick scripts and James Garner's consummate comic skill. For even in his darkest hour, Jim Rockford maintained his sense of humour. Sadly, in Garner's darkest hour, when he was ill and had tired of the role, he suddenly announced he was quitting. He had been doing all his own stunts on the show and had finished up with torn ligaments, sprains, disc trouble and dislocations. He also had to undergo knee surgery, prompting a doctor to pronounce, 'Your legs are in great shape – for a man of 85!' So, although the series still had plenty of life in it, Garner decided to call it a day. Maybe it wasn't such a bad thing for an underdog like Rockford to go out on top.

* In the sixth and final season, Tom Selleck made two appearances as an insufferably perfect private eye, Lance White. It was this role which alerted producers to the comparatively unknown Selleck's potential, and six months later he was starring as Magnum.

REGULAR CAST

Jim Rockford James Garner   Joseph 'Rocky' Rockford Noah Beery
Det. Dennis Becker Joe Santos   Beth Davenport Gretchen Corbett
Angel Martin Stuart Margolin   Gandolph Fitch Isaac Hayes
John Cooper Bo Hopkins   Lt Chapman James Luisi

Creators: Roy Huggins, Stephen J.
  Cannell
Theme music: Mike Post, Pete
  Carpenter
Producers: Charles Johnson, David
  Chase
Executive producers: Stephen J.
  Cannell, Meta Rosenberg

*A Cherokee/Public Arts Production for
  Universal Television*

120 colour 60-minute episodes and 3
  colour 90-minute episodes

US: NBC (Season 1) 13 Sept 1974 - 7
  March 1975 (22 eps)
(Season 2) 12 Sept 1975 - 19 March
  1976 (22 eps)
(Season 3) 24 Sept 1976 - 1 April 1977
(Season 4) 16 Sept 1977 - 24 Feb 1978
  (20 eps)
(Season 5) 22 Sept 1978 - 13 April 1979
  (21 eps)
(Season 6) 28 Sept 1979 - 25 July 1980
  (16 eps)
UK: BBC1 13 Aug 1975 - 31 March 1982

ROCKLIFFE'S BABIES

'Rockliffe is human – so human he makes more mistakes than the
Babies he's supposed to be training up.'   – IAN HOGG

Rockliffe's Babies were five rookie police constables and two young
WPCs, who were being groomed for action on the increasingly
dangerous streets of London in the 1980s. They were assigned to the
Crime Squad of the Metropolitan Police's Victor Tango Division, under
the wing of Detective Sergeant Alan Rockliffe, played by Ian Hogg.

Rockliffe was by no means the ideal babysitter and sometimes
behaved like a bit of a baby himself, throwing tantrums and stamping
his feet. But it was usually to get the best out of his charges who, it has
to be said, often looked eminently more suited to combatting crime than
their wayward boss.

A watchable series but one which didn't exactly push back the
barriers of television.

REGULAR CAST

Det. Sgt Alan Rockliffe Ian Hogg   *PC David Adams* Bill Champion
PC Steve Hood Brett Fancy   *PC Keith Chitty* John Blakey
PC Gerry O'Dowd Joe McGann   *PC Paul Georgiou* Martyn Ellis
WPC Janice Hargreaves Alphonsa Emmanuel   *WPC Karen Walsh* Susanna Shelling
Det. Insp. Charlie Flight Edward Wilson   *Det. Supt Munro* Malcolm Terris

Creator: Richard O'Keefe
Producer: Leonard Lewis

A BBC Television Production

18 colour 50-minute episodes
UK: BBC1 (Season 1) 9 Jan - 27 Feb
  1987 (8 eps)
(Season 2) 8 Jan - 18 March 1988
  (10 eps)

ROCKLIFFE'S FOLLY

Following on from Rockliffe's Babies, Detective Sergeant Rockliffe left the Met. and moved to the country, to Wessex to be precise. He soon noticed the difference. Instead of the hustle and bustle of the city, the pace of rural life was altogether much slower. But if Rockliffe thought this meant that bank robbers made their getaway on bicycle or in a milk float, he was mistaken. Even the country areas have their share of hardened professional villains – it's just that there aren't as many of them as in the metropolis. For as Ian Hogg was told by local police in the course of his research for the spin-off series, 'A day's crime in central London is a year's crime in Devon and Dorset.'

REGULAR CAST

Det. Sgt Rockliffe Ian Hogg   *Det. Insp. Hoskins* James Aubrey
Insp. Yaxley Ian Brimble   *Det. Con. Whitmore* Aaron Harris

Creator: Richard O'Keefe   7 colour 50-minute episodes
Producer: Ron Craddock   UK: BBC1 2 Nov - 14 Dec 1988

A BBC Television Production

ROCKY KING, INSIDE DETECTIVE

An early 1950s crime series, that had a distinct flavour of an amateur dramatic production. It was made by the little DuMont network who barely had two cents to rub together.

So although we saw Roscoe Karns as dedicated New York homicide detective Rocky King, his family were only ever heard but not seen. This was because DuMont, who clearly hoped to make the series and get change out of $100, were not prepared to pay for him to have a wife. One day an actress in the show was asked to double as Rocky's wife, Mabel, but since it was live and there was no time to change wardrobe, she had to speak from off-screen. Over the next few years, Grace Carney became quite a celebrity as the unseen wife. She could be heard from the kitchen preparing Rocky a great meal, but we never saw her bring it in and eat it. She could be hoovering but she never hoovered the lounge.

Rocky also had an invisible son, Junior, who used to shout from his bedroom, and towards the end of the show's run, Roscoe Karns' son, Todd, was brought in as Rocky's sidekick, Detective Hart.

Yet in spite of its shortcomings, Rocky King built up quite a following and ran for nearly five years, making it DuMont's most successful-ever drama.

* Rocky worked out of the 24th Precinct.

REGULAR CAST

Det. Rocky King Roscoe Karns   *Mabel King* Grace Carney
Sgt Lane Earl Hammond   *Det. Hart* Todd Karns

Producers: Lawrence Menkin, Jerry Layton, Charles Speer

A DuMont Production

Approx. 200 monochrome 30-minute episodes
US: DuMont 14 Jan 1950 - 26 Dec 1954

THE ROOKIES

Three young recruits, fresh out of Police Academy, tried to change the world – or at least the methods of policing it. The idealistic trio, Officers Terry Webster, Willie Gillis and Mike Danko, were attached to Station Number Seven of the South California Police Department, under the command of the uncompromising Lieutenant Eddie Ryker. There was an immediate clash of principles. Ryker was a member of the old school, he believed in fighting fire with fire. He knew that the city's low-life talked with guns and knives, not in social statements. But the rookies were undeterred and did their utmost to bring about a more humane attitude towards keeping the peace on the streets.

Willie Gillis left after two seasons and was replaced by Chris Owens for the final year. Further awareness was added by the presence of Mike Danko's wife, Jill, a righteous registered nurse played by Kate Jackson, soon to star in Charlie's Angels. She didn't do much preaching about humanity there...

REGULAR CAST

Officer Mike Danko Sam Melville   *Officer Terry Webster Georg* Stanford Brown
Officer Willie Gillis Michael Ontkean   *Officer Chris Owens* Bruce Fairbairn
Lt Eddie Ryker Gerald S. O'Loughlin   *Jill Danko* Kate Jackson

Creator: Rita Lakin
Producers: Hal Sitowitz, Rick Husky
Executive producers: Aaron Spelling, Leonard Goldberg

A Spelling-Goldberg Production for ABC

68 colour 60-minute episodes

US: ABC (Season 1) 11 Sept 1972 - 19 March 1973 (23 eps)
(Season 2) 10 Sept 1973 - 18 March 1974 (23 eps)
(Season 3) 9 Sept 1974 - 17 March 1975 (22 eps)
UK: ITV From 5 Aug 1972

ROSIE

Constable Penrose was one of the most naive individuals ever to don a police uniform. He was so wet behind the ears you could have grown rice on his lobes.

His TV career began in the BBC comedy The Growing Pains of PC Penrose, where the young rookie was bullied mercilessly by the fearsome Sergeant Flagg. It was set in Yorkshire and created by Roy Clarke, that brilliant observer of Yorkshire life in the hit comedies Last of the Summer Wine and Open All Hours.

Penrose then returned to his home town on compassionate posting and the series title was changed to Rosie, his nickname. Being close to his invalid mum and various girlfriends caused untold problems for the innocent, and he was grateful for the presence of his worldly colleague, PC Wilmot, to rescue him from some embarrassing situations not in keeping with a member of the constabulary.

As with the majority of Roy Clarke's work, Rosie relied on gentle humour rather than belly laughs. Nevertheless it was certainly one of the better attempts at British police comedy.

The Growing Pains of PC Penrose

REGULAR CAST

PC Penrose Paul Greenwood   *Sgt Flagg* Bryan Pringle

Creator: Roy Clarke
Music: Peter Skellern
Producer: Douglas Argent

A BBC Television Production

7 colour 30-minute episodes
UK: BBC1 2 Sept - 14 Oct 1975

Rosie

REGULAR CAST

PC Penrose Paul Greenwood   *PC Wilmot* Tony Haygarth

Producer: Bernard Thompson

A BBC Television Production

20 colour 30-minute episodes

UK: BBC1 (Season 1) 5 Jan - 9 Feb
1977 (6 eps)
(Season 2) 18 May - 6 July 1978 (7 eps)
(Season 3) 7 June - 19 July 1979 (7 eps)

ROYAL CANADIAN MOUNTED POLICE

You could almost hear the programme announcer's chest swelling with pride as, over the opening titles his deep voice boomed, 'Royal Canadian Mounted Police!' The Mounties epitomized everything that was decent and honourable about law enforcers. You never heard of a bent Mountie. They were lumberjacks and they were OK. And of course they always got their man.

This stirring series was actually endorsed by the Mounties and was set in Shamattawa, a base of the RCMP. It was a co-production between the Canadian Broadcasting Corporation, Crawley Films of Canada and the BBC, and it relied heavily on the contribution of Ed Fowlie, the British special-effects man whose film work had included blowing up the Bridge Over the River Kwai. It was his task to make some dogs look like foxes, and to convince viewers that dogs were pulling a sled, when in truth it was being pushed by the crew.

REGULAR CAST

Corporal Jacques Gagnier Gilles Pelletier   *Constable Scott* John Perkins
Constable Mitchell Don Francks

Producers: George Gorman, Harry Horner, Bernard Girard

A CBC/Crawley Films/BBC Television Production

39 monochrome 30-minute episodes
US: Syndicated 1960
UK: BBC 12 July 1960 - 19 May 1961

THE RUTH RENDELL MYSTERIES

'It was my son, Simon, who pointed out that Inspector Wexford is my father and it's true that some of the things Wexford says, a little bit of his philosophy of life, come from him.'   – RUTH RENDELL

Twenty-five years ago, Ruth Rendell was paid a mere £75 advance for her inaugural Wexford tale, From Doon With Death. Since then she has written a further 13 adventures of the gentlemanly policeman and is now firmly established as one of the world's leading crime writers, a reputation enhanced by the television adaptations of her stories.

Although it appears that she did not recognize it at first, her father partly served as a role model for Wexford. 'He was a teacher,' she says, 'a kind, good and very interesting man who would become not exactly cross, but rather displeased if I, or indeed if anybody in his household, would fail to notice things. For him to say, "You're not very observant," would be a reproof, about the greatest form of reproof I as a child could possibly get.'

Detective Chief Inspector Reg Wexford becomes similarly irked by those who do not pick up on clues, although for the most part he also shares the affability of Ruth Rendell's father, as well as his sophistication. Wexford is fond of quoting Shakespeare.

Played by George Baker, Wexford is a large fatherly figure who speaks with a warm regional burr. He works out of the market town of Kingsmarkham in southern England (Romsey in Hampshire is used for filming). He needs broad shoulders, too, for this quiet locale throws up an inordinate number of particularly nasty murders. He is assisted by Detective Inspector Mike Burden, who has spent most of the time being precisely that – a burden. Since the death of his wife, Jean, Burden moped around aimlessly until suddenly marrying his daughter's history teacher, Jenny Ireland. He is supposed to be happy now – but it's hard to tell.

Wexford has a more stable home life with wife, Dora, and occasional visits from his grown-up daughters. He is every inch the doting father, although he is somewhat old-fashioned and does find trouble in bridging the generation gap. And all too often poor Dora finds him preoccupied with work and likely to nip out from their cottage in the dead of night to pursue a vital clue. He likes to eat well, too, something he has in common with George Baker who, early in his acting career, worked in the kitchens of London's Regent Palace Hotel and is still an accomplished cook.

Wexford and Burden are a long way from being the most dynamic crime-fighters on TV. But what they lack in pace and personality, they make up for with good, steady detective work which wears down the culprit – and sometimes the viewer too.

* Wexford does have one up on Morse, Dalgliesh and all the other British detectives – he is a star in Japan.

REGULAR CAST

Det. Chief Insp. Wexford George Baker *Det. Insp. Burden* Christopher Ravenscroft
Dora Wexford Louie Ramsay *Jean Burden* Ann Penfold
Jenny Ireland/Burden Diane Keen *Det. Sgt Martin* Ken Kitson

Wolf to the Slaughter

Wexford receives an anonymous letter which reveals that a girl named Ann has been murdered by someone called Geoff Smith. But Wexford has no idea who either Ann or Geoff Smith are, let alone who sent the letter. And there is no sign of a body.

GUEST STARS:

Christopher Ellison, Raymond Francis, Donald Hewlett
Dramatized by Clive Exton
Director: John Davies

A Guilty Thing Surprised

Wexford and Burden are confronted with another murder in Kingsmarkham. There seems to be no obvious solution and the discovery of the murder weapon merely serves to complicate matters further.

GUEST STARS:

Michael Jayston, Nigel Terry, Catherine Neilson
Dramatized by Clive Exton
Director: Mary McMurray

Shake Hands Forever

When a woman is found brutally murdered, Wexford feels instinctively that there is something amiss with the husband's reaction. But it leads to old Reg being warned off the case, as he has no evidence to support his theory.

GUEST STARS:

Tom Wilkinson, Patrick Drury, June Ritchie
Dramatized by J.E.M. Brooks
Director: Don Leaver

No Crying He Makes

Just before Christmas, a young mother finds to her horror that her baby has been taken from its pram and another almost identical infant left in its place. Wexford is uneasy about the reason for the swap and is even more concerned about the missing baby.

GUEST STARS:

Jane Horrocks, Clive Wood, Christine Kavanagh
Dramatized by Paula Milne
Director: Mary McMurray

No More Dying Then

It is a year since Burden's wife, Jean, died tragically at the age of 36. Burden has rejected everyone since. When five-year-old John Lawrence vanishes, Burden interviews his beautiful red-haired mother and falls for her. But is there a link between John's disappearance and the earlier murder of Stella Rivers?

GUEST STARS:

Celia Gregory, David Sibley, Simon Shepherd
Dramatized by Geoffrey Case
Director: Jan Sargent

A Sleeping Life

A woman is murdered on a canal towpath. But apart from her aged father who is dying in hospital and a drunken aunt, Wexford can't find anyone who has known the woman in the past 20 years.

GUEST STARS:

Sylvia Syms, Imelda Staunton

Dramatized by Roger Marshall
Director: Bill Hays

The Veiled One

Wexford and Burden are called to the scene of a murder. Wexford is preoccupied by the plight of his younger daughter, Sheila, who has been arrested for cutting the perimeter wire at a military base. But he still finds time to wonder why a seemingly harmless home-help should be attacked from behind with a thin length of wire.

GUEST STARS:

Paolo Dionisotti, Camille Coduri, Hugh Lloyd
Dramatized by Trevor Preston
Director: Mary McMurray

Some Lie and Some Die

Pop star Zeno attracts a huge crowd to an outdoor concert, but nearby a pair of lovers discover the mutilated body of a young woman in a quarry. She is identified as Dawn Stoner and investigations reveal that she died in a dress that wasn't hers. And the mystery deepens when Wexford learns that Dawn was an old school friend of Harold Goodbody, now better known as Zeno.

GUEST STARS:

Peter Capaldi, Gemma Jones, Donald
  Sumpter
Dramatized by Matthew Jacobs
Director: Sandy Johnson

The Best Man to Die

It is Jack Pertwee's wedding day but the ceremony is called off when the best man, Charlie Hatton, is found floating face down in the river. Meanwhile Wexford is having problems identifying the body of a young girl found at the scene of a fatal car crash. Is there a connection between the two deaths?

GUEST STARS:

Tracie Bennett, Barbara Leigh-Hunt,
  Tony Haygarth
Dramatized by John Brown
Director: Herbert Wise

An Unkindness of Ravens

When Rodney Williams goes missing, Wexford believes at first that it is a simple case of a wayward husband going off with another woman. Then his car is found abandoned in a neglected side road and it becomes clear that there is a more chilling reason for Williams' disappearance, after two schoolboys find his body buried near the roots of a fallen tree.

GUEST STARS:

Cheryl Prime, Norma West, Deborah
  Poplett
Dramatized by Robert Smith
Director: John Gorrie

Put On By Cunning

Rich and famous flautist, Sir Manuel Camargue, is found drowned in a muddy lake in his own grounds. Everyone believes his death is a tragic accident, but Wexford becomes suspicious when Camargue's fiancee claims that his long-lost daughter, who returned to see her father shortly before

his death, was an imposter. Wexford's trail leads him to America.

GUEST STARS:

Rossano Brazzi, Cherie Lunghi, Beryl
  Reid
Dramatized by Trevor Preston
Director: Sandy Johnson

A New Lease of Death

Thirty years ago, when Wexford was a young detective sergeant, he helped to convict a man who was subsequently hanged for murdering a wealthy old lady. It was Wexford's first murder investigation. Suddenly the case is re-opened when a man of the church, whose son is to marry the killer's daughter, challenges the conviction.

GUEST STARS:

Sharon Maughan, Peter Egan, Dorothy
  Tutin
Dramatized by Peter Berry
Director: Herbert Wise

Murder Being Once Done

While convalescing from surgery, Wexford learns about the chilling murder of a young girl. His unofficial investigation delves into the lives of the people involved and reveals a moving story about adoption.

GUEST STARS:

Michael Elwyn, Polly Adams, Charlotte
  Attenborough
Dramatized by Matthew Jacobs
Director: John Gorrie

From Doon With Death

A passionate relationship, born innocently during schooldays, burns out with disappointment and ultimately murder, as contact is resumed in later life. Adapted from Ruth Rendell's first novel.

GUEST STARS:

Amanda Redman, John Salthouse
Dramatized by George Baker
Director: Mary McMurray

Means of Evil

Wexford investigates the lifestyle of glamorous health food writer Corrine Last, who is linked to rumours of a particularly nasty case of attempted poisoning.

GUEST STARS:

Cheryl Campbell, Patrick Malahide
Dramatized by Peter Berry
Director: Sarah Hellings

Achilles Heel

Wexford, Burden and their wives are on holiday on the Mediterranean, when Wexford becomes increasingly intrigued by the behaviour of a well-heeled young couple, and almost unhealthily obsessed by the strikingly beautiful wife. Back in Kingsmarkham, Wexford discovers that she was the heiress to a local fortune. But now she's dead...

GUEST STARS:

Norman Eshley, Saira Todd
Dramatized by Guy Hibbert
Director: Sandy Johnson

Music: Brian Bennett
Producer: Neil Zeiger
Executive producer: Graham Benson

A TVS Production

UK: ITV
WOLF TO THE SLAUGHTER
4 colour 60-minute episodes 2 - 23 Aug
   1987
A GUILTY THING SURPRISED
3 colour 60-minute episodes 19 June -
   3 July 1988

SHAKE HANDS FOREVER
3 colour 60-minute episodes 23 Sept -
   7 Oct 1988
NO CRYING HE MAKES
One colour 90-minute episode
23 Dec 1988
NO MORE DYING THEN
3 colour 60-minute episodes
22 Oct - 5 Nov 1989
A SLEEPING LIFE
3 colour 60-minute episodes
12 - 26 Nov 1989
THE VEILED ONE
One colour 120-minute episode
17 Dec 1989
SOME LIE AND SOME DIE
3 colour 60-minute episodes
30 Sept - 14 Oct 1990
THE BEST MAN TO DIE
3 colour 60-minute episodes
21 Oct - 4 Nov 1990
AN UNKINDNESS OF RAVENS
2 colour 60-minute episodes
11 - 18 Nov 1990
PUT ON BY CUNNING
One colour 90-minute episode
24 Dec 1990
A NEW LEASE OF DEATH
3 colour 60-minute episodes
29 Sept - 13 Oct 1991
MURDER BEING ONCE DONE
3 colour 60-minute episodes
20 Oct - 3 Nov 1991
FROM DOON WITH DEATH
2 colour 60-minute episodes
10 - 17 Nov 1991
MEANS OF EVIL
2 colour 60-minute episodes
24 Nov - 1 Dec 1991
ACHILLES HEEL
One colour 120-minute episode
Christmas 1991

US: Arts and Entertainment cable
   channel From 1990

THE SAINT

'I always play heroes but I am a coward. I would run miles to avoid a fight.'
                                                              – ROGER MOORE

But there was certainly nothing cowardly about Leslie Charteris' debonair adventurer/sleuth Simon Templar, the man with the ring of confidence above his head. He was so sure of himself that even the show's star Roger Moore was forced to concede: 'The Saint is a bighead.'

Although his expertise was that of a true professional, the Saint was strictly an amateur detective, the perfect gentleman who, no matter how fierce the foe, never had a hair out of place. Handsome, intelligent, witty, no wonder girls the world over found him irresistible. He was a knight in shining armour, something Moore could relate to, having clanked around on set a few years earlier as Ivanhoe. Nicknamed The Saint because of his initials S.T., Templar always left his calling card, a stick man with a halo, usually on a girl's pillow. We were expected to believe that he had made his excuses and left, but the girls invariably wore a smile in their slumbers.

The first Saint story, Meet the Tiger, was published in 1928 and George Sanders appeared in a number of Saint movies in the early 1940s. Louis Hayward and Hugh Sinclair also played Templar on the big screen, while among the radio Saints have been Vincent Price, Brian Aherne and George Sanders' brother, Tom Conway.

The first choice for the TV Templar was Patrick McGoohan, star of Danger Man. But McGoohan is a man of strong principals and morals and turned down the part because he objected to the way the script called for the Saint to have an affair with a different girl each week. He stated at the time: 'I am not against romance on TV but sex is the antithesis of romance. It is phoney, promiscuous sex I am against. Television is a gargantuan monster that all sorts of people watch at all sorts of times and it has a moral obligation to its audience.'

In reality, the restrictions placed on television companies in the early 1960s necessitated that The Saint was a fairly moral show anyway. He was not allowed to maim, kill, shoot or disfigure and, in fist-fights, he had to adhere to the Queensbury Rules, with no kicking below the belt. He was not permitted to be seen picking locks, in case watching children attempted to copy, and he had to give back any ill-gotten money he happened to come by in the course of his escapades.

But production problems did not end with the casting of Roger Moore instead of McGoohan. Always on the lookout for a money-making deal, ATV chief, Lew Grade, took two strong episodes to the US in an attempt to sell the series to NBC. The story goes that NBC Vice-President, Mort Werner, sat in stony silence through the first and hardly had the second one started when he stood up and said, 'Lew, I've never seen so much crap in all my life.' Cynics might have pointed out that with the state of some American TV shows then, that comment meant Lew was on to a winner.

And so it turned out, because The Saint went on to become one of Britain's most lucrative exports to the US. NBC bought 71 black and white programmes for syndication, and they did well enough for the network to order another 43 colour shows in 1967, according them the accolade of a prime-time slot.

With the series being sold to over 80 countries, Roger Moore didn't do too badly either, since his deal gave him a share in world profits. Also, of course, the role led to another nice little earner, James Bond.

The Saint was without doubt one of the best shows of the 1960s, with Moore rescuing damsels in distress, foiling elaborate crimes and still finding time to mock the incompetent Chief Inspector Claud Eustace Teal, who he patronizingly referred to as 'Scotland Yard's finest'. Templar had contacts across the globe – when in New York his police chum was Inspector John Henry Fernack.

The sense of fun that Moore brought to the character on screen spilled over on to the film set. He loved to play practical jokes. One such occasion was when actor Graham Stark was making his debut as a director on an episode. Moore hid in a cupboard, dressed as one of those outlandish Hollywood German movie directors from the 1930s, complete with knee-breeches and jackboots. He waited until Stark called his first 'Action!', which is a big moment for any director, and leaped out of the cupboard screaming, 'Not like zat! You have to shout it like zis, "ACTION!"'

* The reason the Saint drove a Swedish sports car, a Volvo P-1800, was simple. British car giants, Jaguar, refused to lend an E-Type. They reckoned they didn't need the publicity.

* In total, four actors played Claud Eustace Teal. Ivor Dean became the regular, but only after Campbell Singer, Wensley Pithey and Norman Pitt had each played him once in the first season.

REGULAR CAST

Simon Templar Roger Moore   Chief Insp. Teal Ivor Dean
Insp. Fernack Allan Gifford

Creator: Leslie Charteris
Saint theme: Leslie Charteris
Music: Edwin Astley

8 Oct 1964 - 11 March 1965
1 July - 26 Aug 1965
US: Syndicated 1963 - 1966

Monochrome series
Producers: Robert S. Baker, Monty Norman

An ATV Production for New World/ITC

71 monochrome 60-minute episodes
UK: ITV 4 Oct 1962 - 19 March 1964

Colour series
Producer: Robert S. Baker

A Bamore Production for ITC

47 colour 60-minute episodes
UK: ITV 30 Sept 1966 - 2 June 1967
        22 Sept 1968 - 9 Feb 1969
US: NBC 21 May 1967 - Sept 1969

In addition to the Ian Ogilvy version (SEE THE RETURN OF THE SAINT), there was another revival in 1989, starring Simon Dutton, who was actually named after Simon Templar because his mum had been a big fan of The Saint. Alas there weren't many fans of Simon Dutton's Saint, and only a couple of episodes were networked, on 2 and 9 September.

SAM

It wasn't only Starsky who had a partner with fair hair, big eyes and a shiny coat. Officer Mike Breen did too – and his had a cold nose thrown in for good measure. For Mike's partner was a golden labrador retriever police dog, Sam.

Mike and Sam were members of the Los Angeles Police Department (where else?) and formed a successful alliance, although Mike's boss, Captain Tom Clagett, retained serious reservations about the dog's value. But the fact was that Sam was a darn fine sniffer, who could hunt out bodies over great distances...as long as the victim was carrying a pound of sausages or a bone when he was killed.

REGULAR CAST

Officer Mike Breen Mark Harmon   *Capt. Tom Clagett* Len Wayland

Creators: Jack Webb, Dan Noble
Producer: Leonard B. Kaufman
Executive producer: Jack Webb

7 colour 30-minute episodes
US: CBS 14 March - 18 April 1978
UK: ITV 17 July - 21 Nov 1979

SAN FRANCISCO BEAT (US TITLE: THE LINEUP)

Over 20 years before The Streets of San Francisco, Detective Lieutenant Ben Guthrie, and the equally hard-bitten Inspector Matt Grebb, policed the Golden Gate city in this superior cop drama. Produced with the co-operation of the San Francisco Police Department, the series was based on real cases, most of which included an identity parade, known in the US as a lineup. It was very much CBS's answer to Dragnet. After five years, the format changed from half-hours to hour-long episodes and Inspectors Grebb and Fred Asher were replaced by younger models, Dan Delaney and Charlie Summers.

* The show spawned a 1958 film, The Lineup, with Warner Anderson as Guthrie and Emile Meyer as Grebb.

REGULAR CAST

REGULAR CAST

Det. Lt Ben Guthrie Warner Anderson   *Insp. Matt Grebb* Tom Tully
Insp. Fred Asher Marshall Reed   *Insp. Dan Delaney* William Leslie
Insp. Charlie Summers   Tod Barton

Announcer: Art Gilmore

30-minute episodes *A Desilu Production*
    for CBS

60-minute episodes *A Marjeff Production*
    for CBS

183 monochrome 30-minute episodes
    and 18 monochrome 60-minute
    episodes
US: CBS 1 Oct 1954 - 20 Jan 1960
UK: ITV From 26 Sept 1957

SAPPHIRE AND STEEL

Usually associated with writing for more conventional police shows, such as Z Cars and Hunter's Walk, P.J. Hammond came up with this baffling science-fiction yarn about two 'time detectives' codenamed Sapphire and Steel. Their activities would have had Columbo scratching his head and Kojak sucking his lollipop in disbelief.

Sapphire and Steel were elemental beings, who became human to combat space invaders intent on breaking through the time corridor. Dressed all in blue, Sapphire was played by that heavenly body Joanna Lumley, with David McCallum as the cold Steel.

Their adventures took them back and forth through history, to confrontations with Roundhead soldiers from the 17th Century, footmen from the First World War and time travellers from the future.

* The 34 episodes were broken down into six separate stories, the first season being comprised of a six-parter and an eight-parter, and the second season featuring a six-part and a four-part tale.

REGULAR CAST

Sapphire Joanna Lumley   *Steel* David McCallum
Silver   David Collings

Creator: P.J. Hammond
Music: Cyril Ornadel
Producer: Shaun O'Riordan
Executive producer: David Reid

An ATV Network Production

34 colour 30-minute episodes
UK: ITV (Season 1) 10 July - 22 Nov
    1979 (14 eps)
(Season 2) 6 Jan - 5 Feb 1981 (10 eps)
(Season 3) 11 - 26 Aug 1981 (6 eps)
(Season 4) 19 - 31 Aug 1982 (4 eps)

Sarge

Not to be confused with priest detectives like Father Brown and Father Dowling, Sarge was a homicide detective turned priest. Emotionally shattered after his wife was killed by an assassin's bullet meant for him, Sergeant Swanson of the San Diego Police Department entered the priesthood, and three years later was ordained as Father Samuel Patrick Cavanaugh.

His parish was St Aloysius, the same area of town where he had spent nine years on the force. Known to all as 'Sarge', his help was often enlisted by his old pal, Chief of Detectives Barney Verick, especially when his parishioners found themselves on the wrong side of the law. Also featured were rectory cook Kenji Takichi and Valerie, the parish secretary. Sarge was developed from the pilot shows The Badge or the Cross and The Priest Killer, the latter having originally been intended as two episodes of Ironside.

Regular Cast

Father Cavanaugh George Kennedy   *Barney Verick* Ramon Bieri
Valerie Sallie Shockley   *Kenji Takichi* Harold Sakata

Creator: David Levy
Producer: David Levinson
Executive producer: David Levy

A Universal Television Production
13 colour 60-minute episodes
US: NBC 21 Sept 1971 - 11 Jan 1972

Scene of the Crime

Another attempt by American TV to combine detection and audience participation. A murder playlet was halted just before the crucial revelation and guest celebrities were asked to say whodunnit. The host was master of mystery, Orson Welles, and the recurring cast included Greg Evigan from B.J. and the Bear and Steve Kanaly, cowboy Ray Krebbs in Dallas.

Executive producer: Jon Epstein

6 colour 30-minute episodes
US: NBC 30 Sept - 4 Nov 1984

A J.E. Production for Universal

SCHIMANSKI

British viewers who have stayed up until the early hours to catch this German cop series could be forgiven for thinking they were watching the late-night horror movie. For there is more blood and gore in a single episode of Schimanski than Bela Lugosi, Christopher Lee and Peter Cushing managed in a lifetime of nibbling necks and prowling graveyards.

Horst Schimanski is a macho man cop with the Duisburg murder squad. 'Shimmy', as he is nicknamed, is the most eligible bachelor in town, known by everyone, even the local hookers, feared by the underworld – a celebrity who flouts authority and whose wild private life makes front-page headlines. His time is divided between bunk-ups and shoot-outs, for after a heavy session with that night's girl, he goes to work and pumps holes into terrorists, bank robbers and anyone else who happens to be passing.

But there is one problem Shimmy can't solve – how his lips speak German but the words that come out are English. Perhaps it is because the show is dubbed that there is so much gunfire. The language of the bullet is international.

Schimanski is a grossly exaggerated version of The Sweeney's Jack Regan, a comparison encouraged by the fact that the dubbed voice of Schimanski's chief is provided by actor Garfield Morgan, who played Regan's boss, Frank Haskins. But even on a bad day, Regan was never this violent. In some Schimanski episodes, the level is unacceptable. In fact TVS refused to transmit one show because they considered it too violent, even for 12.35 in the morning.

REGULAR CAST

Horst Schimanski Gotz George   *Christian Thanner* Eberheid Feik

Producer: Hartmut Grund

An ECO Production in association with JBTV

Colour 105-minute episodes
UK: ITV 29 Jan - 16 April 1991 (TVS)
(12 eps)

SEAWAY

Nick King was an agent for the Ship Owners Association, an organization responsible for maintaining security along Canada's St Lawrence Seaway. To all intents and purposes, he was a special policeman. Set in Montreal and mainly produced by Canada (Britain's

ATV provided extra funding), it was the costliest-ever Canadian series at the time. But it faded away because its black and white episodes were unable to compete with rival Canadian colour shows. In a desperate bid to save the day, the final two episodes of Seaway were shot in colour. But it was too little, too late.

* Among the guest stars on Seaway was a young Faye Dunaway.

REGULAR CAST

Nick King Stephen Young   *Admiral Fox* Austin Willis

Music: Edwin Astley
Executive producer: Maxine Samuels

An ASP/ATV Production

28 monochrome and 2 colour 60-minute episodes
Canada: CBS 1965
US: Syndicated 1969
UK: ITV 8 April 1967 - 11 July 1970 (Anglia)

SERGEANT CORK

Rather like the chap who invented the wheel, Sergeant Cork was ahead of his time. In Victorian England, just as advanced medicine sometimes still meant eye of toad and crushed newt, so policing methods remained in the Dark Ages. Sergeant Cork wanted to change all that, to convince his superiors that detection technique really had advanced beyond trial by ordeal.

Cork was a member of the recently-founded CID Division of Scotland Yard and favoured the new-fangled scientfic approach to his job. But he and his enthusiastic young sidekick, Detective Sergeant Bob Marriott, were banging their heads against a Victorian brick wall, as they tried to convince their superior, the stubborn Detective Joseph Bird. Fortunately they had an ally in Superintendent Billy Nelson, and when Bird was transferred and replaced by another sympathizer, Superintendent Rodway, Cork was finally able to drag Scotland Yard into the 19th Century.

A fondly-remembered series which was nicknamed H Cabs (in deference to the BBC's Z Cars) to denote Cork and Marriott's most frequent mode of transport, the hansom cab.

REGULAR CAST

Sgt Cork John Barrie   *Sgt Marriott* William Gaunt
Det. Bird Arnold Diamond   *Supt Nelson* John Richmond
Supt Rodway Charles Morgan

Creator: Ted Willis
Producer: Jack Williams

65 monochrome 60-minute episodes
UK: ITV 9 June 1963 - 26 March 1968

An ATV Network Production

SERGEANT PRESTON OF THE YUKON

'Sergeant Preston of the North-West Mounted Police with Yukon King, swiftest and strongest lead dog, breaking the trail in the relentless pursuit of lawbreakers in the wild days of the Yukon.'
— PROGRAMME ANNOUNCER

They didn't come much tougher than Sergeant Preston and his trusted husky, Yukon King, the perfect combination of man and beast. Both were half-breeds. The dog had been raised by a female wolf and rescued by Preston during a lynx attack. For his part, Preston's parentage was a pedigree mix of the Lone Ranger and the Green Hornet, his creators having been the men behind those shows, George W. Trendle and Fran Striker.

Hero and hound kept law and order on Canada's Alaskan border at the turn of the century. Preston was a member of the Royal North-West Mounted Police and rode a mighty black horse called Rex. But his real pal was Yukon King, who he had taught to command a team of huskies, to respect good men and hate the wicked. The dog didn't need telling which were which either – he was obviously studying to be a psychiatrist as well as a crime-fighter.

The majority of the crooks were gold miners or settlers who had come to colonize the wild frontier but no matter how ruthless they appeared, no matter how desperate they were to make their fortune by foul means, they were no match for this man and his dog.

There was one slight problem with production. Richard Simmons, who played Sergeant Preston, explained: 'A harnessed team of dogs is a quivering mass of supercharged energy howling for release, but trained not to move before a verbal command. So the director dared not call out "Action" or the dogs would have bolted with the cast!'

* Sergeant Preston had been an American radio favourite since 1947.

REGULAR CAST

Sgt William Preston Richard Simmons

Creators: George W. Trendle, Fran Striker
Theme music: 'Donna Diana Overture' by Emil Von Reznick

A Wrather Films Production

78 monochrome 30-minute episodes
US: CBS 29 Sept 1955 - 25 Sept 1958
UK: ITV 22 Sept 1959 - 21 June 1961 (ATV)

SERPICO

A real-life crusading New York cop, Frank Serpico had already been the subject of a book and a 1973 film starring Al Pacino, before the TV series came along. Badge number 21049, Serpico worked out of the city's 22nd Police Precinct and was dedicated to exposing corruption, not only in high places but also within the N.Y.P.D. itself. In particular, he was out to nail officers and politicians who were receiving pay-offs from organized crime.

Serpico was a fearless operator, often going undercover with his assistant, Tom Sullivan, to achieve his means. Not surprisingly, he was not over-popular with his fellow cops who branded him a troublemaker. And since he was so determined to enforce law and order, crooks didn't care for him much either – the real Frank Serpico was shot in the face by a drugs pusher and forced to retire from the force on a disability pension. The N.Y.P.D.'s loss was film and television's gain.

REGULAR CAST

Frank Serpico David Birney   *Tom Sullivan* Tom Atkins

Music: Robert Dransin, Elmer Bernstein
Producers: Don Ingalls, Barry Oringer
Executive producer: Emmet G. Larvey Jnr

A Paramount Television Production

15 colour 60-minute episodes
US: NBC 24 Sept 1976 - 28 Jan 1977
UK: BBC1 12 Feb - 26 March 1977

77 SUNSET STRIP

'In the end I admit I stopped learning my lines – they never changed that much anyway.'   — EFREM ZIMBALIST JR

Back in the days when teenagers were dancing to the Everly Brothers and Bobby Darin and trying on their Itsy Bitsy Teeny Weeny Yellow Polka

Dot Bikinis for the first time, 77 Sunset Strip was the hippest show around. It had cool college boys, swinging chicks, an abundance of glamour and excitement and a theme tune that everyone sang along to, clicking their fingers at the appropriate moments. The result was that, despite carping from critics and sometimes the cast about its quality, 77 Sunset Strip was a worldwide triumph for Warner Bros, inspiring a crop of imitators from within the company – Hawaiian Eye, Bourbon Street Beat and Surfside 6.

The show's origins lay in a 1956 episode of the US drama Conflict. Called Anything for Money, it was written by Roy Huggins and starred Efrem Zimbalist Jnr in a solo adventure, as private eye Stu Bailey. For 77 Sunset Strip, Huggins teamed Bailey with Jeff Spencer, played by Roger Smith, as private detectives with their office on Hollywood's famous Strip. Both had been government undercover agents in an earlier life and were experts in judo. They had brains too – Bailey could speak several languages and had once intended to become a college professor, while Spencer possessed a degree in law.

Their cases took them all over the world, yet the show's most popular ingredient was next door to 77, at a swish restaurant called Dino's (a real eating-house named after Dean Martin) where the car park attendant was a jive-talking, laid-back guy by the name of Gerald Lloyd Kookson III, or 'Kookie' to his friends. Kookie was so popular with girls that even the Fonz would have been jealous. But he dreamed of being a private eye and often persuaded Stu and Jeff to let him help out on assignments.

Stu Bailey needed all his mastery of languages to cope with Kookie, who had a crazy vocabulary foreign to any Oxford dictionary. For example, 'piling up the z's' meant 'sleeping'; 'antsville' was 'a crowded room'; 'play like a pigeon' meant 'deliver a message'; and 'keep the eyeballs rolling' suggested 'be on the lookout'. Kookie-talk was copied throughout the high-schools of America as was his other trademark, his habit of constantly combing his hair.

Kookie, in the form of actor Edd Byrnes, became a teen idol. He received 15,000 fan letters a week, Kookie combs and wallets were marketed and in one month alone, he appeared on the cover of 26 magazines. He briefly turned pop star to duet with Connie Stevens for 'Kookie, Kookie, Lend Me Your Comb' and that, too, captured the imagination of the American public, turning into a big hit. Yet ironically in the pilot for Sunset Strip, entitled Girl on the Run, Edd Byrnes had played a psychopathic killer!

Overnight stardom is probably the most difficult phenomenon for either actor or studio to contend with, and invariably causes conflict. Thus Byrnes decided he wanted a bigger role to reflect his new-found fame and eventually walked out on the show. Even before his departure, he had always been at great pains to point out that in reality he was absolutely nothing like Kookie. 'I wear suits and ties in everyday life,' he stated. 'As a matter of fact, I can't stand the garb I wear on 77 Sunset Strip. And I do not comb my hair all the time.'

But his exile was only temporary. A few months later, Byrnes returned to the fold at the start of the fourth season and Kookie was duly promoted to a fully-fledged partner alongside Stu and Jeff, while another heartthrob, J.R. Hale, played by Robert Logan, took over at the parking lot. There had been a third partner for the previous season when Richard Long briefly transferred from Bourbon Street Beat to play Rex Randolph.

It seemed that everything was back to normal. The Warner Bros conveyor belt trundled on relentlessly, the policy of Jeff and Stu starring in alternate episodes increasing output, as crews were able to work on more than one episode at a time. Aside from the leads, secondary characters like racetrack tout Roscoe and the guys' French switchboard operator, Suzanne Fabray, built up their own followings.

However, the rot started to set in. The scripts became more repetitive than ever until, in 1963, in a desperate attempt to halt the decline, Jack Webb was brought in as executive producer, with William Conrad as director. The entire cast – Kookie and all – were axed with the exception of Zimbalist, who set up as a freelance investigator with a new secretary, Hannah. But it was not a successful operation. Webb's remedies merely killed the patient.

The cast weren't too sorry to see the demise of Sunset Strip. Byrnes was type-cast for years afterwards, while Zimbalist said: 'Towards the end, it was only feminine appeal that kept the show going. There was Robert Logan for the teenagers, Edd Byrnes for the young marrieds, Roger Smith for slightly more mature women and me for grandmothers, derelicts and non-walking patients!'

REGULAR CAST

Stu Bailey Efrem Zimbalist Jnr   *Jeff Spencer* Roger Smith
'Kookie' Edd Byrnes   *Roscoe* Louis Quinn
Suzanne Fabray Jacqueline Beer   *J.R. Hale* Robert Logan
Rex Randolph Richard Long   *Hannah* Joan Staley
Lt Gilmore Byron Keith

Creator: Roy Huggins
Theme music: Mack David, Jerry Livingston
Producer: Howie Horowitz
Executive producers: Bill Orr, Jack Webb (Season 6)

A Warner Bros Production

205 monochrome 60-minute episodes
US: ABC (Season 1) 10 Oct 1958 - 29 May 1959 (34 eps)

(Season 2) 2 Oct 1959 - 10 June 1960 (36 eps)
(Season 3) 16 Sept 1960 - 2 June 1961 (38 eps)
(Season 4) 22 Sept 1961 - 29 June 1962 (41 eps)
(Season 5) 12 Oct 1962 - 14 June 1963 (36 eps)
(Season 6) 20 Sept 1963 - 7 Feb 1964 (20 eps)
UK: ITV 9 Dec 1959 - 7 Aug 1964 (Anglia)

SEXTON BLAKE

Tall, slim and virtuous, Sexton Blake, 'The Great Detective', was every inch a British boys' hero. He was created by Hal Meredith (real name Harry Blyth) back in the 19th Century, and starred in a number of minor 20th Century films, beginning with The Clue of the Wax Vesta in 1914. Among the actors who played him were George Curzon and David Farrar, in the 1930's and 1940's respectively.

The TV series was set in the late 1920s and went out as a children's adventure, which meant that most of the mysteries Blake investigated were of a non-violent nature. Blake has often been likened to Sherlock Holmes, mainly because they are of similar build, both have a housekeeper (Blake's equivalent of Mrs Hudson is Mrs Bardell) and both have offices in London's Baker Street. But whereas Holmes has his dark moods which make him so fascinating, Sexton Blake, like the vast majority of Ripping Yarn-type characters, is simply too clean-cut to be true.

On television, Blake's pride and joy was the Grey Panther, a splendid white Rolls-Royce, in which he drove his human assistant, Edward Clark, known to all as 'Tinker', and canine crime-fighter, Pedro the bloodhound.

REGULAR CAST

Sexton Blake Laurence Payne   *Tinker* Roger Foss
Mrs Bardell Dorothea Phillips   *Insp. Cutts* Ernest Clark
Insp. Van Steen Leonard Sachs   *Insp. Cardish* Eric Lander

Producer: Ronald Marriott

An Associated Rediffusion Production

32 colour 30-minute episodes

UK: ITV 25 Sept 1967 - 24 July 1968

A Thames Television Production

28 colour 30-minute episodes
UK: ITV 14 Nov 1968 - 13 Jan 1971

SHADOW SQUAD

A quirky British detective series, immensely popular in the late 1950's, about two private eyes who relied on the office cleaning lady to solve cases.

Former Flying Squad member, Vic Steele, resigned from the police force to set up Shadow Squad, in company with Ginger Smart, an archetypal cockney cheekie chappie. The two took on a wide variety of intriguing assignments until, after 26 episodes, Steele was suddenly dispatched to Australia, never to be seen again. His place was taken by Don Carter, who had been a Detective Inspector with Scotland Yard, and the show went from strength to strength.

Steele, Carter and Smart were able operatives in their own right, but they would have been far less effective without the assistance of the redoubtable Mrs Moggs, the charlady who was better at spotting clues than spotting a pile of dust. The fact that she rarely got round to cleaning their office mattered not, as she polished off cases in no time.

* Among the writers on Shadow Squad was Tony Warren, the man who, a couple of years later, created Coronation Street.

REGULAR CAST

Vic Steele Rex Garner   *Don Carter* Peter Williams
Ginger Smart George Moon   *Mrs Moggs* Kathleen Boutall

Producer: Barry Baker

An Associated Rediffusion Network Production (eps 1-26)

A Granada Television Network Production (eps 27 - 175)

175 monochrome 30-minute episodes
UK: ITV 17 June 1957 - 24 June 1959

SHAFT

Remembered mainly for Isaac Hayes' Academy Award winning theme music, Shaft was the story of an extrovert black New York private detective, whose speed with flip one-liners was matched only by his speed on the trigger. A product of the rough, tough city streets, John Shaft had a liking for trendy clothes, but his tendency to become involved in dangerous missions meant that all too often he dressed to kill. For Shaft could be ruthlessly efficient, a fact recognized by his police contact and friend, Lieutenant Al Rossi.

The series was a spin-off from three highly-acclaimed but fairly violent Shaft movies, also starring Richard Roundtree. Isaac Hayes' theme was written for the first, Shaft (1971), which was succeeded by Shaft's Big Score (1972) and Shaft in Africa (1973).

Sadly, in toning down the violence for television, the producers also toned down Shaft's character, with the outcome that the trail-blazing black came over in shades of grey.

REGULAR CAST

John Shaft Richard Roundtree   *Lt Al Rossi* Ed Barth

Theme music: Isaac Hayes
Music: Johnny Pate
Producer: William Reed Woodfield
Executive producer: Allan Balter

An MGM Television Production

8 colour 90-minute episodes
US: CBS 9 Oct 1973 - 3 Sept 1974
UK: ITV 22 Jan 1974 - 1 Dec 1976

SHANNON (1961)

Described by Columbia as a family series that would concentrate on 'people in trouble, not trouble in people', Shannon focussed on the cases of an amiable insurance investigator with America's Transport Bonding and Surety Company. Joe Shannon travelled in, and worked from, his gadget-laden Buick convertible which, among other items, contained a phone and a tape recorder, state-of- the-art technology for 1961. Shannon's boss, Bill Cochran, was played by Regis Toomey who, with three shows a week to record, found that production time was so short that it paid to keep his hat on throughout the series. It saved valuable minutes on a make-up girl having to powder his bald head...

REGULAR CAST

Joe Shannon George Nader   *Bill Cochran* Regis Toomey

Creator: John Hawkins
Producer: Jerry Briskin
Executive producer: Robert Sparks

*A Screen Gems Production for Columbia
   Pictures Television*

36 monochrome 30-minute episodes
US: Syndicated 1961

SHANNON (1981)

It was hard to believe that Kevin Dobson, so convincing as Bobby Crocker in Kojak, could have allowed himself to be talked into such sentimental clap-trap as this.

He played Jack Shannon, a plainclothes detective with the New York Police Department, who was devastated by the sudden death of his young wife. He got a posting to San Francisco, partly so that he could forget the bitter taste left by the Big Apple, and partly so that his two-year-old son, Johnny, could be brought up by his in-laws, Paul and Irene Locatelli, who lived there.

Jack joined the SFPD's Special Squad of Investigators, where he and his partner, Detective Norm White, reported to Lieutenant Moraga. But of course all the time Jack was out fighting crime, his thoughts were with little Johnny. Don't it just make you wanna weep?

REGULAR CAST

Det. Jack Shannon Kevin Dobson   *Det. Norm White* William Lucking
Lt Moraga Michael Durrell   *Johnny Shannon* Charlie Fields
Paul Locatelli Al Ruscio   *Irene Locatelli* Karen Kondazian

Creator: Albert Ruben
Producers: David J. O'Connell, Alvin Sapinsley
Executive producers: James Aubrey, James McAdams

An Aubrey Company Production for Universal Television

13 colour 60-minute episodes
US: CBS 11 Nov 1981 - 7 April 1982
UK: BBC1 19 Nov 1982 - 2 Sept 1983

THE SHERIFF OF COCHISE

No end of future stars guested as virtual unknowns on this long-running modern Western set in Cochise County, Arizona – Stacy Keach, Charles Bronson, Jack Lord, David Janssen and Michael Landon. Lord, in a far cry from his Steve McGarrett role in Hawaii Five-O, played a convicted killer escorted by the central character, Sheriff Frank Morgan, to a nearby US Marshal. But Lord murdered the marshal and escaped, so Morgan took over the dead man's job in order that he would have the jurisdiction to catch the killer. And from then on, the show was titled US Marshal, to mark Morgan's instant promotion.

The series turned the real Cochise County into something of a tourist attraction, and during the County's 4th of July celebrations in 1957, actor John Bromfield, who played Frank Morgan, was the guest of honour and was sworn in as a bona-fide deputy sheriff.

* The programme's creator, Stan Jones, played a deputy for the first two years but left when Morgan was made up to marshal.

REGULAR CAST

Sheriff/Marshal Frank Morgan John Bromfield   *Deputy Olson* Stan Jones
Deputy Tom Ferguson James Griffith

Creator: Stan Jones
Producer: Mort Briskin
156 monochrome 30-minute episodes

US: Syndicated 1956 - 1960
UK: ITV From 26 Sept 1957

SHERLOCK HOLMES (1951)

It was certainly an unlikely trio of actors who teamed up for this early BBC production about the world's greatest detective. Holmes was played by Alan Wheatley, soon to achieve everlasting notoriety as the evil Sheriff of Nottingham in The Adventures of Robin Hood; Raymond Francis, who went on to star as Chief Superintendent Lockhart in No Hiding Place, played Watson; and Inspector Lestrade was played by Bill Owen, best known as the moth-eaten Compo from Last of the Summer Wine!

The series was live and this caused untold problems for the cast and the stories' adaptor, Miss C.A. Lejeune, who at the time was film critic of the Observer.

Alan Wheatley recalled: 'Miss Lejeune did some things that are just not possible – like not allowing enough time for changes with live television. In one scene, she finished up with a sentence from me and opened the next scene also with a sentence from me "in heavy disguise", with no time at all for a change. I overcame it by playing the first scene out of camera while I was making up in the corner of the set.'

REGULAR CAST

Sherlock Holmes Alan Wheatley   *Dr Watson* Raymond Francis
Insp. Lestrade Bill Owen

EPISODE TITLES

The Empty House
A Scandal in Bohemia
The Dying Detective
Reigate Squires
The Red-Headed League
The Second Stain

Producer: Ian Atkin

A BBC Television Production

6 monochrome 50-minute episodes
UK: BBC 20 Oct - 1 Dec 1951

SHERLOCK HOLMES (1954)

'In my interpretation, Holmes is not an infallible, eagle-eyed, out-of-the-ordinary personality but an exceptionally sincere young man trying to get ahead in his profession. Where Basil Rathbone's Holmes was nervous and highly-strung, mine has a more ascetic quality, is deliberate, very definitely unbohemian and is underplayed for reality.'
– RONALD HOWARD

This was more of a wimpy Holmes. Instead of snorting cocaine, Ronald Howard's version looked as if he was on Mogadon. But if nothing else, it was a different interpretation of the great man, one which was filmed in Paris where the authorities generously provided thousands of cobblestones to build a Victorian street. One episode even took Holmes to the top of the Eiffel Tower. It was a rather eccentric series all round with Archie Duncan, who played Lestrade, insisting on halting filming at 4pm each day for a proper British teatime, while one of the guest stars, Paulette Goddard, caused delays as a result of her superstition towards cemeteries and the colour green. It's a good job she wasn't with Archie Duncan in Robin Hood!

REGULAR CAST

Sherlock Holmes Ronald Howard   *Dr Watson* H. Marion Crawford
Insp. Lestrade Archie Duncan

EPISODE TITLES

The Case of the Cunningham Heritage
Lady Beryl
The Winthrop Legend
The Mother Hubbard Case
The Pennsylvania Gun
The Red-Headed League
The Belligerent Ghost
The Thistle Killer
The Shoeless Engineer
The Shy Ballerina
The Deadly Prophecy
The Split Ticket
Harry Crocker
The Reluctant Carpenter
The Texas Cowgirl
The Laughing Mummy
The Diamond Tooth
Blind Man's Buff
The Greystone Inscription
The French Interpreter
The Vanished Detective
The Careless Suffragette
The Baker Street Nursemaids
The Tyrant's daughter

The Imposter Mystery
The Christmas Pudding
The Jolly Hangman
The Impromptu Performance
The Singing Violin
The Violent Suitor
The Night Train Riddle
The Perfect Husband
The Unlucky Gambler
The Exhumed Client
The Neurotic Detective
The Baker Street Bachelors
The Eiffel Tower
The Haunted Gainsborough
A Case of Royal Murder

Producer: Nicole Millenaire
Executive producer: Sheldon Reynolds

A Guild Films Production

39 monochrome 30-minute episodes
US: Syndicated from 18 Oct 1954

* In 1980, Sheldon Reynolds produced Sherlock Holmes and Dr Watson, a series of 30-minute colour episodes filmed in Poland, with Geoffrey Whitehead as Holmes and Donald Pickering as Watson. The majority of the stories were not adaptations but originals by Reynolds. It was not shown in Britain but did go out on PBS in America.

SHERLOCK HOLMES (1965)

'I first became steeped in Holmes when I was ill in bed with jaundice as a boy. I had my bed piled with old Strand magazines and would read one Conan Doyle story after another.'   – DOUGLAS WILMER

A neat BBC production of the 1960s, with the angular Douglas Wilmer physically perfect for Holmes, marred slightly by Nigel Stock's bumbling Watson, a man who gave the impression that he was barely capable of writing his own name, let alone prescriptions as a qualified doctor. Unlike Ronald Howard, Wilmer was only too aware of Holmes' seamy side, although it was generally restrained in his screen portrayal. He remarked at the time that Holmes' macabre practice of experimenting in a laboratory, beating corpses to find out if the flesh bruised after death, 'might shock even the most hard-boiled of Mods and Rockers'.

REGULAR CAST

Sherlock Holmes Douglas Wilmer   *Dr Watson* Nigel Stock
Insp. Lestrade Peter Madden   *Mrs Hudson* Mary Holder
Mycroft Holmes Derek Francis

EPISODE TITLES

The Illustrious Client
The Devil's Foot
Copper Beeches
The Red-Headed League
The Abbey Grange
The Six Napoleons
The Man With the Twisted Lip
The Beryl Coronet
The Bruce Partington Plans
Charles Augustus Milverton

The Retired Colourman
Lady Frances Carfax

Producer: David Goddard

A BBC Television Production

12 monochrome 50-minute episodes
UK: BBC1 20 Feb - 8 May 1965

(SEE ALSO THE ADVENTURES OF SHERLOCK HOLMES, THE CASES OF SHERLOCK HOLMES, THE HOUND OF THE BASKERVILLES, YOUNG SHERLOCK)

SHE'S THE SHERIFF

An abysmal American comedy, where the idea started out thin and became positively anorexic. Hildy Granger was a blonde mother of two cloying sit-com kids, who took over her late husband's job. Nothing unusual in that except (wait for it) he was the sheriff of a small town in Nevada. So now she's the sheriff. Suzanne Somers as Hildy did a lot of posing and pouting (she was probably waiting for the laughs) as she tried to instil some discipline into her wayward deputies, notably Max Rubin who was after her job. My three-year-old daughter loved it, but happily by the age of five she had outgrown it.

REGULAR CAST

Hildy Granger Suzanne Somers   *Deputy Rubin* George Wyner
Officer Puttnam Lou Richards

Creators: Dan Guntzelman, Steve
  Marshall
Music: Bruce Miller
Producers: Alan Hamel, David
  Goldsmith, Michael Stokes
Executive producer: Mark Rothman

A Lorimar Production

Colour 30-minute episodes
US: Syndicated 1987
UK: BBC1 From 4 Sept 1989

SHOESTRING

One of the best-ever British private eye series, and ample proof that detective shows do not need car chases, shoot-outs and a brutal murder in the first five minutes, to make compelling viewing. Shoestring replaced the gratuitously violent Target and pulled in viewing figures of 23 million on Sunday evenings, because it was so refreshingly different.

A disciple of the Columbo style of menswear, Eddie Shoestring was a scruffy computer expert who had suffered a nervous breakdown, in the process smashing up a £500,000 computer. On the road to recovery, he was taken on by a local radio station in Bristol, Radio West, to do a short phone-in spot where he would attempt to solve callers' problems. At first, station boss Don Satchley was sceptical about the new venture, but as the fame of his 'private ear', as Eddie became known, spread and, more importantly, ratings rocketed, he was converted to the cause. Eddie dealt with all manner of cases, a few missing persons, others more mundane, but the important thing was that they were believable. Realism was not sacrificed for sensationalism – this was Bristol and there were no mass murderers on the loose, no multi-million pound Colombian drug rings, not even alien invaders from Weston-Super-Mare.

Eddie was a mess emotionally and physically. The show's creator, Robert Banks Stewart, described him as 'twitching, manic and irreverent.' He was still walking a tightrope after his breakdown and remained highly-strung, vulnerable and, as Satchley often found to his cost, unpredictable. He drove around in a second-hand Ford Cortina and rented a room from a smart lady lawyer, Erica Bayliss, who offered legal advice and the occasional shoulder to cry on. She was certainly a cut above most television landladies. The other regular in the cast was friendly Radio West secretary, Sonia, played by Liz Crowther, daughter of comedian Leslie Crowther.

But there was no doubting the star of the show. Trevor Eve as Eddie Shoestring was quite brilliant. Comparatively unknown beforehand, he turned in a performance of the highest calibre and instantly became hot property and a somewhat reluctant and unlikely pin-up for the thirtysomethings. But Eve knew what he wanted and, after two series, he knew that he didn't want any more of Shoestring. It was a shame because there appeared to be a lot more mileage left in the character...if not his car. However, Robert Banks Stewart didn't fret. He thought up a new emotionally-scarred private eye – and decided to set him in the sunnier climes of Jersey. He called him Bergerac.

REGULAR CAST

Eddie Shoestring Trevor Eve   *Don Satchley* Michael Medwin
Erica Bayliss Doran Godwin   *Sonia* Liz Crowther

Creator: Robert Banks Stewart
Music: George Fenton
Producer: Robert Banks Stewart

A BBC Television Production

21 colour 50-minute episodes
UK: BBC1 (Season 1) 30 Sept - 16 Dec
    1979 (11 eps)
(Season 2) 5 Oct - 21 Dec 1980 (10 eps)

SHOTGUN SLADE

At a time when Westerns and trendy detectives were all the rage (Maverick, Gunsmoke, Cheyenne, Laramie, 77 Sunset Strip, Hawaiian Eye etc), Shotgun Slade managed to combine the two genres. Slade was a Western detective who solved crimes for banks, insurance companies and Wells Fargo. He rode around on horseback and owned an unusual two-in-one shotgun, which proved extremely useful in extracting information from the tongue-tied. And like all the best detectives, he found that women were eager to queue up for his services. Among the guest stars was Johnny Cash playing a sheriff.

REGULAR CAST

Shotgun Slade Scott Brady

Creator: Frank Gruber
Music: Gerald Fried
Producer: Frank Gruber

A Shotgun/Revue Production for MCA

78 monochrome 30-minute episodes
US: Syndicated 1959 - 1961

THE SILENT FORCE

Ward Fuller, played by old Peyton Place favourite, Ed Nelson, teamed up with Jason Hart and Amelia Cole to form a special strike force of government agents, appointed to tackle organized crime. Most of their work was undercover, as they attempted the highly-dangerous task of infiltrating the 'mob', which ran rackets in Southern California. But they did so without any credibility whatsoever, and this short-lived police series soon turned into Mission Implausible.

REGULAR CAST

Ward Fuller Ed Nelson   *Jason Hart* Percy Rodriguez
Amelia Cole Lynda Day

Creator: Luther Davis
Executive producer: Aaron Spelling

An Aaron Spelling Production

15 colour 30-minute episodes
US: ABC 21 Sept 1970 - 11 Jan 1971
UK: ITV From 16 Sept 1971

SIMON AND SIMON

The only things that A.J. and Rick Simon had in common were that they were brothers and partners in a small-time, impoverished San Diego detective agency. Apart from that, they were like the proverbial chalk and cheese.

A.J. was a product of the 1980s, clean-cut, hard-working, the sort of son that any mother would be proud of. Rick was scruffy, lazy and manic, a throwback to the carefree 1960s, the sort of son that most mothers disown. A.J. avoided the seedy side of San Diego to preserve the crease in his newly-ironed trousers. Rick wore jeans, a T-shirt and scuffed boots. Tramps used to take pity on him. A.J. drove a sparkling convertible and always ensured that his apartment was spotless. Rick rode around in a beat-up old truck and lived in a houseboat that had all the modern trimmings of the Ark.

Leaving aside solving any cases that happened to come their way, A.J.'s greatest problem was persuading Rick to lift his finger to do anything other than pluck his guitar. Even their mum, Cecilia, used to despair, particularly if the agency wasn't paying its way.

The boys' internal rivalry was nothing compared to that with the firm across the street, the Peerless Detective Agency run by the deeply unpleasant Myron Fowler. Myron's daughter, Janet, worked as his secretary but also put in a few hours helping A.J. and Rick on cases, to her father's intense annoyance. However when she graduated from law school and became a district attorney, she often found herself prosecuting Simon and Simon clients. In another twist, Myron retired but occasionally returned to active service, as legman for the Simons.

Mildly amusing at first, downright predictable later, Simon and Simon unaccountably ran for seven years in the US. In Britain it managed the odd spell of several weeks in the summer, when everyone was away on holiday.

REGULAR CAST

Andrew Jackson (A.J.) Simon Jameson Parker   *Rick Simon* Gerald McRaney
Cecilia Simon Mary Carver   *Janet Fowler* Jeannie Wilson
Myron Fowler Eddie Barth

Creator: Philip DeGuere
Producers: Chas Floyd Johnson, John Stephens
Executive producer: Philip DeGuere

A Universal Television Production

152 colour 60-minute episodes and 2 colour 120-minute episodes
US: CBS 24 Nov 1981 - 18 Aug 1988
UK: ITV 19 July 1983 - 6 Sept 1983 (Thames) (8 eps)
1 June - 24 Aug 1984(LWT) (12 eps)
9 June - 14 July 1985 (LWT) (5 eps)

THE SINGING DETECTIVE

A masterful and suitably complex piece from Dennis Potter, about his own Philip Marlow (deliberately spelt without the final 'e'). Superbly played by Michael Gambon, Marlow was a patient in the Sherpa Tensing Ward of a hospital, where he lay in bed covered in the scales and sores of crippling psoriasis, the disease from which Potter himself has suffered for nearly half his life. Racked with pain and anger, Marlow's only comfort rested in the healing hands of the delectable Nurse Mills, as she rubbed cream into vital areas.

Between Nurse Mills' treatments, author Marlow feverishly dreamed about his wife Nicola's betrayal of him, and of his mother's early affair with the villainous Mark Binney. In turn, the action switched to the hero of one of Marlow's novels, a war-time detective (also played by Gambon) investigating the death of a beautiful girl whose body had been dragged out of the River Thames.

As with most of Potter's works, it would take an entire book to describe the plot fully, but suffice to say that The Singing Detective was arguably his finest-ever creation. In addition to sex and drama, there were some classic comedy scenes, especially the sight of a gaggle of doctors and nurses crowded around the foot of Marlow's hospital bed to sing 'Dem Bones, Dem Bones, Dem Dry Bones'. Yet above all The Singing Detective is remembered for the shots of actor Patrick Malahide's bare buttocks, as he romped in the grass with Alison Steadman and the furore they caused among a minority. Most viewers simply turned the other cheek.

MAIN CAST

Philip Marlow Michael Gambon   *Nurse Mills* Joanne Whalley
Mark Binney Patrick Malahide   *Mrs Marlow* Alison Steadman
Nicola Janet Suzman   *Dr Gibbon* Bill Paterson

Writer: Dennis Potter
Director: John Amiel
Producer: Kenith Trodd

A BBC Television Production

6 colour 50-minute episodes
UK: BBC1 16 Nov - 21 Dec 1986

SLEDGE HAMMER!

'Trust me, I know what I'm doing.'

As a plea for calm, this statement by Detective Hammer was on a par with the Captain of the Titanic's assertion that there was absolutely nothing to worry about. For few people in the history of the police force inspired less trust or had less idea what they were doing than Hammer.

Sledge Hammer! (so called partly as a pun on Mike Hammer but also because of his bull-in-a-chinashop approach) was a send-up of all those movies or TV shows where the hero is a trigger-happy, macho cop. He made Dirty Harry look like Postman Pat.

Partnered with the beautiful but ruthless Detective Dori Doreau, Sledge tried to appear in total control, yet in reality he was hopelessly inept. The trouble was he couldn't be classified a harmless buffoon, he was a definite menace to all around him, being over-enthusiastic to the point of wanton violence and only too willing to discharge his gun at random. He was very attached to his gun (he even talked to it) and used it for all sorts of odd jobs. If Hammer was making an omelette, the chances are he would crack the egg by pumping it with bullets. His beliefs placed him just to the right of Genghis Khan – he no doubt advocated the electric chair for unpaid parking fines.

The subject matter is exactly right for parody and would have made a first-class TV movie. But it was difficult to sustain over 33 episodes and Sledge went downhill fast.

REGULAR CAST

Sledge Hammer David Rasche *Det. Dori Doreau* Anne-Marie Martin

Creator: Alan Spencer
Producer: Thomas Kane
Executive Producers: Alan Spencer,
  Robert Lovenheime

A New World International Production

33 colour 30-minute episodes
US: ABC 12 Sept 1986 - 16 June 1988
UK: ITV From 26 Sept 1987 (TVS)

SMALL AND FRYE

We are talking unfunny here. Darren McGavin, TV's first Mike Hammer, was talked into this ropey sit-com about Hammer-like private investigator, Nick Small, whose partner had the capability to shrink to a height of just six inches. His name was, would you believe, Chip Frye – quite appropriate since the show was panned.

Frye's facility resulted from a laboratory accident but it wasn't easy to control. For example, a sudden bout of hiccups could lead to him diminishing in stature at the most inopportune moments. It didn't seem to put off his girlfriend, Phoebe, who was also the office receptionist and Small's daughter. Clearly here was a girl who knew that size isn't everything.

REGULAR CAST

Nick Small Darren McGavin *Chip Frye* Jack Blessing
Phoebe Small Debbie Zipp

Creators: George Schenck, Ron
 Friedman
Producer: Nick Arnold

A Walt Disney Production

6 colour 30-minute episodes
US: CBS 7 March - 15 June 1983

THE SMITH FAMILY

Henry Fonda starred in this American police family drama from the 'Hi, honey, I'm home' stable. Fonda played Detective Sergeant Chad Smith, a dedicated Los Angeles cop for 25 years, and a man equally caring and conscientious at home as he was at the precinct house. The series concentrated on Smith's family life with wife, Betty, daughter, Cindy (18) and sons, Bob (15) and Brian (7), with police action scenes practically non-existent. Thanks to Fonda's skill, it just about managed to avoid toppling over into sentimental slush.

REGULAR CAST

Det. Sgt Chad Smith Henry Fonda   *Betty Smith* Janet Blair
Cindy Smith Darleen Carr   *Bob Smith* Ronny Howard
Brian Smith Michael-James Wixted

Creator: Edmund Hartmann
Music: Franke De Vol
Executive Producer: Don Fedderson

An ABC Production

39 colour 30-minute episodes
US: ABC 20 Jan 1971 - 14 June 1972
UK: ITV From 22 April 1971 (Granada)

THE SNOOP SISTERS

These two were like stereo Miss Marple – a pair of old biddies who were phenomenally successful mystery writers and whose idea of a jolly good wheeze was to poke their noses into other people's crimes. And like that other famous busybody, Jessica Fletcher, they even had a nephew, Lieutenant Steve Ostrowski of the New York Police Department, who vainly battled to keep his favourite aunts out of mischief.

He had no chance. For Ernesta and Gwen Snoop were thrilled at the opportunity to put their keen detective minds to a more practical use than writing novels. And sleuthing was the ideal outlet for their energies. However, at their advanced age, their energies were more mental than physical. These frail old ladies weren't exactly cut out for scaling walls in pursuit of offenders or even crossing roads into the wind. So they relied on their chauffeur, Barney, to act as their bodyguard and legman.

In the US, The Snoop Sisters aired as part of NBC's Wednesday/Thursday Mystery Movie, along with Faraday and Company, Tenafly and Banacek.

Regular Cast

Ernesta Snoop Helen Hayes *Gwen Snoop* Mildred Natwick
Barney Lou Antonio *Lt Steve Ostrowski* Bert Convy

Music: Jerry Fielding
Producer: Leonard Stern
Executive Producer: Douglas Benton

A Universal Television Production

4 colour 90-minute episodes
US: NBC 19 Dec 1973 - 20 Aug 1974
UK: ITV 24 Jan - 21 Feb 1974

SNOOPS

Following in the footsteps of Nick and Nora Charles and Jonathan and Jennifer Hart, came Chance and Micki Dennis, billed as the husband and wife crime-solving team of the 1980s. And that's where they stayed because, although they didn't start sleuthing until September 1989, their show was received with such apathy that they failed in the US even to make it into the 1990s.

Chance and Micki were certainly a curious couple. He was a criminologist and professor of psychology at Georgetown University, while she was assistant to the Deputy Chief of Protocol for the State Department in Washington, D.C. She was also a woman with what is politely known as an inquiring mind. In other words, she was downright nosey. This fascination for crime and intrigue led her and Chance into no end of perilous situations, as they sought to solve murder mysteries with the same regularity that other couples go to the supermarket.

Among the other characters were Micki's chauffeur and minder, Hugo, and Chance's friend, Police Lieutenant Stan Akers, played by John Karlen, (Harvey of Cagney and Lacey).

Smooth, suave, sophisticated and wise-cracking, Chance and Micki should in theory have had a long television career. It wasn't that their show was awful, it was simply that the format had been done so much better before.

REGULAR CAST

Chance Dennis Tim Reid   *Micki Dennis* Daphne Maxwell Reid
Hugo Troy Curvey Jr   *Lt Akers* John Karlen

Creators: Sam Egan, Tim Reid
Music: 'Curiosity' performed by Ray Charles
Producer: David Auerbach
Executive producers: Tim Reid, Andrew Solt, Sam Egan, George Geiger

A Timalove Production in association with the Solt/Egan Co. and Viacom for CBS

13 colour 60-minute episodes
US: CBS 16 Sept - 9 Dec 1989
UK: Channel Four 29 Sept - 22 Dec 1990

SOFTLY, SOFTLY

A spin-off from Z Cars which became equally popular, running for ten years and 264 episodes. Charlie Barlow and John Watt left Liverpool and Newtown to join a regional crime squad, Wyvern, supposedly near Bristol, and were promoted to Detective Chief Superintendent and Detective Chief Inspector respectively. As chance would have it, one of the first people they bumped into was another refugee from Z Cars, former Desk Sergeant Blackitt, now simply Mr Blackitt, accompanied everywhere by his dog, Pandy.

They were soon joined by Detective Inspector Harry Hawkins, a local man who became the series' pin-up, jolly Welshman Sergeant Evans and dour dog-handler PC Henry Snow, another candidate for the award for the most miserable policeman on TV. He preferred dogs to people and went around impersonating a bloodhound. One of his brave alsatians, Inky, was clearly an accomplished actor because in real life he had been sacked as a police dog for going AWOL over a wall. And when Inky was shot in an episode of Softly, Softly, the BBC received so many angry letters that the dog had to appear on Blue Peter to prove that he was still alive and kicking and had only been acting.

In the early 1970s, a number of changes took place. Stratford Johns went off to star in two further spin-off series, Barlow at Large and Barlow (SEE BARLOW AT LARGE), and from 13 September 1972, the show's title was changed to Softly, Softly Task Force. To the end, it remained a quality programme, although in the latter years the action did become somewhat infrequent, with possibly too much time devoted to police politics. Among an excellent team of writers were Elwyn Jones, Alan Plater, Robert Barr and Keith Dewhurst.

* The title Softly, Softly came from the phrase 'Softly, softly catchee monkey'.

REGULAR CAST

Det. Chief Supt Charlie Barlow Stratford Johns
Det. Chief Insp. John Watt Frank Windsor
Det. Insp. Harry Hawkins Norman Bowler   *PC Henry Snow* Terence Rigby
Mr Blackitt Robert Keegan   *Insp. Gwyn Lewis* Garfield Morgan
Det. Con. Stone Alexis Kanner   *Det. Con. Box* Dan Meaden
Sgt Evans David Lloyd Meredith   *Asst Chief Con. Gilbert* John Barron
Chief Con. Calderwood John Welsh   *Chief Con. Cullen* Walter Gotell

Producers: David E. Rose, Leonard Lewis, Geraint Morris

A BBC Television Production

264 monochrome and colour 60-minute
episodes
UK: BBC1 5 Jan 1966 - 15 Dec 1976

* In 1973, Barlow and Watt teamed up for a six-part investigation into the Jack the Ripper murders. Producers were Leonard Lewis and Paul Bonner.

SONNY SPOON

'Sonny Spoon is a private eye with a penchant for operating slightly off-centre.'   – EXECUTIVE PRODUCER STEPHEN J. CANNELL

To put it mildly, Sonny Spoon was eccentric. He was as conventional as Frank Cannon was slim. His 'office' was an out-of-order telephone booth on a busy street in an unnamed American East Coast city, but any similarity with Superman ended there. For when Sonny changed clothing, it wasn't into a cape to fly through the air and save the planet, it was into one of his many disguises to tread the streets and pay the rent.

Part detective, part con artist, Sonny was able to slip into a wide variety of characters to get the job done. One day he would be a Rastafarian, the next a pompous attorney. He had more outfits than Joan Collins.

He survived by keeping his ear to the ground and received a steady supply of information from news vendor Lucius DeLuce. And no matter how formidable the situation, Sonny remained an optimist, always seeing the funny side, which was more than could be said of ambitious assistant D.A. Carolyn Gilder. She made it perfectly clear that, besides not understanding Sonny's antics, she did not approve of them one bit.

REGULAR CAST

Sonny Spoon Mario Van Peebles   *Lucius DeLuce* Joe Shea
Carolyn Gilder Terry Donahoe

Producer: Randall Wallace
Executive producer: Stephen J. Cannell

A Stephen J. Cannell Production in association with NBC

15 colour 60-minute episodes
US: NBC 12 Feb - 16 Dec 1988
UK: British Sky Broadcasting From 8 Sept 1990

SOUTH OF THE BORDER

'TV is always showing us the back streets of Los Angeles. Quite frankly I find the back streets of Deptford far more interesting.'
— Creator Susan Wilkins

Described as the Oxfam version of Cagney and Lacey, South of the Border recounted the adventures of girl private eyes, Pearl Parker and Finn Gallagher, in a less than salubrious area of south-east London. Pearl was black, beautiful and ambitious, Finn was a petty criminal who had just been released from prison after serving two years for theft. Pearl was determined not to end up on dead-end street, like most of her friends, while Finn didn't fancy the prospect of more prison, so they accepted the offer of detective work for lawyer, Milly. It was a tough job for two young girls, their only back-up being the occasional assistance from Pearl's former lover, Fitz, who ran a reggae music shop.

Grittily realistic with some nice light touches, South of the Border was nevertheless possibly a shade too down-beat to achieve mass appeal.

REGULAR CAST

Pearl Parker Buki Armstrong   *Finn Gallagher* Rosie Rowell
Milly Dinah Stabb   *Fitz* Brian Bovell

Creator: Susan Wilkins
Music: Alan Lisk
Producer: Caroline Oulton

A BBC Television Production

15 colour 50-minute episodes
UK: BBC1 (Season 1) 25 Oct - 13 Dec 1988 (8 eps)
(Season 2) 11 May - 22 June 1990 (7 eps)

SPECIAL AGENT 7

Is it a bird, is it a plane, is it a tax return form? Treasury Agent Conroy could turn a blind eye to murderers and international terrorists, he was only concerned with those who attempted to undermine civilization as we know it, by defrauding the US Department of Internal Revenue. He was Taxman.

The series was based on official files, with Conroy working for the Department's Intelligence Bureau. This was one of the few shows where, no matter how heinous the crime, the villain was always more popular than the hero.

REGULAR CAST

Treasury Agent Conroy Lloyd Nolan

A TPA/Revue Production

26 monochrome 30-minute episodes
US: Syndicated 1958 - 1959

SPECIAL BRANCH

Special Branch was a landmark series for British television. Until then, our TV policemen gave the impression that they bought all their clothes at Dunn and Co. and had their hair cut by Sweeney Todd. But instead of the hitherto standard CID attire of subdued colours and styles, Derren Nesbitt's Detective Inspector Jordan wore bright ties and floral shirts, and had long sideboards, very much the fashion at the time. The sight of him may have appalled little old ladies in Worthing, but the fact remained that he was as good a copper as the short back and sides, trilby and raincoat brigade.

Jordan worked for Scotland Yard's Special Branch, a clandestine department designed to safeguard national security. His first boss was Detective Superintendent Eden, followed by Detective Superintendent Inman, but by the third season, all three men had departed. The major new arrivals were Detective Chief Inspector Alan Craven and Detective Chief Inspector Tom Haggerty, another rule-bending modern copper. The final season also introduced a senior civil servant, Strand, whose pompous attitude grated with Haggerty.

REGULAR CAST

Det. Insp. Jordan Derren Nesbitt   *Det. Supt Eden* Wensley Pithey
Det. Supt Inman Fulton Mackay   *Det. Ch. Insp. Craven* George Sewell
Det. Ch. Insp. Haggerty Patrick Mower   *Det. Sgt North* Roger Rowland
Commander Nicols Richard Butler   *Commander Fletcher* Frederick Jaeger
Strand Paul Eddington

Music: Robert Earley
Producer: Reginald Collin (eps 1-7),
   Robert Love (eps 8-26), Geoffrey
   Gilbert (Season 3), Ted Childs
   (Season 4)
Executive producers: Lloyd Shirley
   (Seasons 3,4), George Taylor
   (Season 4)

A Thames Television Network Production
   (Seasons 1,2)

A Euston Films Production (Seasons 3,4)

52 colour 60-minute episodes
UK: ITV (Season 1) 17 Sept - 17 Dec
   1969 (13 eps)
(Season 2) 11 Aug - 4 Nov 1970 (13 eps)
(Season 3) 4 April - 4 July 1973 (13 eps)
(Season 4) 14 Feb - 9 May 1974 (13 eps)
US: Syndicated 1976 (Season 4 only)

SPECIAL SQUAD

A hard-hitting Australian police action drama set in the state of Victoria, with the three principals part of a hand-picked team engaged in a constant battle against the most vicious elements of the Down Underworld. The trio were the athletic and good-looking Davis, junk food addict, Smith, and their dictatorial boss, Anderson. It was the latest in a long line of police series from Crawford Productions, following in the size 11 footsteps of Homicide, Division 4, Matlock Police and Cop Shop. British expertise was provided by Raymond Menmuir who, back in 1970s' Britain, produced The Professionals.

REGULAR CAST

Anderson Alan Cassell   *Davis* John Diedrich
Smith Anthony Hawkins

Theme music: Graeme Lyall
Producer: Raymond Menmuir
Executive producers: Hector Crawford,
   Ian Crawford, Terry Stapleton

A Crawford Production

39 colour 60-minute episodes
Australia: Network 10 From 22 Aug 1984
UK: ITV 17 Jan 1986 - 13 Feb 1988
   (LWT)

SPECIALS

What do a physiotherapist, a bank clerk, a partner in a coach company, a solicitor and a ladies' underwear salesman have in common? They are all 'Specials', five of the 20,000 men and women from different walks of life, who spend their spare time volunteering to keep the peace on the streets of Britain.

The unusual double lives of these Special Constables, or 'hobby bobbies' as they are known, has been dramatized for a new series centred on the fictitious Division S, in the West Midlands. Aiming for authenticity rather than sensational blood and guts, Specials shows them dealing with petty crime and the pressures of community policing.

Among the Specials are man-hungry bank clerk, Viv Smith, who has only joined up because she has a thing about men in uniform. Then there is oddball Freddy Calder, a 38-year-old bachelor who lives at home with his domineering mum. He sells ladies' lingerie by day and joins the Specials after work, chasing up dodgy street-traders and so on. He goes from selling knickers to nicking sellers.

* Specials' co-creator Harry Robertson was a leading member of the 1950s and 1960s pop music scene, under the name of Lord Rockingham. He had a string of hits with Lord Rockingham's XI, including the 1958 British chart-topper, Hoots Mon, before producing Millie's My Boy Lollipop. He also acted as musical director for the likes of Judy Garland and The Beatles.

REGULAR CAST

Freddy Calder Ron Donachie   *Viv Smith* Cindy O'Callaghan
Anjali Shah Kim Vithana   *Bob Loach* Martin Cochrane
John Redwood Brian Gwaspari

Creators: Brian Degas, Harry Robertson
Music: Harry Robertson
Producer: Ian Brindle

A BBC Television Production

12 colour 50-minute episodes
UK: BBC1 from 25 Sept 1991

SPENDER

Played by Geordie actor Jimmy Nail, who attained cult status for his role as boozing, bruising brickie Oz, in Auf Wiedersehen, Pet, Spender was working as a Detective Sergeant with the Metropolitan Police in London, when his unorthodox methods landed him in deep water, and his partner in hospital. So Spender accepted a posting back to his native Newcastle-upon-Tyne, to work undercover on cases the local police are unable to handle because their faces are too well known.

Spender is hardly the ideal candidate for undercover work himself. At well over 6ft tall and a face that appears to have been chiselled from Hadrian's Wall, he hardly blends into the background. He sticks out like a sore thumb in most company, with the possible exception of destitute winos.

His new boss is Superintendent Yelland (unexpected promotion for actor Paul Greenwood, a humble PC in Rosie). Yelland likes to do things by the book and is appalled at the state and tactics of his new recruit, even more so when he finds he is associating with former building society robber, Stick, a man whose etiquette leaves even more to be desired than Spender's. Stick must surely be short for 'stick insect'.

Stick is not quite a reformed character – whenever he passes a building society, he feels that old urge to pull on his mask again – but Spender has a powerful hold over him and Stick often finds himself a reluctant accomplice on some of Spender's more hazardous missions. Spender doesn't carry a gun and is regularly roughed up. The consolation is that a beating won't spoil his looks.

Spender is not just a one-dimensional character. He has a tender side, too, for Newcastle is also home to his family – ex-wife Frances, of whom he is still very fond and who is studying for a degree with the Open University, and two young daughters, Laura and Kate.

Other characters include Spender's occasional colleague, the understanding Detective Sergeant Dan Boyd, and Keith Moreland, a crippled rock guitarist whose music shop Spender uses as a point of contact.

The strength of the show is that, between the action there are some great lines. One of the best occurred when Spender took Stick to a nouvelle cuisine restaurant and the waiter brought the ex-con a plate of rare lamb. Stick looked horrified. 'It is a little pink,' ventured the waiter. 'A little pink?' said Stick. 'A good vet could probably have this bugger on its feet again...'

* At the time of writing, a new series is planned for 1992.

REGULAR CAST

Spender Jimmy Nail   *Supt Yelland* Paul Greenwood
Stick Sammy Johnson   *Det. Sgt Dan Boyd* Berwick Kaler
Frances Denise Welch   *Laura* Dawn Winlow
Kate Lynn Harrison   *Keith Moreland* Tony McAnaney

Creators: Jimmy Nail, Ian La Frenais   8 colour 55-minute episodes
Music: Tony McAnaney   UK: BBC1 8 Jan - 26 Feb 1991
Producer: Martin McKeand

A BBC Television Production

SPENSER: FOR HIRE

Based on the acclaimed novels by Robert B. Parker, Spenser was a product of the 1980s, a yuppie detective. A former football star and police detective now turned Boston private eye, Spenser liked the good things in life – particularly skiing weekends, gourmet cooking and his glamorous girlfriend, Susan Silverman.

But his benign countenance hid a steely determination and a strong set of principles. His sense of morality, though at odds with the tarnished reputations of the people he helped, made him one of the more honourable members of his profession. He was, however, prone to be just a little too righteous, at which times he relied on Susan to keep his ideals in perspective.

If Susan provided him with moral support, he looked to his long-time acquaintance, Hawk, for physical support. Mean, moody, shaven-headed and with eyes that could stare through walls, Hawk was a one-man army. He was so tough he made Mr T look like Bill Cosby.

Spenser, who, like so many private eyes, had no first name, also remained on good terms with his police contacts, homicide commander Lieutenant Martin Quirk and Sergeant Frank Belson.

In the hands of Robert Urich (Dan Tanna in Vega$), Spenser came over as a considerably milder character than in the novels. But even with his claws retracted, this was still a highly watchable series, all the better for the background of a snow-capped Boston winter as a welcome alternative to all those long hot California summers.

REGULAR CAST

Spenser Robert Urich   *Hawk* Avery Brooks
Susan Silverman Barbara Stock   *Lt Martin Quirk* Richard Jackal
Sgt Frank Belson Ron McCarty

Based on characters created by Robert B. Parker
Producers: Dick Gallegly, Robert Hamilton
Executive producer: John Wilder

A John Wilder Production in association with Warner Bros

66 colour 60-minute episodes
US: ABC 20 Sept 1985 - 3 Sept 1988
UK: BBC1 12 Sept 1989 - 28 August 1991

SPOONER'S PATCH

The combination of the writing talents of Johnny Speight (Till Death

Us Do Part) and Ray Galton, who wrote Hancock and Steptoe and Son with Alan Simpson, should have ensured a comedy classic. It didn't.

Set in a suburban police station, this routine comedy was remarkable only for having three different actors in the lead role of Inspector Spooner. Ian Bannen appeared in the pilot programme, Ronald Fraser for the first series and then Donald Churchill for the remainder.

All Spooner wanted was the quiet life, to avoid any dealings with the public so that he could spend more time on the golf course. But the men under his wing made that impossible by their incompetence. Detective Constable Bulsover was the main culprit. He behaved, dressed and drove like his heroes, Starsky and Hutch, and even had his police car painted red and white. Then there was the caustic Killick, fascist Goatman, station hanger-on, Kelly, a persistent pest, and another all-too frequent visitor, irascible traffic warden Mrs Cantaford, played by the marvellous Patricia Hayes.

Only when she and Churchill's Spooner were at loggerheads did the show come close to realizing anything like its potential.

REGULAR CAST

Insp. Spooner (pilot) Ian Bannen *(Season 1)* Ronald Fraser
(Seasons 2,3) Donald Churchill
Det. Con. Bulsover Peter Cleall   *PC Killick* John Lyons
PC Goatman Norman Rossington   *Mrs Cantaford* Patricia Hayes
Kelly Dermot Kelly

Creators: Ray Galton, Johnny Speight   18 colour 30-minute episodes
Producer: William G. Stewart   UK: ITV 16 July 1979 - 24 Aug 1982

An ATV Network Production

STAND BY FOR CRIME

Whodunnits were extremely popular in the early days of American television and this one was like a primitive Opportunity Knocks, with the action being stopped at the vital moment and viewers asked to phone in and nominate their favourite murderer. The on-screen inquiries were conducted by Inspector Webb, until he was replaced by Lieutenant Anthony Kidd of the homicide squad and his assistant, Sergeant

Kramer. Kidd was played by Myron Wallace who later defected to journalism, changed his name to Mike and became one of America' s best-known faces in news programmes like 60 Minutes.

REGULAR CAST

Insp. Webb Boris Aplon   *Lt Kidd* Myron Wallace
Sgt Kramer George Cisar

An ABC Production   33 monochrome 30-minute episodes
US: ABC 11 Jan - 27 Aug 1949

STAR COPS

Wherever Man goes, crime follows. That applies to Space, too, and was the reason behind the formation of Star Cops. Under the watchful, and sometimes vengeful, eye of professional detective Nathan Spring, the International Space Police Force was an inter-galactic Sweeney, responsible for maintaining law and order in the year 2027. Initially composed of part-time volunteers, the team policed five manned space stations and settlements on the Moon and Mars, investigating cases ranging from murder to minor theft. The squad included Australian Pal Kenzy, young Japanese scientist Anna Shoun and American flight engineer David Theroux.

Star Cops was the brainchild of Chris Boucher, who had written scripts for Shoestring, Juliet Bravo and Bergerac. If he had posted Bergerac to Mars, you could be sure that the first person he would have bumped into would have been Charlie Hungerford, developing a promising crater site for a block of holiday apartments.

REGULAR CAST

Nathan Spring David Calder   *David Theroux* Erick Ray Evans
Pal Kenzy Linda Newton   *Anna Shoun* Sayo Inaba

Creator: Chris Boucher   9 colour 55-minute episodes
Theme music: Justin Hayward   UK: BBC2 6 July - 31 Aug 1987
Producer: Evgeny Gridneff

A BBC Television Production

STARSKY AND HUTCH

'I directed an episode of Starsky and Hutch in which a man fell five storeys to his death. "Oh no," said the network, "you can't have that. Take it out." I refused. So the network said, "OK, keep it in but he only falls three storeys."'
— DAVID SOUL

Starsky and Hutch were the ultimate 'good buddies', two plainclothes Los Angeles cops whose relationship was so intense that to some observers it bordered on the unnatural. They cared for each other like brothers – if they had got any closer they would have been joined at the hip. But this bond was no bad thing for police partners, because it meant that if one was in trouble, he could always rely on the other to bail him out.

And Detectives Dave Starsky and Ken Hutchinson, played by Paul Michael Glaser and David Soul respectively, had plenty of opportunity to practise heroics, since their beat was the roughest area of L.A., home to the dregs of the city's low-life – drug pushers, pimps, prostitutes and street muggers. It wasn't as if the pair of them went around incognito. Starsky's vivid red and white 1974 Ford Torino drew attention to itself even when stationary, let alone when it was racing through the streets, tyres screeching, in pursuit of suspects. After a week the tyres must have been as bald as Kojak's head.

Starsky and Hutch were freewheeling bachelors. Starsky was loud, streetwise and with a taste for junk food, while Hutch preferred health food and was more pensive and softer-spoken. But there was nothing quiet about the action, as the fearless duo specialized in shoot-outs and car chases, displaying an alarming tendency to dive on car roofs and bonnets for the slightest reason. One was left with the impression that if they were changing the oil, the first thing they would do was leap onto the bonnet. It was a trend that was copied worldwide, so that a South London council had to lower a wall after young Starsky and Hutch fans used it as a launchpad to jump on parked cars.

The anti-violence brigade were not pleased with the show, either, and a prolonged campaign resulted in a noticeable toning-down of the action scenes from the third season onwards. What was left was an excruciating sentimentality between the two. At one stage there seemed a very real possibility that they would join hands and skip off into the California sunset together. And when Starsky was lying on his death bed, victim of a gunman's bullet, Hutch's bedside grieving was worse than anything from Dr Kildare.

With guest stars such as Joan Collins, and colourful supporting characters including their superior, fiery Captain Harold Dobey, and prime informant, the flash, jive-talking Huggy Bear, who knew that if he didn't talk he would end up inside, Starsky and Hutch was a huge success on both sides of the Atlantic. The one to derive most benefit from its strong youth appeal was blond-haired David Soul, who became a pin-up and embarked on a profitable music career, with five songs in the British top 20 including two chart toppers, Don't Give Up On Us and Silver Lady. Soul had actually started out as a singer rather than an actor and for some reason used to cover his face in a ski mask, which won him the contract to become The Covered Man, resident singer on America's Merv Griffin Show. Soul's singing prowess has made him the number one singing detective of all time, fighting off such opposition as Bruce Willis, Telly Savalas, Dennis Waterman, Lee Marvin and Don Johnson. And we all know that when he tenderly sang Don't Give Up On Us, he was really singing it to Starsky.

But possibly the series' most lasting impression was on policemen's mode of attire. Instead of wearing suits and ties to work, young detectives suddenly wanted to dress like Starsky and Hutch. It was a drop in standards that was rightly deplored. Merseyside police chief Ken Oxford complained: 'When the Starsky and Hutch series was showing, police on patrol duty were adopting sunglasses and wearing their gloves with the cuffs turned down. They also started driving like bloody maniacs.'

REGULAR CAST

Det. Dave Starsky Paul Michael Glaser   *Det. Ken Hutchinson* David Soul
Huggy Bear Antonio Fargas   *Capt. Harold Dobey* Bernie Hamilton

Creator: William Blinn
Music: Lalo Schifrin, Tom Scott, Mark Snow
Producer: Joseph T. Naar
Executive producers: Aaron Spelling, Leonard Goldberg

A Spelling-Goldberg Production for ABC

88 colour 60-minute episodes
US: ABC (Season 1) 10 Sept 1975 - 21 April 1976 (22 eps)
(Season 2) 25 Sept 1976 - 16 April 1977 (23 eps)
(Season 3) 17 Sept 1977 - 17 May 1978 (22 eps)
(Season 4) 12 Sept 1978 - 15 May 1979 (21 eps)
UK: BBC1 23 April 1976 - 4 Dec 1981

STATE TROOPER

Trooper Rod Blake was the chief investigator for the Nevada State Police and as such, could travel all over the state in hot pursuit of robbers, kidnappers and murderers. Much of his work was undercover, no mean feat for gangling Rod Cameron, king of American police syndicated series (SEE CITY DETECTIVE,

CORONADO 9). State Trooper was the longest running of the three, much of its appeal being down to the fact that it was based on real Nevada police files.

REGULAR CAST

Trooper Rod Blake Rod Cameron

Producer: Richard Irving

An MCA/Revue Production

104 monochrome 30-minute episodes
US: Syndicated Jan 1957

STONE

From the prolific stable of Richard Levinson and William Link (Columbo, Murder, She Wrote, Mannix and many more) came Stone, Dennis Weaver's follow-up to McCloud. With echoes of Joseph Wambaugh, Daniel Stone was a Detective Sergeant and also a best-selling novelist. His was a familiar face on TV as he did the rounds promoting his books, all of which recounted his own experiences on the force. Stone was adept at juggling his two diverse careers. He wrote in his spare time and was still one of the squad's most competent detectives, thus defusing the arguments of his would-be detractors, among them police chief Paulton. Even if Stone's books were borrowed from Wambaugh, it wasn't a bad series, which surprisingly only ran to 11 episodes.

* Dennis Weaver's own son, Robby, played rookie detective Buck Rogers – in the 20th century.

REGULAR CAST

Det. Sgt Daniel Stone Dennis Weaver   *Chief Paulton* Pat Hingle
Det. Buck Rogers Robby Weaver

Creators: Richard Levinson, William Link
Music: Mike Post, Pete Carpenter
Producer: J. Rickley Dumm
Executive producer: Stephen J. Cannell

A Stephen J. Cannell Production for Universal

11 colour 60-minute episodes
US: ABC 14 Jan - 17 March 1980
UK: BBC1 15 Oct - 10 Dec 1980

THE STRANGE REPORT

Some detectives arrive at the scene of a crime by car, others turn up on foot, the wealthy ones travel by jet, while McCloud used to get on his horse. But Adam Strange had arguably the most unusual mode of transport of all – he rode around in an unlicensed, black London taxi.

Adam Strange, a rare television role for respected film actor Anthony Quayle, had retired from his job as a Home Office criminologist to work as a freelance, investigating crimes that had baffled the finest brains of Scotland Yard, or cases which were considered too sensitive for the British government to become involved in. Strange's base was a Paddington flat, fitted with its own laboratory which he shared with his young American friend, Hamlyn Gynt, a museum researcher. Further help was provided by Strange's next-door neighbour, Evelyn McLean.

This was among ITC's finest series and one which did well in Britain and America.

REGULAR CAST

Adam Strange Anthony Quayle   *Hamlyn Gynt* Kas Garas
Evelyn McLean Anneke Wills

Music: Roger Webb
Producer: Robert Berger
Executive producer: Norman Felton

An Arena Production for ITC

16 colour 60-minute episodes
UK: ITV 21 Sept 1968 - 28 Dec 1969
US: NBC 8 Jan - 10 Sept 1971

THE STRANGER

A bizarre mystery series about a man with no name who, purely out of the goodness of his heart, helped out victims of crime by clever detective work. He never accepted payment for his services and, at the satisfactory conclusion of each case, he disappeared into the darkness, Lone Ranger-like, his anonymity intact.

REGULAR CAST

The Stranger Robert Carroll

A DuMont Production

34 monochrome 30-minute episodes
US: DuMont 25 June 1954 - 11 Feb 1955

STRANGERS

An excellent British police series which furthered the career of eccentric Detective Sergeant George Bulman, first seen in a thriller, The XYY Man, and eventually to progress to his own series (SEE BULMAN).

Here Bulman was joined by Detective Constable Derek Willis (also in The XYY Man) and Detective Constable Linda Doran to form Unit 23, a squad of officers posted to Northern England, to go undercover in towns where the local police were too well-known. Because they were outsiders with unfamiliar faces, they were called 'strangers'. Bulman's co-commander of the team was an experienced local man, Detective Sergeant Singer.

By the third season, WDC Frances Bennett had succeeded WDC Doran, and Bulman and Co. were christened the Inter City Squad, under the command of grim Scottish Detective Chief Superintendent Lambie, played by Mark McManus in a fine rehearsal for his role as Taggart. The new squad's aim was to solve crimes nationwide, by cutting through the red tape and officialdom which often prevents neighbouring forces from co-operating effectively. Another new character was William Dugdale of the British Secret Service, who would reappear in Bulman.

For all his quirks, Bulman was promoted to Detective Chief Inspector, where his highly individual approach contrasted even more sharply with the forceful Lambie. Strangers was vastly under-rated. It had good rounded characters and, in Fiona Mollison as WDC Bennett, possessed one of the most arresting policewomen for many a year.

REGULAR CAST

Det. Sgt Bulman Don Henderson   *Det. Sgt Willis* Dennis Blanch
Det. Sgt Singer John Ronane   *Det. Chief Supt Lambie* Mark McManus
WDC Doran Frances Tomelty   *WDC Bennett* Fiona Mollison
William Dugdale Thorley Walters

Creator: Murray Smith
Music: Mike Moran
Producer: Richard Everitt

A Granada Television Network Production

32 colour 60-minute episodes
UK: ITV (Season 1) 5 June - 17 July
1978 (7 eps)
(Season 2) 9 Jan - 6 Feb 1979 (5 eps)
(Season 3) 14 Oct - 25 Nov 1980 (7 eps)
(Season 4) 25 Sept - 30 Oct 1981 (6 eps)
(Season 5) 8 Sept - 20 Oct 1982 (7 eps)

THE STREET

An innovative police drama, which eavesdropped on two pairs of officers in Newark, New Jersey, who shared car 260 on their respective eight-hour shifts. Shot on video on location, often with hand-held cameras, the series had a documentary feel to it and, for added authenticity, four genuine patrol officers attended filming to advise on police procedures and attitudes. The fictional cops were the street-wise Bud Peluso and the more reserved Arthur Scolari, who worked the 3pm - 11pm shift, and veteran Jack Runyon and his ambitious black partner, Shepard Scott, who took over between 11pm and 7am. The Street was transmitted daily in the US.

REGULAR CAST

Bud Peluso Bruce MacVittie   *Arthur Scolari* Stanley Tucci
Jack Runyon Ron Ryan   *Shepard Scott* Michael Beach

Creators: John Mankiewicz, Daniel Pyne
Executive producers: John Mankiewicz, Daniel Pyne, Robert Pittman

A Newark Production with Quantum Media TV

40 colour 30-minute episodes
US: Syndicated 12 April - 29 July 1988
UK: Channel 4 5 Nov 1988 - 3 May 1989
7 July 1991 - 8 Sept 1991

STREET HAWK

Knight Rider on two wheels! Jesse Mach was an accomplished police motorcycle officer, until he suffered a permanent knee injury after being left for dead by drug smugglers. So he reluctantly accepted a quiet, no thrills job in the police department's public relations unit.

Then he was approached by Norman Tuttle, a research engineer for the Federal Government. Tuttle could fix Jesse up with an operation to restore his knee, but only on condition that the daredevil motorcyclist applied his riding talents to Tuttle's new creation, 'Operation Street Hawk'...for life.

'Operation Street Hawk' was a clandestine government project, in which man and motorcycle were tested in crime-fighting situations which would normally have involved the police department. They were controlled experiments with the hope that, in the future, every police department would have a 'Street Hawk' on the street.

'Street Hawk' was no ordinary motorcycle. Jet-black, turbo-designed, sleek, low and fast, it was equipped with hyper-thrust which could throw the machine 30 metres in the air. It had a hydraulic suspension system to adjust for off-street use and, most important of all, an advanced weaponry including a barrel that could neutralize, stun and immobilize the enemy with laser particle beams. It was a far cry from the old British bobby's push-bike.

Jesse's identity, which had to remain secret, was hidden by a computerized helmet, equipped with digital readout. Jesse and Tuttle worked as a team, with Tuttle operating the computer control centre that monitored the technical functions of 'Street Hawk' and warning Jesse of impending dangers. The impulsive Jesse's other guiding light was his police department boss, Commander Leo Altobelli, who constantly had to remind him that officially he was no longer working for the department and should therefore steer clear of police investigations.

Aimed primarily at a teenage audience, Street Hawk was harmless escapism, but proved no match for Michael Knight and KITT. After 13 episodes, Jesse Mach was free to return to PR.

REGULAR CAST

Jesse Mach Rex Smith   *Norman Tuttle* Joe Regalbuto
Leo Altobelli Richard Venture

Creators: Bob Wolterstorff, Paul Belous
Producers: Steve Cragg, Burton Armus,
   Karen Harris
Executive producers: Bob Wolterstorff,
   Paul Belous

An MCA TV/Universal Production

One colour 90-minute episode and 12
   colour 60-minute episodes
US: ABC 4 Jan - 16 May 1985
UK: ITV 7 March - 11 April 1985 (6 eps)
23 Dec 1985 - 4 Sept 1986 (7 eps)
(Thames)

THE STREETS OF SAN FRANCISCO

'Mike Stone and Steve Keller were true partners in every sense of the word. They worked together as equals. Steve respected Mike's experience and Mike respected Steve's training.' – MICHAEL DOUGLAS

Karl Malden as Detective Lieutenant Mike Stone and Michael Douglas as Detective Inspector Steve Keller, formed one of the best-loved TV cop partnerships of the 1970s. Totally different from, and superior to the Starsky and Hutch 'buddies', Stone and Keller had a relationship which was more like father and son.

Mike Stone had 23 years' service on the force – you could tell he was an old-fashioned cop because he usually wore a hat. A widower (his daughter, Jean, was featured sporadically), he worked out of the Bureau of Inspectors Division of the San Francisco Police Department. He was teamed with 28-year-old Steve Keller, one of the new breed of college-educated cops.

Few detective shows have had better actors in the lead roles than Malden and Douglas and the result was a thoroughly realistic action show, greatly enhanced by the fact that it was filmed on location. The city's steep streets are just made for car chases. And some scenes were filmed in real San Francisco Police Department buildings, such as the morgue.

After four highly successful seasons, Michael Douglas left. The storyline had Keller going off to become a teacher and Stone finding a new partner, the athletic Dan Robbins, for what turned out to be the final year. The reason behind Douglas's departure was simple. He had just produced the award-winning Jack Nicholson movie, One Flew Over the Cuckoo's Nest, and saw his future in films. Unlike many others who flee from long-running shows in the hope of attaining movie stardom, Michael Douglas has been proved right.

* The Streets of San Francisco was based on characters from the novel Poor, Poor Ophelia by Carolyn Weston.

REGULAR CAST

Det. Lt Mike Stone Karl Malden   *Det. Insp. Steve Keller* Michael Douglas
Det. Insp. Dan Robbins Richard Hatch   *Jean Stone* Darleen Carr
Lt Lessing Lee Harris   *Sgt Sekulovich* Art Passarella
Officer Haseejian Vic Tayback

Music: John Elizade, Pat Williams
Producers: John Wilder, Cliff Gould, William Yates
Executive producer: Quinn Martin

A Quinn Martin Production for ABC

120 colour 60-minute episodes
US: ABC (Season 1) 16 Sept 1972 - 12 April 1973 (27 eps)
(Season 2) 13 Sept 1973 - 14 March 1974 (23 eps)
(Season 3) 12 Sept 1974 - 13 March 1975 (23 eps)
(Season 4) 11 Sept 1975 - 3 June 1976 (23 eps)
(Season 5) 30 Sept 1976 - 16 June 1977 (24 eps)
UK: ITV 19 Nov 1973 - 24 June 1980

STRIKE FORCE

'The years since The Untouchables have not dimmed the glitter in his stern blue eyes nor softened the clench in his jaw as he contemplates the disgusting fact that some criminals are still walking around in lead-free condition.'
— ROBERT MACKENZIE, TV GUIDE ON ROBERT STACK

Twenty years on from The Untouchables, actor Robert Stack may have been ready for his bus pass, but he still managed to convey that steely presence that put the fear of God into the gangsters of the prohibition era. In Strike Force, he played Captain Frank Murphy, head of a crack unit within the Los Angeles Police Department, created to tackle seemingly impenetrable investigations. These were cases that had proved too hot to handle for ordinary cops – bombers, terrorists and assassins. Murphy and his men took on one case at a time and often resorted to undercover tactics to prise out the guilty.

But it was a tired format, not worthy of its star.

REGULAR CAST

Capt. Frank Murphy Robert Stack   *Det. Paul Strobber* Dorian Harewood
Lt Charlie Gunzer Richard Romanus   *Det. Rosie Johnson* Trisha Noble
Det. Mark Osborn Michael Goodwin   *Dep. Commissioner Herbert Klein* Herb Edelman

Creator: Lane Slate
Producers: Joe Naar, Michael Fisher
Executive producer: Aaron Spelling

*An Aaron Spelling/Metromedia
Production for ABC*

19 colour 60-minute episodes
US: ABC 13 Nov 1981 - 24 Sept 1982

STRYKER OF SCOTLAND YARD

Although filmed in Hollywood, this 1950s crime show was, as the title implies, about one of the foremost denizens of Scotland Yard – the honourable and dependable Chief Inspector Robert Stryker. Assisted by Sergeant Hawker, he tackled diamond thieves, bank robbers and other fiendish villains. But none of them was a match for Stryker of the Yard.

REGULAR CAST

Ch. Insp. Stryker Clifford Evans   *Sgt Hawker* George Woodbridge

39 monochrome 30-minute episodes US: Syndicated 1957
UK: From 2 Nov 1961 (ATV)

SURFSIDE 6

Another of Warner Bros' clone detective series around the start of the 1960s. This one was a poor man's 77 Sunset Strip, with the familiar ingredients of three handsome young private eyes, beautiful women, an exciting city and plenty of sun, sea and surf.

The main difference was that the setting for Surfside 6 was the east not the west coast of America – Miami, to be precise. In those days Miami came across as a fun city, nothing like the sleazy picture painted by Crockett and Tubbs. This was Miami Nice.

The toy-boy tecs were Ken Madison, a refugee from another Warner show, Bourbon Street Beat, Dave Thorne, a former lawyer who turned his back on New York and the militant District Attorney he worked for, and Sandy Winfield II, who abandoned his dad's business on Wall Street for the thrill of being a sleuth in Miami.

They lived and operated from a boat called 'Surf Side', moored at Dock 6 – hence the title. Anchored next to it was a yacht owned by the elegant Daphne Dutton and nearby was the lavish Fountainebleau Hotel, where Cha Cha O'Brien worked as a singer in the curiously-named Boom Boom Room. Both ladies were to figure frequently in the boys' adventures, usually as nothing more than a glossy backdrop. For in 1960, women in television dramas hadn't progressed much from the years when all they ever did was trip and twist their ankle at a crucial moment in a Western.

REGULAR CAST

Ken Madison Van Williams   Dave Thorne Lee Patterson
Sandy Winfield II Troy Donahue   Daphne Dutton Diane McBain
Cha Cha O'Brien Margarita Sierra   Lt Snedigar (Season 1) Donald Barry
Lt Gene Plehan (Season 2) Richard Crane

Producer: Jerome L. Davis
Executive producer: William T. Orr

A Warner Bros Production

73 monochrome 60-minute episodes US:
ABC (Season 1) 3 Oct 1960 - 22 May
1961 (33 eps)
(Season 2) 18 Sept 1961 - 25 June
1962 (40 eps)
UK: ITV 27 Oct 1962 - 5 Jan 1963
(13 eps)

SUTHERLAND'S LAW

After playing Glasgow hood Charlie Endell opposite Adam Faith in
Budgie, Iain Cuthbertson switched to the right side of the law for this
gentle series about procurator-fiscal John Sutherland. Under Scottish
law, the police don't prosecute – they take their evidence to the
procurator-fiscal who is thus a combination of district attorney and
investigative prosecutor. John Sutherland was one such law-enforcer in
a Highland fishing town on the west coast of Scotland. He could spot a
red herring a mile off. His cases proved surprisingly popular, even
among English city dwellers, mainly because they afforded the
opportunity to wallow in the glorious Scottish scenery, something
normally reserved for holiday programmes.

REGULAR CAST

John Sutherland Iain Cuthbertson

Creator: Lindsay Galloway
Producer: Neil McCallum

A BBC Scotland Production

47 colour 50-minute episodes

UK: BBC1 (Pilot) 23 Aug 1972
(Season 1)6 June - 5 Sept 1973 (13 eps)
(Season 2) 15 May - 1 Oct 1974 (13 eps)
(Season 3) 27 May - 15 July 1975
 (8 eps)
(Season 4)6 July - 31 Aug 1976 (12 eps)

S.W.A.T.

Following the inner-city riots of the late 1960s, S.W.A.T. teams
sprang up in a number of large American conurbations. The initials
stood for Special Weapons and Tactics and the squads' brief was to
crush disturbances that were too violent for ordinary police officers to
deal with.

Originating from an episode of The Rookies entitled S.W.A.T., the
series was roundly condemned for its violence. Given the nature of the
subject matter, this was scarcely surprising, as the S.W.A.T. team had
enough weapons to repel an invading army, let alone a couple of
hundred rioters.

The squad were all Vietnam veterans and wore combat jackets. They were pretty much like the A-Team and even travelled in a similar specially-equipped van. The Commanding Officer was Lieutenant Dan 'Hondo' Harrelson and he was supported by Sergeant David 'Deacon' Kay (the official observer), Dominic Luca (the ace marksman), Jim Street (the scout) and T.J. McCabe (back-up). Although for the most part, the instructions seemed to be 'shoot anything that moves and even if it doesn't, fill it with lead just to make sure', Harrelson did occasionally recognize his responsibilities and attempt to restrain the younger trigger-happy officers. But California residents lived in fear – they never knew whether a neighbourly dispute over repairing a garden fence could lead to a visit from the S.W.A.T. team.

But for all their arsenal, the S.W.A.T. boys were unable to wipe out the anti-violence lobby and after 34 episodes and a lot of complaints, the show was cancelled.

REGULAR CAST

Lt Dan Harrelson Steve Forrest   *Sgt David Kay* Rod Perry
Officer Dominic Luca Mark Shera   *Officer Jim Street* Robert Urich
Officer T.J. McCabe James Coleman

Creator: Robert Hamner
Theme music: Barry De Vorzon
Producers: Robert Hamner, Barry
 Shear, Gene Levitt
Executive producers: Aaron Spelling,
 Leonard Goldberg
A Spelling-Goldberg Production for ABC

34 colour 60-minute episodes
US: ABC 24 Feb 1975 - 29 June 1976
UK: ITV 4 Dec 1976
10 July - 2 Oct 1981 (LWT)

THE SWEENEY

'If our critics had been right, shopping precincts would have been full
of marauding OAPs beating the rest of us over the head with pension
books.' –   PRODUCER TED CHILDS

In the wake of Dr William Belson's 1977 survey, which suggested that boys exposed to high levels of TV violence were more likely to commit serious crimes than others, The Sweeney came under heavy fire. But producer Ted Childs leapt to its defence, pointing out that half the shows' fans were over 60 and there hadn't yet been any marked upsurge in geriatric crime.

Along with its BBC imitator, Target, The Sweeney was a prime candidate for concern. Both the action and the language were strong. Dockers were known to blush. It was also brilliant.

The title The Sweeney was derived from Sweeney Todd, cockney rhyming slang for the Flying Squad, a section of the Metropolitan Police which specializes in sorting out armed robbers. And on television they weren't fussy about how they did it. The main characters, Detective Inspector Jack Regan (played by John Thaw, later to become the infinitely more refined Inspector Morse), and Detective Sergeant George Carter (played by Dennis Waterman), pulled no punches. They were determined to nail villains by hook or by crook. They didn't just bend the rule book, they tore it into little pieces.

There was nothing Regan and Carter enjoyed more than a hearty punch-up to catch a gang of security van raiders in the act, then down the boozer for a couple of pints to celebrate. Dennis Waterman seemed to revel in the fight scenes, his brother Peter having been a professional boxing champion. But Dennis admitted that he couldn't handle a gun as well as George Carter – he is so short-sighted he would never have made a bobby on the beat, let alone a sharpshooter.

The programme was thoroughly researched for authenticity, with a former Flying Squad officer, Jack Quarrie, advising the writers on police procedures. He also helped with Parliamo Sweeney, as viewers learned a whole new language of crime slang – 'blag' (armed robbery), 'readies' (money), 'snout' (informant) etc. Understandably the real police were none too impressed, especially by detectives whose idea of questioning suspects was to pin them against a wall and pummel them into confession. It was not terribly good for the image of the boys in blue.

The Sweeney was made by Euston Films – on the cheap. They worked out of Colet Court, an old school in Hammersmith, West London, using the phone in the pub across the road, and often buying the props they needed for the next scene with whatever cash the producer had in his back pocket. In the first series, each episode was completed in just ten days and on a budget of as little as £40,000. But after a slow start, its popularity grew to the extent that it spawned two feature films and ran for four series, seeing off all opposition, including Kojak and Starsky and Hutch. It is still frequently repeated 13 years on, even though Regan and Carter look a bit daft now, in those kipper ties and flared trousers.

Regan, who Carter always called 'guv', was the more volatile of the two hotheads and sometimes had to be restrained by his younger colleague. He was hard-working, hard-drinking, impatient and frequently frustrated. His wife had left him after years of coming second to villains and now, apart from the odd one-night stand, his main companion was Carter. Like Regan, Carter, a sharp cockney who could easily have ended up on the wrong side of the law, was to lose his wife. Played by Stephanie Turner, later to become the star of

Juliet Bravo, she died. This gave the two men the opportunity to study together the pitfalls of life through the bottom of a beer glass, and eye up the local talent at the same time. Endeavouring to keep them in line was Chief Inspector Frank Haskins who, although appreciative of their work, seldom approved of the manner in which they went about it. As a result, Haskins and Regan did not always see eye to eye.

It all came to a head in the final episode, Jack or Knave, when Regan was arrested on suspicion of having taken bribes, while a Detective Sergeant back in 1968. He was thrown in a cell and although freed, the experience left him more bitter than usual. He told Haskins and Carter in no uncertain terms: 'I am utterly and abjectly pissed off with this little lot. I've given the best years of my life to the job. I've got 18 bloody commendations if you include the one I didn't get yesterday. And how does this wonderful police force show its gratitude for all my years of unstinting effort? It bangs me up in a cruddy little cell like a cheap little villain. I'm going to have to be re-instated. And what do you bunch of bleeding, double-dyed hypocrites do now? You want me to crawl back to work and be very grateful that I didn't get nicked for something I didn't do. Well you can stuff it.'

And that was that.

For all its blood and thunder approach, a feature of The Sweeney was its earthy humour, notably the repartee between Regan and Carter. Morecambe and Wise appeared in one episode, and there were the special lines of dialogue that every writer would try to include. The favourite was: 'Get yer trousers on, you're nicked.'

* Both John Thaw and Garfield Morgan, who played Haskins, had previously served in the force. Thaw was Detective Constable Elliott in Z Cars and Morgan appeared as Detective Chief Inspector Lewis in Softly Softly.

REGULAR CAST

Det. Insp. Jack Regan John Thaw   *Det. Sgt George Carter* Dennis Waterman
Chief Insp. Frank Haskins Garfield Morgan

Creator: Ian Kennedy Martin
Theme music: Harry South
Producer: Ted Childs
Executive producers: Lloyd Shirley, George Taylor

A Euston Films Production for Thames Television

52 colour 60-minute episodes
UK: ITV (Season 1) 2 Jan - 27 March 1975
(13 eps)
(Season 2) 1 Sept - 24 Nov 1975 (13 eps)
(Season 3) 6 Sept - 20 Dec 1976 (13 eps)
(Season 4) 7 Sept - 28 Dec 1978 (13 eps)
US: Syndicated 1976

SWITCH

Hot on the heels of The Sting came this light crime caper, starring Robert Wagner as former con man Pete Ryan and Eddie Albert as retired cop Frank McBride. They teamed up to open a detective agency in Los Angeles, that specialized in pulling 'switches' on con men, craftily turning the tables so that the swindlers ended up as the swindled. The agency's secretary, Maggie, was played by Sharon Gless. Ryan and McBride needed help for their elaborate ruses and so enlisted the services of Malcolm Argos, a one-time petty thief and con artist who had given up a life of crime to open a restaurant.

But by the middle of the second season, there were fewer con tricks and the show adopted a more conventional private eye format. It remained worth watching for the performances of Wagner and Albert.

REGULAR CAST

Pete Ryan Robert Wagner   *Frank McBride* Eddie Albert
Malcolm Argos Charlie Callas   *Maggie* Mindi Miller

Music: Stu Phillips, Glen A. Larson
Producers: Leigh Vance, Jack Laird, John Guss, Paul Playdon John Peyser
Executive producers: Glen A. Larson, Matthew Rapf

A Universal Television Production

One colour 90-minute episode and 70 colour 60-minute episodes US: CBS (Season 1) 9 Sept 1975 - 6 April 1976 (25 eps)
(Season 2) 21 Sept 1976 - 3 April 1977 (24 eps)
(Season 3) 23 Sept 1977 - 20 Aug 1978 (22 eps)
UK: Channel Four From 19 March 1983

TAGGART

'I suppose I can be tough in real life. I wouldn't take a step back from anybody, put it that way. In Glasgow, if you don't show front, you're not regarded. I wouldn't go up to anybody and say, d'you wanta fight? But if it comes, well...' –   MARK MCMANUS

Granite-faced Detective Chief Inspector Jim Taggart is one of the toughest men on screen. The only time the tetchy 'tec ever smiles is when he learns that there has been another gruesome murder on his

Glasgow patch, the Northern Division. And Mark McManus, the actor who has turned Taggart into one of Glasgow's favourite sons, is no shrinking violet either. The son of a miner, he once earned his living boxing in Australia, until he was mismatched with a local Aborigine giant. Now his broken nose and craggy face are held together by a total of 140 stitches – a legacy of his boxing days. His native Glasgow is a hard city and the naturally amiable McManus can be a hard man.

McManus and Taggart are stars in over 30 countries, almost everywhere except the United States, where they are worried about being unable to decipher the thick Glasgow accents. Even those living south of Carlisle could sometimes do with sub-titles.

Taggart is a superb character who has really caught the imagination of the Scottish public. McManus admits: 'In some pubs in Glasgow, they still dash out the back door when I walk in 'cos they think I'm one of the bizzies!'

Created by Glenn Chandler, Taggart is tough and cynical. He has seen it all. Another day, another body. He is completely obsessed with work and is blinkered to the needs, interests or sensitivities of everyone around him. His long-suffering wife, Jean, confined to a wheelchair for over 20 years since the birth of their only child, Alison, has given up hope of seeing him return home at a sensible hour. And when he is there, he has the conversation of a Trappist monk.

He's not much more fun at work. Taggart's first assistant was Detective Sergeant Peter Livingstone, a middle-class graduate from Edinburgh. He and Taggart, working-class and Glasgow through and through, did not get on. It did not help that Livingstone and Jean Taggart shared a love of the arts, whereas Taggart thinks Gilbert and Sullivan were the full-backs in the Rangers' 1948 Cup winning team!

Livingstone's replacement since 1987 has been Detective Sergeant Mike Jardine, a non-drinking Christian. This to Taggart is like red rag to a bull, for there are few things that irk him more than leaning on the bar of a rough Glasgow pub and having to order an orange juice for his partner. Actor James Macpherson, who plays Jardine, comments: 'Taggart used to rib Jardine a lot in the early days but now they get on better. Taggart still tells him off but there's more respect now. Young Jardine has shown him he can do the business – even if he is still pretty unsuccessful with women.'

Mark McManus modelled Taggart on two uncompromising policemen he knows. 'They're big guys and pretty horrific characters,' he says. To gain an insight into their work, he toured Glasgow with them at night. 'Most of the cases they dealt with were fights and hooliganism but once when they went to look into the possible death of an old lady who hadn't been seen for four days, they wouldn't let me out of the car. And what they saw when they eventually found the body, made one of these hard guys actually physically sick.' McManus also constantly keeps one ear open for Glasgow street talk, rightly believing that the city itself is an important factor in the show's success. However, it must have been difficult for the city fathers to make out a good case for Glasgow being European City of Culture for 1990, when Taggart keeps stumbling across mutilated bodies down every alley.

Much of the programme's popularity is down to the location filming, although this has been known to cause problems. Harriet Buchan, who plays Jean Taggart, remembers: 'One time there was a fire alarm where we were filming. When the police arrived, they were terribly mixed up because there were all these pseudo policemen everywhere!'

But what really puts Taggart head and shoulders above most other detective shows is the delicious black humour. One memorable scene saw Jean lying in a coma after an accident and doctors trying everything to make her regain consciousness. Finally, her bad-tempered husband arrived at the hospital and started haranguing a nurse in his familiar style. The moment Jean heard that voice, she came round. Wonderful stuff. America, you don't know what you're missing.

* Away from murder cases, Mark McManus pursues the more gentle hobby of butterfly breeding. Taggart would probably pull the wings off.

REGULAR CAST

Det. Chief Insp. Taggart Mark McManus   *Det. Sgt Livingstone (1983-7)* Neil Duncan
Det. Sgt Jardine (1987-) James Macpherson   *Supt McVitie* Iain Anders
Jean Taggart Harriet Buchan   *Dr Andrews* Robert Robertson

Creator: Glenn Chandler
Music: Mike Moran
Theme sung by: Maggie Bell
Producer: Robert Love

A Scottish Television Network Production

42 colour 60-minute episodes and 4 colour 90-minute episodes

EPISODE TITLES

UK: ITV
Killer 6 - 20 Sept 1983 (3 eps)
Dead Ringer 2 - 16 July 1985 (3 eps)
Murder in Season 23 July - 6 Aug 1985 (3 eps)
Knife Edge 24 Feb - 10 March 1986 (3 eps)

Death Call 2 - 16 Sept 1986 (3 eps)
The Killing Philosophy 15 - 29 April 1987 (3 eps)
Funeral Rites 9 - 23 Sept 1987 (3 eps)
Cold Blood 31 Dec 1987 (One 90 min. ep)
Dead Giveaway 7 - 21 Sept 1988 (3 eps)
Root of Evil 28 Sept - 12 Oct 1988 (3 eps)
Double Jeopardy 30 Dec 1988 (One 90 min. ep)
Flesh and Blood 5 - 19 Sept 1989 (3 eps)
Love Knot 1 Jan 1990 (One 90 min. ep)
Hostile Witness 1 - 15 March 1990 (3 eps)
Evil Eye 4 - 18 Sept 1990 (3 eps)
Death Comes Softly 3 - 17 Dec 1990 (3 eps)
Rogues Gallery 31 Dec 1990 (One 90 min. ep)
Nest of Vipers Nov 1991 (3 eps)

TAKE A PAIR OF PRIVATE EYES

Written by Peter O'Donnell, who in the 1960s was the author of newspaper strip cartoons Garth in the Daily Mirror and Modesty Blaise in the London Evening Standard, this light detective series revolved around the activities of a husband-and-wife sleuthing team.

Hector Frayne had retired after a life of undetected crime but his hobby was keeping an elaborate filing system on crooks and their methods. This criminal information index proved invaluable to his son, Ambrose who, with the help of French wife, Dominique, ran an agency for the recovery of stolen property. So, card in hand, they set out to track down missing loot for their clients.

REGULAR CAST

Ambrose Frayne Derek Fowlds   *Dominique Frayne* Jeanne Roland
Hector Frayne Sam Kydd

Creator: Peter O'Donnell
Producer: Alan Bromly

6 monochrome 55-minute episodes
UK: BBC2 10 April - 15 May 1966

A BBC Television Production

TALLAHASSEE 7000

Walter Matthau (no less) starred in and narrated this moderate Miami Beach-based series about Lex Rogers, an agent-cum-troubleshooter for the Florida Sheriff's Bureau. Tallahassee 7000 was the Bureau's phone number.

REGULAR CAST

Lex Rogers Walter Matthau

Music: Irving Friedman

26 monochrome 30-minute episodes
US: Syndicated 1959

A Columbia/Screen Gems Production

TARGET

As defined in this hard-hitting British police drama, a target was 'a person active in the commission of a serious crime.' It starred Patrick Mower as the unscrupulous Superintendent Steve Hackett, a detective with a regional police force covering an unidentified large port in the South of England. Hackett was one of the new breed of 1970s' TV cops – trendy, brash and deeply unpleasant. Even though he was dealing with smugglers, murderers and bombers, he and his team rarely came across as being much better than the villains.

Target was the BBC's answer to The Sweeney but whereas it exceeded its ITV rival in terms of violence, it desperately lacked The Sweeney's humour. The first series was so poorly received that it was cut short because of protests about the unwarranted level of violence and the second, and final, season was toned down considerably.

Before Target began, Patrick Mower claimed: 'I know a lot of policemen. They're always asking me to open fetes.' I doubt if he had as many requests afterwards.

REGULAR CAST

Det. Supt Steve Hackett Patrick Mower   *Det. Chief Supt Tate* Philip Madoc
Det. Sgt Louise Colbert Vivien Heilbron   *Det. Sgt Frank Bonney* Brendan Price
Det. Con. Dukes Carl Rigg

Music: Dudley Simpson
Producer: Philip Hinchcliffe

A BBC Television Production

22 colour 50-minute episodes
UK: BBC1 (Season 1) 9 Sept - 11 Nov
1977 (9 eps)
(Season 2) 15 Sept - 8 Dec 1978 (13 eps)

TARGET: THE CORRUPTORS

Crusading newspaperman, Paul Marino, and his undercover agent, Jack Flood set out to expose corruption in low places – prostitution, protection rackets and fraud. Flood was the Roger Cook of his day, infiltrating crooked businesses, run by gangsters, and supplying Marino with the material both for his newspaper revelations and to pass on to the police. These guardians of justice were based on articles by Lester Velie and the series featured a fine array of guest stars, among them Walter Matthau, Peter Falk, Jack Klugman and Ed Asner who, as Lou Grant, was to be a campaigning journalist in his own right.

REGULAR CAST

Paul Marino Stephen McNally   *Jack Flood* Robert Harland

Music: Herschel Burke Gilbert, Rudy Schrager

A Velie-Burrows-Ackerman Production in association with Four Star and ABC

35 monochrome 60-minute episodes
US: ABC 29 Sept 1961 - 21 Sept 1962

TECX

A disappointing British drama about three young, ambitious Brussels-based private detectives, who attempted to reduce the EC crime mountain. Chris Tierney, a former student, grape picker and teacher was persuaded by Italian wine businessman, Fabio Cavalcanti, to join in his latest venture, TECX. A Raymond Chandler addict, Cavalcanti had come to the conclusion that private detective work was more exciting than the wine industry. And he didn't need to show much bottle, since they concentrated on guile rather than guns.

The third member of the team was to be Anna Holz, who worked for Brussels lawyers, Souverain Associates. Isabelle Souverain believed that her practice would be boosted if she were able to call on a discreet detective agency and so, when she was approached by Cavalcanti and Tierney, she decided to give TECX a test case. They passed with flying colours and continued to work mainly for Souverain and her colleague, Kate Milverton, on cases in Holland, France and the United Kingdom as well as in Belgium.

Well-intentioned but uninspiring, TECX merely re-inforced the British belief that nothing that comes out of Brussels is worth paying the slightest attention to.

REGULAR CAST

Chris Tierney Ron Spendlove   *Fabio Cavalcanti* Urbano Barberini
Anna Holz Ulrike Schwarz   *Kate Milverton* Jenny Agutter
Isabelle Souverain Stephane Audran

Producer: Simon Channing-Williams
Executive producer: Ted Childs

*A Central Films Production for Central
Independent Television*

13 colour 60-minute episodes
UK: ITV 22 March - 11 July 1990

THE TELLTALE CLUE

Despite its corny title, this was an ingenious show, which examined detective work in the minutest detail and thereby not only proved entertaining to American viewers of the mid-1950s but informative too. Detective Lieutenant Richard Hale was the head of criminology with the Metropolitan Homicide Squad in a large, unidentified city. Presented with what appeared to be a perfect crime, Hale would use the latest scientific methods plus his own analytical mind to unearth that telltale clue, which would bring about the villain's downfall. A good man to have on your side.

REGULAR CAST

Det. Lt Richard Hale Anthony Ross

A CBS Production

12 monochrome 30-minute episodes
US: CBS 8 July - 23 Sept 1954

TENAFLY

With most TV detectives, the only thing more important than that day's work is the next day's work. Harry Tenafly was different – he made his family (wife Ruth and son Herb) the major consideration in his life. Harry was a black private detective with Hightower Investigations Inc., operating out of the crime capital of television, Los Angeles. The action was split between home and office.

His first case was to solve the murder of the wife of a chat show host and in his subsequent investigations he came to rely on his friend at the L.A.P.D., Lieutenant Sam Church, to bail him out of tight situations.

Tenafly was part of the NBC Mystery Movie but only ran to five episodes. Perhaps it was because at a time of gimmick detectives, Harry's only gimmick was that he was nondescript. And it didn't help having a surname that sounded as if it carried some deadly tropical disease.

REGULAR CAST

Harry Tenafly James McEachin   *Ruth Tenafly* Lillian Lehman
Herb Tenafly Paul Jackson   *Lt Sam Church* David Huddleston

EPISODE TITLES

Tenafly
The Cash and Carry Caper
Joyride to Nowhere
Man Running
The Window That Wasn't

Music: Gil Melle
Producer: Jon Epstein
Executive producers: Richard Levinson,
   William Link

A Universal Television Production

5 colour 90-minute episodes
US: NBC 10 Oct 1973 - 6 Aug 1974
UK: ITV From 3 Jan 1974

TENSPEED AND BROWN SHOE

Starring dancer Ben Vereen and the lanky Jeff Goldblum and launched amid Twin Peaks-like hype, Tenspeed and Brown Shoe turned out to be too much of an acquired taste for mass consumption. It was certainly off-beat, the partnership being the oddest couple since...The Odd Couple.

Vereen played E.L. Turner, a likeable con-man who needed the honest employment of private detective work to fulfil the conditions of his parole. He was nicknamed 'Tenspeed' because he was hot on his toes. A master of disguise, he missed no opportunity to go undercover, posing as such diverse persona as a psychiatrist, a priest and Pele!

His partner was Goldblum's Lionel Whitney, christened Brown Shoe, an old American term for a stockbroker. He lived with his head in the clouds (with Goldblum's height, almost literally) and abandoned his respectable city job to pursue a more romantic career as a detective. A fan of old Bogart movies, he saw himself as Sam Spade and polished his technique by reading detective novels featuring his hero, Mark Savage. The author's name on these books was Stephen J. Cannell, the show's creator, who even appeared on the back covers, pipe in hand.

The pair worked from an office near Sunset Boulevard in Los Angeles, with Tenspeed continuing to get up to his old tricks, despite faithfully promising Brown Shoe otherwise. But in time, the wide-eyed innocent Brown Shoe came to accept his colleague's deviousness. He was simply happy to be a private eye, all the more so since many of his cases took a leaf out of Mark Savage's books, right down to a recurring villain, Tommy Tedesco.

REGULAR CAST

E.L. Turner ('Tenspeed') Ben Vereen   *Lionel Whitney ('Brown Shoe')* Jeff Goldblum
Tommy Tedesco Richard Romanus

Creator/Executive producer: Stephen J. Cannell

10 colour 60-minute episodes
US: ABC 27 Jan - 27 June 1980

A Paramount Television Production

THE THIN MAN

The prototype for countless similar models, the most blatant copy being Hart to Hart, the adventures of Nick and Nora Charles broke new ground when they first appeared on the big screen in 1934. That Thin Man movie was just about the first production to show a wisecracking, affectionate marriage instead of the more commonplace sarcastic marital barbs. Incidentally, the 'thin man' was not Nick but another character in the film. The stars were William Powell and Myrna Loy, who went on to portray the couple created by Maltese Falcon author, Dashiell Hammett, in five further movies through till 1947. Nora Charles was reputedly based on Hammett's real-life love, Lillian Hellman.

Nick and Nora came to television in the late 1950s, with Peter Lawford and Phyllis Kirk in the lead roles. The Charles lived in an opulent apartment on New York's Park Avenue, with their wire-haired fox terrier, Asta (Hart to Hart even lifted the dog!). They were fabulously rich and moved in the city's most elite circles. No social gathering of any repute was complete without the presence of Nick and Nora Charles.

Nick (real name Nicholas Charalambides) had been a private eye with the Trans-American Detective Agency but, on marrying Nora had decided to retire gracefully. However, he was still plagued by his old underworld associates, the most persistent of whom was Beatrice Dane, a beautiful con-artist who also used the name Blondie Collins. Nick found it hard to give up old habits, and so he and Nora became amateur detectives, solving crimes for the sheer hell of it. And of course they were infinitely more competent than the police, perhaps not surprising when one notes that Lieutenant Ralph Raines was played by Stafford Repp, the oafish Chief O'Hara from Batman. Asta joined in, too, and often unearthed more than a bone in his efforts to prove he was as good as a bloodhound.

The Thin Man was an enjoyable example of light sleuthing, but the television show's reputation has suffered through being compared unfavourably to the films. William Powell and Myrna Loy were a hard act to follow.

REGULAR CAST

Nick Charles Peter Lawford   *Nora Charles* Phyllis Kirk
Beatrice Dane Nita Talbot   *Lt Ralph Raines* Stafford Repp
Lt Steve King Tol Avery   *Lt Harry Evans* Jack Albertson

An MGM Television Production

78 monochrome 30-minute episodes

US: NBC 20 Sept 1957 - 26 June 1959

UK: BBC 22 Dec 1957 - 20 July 1958

THE THIRD MAN

'What would have happened if Harry Lime had lived? What sort of a man would he have become in the world of today – away from the intrigue, black market and sewers in end-of-war Vienna?'

That was the question posed by Radio Times in the autumn of 1959, to herald the arrival of a new version of Graham Greene's famous character. Michael Rennie's TV portrayal differed greatly from both the novel and the memorable 1949 film, starring Orson Welles. There, Lime was an evil manipulator who was actually killed off at the end of the movie. On TV he was genial, suave and debonair – more a Lime cordial.

The original Harry Lime could never have been described as a detective, but on the small screen he travelled the world solving mysteries and helping waifs and strays. Harry had an eye for a pretty face while in turn, girls were instantly attracted by his looks and money.

He was the head of a major import-export company – Harry Lime Ltd in London, Harry Lime Inc. in New York and similar organizations in most of the world's capitals. He specialized in acquiring valuable objets d'art. The treasurer of his companies was the prissy Bradford Webster, who served as Lime's unofficial manservant, and Harry also had many dealings with Scotland Yard's Arthur Shillings, a fervent admirer of the millionaire. Shillings was played by Rupert Davies who, the following year, would cross the English Channel to become Maigret.

The Third Man was a joint Anglo-American production, with half of the episodes filmed at Shepperton Studios in England, and the other half in Hollywood. With its jaunty theme music, the series was a winner with British audiences, a classy forerunner to The Saint.

* In the US, Orson Welles also made a 1950s radio version of The Third Man.

REGULAR CAST

Harry Lime Michael Rennie   *Bradford Webster* Jonathan Harris
Arthur Shillings Rupert Davies

Theme music: Anton Karas
Producers: Felix Jackson, Vernon Burns

A BBC Television Production in association with National Telefilm Associates of America and the British Lion Film Corporation

77 monochrome 30-minute episodes
UK: BBC 2 Oct 1959 - 30 Dec 1964
US: Syndicated Autumn 1960

THIS MAN DAWSON

Most reputable actors like to research a part beforehand, but few can have been granted the access afforded to Keith Andes for his role as police department official, Colonel Frank Dawson. Andes was allowed to sit in on the three-man panel which screened applicants for the Los Angeles Police Department, and on more than one occasion it was he who cast the deciding vote! Imagine if they had let Raymond Burr train by defending a few murder suspects! Andes' experiences were put to good use, as he and Dawson embarked on a mission to rid the city of political and corporate corruption.

REGULAR CAST

Col. Frank Dawson Keith Andes

Producers: William Conrad, Elliot Lewis

A Ziv Production

39 monochrome 30-minute episodes
US: Syndicated 1959

TIGHTROPE

Secrecy was the name of the game for the police undercover agent in Tightrope. He had no identity (although he was sometimes referred to as 'Nick', a good name for a policeman) and did his utmost to protect his anonymity, while endeavouring to infiltrate organized crime. Throughout his work, for which he always wore his gun behind his back, he walked a dangerous tightrope, since he ran the risk of being shot by his police colleagues, many of whom were unaware that he was on their side and not a criminal. A hard-hitting gangster series which was eventually cancelled because of protests about the level of violence.

REGULAR CAST

Undercover agent Mike Connors

Creators/Producers: Clarence Greene, Russell Rouse

A Screen Gems Production for Columbia

37 monochrome 30-minute episodes
US: CBS 8 Sept 1959 - 13 Sept 1960

T.J. HOOKER

With a shaggy wig on his head, William Shatner made sure that he didn't 'baldly go' into the police precinct house, as good guy cop, T.J. Hooker.

Hooker had been a detective but switched to street duty with special responsibility for the Academy Precinct, where he acted as a shining example to young recruits. Hooker was an American Dixon of Dock Green, ever ready to preach the values of traditional policing and saying that it was never like this in the old days. He could probably remember when the whole of Los Angeles was fields.

His prime proteges were his enthusiastic new rookie partner, Vince Romano, and trainee officer, Stacy Sheridan. He had to keep on the right side of Stacy since her father was Hooker's stern superior. With a hint of nepotism, Stacy progressed to a beat of her own, on which she was accompanied by veteran officer, Jim Corrigan.

Although on the force he was a paragon of virtue, dedicated to upholding policing standards, Hooker had led a chequered life. His former partner had been killed in the line of duty and Hooker's marriage had ended in divorce, but he remained on amicable terms with ex-wife Fran. His two daughters, Cathy and Chrissie, appeared on the show from time to time as well.

Other guest stars were more surprising. The Beach Boys did a spot, as did Jerry Lee Lewis, while Shatner's old Star Trek sidekick, Leonard Nimoy, was beamed down to play a distraught cop whose daughter had been raped.

But the occasional 'spot the famous face' was insufficient to make T.J. Hooker rise above mediocrity. Ultimately it was only worth watching for the gorgeous Heather Locklear, and to see whether Shatner's hair ever moved.

REGULAR CAST

Sgt T.J. Hooker William Shatner   *Officer Stacy Sheridan* Heather Locklear
Officer Vince Romano Adrian Zmed   *Capt. Sheridan* Richard Herd
Officer Jim Corrigan James Darren   *Fran Hooker* Lee Bryant
Cathy Hooker Susan McClung   *Chrissie Hooker* Nicole Eggert

Creator: Rick Husky
Producer: Jeffrey Hayes
Executive producers: Aaron Spelling, Leonard Goldberg

A Spelling/Goldberg Production for Columbia Pictures Television
78 colour 60-minute episodes
US: ABC 13 March 1982 - 14 Sept 1985
UK: ITV 16 April 1983 - 6 Dec 1985

TODAY'S F.B.I.

An updated version of an old favourite (SEE THE F.B.I.) and again produced with full Bureau approval, which meant that the agents came over as whiter than white. The extent of their faults was maybe once failing to give up their seat on the bus to an old lady.

The new hero was Ben Slater, a member of the F.B.I. for 20 years and the leader of a team of bright-eyed and bushy-tailed agents. These comprised the athletic Al Gordean, eager Nick Frazier, who liked to indulge in undercover work, Maggie Clinton, a psychologist who was also a crack shot when she had a mind to be, and former marine intelligence officer, Dwayne Thompson.

Even though the episodes were based on real case files, the characters were so wooden that the show never looked like repeating the success of its predecessor. Today's F.B.I. was yesterday's idea.

REGULAR CAST

Ben Slater Mike Connors *Al Gordean* Richard Hill
Nick Frazier Joseph Cali *Maggie Clinton* Carol Potter
Dwayne Thompson Harold Sylvester

Creator: Jerry Ludwig
Producer: Fred Caruso
Executive producer: David Gerber

A Columbia Pictures Television Production for ABC
13 colour 60-minute episodes
US: ABC 25 Oct 1981 - 14 Aug 1982

TOMA

Like Serpico, Toma was modelled on the experiences of a real-life city cop – in this case, Detective David Toma of the Newark, New Jersey, Police Department. In fact the real David Toma actually made guest appearances on the show.

Toma's forte was undercover work. A master of disguise, he worked alone to bust big crime syndicates, his courage and highly individual approach elevating him to something akin to celebrity status. As with most personality cops, he continually fought the system and was a thorn in the side of his boss, Inspector Spooner. His wife Patty worried about him too – she had two young children, Jimmy and Donna to raise, and knew only too well the deadly nature of Toma's line of inquiry.

The series was well received but closed after just one season because actor Tony Musante, who played the title role, found the production schedule too hectic. ABC intended bringing the show back with a new actor and were going to call it Toma Starring Robert Blake. But instead they tampered with the format, moved it to Los Angeles and re-titled it Baretta. (SEE BARETTA)

REGULAR CAST

Det. David Toma Tony Musante   *Insp. Spooner* Simon Oakland
Patty Toma Susan Strasberg   *Jimmy Toma* Sean Manning
Donna Toma Michelle Livingston

Creator: Roy Huggins
Executive producers: Stephen J.
  Cannell, Roy Huggins, Jo Swerling Jnr

24 colour 60-minute episodes
US: ABC 4 Oct 1973 - 6 Sept 1974
UK: ITV From 2 Aug 1984

A Universal Television Production

TOUCAN TECS

'One can do it well, Toucan do it better!'

That was the motto of Zippi and Zac, a pair of trouble-shooting toucans ready at a moment's notice to fly round the world to help animals in distress, for this children's animation series. They were a bit like The Persuaders but with finer plumage. In complete detective gear, down to the magnifying glass, and helped by their butler, Samson the snail, these feathered felon-fighters investigated such mysteries as why all the clocks in Switzerland had stopped, causing grief to the local goats. These were arguably the only TV detectives with a pronounced liking for millet.

VOICES

Peter Hawkins, Kate Lee, Tony Robinson, Phil Whitchurch Creator: Peter Lawson

Writer: Elizabeth Laird
Music: Ernie Woods
Director: Gary Hurst

A Cartwn Cymru Production for Yorkshire Television

5 colour 15-minute episodes
UK: ITV 7 Jan - 4 Feb 1991

TRAVELLING MAN

'I went out with a woman detective from a drug squad. She told me that she and her colleagues frequently handled very large sums of money and often joked about ripping off the authorities.'
– CREATOR ROGER MARSHALL

That meeting gave writer Roger Marshall, who had penned some of the best episodes of The Sweeney, the inspiration for Travelling Man , a 1980s' version of The Fugitive.

The Kimble in this instance was Lomax, a former Detective Inspector with the Metropolitan Police Drug Squad, who had been wrongly imprisoned for two years after a drugs heist went wrong and the £100,000 proceeds disappeared. His release was hardly cause for celebration. His wife Jan had left him and his teenage son, Steve, was in hiding somewhere along the network of England's canals.

Lomax was in great demand – from the underworld, a persistent crime reporter named Robinson, and the police, who remained convinced that he had stashed away the missing £100,000. For his part, Lomax was determined to clear his name and find his drop-out son, so he set off on a narrow boat (ironically called 'Harmony') to track down the villain who framed him.

With the excellent Leigh Lawson as Lomax, Travelling Man made for compelling viewing, with the unusual canal backdrop an added bonus. Roger Marshall explained his reasons for choosing that setting. 'The canals have a mini-culture all their own. There is a gypsy-like quality about the way in which bargees live. And it is different.' That in itself was recommendation enough.

REGULAR CAST

Lomax Leigh Lawson   *Robinson* Terry Taplin

Creator: Roger Marshall
Music: Duncan Browne
Producer: Brian Armstrong
Executive producer: Richard Everitt

A Granada Television Network
* Production*

13 colour 60-minute episodes
UK: ITV (Season 1) 7 Nov - 12 Dec 1984
  (6 eps)
(Season 2)3 Sept - 15 Oct 1985 (7 eps)

TREASURY MEN IN ACTION

Young James Dean cut his acting teeth on this live action drama of the early 1950s. And he was not alone, for among other guest stars in the programme's five-year run were Grace Kelly, Lee Marvin and Charles Bronson.

Based on real cases from the files of the US Treasury Department, it starred Walter Greaza who was simply billed as 'The Chief'. This was because he played the chief of whichever departmental division was involved in that week's investigation, and thus appeared as several different characters overall.

The Chief's job was to seek out those who attempted to defraud the Treasury – counterfeiters, tax evaders etc – and since he was always successful, the series earned widespread praise from his real-life counterparts, to the extent that genuine government officials occasionally put in an appearance.

REGULAR CAST

The Chief Walter Greaza

An ABC Production

Monochrome 30-minute episodes
US: ABC/NBC 11 Sept 1950 - 30 Sept 1955

TUCKER'S WITCH

At last, a witch detective! This mix of Bewitched and The Thin Man centred around the exploits of husband and wife, Rick and Amanda Tucker, who ran a private detective agency. Rick was relatively normal, but when Amanda couldn't crack a case, she resorted to witchcraft. Unfortunately she wasn't very competent and, despite the assistance of standard witch's cat, Dickens, and her mother, Ellen Hobbes, who was also a witch, a number of her spells failed to have the desired effect. Other characters included Marcia Fulbright, the Tuckers' secretary, and their arch enemy, homicide detective, Sean Fisk, who understandably preferred more conventional methods of detection.

Alas the show had little magic and after a short spell, disappeared.

REGULAR CAST

Rick Tucker Tim Matheson   *Amanda Tucker* Catherine Hicks
Ellen Hobbes Barbara Barrie   *Marcia Fulbright* Alfre Woodard
Lt Sean Fisk Bill Morey

Creators: William Bast, Paul Huson
Producers: Bernie Kukoff, William Bast,
Steve Kline, John Thomas Lennox
Executive producers: Philip Mandelker,
Leonard Hill

A TCF Production for CBS

13 colour 60-minute episodes
US: CBS 6 Oct 1982 - 8 Aug 1983
UK: ITV 23 June - 10 Nov 1986 (Thames

21 BEACON STREET

The only thing that distinguished 21 Beacon Street from countless other detective shows of the period, was that the hero, Dennis Chase, was no glory-seeker. Whereas on Sunset Strip, Bourbon Street, Surfside 6 etc, the private eye always got his man, Chase was so modest that, having unravelled the mystery, he would pass the information on to the police and let them move in for the kill.

The title was derived from the Boston address where private investigator Chase and his team worked tirelessly to crack cases. His staff was made up of law school graduate Brian, Jim, who specialized in dialects, and the sexy Lola, who utilized her obvious assets to extract information from the most unwilling sources. Before long, she was in better shape than the show.

REGULAR CAST

Dennis Chase Dennis Morgan   *Lola* Joanna Barnes
Brian Brian Kelly   *Jim* James Maloney

A Filmways Production for NBC

34 monochrome 30-minute episodes

US: NBC/ABC 2 July 1959 - 20 March 1960

21 JUMP STREET

An elite unit of baby-faced cops went back to school to combat the world of teenage crime, in this popular, youth-orientated American police drama. Based on a genuine top secret police mission, four rookies posed as tough teenagers and risked their lives to infiltrate circles of high-school criminals.

The series dramatized the everyday situations faced by the officers. Tantalized by the chance to relive the innocence of their youth, the cops were jolted by the harsh reality of crime-busting. In addition to experiencing once again study halls, adolescent romances and authoritarian teachers (but no maths homework), the cops also found themselves vulnerable to the controversial issues confronting teenagers in the 1980s. With their headquarters in an abandoned chapel at 21

Jump Street, this undercover force delved beyond the crimes to explore and understand the reasoning and relationships of the youths involved.

The team leader was the firm but understanding Captain Adam Fuller. His recruits were fresh-faced Tommy Hanson, a recent police academy graduate, who had to reconcile his formal training with the real world; Judy Hoffs, a beautiful black woman from Chicago who rejected her upper middle-class roots to be a cop; H.T. Ioki, a Japanese immigrant who learned to speak English by watching television; and Doug Penhall, an inflammable officer, who might just as easily have become a criminal but preferred the job security of the police force. When actor Johnny Depp, who was cast as heart-throb Hanson, left to pursue a movie career, he was replaced by a similar model played by Richard Grieco.

REGULAR CAST

Captain Adam Fuller Steve Williams   *Officer Tom Hanson* Johnny Depp
Officer Doug Penhall Peter DeLuise   *Officer Judy Hoffs* Holly Robinson
Officer H.T. Ioki Dustin Nguyen

Creators: Patrick Hasburgh, Stephen J. Cannell
Producer: Steve Beers
Executive producer: Patrick Hasburgh

A Stephen J. Cannell Production for Columbia Pictures Television and the Fox Broadcasting Company

105 colour 60-minute episodes
US: FBC 12 April 1987 - May 1991
UK: British Sky Broadcasting From 3 Sept 1989

TWIN PEAKS

'It's all about secrets. You just sort of picture this kind of darkness and this wind going through the needles of these Douglas firs and you start getting a bit of a mood coming along...little by little you are sucked in. And hopefully you want to go back and feel the mood and the sense of place each week.' –   DAVID LYNCH

Twin Peaks arrived with enough publicity to suggest that it was at least the Second Coming. Hailed by creator David Lynch as 'a Peyton Place for the 1990s', it gripped America with the biggest cliffhanger since JR was shot in Dallas, and introduced a new kind of detective to television – the compulsive cherry pie-eater.

At first, 30 million Americans were hooked by this bizarre murder mystery. Each week Peakies, or Tweakies as the fans of the series came to be known, gathered around their sets, munching cherry pie and doughnuts in the same way as the show's two lawmen, and tried to work out which of Twin Peaks' oddball residents killed Laura Palmer. It was the most talked-about programme in years.

The distinctive dialogue caught on so that Peakspeak swept the nation. Fans wore 'I Killed Laura Palmer' T-shirts to viewing parties and even the haunting theme music became a hit. Meanwhile the real Twin Peaks, the sleepy two-traffic-light town of Snoqualmie, Washington State, some 30 miles from Seattle, had suddenly become a tourist attraction. One local bemoaned: 'The big change in this town, which everybody is talking about and worried about, is Californians. They just seem to be everywhere in this valley.'

Reviewing the opening episode, Time Magazine wrote that Twin Peaks was 'like nothing you've seen in prime time – or on God's earth.'

So what was all the fuss about? Twin Peaks was the invention of former Hill Street Blues writer, Mark Frost, and cult film director, David Lynch, the man responsible for such excursions into the mind as Eraserhead, The Elephant Man and Blue Velvet. They set their surreal whodunnit in the mist-shrouded Pacific sawmill town of Twin Peaks (population 51,201 and falling), peopled by strange characters who talk in cryptic dialogue and who have dark secrets to hide. And their guilt, passions and personality complexes come to the surface when the naked body of 17-year-old high school prom queen, Laura Palmer, is washed ashore at the local lake, wrapped in a plastic bag.

But before Harry S. Truman, the local sheriff, can begin his investigations, another victim of torture and rape is discovered, so FBI agent Dale Cooper is called in to take over the case. To describe agent Cooper as 'quirky' is like calling Einstein 'bright'. Cooper has strange dreams about midgets, dictates his thoughts on everything (from the area's fir trees to the latest clue) into a pocket tape recorder, for his unseen assistant Diane, and has a fetish for cherry pie. He also coined America's catchphrase of 1990 : 'That's a damned fine cup of coffee!'

Cooper and Truman set out to find the murderer, in the process laying bare the town's secrets. Why does the deputy sheriff burst into tears whenever he sees a dead body? Why is a one-eyed woman obsessed with curtains? Why does a woman carry a pet log? Why does the dwarf talk backwards? And what is the significance of the local Lolita's ability to tie a knot in a cherry stalk with her tongue?

The British consider themselves immune to hype, but the fanfare announcing Twin Peaks initially proved deafeningly irresistible. For the first couple of weeks, fans furiously debated who killed Laura Palmer. Was it Diane, the stag's head on the table at the bank, Douglas firs, or David Lynch himself? By the third week, doubts had started to set in. Was it really that good? After all, nobody ever referred to Peyton Place as a masterpiece. By the fourth, many viewers were bored and confused, particularly on learning that the identity of the culprit would not be revealed for months. By the fifth, a good number, although they weren't prepared to admit it, had secretly switched to the Polish film with sub-titles, on Channel four. Twin Peaks had peaked.

They held out longer in America, but early in 1991 ratings began to fall faster than the show's famous fir trees. When ABC announced that it was shelving the last few episodes, diehards protested by staging a rally, wearing eye-patches and carrying logs and cherry pies. But they were in a minority. For even by the time the guilty party was revealed (it was her dad, Leland), few people gave a damn who killed Laura Palmer.

EXAMPLES OF PEAKSPEAK

'Who's the lady with the log?' – Cooper 'We call her the log lady.' – Truman

'I've got one man too many in my life, and I'm married to him.' – Shelly Johnson, waitress at the Double R Diner

'Don't drink that coffee. There was a fish in the percolator.' – Sawmill foreman, Pete Martell, to Cooper and Truman

'Diane, I'm holding in my hand a small box of chocolate bunnies.' – Cooper, dictating to his secretary

* Actor Kyle MacLachlan, who played agent Cooper, can't stand cherries and refused to eat them. Instead, technicians had to use a special food dye to make berries look like Cooper's beloved cherries. MacLachlan explained: 'Apple pie is my favourite pie. But they couldn't make that look like cherries. Instead they gave me berry pie. I could just about cope with that.'

REGULAR CAST

Agent Dale Cooper Kyle MacLachlan   Sheriff Truman Michael Ontkean
Catherine Martell Piper Laurie   Shelly Johnson Madchen Amick
Audrey Horne Sherilyn Fenn   Benjamin Horne Richard Beymer
Pete Martell Jack Nance   Log lady Catherine Coulson

Creators: David Lynch, Mark Frost
Music: Angelo Badalamenti
Producer: Harley Peyton
Executive producers: David Lynch, Mark Frost

A Lynch/Frost Production for Spelling Entertainment and ABC

2 colour 90-minute episodes and 28 colour 60-minute episodes
US: ABC From 8 April 1990
UK: BBC2 (Season 1) 23 Oct - 11 Dec 1990 (8 eps)
(Season 2) 8 Jan 1991 - 18 June 1991

THE UNTOUCHABLES

> 'What drives Eliot Ness? Partly because he's bringing home only
> 2,500 bucks a year to support his family and kids while bent cops are
> taking thousands a week in bribes from Capone and his henchmen.'
> – ROBERT STACK

With all due respect to Batman, Eliot Ness was probably the most feared
TV crime-fighter of all time. Cold-eyed and unsmiling, he and his elite
band of agents strode where other law enforcers feared to tread, and
took on the crime barons of Chicago in the bullet-riddled days of
Prohibition. Accompanied by a hail of machine-gun fire and a screech
of tyres, Ness and his men would leap into action to bring either to
justice or to the morgue, another ruthless gangster intent on controlling
the city.

The real Eliot Ness was a treasury department gangbuster who had
been instrumental in breaking Al Capone's stranglehold on Chicago, in
1931. A Chicago newspaper had dubbed Ness and his incorruptible
squad 'the Untouchables' as they were just about the only ones in the
city not open to bribes. Ness later wrote his autobiography and it was
this which was dramatized into a faithful two-part account of the
Capone caper, The Scarface Mob, and which aired in the US on Desilu
Playhouse in April 1959.

Robert Stack, an accomplished movie actor over the previous 20
years, took the part of Ness and the programme was so successful that it
was developed into a series from the following October. Here television
started to stray from fact, because in real life Ness had disbanded the
Untouchables after bringing Capone to heel, but for the series they
carried on relentlessly tackling new foes. Capone had been sent down in
the April special so the series proper opened with the power struggle
between his two top lieutenants, Jake 'Greasy Thumb' Guzik and Frank
'The Enforcer' Nitti. Among other hoods rounded up by the
Untouchables were such quaint characters as Mad Dog Coll, Dutch
Schultz, Bugs Moran (in whose garage the St Valentine's Day massacre
took place) and Ma Barker. This last arrest infuriated the FBI, who had
actually been the ones responsible for nailing Ma Barker and wanted the
world to know it.

This was not the only area in which the show tampered with fact –
indeed the real Ness rarely used a gun. So many groups objected to
various facets of the stories that eventually Desilu Productions stated at
the end of each episode that certain segments of the programme had
been 'fictionalized'.

The estate of Al Capone sued the show for a million dollars, for
using Capone's name and likeness for profit; US prison officials
objected to scenes apparently showing Capone being treated favourably

in the Atlanta Penitentiary, but the most persistent complaints came from Italian-Americans. They were livid that virtually all the gangsters were given Italian names. The Federation of Italian-American Democratic Organizations attacked the programme's sponsor, L and M cigarettes, and launched a boycott of L and M products. Finally Desilu agreed to a four-point plan. There would be no more fictional hoods with Italian names; there would be greater stress on the role of one of Ness's sidekicks, Enrico Rossi, as a law enforcer; the show would emphasize the 'formidable influence' of Italian-Americans in reducing crime; and further emphasis would be put on the 'great contributions' made to US culture by Americans of Italian descent.

Excessive violence was another cause for concern. There were usually three full-blooded shoot-outs per episode, plus an incalculable number of lesser woundings, and with estimates that the series was watched by up to eight million youngsters, there were grave fears that they would begin to identify with the criminals. This was underlined when a juvenile gang in Cleveland called itself 'the Untouchables'.

A group which surveyed night time television in Los Angeles during the week beginning 12 November 1960 counted: 144 murders, 143 attempted murders, 52 justifiable killings, 14 druggings, 12 jailbreaks, 36 robberies, 6 thefts, 13 kidnappings, 6 burglaries, 7 cases of torture, 6 cases of extortion, 5 cases of blackmail, 11 planned murders, 4 attempted lynchings, 1 massacre scene with hundreds killed, 1 mass murder of homesteaders, 1 planned mass murder by arson, 3 scenes of gangland shootings, 1 other mass gun battle and 1 programme with over 50 women kidnapped. These weren't all from The Untouchables (well, not in one episode anyway) but nevertheless the level of violence was toned down towards the end of the show's four-year run.

Ness became more human and investigators from other government bureaus were introduced, including Barbara Stanwyck as a lieutenant from the Bureau of Missing Persons. But with the arrival of the softly, softly approach, the show lost much of its appeal. For the great joy of The Untouchables was watching these vicious gangsters receive their comeuppance. The good guys were good and the bad guys were bad. There were no grey areas, no room for claims of wrongful arrest, no social workers around to claim that Mad Dog Coll only behaved the way he did because he was deprived of an extra helping of ice cream as a child.

Eliot Ness's widow, Elizabeth, said in 1959 that she approved of Stack's portrayal of her late husband. 'He has the same quietness of voice, the same gentle quality that characterized Eliot. He smiles less but Mr Stack has been given less to laugh at than Eliot found in real life.'

* Desi Arnaz, head of Desilu, magnanimously hired Walter Winchell as the show's narrator, even though Winchell had branded Lucille Ball (Arnaz's wife) a communist during the McCarthy witch-hunts.

REGULAR CAST

Eliot Ness Robert Stack   *Agent Enrico Rossi* Nick Georgiade
Agent William Youngfellow Abel Fernandez   *Agent Martin Flaherty* Jerry Paris
Agent Lee Hobson Paul Picerni   *Agent Rossman* Steve London
Agent Cam Allison Anthony George   *Al Capone* Neville Brand
Frank Nitti Bruce Gordon   *Narrator:* Walter Winchell

EPISODE TITLES
(with major guest stars)

The Empty Chair
The George 'Bugs' Moran Story
Noise of Death (with J. Carrol Naish)
Ma Barker and Her Boys
You Can't Pick a Number
The Jake Lingle Story (with Jack Lord)
Ain't We Got Fun
The Vincent 'Mad Dog' Coll Story (with
    Clu Galager)
Mexican Stakeout
The Artichoke King
The Tri-State Gang (with William
    Bendix)
The Dutch Schultz Story
Underground Railway (with Cliff
    Robertson)
Syndicate Sanctuary
Star Witness (with Jim Backus)
One Armed Bandit
The St Louis Story
The Big Squeeze
Little Egypt
Unhired Assassin
The White Slavers
Three Thousand Suspects
The Doreen Maney Story
Portrait of a Thief
The Underworld Bank (with Peter Falk)
Head of Fire, Feet of Clay
The Frank Nitti Story
A Seat on the Fence
The Jack 'Legs' Diamond Story
The Rusty Heller Story (with Elizabeth
    Montgomery)
The Waxey Gordon Story
The Mark of Cain
The Otto Frick Story
Nicky
The Big Train
The Purple Gang
The Kiss of Death Girl
The Larry Fay Story

The Tommy Karpeles Story
The Masterpiece
Augie 'The Banker' Ciamino (with
    Keenan Wynne)
The Organization (with Richard Conte)
Jamaica Ginger
The Underground Court
The Nick Moses Story
The Antidote (with Telly Savalas)
The Lily Dallas Story
Murder Under Glass
Testimony of Evil
Ring of Terror
Mr Moon
Death for Sale
Stranglehold (with Ricardo Montalban)
The Seventh Vote
The Nero Rankin Story
The King of Champagne (with Barry
    Morse)
The Nick Acropolis Story (with Lee
    Marvin)
90 Proof Dame
Tunnel of Horrors
Power Play (with Wendell Corey)
The Matt Bass Scheme (with Telly
    Savalas)
Loophole (with Jack Klugman)
The Troubleshooters (with Peter Falk)
The Genna Brothers
Hammerlock
Jigsaw
Mankiller City
Without a Name
Canada Run
Fall Guy
The Silent Partner
The Gang War
The Whitey Steele Story
Takeover (with Robert Loggia)
The Death Tree (with Charles Bronson)
The Stryker Brothers

EPISODE TITLES *continued*
(with major guest stars)

Element of Danger (with Lee Marvin)
The Maggie Storm Story
Man in the Middle
Downfall
The Case Against Eliot Ness
The Ginnie Littlesmith Story
The Contract
Pressure
The Monkey Wrench
Arsenal
The Chess Game
The Night They Shot Santa Claus
The Pea (with Frank Gorshin)
Cooker in the Sky
The Economist
A Taste of Pineapple
The Snowball (with Robert Redford)
Elegy (with Barbara Stanwyck)
Bird in the Hand
Come and Kill Me
The Eddie O'Hara Story
An Eye for an Eye (with Jack Klugman)
Search for a Dead Man (with Ed Asner)
A Fist of Five (with Lee Marvin)
The Floyd Gibbons Story (with Dorothy Malone)
Doublecross
The Speculator (with Telly Savalas)
Jake Dance
Blues for a Gone Goose (with Robert Duvall)
Globe of Death

Junk Man
Man in the Cooler
The Butcher's Boy
The Spoiler
One Last Killing
The Giant Killer
The Charlie Argos Story (with Robert Vaughn)
The Jazz Man
The Torpedo
Line of Fire (with Ed Nelson)

Music: Wilbur Hatch, Nelson Riddle
Producers: Howard Hoffman, Alan A. Armer, Alvin Cooperman, Lloyd Richards, Fred Freigberger, Charles Russell
Executive producers: Jerry Thorpe, Leonard Freeman, Quinn Martin

A Desilu Production for ABC

117 monochrome 60-minute episodes
US: ABC (Season 1) 15 Oct 1959 - 28 April 1960 (28 eps)
(Season 2) 13 Oct 1960 - 8 June 1961 (31 eps)
(Season 3) 12 Oct 1961 - 5 July 1962 (28 eps)
(Season 4) 25 Sept 1962 - 21 May 1963 (30 eps)
UK: ITV 14 April 1966 - 5 April 1969 (Anglia)

* A hit 1987 film The Untouchables starred Kevin Costner as Eliot Ness, with Sean Connery and Robert De Niro.

VAN DER VALK

'One of the reasons I like Van Der Valk is that I see some of myself in him. You never quite know how he's going to react, he's unpredictable.'
– BARRY FOSTER

Piet Van Der Valk had two things going for him. One, he was Dutch and that made him unique among TV detectives and two, he had the good fortune to be introduced each week by the most successful of all detective show themes, Eye Level. Written by Dutchman, Jan Stoeckhart, (who assumed the English nom de plume of Jack Trombey) and recorded by the Simon Park Orchestra, Eye Level spent four weeks at the top of the UK charts in 1973.

Otherwise, Van Der Valk was fairly nondescript. Based on the books by Nicholas Freeling and played by Barry Foster, he was a detective with the Amsterdam CID Division, eventually slowly working his way up to the rank of Commissaris. Impulsive, moody and a maverick lacking in diplomacy and political tact, he was not exactly tailor-made for rapid promotion, but there could have been other reasons. For, although he claimed to be a thinking detective, he singularly failed to spot that his French wife, Arlette, to whom he insisted he was devoted, had three different heads over the years. During the first two seasons in the 1970s, she was played by Susan Travers, in the third season by Joanna Dunham and then on the show's return after a fourteen-year absence in 1991, by Meg Davies. It doesn't say much for his powers of observation. No wonder he kept a photo of her on his office desk – it was to remind him which Arlette he was married to that week.

Nor had he noticed that his boss, Hoof Commissaris Samson, had also undergone a head transplant, from Nigel Stock to Ronald Hines. Mind you, Van Der Valk wouldn't have been allowed into the British police force anyway. He was too short. His eye level was considerably lower than most people's, which was why he used to ask suspects to sit down before he questioned them.

In the original hour-long series, Van Der Valk's almost total lack of charisma was compensated for by some sharp scripts and the atmospheric Amsterdam backdrop of canals, bridges, drug pushers and pimps. When it suddenly returned in 1991, Amsterdam was still the same, but the two-hour stories were flabby and compared most unfavourably with those of Morse, Dalgliesh, Taggart and even Wexford.

Now a tetchy 59-year-old, with his curly hair growing ever whiter, Van Der Valk had acquired a policeman son, Wim (it was surely short for Wimp) as well as a new wife. But the revival was a pale imitation. Time had caught up with him. He looked ready for his canal bus pass.

* Author Nicholas Freeling had killed off Van Der Valk before the TV series became popular. He had him shot dead and devoted a novel to the widow Arlette's hunt for the sniper.

REGULAR CAST

Van Der Valk Barry Foster
Arlette (Seasons 1 and 2) Susan Travers *(Season 3)* Joanna Dunham *(Season 4)* Meg Davies
Samson (Seasons 1 - 3) Nigel Stock *(Season 4)* Ronald Hines
Wim Richard Huw

Creator: Nicholas Freeling
Theme music: Jack Trombey
Producers: Michael Chapman (Season 1) Robert Love (Season 2) Geoffrey Gilbert (Season 3) Chris Burt (Season 4)
Executive producers: Lloyd Shirley (Seasons 1 - 4), George Taylor (Season 3), Brian Walcroft (Season 4)

Seasons 1 and 2 produced by Thames Television
Season 3 by Euston Films
Season 4 an Elmgate Production for Thames Television

25 colour 60-minute and 4 colour 120-minute episodes
UK: ITV (Season 1) 13 Sept - 18 Oct 1972 (6 eps)
(Season 2) 29 Aug - 10 Oct 1973 (7 eps)
(Season 3) 5 Sept - 21 Nov 1977 (12 eps)
(Season 4) 16 Jan - 6 Feb 1991 (4 eps)

VEGA$

Robert Urich hit the jackpot as Las Vegas private eye, Dan Tanna. The colourful casinos with their roulette, blackjack and poker made for such a different setting that Vega$ became a huge hit, running for three seasons.

Basically, Tanna was very much the standard handsome, wisecracking P.I. but Urich's charm lifted the character onto a higher level. In his jeans and sports car (a vintage red Thunderbird), Tanna cruised around the city earning a healthy living. For crime was so rife in Las Vegas (Tanna investigated a murder a week) that anyone connected with solving it found there was more than enough to go round.

Tanna's office was part of the Desert Inn Hotel, owned by millionaire Philip Roth, to whom Tanna was on a retainer. Roth was also the proprietor of a number of other large Vegas hotels.

The glamorous scenario was enhanced by Tanna's two sexy showgirl assistants – Beatrice Travis, his secretary, and Angie Turner, his somewhat vacant receptionist, whose brain was often out to lunch even if the rest of her wasn't. And helping out as legmen were Binzer, a reformed crook, whose enthusiasm sometimes masked his incompetence, and Red Indian Eli Two Leaf. Dan Tanna's first contact at the Las Vegas Police Department was Sergeant Bella Archer, but she was succeeded at the end of the first season by Lieutenant David Nelson.

A highly-popular series on both sides of the Atlantic, even though the body count made Vegas slightly less appealing as a holiday destination than Beirut.

REGULAR CAST

Dan Tanna Robert Urich	*Philip Roth* Tony Curtis
Beatrice Travis Phyllis Davis	*Angie Turner* Judy Landers
Bobby Borso ('Binzer') Bart Braverman	*Sgt Bella Archer* Naomi Stevens
Lt David Nelson Greg Morris	*Eli Two Leaf* Will Sampson

Creator: Michael Mann
Music: Dominic Frontiere
Producers: Alan Godfrey, E. Duke Vincent
Executive producers: Aaron Spelling, Douglas S. Cramer

A Spelling-Cramer Production for ABC

67 colour 60-minute episodes
US: ABC (Season 1) 20 Sept 1978 - 9 May 1979 (22 eps)
(Season 2) 19 Sept 1979 - 18 June 1980 (22 eps)
(Season 3) 5 Nov 1980 - 3 June 1981 (23 eps)
UK: ITV 17 Nov 1978 - 21 Nov 1981

VENDETTA

The majority of TV detectives dream of waking up next to a beautiful blonde but Danny Scipio was more likely to wake up next to a horse's head. For Danny was a Mafia hunter.

His hatred of the 'brotherhood' was deep-rooted – he had witnessed the murder of his parents by the Mafia when he was just ten. In 1957 an Anti-Mafia Commission was established in Rome, to fight the spread of evil on a world-wide scale. An advertisement was placed for a man to head it. There was only one reply – Danny Scipio.

With the help of fellow Commission agent, Angelo James, and US District Attorney Mike Hammond, Scipio set out to eliminate the Mafia by any means, his crusade taking him across the continents of the world, as far afield as South America, Algeria and Spain.

However all of these countries bore an uncanny resemblance to Malta where the series was filmed, and which doubled for the rest of the world.

At first this action series was ridiculed for suggesting that the Mafia operated outside Sicily, but critics were forced to eat their words as evidence emerged that the Mafia was even active in Britain at the time, especially Glasgow.

Not the most demanding of shows, but Italian actor Stelio Candelli appealed to women as Danny Scipio. And it was worth watching to see George Cole playing an Italian police chief.

REGULAR CAST

Danny Scipio Stelio Candelli   *Angelo James* Neil McCallum
Mike Hammond Kieron Moore

Creators: Brian Degas, Tudor Gates
Producers: Anthony Coburn, William
  Slater

A BBC Television Production

35 monochrome 50-minute episodes
UK: BBC1 (Season 1) 4 Nov 1966 -
  27 Jan 1967 (13 eps)
(Season 2) 21 June - 13 Sept 1967
  (12 eps)
(Season 3) 1 July - 2 Sept 1968 (10 eps)

WALKING TALL

A bit like Death Wish meets Green Acres, Walking Tall revolved around Sheriff Buford Pusser, a guy who was larger than life in every respect. A colossus of a man, his idea of law enforcement was not a quiet chat about responsibility to society and the need to uphold decent standards of behaviour, he favoured whacking perpetrators over the head with a four-foot club, which he called his 'pacifier'.

Understandably, vigilante Pusser was not the most popular of men in rural McNeal County, Tennessee, where he held office. The local villains had been trying to dispose of him for years – one assassination attempt had instead killed his wife, Pauline, leaving Pusser to raise two young children single-handed, with a little help from his father, Michael.

The scenario sounds far-fetched, the invention of some Hollywood scriptwriter on a bad day, but in fact there was a real Buford Pusser and he had been the subject of a 1973 film, Walking Tall, starring Joe Don Baker. Bo Svenson took over in two sequels and played the role on TV.

Buford Pusser was to have played himself in the third movie but was mysteriously killed in a car crash, the nature of which led to rumours that his underworld enemies had finally got even with him.

REGULAR CAST

Sheriff Buford Pusser Bo Svenson   *Michael Pusser* Rad Daly
Deputy Grady Spooner Jeff Lester   *Deputy Aaron Fairfax* Harold Sylvester

Executive producer: David Gerber

*A Columbia Pictures Television
Production for NBC*

7 colour 60-minute episodes
US: NBC 17 Jan - 6 June 1981

THE WALTER WINCHELL FILE

Before narrating The Untouchables, hard-hitting American newspaper columnist, Walter Winchell, the man famous for always wearing his hat on screen, presented his own crime anthology series. The episodes were dramatized from real stories that Winchell had uncovered during his days as a crime reporter in New York. There was no regular cast.

Host/narrator: Walter Winchell

A Desilu Production for ABC   26 monochrome 30-minute episodes
US: ABC 2 Oct 1957 - 28 March 1958

WATERFRONT BEAT

A new British crime series with the emphasis firmly on office furniture. The police of the Liverpool Dockside Division never seem to turn a hair if a £100,000 payroll is stolen, but they'd be out in force with a S.W.A.T. team for back-up, if a consignment of paper clips went missing. And no doubt the arrival of a batch of 1992 desk-top diaries, with metric conversion tables and major sporting events of the year, would warrant a police escort through the city!

Waterfront Beat aimed to be realistic, but was so realistic at first that it sent viewers to sleep. People who switch on to a cop show do not want to listen to arguments among officers as to who has got the biggest desk and who has the best view from the window. They can listen to all that in their own office.

After the first season, producers were told that the concentration on the 'personal and office problems of policemen' was a turn-off, and so the order went out to step up the action when the show returned. Therefore in the second series, while there was still an unhealthy amount of talk about filing cabinets and notice boards, at least there was some excitement too, with armed robbery and river piracy.

Waterfront Beat could have been a good police show. From the mesmeric silent opening scenes, it was excellently produced by Phil Redmond, creator of Brookside and Grange Hill, and the acting was faultless.

Head of the Dockside Division was Detective Chief Superintendent Don Henderson, a whizz-kid cop with a bad back and a dead wife (she was killed in a car crash at the end of the first series). He had a good knowledge of media-speak but abhorred red-tape. Among the other characters were Henderson's major adversary, the pompous Superintendent Peter Fallows, naive rookie PC Ronnie Barker, and ladies' man Detective Sergeant Don 'Macker' McVay.

What with Don Henderson and Ronnie Barker, I can't help thinking the producers chose the character names by flicking through the actors' directory, Spotlight. I eagerly awaited the appearance of WPC Lulu,

Detective Inspector Engelbert Humperdinck and Detective Sergeant Liberace...

REGULAR CAST

Det. Chief Supt Don Henderson John Ashton
Det. Supt Frank Mathews Geoffrey Leesley   *Supt Peter Fallows* Rupert Frazer
PC Ronnie Barker Brian McCardie   *Asst Chief Constable* Denis Lill
WDS Jackie Byrnes Eve Bland   *WDC Jane Long* Helena Little
Det. Sgt McCarthy (Season 1) Owen Teale   *Det. Sgt 'Macker' McVay* Mark Moraghan
Sgt Trevor Simon Stuart Golland

Creator: Phil Redmond
Music: Steve Wright
Producer: Phil Redmond

A New Media Age Production for BBC Television

16 colour 50-minute episodes
UK: BBC1 (Season 1) 6 Jan - 24 Feb
  1990 (8 eps)
(Season 2) 2 Jan - 20 Feb 1991(8 eps)

WHISPERING SMITH

Detective Tom 'Whispering' Smith actually existed. He is credited with being the first police detective to introduce modern analytic crime-busting techniques to the old West. Based on real cases from the files of the Police Department at Denver, Colorado, the series was set in the 1870s, with Smith played by Western favourite, Audie Murphy, and singer-turned-actor, Guy Mitchell, as his sidekick Detective George Romack. But Mitchell was singing the blues after breaking a shoulder during filming, with only seven episodes completed. As a result, production was postponed for 18 months.

* That was not the only fate to befall the show. Actor Sam Buffington, who played Chief John Richards of the Denver Police Department, died in the course of filming and thus only appeared in a couple of episodes.

REGULAR CAST

Det. Tom 'Whispering' Smith Audie Murphy   *Det. George Romack* Guy Mitchell

Music: Richard Shores, Leo Shuken
Producers: Herbert Coleman, Willard Willingham
Executive producer: Richard Lewis

A Whispering Smith Company Production in association with Revue

25 monochrome 30-minute episodes
US: NBC 15 May - 18 Sept 1961

WHIZ KIDS

The Hardy Boys with software, Whiz Kids followed a group of juvenile computer buffs who used their expertise to practise as amateur detectives. Their leader was Richie Adler, who had his own talking computer, Ralf, a mechanical sleuth capable of outwitting Jessica Fletcher. Accompanied by his fellow pupils from Canyon High School, Hamilton Parker, Alice Tyler and Jeremy Saldino, Richie picked up information about likely investigations from Llewellyn Farley Jnr, a reporter with the Los Angeles Gazette. Farley's brother-in-law was Lieutenant Neal Quinn of the L.A.P.D. computer unit who, although he expressed irritation, was perfectly prepared to provide the kids with access to police computer information. It could only happen in television!

REGULAR CAST

Richie Adler Matthew Laborteaux   *Llewellyn Farley Jnr* Max Gail
Lt Neal Quinn A. Martinez   *Hamilton Parker* Todd Porter
Alice Tyler Andrea Elson   *Jeremy Saldino* Jeffrey Jacquet

Producer: Bob Shayne
Executive producer: Philip DeGuere

A Universal Television Production

8 colour 60-minute episodes
US: CBS 5 Oct 1983 - 2 June 1984
UK: ITV 10 March - 14 July 1984

WHO-DUN-IT

Gary Raymond starred as Inspector Jeremy Moon, in this series of mystery plays set in the 1930s. Each week, the action would stop just before the revelation of the murderer and Moon would ask the viewers to say whodunnit. Not a terribly original idea but extremely well made.

REGULAR CAST

Insp. Jeremy Moon Gary Raymond

Producer: Jack Williams

An ATV Network Production

13 colour 60-minute episodes
UK: ITV 19 Aug - 11 Nov 1969

WHODUNNIT

Popular British light entertainment show of the 1970s in which a panel of celebrity sleuths witnessed a murder mystery playlet and had to guess the culprit by rigorously cross-examining the suspects. The host was one-time Dr Who, Jon Pertwee, and among the regular panelists were Patrick Mower and Anouska Hempel.

* The format briefly transferred to the US with the addition of a game show element. Members of the public competed, too, and if any contestant identified the murderer before the panel, he or she won $10,000. The celebrity expert was F. Lee Bailey, the host Ed McMahon and the murder victims included Erik Estrada and Jack Klugman.

Creators: Jeremy Lloyd, Lance Percival
Producer: Anthony Parker

A Thames Television Network Production

48 colour 45-minute episodes
UK: ITV 15 Aug 1972 - 26 June 1978

Music: Fred Werner
Producers: Doris Quinlan, Joel Stein
Executive producer: Martin Starger

An NBC Production

6 colour 30-minute episodes
US: NBC 12 April - 17 May 1979

WILDE ALLIANCE

A home-grown Thin Man/Hart to Hart which spotlighted the adventures of successful detective novelist, Rupert Wilde, and his wife, Amy. From their luxurious country home, this sporty couple somehow managed to keep stumbling across the type of baffling mysteries that Rupert invented for the characters in his books. Alas there simply wasn't as much excitement in Harrogate as California so that, despite the efforts of the two leads, the series never really caught on and was terminated after one season.

REGULAR CAST
Rupert Wilde John Stride   *Amy Wilde* Julia Foster

Creator: Ian Mackintosh
Executive producer: David Cunliffe

A Yorkshire Television Network Production

13 colour 60-minute episodes
UK: ITV 17 Jan - 11 April 1978

WISEGUY

The police pension must really be something. Undercover cop Vinnie Terranova spent a year in jail just so that he could establish his street credibility and infiltrate the mob on behalf of the Organized Crime Task Force. What dedication to duty!

Vinnie is a street-smart, savvy 'wiseguy' cop, whose unique background and personality make him the perfect choice to become a 'deep sleeper' for the O.C.T.F., a man poised to walk the delicate and dangerous line between undercover work and underworld crime. His fellow agent is Frank McPike, while the O.C.T.F. communications centre is run by Lifeguard, a colourful, long-haired paraplegic.

The story began with Vinnie, whose cover is known by only the highest echelon police, being assigned to infiltrate the criminal organization headed by syndicate boss, Sonny Steelgrave. In no time at all, Vinnie not only befriended the Mafia kingpin, he swiftly moved up through the ranks as Sonny's number-one wiseguy. As the FBI said to Vinnie: 'We've never had an agent in this deep before.'

Vinnie, whose brother is a priest, has gone on to tackle many other investigations from the inside, including one about corruption in the music business which featured Glenn Frey, formerly with The Eagles, and Debbie Harry.

Wiseguy's appeal rests on the broad shoulders of mean and moody-looking Ken Wahl, who plays Vinnie. Having co-starred with Bette Midler in the movie Jinxed and with Paul Newman in Fort Apache: The Bronx, Wahl has built up quite a reputation here, particularly with teenage viewers.

Wiseguy is still being shown on British Sky Broadcasting, but in the States, Vinnie Terranova has been released from undercover operations and is back on terrafirma.

REGULAR CAST

Vinnie Terranova Ken Wahl   *Sonny Steelgrave* Ray Sharkey
Frank McPike Jonathan Banks   *Lifeguard* Jim Byrnes

Creators: Stephen J. Cannell, Frank Lupo
Producers: Les Sheldon, Rod Holcomb
Executive producer: Stephen J. Cannell

A Stephen J. Cannell Production for CBS

US: CBS 16 Sept 1987 - 8 Dec 1990
UK: British Sky Broadcasting From 10 Sept 1989

67 colour 60-minute and 2 colour 120-minute episodes

WOLF

Framed in a drug deal in which a fellow officer died, undercover cop Tony Wolf was fired and spent two years hiding in disgrace. Eventually he returned to the San Francisco wharf neighbourhood of his childhood, determined to put his life back together, repair the family's dilapidated old fishing boat and also mend his relationship with his embittered father, Sal Lupo.

The three little pigs were happier to see the Big Bad Wolf than Sal was to be reunited with his son, but the rest of the North Beach community offered a warmer welcome, especially lifelong friend Connie Bacarri, who combined running a cafe with raising teenage daughter Angeline.

However, Tony's hopes of a peaceful new life were shattered when he was persuaded to turn private investigator on behalf of attorney Dylan Elliott, the man who helped to force him out of the police department. Despite their mutual aversion, Elliott recognized Wolf's skills and they came to an uneasy working arrangement – in exchange for his help with particularly sensitive cases, Elliott would campaign towards clearing Wolf's name. But Wolf was not a howling success and was dropped after 11 episodes.

REGULAR CAST

Tony Wolf Jack Scalia		*Dylan Elliott* Nicolas Surovy	
Sal Lupo Joseph Sirola		*Connie Bacarri* Mimi Kuzyk	
Angeline Bacarri J.C. Brandy		*Capt. Barnett* Don Hood	

Creators/Executive producers: Rod Holcomb, David Peckinpah

A CBS Production

One colour 120-minute episode and 10 colour 60-minute episodes
US: CBS 13 Sept 1989 - 28 June 1990
UK: ITV 9 April - 18 June 1991 (Yorkshire TV)

YELLOWTHREAD STREET

Hong Kong is said to be the most exciting city on earth – and also the most dangerous if you're a cop. Just staying alive is the name of the game for crime-fighters. It should have been the perfect setting for a great action series but, sadly, Yellowthread Street had all the appeal of a two-day old Chinese takeaway.

Filmed entirely on location in Hong Kong, with a vast budget and a prestigious international cast, it had the makings of a sure-fire hit. But something, somewhere went horribly wrong. Confucius would have had a saying for it.

The series was adapted from the novel by former Hong Kong journalist, William Marshall, and focussed on the cases of seven detectives in the Yellowthread Street precinct of the Royal Hong Kong Police Force, as they battled against multifarious crime syndicates and domestic upheavals around Hong Kong and the New Territories. It promised to show every facet of contemporary Hong Kong, from the seedy to the sumptuous.

Heading the task force was the introverted Chief Inspector Alex Vale. He was backed by Detective C.J. Brady, a man whose adrenalin constantly ran on overdrive; the attractive but distant Detective Kelly Lang; cocky Detective Nick Eden; ex-Vietnamese refugee, Detective Eddie Pak; a flippant Australian, Detective Peter Marenta; and a real tough cookie, gum-chewing Detective Jackie Wu, a girl bent on proving to her Triad gang family that resorting to crime was not the only way to escape poverty.

But none of the characters caught on and even the introduction of American guest stars Bill McKinney and Kaz Garas did little to stir viewers' apathy. The plots were so ridiculous too – all that talk of the yellow peril. In the end, Yellowthread quickly became a one-way street to oblivion.

REGULAR CAST

Vale Ray Lonnen   *Brady* Mark McGann
Kelly Catherine Neilson   *Eden* Bruce Payne
Pak Tzi Ma   *Marenta* Robert Taylor
Wu Doreen Chan

Music: Roger Bellon
Producer: Ranald Graham
Executive producer: Keith Richardson

A Yorkshire Television Network Production
13 colour 60-minute episodes
UK: ITV 13 Jan - 7 April 1990

YOUNG SHERLOCK

A worthy attempt to suggest that Sherlock Holmes was just as brilliant a detective even before he was old enough to smoke a pipe. Aimed primarily at children, the serial saw young Holmes investigate The Mystery of the Manor House, and may conceivably have given Steven Spielberg the inspiration for his film Young Sherlock Holmes and the Pyramid of Fear, which followed four years later. One of the many areas in which this idea scored over the movie was that it resisted the temptation to include a young Watson, not even playing doctors and nurses in his short trousers.

REGULAR CAST

Sherlock Holmes Guy Henry

Writer: Gerald Frow

Producer: Pieter Rogers
Executive producer: Michael Cox

A Granada Television Network Production

One colour 60-minute episode and 7 colour 30-minute episodes
UK: ITV 31 Oct - 19 Dec 1982

Z CARS

'I was confined to bed with mumps and to pass the time I started monitoring police messages. Listening in, I got a vastly different impression of the police than that given on Dixon of Dock Green.'

– Z CARS' CREATOR TROY KENNEDY MARTIN

Z Cars revolutionized the image of the British policeman. Before 1962, the British bobby had been epitomized on TV by the homely Dixon of Dock Green, an officer whose main job in life was to tell young boys the time and have a reassuring cup of tea with old ladies. That may have been all very well in 1955 when Dixon started, but by the early Sixties, the world was changing. The teenager had been invented and, rightly or wrongly, old traditions were being abandoned.

In cities across the UK, tower blocks were springing up, concrete ghettos that were to become havens of crime. As the face of Britain changed, so, out of necessity, did the police. Z Cars was the first British series to show the human side of the police, warts and all.

It was set in fictionalized Liverpool, where Seaforth became Seaport and Kirkby New Town was shortened to Newtown. Neither the residents nor the police were presented as paragons of virtue. Young PC Bert Lynch (who was to become a stalwart of the show's 16-year run, rising steadily through the ranks) marked his debut by poking his head through a car window to ask the result of a horse race. Meanwhile PC Bob Steele was seen arguing with his wife, who had bruises from an earlier row. And a stain on the wall commemorated the spot where Steele had thrown the previous night's dinner. Both incidents may sound mild today, but viewers and police authorities alike were outraged then.

Complaints flooded in after the very first programme, and the Chairman of the Police Federation claimed that it had harmed the status of the police, to depict them as wife-beaters and gamblers. It got worse. The Chief Constable of Lancashire, having failed in an attempt to get the show taken off air, withdrew the co-operation of his force in protest. Lancashire police also objected to the Z Cars' coppers' bad table manners.

The character who created the biggest fuss was Newtown nick's bully boy, Detective Inspector Charlie Barlow, played by Stratford Johns. A bear of a man, he favoured verbal and, occasionally, physical violence, when conducting an interrogation. It was like going ten rounds with Henry Cooper, except Barlow didn't cut quite so easily over the eye. He was an intimidating sight – even the cockiest of Scousers were wary of taking liberties with him.

It was Stratford Johns' idea to make Barlow so abrasive. 'I was annoyed that the police had always been portrayed as pipe-smoking bunglers who occasionally stumbled over a corpse,' he says. 'I was bored with it. I had two lines as a detective in a Rod Steiger film, Across the Bridge, in which I was supposed to indicate that I wasn't overpowered by Steiger. I brought a little reality in to it, did a rather bad-tempered act. It got a good reaction.

'So I tried it on Z Cars. The producer said, "Why are you doing it like that?" I said, "Barlow went home last night, had a row with his wife, got out of bed, went downstairs and drank half a bottle of Scotch, sitting on his own. He went back to bed and got up with a hangover." They liked it and bad-tempered Barlow was born.'

Barlow's foil was the gentler Detective Sergeant John Watt and together they made the perfect team, the classic police combination. Barlow would rough them up, then kindly Watt would step in and the suspect, relieved that there was no blood spilt, would spill the beans instead.

The plainclothes boys were seen driving around in patrol cars Z Victor One and Z Victor Two. The early occupants included PCs Jock Weir, 'Fancy' Smith, Bert Lynch, Bob Steele and David Graham, the last-named played by Chariots of Fire writer, Colin Welland, in one of his first TV breaks. The Desk Sergeant was Twentyman but when actor Leonard Williams died of a heart attack a few months into the series, he was replaced by Robert Keegan as Desk Sergeant Blackitt.

After just two months, Z Cars, with its catchy theme tune, had built up an audience of 14 million, but a month later Troy Kennedy Martin abandoned his 'baby'. His original idea had been to show that in some instances, crime can pay, that the police don't catch all the crooks. But this was too subversive for the BBC, who insisted that the villains had to be arrested, so that justice could be seen to be done.

But Z Cars continued without its creator – for another 16 years, totalling 667 50-minute episodes in all, a mixture of two 25-minute programmes a week or standard full-length shows.

Naturally there was a huge turnover in personnel, particularly after Barlow, Watt and Blackitt departed to tread Softly, Softly in 1966. Among the actors given early breaks on Z Cars were Brian Blessed,

Leonard Rossiter, Dame Judi Dench (she played a policewoman in one episode) and even Geoffrey Hayes, presenter of the long-running children's favourite, Rainbow. He played DC Scatliff but there was no sign of Zippy, George and Bungle. Perhaps they were on traffic duty. The series was also a valuable breeding ground for writers, with such frequent contributors as John Hopkins, Robert Barr, Alan Plater and Allan Prior.

Z Cars maintained its high standards right to the end. It broke the mould of British police drama. Without it, there would never have been The Sweeney or The Bill. (SEE ALSO SOFTLY, SOFTLY, BARLOW, BARLOW AT LARGE)

REGULAR CAST

Det. Insp. Charlie Barlow Stratford Johns   *Det. Sgt John Watt* Frank Windsor
PC Jock Weir Joseph Brady   *PC 'Fancy' Smith* Brian Blessed
PC Bert Lynch James Ellis   *PC Bob Steele* Jeremy Kemp
PC David Graham Colin Welland   *PC Sweet* Terence Edmond
Desk Sgt Twentyman Leonard Williams   *Desk Sgt Blackitt* Robert Keegan
Det. Supt Miller Leslie Sands   *Det. Sgt Stone* John Slater
Det. Insp. Goss Derek Waring   *Det. Insp. Bamber* Leonard Rossiter
Det. Con. Scatliff Geoffrey Hayes   *PC Newcombe* Bernard Holley
PC Quilley Douglas Fielding   *Det. Con. Skinner* Ian Cullen
Det. Insp. Witty John Woodvine   *Det. Insp. Hudson* John Barrie
Det. Insp. Todd Joss Ackland

Theme music played by: Johnny Keating
Creator: Troy Kennedy Martin
Producers: David Rose, Richard Beynon, Ronald Travers, Ron Craddock

A BBC Television Production
667 monochrome and colour, 25-minute and 50-minute episodes
UK: BBC1 2 Jan 1962 - 20 Sept 1978

ZERO ONE

Alan Garnett, hero of the 1960s drama series Zero One, was television's airline detective, an investigator hired by various airlines to prevent in-flight crime.

Zero One is the call sign of the International Air Security Board, an organization with a representative at every major airport in the world. Garnett was the London chief, backed by his assistant, Jimmy Delaney, and secretary, Maya.

The show was a co-production with MGM but it failed to take off in the States. This was because airline crime tended to concentrate on hijackings, bombs-on-board and crashes and this scared off potential sponsors, not just the airlines themselves, but food companies with hefty airline contracts. However, the subject matter proved a positive advantage in Canada, where Zero One was sponsored by General Motors, who clearly relished the opportunity to illustrate that it was safer to travel by car than by air.

* Among the guest stars on Zero One was Margaret Rutherford.

REGULAR CAST

Alan Garnett Nigel Patrick   *Maya* Katya Douglas
Jimmy Delaney Bill Smith

Producer: Lawrence P. Bachman

A BBC/MGM Television Production

39 monochrome 25-minute episodes
UK: BBC 3 Oct 1962 - 16 Dec 1964
US: Syndicated 1964

DETECTIVE NOTES

LONGEST-RUNNING DETECTIVE SHOWS (YEARS)

DIXON OF DOCK GREEN	21
Z CARS	16
HAWAII FIVE-O	12
DRAGNET	11
SOFTLY, SOFTLY	10
BERGERAC	10
TOM LOCKHART	10*
THE FBI	9
MAGNUM, P.I.	8
MANNIX	8
A MAN CALLED IRONSIDE	8

* This total includes all three Lockhart series (Murder Bag, Crime Sheet, No Hiding Place).

** The Bill, Hunter and Murder, She Wrote have all so far totalled 7 years, and are still going strong.

STARS WHO MADE IT BIG AFTER PLAYING DETECTIVES

Patrick Swayze (RENEGADES)
Kim Basinger (DOG AND CAT)
Michelle Pfeiffer (B.A.D. CATS)
Burt Reynolds (HAWK, DAN AUGUST)
Michael Douglas (STREETS OF SAN FRANCISCO)
Lee Marvin (M SQUAD)
Charles Bronson (MAN WITH A CAMERA)
Walter Matthau (TALLAHASSEE 7000)
Johnny Depp (21 JUMP STREET)

TOP TEN DETECTIVE CATCHPHRASES

'And hey, let's be careful out there' – Phil Esterhaus
'Book 'em, Dano' – Steve McGarrett
'Who loves ya, baby' – Kojak
'Ten-four' – Dan Mathews
'Ah, just one more thing...' – Columbo
'Evenin' all' – George Dixon
'To the Batmobile' – Batman

'Just the facts, ma'am' – Joe Friday
'There you go' – McCloud
'Goodnight America, wherever you are' – Jack Killian

TEN DETECTIVES I WOULDN'T WANT TO MEET IN A DARK ALLEY

The S.W.A.T. team
Robert McCall, the Equalizer
Norm Buntz
Eliot Ness
Frank Cannon (in a narrow alley)
Sledge Hammer
Frank Ballinger
Bodie and Doyle
Mannix
Richard Kimble (with my arm behind my back)

TEN BEST DETECTIVE GIMMICKS

Columbo's raincoat
Kojak's lollipop
Kookie's comb
Lord Peter Wimsey's monocle
McCloud's horse
Bulman's nasal spray
Lockhart's snuff box
Amos Burke's Rolls-Royce
Ironside's wheelchair
Miss Marple's knitting

THE TEN MOST MISERABLE DETECTIVES

Steve McGarrett
Madigan
Inspector Morse
Henry Snow (Softly, Softly)
Taggart
Adam Dalgliesh
Frank Marker
Charlie Barlow
Harry-O
David Ross (The Outsider)

THE TEN BEST-DRESSED DETECTIVES

Maddie Hayes
Christine Cagney
Remington Steele
Amos Burke
Simon Templar
Hercule Poirot
Batman
Sonny Crockett
Michael Shayne
Kojak

THE TEN WORST-DRESSED DETECTIVES

Columbo
Norm Buntz (Belker had the excuse he was
    undercover)
Frank Marker
George Bulman
Jason King
Starsky and Hutch
Mary Beth Lacey
Spender
Shoestring
Frank Cannon

CHRONOLOGY

(Some of the major detective show landmarks)

1 Sept 1949	Martin Kane, Private Eye (US)	23 Nov 1969	Paul Temple (UK)
7 Oct 1949	Man Against Crime (US)	16 Sept 1970	McCloud (US)
14 Jan 1950	Rocky King, Inside Detective (US)	14 Sept 1971	Cannon (US)
11 Sept 1950	Dick Tracy (US)	15 Sept 1971	Columbo (US)
22 Dec 1950	Charlie Wild, Private Detective (US)	29 Sept 1971	McMillan and Wife (US)
		5 April 1972	Lord Peter Wimsey (UK)
5 Oct 1951	Mark Saber (US)	13 Sept 1972	Van Der Valk (UK)
20 Oct 1951	Sherlock Holmes (UK)	16 Sept 1972	The Streets of San Francisco (US)
16 Dec 1951	Dragnet (US)	25 Sept 1973	Police Story (US)
13 Nov 1954	Fabian of the Yard (UK)	24 Oct 1973	Kojak (US)
9 July 1955	Dixon of Dock Green (UK)	12 Sept 1974	Harry-O (US)
Sept 1955	Highway Patrol (US)	13 Sept 1974	The Rockford Files (US)
16 Sept 1957	Murder Bag (UK)	13 Sept 1974	Police Woman (US)
20 Sept 1957	M Squad (US)	2 Jan 1975	The Sweeney (UK)
20 Sept 1957	The Thin Man (US)	17 Jan 1975	Baretta (US)
21 Sept 1957	Perry Mason (US)	23 Jan 1975	Barney Miller (US)
28 Sept 1957	The New Adventures of Charlie Chan (UK)	3 Sept 1975	Starsky and Hutch (US)
		3 Oct 1976	Quincy, M.E. (US)
9 June 1958	Dial 999 (UK)	5 June 1978	Strangers (UK)
22 Sept 1958	Peter Gunn (US)	20 Sept 1978	Vega$ (US)
30 Sept 1958	Naked City (US)	25 Aug 1979	Hart to Hart (US)
10 Oct 1958	77 Sunset Strip (US)	30 Sept 1979	Shoestring (UK)
16 Sept 1959	No Hiding Place (UK)	11 April 1980	The Gentle Touch (UK)
7 Oct 1959	Hawaiian Eye (US)	30 Aug 1980	Juliet Bravo (UK)
15 Oct 1959	The Untouchables (US)	11 Dec 1980	Magnum, P.I. (US)
31 Oct 1960	Maigret (UK)	15 Jan 1981	Hill Street Blues (US)
17 Sept 1961	Car 54, Where Are You? (US)	18 Oct 1981	Bergerac (UK)
		24 Nov 1981	Simon and Simon (US)
2 Jan 1962	Z Cars (UK)	13 March 1982	T.J. Hooker (US)
4 Oct 1962	The Saint (UK)	25 March 1982	Cagney and Lacey (US)
9 June 1963	Sergeant Cork (UK)	8 April 1983	P.D. James (UK)
23 Jan 1965	Public Eye (UK)	6 Sept 1983	Taggart (UK)
20 Feb 1965	Sherlock Holmes (UK)	26 Jan 1984	Mickey Spillane's Mike Hammer (US)
19 Sept 1965	The FBI (US)	24 April 1984	The Adventures of Sherlock Holmes (UK)
5 Jan 1966	Softly, Softly (UK)		
14 Sept 1967	Ironside (US)	16 Sept 1984	Miami Vice (US)
16 Sept 1967	Mannix (US)	18 Sept 1984	Hunter (US)
9 Sept 1968	The Cases of Sherlock Holmes (UK)	30 Sept 1984	Murder, She Wrote (US)
21 Sept 1968	The Strange Report (UK)	16 Oct 1984	The Bill (UK)
26 Sept 1968	Hawaii Five-O (US)	26 Dec 1984	Miss Marple (UK)
9 March 1969	Department S (UK)	5 March 1985	Moonlighting (US)
17 Sept 1969	Special Branch (UK)	6 Jan 1987	Inspector Morse (UK)
26 Sept 1969	Randall and Hopkirk (Deceased) (UK)	2 Aug 1987	The Ruth Rendell Mysteries (UK)

8 Jan 1989	Agatha Christie's Poirot (UK)	8 April 1990	Twin Peaks (US)
22 Jan 1989	Campion (UK)	8 Jan 1991	Spender (UK)
		25 Sept 1991	Specials (UK)